BLOCKADES OR BREAKTHROUGHS?

# Blockades or Breakthroughs?

## Aboriginal Peoples Confront
## the Canadian State

Edited by

YALE D. BELANGER
and
P. WHITNEY LACKENBAUER

McGill-Queen's University Press
Montreal & Kingston • London • Ithaca

© McGill-Queen's University Press 2014

ISBN 978-0-7735-4390-4 (cloth)
ISBN 978-0-7735-4391-1 (paper)
ISBN 978-0-7735-9612-2 (ePDF)
ISBN 978-0-7735-9613-9 (ePUB)

Legal deposit fourth quarter 2014
Bibliothèque nationale du Québec

Printed in Canada on acid-free paper that is 100% ancient forest free
(100% post-consumer recycled), processed chlorine free

This book has been published with the help of a grant from the Canadian
Federation for the Humanities and Social Sciences, through the Awards
to Scholarly Publications Program, using funds provided by the Social
Sciences and Humanities Research Council of Canada.

McGill-Queen's University Press acknowledges the support of the Canada
Council for the Arts for our publishing program. We also acknowledge the
financial support of the Government of Canada through the Canada Book
Fund for our publishing activities.

Library and Archives Canada Cataloguing in Publication

Blockades or breakthroughs?: Aboriginal peoples confront the Canadian
state/edited by Yale D. Belanger and P. Whitney Lackenbauer.

Includes bibliographical references and index.
Issued in print and electronic formats.
ISBN 978-0-7735-4390-4 (bound). – ISBN 978-0-7735-4391-1 (pbk.). –
ISBN 978-0-7735-9612-2 (ePDF). – ISBN 978-0-7735-9613-9 (ePUB)

1. Native peoples – Canada – Government relations – Case studies.
2. Native peoples – Canada – Claims – Case studies. 3. Direct action –
Canada – Case studies. 4. Government, Resistance to – Canada – Case
studies. 5. Canada – Ethnic relations – Case studies. I. Lackenbauer,
P. Whitney, author, editor II. Belanger, Yale Deron, 1968–, author, editor

E78.C2B56 2014          323.1197'071          C2014-904854-8
                                              C2014-904855-6

This book was typeset by Interscript in 10.5/13 Sabon.

# Contents

# Acknowledgments

This project began in 2004 after a chance meeting of the editors at the University of Saskatchewan. Whitney was completing a postdoctoral fellowship with Professor Jim Miller, while three doors down the hallway in Kirk Hall, Yale was working as an assistant professor in the Political Science Department. For the next four months, these offices incubated long discussions, which generated the idea for this book.

During the next few years, the project gathered momentum despite moves to new positions – Whitney to St Jerome's University in the University of Waterloo and Yale to the University of Lethbridge. The contributors signed on in 2007, and the manuscript eventually found a home with McGill-Queen's University Press under the keen eye of Mark Abley, whom we thank wholeheartedly for believing in this project. We also owe special gratitude to the seven authors whose contributions appear in this book for their fine work, for their openness to reworking their chapters to fit with our vision, and above all else, for their patience. Thanks to the anonymous peer reviewers for the press and to Timothy Winegard and Jennifer Arthur-Lackenbauer for substantive suggestions that shaped and improved this volume. We hope that this book, in its published form, meets their expectations. Our sincerest appreciation also goes to Robert Lewis for his meticulous copyediting, which greatly improved the text. Yale would like to thank Gabrielle Weasel Head and Madeleine Baldwin (Lethbridge) for their assistance in reformatting citations, resolving several critical copyediting issues, and fact checking as this project wound its way into publication. He also expresses his gratitude to Concordia University's First Peoples Studies Program and to the University of Ottawa for their collective invitation to speak, respectively, in the lecture series In Collaboration with Dialogue and in the Aboriginal Conference

Series in October 2012. Panel moderators and audience members at both talks generated important questions and comments, which informed this book's newly crafted introduction. We apologize to anyone whom we may have inadvertently overlooked.

This work could not have been produced without the financial support of the Federation for the Humanities and Social Sciences' Awards to Scholarly Publication Program, a University of Lethbridge Research Dissemination Grant, and a St Jerome's University Aid to Scholarly Publication Grant. This book also benefited from a University of Lethbridge study leave grant and a St Jerome's University faculty research grant.

Finally, we extend our special thanks to Tammie-Jai Belanger and Jennifer Arthur-Lackenbauer. What can we say that has not already been said (or written, for that matter)? Throughout the writing and publication process, they both remained a source of inspiration; their encouragement and support enabled the completion of this work.

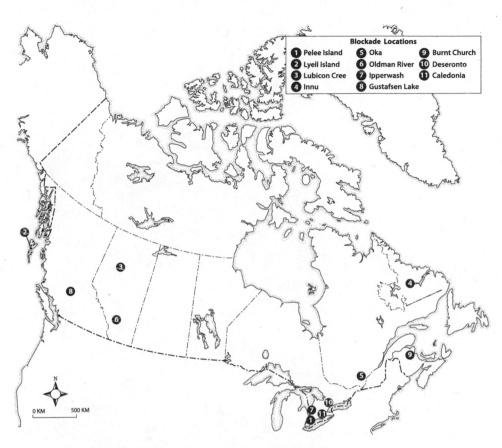

Locations of the blockades and occupations covered in this book.
Maps have been drawn by Jennifer Arthur-Lackenbauer unless otherwise stated.
Please note that all maps are for illustrative purposes only.

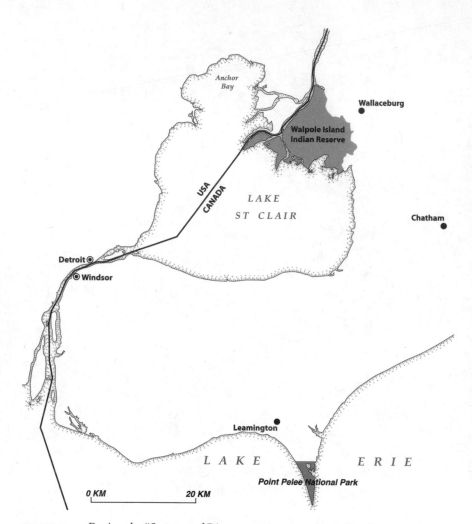

CHAPTER 1 During the "Summer of Discontent" in 1922, the Caldwell First Nation – the only recognized Indian band in southern Ontario without a reserve base – claimed Point Pelee and attempted to occupy an area close to the boundary of Point Pelee National Park.

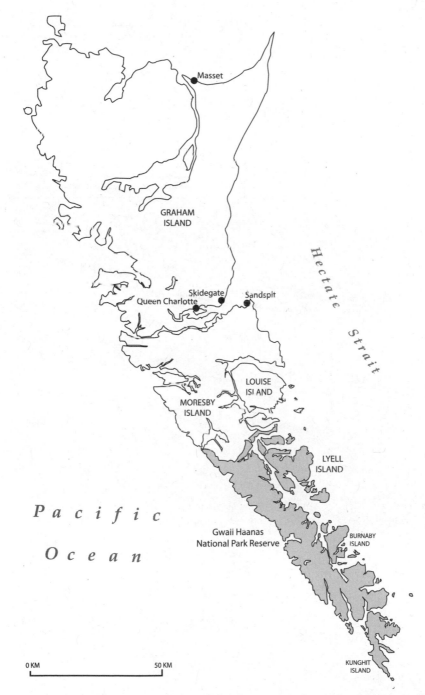

**CHAPTER 2** Map of Haida Gwaii showing key locations in the Haida action on Lyall Island and environmental activism aimed to end clear-cut logging on South Moresby.

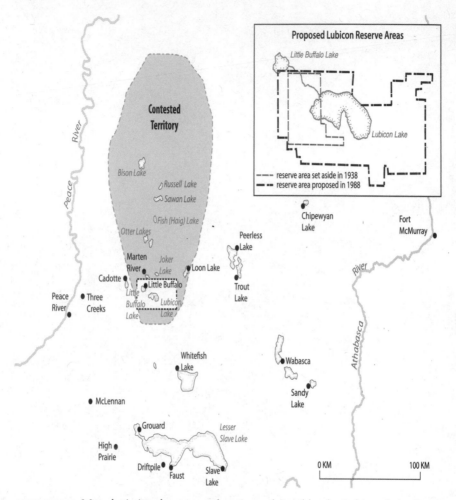

CHAPTER 3 Map depicting the contested territory claimed by the Lubicon Lake Cree in northern Alberta, as well as reserve areas proposed in 1938 and 1988.

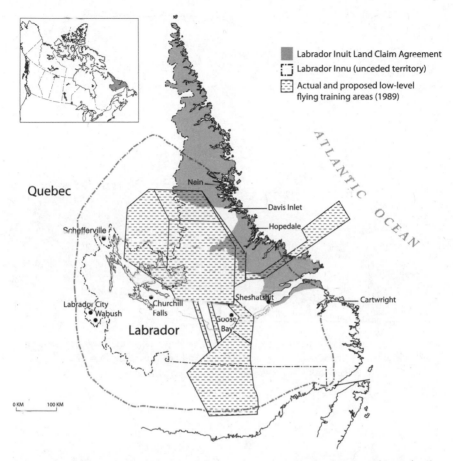

Quebec

Nain

Davis Inlet

Hopedale

Schefferville

Sheshatshit

Cartwright

Labrador City
Wabush

Churchill
Falls

Goose
Bay

Labrador

ATLANTIC OCEAN

0 KM        100 KM

CHAPTER 4 The Goose Bay low-level flying controversy involved Innu and Inuit lands in Labrador and eastern Quebec.

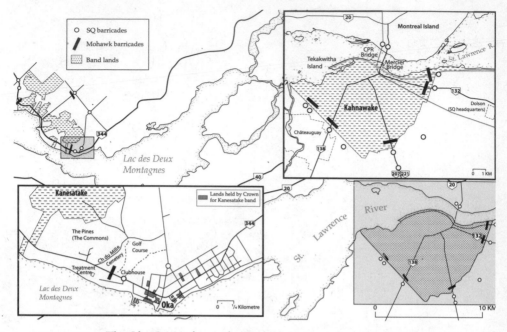

CHAPTER 5 The Oka Crisis of 1990 featured an eleven-week armed standoff between Mohawk Warriors, the Quebec provincial police, and the Canadian Forces on the Kanesatake and Kahnawake Mohawk territories.

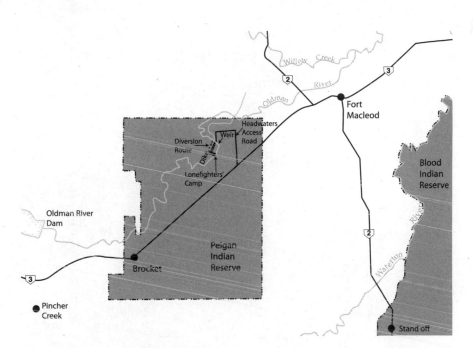

CHAPTER 6 In 1990, the Lonefighters established a blockade to divert the Oldman River on the Peigan reserve of the Piikani Nation of southern Alberta.

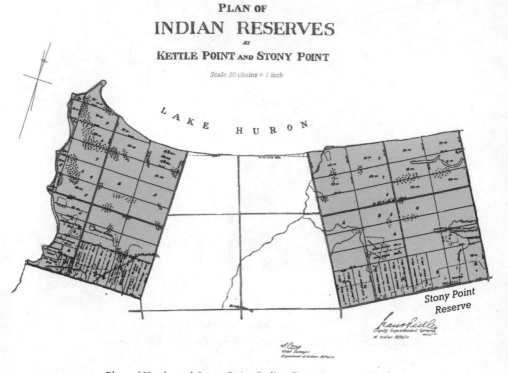

PLAN OF
# INDIAN RESERVES
AT
KETTLE POINT AND STONY POINT

Scale 20 chains = 1 inch

CHAPTER 7  Plan of Kettle and Stony Point Indian Reserves, 1900. Both reserves comprised the officially recognized land base of the Kettle and Stony Point Band.
*Source*: Aboriginal Affairs and Northern Development, Indian Lands Registry.

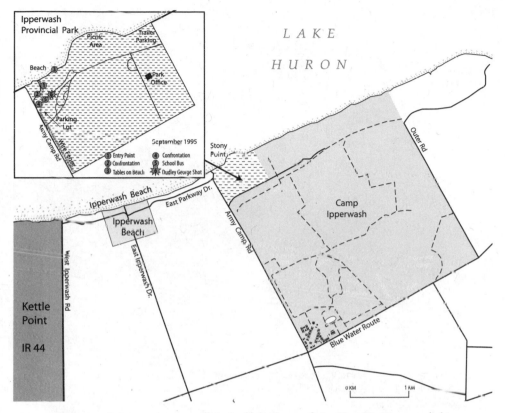

CHAPTER 7 In 1995, a group calling itself the Stoney Point First Nation occupied Camp Ipperwash and Ipperwash Provincial Park. Native protestor Anthony O'Brien (Dudley) George was killed during a confrontation with the Ontario Provincial Police on 6 September (see inset map).

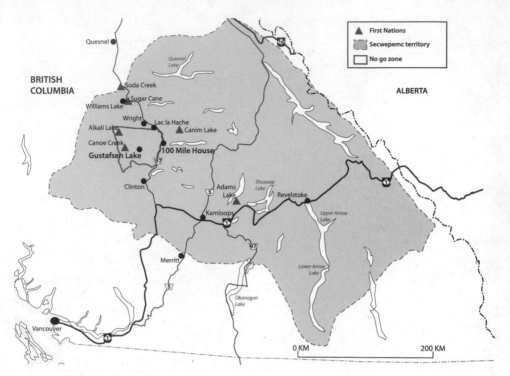

CHAPTER 8 The traditional territory of the Secwepemc (or Shuswap) people, depicting the various First Nations and the "no go zone" demarcating the area around the 1995 Gustafsen Lake standoff.

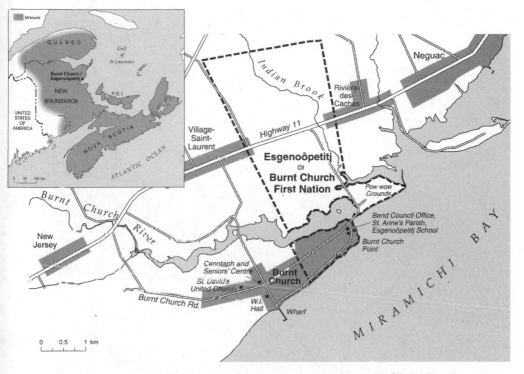

CHAPTER 9 The blockades and confrontations associated with the fishing dispute at Burnt Church involved the Burnt Church First Nation (Esgenoôpetitj in Mi'kmaq) and the settler village of Burnt Church. The communities are built side by side on Miramichi Bay in northeastern New Brunswick or Mi'kma'ki (traditional Mi'kmaw territory). Maps created by the GIS and Cartography Office, Department of Geography, University of Toronto.

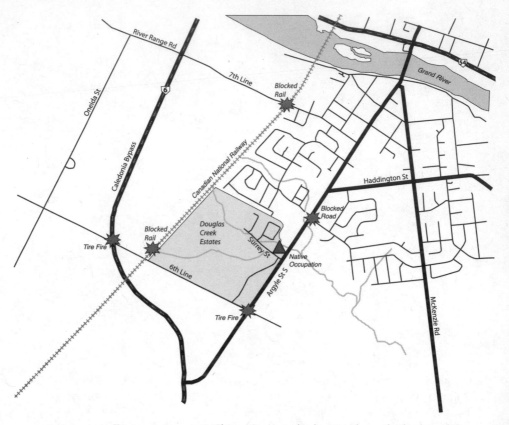

CHAPTER 10 From 2006 to 2008, Shawn Brant and other members of a faction of the Mohawks of the Bay of Quinte set up rail and highway blockades, and occupied a gravel quarry, to assert Mohawk sovereignty over the disputed Culbertson Land Tract. The map shows the location of Mohawk blockades established in the early morning on the National Day of Action, 29 June 2007.

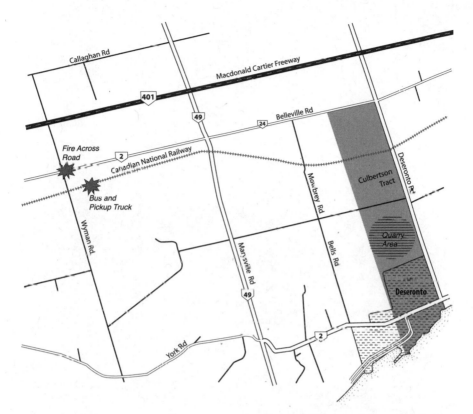

CHAPTER 11 Beginning in February 2006, Aboriginal protestors established barricades along Highway 6 near the Six Nations Reserve south of Caledonia, Ontario, to protest the construction of a new subdivision (Douglas Creek Estates) on disputed lands.

## BLOCKADES OR BREAKTHROUGHS?

Aboriginal peoples have a pre-occupation. It is of land. They occupied land in North America prior to others' arrival on its shores. Over the past 250 years Aboriginal people have been largely dispossessed of their lands and resources in Canada. This dispossession has led to another Aboriginal pre-occupation. It is with land. It is crucial to their survival as peoples. Its loss haunts their dreams. Its continuing occupation and/or reoccupation inspires their visions.

John Borrows, "Crown and Aboriginal Occupations of Land: A History and Comparison," paper prepared for the Ipperwash Inquiry, 15 October 2005, 3

# Introduction

YALE D. BELANGER
and P. WHITNEY LACKENBAUER

Oka, Ipperwash, Caledonia.

Blockades, masked warriors, police snipers.

Why?

Canada's failure to address and resolve the legitimate claims of First Nations.

Imagine your new neighbour comes into your backyard and fences off half of it. Then he sells it to someone down the street. This new neighbour tells you he got a good deal, but he won't say how much he got. Then he says that he'll take care of the cash – on your behalf, of course.

Maybe he even spends a little on himself.

You complain. He denies he did anything wrong.

What would you do?

Go to the proper authorities? Turns out that the authorities and their agencies work for him.

Sue him? He tells you that none of the lawyers can work for you – he's got every one in town working for him. When he finally lets a lawyer work for you, it turns out that he can afford five of them for every one you can afford.

Finally, he says: Okay, I'm willing to discuss it. But first you have to prove I did something wrong. Oh, and I get to be the judge of whether you've proved it. And, if you do prove it, I get to set the rules about how we'll negotiate. I'll decide when we've reached a deal, and I'll even get to determine how I'll pay the settlement out to you. Oh, and I hope you're in no rush because this is going to take about twenty or thirty years to settle.

Sounds crazy?

Welcome to the world of Indian Specific Claims – currently, everything is done on Canada's terms, and the government is both defendant and judge.

With few resources allocated to finding solutions, reaching a settlement can often take twenty or more years from the time a First Nation comes forward

with a claim. Despite the amazing hurdles, almost 300 claims have been settled. In every case where they have been settled, it has meant an immediate
improvement in the lives of First Nations people. It has also strengthened relations between Canada and those First Nations and between those First
Nations and the communities that surround them. Settling outstanding claims
is not only the just thing to do – it is the smart thing.

Close to 900 claims sit in the backlog. Things are getting worse rather than
better. First Nations have been patient – incredibly patient – but their patience is
wearing thin ...

The choice is clear.

Justice, respect, honour.

Oka, Ipperwash, Caledonia.

*Negotiation or Confrontation: It's Canada's Choice*


This excerpt comes from the December 2006 final report of the Standing Senate Committee on Aboriginal Peoples, entitled *Negotiation or
Confrontation: It's Canada's Choice*, which treats the federal "specific
claims" process. The committee argued that a structurally flawed process had left First Nations "extremely frustrated," and it feared that
"failing to find the political will to act appropriately" on Aboriginal
claims "could invite confrontations." Representatives from West Coast
First Nations made this clear. "Make no mistake about it," the British
Columbia Specific Claims Committee warned. "Unless real reform occurs soon, it is only a matter of time before incidents like Oka, Ipperwash and Caledonia occur in communities across British Columbia.
Time is running out. Our patience is wearing thin." Debbie Abbott of the
Union of British Columbia Indian Chiefs advised that "if the current
situation persists, there are only two options left – litigation or confrontation – both of which are costly not only in terms of resources and time
but also to the successful building and sustaining of relationships between B.C. First Nations and Canada."[1] The same logic applied to relationships across the country.

The threat of blockades and occupations remains a powerful political
tool – and a source of consummate concern for some national security
experts. When the federal government mounted its extensive security
operation to safeguard the G8 and G20 summits in 2010, retired military officer Douglas Bland, Queen's University chair of Defence Management Studies, cautioned that the most significant threat to the summit
and to the Canadian economy more generally might be blockades by

Aboriginal groups. "It's a very dangerous situation," Bland said. "The Canadian economy is very vulnerable ... More than 25 per cent of our GDP comes from exports of raw materials, but especially oil, natural gas and electricity to the United States. It's undefended and undefendable infrastructure ... [that] run[s] through aboriginal territories. It would take a very small number of people very little time to bring [it] down." Al Jazeera reporter Jon Elmer noted that "Canada's indigenous communities have shown the will and potential to grind the country's economic lifelines to a halt through strategically placed blockades on the major highways and rail lines that run through native reserves well outside of Canada's urban landscape." This tactic gave Aboriginal blockaders and occupiers major "leverage" to influence the socio-economic and political well-being of Canadians. As for motive, Bland suggested that the dismal social conditions plaguing Aboriginal communities contained all "the root causes which can be the fuel for an insurgency."[2]

When the state casts Aboriginal groups as revisionist actors or insurgents who are discontent with an unfavourable situation and seeking ways to increase their resources and status, it assumes the role of a status quo actor determined to secure its political authority and legal claim to resources. As John Borrows warns, however, such an approach necessitates obscuring a complex history typified by "Non-indigenous peoples [using] physical occupation to secure lands and resources in far greater numbers than Indigenous peoples have employed this device."[3] When the state's approach and this Indigenous history are combined, a contentious and potentially violent theatre develops in which opposing forces may fight to guard their interests from competing claims. Constructing a group of Canadian citizens as a threatening other, especially those fighting for recognition of Aboriginal land rights, is fraught with political dangers. Controversy erupted, for instance, over a draft of Canada's army field manual on counterinsurgency operations, released in 2007, which mentioned the Mohawk Warrior Society as a case study in insurgency. "The rise of radical Native American organizations, such as the Mohawk Warrior Society, can be viewed as insurgencies with specific and limited aims," one passage stated. "Although they do not seek complete control of the federal government they do seek particular political concessions in their relationship with national governments and control (either overt or covert) of political affairs at a local/reserve ('First Nation') level, through the threat of, or use of, violence."[4]

After the excerpt was made public by media reports, Aboriginal leaders denounced the inclusion of their organizations and demanded an apology for being likened to groups such as Hezbollah, Hamas, and the Taliban. Defence Minister Gordon O'Connor issued a statement in the House of Commons promising that the reference would be removed from the final draft. "The withdrawal of the topic [from] the counterinsurgency manual was typical of the reaction by government for fear of upsetting the precarious status quo of relations in the country right now," Bland explained. "It is an example of a trend in Canadian political leadership. There is a great reluctance to name, point to, suggest that we have an internal security problem in Canada based in either the aboriginal communities or in what the Royal Canadian Mounted Police call the aboriginal based criminal organisations."[5]

In the autumn of 2010, the Aboriginal Peoples Television Network broke the news that the military planned to also formally apologize for including the Mohawk Warrior Society in the 2007 draft document. "We want to make sure that [the apology is] delivered in a proper format with a proper amount of respect and from the proper level," military spokesperson Major Martell Thompson told reporters.[6] "I can't wait for it to become a reality," former Akwesasne chief Cheryl Jacobs said. "The black brush-stroke across all Aboriginal people in Canada will go in reverse."[7] Other commentators were appalled at this announcement. Bland insisted that the military did not owe the Warriors, or the broader First Nations community, for that matter, any apology for labelling the Warriors as insurgents:

An insurgency is defined in political texts and in the Oxford English Dictionary as "a rising in active revolt" by a segment of society against "the sovereign state." Here "sovereign" is taken to mean the authority of the state to govern itself ... Stating that some aboriginal organizations in Canada are in disputes with the government of Canada over who is sovereign where and in what circumstances is again, an obvious comment on today's reality of Canadian/aboriginal relationships across the land. We need only look at Oka, Cornwall Island, the "smoke shack" tobacco controversy, the Innu challenges to the government of Quebec, and, of course, the shocking events on both sides at Caledonia.

... The various so-called Warrior Societies proclaim in their several websites that their organizations are armed forces meant to act as a type of militia in the defence of First Nations communities and their rights. They are, arguably, an open challenge to the sovereignty of Canada, unless, of course, Canada surrenders in some fashion its right and responsibility to defend all Canadian territory and all Canadian citizens, including every reserve and all aboriginal people, to the self-appointed Warrior Societies.

In Bland's view, this sorry scenario revealed "the government's apparent preference to cede its sovereignty to every First Nations challenge – including this one." In his assessment, this thinking would "surely inflame disputes" and make military training for domestic counterinsurgency operations all the more necessary.[8]

This idea seemed particularly disconcerting, given that the summer of 2010 marked the twentieth anniversary of the Oka confrontation. At the heart of what was dubbed the "Indian Summer" of 1990, the seventy-nine-day crisis (the product of a centuries-long land dispute) subsumed the Kahnawake and Kanesatake communities, the Quebec provincial government, and the Oka Township. Following an exchange of gunfire between the occupiers and the Sûreté du Québec (Quebec provincial police) that left one officer dead, Ottawa mobilized the Canadian Forces to aid the civil authorities – a decision that ensured the dispute remained front-page news for its duration.[9] When the smoke settled, Prime Minister Brian Mulroney was faced with the prospect of negotiating with what many in the media dubbed "Indian" terrorists. Otherwise, he anticipated future blockades and occupations. He opted to establish a $350 million Royal Commission on Aboriginal Peoples (1991–96) to contextualize the historic and contemporary Aboriginal-Canada relationship and to produce recommendations for improving this relationship and for defusing potential further violence.

Oka captured the Canadian public's attention and remains for many *the* symbol of Aboriginal resistance through direct action, which Aboriginal people continue to employ as a caution to neighbouring non-Native peoples of the consequences associated with ignoring their demands.[10] Notwithstanding its lasting impact and the confidence in the political potency of such actions, demonstrated by Aboriginal people at such places as Oka and Goose Bay, the Oldman River Dam, Ipperwash, and Burnt Church, blockades and occupations are all too frequently portrayed in singular terms, as though underlying grievances, local contexts, and Aboriginal histories can be reduced to one or two basic forms. Overlooked in such instances is Sandra Tomson's conclusion that "a major difference between blockades and occupations of non-Aboriginal and Aboriginal people is that the former is theft (i.e., unjust) and the latter is reclaiming what was stolen from them (i.e., just)."[11] Misrepresenting the complexity and variability of Aboriginal political responses to the Canadian state tends to unfairly single out Aboriginal people for "using so-called blockades and re-occupations of land to secure their land," which are but two of the various tactics for retaining or regaining their lands.[12] It also begs several questions: Why do some Aboriginal groups blockade whereas others do not? How do blockades relate to other political tactics? How do blockades relate to internal political tensions? How do blockades affect intragroup tensions?[13] The question of what drives Aboriginal direct action, and what participants in these activities (including Aboriginal and non-Aboriginal actors) ultimately hope to accomplish, warrants more critical investigation from a scholarly perspective than it has received to date. Clarifying these objectives is our goal.

At its core, this book seeks to provide readers with an improved understanding of why Aboriginal peoples blockade and occupy lands, the processes of decision making and of escalation and de-escalation during these events, and the outcomes for both Aboriginal and state actors. Direct action is both instrumental and symbolic. It is both a means to reshape power and authority[14] and a means "to inspire individual and collective ethnic pride and to raise ethnic consciousness."[15] Taking our lead from the Royal Commission, which accurately predicted subsequent events in its 1996 report, this text's contributors were asked to prepare a case study to interrogate precisely the chain of events that led to a particular blockade or occupation. Whereas the Royal Commission's historical narrative detailed the impacts of systemic colonial processes upon Aboriginal-newcomer relations, it cast only a faint light on the specific sequence of events that led Kanesatake citizens to blockade a road into their community and on what ultimately precipitated other blockades and occupations. Accordingly, we asked each contributor to reflect on the importance of blockades and occupations as forms of direct action and political mobilization, viewed from both symbolic and practical perspectives.[16] As the case studies show, blockades and occupations – or the threat of direct action – have supplied Aboriginal leaders with an instrument that some people believe has the potential to penetrate the public sphere while promoting postcolonial consciousness.

The eleven case studies in this book evaluate specific examples by situating disputes in historical context, by examining the reasons Aboriginal groups used to justify their (re)occupation of lands or erection of blockades, by assessing state strategies adopted to respond to confrontations, and by analyzing media labels and frames applied to both Aboriginal and state responses. In sum, we seek to answer the following question: do blockades and occupations achieve anticipated breakthroughs?

## WHY BLOCKADES AND OCCUPATIONS?

There is no consensus about what leads to blockades or causes occupations to develop. Few commentators have convincingly analyzed response strategies, and few individuals have scrutinized more than a handful of events to gauge the effectiveness of blockades and occupations. What Aboriginal and non-Aboriginal peoples can agree upon is that those employing blockades and occupations must believe them to be effective strategies or tactics for achieving a desired end state.

Oka is arguably the go-to event for most journalists and academics interested in elaborating upon Aboriginal direct action because it is so well documented. Frequently overlooked are blockades and occupations dating back to 1968. That year, roughly 100 Iroquois from Akwesasne and Kahnawake blocked and occupied Cornwall's Seaway International Bridge spanning Ontario and New York State to protest Canada's refusal to uphold the Jay Treaty of 1794. This specific moment of direct action combined with the American Indian Movement's (AIM) coincident rise to capture the public's attention. AIM initially generated a fair amount of publicity for challenging the Minneapolis Police Department's affinity for racial profiling, which in turn led to high Indian incarceration rates. It went national in 1969 by participating in the Alcatraz Island occupation and by 1972 was capable of assembling 2,000 participants for its Trail of Broken Treaties caravan to Washington, DC, to raise awareness and to protest the United States refusal to honour 371 treaties agreed to with Indian nations prior to 1870. A seven-day sit-in ensued that resulted in damage to the Bureau of Indian Affairs building and the ensuing appropriation of thousands of government files that would have likely justified Indian claims of government duplicity.[17] It also hurt AIM's credibility. AIM's notoriety peaked in 1975 after its initial nonviolent efforts to curtail tribal government violations of the rights of Oglala Reservation traditionalists devolved into a civil war that claimed at least sixty-one lives.[18] AIM justified its political stance and aggressive tactics by citing a history of overtly hostile US government actions against Indians, which in turn generated extensive media coverage and academic attention.

On the surface, American Indians and Canada's Aboriginal peoples claimed a shared colonial history, and journalists from Canada consequently tended to frame Aboriginal-led action as similarly contentious and inherently confrontational. Lost in the hyperbole was a concentrated attempt to ascertain Aboriginal motivations for blockades and occupations. This was evident at the Seaway International Bridge blockade and occupation, where action leaders cited federal policies of neglect as catalytic. Noticeably, the fourth estate dislocated recent events from a history of bureaucratic and social disregard and applied similar social theories anchored by a collective societal belief that Canada was lawfully in occupation of its contiguous national lands, which in turn undermined Aboriginal claims to land and resources. That journalists were confused by or uninformed of this tumultuous history is not surprising: the Seaway International Bridge event and subsequent blockades and occupations occurred at a time when newly elected prime minister Pierre Elliott Trudeau was publicly advocating his "just society" proposal of English-French harmony within a united Canada, which in addition also anticipated Indian and Inuit integration.[19] The next year, Trudeau and his minister of Indian affairs, Jean Chrétien, proposed a new Indian policy.[20] Known as the White Paper (the standard name of formal policy documents but in this case with an unfortunate racial connotation), it would have quashed the flawed but longstanding legal relationship enshrined in treaties and the Indian Act.[21]

Even though publicly it seemed that Canadian politicians were reconciled to dealing with Aboriginal issues in a transparent and progressive manner, Aboriginal leaders organized collectively to present a time-honoured treaty message of equal coexistence with the Crown. Some expressed a cautious optimism, but the majority were concerned with the government's reliance on the historic language of protection and inclusion (read as assimilation).[22] Trudeau took great pains to deflect criticisms by highlighting that Indians and Inuit failed to accept "the full rights of citizenship" and by arguing that the government should not be blamed for Aboriginal difficulties.[23] In the face of stiff Aboriginal resistance, the government retracted the White Paper within eighteen months, but it remained important for two reasons. First, Trudeau's White Paper agenda inadvertently tabled a call to arms to Aboriginal people to halt a policy of legislative termination – an issue around which most Aboriginal people nationally could rally. Second, Aboriginal leaders quickly learned that collective action could influence policy – and their success affirmed that the federal government would have to consider the impact of a potentially hostile reaction prior to forging new policies.

## RESISTANCE, ACTIVISM, AND PROTEST: GAUGING THE ANALYTICAL FRAMEWORKS

For Christa Scholtz, the 1960s represents "an important qualitative change in indigenous political history" when "indigenous political organizations expanded their repertoires to include collective action through public protest. Land rights became the central symbol around which disparate indigenous groups could unite and find a common voice. Once indigenous people demonstrated in a public way that they could unite behind a common agenda, indigenous people began to matter in the policy process in a way they never had before."[24] In both Canada and the United States, Indigenous peoples confirmed the power of collective activism in drawing attention to a cause and to groups marginalized within existing political structures.[25] The key difference, and it is notable, is that in the United States AIM executed public spectacles to simultaneously attract new supporters and dislodge Americans from their colonial perch, whereas Aboriginal blockades and occupations in Canada were intended to confront assimilation and challenge centuries of colonial oppression embedded in land policies that assigned Canada territorial sovereignty and thus absolute autonomy. But according to the literature, Aboriginal blockades and occupations went beyond protesting the government's unilateral actions. They were useful for reminding politicians (and perhaps even the participants) of the oft-forgotten history of Aboriginal diplomacy, of Aboriginal people's role in Canada's evolution, and most important, of their collective desire to remain "partners in Confederation," to quote the Royal Commission.[26] Reflecting on this history, legal scholar Robert Williams asserts that Native people were "active facilitators of the many multicultural accommodations that Europeans found absolutely essential for survival on a colonial frontier."[27] Trudeau's failure to consult Aboriginal leaders prior to tabling the 1969 White Paper suggested to them that diplomacy had failed and that in seeking to eliminate the Indian problem, federal officials embraced a political expediency that trumped both engaging in ongoing dialogues and building or maintaining political and economic relationships.

This realization was anything but new to Aboriginal leaders, who had been resisting colonial policies since Canadian Confederation in 1867. In many cases, they watched as a federal government responsible for Indian affairs distanced itself from conversing substantively with Aboriginal leaders, now confined to reserves and increasingly aware that the treaties lacked political weight in Ottawa.[28] A "father knows best" attitude came to dominate in Canada, as did a federal certainty in civilization's benefits that underlay assimilation policies.[29] The Indian Affairs Department, established in 1880 to administer the Indian Act of 1876, compelled most Aboriginal communities to abandon traditional governance practices,[30] which in turn paved the way for the construction of

residential schools that ensured Aboriginal children's removal and isolation from the influence of their homes, families, traditions, and cultures,
thus promoting their final assimilation.[31] The resistance to many policies
that did occur tends to be disregarded due to its unassuming nature.
It combined subtle methods that included keeping children home from
residential schools and forming the political organizations that emerged
in the late nineteenth and early twentieth centuries to challenge the
Canadian government.[32] They tended to reflect Michel Foucault's belief
in the need to employ productive and effective mechanisms, rather than
negative resistance techniques, in order to renew historic relationships.[33]
Philosopher James Tully suggests that this paradoxical approach of utilizing resistance for purposes of renewal revealed a form of diplomacy
that enabled Aboriginal peoples to actively resist the extra-community
exercise of control without arousing suspicion or antagonizing one of
several negotiating partners.[34]

As alternate forms of resistance, blockades and occupations are direct
resistance strategies for reasserting sovereignty over a homeland, and
they are influenced by what geographer David A. Rossiter describes as a
cultural logic rooted in specific epistemologies that inform conceptions
of land and its cultural centrality.[35] A case in point was Akwesasne chief
Mike Mitchell's decision to pursue the combined blockade-occupation
of the Seaway International Bridge, which simultaneously protested
Canadian and American indifference and asserted nationhood status.
The Jay Treaty, signed between Great Britain and the United States in
1794, was the catalyst, specifically the promise in article 3 to respect
"Indians'" long-established systems and practices such as trade and
commerce and their mobility between territories. Mitchell maintained
that both Canadian and American officials ignored this provision. US
officials, according to Mitchell, countered that the War of 1812 abro-
gated the treaty, which allowed border guards on both sides to illegally
restrict the movement of those individuals identified as illegal aliens,
whom Canadian officials considered citizens under federal laws. Mitchell
stated that such actions violated this and other treaties that illustrated an
intricate history of economic, political, and social relationships between
the Mohawks and European powers dating to 1617. "We don't want to
be a Canadian citizen," he claimed. "We don't want to be an American
citizen. They told us a long time ago that we were North American
Indians and today we feel this way too. We feel this way because we
think this reservation is ours, and it does not belong to the white man.
It's the only part that we still have left."[36] Centring out the Canadian

Department of Indian Affairs and Northern Development as the main culprit, Mitchell identified its aptitude at impeding his (and other) community's attempts to foster a dialogue with the federal Crown.[37] Following the brief occupation-blockade, an Indian Affairs employee attending a meeting at Akwesasne witnessed Mitchell and other community members express their desire to renew old political relationships. In this case, a combined blockade-occupation was employed to explicitly challenge Canadian authority with the aim of restoring original covenants by stressing internation dialogues and treaty relationships.

The mainstream media, however, did not probe this history and accordingly framed the event as a protest. The simple language of protest and activism cannot adequately capture the importance of blockades and occupations as acts of empowerment and thus fails to recognize the attendant historical and social circumstances leading to the events in question. Simplifying these value-laden acts by casting them as simple reactionary protests also undermines their perceived worth as expressions of nationalism and anticolonial defiance. The work of sociologists Howard Ramos and Rima Wilkes highlights the difficulties faced when conflating protest and direct action. Ramos explores Canadian Aboriginal protest activities, which he defines as movements enacted and organized "outside the dominant institutions, with the intention of engaging or challenging power holders," although he does so without fully defining the contours of what protest means.[38] Wilkes's work explores Aboriginal mobilization from 1981 to 2000 and finds that blockades were the most common tactic (48.1%), followed by marches and/or demonstrations (20.3%) and by occupations of lands or buildings (8.3%).[39] However, she casts a wide net, ensuring that all potential forms of direct action are integrated, including boycotts, violence and destruction of property, and fish- or log-ins.

Reliance on terms such as "activism" and "protest" can lead us to inaccurately interpret Aboriginal actions as token acts of political defiance rather than as deliberate strategies with explicit outcomes. As Borrows identifies, it also undermines the value of these tools, which are located within an ongoing tradition of diplomacy used by Aboriginal groups seeking to retain the "occupation of areas to which they maintain or claim rights."[40] As popular analytical buzzwords, they can also obscure the role of cultural politics in defending or reinstating endangered lifestyles. We must note that not all Aboriginal blockades and occupations are well thought out or enjoy widespread acceptance as part of a historically or culturally grounded protest tradition. Generating understanding demands that we train our lens on material restraints that affect organizing at the community level, evaluating both how these issues were understood at the community level and dealt with by Canadian policymakers and how the media interpreted them. Academics seeking to understand Aboriginal resistance must exercise caution, for as political scientist James Scott has demonstrated, oppressed peoples resist strategically.[41] Further muddying the waters is the fact that these forms of resistance often appear to be supportive of the status quo, whereas other forms may appear more overt and aggressive. Often overlooked is that these strategies can coalesce to forge a broad macro-strategy that helps to identify new sites of opposition.[42] Blockades and occupations may therefore be better understood if they are recognized as celebrated nationalist tactics rather than subsumed by umbrella terms such as "protest" and "activism."

Arguably, Akwesasne and later blockades and occupations may appear on the surface to be protests that challenge institutional deficits such as the Indian Act or the American and Canadian governments' failure to abide by the Jay Treaty's provisions, to name two examples. But they also represent an ideological instrument anchored by a desire to re-establish lines of communication and thus reanimate dormant political relationships. Consequently, a subtle but unyielding resistance to Canadian norms is evident that although aimed at preserving social and political autonomy is not intended as an inherently secessionist strategy, a stance that confounds most non-Aboriginal individuals. This was evident in 1967 when the celebrated American community organizer Saul Alinsky visited the Mnjikaning First Nation (Rama Reserve) adjacent to Orillia in Ontario.[43] Speaking with a group of youths who were interested in developing strategies to persuade the federal government to revise the Indian Act, Alinsky advocated organizing, agitating, and unleashing decades of frustration through political protest. Espousing an organizing philosophy of "utilizing the power of one part of the power structure against another part," he became irritably perplexed by the participants' support for dialogue over aggression.[44] Aboriginal rights advocate Duke Redbird respectfully contested Alinsky's ideas by advocating for nonmilitant collaborative approaches to social change that encouraged the operation of First Nations governments that were independent of the Canadian political system. In a video that captured the exchange, a noticeably aggravated Alinsky clearly did not comprehend Redbird's insistence on nation-to-nation dialogue, even when Redbird articulated his concerns that opting to join the dominant system would compromise each Aboriginal group's ability as an independent nation to at once defy *and* engage Canada. As Redbird stated, "once you take on the trappings of the white man you become a white man."[45]

Academics and journalists alike failed to identify this approach to relationship maintenance and rebuilding. Despite this oversight, some of the early work exploring what was then considered to be the Indian protest movement was insightful. The National Film Board's thirty-eight-minute documentary *You Are on Indian Land* (1969) critically interrogated the troubled history leading up to the Akwesasne's Seaway International Bridge blockade and occupation.[46] Laurentian University professor J.W.E. Newberry's pamphlet *The Spirit of Indian Protest* (1975) sought to elaborate upon AIM's influence on those participating in Kenora's Anicinaabe Park occupation in 1974.[47] These investigations were historically driven analyses that offered qualified support of Aboriginal groups employing direct action. During the next decade, journalists would produce the majority of the pre-Oka (1990) material exploring Aboriginal direct action. In the wake of Oka, works such as Geoffrey York and Loreen Pindera's *People of the Pines* (1991) and documentary films like Alanis Obomsawin's *Kanesatake: 270 years of Resistance* (1993) influenced academics to explore direct action in a systematic way.[48] Compared to previous studies, these statements were analytically expansive, were accessible, and offered a dialogical starting point for improving our collective understanding of events. Slowly, additional academically oriented materials exploring specific cases began to materialize in the form of journal articles, book chapters, and monographs. What we found in our review of the literature was that despite the choice to investigate Aboriginal direct action, this increased academic attention often tended to gloss over the degree of internal Aboriginal organization, strategic complexity, and the actual tactics employed at each event.

New scholarship is pointing to more comprehensive analyses. Borrows contends that the failure to evaluate settler use of blockades and occupations to illegally assert sovereignty over contested lands undermines our understanding both of Aboriginal blockades and occupations as central diplomatic tools and of how historical events influence contemporary acts that Canadian officials portray as rebellion.[49] A 2010 collection edited by Leanne Simpson and Kiera Ladner offers valuable Aboriginal perspectives on the sense of empowerment that grew out of direct action.[50] In that volume, political scientist Peter Russell argues that blockades and occupations are "flashpoint events" that can aid in forging just relations between Aboriginal peoples and the state.[51] Ravi de Costa and Tristan Knight concur, adding that to achieve justice Aboriginal people may be better off escalating events.[52] Laura Devries's 2011 work on Caledonia demands that we reassess law and order and land ownership through the prism of cultural relativity and, as John Ralston Saul would argue, that we consider the Métis identity of Canada that materialized from past relationships between Aboriginal peoples and the state in their efforts to ensure equitable territorial access and just treatment.[53] As this brief review suggests, the scholarship on blockades and occupations has developed and improved over time, informing our collective understanding of Aboriginal direct action. The following section elaborates on this understanding.

## FRAMING BLOCKADES AND OCCUPATIONS

Blockades and occupations are instrumental and symbolic, a means to reshape the spatiality of power and authority.[54] As Joanne Nagel demonstrates in her examination of the Red Power movement, American Indian activism in its various forms has the power "to inspire individual and collective ethnic pride and to raise ethnic consciousness," particularly for those who witness or participate in action.[55] Her analyses, however, reflect a tendency in the literature to assess antagonist-protagonist actions and to weigh outcomes with the simple goal of identifying a winner. Parties are thus portrayed in straightforward ways that border on stereotype. This is particularly evident in the regular use of the concepts of "warrior" and "state hegemon." The warrior and the militant stories that warriors tell engender a masculine and universalizing image of direct action. Although informative in its own right, this perspective can lead to the presentation of a one-dimensional image that conceals deeper debates within Aboriginal communities about the warrior's efficacy and representativeness.[56] As the late Gail Valaskakis observed, the media at Wounded Knee and Oka "mapped modern warriors onto the contours of Native resistance in representations of armed conflict and expressions of Native radicalism that resonated across the deeply rooted borders separating Native and other North Americans."[57]

Warrior societies have since become closely associated with blockades and occupations, something that both the media and certain academics perpetuate. Taiaiake Alfred's work is a good example. Alfred claims that warrior societies are best characterized as traditional security forces that are both authentic and organic expressions of "timeless indigenous values" and whose membership, strategy, and tactics are "bound to the territory and community ... they exist to protect ... from external threats."[58] This commentary is certainly accurate insofar as it reflects various communities' longing to protect their traditional lands from legislative and physical encroachment. It also speaks shrewdly to the warriors' potential utility in reanimating dormant nation-to-nation political relationships. These and similar sentiments, however, downplay the fact that not all Aboriginal communities claim warrior societies historically or currently. They also obscure debates within Aboriginal communities about the warriors' value and militancy more generally. To some people, warriors embody Aboriginal military, political, and spiritual tradition and positively (re)assert Aboriginal sovereignty using the language of nationhood and agency. To others, they are lawless thugs whose militant ideology and self-interest undermine the very Aboriginal nationalisms they claim to represent.[59] Furthermore, not all people participating in direct action consider themselves to be warriors.

The warrior image operates in juxtaposition to the pervasive state hegemon framework, which highlights the state's role in dominating and oppressing Indigenous peoples. It also treats the state as an absolute force and thus analytically privileges its power. "Where the role of the respective organs of the state is differentiated, what is emphasized is the degree to which all speak with the same voice and work to reinforce the colonial and paternalistic patterns of the other," Scholtz observes. "The danger of this tradition is to adopt an intellectual bias where the state is all-powerful, so the worth of looking at the state in a more critical and differentiated way to find contestation within it, is negligible."[60] For this reason, Canadian society as a whole is necessarily oppressive and dominant, perpetuating Aboriginal peoples' physical and psychological oppression, and any attempts by Aboriginal groups to interact through a negotiated framework simply results in negotiating one's inferiority.[61] As with postcolonial studies more generally, literature employing the state hegemon framework tends to situate Aboriginal society opposite non-Aboriginal society in a binary relationship, thus limiting the possibility of discovering hybrid or shared space. This limitation makes interaction difficult and compromise inherently self-destructive.[62] It also (re)produces or perpetuates "ideological walls around cultures" that "minimize points of cultural convergence."[63] History is thus distilled into "the simple narrative structure of a protagonist's conflict with, and eventual triumph over, opposing forces," which "renders invisible the complexity of historical interactions and the diversity of social groups." Yet one can argue that "the colonial encounter" is characterized by precisely these "multiple identities, the diverse and conflicting interests, and the ambiguities and incompleteness of domination and resistance."[64] False dichotomies can lead to overly simplistic understandings, undermining our ability to comprehend a larger and more complex story.[65]

It is also interesting to note that the analyses of blockades and occupations tend to reflect the ideological grounding of analysts in terms of Aboriginal-state relations, which according to historian Jim Miller fall into one of three categories. The first approach is to adopt the two-row wampum metaphor, which envisions Canada and First Nations as distinctive self-governing entities travelling side by side without interfering in one another's affairs. Championed by most First Nations organizations, including the Assembly of First Nations, and formally articulated in the Royal Commission's final report, this approach encourages the acknowledgment of coexisting sovereignties. The second approach, assimilation, "appeals both to those who think that cultural homogenization is inevitable in a highly technological world ... and to those who long for a dramatic, comprehensive, and final resolution of the challenges that arise from cultural diversity."[66] Critics of this argument highlight a four-century history of failed policy and the linked cultural, political, and economic damage exacted on Aboriginal communities. Finally, the "citizens plus" approach posits that First Nations possess all the rights of Canadian citizenship *plus* those derived from their prior occupancy and historic claims. As a result, First Nations and other Canadians share a common citizenship – a middle ground on which to develop a cooperative relationship – in a context of additional accommodation of Aboriginal rights.[67] In each case, however, we still see a strict comparative model in place, whether it is two self-determining agents gauging each other's political motives, one people attempting to culturally absorb the other, or two peoples attempting to establish an accommodating middle ground. It is therefore not surprising that the literature reads warrior versus state hegemon.

The Aboriginal challenge to Canadian sovereignty, in which protestors identify "Indian space" and confront state authority, is what marks blockades and occupations as forms of legal and political *crises* from a non-Aboriginal perspective. Reconciling Aboriginal cultural and legal logic with state law and order constructs has proven a complex task. Like Canadian officials, some proponents of a state-defined "law and order" framework portray blockades and occupations as illegal forms of dissent and Aboriginal participants as Canadian citizens thus subject to state laws. (Canadian officials likewise deem blockades and occupations

illegitimate strategies.) According to this argument, societies operate efficiently only when one colour-blind law applies equally to everyone. But
as Borrows suggests, one can also make the claim that blockades are also
about *bringing* law and order and that they must be considered logical
and appropriate responses to non-Aboriginal newcomers' illegal occupation of traditional Aboriginal homelands. Systemic forces frequently
overwhelm Aboriginal leaders and their communities while simultaneously keeping the dominant society from acknowledging and addressing
legitimate grievances. This situation requires that Aboriginal people negotiate a better deal with Canada in the hopes of improving local well-
being, but when this approach fails (which many activists intimate is
inevitable), they must aggressively confront the state to force change.[68]

The scholarly literature on major judicial decisions in Canada indicates that the law has historically failed the colour-blind test and that
Aboriginal blockaders and occupiers may indeed rightfully claim both
the moral and, perhaps more important, the legal high ground. Beginning
with the Supreme Court of Canada's 1973 Calder decision affirming the
existence of an Aboriginal right tied to the land,[69] court decisions have
elaborated on this concept, compelling the federal government to interpret treaties more broadly,[70] protect Indians and their property from
dispossession,[71] and consult First Nations communities about their
traditional lands and resources in seeking mutual accommodation.[72]
Judicial reasoning has also concluded that the Crown's intent during the
treaty process was to establish an effective law and order regime that
protected the interests of the First Nations[73] and thus placed an overarching fiduciary duty on the Crown.[74] The Supreme Court has repeatedly
declared that treaties are not contracts or pacts bound by international
law but unique (*sui generis*) accords requiring a fair and liberal interpretation that is not restricted to British/Canadian legal frameworks.[75]

Despite landmark court decisions, the federal government maintains
policies that make it onerous for Aboriginal leaders to obtain legitimate
and political recognition of their rights. Given the snail's pace and the
costs associated with litigating what are, in many cases, claims dating
back generations, legal scholar Bradford Morse has concluded that
extra-judicial remedies (such as direct action tactics) are the only viable
options for Aboriginal peoples seeking political change.[76] Through court
cases and land claim proceedings, Aboriginal leaders consistently argue
that their communities need a secure land base. Accordingly, blockades
and occupations are deemed an appropriate response to non-Aboriginal
people's illegal occupation of traditional homelands. These power

struggles over national boundaries and territorial control, Alfred asserts, "are inherently *political* and should not be viewed as legal or policing issues – a legalist perspective devoid of historic and political context skews the analysis toward legitimating an exercise of power by the state that is not founded on factual or morally defensible principles."[77]

As geographer Nicholas Blomley tidily summarizes, blockades and occupations are complex events that become increasingly incomprehensible when framed by simple dichotomies:

> The blockade does not operate only in the material world of physical movement. It must also be considered in terms of the meanings it endows and with which it is freighted. As a blockade reflects deeply rooted disputes, it is not surprising that the blockade itself will be cast in different ways by opposing groups ... For those behind it, the blockade has a symbolic effect to the extent that it marks out two spaces. In an immediate sense, it maps out a boundary and, in so doing, distinguishes an "Indian" space from a "Euro-Canadian" space. Presumably, there are two audiences to which the claim of such a demarcation is directed. To the dominant society, the claim is an assertion of place, implying a Native rejection of generations of systematic racism, territorial dispossession, and economic marginalization. To the First Nations, the claim is one of shared aspirations and identity as well as principled defiance. To be able to assert some claim to, and control over, space (albeit temporarily) through a blockade both relies upon, and further sustains, First Nations claims to unabrogated sovereignty over specific territory.[78]

This complexity demands equally complex responses from all involved once the barricades go up or the land is (re)occupied. As an example, political scientist C. Radha Jhappan has suggested that Aboriginal people participating in direct actions "use symbols which appeal to society's general sense of justice and fairness" when publicizing their grievances. This underscores the perceived importance of securing public support for addressing alleged injustices, securing space for groups and issues on the political agenda, attracting allies, and creating a sense of urgency. A resulting contest for broader societal support can conversely lead to "adverse public sentiment, particularly if the group is seen to be demanding special treatment or rights, and it may even mobilize opposition among other groups." Jhappan concludes that the militancy of the Oka Crisis in

1990 crossed "the imaginary line of legitimacy" and enabled the federal government to "reverse the terms of discourse and itself invoke the symbols and values of law and order, justice and fairness." By extension, groups had to recognize that "publicity is a double-edged sword: it can be a source of power, but it is a treacherous weapon once turned against its wielder."[79] Some Aboriginal commentators have even questioned the motives of self-proclaimed warriors and their claims to speak on behalf of their and other communities. As Aboriginal philosopher Dale Turner warns, Aboriginal peoples must always remain cognizant that the "need to explain ourselves to the dominant culture arises primarily for political reasons" and that "Aboriginal peoples must be more cautious about what they do with their ways of knowing the world, and especially with how they develop legal and political strategies for asserting, defending, and protecting the rights, sovereignty, and nationhood they still believe they possess."[80]

Further confusing onlookers are state responses to blockades and occupations, which further suggest that there are often two different rulebooks at play: one for Aboriginal peoples and one for the rest of society. Aboriginal activists who break the law are not held to account because of their alleged special status, something that political scientist Tom Flanagan and others have decried as arising from race-based laws. When state authorities agree to blockaders' and occupiers' demands, certain commentators denigrate them for succumbing to blackmail. Aboriginal communities that choose to seek resolutions within the system's land claims processes can also be disadvantaged by individuals and groups that challenge Canadian laws and redirect attention and resources away from communities that are working through government-prescribed political and legal channels. Aboriginal people have found it difficult to negotiate a better deal with Canada to improve local well-being. The issues are more than just conceptual. The Supreme Court has acknowledged that unjust colonial appropriation of sovereign Aboriginal lands has occurred. To legitimize direct action tactics, critics of the status quo can combine this ruling with evidence of the federal government's historic assimilationist mission and its failure to recognize and respect Aboriginal rights.

Supporters of direct action tactics suggest that Aboriginal participants cannot simply be criminalized and dealt with by police. With this context in mind, it appears that blockades and occupations can rightly be conceived, as Borrows contends, as actions designed to prevent outsiders from entering *their* territories rather than exclusively as acts of violence against the Canadian state, with occupations being *reposses-sions* of lands within traditional territories.[81]

### THE COMPARATIVE CASE STUDY APPROACH

A comparative methodology can facilitate systematic analysis of whether blockades and occupations permit Aboriginal groups to break an unfa-vourable status quo, overcome structural obstacles, and achieve their goals. For example, although crises begin for non-Aboriginal leaders when the barricades go up or the occupation commences, the underlying issues for Aboriginal community members can be rooted in decades or even centuries "of dissension and exclusion."[82] Each chapter in this book therefore provides background information on the Aboriginal commu-nity or groups, their relations with the state, and the relevant conflict that led to direct action. The authors also evaluate the Aboriginal leadership and community dynamics that led to the occupation or blockade. Blomley suggests that "to the extent that it signals a deliberate defiance of the established codes of political conduct (the petition, quiet diplomacy, etc.), combined with a deliberate attempt to draw public and state atten-tion to a specific set of concerns, the blockade can be best thought of as a form of 'strategic militancy' rather than as a random and unplanned act."[83] If this holds true, who specifically decided upon direct action, and why? What was the immediate source of dissatisfaction or frustration? What were the objectives, and what was the anticipated response?

Hypothetically, the narrower and more localized the Aboriginal group's demands, the greater the likelihood that it received sympathetic media coverage and popular support. The Lubicon Cree, Haida, Innu, and Mi'kmaq, for example, adhered to an original plan that called for spe-cific outcomes. In these cases, an internally selected and publicly identifi-able group of community members led the direct action. In other cases, the lines of authority were less clear. Shifting political demands at Oka grew from localized interests in protecting a white pine forest to sweep-ing demands that the Canadian state recognize Mohawk sovereignty. Other cases reveal similar expansionist dynamics and competing inter-ests at play. From a constructivist perspective, this divergence in priori-ties suggests that Aboriginal rights conflicts are power contests to define the political and geographical location and scale of decision-making authority. Bruce D'Arcus explains:

> From this perspective, boundaries – like the spaces they delineate –
> are not only socially constructed, but criss-cross our worlds in

myriad complex and overlapping ways. Politics thus revolve not just around the transgression of *a* boundary, but also in the reconfiguration of relationships *between* different kinds of boundaries. A sense of this rather abstract notion is conveyed in Neil Smith's concept of the production of scale ... [within which] different actors wage politics as they seek to define the scope or extent of a set of social relations. Scale is thus a bounded space: a temporarily frozen set of socio-spatial relations. When such settled relations are upset – as in the case of a political movement, for example – conflict results over who will be most effectively able to transcend those relationships, and who will be subsequently contained by them. Only by transcending the immediate realm of settled social relations, and thus of particular crystallizations of power, can marginalized groups effectively change such conditions.[84]

Theoretically, non-Aboriginal support should wane as demands escalate to incorporate broader goals – including explicit articulations of Aboriginal sovereignty – geared at broader political transformation.[85]

But is broad political transformation the underlying goal of groups that decide to adopt direct action tactics? Are blockades and occupations therefore rationalized in terms designed to fundamentally challenge powerful groups and political structures, or are they constrained to focus on particular local situations and specific outcomes? Commentators frequently place the timing of occupations and blockades on a graduated scale of protest activities that challenge state authority, beginning with lobbying politicians and public rallies and culminating with physical action. Borrows notes that "this form of resistance or insistence usually occurs only if other avenues of relief are exhausted."[86] Few scholars have critically analyzed this escalation as a decision-making process based upon success or failure in the formal land claims or political processes or in lower-level actions of protest, such as lobbying or court action. Factors such as timing, publicity, and the intention to provoke a government response must also be weighed.[87]

These case studies confirm that most blockades started in response to local situations and sought specific local outcomes. The Haida blockade was designed to protect South Moresby from clear-cut logging. The Innu occupied bombing ranges and runways in response to government plans to expand military operations that they believed would destroy their environment and way of life. The Lubicon Lake Crees' blockade sought a halt to oil exploration until their Aboriginal title and sovereignty were recognized. In the case of Oka, the original occupiers' intention was to block development of a white pine forest and safeguard this long-contested site. The Lonefighters mounted their resistance to stymie the Alberta government's plans to construct a reservoir on traditional lands. The Stoney Pointer faction's decision to occupy Camp Ipperwash was borne of decades of frustration over the military's unwillingness to return a reserve that it had seized during the Second World War. The Gustafsen Lake standoff began with claims to a specific site on privately owned ranchlands. The series of actions at Burnt Church (Esgenoôpetitj) was over specific fishing rights, one element of which related directly to local employment. The Bay of Quinte protests were aimed at halting the development of contested Mohawk lands, whereas the Caledonia occupiers demanded the return of the Douglas Creek Estates property and a land claim settlement to consolidate their gains, having submitted successive land claims over three decades before taking direct action.

Leadership and support are also pivotal to understanding how questions of power and authority played out, which begs several questions: Who established themselves as the leaders or spokespersons for the action? Did the blockade or occupation enjoy widespread support within the community, or did it represent the actions of a "renegade" or dissent group? What rationale did leaders offer for pursuing direct action, both within the community and to the outside media? How did the elected band, or First Nation, leadership respond?

Christa Scholtz's comparative study of Indigenous land claim negotiations notes that the ability of Aboriginal groups to leverage their power into political gains depends upon variables such as internal cohesion within the claimant group and the sequencing of political mobilization prior to a "crisis."[88] As we suggested, scholarship often sets up binary relationships between the state and a First Nation as though both sides were monolithic actors, yet factionalism is a reality of political life in Aboriginal communities, as it is in Canadian politics. Internal dynamics complicate relationships. In theory, the degree of cohesiveness in the Aboriginal community should influence decision making and outcomes. A group beset with internal division and strife that fails to present a united front will undermine the credibility of those taking direct action. Taiaiake Alfred and Lana Lowe suggest this in their study on warrior societies, which they conclude usually have "an adversarial or tense relationship with the elected band councils." Concurrently, they suggest that Aboriginal people who disagree with militant tactics "are sought out and highlighted; their voice becomes the rational, legitimate voice of the community, while the indigenous warrior is described as 'self-appointed' or 'self-proclaimed.'"[89] In this sense, contests for legitimacy and efforts to discredit militants stem from within – not just from outside – local First Nation communities.

In each case study, we asked the author(s) to identify *which* Aboriginal community members decided to pursue direct action and why. In a few cases, there was widespread community support for blockades or occupations. For instance, the Innu protests over low-level flying enjoyed nearly universal support from the local Innu community, as did the Haida protests at Moresby Island and the Lubicon Lake blockade. In other cases, elected chiefs and band councils distanced themselves from the direct action and insisted that a "renegade" or dissent group directed it. In the case of Ipperwash, for example, the officially recognized Kettle and Stony Point First Nation openly challenged the claims of the Stoney Pointer faction, which occupied the military camp and neighbouring provincial park. At Kanesatake, the Mohawk Warrior Society did not enjoy the support of some community members in either its claims to authority or its actions. Mohawk communities were split between traditional and Indian Act band councils, moderates, traditionalists who opposed the Warriors, and the Warriors themselves. The overlap of "membership" and multifaceted personal agendas complicated matters further. Likewise, the Piikani Lonefighters, the protestors at Gustafsen Lake, and Shawn Brant and his Tyendinaga supporters failed to secure community support. In some cases, band councils openly challenged their actions, questioned their legitimacy, and advocated existing political and legal channels to seek desired outcomes. The inability to present a united front can be used to undermine the credibility of those taking direct action. If this is the case, does challenging the state serve as a catalyst for greater unity or division within a community or Aboriginal group? If division or opposing viewpoints are noted, with whom do states negotiate? Who is considered the proper claimant group among all the actors? Can the negotiators ensure compliance with a negotiated settlement?[90]

In most cases, federal government officials negotiated with elected band councils and were careful not to convey political legitimacy on "dissident" groups that acted without clear community support. This fitted with the Canadian state's position as a status quo political actor that intervenes to protect its sovereign territory, political authority, and legal integrity when Aboriginal groups seek, as "revisionist actors," to shock the system and disrupt the status quo. The state, however, is not a monolith: it consists of multiple layers of government, bureaucratic actors in a range of departments and branches at each level, and various agencies such as the military and police forces that are authorized to maintain order and control. "In the real world of politics and administration," policy scholar Leslie Pal explains, "there are multiple decision-makers with conflicting perspectives and priorities, information is in short supply or contradictory, and everything has to be done immediately." Decision makers often "muddle through" rather than adhering to rational decision-making models.[91] Did state authorities tend to adhere to a clear strategy in responding to similar crises, or did they make incremental decisions in an ad hoc fashion as events unfolded? The case studies suggest the latter: that ad hockery and incrementalism rather than coherent strategies explained government behaviour in most cases. Seldom did government officials have a clear political plan when lands were occupied or blockades went up.

Aboriginal issues become increasingly complex when we add to the mix the regional nature of Confederation.[92] Although the federal Indian affairs minister offered to initiate a special process to negotiate the Haida claim to the South Moresby region, the province declined this overture and refused to acknowledge the concept of Aboriginal title in British Columbia. The federal government's views of the Lubicon Cree claim also differed from those of the Alberta premier. During the Oldman River and Caledonia standoffs, federal officials watched from the sidelines as provincial officers negotiated with activists. Similarly, federal officials tried to avoid involvement in the Oka negotiations, despite repeated appeals from the provincial government, and refused to intervene in the Stoney Pointers' occupation of Ipperwash Provincial Park after the military abandoned the adjoining army camp. They also refused to acknowledge Caledonia as a land claim despite the Six Nations' submission of twenty-nine specific land claims between 1975 and 2006. Provincial officials who frequently noted that the underlying issues (particularly Aboriginal title claims) were federal jurisdiction criticized this hands-off approach. As a consequence, jurisdictional "buck passing" put provincial officials in the awkward position of having to enter negotiations in order to resolve the disputes without complete knowledge of or jurisdiction over the core issues.

In several cases, politicians preferred to abdicate practical responsibility for managing the blockades and occupations to military and police authorities rather than dealing directly with underlying Aboriginal title and rights issues. At Gustafsen Lake and Ipperwash, for example, politicians were quick to brand the protestors as criminals and a law enforcement responsibility (although at Gustafsen Lake this may have indeed been the case). When political discussions broke down, practical negotiations devolved to mobilizing police and soldiers on the ground.

Without mandates to address underlying issues, these confrontations were reduced to law enforcement or military engagements, with negotiations focused on containing violence and on terms of surrender. For example, after the Sûreté du Québec's raid at Kanesatake ended in disaster, the military was left to manage the highly volatile situation at Oka. In this case, the Canadian Forces helped to stabilize the situation and prevent further loss of life. The Ontario Provincial Police's (OPP) intervention at Ipperwash, however, created instability and resulted in bloodshed. The circumstances surrounding Dudley George's death have spawned a large body of literature on the role of police in handling Aboriginal occupations and protests and on the need for "measured responses."[93] The "colour of right" principle also influenced police behaviour, leading to elastic applications of the law and of policing in various cases.[94] At Caledonia, the OPP refused to act on the court injunction for the removal of the protestors and watched the situation devolve into violence between Aboriginal and non-Aboriginal factions.

Although the decision to resort to direct confrontation – including the threat of violence – is often depicted as a natural or inevitable response to government aggression, various case studies reveal ongoing debates within communities about the desirability and utility of heightened militancy. Sarah King, for instance, reveals that Mi'kmaq took action at Burnt Church with various goals in mind: "creating livelihoods within their community, having their rights recognized, re-establishing Mi'kmaw sovereignty over Mi'kmaw territory." Community members expressed diverse opinions about how they should secure government recognition for their fishery but disagreed on tactics and whether the sovereigntists were correct in opposing both the Canadian government and the elected band council. Furthermore, there was a constant debate within the overarching Mi'kmaw community about the appropriateness of strategic violence. This complexity was lost in media reporting, which failed to distinguish between those youth and sovereigntists who pressed for more militant confrontation and those elders who worried about the negative repercussions of violent action.

Historian Ken Coates reminds us that, despite longstanding grievances, violence has been rare and that most blockades – however "noisy and angry" – have been resolved peacefully. He applauds First Nations' leadership for this outcome:

There is a great deal of anger and frustration in many Aboriginal communities. Young men, often disconnected from both traditional activities and the modern economy, are very upset with the status quo, which typically leaves the social and economic burden for unresolved issues on the backs of First Nations people and communities. Over the past few decades, Warrior Societies have become more active, with young people practicing with firearms and organizing for more direct action. Despite the frustration, the opportunities, and the specific crises that had the potential to spark violent protests, however, very little has occurred. That such violence has not materialized is one of the most important, yet little appreciated, aspects of contemporary Canadian society.

He also celebrates elders, traditional chiefs, and elected officials for working "extraordinarily hard to keep the lid on First Nations protests" and for managing pressures for urgent action in their communities. "They also know that violence would not produce a better solution (and that peaceful blockades can often attract attention)," he observes. "Far from the glare of the media and well out of the view of most Canadians, First Nations leaders have done this country and their communities an enormous service. They have pursued peace where violence was possible. They have sought negotiated settlements when conflict seemed inevitable. They have kept their young people focused on the long-term interests of the community."[95]

What role do elders and younger community members play in confrontations? Coates's comments resonate with the existing literature, which suggests that internal divisions over militancy are attributable, at least in part, to a generation gap. Alfred and Lowe observe that, in the media, "indigenous people, particularly the youth, are portrayed as angry and inherently violent, prone to drug abuse, drunkenness, suicide, shootings, gang fights, assault, and murder." In the context of poverty, lack of education, unemployment, and poor prospects for the future, Indigenous youth are described as "a 'tinderbox' or a 'powder keg' ready to explode into violence against unsuspecting Canadians" because "they have nothing to lose."[96] The more peaceful, controlled blockades and occupations analyzed in the case studies were guided by elders and experienced community leaders, as David A. Rossiter, Tom Flanagan, and P. Whitney Lackenbauer demonstrate for the Moresby Island, Lubicon, and Goose Bay actions. In each of these cases, youth played integral roles but did not seek to appropriate the agenda or dominate the media spotlight.

But were cases of heightened militancy, as stated by journalist Rudy Platiel, examples of "young natives" seizing opportunities "to rebel, particularly against white authority, in the name of upholding their people's rights"?[97] The evidence presented in this book suggests that the more confrontational and violent blockades and occupations were not led by radical youth but by individuals in their mid-thirties or older who liberally adopted the language of cultural preservation and genocide to justify their actions. The exploits of Lasagna, Dudley George, Wolverine, Milton Born With A Tooth, and Shawn Brant have turned these individuals into Aboriginal folk heroes in some circles. Further scrutiny, however, shows that their agendas did not align with those of their broader communities – particularly those of elected band councils. The most aggressive protestors were alienated within their own communities and, in most cases, were kept at arm's length from negotiations that achieved political objectives.[98] In some cases, they were the actors whom "silk-shirts" (people who distanced themselves from tactical action) considered expendable to protect and promote profit and economic agendas.

The authors also explore the scope and nature of the tactics employed by all sides of the dispute: What strategies were developed in anticipation of certain actions? And how were the pressures associated with each phase of the action handled in practice? Scholars have long investigated crisis behaviour to better understand why some crises lead to physical challenge whereas others are resolved nonviolently and why some are prolonged whereas others are short in duration. The first issue is defining the event itself: What is the perceived threat to basic values, how much time do decision makers have to respond, and what is the likelihood of violence? Is this a crisis related to land and resources or to political legitimacy and sovereignty more generally? Is it local or national in scope? Does this change over time? What are the desired ends, goals, and objectives of the various actors? Can desired outcomes best be attained through bargaining, negotiations, the threat of force, or force itself?

Because blockades and occupations are based upon accusations of injustice, state actors must gauge the thresholds of potential violence that Canadian society – a democratic, pluralistic society – will tolerate in response. This potentially constrains their range of options more than would be the case in more ideologically monolithic societies. What containment strategies do government authorities adopt to prevent these challenges from eroding their legitimacy on the national or international stage? What are the legal, political, and moral constraints on state behaviour? Blockades and occupations are obviously confrontational, but are they used as part of a strategy of compromise and negotiation? If so, under what conditions and in what contexts are the various actors willing to negotiate and what influences the form and pace of these negotiations? Christopher Alcantara observes that trust relationships aid in determining the speed of negotiations, thereby allowing negotiators to propose ideas outside of the formal negotiating process without fear of recrimination or public embarrassment.[99] Can these and like relationships be created and maintained? How and why do the various participants' expectations about the outcomes of particular courses of action change over time? Why do state authorities use force in some situations and choose to negotiate outcomes in others? In short, how and why do state and Aboriginal responses vary?

In understanding political and popular responses to blockades and occupations, it is also vital to discern how the news media (print and electronic) as well as the main protagonists depict these confrontations. Scholarly studies typically criticize the media for their racist coverage of Aboriginal people's issues, depicting journalists as "agents and handmaidens of dominant groups whom they are challenging"[100] – in sum, as colonial instruments working with central governments and corporate Canada. Many Aboriginal people believe that the press consistently portrays them in a negative, biased, sensationalizing manner, which creates and perpetuates misperceptions of Aboriginal violence and hostility.[101] Yet Aboriginal groups also recognize that the media can convey broader-based critiques of state power that mobilize support beyond their local group and geographical area, validate their claims, and influence power relationships.[102] The media have the potential to carry expanding narratives to large audiences, thereby educating people as events unfold, which allows participants in blockades and occupations to reach would-be allies outside of their local group and geographical area. Broadening the scope of the conflict through media engagement can draw in or estrange contestants, thus changing the power relationships.[103]

The following chapters offer insights regarding the media's role in shaping blockades and occupations. What media strategies do Aboriginal groups, opposing groups, and governments adopt? What core issues are emphasized or debated, and whose voices are granted standing? Are Native actions depicted as rational and grounded in historical injustice or as reactive and self-serving? Do the media distinguish internal conflicts within Native communities from conflicts between Aboriginal people and broader Canadian society? Do these internal dynamics become a key part of the public story, and does this deflect attention or blur the preferred issue frame?[104] To whom is the moral high ground accorded? Furthermore, some commentators have identified differences between local and national media coverage, suggesting that the national media tend to be more sympathetic to Native direct action. Does the evidence bear this out? Whom do the media hold responsible for the respective blockade or occupation, and how is the eventual outcome depicted?

If one of the strategic objectives for Aboriginal protestors in mounting blockades and occupations is to draw attention to a cause that has failed to gain traction through official legal and political channels, they usually succeed. Many Aboriginal groups have considered the media an integral aspect of their confrontation strategy. At Oka, for instance, the Mohawk Warrior Society established an organized media campaign complete with an office housing fax machines, cell phones, and a media greeting lounge. The Warriors regularly circulated flyers and media reports akin to those of the Canadian Forces.[105] The Lonefighters prepared and circulated a detailed press package prior to establishing their occupation, thereby publicly communicating their goals while temporarily undermining the government press agents' ability to respond. Similar strategies are evident in other cases.

The case studies in this volume suggest that, in the short term at least, Aboriginal groups met with mixed success in their efforts to convince reporters to disseminate their message and frame the debate in ways that were sympathetic to their aspirations. Consequently, the media were no more of a monolith than government or Aboriginal peoples. In some cases, journalists echoed the law and order message pronounced by state authorities *and* displayed the racist tendencies typically described by academic commentators analyzing media coverage of Aboriginal issues. For example, reporters tended to side with the positions articulated by federal, provincial, and elected First Nation officials during the Oldman River, Gustafsen Lake, and Tyendinaga conflicts. In other cases, such as the Haida, Innu, Lubicon Cree, and Stoney Pointer actions, the national and international media sided with the underdog. The evidence does not show that the media were inherently biased for or against Aboriginal claims or direct action tactics – as long as the latter did not devolve into open violence. In all cases, however, coverage tended to be reactive.

Although journalists sought out competing voices to frame their stories, they seldom situated the confrontations (or the claims upon which they were based) in rigorous historical and political contexts. Narrative frames were often binary, distilling complex histories, competing "truth" claims, and social contexts into law and order narratives that pitched state authorities against Aboriginal protestors. But this did not mean that all journalists sided with government, succumbed to simple sensationalism, or slavishly adhered to a single frame or opinion. Initially, journalists supported the Lonefighters and the Tyendinaga activists, although this backing shifted once reporters became aware of both the ad hoc nature of the protests and the activists' desire for confrontation. Some diligent journalists probed deeper and discussed internal dynamics within Aboriginal communities, such as Piikani divisions over the Lonefighters, the Stoney Pointers' relationship with the Kettle and Stony Point First Nation, and Shawn Brant's strained relations with the chief and council of the Bay of Quinte Mohawks. In the Oka, Ipperwash, and Caledonia cases, some reporters actually conferred legitimacy on activists who did not enjoy support from band leadership or their communities at large. These protestors were often the outcasts of their own communities and acted independently of political, social, and community consensus. Whether this was an unintentional outcome of superficial journalism or a conscious attempt to give political voice and credibility to protestors who did not enjoy the support of government or Aboriginal authorities remains open to interpretation.

Analysis of media coverage must also grapple with local, regional, national, and international scales. In some cases, like the debate on low-level flying in Labrador, there were marked differences between national and international coverage, which generally sympathized with the Innu and their supporters, and local and regional coverage, which was comparatively critical of their cause. In the case of Oka, the English-language media tended to be more supportive of the Mohawk Warriors than did the French-language media. The lack of uniformity of regional coverage makes it difficult to determine whether the eastern affiliates covered the issues better than did their western colleagues and whether media-concentrated provinces like Ontario and British Columbia provided more inclusive coverage. Media coverage was, to put it colloquially, hit and miss, depending upon available resources, reporter initiative, and conflict duration. Therefore, the assumption that the media are racist and/or opposed to Aboriginal agendas is overly simplistic, and more scholarly work in this area is sorely needed.

## CHAPTER OVERVIEW

The purpose of this book is to evaluate whether Aboriginal direct action leads to the anticipated breakthroughs. Did Aboriginal protestors/occupants accomplish their goals or achieve partial victories, or did they fail? Do blockades and occupations represent a practical way for Aboriginal groups to break an unfavourable status quo and bring about positive outcomes?

There is no clear verdict. Some blockades and occupations were more successful than others, measured according to stated Aboriginal political, social, economic, environmental, and spiritual outcomes. In many cases, gauging success depends upon which element or group of Aboriginal individuals one chooses to privilege. Some actions were well planned, whereas others were ad hoc and poorly led, but all were seen as an alternative to the institutionalized land claims process and to unresponsive federal and provincial policies. Some fulfilled their organizers' desired outcomes, whereas others failed miserably. Furthermore, when conflicts turned violent, the achievements must be tempered against the loss of life, indicating that these protests also must be evaluated in relation to their social and political ramifications. Did they strengthen community resolve or widen existing social and political divides? It is equally important, but more difficult to discern, how these direct actions have influenced future generations' self-esteem[106] and approaches to community-based advocacy.

In the first chapter, historian John Sandlos documents the occupation of Point Pelee National Park in 1922 by members of the Caldwell First Nation who were seeking to repopulate a traditional site and, based on historic occupancy, to secure greater permanent access to the park. In doing so, he reminds us that as far back as the 1920s, blockades and occupations could be tools of direct action. Sandlos sheds light on the historically dynamic political nature of blockades and occupations and shows how participants' internal conflicts undermined their message, foreshadowing what would become a normative issue confronting later Aboriginal blockaders and occupiers. Federal officials exploited this weakness and challenged the validity of Aboriginal land claims in the highly populated southern Ontario region coveted by cottagers. Eighty years after this abortive attempt to occupy Point Pelee, the Caldwell Band's claims remain unresolved and still dominate the community's political agenda, and the themes Sandlos raises set the stage for subsequent analyses.

Geographer David A. Rossiter follows with his analysis of the Haida's 1985 blockade of a logging camp access road on Lyell Island in the South Moresby region of the Queen Charlotte Islands in British Columbia (since renamed Haida Gwaii), a planned blockade that eschewed violence and united regional community members. This fundamentally peaceful protest nevertheless led to dozens of arrests and forced provincial officials to consider establishing a provincial Aboriginal land claims process. A cautionary tale emerged concerning the media's penchant for distilling a complex array of dynamic relationships into simple frames. In this instance, the media refined the multifaceted socio-political and socio-economic dialogues driving the participants' actions into an image of a historic people of the woods seeking reintegration into their natural environment. The media's inability to consider the Haida through the dual lenses of history and modernity was debilitating for the Haida, who were forced to modify their political strategies to better advance their claims. International scrutiny and federal government pressure ultimately forced British Columbia to turn South Moresby over to Parks Canada, which created South Moresby National Park in 1987. Provincial and national media support for the Haida cause was unable to counter the popular image of "the natural environment of the islands" as "all but divorced from Haida culture, except where it might serve as an aesthetic backdrop through reference to tradition and harmony with nature." Accordingly, although the Haida and their supporters successfully achieved a key objective in preventing the extraction of old-growth forests by the logging industry, they failed to realize their goal of expressing and achieving sovereignty over their homeland. The Haida role in joint management of Gwaii Haanas National Park and the Haida Heritage Reserve resulted in partial control of land and resources, but their larger land claim remains unresolved.

This was also the case with the Lubicon Lake Cree, whose brief blockade of October 1988 achieved a short-term political breakthrough but did not translate into long-term political gains. In chapter 3 political scientist Tom Flanagan critically examines Lubicon Cree attempts to secure federal and provincial recognition of territorial sovereignty and to protect their lands from development. Lubicon leaders had neither negotiated nor signed a treaty and as a result remained unconvinced that their Aboriginal rights to their traditional lands had been extinguished. Provincial and federal officials appeared to agree with this assessment when they met with Lubicon leaders in the mid-1980s to discuss this issue. But when court actions failed to support the Lubicon title case or an injunction against resource development, they adopted "tactics of political guerrilla warfare" to assert jurisdiction over their traditional territory. Flanagan is critical of Chief Bernard Ominayak's reliance on outside advisors' strategic advice and concludes that he and his associates' lack of experience and their ideological orientation were obstacles to practical solutions. This in turn led federal officials to abandon negotiations once it became evident that no agreement was imminent. The Royal Canadian Mounted Police (RCMP) quickly dismantled a brief five-day blockade of four main roads in October 1988. Favourable media coverage due in part to an extensive network of Canadian and international supporters was augmented by the Alberta premier agreeing with some of their demands. Negotiations with the federal government soon bogged down in a stalemate, and 117 band members opposing Chief Ominayak broke away to form the Woodland Cree First Nation. The new band soon settled a specific claim with the federal government, whereas the Lubicon Cree remain the only Native community in north-central Alberta that has not settled its claims. In Flanagan's final assessment, despite a promising beginning and provincial and international support, the Lubicon "snatched defeat from the jaws of victory."

Unsettled claims also lay behind the Innu protests over low-level flying in Labrador and eastern Quebec. In chapter 4 historian P. Whitney Lackenbauer's analysis of this case highlights how peaceful direct action can reap community benefits even if it does not achieve its political objectives. In the Innu protests, group cohesiveness and an uncomplicated political-protest agenda that embraced a forthright demand to end low-level flying denied authorities the chance to obscure the Innu's message. The Sheshatshit Innu community appeared to have two main goals: first, to stop the proposed creation of a NATO training centre that would have expanded the military presence at Goose Bay and the tempo of air force operations over Nitassinan, their traditional territory; second, to exercise traditional rights over an unceded area linked to the Innu land claim. The national media found the Innu message easily digestible, which enabled the story to be told in simple terms. The resultant "David versus Goliath" narrative inevitably pitted the resources-deficient Innu against Canada and the international military complex represented by NATO. Low-level flying continued, and the various Innu blockades that occurred between 1987 and 1990 produced a striking degree of community unity as well as a sense of personal empowerment. This case highlights the important role of women and elders in mobilizing their neighbours and how mounting peaceful occupations can garner favourable national and international media support. This direct action factored little in the NATO decision not to establish the training centre, and the Innu did not succeed in halting low-level flying or in securing official acknowledgment of their territorial sovereignty. All the same, community members believed that their activism had made a difference, and it represented an intangible breakthrough by fostering a sense of collective purpose and unity. This advanced a broader social aim: to create and sustain a safe environment on the land in which their people could nurture their ailing communities back to health.

Whereas the preceding case studies were nonviolent, the following series of blockades and occupations featured armed militants confronting state authorities. Beginning with his analysis of the seventy-nine-day

Oka standoff between the Quebec provincial police and the Canadian Forces, on one side, and the Kanesatake and Kahnawake Mohawk communities near Montreal, on the other, Lackenbauer focuses on the Mohawks' shifting political objectives and the military's strategy on the ground. The goal of the initial protests at Kanesatake was to protect a white pine forest called "the Pines," and it was quickly engulfed by larger political issues of Mohawk sovereignty, the Mohawk Warrior Society, and land claims more generally. Even though the Mohawks projected a united front to the media, internal voices ranged in opinion from those who sought a peaceful reclamation of disputed lands to those like the Warriors who demanded formal recognition of Mohawk sovereignty. Bogged down in jurisdictional squabbles on the other side of the barricades, the federal and provincial governments refused to concede to escalating Mohawk demands and abdicated to the Canadian Forces practical responsibility for managing the crisis. Although the local land dispute at Kanesatake was the product of a long and tortured history, the Warriors' decision to blockade the Mercier Bridge proved "a bridge too far." The blockades at Oka prevented the golf course from expanding onto the Pines. In this sense, direct action was successful and was clearly "a watershed for the Warrior movement." The Warrior rhetoric and tactics on display at Oka have also become quintessential images of Aboriginal activism in Canada. Yet the political outcomes were less decisive. The crisis may have served as a catalyst for promises of Aboriginal self-government and federal Indian Affairs policy reform, as well as Canada's largest royal commission, but it did not resolve deep political and social divisions within the Mohawk communities. This chapter reveals how Aboriginal sovereignty and nationalism can be mobilized as a powerful driver to challenge government control, but it also shows that violent militancy opens the door for the state – in this case, the military – to turn the tables, generate public support, and project itself as the legitimate, moderate actor in a volatile situation.

In chapter 6 Native studies scholar Yale Belanger evaluates western Canada's first conflict-driven blockade to attract national media attention. Overshadowed by the more sensational events occurring at Oka in the summer of 1990, the Peigan Lonefighters' resistance to Alberta construction workers and later the RCMP's entry into the Peigan Reserve of the Piikani Nation highlighted the fragility of local political equilibrium. What began as the Lonefighters' public protest to raise awareness about the potential environmental impacts of a local water diversion project escalated into an occupation of a portion of their own reserve and a fight for local political legitimacy. In addition to irritating several elders' groups and the band council, the Lonefighters' activities compelled the RCMP's mobilization, leading to a potentially dangerous situation, and amplified provincial political resolve to end the dispute at all costs. Since the Lonefighters sought provincial retreat and return of the contested land, their claims of success must be reconsidered in light of the occupation's detrimental impact on local kinship relations. Adding insult to injury, the Piikani Band Council's legal success in a lawsuit launched against the Alberta government further catalyzed the resistant Lonefighters. In 2001 the Peigan were awarded $64.3 million. Moreover, an environmental impact assessment of the Oldman River Valley was agreed to, as was guaranteed Piikani participation in the Oldman Dam Hydro Project, the establishment of a joint provincial-Piikani committee on economic development initiatives, and the use of Piikani labour and resources for canal maintenance. Recent years have witnessed the healing of kinship ties, even though disputes surrounding the settlement money have further disrupted local social and economic development.

The Ipperwash case also reveals deep-seated internal divisions within the local Aboriginal community that complicated decision making and led to a violent – and tragic – confrontation in September 1995. In chapter 7 Lackenbauer and anthropologist Victor Gulewitsch re-examine the complex events leading up to and surrounding the death of Aboriginal activist Dudley George at Ipperwash in September 1995. This represented the culmination of a six-decade-long dispute between the Kettle and Stony Point First Nation, a splinter group declaring itself to be a distinct Stoney Point First Nation, and the federal and Ontario governments over former reserve lands sold and appropriated before and during the Second World War. The goal of the Stoney Pointer faction that occupied the army camp and then Ipperwash Provincial Park was to reclaim land, which its members believed was rightfully theirs. The second goal was to achieve First Nation status separate from the Kettle and Stony Point First Nation. Although internal divisions within the local Aboriginal community confused government decision making, the complicity of the Ontario Provincial Police in the death of protestor Dudley George generated unprecedented media inquiry and a provincial inquiry. The subsequent process of allocating responsibility for the tragedy placed the blame squarely on government officials and the police, downplayed competing Aboriginal relationships, and yielded an outcome that might imply the blockade was successful. In 2009 the province formally signed over control of Ipperwash Provincial Park to the Kettle and Stony Point

First Nation and will do the same with the former Camp Ipperwash lands once they are remediated. The Stoney Pointers have not been officially recognized as a distinct band, and the distinction between "Kettle Pointers" and "Stoney Pointers" remains, but the community seems to have bonded over the Ipperwash Inquiry's final recommendations and over the official transfer of the park, which will be environmentally protected and will remain sacred ground to be used recreationally by all local peoples.

If Ipperwash was a tragic success, the Gustafsen Lake standoff was an unmitigated failure for the self-proclaimed "Defenders of the Shuswap Nation." Concurrent to the events at Ipperwash during the summer of 1995, the conflict between the Defenders of the Shuswap Nation, who were seeking to establish sovereignty over the Gustafsen Lake/Ts'peten Sundance site, and the RCMP was front-page news. In chapter 8 religious studies scholar Nick Shrubsole and Lackenbauer discuss how the occupiers, who came from across North America, saw themselves as the rightful heirs to a Sundance site that had never been ceded by hereditary chiefs. Their explicit goals included investigations into general land transactions involving Aboriginal lands across Canada, a meeting with the queen to revisit treaty obligations, and guarantees that their religious freedom would be protected at the site. At no time did the Defenders of the Shuswap Nation enjoy the support of local First Nation leaders, who the occupiers consequently dismissed as sellouts to colonial authority. The occupation's leaders also failed to convince the media of their violent tactics' legitimacy, and federal officials refused to negotiate at gunpoint. A skilful government "smear campaign" and RCMP (and clandestine Canadian Forces) intimidation tactics achieved their desired effects, and the standoff ended without fatalities. Subsequent trial proceedings revealed that the occupiers failed to represent a united front, despite the strong rhetoric expressed during the confrontation, and that personal agendas clearly influenced the pretext and form of collective action. In the end, the occupiers did not succeed either in establishing their sovereignty over Gustafsen Lake or in protecting the Sundance site.

The outcome at Burnt Church (Esgenoôpetitj) does not lend itself to such a clear assessment. While the Ipperwash Inquiry was unfolding, the Supreme Court of Canada in 1999 affirmed the legitimacy of two treaties signed between the Mi'kmaq and British authorities in 1760 and 1761.[107] In chapter 9 Sarah J. King describes how the court's recognition of the Mi'kmaw treaty right to fish and earn an income prompted some Mi'kmaq at Burnt Church (Esgenoôpetitj), New Brunswick, to take immediately to the ocean. Non-Aboriginal commercial fishers were troubled by the threat that this appeared to represent to local resources – and to their own livelihoods. The two groups violently clashed, leading to altercations between commercial fishers and Mi'kmaw fishers and activists, the chasing and sinking of Aboriginal boats, and the arrest of Aboriginal fishers. Yet King carefully explains that what occurred was neither simply a blockade nor an occupation. Supported by other activists and Warriors who engaged the federal government on the waters of Miramichi Bay, Mi'kmaq blockaded roads and occupied lands and eventually signed an agreement allowing the federal government to regulate their fishery, much to some community members' dissatisfaction. Regardless of this controversial outcome, many people emphasized that by taking action as members of the physical and political landscape, insisting on participating in the fishery, and attempting to revitalize their community, the Mi'kmaq at Burnt Church (Esgenoôpetitj) experienced an important breakthrough – even if their hopes for a Mi'kmaq-managed fishery are not yet realized.

In chapter 10 Belanger chronicles two decades of blockades and occupations by members of the Mohawks of the Bay of Quinte near Kingston, Ontario. Led primarily by activist Shawn Brant, a small group of disaffected followers critical of the band council's strategy for engaging federal, provincial, and municipal officials blockaded railways and highways in protest. The protestors and the band council each proclaimed its actions to be an appropriate exercise of Mohawk sovereignty, but internal conflict undermined the political and social legitimacy of both sides. Starting slowly with small-scale marches and protests, Brant's actions frustrated band council members by threatening local economic interests, and he was consequently vilified as an unpredictable leader whose scattershot approach to civil disobedience challenged his outwardly sovereigntist claims. Direct action was not implemented with specific outcomes in mind, and little thought was given to its lasting impact. Finally, even though several actions and protests undertaken by the Bay of Quinte Mohawks overlapped with events unfolding at Caledonia, little camaraderie was evident between the various protest groups, and there was no attempt to foster extra-community partnerships. On one level, Brant and his followers accomplished little beyond alienating fellow community members and tarnishing the community's reputation. On a more analytical level, Belanger suggests that these protests could be considered breakthroughs, as local development of contested land was temporarily halted. Brant and his followers came to be seen as social and political outsiders and thus a threat to both First Nations and regional safety and stability. The events at Oka and Caledonia induced governments to purchase contested lands and address Aboriginal concerns; something that did not occur at Tyendinaga, and the protests only delayed existing – and compromised potential – land claims.

The final chapter, by Timothy Winegard, examines the events that began at Caledonia in 2006 when unarmed protestors from the Six Nations of the Grand River barricaded the entrance to a partially built subdivision. The issues surrounding this disputed land soon gave way to Aboriginal and non-Aboriginal protests that consumed the town of Caledonia and attracted intense media attention for more than three years. After various community groups formed, non-Caledonia residents and racially motivated outsiders took leadership of the non-Aboriginal protests, which became increasingly confrontational. Local business owners and residents watched helplessly in the shadow of a submissive OPP force as the governments of Canada and Ontario squabbled over jurisdiction. Journalists and other commentators questioned the application of a two-tiered policing system.[108] The blockade and civil unrest at Caledonia halted the subdivision's construction, and the province bought the disputed land with the intention of turning it over to the Six Nations. Nevertheless, protest and violence wrought by small opposing groups, without consensus or sweeping support from the majority of community members and leadership, came to overshadow the land claim and typify the situation at Caledonia. This may prove to be the enduring legacy of the dispute. Since the 1830s, the Six Nations and the residents of Caledonia had generally enjoyed a cordial relationship. Many inhabitants of both communities believe that the damage to this relationship will take generations to reconcile and heal. From this standpoint, the end did not justify the means. Perhaps most important, Winegard concedes, it seems that the general Canadian society is becoming increasingly disillusioned with Aboriginal barricades, while losing patience and faith with current government policy and its application.

NOTES

1 Debbie Abbott, in Standing Senate Committee on Aboriginal Peoples, *Negotiation or Confrontation: It's Canada's Choice*, final report, Senate, Ottawa, December 2006, iii–iv, 33–4. The British Columbia Specific Claims Committee is comprised of the Aboriginal Council of British Columbia,

the Union of BC Indian Chiefs, the Treaty 8 Tribal Association, the Nlaka'pamux Nation Tribal Council, and the Alliance of Tribal Nations. For their views, see Grand Chief Ken Malloway to Hon. Jim Prentice, 12 June 2006, http://gsdl.ubcic.bc.ca/collect/firstna1/import/BC%20 Specific%20Claims%20Committee%20(2007)/Digital%20Kit/Letter%20 from%20BCSCC%20to%20Minister%20Jim%20Prentice_June%20 2006.pdf.

2 Douglas Bland, in Jon Elmer, "Canada's Brewing Insurgency," *Al Jazeera*, 26 June 2010, http://english.aljazeera.net/focus/2010/06/ 20106238405246236.html.

3 John Borrows, "An Analysis of and Dialogue on Indigenous and Crown Blockades," in *Philosophy and Aboriginal Rights: Critical Dialogues*, ed. Sandra Tomsons and Lorraine Mayer, 101–23 (Toronto: Oxford University Press, 2013), 114.

4 Bill Curry, "Forces' Terror Manual Lists Natives with Hezbollah," *Globe and Mail*, 30 March 2007.

5 Douglas Bland, in Elmer, "Canada's Brewing Insurgency." See also Jorge Barrera, "Military to Say Sorry for Mohawk Inclusion in Counter-insurgency Manual," *APTN National News*, 7 December 2010, http://aptn. ca/news/2010/12/07/military-to-say-sorry-for-mohawk-inclusion-in-counter-insurgency-manual; and J.L. Granatstein, "No Need to Apologize," *The Dispatch: Quarterly Review of the Canadian Defence and Foreign Affairs Institute*, Spring 2011, 6–7.

6 Martell Thompson, in "Mohawk Warriors to Get Military Apology," *CBC News*, 21 December 2010, http://www.cbc.ca/news/canada/montreal/ story/2010/12/20/mohawk-military-apology.html.

7 Cheryl Jacobs, in Barrera, "Military to Say Sorry."

8 Douglas Bland, "Merely Stating the Obvious," *Ottawa Citizen*, 30 December 2010.

9 See generally Warren Skea, "The Canadian Newspaper Industry's Portrayal of the Oka Crisis," *Native Studies Review* 9, no. 1 (1994): 15–31; and Geoffrey York and Loreen Pindera, *People of the Pines: The Warriors and the Legacy of Oka* (Toronto: McArthur and Company, 1991).

10 There is a significant literature base at this stage even if it remains fairly scattered in terms of both its geographic and conceptual scope. See this book's selected bibliography as a starting point.

11 Sandra Tomson, in Borrows, "Analysis," 113.

12 Ibid., 101.

13 Nicholas Blomley, "'Shut the Province Down': First Nations Blockades in British Columbia, 1984–1995," *BC Studies* 111 (Autumn 1996): 5–35 at 11.

14  Ibid., 29.

15  Joanne Nagel, "American Indian Ethnic Renewal: Politics and the
    Resurgence of Identity," *American Sociological Review* 60, no. 6 (1995):
    947–65 at 957–8.

16  Blomley, "'Shut the Province Down,'" 17. See also Mark Anderson and
    Carmen Robertson, "The 'Bended Elbow' News, Kenora 1974: How a
    Small-Town Newspaper Promoted Colonization," *American Indian
    Quarterly* 31, no. 3 (Summer 2007): 410–40; Elizabeth Furniss, *The
    Burden of History: Colonialism and the Frontier Myth in a Rural
    Canadian Community* (Vancouver: UBC Press, 1999); and Skea,
    "Canadian Newspaper."

17  See generally Vine Deloria Jr, *Behind the Trail of Broken Treaties: An
    Indian Declaration of Independence* (New York: Dell, 1974); Charles
    Wilkinson, *Blood Struggle: The Rise of Modern Indian Nations*
    (New York: Norton, 2005), 139–43; and Paul Chaat Smith and Robert
    Allen Warrior, *Like a Hurricane: The Indian Movement from Alcatraz to
    Wounded Knee* (New York: New Press, 1996).

18  This figure is drawn from Ward Churchill, *Indians Are Us? Culture and
    Genocide in Native North America* (Monroe, ME: Common Courage,
    1991), 197–206. The most detailed treatment of this event is Peter
    Matthiessen, *In the Spirit of Crazy Horse: The Story of Leonard Peltier
    and the FBI's War on the American Indian Movement* (New York: Penguin,
    1992). See also Russell Means, *Where White Men Fear to Tread: The
    Autobiography of Russell Means* (New York: St Martin's Press, 1995);
    Ward Churchill and Jim Vander Wall, *Agents of Repression: The FBI's
    Secret War against the Black Panther Party and the American Indian
    Movement* (Boston, MA: South End, 1990); and Smith and Warrior, *Like
    a Hurricane*.

19  See Sally Weaver, *Making Canadian Indian Policy: The Hidden Agenda,
    1968–79* (Toronto: University of Toronto Press, 1981).

20  Ibid. See also Harold Cardinal, *The Unjust Society: The Tragedy of
    Canada's Indians* (Edmonton: Hurtig, 1969).

21  For this argument, see Yale D. Belanger and David R. Newhouse,
    "Reconciling Solitudes: A Critical Analysis of the Self-Government Ideal,"
    in *Aboriginal Self-Government in Canada: Current Trends and Issues*, ed.
    Yale D. Belanger, 1–19 (Saskatoon: Purich, 2008); Yale D. Belanger and
    David R. Newhouse, "Emerging from the Shadows: The Pursuit of
    Aboriginal Self-Government to Promote Aboriginal Well-Being," *Canadian
    Journal of Native Studies* 24, no. 1 (2004): 129–222; and David R.
    Newhouse, Kevin Fitzmaurice, and Yale D. Belanger, *Creating a Seat at the*

*Table: Aboriginal Programming at Canadian Heritage – A Retrospective Study for Canadian Heritage* (Ottawa: Canadian Heritage, 2005).

22 See, for example, Peter McFarlane, *Brotherhood to Nationhood: George Manuel and the Making of the Modern Indian Movement* (Toronto: Between the Lines, 1993); George Manuel and Michael Posluns, *The Fourth World: An Indian Reality* (Toronto: Collier Macmillan Canada, 1974); Harold Cardinal, *The Rebirth of Canada's Indians* (Edmonton: Hurtig, 1977); and Cardinal, *Unjust Society*. It is notable that Cardinal does not see through this smokescreen.

23 Pierre Elliott Trudeau, in Ron Graham, ed., *The Essential Trudeau* (Toronto: McClellend and Stewart, 1998), 16–20.

24 Christa Scholtz, "Negotiating Claims: Recognition, Citizenship, and the Emergence of Indigenous Land Claim Negotiation Policies in Australia, Canada, New Zealand, and the United States" (PhD diss., Princeton University, 2004), 66.

25 Joanne Nagel, *American Indian Ethnic Renewal: Red Power and the Resurgence of Identity and Culture* (New York: Oxford University Press, 1997).

26 Royal Commission on Aboriginal Peoples, *Partners in Confederation* (Ottawa: Canada Communications Group, 1993).

27 Robert A. Williams, *Linking Arms Together: American Indian Treaty Visions of Law and Peace, 1600–1800* (New York: Routledge, 1999), 59.

28 J.R. Miller, *Compact, Covenant, Contract: Aboriginal Treaty-Making in Canada* (Toronto: University of Toronto Press, 2009).

29 E. Brian Titley, *A Narrow Vision: Duncan Campbell Scott and the Administration of Indian Affairs in Canada* (Vancouver: UBC Press, 1986).

30 See generally John Leslie and Ron Maguire, *The Historical Development of the Indian Act* (Ottawa: Treaties and Historical Research Centre, Department of Indian Affairs and Northern Development, 1978); and John Goikas, "The Indian Act: Evolution, Overview, and Options for the Amendment and Transition," in *For Seven Generations: An Information Legacy of the Royal Commission on Aboriginal Peoples*, ed. Royal Commission on Aboriginal Peoples, CD-ROM (Ottawa: Canada Communications Group, 1996).

31 See generally J.R. Miller, *Shingwauk's Vision* (Toronto: University of Toronto Press, 1998); and John S. Milloy, *"A National Crime": The Canadian Government and the Residential School System, 1879–1986* (Winnipeg: University of Manitoba Press, 1999).

32 There is substantial scholarly material examining the evolution of Aboriginal organizing in Canada that demonstrates most organizational

leaders were cognizant of how their actions and political agendas would be perceived by Canadian politicians and therefore crafted their agendas carefully so as not to risk alienating government officials, while also ensuring their access to key policymakers and politicians. For an overview of the literature and how Indian leaders of the late nineteenth and early twentieth centuries responded to government oppression, see Yale D. Belanger, "Seeking a Seat at the Table: A Brief History of Indian Political Organizing in Canada, 1870–1951" (PhD diss., Trent University, 2006).

33  Michel Foucault, in Paul Rabinow, ed., *The Foulcault Reader: An Introduction to Foulcault's Thought* (London: Penguin, 1991).

34  James Tully, *Strange Multiplicity: Constitutionalism in an Age of Diversity* (New York: Cambridge University Press, 1995), 23.

35  David A. Rossiter, "The Nature of Protest: Constructing the Spaces of British Columbia's Rainforests," *Cultural Geographies* 11 (2004): 139–64. See also David A. Rossiter and Patricia K. Wood, "Fantastic Topographies: Neo-liberal responses to Aboriginal Land Claims in British Columbia," *Canadian Geographer* 49, no. 4 (2005): 352–66. For a discussion of the role of epistemology in guiding our understanding of our environment and historical interface with others, see Vine Deloria Jr, *God Is Red: A Native View of Religion* (Golden, CO: Fulcrum, 1994); Sakej Youngblood Henderson, "*Ayukpachi*: Empowering Aboriginal Thought," in *Reclaiming Indigenous Voice and Vision*, ed. Marie Battiste, 248–78 (Vancouver: UBC Press, 2000); and Yale D. Belanger, "Epistemological Distinctiveness and the Use of 'Guided History' Methodology in Writing Native Histories," *Indigenous Nations Studies Journal* 2, no. 2 (Fall 2001): 15–36.

36  Mike Mitchell, in Mort Ransen, *You Are on Indian Land* (Ottawa: National Film Board of Canada, 1969).

37  See E. Palmer Patterson, "Andrew Paull and the Canadian Indian Resurgence" (PhD diss., University of Washington, 1962); Paul Tennant, *Aboriginal Peoples and Politics: The Native Land Question in British Columbia, 1849–1989* (Vancouver: UBC Press, 1990); J.R. Miller, "Petitioning the Great White Mother: First Nations' Organizations and Lobbying in London," in *Reflections on Native-Newcomer Relations*, ed. J.R. Miller, 217–41 (Toronto: University of Toronto Press, 2004); Keith Thor Carlson, "Rethinking Dialogue and History: The King's Promise and the 1906 Aboriginal Delegation to London," *Native Studies Review* 16, no. 2 (2005): 1–38.

38  Howard Ramos, "What Causes Canadian Aboriginal Protest? Examining Resources, Opportunities and Identity, 1951–2000," *Canadian Journal of Sociology* 31, no. 2 (2006): 211–34 at 226, 212n3.

39 Rima Wilkes, "A Systematic Approach to Studying Indigenous Politics: Band-Level Mobilization in Canada, 1981–2000," *Social Science Journal* 41, no. 3 (2004): 447–57.

40 Borrows, "Analysis," 104.

41 James Scott, *Domination and the Arts of Resistance* (New Haven, CT: Yale University Press, 1990).

42 Dorinne Kondo, *About Face: Performing Race in Fashion and Theater* (London: Routeledge, 1997).

43 Peter Pearson, *Encounter with Saul Alinsky – Part 2: Rama Indian Reserve* (Ottawa: National Film Board of Canada, 1967).

44 Saul D. Alinsky, *Rules for Radicals: A Practical Primer for Realistic Radicals* (New York: Vintage, 1972), 148.

45 Pearson, *Encounter with Saul Alinsky.*

46 Ransen, *You Are on Indian Land.*

47 J.W.E. Newberry, *The Spirit of Indian Protest* (Canadian Association in Support of the Native Peoples, 1975).

48 York and Pindera, *People of the Pines*; Alanis Obomsawin, *Kanesatake: 270 years of Resistance* (Ottawa: National Film Board of Canada, 1993).

49 Borrows, "Analysis"; John Borrows, "Crown and Aboriginal Occupations of Land: A History and Comparison," paper prepared for the Ipperwash Inquiry, 15 October 2005, http://www.attorneygeneral.jus.gov.on.ca/inquiries/ipperwash/policy_part/research/index.html.

50 Leanne Simpson and Kiera L. Ladner, eds, *This Is an Honour Song: Twenty Years since the Blockades* (Winnipeg: Arbeiter Ring, 2010).

51 Peter H. Russell, "Oka to Ipperwash: The Necessity of Flashpoint Events," in Simpson and Ladner, eds, *This Is an Honour Song*, 29–46.

52 Ravi de Costa and Tristan Knight, "Asymmetric Encounters in Native Canada," *American Review of Canadian Studies* 41, no. 3 (2011): 212–27.

53 Laura Devries, *Conflict in Caledonia: Aboriginal Land Rights and the Rule of Law* (Vancouver: UBC Press, 2011). See also John Ralston Saul, *A Fair Country: Telling Truths about Canada* (Toronto: Viking Canada, 2008).

54 Blomley, "'Shut the Province Down,'" 29.

55 Nagel, "American Indian Ethnic Renewal," 957–8.

56 Gail Guthrie Valaskakis, *Indian Country: Essays on Contemporary Native Culture* (Waterloo, ON: Wilfrid Laurier University Press), 39. See also Libby R. Tronnes, "'Where Is John Wayne'? The Menominee Warriors Society, Indian Militancy, and Social Unrest during the Alexian Brothers Novitiate Takeover," *American Indian Quarterly* 26, no. 4 (Fall 2002): 526–58 at 541.

57 Valaskakis, *Indian Country*, 36.

58  Taiaiake Alfred and Lana Lowe, "Warrior Societies in Contemporary
    Indigenous Communities," paper prepared for the Ipperwash Inquiry,
    May 2005, 13, 36, http://www.attorneygeneral.jus.gov.on.ca/inquiries/
    ipperwash/policy_part/research/index.html.
59  Akwesasne resident and author Douglas George-Kanentiio is unflinching
    in this assessment. See Douglas M. George-Kanentiio, *Iroquois on Fire:
    A Voice from the Mohawk Nation* (Lincoln: University of Nebraska Press,
    2008). See also John C. Thompson, "The Long Fall of the Mohawk
    Warriors," paper for the Mackenzie Institute for the Study of Terrorism,
    Revolution and Propaganda, Toronto, 2006, http://www.numberswatchdog.
    com/THE%20LONG%20FALL%20OF%20THE%20MOHAW%20
    WARRIORS.htm; and Rick Hornung, *One Nation under the Gun*
    (Toronto: Stoddart, 1991).
60  Scholtz, "Negotiating Claims," 23.
61  Kiera L. Ladner, "Negotiated Inferiority: The Royal Commission on
    Aboriginal People's Vision of a Renewed Relationship," *American Review
    of Canadian Studies* 31, nos 1–2 (2001): 241–64.
62  See Lynette Russell, "Settler Nation: Contemporary Constructions and
    Visual Expressions of Australian National Identity," paper presented at the
    Second Annual Conference of the International Social Theory Consortium,
    University of Sussex, 5–7 July 2001.
63  Alan Cairns, *Citizens Plus: Aboriginal Peoples and the Canadian State*
    (Vancouver: UBC Press, 2000), 98.
64  Furniss, *Burden of History*, 18. See also P. Whitney Lackenbauer,
    "Vanishing Indian, Vanishing Military: Military Training and Aboriginal
    Lands in the Twentieth Century" (PhD diss., University of Calgary, 2004).
65  Leroy Little Bear, "Jagged Worldviews Collide," in *Reclaiming Indigenous
    Voice and Vision*, ed. Marie Battiste, 77–85 (Vancouver: UBC Press, 2000);
    Leroy Little Bear, "Aboriginal Relationships to Land and Resources," in
    *Sacred Lands: Aboriginal World Views, Claims, and Conflicts*, ed. Jill
    Oakes et al., 15–20 (Edmonton: Canadian Circumpolar Institute, 1998);
    Leroy Little Bear, *Discussion* (Calgary: Glenbow Museum, 1995), 7;
    Leroy Little Bear, "Relationship of Aboriginal People to the Land and the
    Aboriginal Perspective on Aboriginal Title," in *For Seven Generations:
    An Information Legacy of the Royal Commission on Aboriginal Peoples*,
    ed. Royal Commission on Aboriginal Peoples, CD-ROM (Ottawa: Canada
    Communications Group, 1996), cited in Royal Commission on Aboriginal
    Peoples, *Treaty Making in the Spirit of Co-Existence: An Alternative to
    Extinguishment* (Ottawa: Canada Communications Group, 1994).

66  J.R. Miller, *Lethal Legacy: Current Native Controversies in Canada*
    (Toronto: McClelland and Stewart, 2004), 280.

67  Ibid., 281–2.

68  Taiaiake Alfred, *Wasáse: Indigenous Pathways of Action and Freedom*
    (Toronto: University of Toronto Press, 2005). In the United States, Ward
    Churchill is perhaps best known for his aggressive stance and calls to arms.

69  *Calder v. British Columbia (Attorney General)* [1973] SCR 313.

70  *R. v. Sparrow* [1990] 1 SCR 1075. See W.I.C. Binnie, "The Sparrow
    Doctrine: Beginning of the End of the Beginning," *Queen's Law Journal* 15
    (1990): 217–53; and Andrea Bowker, "*Sparrow*'s Promise: Aboriginal
    Rights in the B.C. Court of Appeal," *University of Toronto Faculty of Law
    Review* 53, no. 1 (1995): 1–48.

71  *R. v. Marshall (No. 1)* [1999] 3 SCR 456. See J.R. Miller, "History, the
    Courts and Treaty Policy: Lessons from Marshall and Nisga'a," in
    *Aboriginal Policy Research: Setting the Agenda for Change*, ed. Jerry P.
    White, Paul Maxim, and Dan Beavon, vol. 1, 29–44 (Toronto: Thompson
    Educational, 2004).

72  *Taku River Tlingit First Nation v. Ringstad*; and *Haida First Nation v. BC*.
    For a detailed discussion outlining the specific details of the movement of
    these two cases from the BC Provincial Court to the Supreme Court of
    Canada, see Michael Lee Ross, *First Nations Sacred Sites in Canada's
    Courts* (Vancouver: UBC Press, 2005).

73  *Mitchell v. Peguis Indian Band* [1990] 2 SCR 85. See Kent McNeil, "Self-
    Government and the Inalienability of Aboriginal Title," *McGill Law
    Journal* 47, no. 3 (2002): 473–510 at 478–9.

74  *Guerin v. The Queen* [1984] 3 SCR 335. See James I. Reynolds, *A Breach
    of Duty: Fiduciary Obligations and Aboriginal Peoples* (Saskatoon: Purich,
    2005). Two East Coast cases have upheld the provisions of a 1761 treaty
    enabling Mi'kmaw fishers to obtain a livelihood through the sale of their
    annual catch and recognizing the right of Native people in New Brunswick
    to log Crown lands. For an excellent historical overview of the meaning of
    the treaties to the Mi'kmaq, see William C. Wicken, *Mi'Kmaq Treaties on
    Trial: History, Land, and Donald Marshall Junior* (Toronto: University of
    Toronto Press, 2002). See also *R. v. Sappier; R. v. Gray* [2006] 2 SCR 686.

75  Yale D. Belanger, *Ways of Knowing: An Introduction to Native Studies in
    Canada*, 2nd ed. (Toronto: Thompson Nelson, 2014), 78–9.

76  Bradford W. Morse, "Permafrost Rights: Aboriginal Self-Government and
    the Supreme Court in *R. v. Pamajewon*," *McGill Law Journal* 42, no. 4
    (1997): 1012–32.

77 Alfred and Lowe, "Warrior Societies," 3.

78 Blomley, "'Shut the Province Down,'" 24.

79 C. Radha Jhappan, "Indian Symbolic Politics: The Double-Edged Sword of Publicity," *Canadian Ethnic Studies* 22, no. 3 (1990): 19–39 at 35.

80 Dale Turner, *This Is Not A Peace Pipe: Toward a Critical Indigenous Philosophy* (Toronto: University of Toronto Press, 2006), 73.

81 See, for example, Alfred and Lowe, "Warrior Societies," 56.

82 Valaskakis, *Indian Country*, 37.

83 Blomley, "'Shut the Province Down,'" 16.

84 Bruce D'Arcus, "Contested Boundaries: Native Sovereignty and State Power at Wounded Knee, 1973," *Political Geography* 22, no. 4 (2003): 415–37 at 419.

85 Steven E. Silvern, "Scales of Justice: Law, American Indian Treaty Rights and the Political Construction of Scale," *Political Geography* 18, no. 6 (1999): 639–68 at 641.

86 Borrows, "Crown and Aboriginal Occupations," 4.

87 Jhappan, "Indian Symbolic Politics," 23.

88 Scholtz, "Negotiating Claims," 11, 23–4.

89 Alfred and Lowe, "Warrior Societies," 44.

90 Scholtz, "Negotiating Claims," 58–9.

91 Leslie A. Pal, *Beyond Policy Analysis: Public Issue Management in Turbulent Times* (Scarborough, ON: Nelson Education, 1997), 20–1.

92 Stephen Brooks, *Canadian Democracy: An Introduction*, 4th ed. (Toronto: Oxford University Press, 2004), 95–7.

93 See, for example, the research papers commissioned by the Ipperwash Inquiry at http://www.attorneygeneral.jus.gov.on.ca/inquiries/ipperwash/policy_part/research/index.html.

94 Don Clairmont and Jim Potts, "For the Nonce: Policing and Aboriginal Occupations and Protests," paper prepared for the Ipperwash Inquiry, May 2006, 9–10, http://www.attorneygeneral.jus.gov.on.ca/inquiries/ipperwash/policy_part/research/index.html.

95 Ken Coates, "The Peaceful Struggle of Canada's First Nations," *The Mark*, 21 September 2010, http://pioneers.themarknews.com/articles/2476-the-peaceful-struggle-of-canadas-first-nations/#.UwfQVP2A2oo.

96 Alfred and Lowe, "Warrior Societies," 35. For an extreme example, see Kloi, "War against the Machines," *Redwire Magazine*, October 2007, 10–11. *Redwire Magazine* is produced by a Native youth media society funded by the federal Department of Canadian Heritage, and although the editor distances himself from Kloi's message, which is "deemed illegal by our enemies, agents of the Canadian colonial police state," the article

asserts that corporations and governments have conspired to destroy Mother Earth for profit. "It is up to us to take back some of this power and control and use it for good," Kloi urges young Aboriginal readers. "We can start by waging war against the machines," striking out at industrial targets using "smart, modern warfare tactics and strategies." These sabotage operations – from road spiking to blockades to destroying bridges and power lines – would perpetuate "a long history of proud warrior histories."

97  Rudy Platiel, in Blomley, "'Shut the Province Down,'" 15.

98  Scholtz, "Negotiating Claims," 58–9.

99  Christopher Alcantara, "Explaining Aboriginal Treaty Negotiation Outcomes in Canada: The Cases of the Inuit and the Innu in Labrador," *Canadian Journal of Political Science* 40, no. 1 (2007): 185–207 at 202.

100  W.A. Gamson and G. Wolfsfeld, "Movements and Media as Interacting Systems," *Annals of the American Academy of Political and Social Science* 528 (1993): 114–25 at 119.

101  See A. Khaki and K. Prasad, *Depictions and Perceptions: Native Indians and Visible Minorities in the Media* (Vancouver: Page Master Services, 1988); and M. Grenier, *Critical Studies in Mass Media* (Toronto: Butterworth, 1992). The Royal Commission's final report, for example, discussed the harm caused by "misinformation, sweeping generalizations, and galling stereotypes," which tend to produce fearful images related to Native people, land, and resource issues. Royal Commission on Aboriginal Peoples, *Final Report*, 5 vols., Ottawa, 2006, vol. 3, 623, 634. See also Sandra Lambertus, *Wartime Images, Peacetime Wounds: The Media and the Gustafsen Lake Standoff* (Toronto: University of Toronto Press, 2004), 5.

102  Gamson and Wolfsfeld, "Movements and Media," 116–17.

103  For example, some Aboriginal groups have successfully used the media to attract sympathetic international attention to their cause, thus striking at the "Achilles heel" of Canada's reputation as a good international citizen. Andrew F. Cooper and P. Whitney Lackenbauer, "The Achilles Heel of Canadian Good International Citizenship: Indigenous Diplomacies and State Responses in the Twentieth Century," *Canadian Foreign Policy Journal* 13, no. 3 (2007): 99–119. Ronald Niezen in particular has identified how the Quebec Cree used the "politics of embarrassment" to generate public sympathy and stymie major provincial hydro-electric projects. See, for example, Ronald Niezen, *Defending the Land: Sovereignty and Forest Life in James Bay Cree Society* (Boston, MA: Allyn and Bacon, 1998); and Ronald Niezen, "Recognizing Indigenism: Canadian Unity

and the International Movement of Indigenous Peoples," *Comparative Studies in Society and History* 42, no. 1 (2000): 119–48. See also Noel Castree, "Differential Geographies: Place, Indigenous Rights and 'Local' Resources," *Political Geography* 23, no. 2 (2004): 133–67.

104 Gamson and Wolfsfeld, "Movements and Media," 123.

105 On this strategy, see Timothy Winegard, *Oka: A Convergence of Cultures and the Canadian Forces* (Kingston: Canadian Defence Academy Press, 2008).

106 See Simpson and Ladner, eds, *This Is an Honour Song*.

107 See Wicken, *Mi'kmaq Treaties on Trial*; and Ken Coates, *The Marshall Decision and Native Rights* (Montreal and Kingston: McGill-Queen's University Press, 2000).

108 See, for example, Christie Blatchford, *Helpless: Caledonia's Nightmare of Fear and Anarchy, and How the Law Failed All of Us* (Toronto: Doubleday Canada, 2010).

I

# Point Pelee's Summer of Discontent

JOHN SANDLOS

The trouble began at Point Pelee in the late spring of 1922, at the end of the seasonal songbird migration that has made this national park in southwestern Ontario so famous. In early June, a group of fifteen Chippewa people from the Caldwell First Nation moved to a small cabin at the edge of the park boundary and declared that they were reclaiming the area as their reserve. If this move did not provide enough difficulty for Park Superintendent Forest Conover, a rumour had spread throughout the region that an additional 1,500 Native people from the surrounding area were set to march on the park to bolster the strength of the park occupation. By 9 June, Constable E.G. Weeks of the Royal Canadian Mounted Police (RCMP) had arrived to investigate and discuss the situation with the protestors. According to Constable Weeks, one of the Native leaders at the site, John Dodge, claimed that his unregistered Caldwell Band had never signed a treaty surrendering Point Pelee and had a well-documented claim to the park and surrounding area (including Pelee Island). According to Dodge, the rest of the band of 300 Natives, currently dispersed throughout the region surrounding Point Pelee, would arrive at the park in the next week and take up permanent residency within. Constable Weeks reported that the situation was tense: Dodge may have presented the planned occupation in a nonthreatening manner, but undoubtedly "the Band would resent any interference with their taking up residence within the Park." For Dodge, the planned occupation of the park was meant to draw attention to the specific land claim issue and also the general poor treatment of the band at the hands of the government.[1]

These events represent only the beginning of the Caldwell First Nation's attempt to occupy an area close to the boundary of Point Pelee National

Park, but the story is already unique in many ways. Amid the recent spate of historical literature devoted to the exclusion of Native people from national parks and other forms of protected areas in North America, not one study has traced an attempt by Native people to occupy a national park or protected area as an overt protest strategy prior to the Second World War. In general, historians have uncovered examples where Native (and non-Native) groups expelled from parks and protected areas have challenged state authority using tactics resembling E.P. Thompson's concept of the moral economy among the British rural underclass or James Scott's "everyday forms of resistance" within peasant societies.[2] Accordingly, illegal acts such as poaching, timber theft, and setting forest fires were not acts of ignorant law breaking (as the authorities of the day viewed them) but often represented a persistent and deeply rooted critique of arbitrary state authority in rural and hinterland regions.[3] A plan to occupy a national park might be similar to these everyday forms of protest in its basic challenge to state authority, but as a protest tactic it more closely resembles occupations and blockades that we associate with Native activism in the United States after the civil rights era, beginning with the Alcatraz and Wounded Knee standoffs in the early 1970s.[4] Although it is easy to dismiss the Point Pelee occupation as an isolated case (one that largely failed in its short-term goals, as we shall see), it does reveal that more recent standoffs in Canada, such as Temagami, Oka, Gustafsen Lake, the tragic Ipperwash Provincial Park protest, and Caledonia, have at least some historical precedent prior to the Second World War. The Point Pelee case also suggests that at least one Native group did employ a diverse array of protest strategies beyond the rubric of everyday resistance. In addition, subsequent events at Point Pelee, including police mobilization, the publication of sensational media articles that ultimately denigrated the protests, and the inability of Native leaders to mobilize their band in support of the protest, provide some possible clues as to why park occupations remained extremely rare until the more recent past.

The Caldwell First Nation's claim to Point Pelee National Park (and Pelee Island) was rooted in occupancy of the area that most likely began shortly after the general spread of Chippewa groups (alternatively Anishanaabeg or Ojibwa) into the far southwestern region of Ontario in 1701, when a treaty brought peaceful relations with the Haudenosaunee.[5] The precise date of settlement is unknown, but scattered records suggest Native occupation as early as the 1730s.[6] Certainly, the Caldwell First Nation occupied Point Pelee by the time the British Crown and local chiefs from the Chippewa, Ottawa, Pottawatomi, and Huron Nations signed Treaty 2 in 1790. This agreement ceded to the Crown a huge swath of land from just east of London to Windsor and Amherstberg in the west in exchange for £1,200 in cash payments and several small reserves. However, the chiefs from Point Pelee – Quineseas Caldwell and Midwayosh Caldwell – did not attend the signing ceremony and did not agree to any cession of land. Moreover, the British authorities had apparently promised the Caldwell Band formal title to Point Pelee and Pelee Island as a reward for their military role in the War of 1812.[7] By the 1830s, as non-Native settlers began to crowd into the region, the Crown assumed that the land had been surrendered. Over the next three decades, increasing settlement on Point Pelee had largely forced the Caldwell First Nation off its land, with Chief William Caldwell claiming that most of his people had moved on because the whites had "misused" them. As early as 1861 only five Native families continued to live at Point Pelee; the rest had dispersed to reserves and townships in the surrounding area.[8]

Despite this diaspora, the Caldwell Band leaders continually pressed their claim to Point Pelee and Pelee Island throughout the 1880s and 1890s. In 1881 Chief William Caldwell wrote directly to Prime Minister John A. Macdonald on the matter, but his petition was quickly rejected.[9] By 1884 Indian Affairs had adopted a policy that the Caldwell Band should accept the department's offer of land on the Walpole Island Reserve in the St Clair River or be left to its own devices.[10] The band leaders thought the Walpole Island lands would be wet and unhealthy for their people and continued to press the claim to Point Pelee.[11] In 1892 Chief Robert Caldwell produced pamphlets for federal members of Parliament informing them of his people's claim to Point Pelee and Pelee Island.[12] Three years later, Duncan Campbell Scott, the acting assistant deputy of Indian affairs, attempted to grant the Caldwell Band a block of farmland on Point Pelee adjacent to the non-Native farmers, in addition to a portion of the marshlands, in return for the surrender of Pelee Island.[13] Scott's superiors rejected his proposal due to the purported high cost of the land and because much of the proposed marshland tract had been leased to the South Essex Gun Club for hunting purposes.[14] At the end of the century, the Caldwell Band remained without a home, dispersed among the small reserves and non-Native communities in the surrounding area.

Ironically, Point Pelee's newer non-Native settlers also retained only the most tenuous claim to the land they had inhabited. In 1799 the federal government designated much of the point as a naval reserve and did not officially recognize the claims of the Pelee squatters to their homesteads until 1881.[15] Despite obtaining formal title to their lands, the creation of the national park in 1918 brought severe consequences for the local economy of the squatters. Although their lands were not included in the park, the federal government convinced its provincial counterpart to designate private lands outside the park as a game preserve, thus prohibiting muskrat trapping – an important source of income for the homesteaders – anywhere within Point Pelee's marshes. At the same time, the federal Parks Branch allowed members of a local hunting club, the Essex County Wildlife Association (descendant of the aforementioned Essex Gun Club), to hunt ducks in the park. The conflict between the sport hunting and homesteading factions was intense – so much so that vague death threats were directed at Park Superintendent Forest Conover. Even after the Parks Branch recognized the contradictory nature of its policy and allowed muskrat hunting in 1920, a debate rife with overtones of class conflict continued unabated among the trappers and sport hunters. By the time of the occupation in 1922, Point Pelee was already a powder keg of competing interests in the local landscape.[16] Indeed, one police report speculated that it was actually the settlers who were encouraging the Native claim to the park because "they resent the Government's action to prohibit shooting & trapping on the Park property."[17]

The idea for an organized protest at Point Pelee originated at a meeting of the Caldwell Band held on 14 March 1922 at Alvinston under the leadership of Chief Moses Caldwell (likely a hereditary chief, as Sergeant A. Birtwistle of the RCMP claimed he was never elected). Here the band discussed the details of its 35,000 acre claim on Point Pelee and agreed to meet at the park close to 15 May. The band ultimately failed to converge on this date, apparently because of "matters concerning the commissary department and finances."[18] Chief Caldwell arrived at Point Pelee on 20 May and waited in vain for more members of the band to arrive. On 12 June, however, the local press reported that nineteen Native families had moved to an area near the park boundary and were camped under the leadership of Archibald (Archie) Dodge (although this number may have been exaggerated, as police reports suggested there were only nineteen individuals). More important, local rumours began to spread that a much larger band had been sighted at Leamington and Wheatley, within a day's march of Point Pelee. The local press declared that the "invasion" of Point Pelee by a force of 300 "Petawba Indians" from Walpole Island and Alvinston was "momentarily expected."[19]

The relevant authorities – the Parks Branch, Indian Affairs, and the police – were clearly determined to prevent any further protests as rumours of the impending Native occupation and the actual number of families camped at Point Pelee began to escalate. In part, authorities such as Superintendent Conover were concerned that the Pelee protest might be an extension of "troubles" that had occurred two weeks earlier on the nearby Brantford Six Nations Reserve. According to local and international press reports, reserve residents pelted local court officials with "missiles" in defiance of an eviction order against a local "squatter" named Vyse, asserting the right of the local First Nations government to control the dispensation of leases for reserve land.[20] To prevent similar problems from erupting at Point Pelee, James Harkin, the commissioner of national parks, ordered Superintendant Conover to reject the Caldwell Band's claim to the park and to designate any Natives who entered the park as trespassers.[21] Duncan Campbell Scott, the now deputy superintendant of Indian affairs, similarly dismissed the grievances of the Caldwell Band and wasted little time requesting a heavy RCMP presence "to prevent trespass on the park and to have the Indians dispersed."[22] A.W. Duffus, the commanding officer for the RCMP's Western Ontario District, quickly dispatched four officers to guard the park. Although Duffus played down sensational press reports about the severity of the occupation, he emphasized that police were ready to quell any disturbance that might arise, suggesting he could mobilize eighteen officers within eight hours if need be.[23] At the actual site of the protest, the police officer in charge, Sergeant A. Birtwistle, threatened the Natives residing at the edge of the park in no uncertain terms: "if there were trouble between your tribe and the Canadian Government," he declared, "I can assure you that it would not be to your advantage." If such a firm police presence was not enough to quell the disturbance, two local First World War veterans, Major M.B. Twomey and Colonel William T. Gregory, offered to raise an armed force of 2,000 militia to meet the Native invasion force head on.[24]

In retrospect, the offer of a military contingent was more akin to breaking a butterfly on a wheel than it was a rational response to the prospect of conflict at Point Pelee. No large contingent of Native protestors ever arrived at the point. As the police gathered evidence, they quickly dismissed as an unfounded rumour the notion that a large contingent of Natives was marching purposefully along the rural back roads of southern Ontario toward a standoff at the national park.[25] In addition, the police emphasized the relative quiet of the protest at the park boundary, its apparent lack of popular appeal, and its origins as the work of a few so-called troublemakers. After the initial few days of heightened concern, the police reports repeatedly suggested that all was calm at Point Pelee. Only two families, Jackson Dodge's and John Dodge's, had settled into a rental shack on the property of the homesteader James Grub. To the eyes of patrolling RCMP officers, the Grub property was hardly a hotbed for radical political activity, as the women wove baskets from black ash to sell and the older children worked in nearby onion fields.[26]

Despite the relative quiet, the police immediately set about investigating whether the Pelee protest was the product of broader Native discontent in the region. Throughout the summer, officers patrolled surrounding reserves to assess levels of support among local Native communities for the Pelee group. On 13 June, Sergeant Birtwistle travelled to the Walpole Island Reserve (one possible point of origin for the march, as some members of the itinerant Caldwell Band resided there) and reported that the Pelee protest was solely the work of the Dodge families and Chief Moses Caldwell. According to Birtwistle, the Walpole Island people regarded Caldwell as a "regular old trouble maker" who, having been deposed as chief of his nontreaty band in an election, was using the protest to regain the support of his people. The Dodges, in turn, were just "roving non-treaty Indians" who locals referred to as "scabs." Birtwistle went to great pains to demonstrate that the Walpole Island people did not support the Pelee protests, even checking the minutes of the band council meetings for any relevant references or plans. He concluded that "there is not an Indian on the Reserve who is the least interested or connected with this claim to Point Pelee, [and] they all appear to be highly amused over the affair and the stir that it has caused."[27] The premise of Birtwistle's report is somewhat questionable: unlike the dispersed Caldwell Band, the residents of Walpole Island already had a reserve and maintained no direct interest in the issue. However, a subsequent police report reiterated the same theme, emphasizing that there was no widespread support for the Pelee claim on other reserves in the region.[28]

The RCMP nevertheless remained cautious and concerned that the very small protest at Point Pelee might expand into a much broader demonstration. At the end of June, Chief Caldwell moved to the site again, and police took this as a sign that families would arrive soon from Walpole Island to settle permanently near the park boundary.[29] At the same time, Jackson Dodge, who resided only intermittently near the park due to frequent medical treatments in London to mitigate the effects of being gassed in France with the Canadian Expeditionary Force, claimed that a large group of Caldwell Band members would arrive soon from Alvinston to take up lands adjacent to the park. The police and park officials continued to patrol the park and surrounding area throughout the end of June as local rumours continued to circulate that the larger Caldwell Band and its supporters were somewhere marching toward the park in search of trouble.[30] There was, however, no influx of new protestors throughout the summer months. According to the police, the Dodge family members continued to make baskets and work the onion fields as the summer faded into autumn. By the middle of October, both the Dodge families and Moses Caldwell had moved on.[31]

Tensions in the local area likely remained high throughout the summer because the Canadian and American press descended on the region and began to produce sensational reports on the potential for a standoff in the park. On 15 June the *Ottawa Morning Journal* reported that, even though no large band of protestors was on the roads leading to Point Pelee, Sergeant Birtwistle would soon "demand a showdown when he meets the chief and leading members of the tribe there [at Wallaceburg] today." Contrary to police reports on the situation, the article claimed that the RCMP were bracing for the protestors to begin their "pilgrimage" and that the meeting was called to "bring matters to a head and decide the question once and for all."[32] Another clipping from the police case file suggests falsely that on 18 June the protestors already at Point Pelee had "seized the twelve square miles of government park land," while "somewhere on the road between the Walpole Island Reserve and Leamington, marches the main body of the Petawabas [*sic*], led by their chief, for whom the police were waiting." The article concludes with an image of a looming battle, claiming potential bloodshed as police reinforcements flooded in from Toronto to confront the protestors and evict them from the park.[33] The most outrageous account of the rumoured standoff was printed in the American socialist newspaper the *New York Call*. The article claimed that the entire Native population of the reserves at Alvinston and Walpole Island, led by Chief Moses Caldwell and John Dodge, were somewhere on the rural back roads and marching on the park. Invoking the image of Tecumseh (seemingly unaware that he was a British ally during the War of 1812), the paper produced an overexcited account of a Native army on its way to fight government forces for possession of Point Pelee, all the more remarkable because it ran completely counter to the reality of the situation:

> It is a different kind of "invasion" from that remembered by old
> residents here. There has been no beating of drums, war paint,
> and stealthy marauding. The Indians are coming down the roads,

straggling along, obediently obeying the instructions of a squad of
mounted police and minding the government's official order
against entering Point Pelee, which is a peninsula extending out
into Lake Erie and containing some of the best farming and
hunting grounds in Ontario.

The old men – the ancient medicine men – are in control of the
young bucks, who follow behind with their squaws and papooses.

As night fell today the lights of campfires were to be seen at Sea
Cliff; the smell of dried meat roasting over the blaze was in the
air, and the shadowy outlines of groups of bronze-faced bucks,
stoically smoking – not the long pipes of the olden days, but short-
stemmed British briars and even cigarettes – brought back to old
times here the days when Pottawatomie and Ojibway pow-wows
threw fear into the hearts of every white man.

The pow-wow will continue for a week. Then the chiefs will
meet the government officials under the trees in a final parley.

Then will come the test – whether the American [Indian] has
been so subdued that he will take the decision of the white man
in sorrow and resignation or whether he still has the flaming spirit
that years ago bade him put on his war paint and fight.[34]

Clearly, for many journalists, the potential for drama in the form of a
melee at Point Pelee proved far more interesting than the issues that led
to the protest in the first place.

Some Canadian papers, most notably the *Toronto Daily Star* and the
*Toronto Globe*, avoided and decried the sensationalism among their
peers, but for most the temptation to invoke stereotypical and colourful
imagery of Native people outweighed the imperative to report accurately on the political context surrounding the protest.[35] In the nation's capital, the *Ottawa Morning Journal* undoubtedly stoked fears among senior
civil servants with this headline on 12 June: "Redskins Are Ready to
Fight the Whites."[36] Even the *Windsor Border Cities Star*, despite providing the most sustained and in-depth coverage of the Point Pelee protests,
ran a column by Findsomore Cooper that simultaneously satirized the
Wild West imagery in the other papers and trivialized Native grievances
over Point Pelee. Cooper facetiously quoted from a fictional letter written by Major Twomey, erstwhile organizer of the local militia response,
to Sears Roebuck in an attempt to mail-order antagonists for the looming conflict: "Situation here serious. We must have the Indians. Kindly
quote at once your best price on 85 bucks and squaws at time of wiring.

This is a last resort. We cannot hold out much longer. Ship f.o.b. Chicago, fully equipped with canoes, tomahawks and scalp knives." With no contingent of Native marchers having arrived at the site by 15 June, Cooper concluded that the invasion of Point Pelee was finally over: "so endeth the Battle of Pelee Point – a valiant victory for all those who did take part, beside which the deeds at Thermopylae and of Horatius at the Bridge shall now pass into everlasting insignificance." For Cooper, it was far more important to denigrate the Point Pelee protestors for their failure to live up to media hype than to critically examine the issues that prompted a small number of Natives to camp at the edge of the national park.[37]

Undoubtedly, some of the journalists who produced such outrageous accounts of the Pelee protests were influenced by the cultural tendency, prevalent in the early twentieth century, to romanticize precontact Native life as a symbolic counterculture to an increasingly urban and industrial life in North America. Authors, painters, and photographers such as Ernest Thompson Seton, Edwin Curtis, Edmund Morris, and Grey Owl celebrated the traditional Natives as exemplars of a noble warrior culture that lived in harmony with the natural world.[38] The invocation of images of latter-day Indian warriors was also apparently common in the press during this period. Fred O. Loft, president of the League of Indians of Canada, commented to the the *Toronto Globe* on his surprise at the large number of exaggerated and fanciful "Indian uprising" stories that had emerged in the newspapers during the previous six months.[39] Some of these celebrations of Native primitiveness employed relatively positive (albeit cartoonish) stereotypes, but they also tended to ignore the pressing political grievances of contemporary Natives, often dismissing groups or individuals as drunken, dirty, or lazy when they failed to live up to expectations of primitive perfection. In the case of Point Pelee, the largely fabricated press reports suggesting looming violence in the form of a Buffalo Bill's Wild West Show with live ammunition undermined a legitimate protest by subsuming its key issues within apolitical and romanticized popular images that would appeal to a mass audience.

If the Point Pelee protest was not the revival of the Wild West that the press had hoped for, can it simply be dismissed as the isolated and unsuccessful actions of a few malcontents? As with many document-driven histories of Native people, the voices of the protest's main protagonists – their practical goals, their political motivations, and their reactions to changing circumstances – are subsumed within an archival record that privileges the perspective of police and government officials. However,

the police and media reports do contain background information and
first-hand accounts of conversations with protestors that suggest a highly organized attempt to mobilize a very scattered band in support of the
claim. On 12 June, Sergeant Birtwistle discussed the protest with twenty-
three-year-old Archie Dodge (the apparent head of the two Dodge families at Point Pelee), who claimed the Caldwell Band had never planned
to take violent possession of the park but had hoped to assemble at the
site to draft a petition to the Department of Indian Affairs pressing
for "the restoration of their deprived rights to the Point Pelee Indian
Reserve." Failing that, Dodge claimed he would press the matter with
Indian Affairs on his own.[40] Chief Moses Caldwell similarly claimed in
a press interview that his band possessed no arms and had never intended to forcibly occupy the park. Caldwell was unwavering, however,
in his claim that the Crown had granted his band the territory of Point
Pelee and that "the government had absolutely no authority for their action in taking the land and making it a national park." The case, Caldwell
claimed, would be decided through arbitration based on documentation
proving his band's title to the point.[41] Another member of the encampment at Point Pelee, John Dodge, told the press that his people wanted
"no trouble" but would simply use the gathering at Point Pelee as an
opportunity to educate band members about the land claim and decide
on the best course of action. As with other participants in the protest, Dodge eloquently articulated his people's claim to land within the
national park:

> We are not squatters. We are simply coming home. The land is
> ours. More than 60 years ago, our fathers were here and camped
> on the same property to which we are returning now. It was ours
> then. It is ours now.
>
> If they will see our side of the story and send along government
> officials with their documents to compare with ours, we will get to
> the bottom of the matter. We think our deeds are proof positive of
> ownership. If they are not, then we want to be shown where we
> are wrong. We must know where we are wrong before we leave the
> territory. When the Chief arrives from Point Pelee with the plans
> he showed us at Alvinston, there must be a decision one way or the
> other. We do not want anything that does not belong to us. We are
> just returning to our homes. The log cabins which were built by
> our fathers have long since disappeared. At the present time we are
> living in a place which is rented from the owner of the house –

built on our own land. This land was given to us by the British Government. I am a direct descendant of Tecumseh, ally of the British in the war of 1812. We do not want any differences of opinion over this question. All we ask for is a fair conference between representatives of the Canadian Government and our own Council. I think that this is only fair.[42]

Far from donning war paint and brandishing tomahawks, Chief Caldwell and the Dodge families hoped that a mass rally of band members either within or at the edge of Point Pelee National Park would bring about serious consideration of their claim to the area.

Given the obvious commitment of its leadership to the cause of reclaiming Point Pelee, why did the Caldwell Band fail to mobilize behind its chief and the Dodge families? In the short term, there is no doubt that the tragic death of Chief Caldwell's son Peter in a car accident as he returned from travels in Mexico in mid-June to participate in the protest caused the band's leadership to delay the march on Point Pelee. Caldwell in particular was consumed with grief and with the need to raise $125 to repatriate his son's body. Despite the fact that band members were preoccupied with the planned funeral at Alvinston, Jackson Dodge assured the press that they would set out for Point Pelee "at once" after the proper traditional rites had been administered.[43]

For reasons that are unclear, the planned march never took place. It is possible that the sudden influx of police into the area, with frequent motorcycle patrols and two RCMP officers wearing full red tunics guarding the entrance to the park, may have intimidated potential protestors to the point where they decided to stay home.[44] The exaggerated predictions of violence associated with the sensational press reports may also have persuaded potential protestors that trigger-happy law enforcement officials and citizen militias awaited them on the long road to Point Pelee. The subsequent police patrols into the surrounding reserves, complete with invasive searches of local government records and dismissive conversations between police and Native people about the validity of the Pelee claim, possibly convinced Caldwell Band members and potential allies that the government was not ready to grant any substance to their grievances. Certainly the police went out of their way to criticize the substance of the Caldwell Band's claim to Point Pelee, rejecting the validity of the documents that Moses Caldwell presented as the legal foundation of the band's ownership of the area.[45] No matter how committed the Caldwell Band was to pressing its claim on Point Pelee, its members likely came to realize that federal parks officials and law enforcement agents were not willing to seriously entertain a challenge to their authority over a protected area that conservationists throughout North America regarded as critical habitat for migratory birds, an emerging jewel in the crown of a national parks system that was slowly expanding eastward.[46]

Practical considerations also undoubtedly played a role in the decision to finally end the protest and abandon the cabin that the Dodge families had occupied near the park boundary. With the advent of autumn and the end of both the tourist market for baskets and the work in the onion fields, the question of how to support the protesting families loomed large. As early as the end of June, Jackson Dodge asked Constable R.E. Nelson of the RCMP whether the protestors would have any right to hunt for food and trap in the park. Constable Nelson answered that "the Park Regulations did not allow Indians any more rights than any one else," neglecting the fact that select groups of non-Natives were already allowed to hunt and trap within the park boundary.[47] At the end of October, Constable Nelson reported that the Dodge families "had expected that they would be allowed to hunt and trap on the Park during the coming Winter, but on being informed by us on our last patrol that they would not be allowed to do so, they decided to return to the Alvinston district."[48] Facing the prospect of a cold winter with no possibility of making a living off of local resources, the Dodge families decided to end their protest and return to their former homes.

The collapse of the 1922 protest did not suggest any wavering of the Caldwell Band's long-term commitment to the Point Pelee claim. Indeed, the band pressed its case intermittently over the next seventy years until the shifting politics of federal relations with First Nations communities gave them some hope of success. The band's online history of the claim suggests that Archie Dodge, now a chief, remained true to his earlier promise and continued to press the land claim with the federal government throughout the 1920s, enlisting the support of local politicians and the federal Indian agent. The Kent and Lambton County Councils even passed resolutions in 1923 supporting the provision of a land base for the Caldwell Band. In 1974 Chief Carl Johnson publicly proclaimed the Caldwell Band's historic right to land on Point Pelee and Pelee Island. The Department of Indian Affairs rejected the claim, arguing that the Caldwell Band's rights to the area and been extinguished by the 1790 treaty. The band attempted again in 1987 to press a formal land claim, but it was not until 1996 that the federal government agreed to negotiate under the framework of the Specific Claims Policy.[49] In 1998 the two parties reached an agreement-in-principle that included cash compensation for goods allotted in the treaty and funds to buy private lands in the area as an alternative to a reserve on Point Pelee and Pelee Island.[50] However, implementation of the agreement was complicated by the fact that local non-Native citizens opposed the creation of a reserve. They created an organization, the Chatham-Kent Community Network, to lobby the federal government and launched a legal challenge to the historical validity of the claim.[51] Even the Caldwell Band was divided internally on the provisions of the agreement-in-principle, and the minister of Indian affairs nullified the results of a referendum on the issue in 2003 due to voting irregularities. In 2006 the federal government and the Caldwell Band returned to the negotiating table and in January 2010 reached an agreement-in-principle providing the band with $105 million and thirty years to select reserve lands (with the current chief and council favouring an urban reserve in Leamington near Point Pelee). The Caldwell First Nation ratified the agreement with an overwhelmingly positive referendum vote in August 2010.[52] In a separate initiative, Parks Canada attempted to forge a closer relationship with the Caldwell First Nation, inviting band members to participate in the annual cull of the exploding white-tailed deer population within Point Pelee National Park.[53] For seventy years since the abortive attempt to occupy the edge of the park boundary in 1922, the issue of the Point Pelee land claim has dominated the Caldwell Band's political agenda.

Throughout the complicated history of controversy over the Pelee land claim, the Caldwell First Nation never again attempted to organize anything resembling the direct action protest of 1922. The protest therefore does not represent a persistent history of radicalism on the part of the band but was one among many strategies, including more mainstream tactics such as petitions and the filing of land claims, that the Caldwell Band used to press its rights to Point Pelee. Yet it is still possible to see in the original Point Pelee protest a tentative attempt to develop an alternative strategy to the failed formal petitions of the 1890s or more coded forms of everyday resistance that Native people had used in other national parks, one that has more in common with the direct action campaigns of Native advocacy groups in the era after the Second World War. The analogy with more recent protests influenced by the Red Power movement is not exact: nobody was armed at Point Pelee, and there was, in the end, no confrontation between the police and protestors. But in a period when the Department of Indian Affairs administered Canada's Native people through the lens of extreme paternalism, the emergence of a direct action campaign – even one that is a shadow of later protests in terms of its intensity – represents a significant evolution in the array of tactics that First Nations used to press their grievances about lands appropriated for the purposes of national and provincial parks. If the Point Pelee protest of 1922 was limited in size and result, it did at least briefly provoke fear and concern among federal authorities, a portent of events that would unfold decades later as Native people set up blockades and occupations in other national parks and protected landscapes that they had once regarded as home.

NOTES

The author wishes to acknowledge a postdoctoral fellowship for research on this chapter from the Social Sciences and Humanities Research Council of Canada and a visiting fellowship for the final stages of writing and editing from the Rachel Carson Center for Environment and Society. Special thanks to Lianne Leddy for offering crucial advice and commentary.

1 Const. E.G. Weeks, RCMP, "Report Re – Patrol to Point Pelee National Park," 10 June 1922, RG 18, vol. 3295, file HQ-1034-0-2, Library and Archives Canada (LAC).

2 E.P. Thompson, *Whigs and Hunters: The Origin of the Black Act* (New York: Pantheon, 1975); James C. Scott, *Weapons of the Weak: Everyday Forms of Peasant Resistance* (New Haven, CT: Yale University Press, 1985). For an important overview of the conflict between national parks and local people in Africa, with a theoretically sophisticated use of Thompson's moral economy as a framing principle, see Roderick P. Neumann, *Imposing Wilderness: Struggles over Livelihood and Nature Preservation in Africa* (Berkeley: University of California Press, 1998).

3 See Theodore Binnema and Melanie Niemi, "'Let the Line Be Drawn Now': Wilderness, Conservation and the Exclusion of Aboriginal People from Banff National Park in Canada," *Environmental History* 11, no. 4 (October 2006): 724–50; Philip Burnham, *Indian Country, God's Country: Native Americans and the National Parks* (Washington, DC: Island, 2000); Karl Jacoby, *Crimes against Nature: Squatters, Poachers, Thieves and the Hidden History of American Conservation* (Berkeley: University of California Press, 2001); Robert H. Keller and Michael F. Turek, *American Indians and National Parks* (Tucson: University of Arizona Press, 1998); Jean Manore, "Contested Terrains of Space and Place: Hunting and the Landscape Known as Algonquin Park, 1890–1950," in *The Culture of*

*Hunting in Canada*, ed. Jean Manore and Dale Miner, 121–47 (Vancouver: UBC Press, 2007); John Sandlos, "Federal Spaces, Local Conflicts: National Parks and the Exclusionary Politics of the Conservation Movement in Ontario, 1900–1935," *Journal of the Canadian Historical Association* 16, no. 1 (2005): 293–318; John Sandlos, *Hunters at the Margin: Wildlife Conservation in the Northwest Territories* (Vancouver: UBC Press, 2007); John Sandlos, "Not Wanted in the Boundary: The Expulsion of the Keeseekowenin Ojibway Band from Riding Mountain National Park," *Canadian Historical Review* 89, no. 2 (2008): 189–221; Mark David Spence, *Dispossessing the Wilderness: Indian Removal and the Making of the National Parks* (Oxford: Oxford University Press, 1999); and Louis Warren, *The Hunter's Game: Poachers and Conservationists in Twentieth Century America* (New Haven, CT: Yale University Press, 1997). For the more complicated application of the wilderness ideal to Alaskan Natives, see Theodore Catton, *Inhabited Wilderness: Indians, Eskimos and National Parks in Alaska* (Albequerque: University of New Mexico Press, 1997).

4 For a general overview of historical patterns of Aboriginal resistance strategies, see Bruce W. Hodgins, Ute Lischke, and David T. McNab, eds, *Blockades and Resistance: Studies in Actions of Peace and the Temagami Blockades of 1988–89* (Waterloo, ON: Wilfrid Laurier University Press, 2003).

5 Jonathan Rose, "Without Reservation: The Chatham-Kent Community Network and the Caldwell First Nation Land Dispute" (MA Thesis, Trent University, 2008).

6 Neal Ferris, "Continuity within Change: Settlement-Subsistence Strategies and Artifact Patterns of the Southwestern Ontario Ojibwa, A.D. 1780–1861" (MA thesis, York University, 1989).

7 For a summary of the basis of the Caldwell Band's claim, see "Statement of Chief William Caldwell," sent under a cover note from supporter J.G. Schleihauf, 17 December 1881, and a second memo to the Superintendent of Indian Affairs sent under a cover note from J.G. Schleihauf, 3 October 1882, RG 10, vol. 2043, file 8986, part 3, LAC. See also Aboriginal Affairs and Northern Development Canada, "Negotiations on the Caldwell First Nation's Specific Land Claim – January 2007," http://www.aadnc-aandc.gc.ca/eng/1100100030384/1100100030385.

8 For a summary, see Rose, "Without Reservation," 26–31. See also memo to the Superintendent of Indian Affairs sent under a cover note from J.G. Schleihauf, 3 October 1882, RG 10, vol. 2043, file 8986, part 3, LAC.

9 See Caldwell's statement sent under a cover note from supporter
   J.G. Schleihauf, 17 December 1881, RG 10, vol. 2043, file 8986, part 3,
   LAC. The rejection came in a letter from an unidentifiable signatory,
   4 January 1882, RG 10, vol. 2043, file 8986, part 3, LAC.

10 Absolom Dingman, Inspector of Indian Agencies and Reserves, to
   L. Vankoughnet, Deputy Superintendant of Indian Affiars, 5 February
   1884, RG 10, vol. 2043, file 8986, part 3, LAC.

11 For the refusal to go to Walpole despite Absolom Dingman's exhortations,
   see a retrospective memo from Hayter Reed, Commissioner of Indian
   Affairs, to Minister of Indian Affairs Thomas Mayne Daly, 22 May 1895,
   RG 10, vol. 2043, file 8986, part 3, LAC.

12 Robert Caldwell, "Review of the Facts Regarding the Ownership and
   Disposal of Point au Pelee Island," 31 May 1892, RG 10, vol. 2043,
   file 8986, part 3, LAC.

13 See summary in memo signed by Hayter Reed, Commissioner of Indian
   Affairs, 3 January 1896, RG 10, vol. 2043, file 8986, part 3, LAC.

14 For the cost issue, see Reed to Minister of Indian Affairs Daly, 24 February
   1896, RG 10, vol. 2043, file 8986, part 3, LAC. For the Essex Gun Club
   lease, see Assistant Secretary of the Department of the Interior to J.D.
   McLean, Acting Secretary, Department of Indian Affairs, 12 May 1897,
   RG 10, vol. 2043, file 8986, part 3, LAC.

15 Alex Baird recognized the claims in a Dominion land survey conducted
   in the autumn of 1881. RG 84, vol. 478, file 1509, part 1, LAC. See also
   "Squatters' Holdings as per Plan by Baird, D.L.S.," RG 84, vol. 478,
   file 1509, part 1, LAC.

16 Sandlos, "Federal Spaces, Local Conflicts."

17 Sgt A. Birtwistle to A.W. Duffus, Officer Commanding, Western Ontario
   District, Royal Canadian Mounted Police, 15 June 1922, RG 18, vol. 3295,
   file HQ-1034-0-2, LAC.

18 Edward E. McCammon, "Son of Chief Dies; Indian Raid Delayed,"
   *Windsor Border Cities Star*, 13 June 1922, A1.

19 Canadian Press, "Mounted Police to Curb Indians," *Windsor Border Cities
   Star*, 12 June 1922, A1.

20 See Forest Conover to James B. Harkin, Parks Commissioner, 20 May
   1922, RG 10, vol. 2043, file 8986, part 1A, LAC. For press coverage, see
   "Indians Threaten on Canada Reserve," *New York Times*, 12 May 1922,
   13; "American Indians: Trouble over Canadian Lands," *Brisbane Courier*,
   17 May 1922, 5.

21 Harkin's order is mentioned in Const. E.G. Weeks, RCMP, "Report Re –
   Patrol to Point Pelee National Park," 10 June 1922, RG 18, vol. 3295,
   file HQ-1034-0-2, LAC.

22  Scott to Cortlandt Starnes, 12 June 1922, RG 18, vol. 3295,
    file HQ-1034-0-2, LAC.

23  Duffus to Starnes, 12 June 1922, RG 18, vol. 3295, file HQ-1034-02, LAC.

24  A. Birtwistle, in Edward E. McCammon, "Keep Off Pt. Pelee, Indians Told;
    March of Tribesmen Deferred," *Windsor Border Cities Star*, 13 June
    1922, A1.

25  "Indian Invasion of Point Pelee Is Only a Myth," *Toronto Daily Star*,
    14 June 1922, A1.

26  See Birtwistle to Duffus, 13 June 1922, 19 June 1922, 21 June 1922,
    24 June 1922, RG 18, vol. 3295, file HQ-1034-02, LAC.

27  Birtwistle's patrol to Walpole Island is summarized in a report to Duffus,
    15 June 1922, RG 18, vol. 3295, file HQ-1034-02, LAC.

28  Sgt A. Birtwistle to Duffus, 3 August 1922, RG 18, vol. 3295,
    file HQ-1034-02, LAC.

29  Birtwistle to Duffus, 24 June 1922, RG 18, vol. 3295, file HQ-1034-02,
    LAC.

30  The reports from the middle to the end of June mention the rumours of a
    mass protest but emphasize that all was quiet in the region. See Birtwistle
    to Duffus, 13 June 1922, 15 June 1922, 19 June 1922, 21 June 1922,
    24 June 1922, RG 18, vol. 3295, file HQ-1034-02, LAC.

31  Constable R.E. Nelson to Duffus, 27 June 1922, RG 18, vol. 3295,
    file HQ-1034-02, LAC.

32  "Call Indians' Hand; Point Pelee Affair," *Ottawa Morning Journal*,
    15 June 1922. Clipping with no author listed found in RG 18, vol. 3295,
    file HQ-1034 02, LAC.

33  "Indians Seize Park Land at Point Pelee," 16 June 1922. The name of the
    newspaper is handwritten on the clipping, but only the word "Gazette"
    is legible. The clipping was found in the case file, RG 18, vol. 3295,
    file HQ-1034-02, LAC.

34  "Indian Tribes on War March to Reclaim Ontario Lands," *New York Call*,
    14 June 1922. The clipping was found in the case file, RG 18, vol. 3295,
    file HQ-1034-02, LAC.

35  "Indian Invasion of Point Pelee Is Only a Myth," *Toronto Daily Star*,
    14 June 1922, A1; "Looking for an Indian Invasion at Point Pelee,"
    *Toronto Daily Star*, 15 June 1922, A3; "Guarding Park from Incursion of
    Indian Band," *Toronto Globe*, 13 June 1922, 3 (Lifestyle); "Point Pelee
    'Invasion' Believed to be Averted," *Toronto Globe*, 14 June 1922, 3 (News).

36  "Redskins Are Ready to Fight the Whites," *Ottawa Morning Journal*,
    12 June 1922. The clipping was fround in RG 10, vol. 2043, file 8986,
    part 1A, LAC. This newspaper did temper its tone in the article on 15 June,
    cited in note 32 above.

37 Findsomore Cooper, "Just One Thing Ruined Mutiny – Indians Scarce," *Windsor Border Cities Star*, 15 June 1922, A3.

38 See Ernest Thompson Seton, *The Gospel of the Redman: An Indian Bible* (London: Psychic, 1970); Arthur Heming, *Spirit Lake* (New York: MacMillan, 1907); and Grey Owl, *The Men of the Last Frontier* (London: Country Life, 1934). For an overview, see S. Elizabeth Bird, *Dressing in Feathers: The Construction of the Indian in American Popular Culture* (Boulder, CO: Westview, 1996); Joe Sawchuck, ed., *Images of the Indian: Portrayals of Native People* (Brandon, MB: Bearpaw, 1995); and Daniel Francis, *The Imaginary Indian: The Image of the Indian in Canadian Culture* (Vancouver: Arsenal Pulp, 1993).

39 Fred O. Loft, in "Guarding Park from Incursion of Indian Band," *Toronto Globe*, 13 June 1922, 3 (Lifestyle). Loft made no specific mention of the previously mentioned protest that had reportedly occurred on his own Six Nations Reserve at Brantford in June, so it is difficult to determine whether he would have classified this incident as one of the mythical uprisings.

40 Birtwistle to Duffus, 13 June 1922, RG 18, vol. 3295, file HQ-1034-02, LAC.

41 Birtwistle's patrol to Walpole Island is summarized in a report to Duffus, 15 June 1922, RG 18, vol. 3295, file HQ-1034-02, LAC. Caldwell is quoted in Edward E. McCammon, "Indians to Press Point Pelee Claim," *Windsor Border Cities Star*, 15 June 1922, 1.

42 John Dodge, in Edward E. McCammon, "Son of Chief Dies; Indian Raid Delayed," *Windsor Border Cities Star*, 13 June 1922, A1, A13.

43 Ibid., A1.

44 Reference to the police guarding the park in full tunic was found in "Point Pelee 'Invasion' Believed to Be Averted," *Toronto Globe*, 14 June 1922, 3 (News).

45 See, in particular, Birtwistle to Duffus, 15 June 1922, RG 18, vol. 3295, file HQ-1034-02, LAC.

46 For the international conservationist support behind Point Pelee and migratory bird conservation, see Kurkpatrick Dorsey, *The Dawn of Conservation Diplomacy: U.S.-Canadian Wildlife Protection Treaties in the Progressive Era* (Seattle: University of Washington Press, 1998).

47 Constable R.E. Nelson to Duffus, 27 June 1922, RG 18, vol. 3295, file HQ-1034-02, LAC.

48 Constable R.E. Nelson to Duffus, 27 October 1922, RG 18, vol. 3295, file HQ-1034-02, LAC.

49 Caldwell Head Office, "History of the Caldwell Band," http://www.oocities.org/athens/rhodes/6024/detailed.htm.

50  Aboriginal Affairs and Northern Development Canada, "Fact Sheet: Caldwell First Nation Specific Claim," http://www.aadnc-aandc.gc.ca/aiarch/mr/nr/s-d2006/02788bk-eng.asp.

51  Rose, "Without Reservation."

52  "Caldwell First Nation Approves Land Claim Offer," CBC News, 23 August 2010, http://www.cbc.ca/news/canada/windsor/story/2010/08/23/windsor-caldwell-treaty-settlement.html; Aboriginal Affairs and Northern Development Canada, "Fact Sheet"; Aboriginal Affairs and Northern Development Canada, "Canada and the Caldwell First Nation Reach Major Milestone in Claim Settlement Process," 18 January 2010, http://www.aadnc-aandc.gc.ca/eng/1100100016076/1100100016077; Elmwood Shreve, "Caldwell First Nation Gets $105M Offer," London Free Press, 19 January 2010, http://www.lfpress.com/news/london/2010/01/18/12520196.html.

53  Sharon Hill, "Caldwell First Nation Joins 8th Cull of Point Pelee Deer," Windsor Star, 24 January 2009, http://www2.canada.com/windsorstar/news/story.html?id=9480fbfc-0229-4e73-8b91-025bd76e853c.

# The Nature of a Blockade: Environmental Politics and the Haida Action on Lyell Island, British Columbia

DAVID A. ROSSITER

On 30 October 1985 a small group of Haida blocked access to a logging camp on Lyell Island in the South Moresby region of the Queen Charlotte Islands off the west coast of British Columbia – islands that the Haida call Haida Gwaii ("islands of the people").[1] Explaining the decision to set up a blockade on the only road in or out of the camp, the chief of the Council of the Haida Nation, Miles Richardson, declared, "We can't just sit back and have our homelands consistently pushed aside because of the interests of others."[2] Within a week, two dozen Haida had taken up occupation at the blockade near Sedgwick Bay, their presence bringing an effective halt to industrial activity on the south side of the island.[3] Although the affected logging contractor, Haida Gwaii resident Frank Beban, was adamant that he did not "want to have a confrontation," as the Haida were his "friends,"[4] on 9 November the legal proceedings initiated by Western Forest Products resulted in an injunction against the Haida requiring the removal of the blockade.[5] Despite the court order, the Haida remained on the road. The following week, members of the Royal Canadian Mounted Police (RCMP) arrested three Haida elders for maintaining the action.[6] A flurry of legal activity and arrests continued over the next several weeks,[7] and by the end of the month, seveny-two Haida had been arrested for blockading the road on Lyell Island in their bid to stop the harvest of its timber through clear-cut forestry.[8] As the action simmered throughout the winter and several more people were arrested, it became clear that unchallenged industry access to the timber resources of the region was a thing of the past.[9]

In several ways, the blockade was effective. The Haida action was in response to the BC government's decision to permit the resumption of industrial logging on Crown lands in the area,[10] despite official assurances that logging would be suspended on Lyell Island while negotiations regarding the preservation of the whole South Moresby region were ongoing between government, industry, environmental groups, and the Haida.[11] As partners in a decade-old coalition fighting to preserve South Moresby from industrial development, the Haida had decided, in the words of Elizabeth May, "to do whatever it took to stop the logging on Lyell."[12] They could no longer stand by and watch as the resources of their homeland were stripped and carted away while politicians debated the merits of preservation from industrial activity. Highlighting issues of environmental preservation and Aboriginal land and resource rights through extensive media coverage, the blockade helped to draw both domestic and international attention to the cause of protecting South Moresby – attention that, in the short term, slowed the rate of cut on Lyell Island and, ultimately, helped to force a deal between federal and provincial governments that led to the establishment of South Moresby National Park in the spring of 1987.[13] Thus it is fair to say that the blockade played a significant role in achieving the goal of preserving the South Moresby region of Haida Gwaii from industrial development.

However, there is a difficult irony buried in this seemingly positive outcome. The Haida who risked arrest at the blockade had aided environmental activists in achieving their goal, but the creation of a park did not bring them any concrete progress on the issue of Aboriginal title to and control over their homeland. Indeed, the establishment of a national park on Haida-claimed territory struck many members of the Haida Nation as a continuation of colonial land relations, where decisions are made and imposed from afar. Although this situation was somewhat tempered in 1993 with the drafting of an agreement between the Council of the Haida Nation and the federal Department of the Environment that would guide management at the renamed Gwaii Haanas National Park (islands of beauty and wonder), the Haida claim to Haida Gwaii remains unsettled to this date.[14] To claim, then, that the creation of the park marked "paradise won," to quote the title of May's volume on the South Moresby campaign, might be a somewhat limited reading of the outcome of both the Haida blockade and the larger conflict over the South Moresby region.

In this chapter, I aim to untangle the Haida position from that of the larger preservationist coalition that fought successfully for the protection

of the southern third of the Queen Charlotte Islands. Following an overview discussion of the Charlottes' historical and political geographies,
I demonstrate that whereas the Haida and their local supporters articulated a position that intertwined the vitality and presence of Aboriginal
culture with a locally complex natural environment, the discourse of
support that emerged at the provincial, national, and international levels
largely seized on particular qualities of that environment (uniqueness,
wilderness) to argue for its protection from industrial activity. I claim
that this had the effect of both marginalizing the Haida's key demand
for control over their homelands in the national debate and appropriat-
ing Aboriginal lands in the service of an idealized national geographical
imagination where pristine nature reserves sit in counterpoint to the urban complexes that dominate most people's lives. In making this argument, I assert that the Haida at Lyell Island therefore had an early
experience with the mixture of environmental and Aboriginal politics
that would come to mark British Columbia's "war in the woods" during
the Clayoquot Sound and Great Bear Rainforest conflicts of the 1990s.[15]
I conclude by suggesting that the tension that marks the political ecology
of Crown forest lands in coastal British Columbia is a local manifestation of a broader epistemological conflict concerning the definition of
nature and culture that lies at the heart of Aboriginal claims to land
and resources.

## MAKING ISLANDS:
### HAIDA GWAII AND THE QUEEN CHARLOTTES

Despite the fact that they lie at precisely the same coordinates on the
map and mirror one another in climate, topography, flora, and fauna,
Haida Gwaii ("islands of the people") and the Queen Charlotte Islands
have quite different historical geographies. In the words of Haida artist
and activist Bill Reid, for millennia the islands of the people "lay secure
in their isolation, protected by the sea even from the ice that swept south
to cover most of the continent. Because of this isolation these islands
gave birth to many unusual, in some cases unique, kinds of animal and
plant life. And when about ten thousand years ago some newcomers
penetrated their isolation, arriving by sea or being coaxed out of a clam-
shell by Raven, they too were transformed into a people as unusual and
in some ways as unique as their environment – the Haida."[16] To the
Haida, this ten-thousand-year bond between people and place remains
intact and strong. Indeed, a recent edited collection on the natural and
human history of the islands demonstrates that the Haida and their

homeland have evolved in intimately intertwined ways, with climate, flora, and fauna shaping political and material culture and with Haida settlement patterns and resource use shaping local topographies and ecologies.[17] Although the imposition of colonial land relations in the late nineteenth century changed modes of work and interaction with the environment and disease killed many, and although cultural practices such as the potlatch and local education were banned or hampered by the federal government, the Haida maintained a presence on their islands, one that grew ever stronger as the twentieth century wore on.[18] On Haida Gwaii, then, people and their environment have become so intertwined over the millennia that one cannot be adequately understood without the other.

The ongoing and durable physical use and occupation of the islands by the Haida have imbued them with a sense of sovereignty over their homeland. This sense is well captured in the words spoken by elder Ethel Jones as she faced arrest at the Lyell Island blockade: "At this moment we want our island back. There's no written statement anywhere that we signed this land over to the government."[19] Despite its outward simplicity, Jones's remark captures both the frustration felt by the Haida over the treatment of their homeland and a sense of the legal and political terrain the action would ultimately expose. And the frustration had been simmering for generations. Noting the longevity of the Haida claim to the islands during a hearing on the legality of the blockade, Council Chief Richardson declared: "Our people have been trying to get this issue dealt with for more than 100 years. We have transcribed testimony from 1913 on precisely this issue ... For us to exist as a people, for us to exist as a culture, there has to be a place on our homelands, on our domain, our only place in this world, on our islands that is left unspoiled."[20] Thus, through an understanding of culture and nature on the islands as mutually constitutive, and of Haida use and occupation as durable and long-asserted, Haida Gwaii and its long-time inhabitants are rendered as one. For Reid, Jones, and Richardson, then, Haida Gwaii stands as the centre of their people's world, a world never ceded to foreign powers and certainly not one to be relegated to the past.

The Queen Charlotte Islands represent something quite different. Their history began in the late eighteenth century when Europeans voyaging in the name of commerce and empire encountered the archipelago. Named and mapped by British captain George Dixon in 1787, over the following century and a half, the Charlottes were constructed within, and thereby contributed to, a developing British (and, more generally, European) colonial and commercial geographical imagination.[21] Dixon's cartography brought the islands into view for distant interests at the end of the eighteenth century through what Daniel Clayton has called, in referring to similar processes on Vancouver Island to the south, an imperial fashioning – a rendering of space steeped in scientific and commercial discourses that positioned the island in relation to the centre of empire.[22] It was a remote frontier, a wild place inhabited by an uncivilized people, but it held out the promise of certain wealth. As both Bruce Braun and Jason Grek-Martin have recently shown, by the end of the nineteenth century, and following upon British Columbia's entry into the Canadian federation, interest had developed in the natural resource potential of the islands. The interest in the mineral, timber, and marine resource potential of the region led to natural and cultural surveys, most famously those of federal geologist George Dawson in the 1870s, which marked both nature and culture in terms congruent with the development of a pan-Canadian settler society. By obscuring entrenched Aboriginal geographies and highlighting extractable commodities, while denying the possibility of an Aboriginal future, such renderings set the islands up as awaiting development by an incoming civilization; these were the spaces of a fading people, spaces that awaited the industrious settler who would be the backbone of the Canadian nation.[23]

The claims to Haida Gwaii by outsiders of European background have been largely effective, coming under significant scrutiny only in the past three decades. Prior to a surge in Aboriginal political power in the 1970s (one concomitant with an emergent environmental activism),[24] Crown claims to the islands seemed solid. Notwithstanding Native testimony to the McKenna-McBride Commission of 1913–16 (the testimony referred to by Richardson above) asserting ongoing Aboriginal possession and occupation of lands that successive colonial and provincial governments claimed for the Crown,[25] colonial development proceeded on the islands and accelerated as the twentieth century progressed. Following the Second World War, for example, the landscapes of Haida Gwaii were caught up in the labour politics of postwar industrial forestry when crews of Scandinavian loggers organized a union.[26] Over the following decades, the entrenchment on the islands of an economy and society based upon the extraction of raw resources for export, timber in particular, saw Haida Gwaii drawn ever more into the industrial system that has marked the province's development for well over a century. By the early 1980s, successive provincial governments, both New Democratic and Social Credit, consistently refused to acknowledge Aboriginal title to lands in British Columbia in the face of claims, thereby ratcheting up frustrations through a refusal to negotiate.[27] Indeed, in the midst of tensions on Lyell, the province's intergovernmental relations minister, Garde Gardon, went so far as to compare Haida claims to the separatist movement in Quebec: "We firmly believe in freeing natives from the shackles of the federal bureaucracy ... But we do not agree with native sovereignty beyond the Parliament of Canada under any circumstances. I don't think it is appropriate to take a separatist position as adopted by the Government of Quebec."[28] Despite the position of BC governments, the institutional context of Aboriginal rights to land and resources underwent significant change during the same period. Beginning with the Calder decision of 1973, in which the Supreme Court of Canada recognized the existence of Aboriginal title in rendering a decision (albeit unfavourable) on the Nisga'a Nation's claim to the territory around the Nass Valley in northern British Columbia, and continuing through the recognition and entrenchment of Aboriginal peoples and rights in the Constitution Act of 1982, First Nations in Canada gained some institutional support for their claims.[29] It was into this tense context that the Haida launched the drive to reconcile the Queen Charlotte Islands with their homeland of Haida Gwaii.

## SOUTH MORESBY: A PLACE TO PROTECT

The tensions over resource use and claims of ownership that exist between the two sets of islands outlined above were forced into the open in 1974. In that year, a coalition was formed between the Haida and several environmental activists aimed at ending clear-cut logging on the southern half of Moresby Island and surrounding smaller islands. In her history of the South Moresby campaign, May presents an intimate account of the humble beginnings of an environmental movement. In her telling, in the middle of a spring night at a cabin on the northern tip of the islands, two young acquaintances, one Haida and the other an American expatriate now resident on the islands (it was his cabin), hatched a plan to preserve forever the archipelago's remaining old-growth forests. Logging had occurred throughout much of the north, but the southern half remained largely intact. Strategically leaving aside enough prime forest to satisfy industry in the short term while negotiations would be undertaken, the pair designated the bottom third of the archipelago as the target for protection. The next morning they presented their South Moresby Wilderness Proposal to an assembled group of friends. Dubbing their fledgling group the Islands Protection Society, they launched a formal coalition and vehicle for change.[30] For the non-Aboriginal environmentalists, at stake were wilderness landscapes and wildlife, with all of their attendant values and symbols: pristine environments as the counterpoint to the spaces of urban industrial capitalism.[31] For the Haida, the cessation of logging was sought as part of an assertion of sovereignty and control over their homeland. In the end, suggests Robert Keller, although each side's end goals were different (if not entirely incompatible), both the environmental activists and the Haida deemed their respective partner to be a useful ally.[32]

The twelve-year saga that ultimately led to the establishment of South Moresby National Park in the spring of 1987 included lobbying all and sundry stripes of politicians, both federal and provincial; public protest at legislatures and conferences; media exposure, both coverage and promotion; and throughout it all, the garnering of substantial national and international support.[33] In many ways, however, the centerpiece of the campaign was the publication by the Islands Protection Society of the volume *Islands at the Edge*.[34] Although laid out much like a coffee table book, it is more than a mere aesthetically pleasing curiosity. Part natural history essay, part social critique, and throughout passionate in its advocacy of the preservation of the South Moresby region, the volume seems to hold the various threads of the Native-environmentalist alliance together seamlessly. An introductory essay by Bill Reid,[35] which paints the islands and the Haida as one, leads into a discussion of natural history and of Haida Gwaii as the Canadian Galapagos,[36] which gives way to an explanation of the Islands Protection Society's position and politics.[37] Throughout, photographs of both stunning landscapes and their fall at the hands of industrial logging complement the essays. As a prime tool in the campaign to protect South Moresby, *Islands at the Edge* made a powerful case for the preservationist position, and its combination of aesthetic appeal and scientific argument was attractive enough to sell out the first printing in less than a month.[38]

A second glance, however, reveals that an ultimate highlighting of "nature" (old-growth forests, mountain vistas, exotic marine life) over "culture" (Haida as symbiotically related to the islands) dominates the volume. After Reid's eloquent defence of a place and its peoples, much of the remaining text and accompanying images pit a precious and complex wilderness against the rapacious appetite of industrial capitalism. Only in the final paragraphs of the penultimate essay does John Broadhead, a leader of the Islands Protection Society, revive the theme of culture and environment in intimate interaction and mutual definition.

He does so by quoting Chief Sealth of the Duamish tribe: "This we know: the earth does not belong to man, man belongs to the earth. This we know. All things are connected like the blood that unites one family. All things are connected. Man did not weave the web of life, he is merely a strand in it. Whatever he does to the web, he does to himself."[39] When coupled with Reid's essay, then, Broadhead's presentation of these words clearly demonstrates that the leaders of the Islands Protection Society were sensitive to Haida claims to the islands as the place of a living and thriving culture. However, the dominant representation throughout the book of a pristine natural environment under threat has the effect of marginalizing the importance of Haida land claims; within the cultural politics of nature, the Haida voice was being pushed aside by the loud and clear discourse of ecology and romantic appeals to a pristine, non-human natural world. As studies of the subsequent antilogging campaigns in Clayoquot Sound and the Great Bear Rainforest have shown, such marginalization would come to characterize British Columbia's "war in the woods" throughout the 1990s as well.[40] And, as I will now demonstrate, it formed a prominent part of provincial, national, and international responses to the Haida blockade.

## NATURE AT THE BLOCKADE

The decision of the Haida to block the road that Frank Beban's crew used to reach its logging camp on the south side of Lyell Island was taken in response to the apparent betrayal of the preservationist coalition by the provincial government of William Bennett. Having earlier that year convinced the federal environment minister, Tom McMillan, to commit to the idea of a national park (along with millions of dollars for its establishment)[41] and having also won the provincial environment minister, Austin Pelton, over to the idea, members of the Islands Protection Society felt that they had momentum on their side. Now all that remained was to convince Bennett and the rest of his Cabinet. It would be a hard sell. Swayed by arguments about loss of jobs and provincial revenues if a park was established, Bennett and the Cabinet sided with industry, and in the middle of October 1985 new logging permits were issued for the old-growth timber on the south side of the island. Both the Haida and the environmental activists were infuriated.[42] For the activists, many of whom were veterans of environmental campaigns in other parts of British Columbia and beyond, the betrayal was marked by the seeming failure of years of lobbying and networking; trust had been broken and personal relationships strained.[43] For the Haida, the sense of betrayal was equally as visceral. In their case, however, the broken trust ran right to the heart of the Haida relationship with the Crown. "The Government has betrayed us," declared Council Chief Richardson days before the beginning of the blockade. Determined to stop the rending of Haida culture from its homeland, he vowed, "We'll be prepared to do what we have to do to uphold the position our people have taken. We will be there. We will be there."[44] The Haida were set to take on the full spotlight in the exploding debate over the future of South Moresby.

As Nicholas Blomley notes in his survey of First Nations blockades in British Columbia, such actions are "intensely spatial" forms of resistance and political protest, where drawing a line and controlling space serve as both instrumental and symbolic declarations of sovereignty.[45] On Lyell Island the instrumental effect of the Haida blockade was significant. The immediate on-the-ground goal of preserving old-growth forests met with relative success. Upon initiation of the blockade (essentially a camp with people blocking the road to approaching vehicles and crews), all work ceased on the south side of Lyell.[46] And over the next ten days, while Western Forest Products filed an injunction against the Haida, the blockade action also forced the question of Aboriginal title in the province back into the political spotlight.[47] Testifying in a Vancouver court, Council Chief Richardson and other Haida argued that their people had relied upon the resources of Haida Gwaii for millennia and that modern industrial practices were undermining the health of their homeland and culture. They made a case for the Haida as rightful owners of the archipelago.[48] Against this position, lawyers for the logging company replied that their client had secured cutting rights from the government and simply wanted to get its crews to work; the Haida blockade was interrupting its legal right to do business.[49] On 8 November, Justice Harry McKay ruled that the Haida must not obstruct the loggers while they went to work on the road.[50] In this first round, the arguments of industry, as backed by the state's institutions, won the day. However, the Haida had thrown a major wrench into the plans to log the south side of Lyell Island and had forced their land claim into the spotlight all in one fell swoop.

In coming to his decision, McKay laid out the political ecology of the lands and forests at the blockade. Despite sympathizing with the passionate testimony offered by members of the Haida Nation, McKay ultimately saw himself confined by the legal framework of the state and its institutions: "I could reserve (my decision), but I want to face the Haida who spoke so eloquently. I have been moved and impressed. I have come to the conclusion that, on law, I have no alternative but to grant the injunction."[51] The forests under discussion were claimed by the Crown as natural resources to be exploited for provincial development, a claim that seemed durable after more than a century of assertion and entrenchment through discourse and practice.[52] McKay declared himself hostage to this entrenched political ecology, stating simply, "I am doing my best to administer the law but I do not make government. If I did, I would be stepped on very quickly."[53] With an injunction granted against them, the Haida's ability to continue to hold up logging activity was in doubt. It was becoming clear that their nation's objectives could not be advanced through established legal channels. Nevertheless, the Haida remained determined. Upon hearing the judge's verdict, Richardson replied, "We knew we were right when we went in (the court) and now we have an important decision to make. One thing is that we're unified on this and we'll consider it seriously."[54] To maintain their protection of Lyell's old-growth forests, the Haida would now be faced with the clear prospect of arrest.

After allowing workers access to the camp as a show of goodwill in the days following the injunction (and in the wake of concerns expressed by members of the RCMP),[55] the Haida resumed the blockade on 15 November. Among the Haida were several elders, all of whom felt that the risk of arrest was worth it if the Haida claim was advanced through the action. Sixty-seven-year-old Ada Yovanvic summed up her stoic attitude about the possibility of time in jail: "It doesn't really matter as long as I have some fancy work to do. I don't mind at all. Otherwise, I wouldn't be here." Betraying a sense of sadness, she concluded, "It's too bad it had to come to this kind of confrontation."[56] And so the arrests began. First to go on 17 November were the three elders: Watson Price, eighty; Ethel Jones, sixty-five; and Yovanic. They were charged with mischief and then released on the condition that they not return to Lyell Island.[57] The following day, ten more Haida were arrested and taken from the blockade. Unbowed, Frank Collison, speaking on behalf of the Council of the Haida Nation, declared, "We are bringing in more people. We are taking quite a number from Masset – about eight or ten – and others from Skidegate."[58] Thus, in the weeks leading up to Christmas, logging was interrupted (but not halted altogether), and judges and police officers were forced to consider the legal, political, and moral standing of the Haida claim in their reactions to the ongoing blockade.[59] Chief Justice Allan McEachern of the Supreme Court of British Columbia acknowledged some of the unease that the conflict had cast over the legal institutions of British Columbia and Canada when he felt compelled to state that the Haida at the blockade were "not criminals in the usual sense."[60] As the action and arrests continued (including the arrest of Svend Robinson, a member of the federal Parliament for the New Democratic Party),[61] the road remained free of violence, and the Haida started to win the support of many British Columbians.[62] The blockade had helped the Haida to put their claim in the political stoplight in a favourable manner.

The dispute continued throughout December, and as the arrests mounted, so did support from outside the province and a corresponding spotlight on the conflict and its prime players. The Assembly of First Nations offered financial support to the Haida,[63] churches voiced their backing for a struggle that was labelled a "human rights issue,"[64] and the federal Indian affairs minister, David Crombie, offered to initiate a special process to negotiate the Haida claim to the South Moresby region outside of the normal limit of six concurrent treaty negotiations (at the time the limit had been reached) allowed by federal legislation. The province, however, declined the federal offer[65] or, indeed, to even acknowledge the concept of Aboriginal title to Crown lands on South Moresby or elsewhere in British Columbia, going so far as to seek an injunction barring the Haida from even approaching Lyell Island.[66]

As 1986 began, it appeared that sparks would again fly after a hiatus in tensions over the Christmas holidays.[67] And then a bombshell hit the provincial government: Forest Minister Thomas Waterland was forced to resign from Cabinet after revelations surfaced that he had a $20,000 stake in a pulp mill partnership that was dependent upon timber from the South Moresby region.[68] Given the events of the previous few months, the optics were terrible. The subsequent political firestorm caused Premier Bennett to announce a moratorium on all logging on Lyell Island until the province's Wilderness Advisory Committee had delivered a final set of recommendations later that spring. When it released its report in March, the committee called for the preservation of about 90 per cent of what the Islands Protection Society had requested, the excluded 10 per cent including Lyell Island. On that basis, in July the provincial government again issued cutting permits for the island, causing nine Haida leaders to renounce their citizenship. However, this would be industry's last gasp. In the end, the international scrutiny brought to bear on the province (particularly through Vancouver's hosting of the

World Exposition in the summer of 1986), combined with pressure from the federal government, ultimately forced the province to agree to turn South Moresby over to Parks Canada for the creation of South Moresby National Park (not without compensation, of course).[69]

In light of the above summary of a complex set of events, one can argue that the instrumental effects of the blockade included a significant disruption of the rate of logging on Lyell Island and a concomitant highlighting of the legal, political, and moral terrain of Haida claims to Haida Gwaii, with both spurring on the creation of the national park. But what of the symbolic effects of the blockade? Here, I suggest that a reading of expressions of support for the Haida – provincial, national, and international – reveals a discourse wherein the environment of South Moresby is torn from its local context and appropriated in the name of national and international values and objectives. As Matthew Sparke notes in his discussion of the Giktsan claim in northern British Columbia, powerful representations of space and environments made in the name of the nation and state have shaped the colonial geographies that underlie current experience.[70] And, as Bruce Braun and others have demonstrated, much of the preservationist discourse that characterized the Clayoquot Sound and Great Bear Rainforest conflicts identified the landscapes under threat from clear-cut logging as a pristine, nonhuman natural environment to be preserved as a national (and international) heritage.[71] In failing to seriously recognize and treat the contested lands as claimed Aboriginal territory, environmental groups (led by Greenpeace) invited accusations of practising a form of environmental colonialism throughout the "war in the woods" that marked the province in the 1990s.[72] It would only be as the millennium turned and a comprehensive land use plan was negotiated for the province's mid-coast that environmental and Aboriginal politics would find some sort of reconciliation in the coastal forests.[73] With the case of Lyell Island, it is possible to catch an early glimpse of this fundamental tension in the cultural politics of nature in the province.

At the provincial and national levels, support for the Haida was voiced in terms of the worthy objective of preserving the South Moresby region. Editors of major metropolitan newspapers lined up on the side of the Haida and the Islands Protection Society soon after the blockade began. Editorials and columns came to the defence of "a special place ... unique on the face of the earth"[74] and of a "natural heritage" in need of preservation.[75] Writers of letters to editors at the same newspapers bemoaned the embarrassment that the BC government was inviting upon the province and nation in failing to protect such a rich and unique ecological area.[76] And, in perhaps the most seamless shift between support for the Haida and a national appropriation of South Moresby's spectacular landscapes, during daily question period in the House of Commons, John Turner, leader of the federal Liberal Party and the Official Opposition, demanded to know why Prime Minister Brian Mulroney of the Conservative Party was standing by as Haida lands were being destroyed and when he would take action to preserve this "priceless national treasure."[77] The mountainous old-growth landscapes of the archipelago had captured the national geographical imagination. Although the on-the-ground campaigners from the Islands Protection Society had an intimate understanding of their partners' and neighbours' relationship with the environment of the islands, it was lost in translation to the national stage. Thus, to many of the voices clamouring for South Moresby's preservation, the creation of a national park made perfect sense; the trees would be saved, thereby both placating the Haida and reserving for the nation an exotic landscape that promised escape from the urban reality of many people's lives.

In their appeal to the BC government to preserve the islands, a coalition of Canadian environmental groups took the campaign international. Recognizing the political utility of garnering support beyond Canada, the group sought to promote Haida Gwaii as the Canadian Galapagos and achieve its protection as a United Nations heritage site.[78] American politicians,[79] Australian environmental activists,[80] and prominent international forest scientists,[81] to name a few, had already spoken out in support of the Haida's objective of halting the logging. In each case, the rationale rested upon ecological terms; the ancient forests of South Moresby were rendered as distinctly nonhuman space. By approaching the United Nations for heritage designation largely on environmental grounds, the unique ecology of the islands constituting a "world treasure,"[82] the coalition was taking the final step in solidifying support for wilderness protection in the archipelago. In the process, however, the natural environment of the islands was all but divorced from Haida culture, except where it might serve as an aesthetic backdrop through reference to tradition and harmony with nature.[83] Thus, in the discourse of international support that emerged in the wake of the blockade and ultimately pushed the BC government to negotiate the terms of a national park, the islands were portrayed as a resolutely natural system; a chance to champion a modern symbiosis of culture and environment, a renaissance of Haida Gwaii, quietly slipped by.

## CONCLUSION:
## FROM SOUTH MORESBY TO GWAII HAANAS

When, in early July 1987, the BC government signed 145,000 hectares of the Queen Charlotte Islands over to the federal government for the creation of South Moresby National Park, it seemed that the dream concocted by those two young men one night years ago had come to an almost impossible fruition. An entrenched logging industry and intransigent provincial government had bowed to public pressure (however reluctantly) and agreed to the preservation of virtually the entire area called for in the pair's original South Moresby Wilderness Proposal. It was an impressive achievement, but the victory was only partial. Although the Haida's action in blockading the logging road on Lyell Island had the effect of obstructing extraction and putting the politics of land in the region on wide display, their ultimate goal of expressing and achieving sovereignty over the Haida homeland was not fully realized.

The blockade certainly helped to push the politics of Native land claims in British Columbia into a spotlight from which it has not since retreated. The land use arrangement that emerged in the summer of 1987, however, came nowhere near to meeting Haida requirements for territorial control. In place of the BC government and its Department of Forests as overseers, the Haida had inherited the Canadian government and its Department of Parks. Not content to let the issue lie there, the Haida would work with federal officials over the next six years to create a joint management plan. In 1993 the Gwaii Haanas Agreement was signed and the park renamed Gwaii Haanas National Park and Haida Heritage Reserve. Although this move went some way toward returning control of land and resources to the Haida Nation,[84] it cannot be considered a final resolution. Indeed, the Haida have continued to be at the forefront of the land claims issue in British Columbia, pursuing their comprehensive claim and forcing legal decisions that have required governments and industry to consult and partner with Native peoples in claimed, but as yet untreatied, territories.[85]

The tale of the South Moresby campaign and of the place of the Haida blockade of Lyell Island within it lays bare a tension that must be addressed in choosing between what scholars have come to regard as the "two-row wampum" and "citizens plus" approaches to the resolution of Aboriginal social and territorial grievances.[86] Renderings of nature and society by different cultures are often difficult to reconcile. With the signing of the Gwaii Haanas Agreement in 1993, the situation in the southern third of the archipelago took on some of the tones of a "citizens plus" arrangement. The Haida serve as full and equal partners in decision making and resource use, with members of their nation occupying most of the on-the-ground management positions.[87] However, ultimate control of the park rests with the minister of the Crown responsible for national parks, and the continuation of the Haida claim to all of Haida Gwaii is evidence that the relationship remains uneven in the eyes of the Haida. That, after almost three decades of confrontation and negotiation, the dispute over ownership of the islands still lingers testifies to the difficulty of forging an adequate "citizens plus" arrangement over hotly contested lands and resources.

In the case at hand, this difficulty manifested itself in, among other things, the cultural politics of nature evident in the campaign to preserve South Moresby. Although on the surface both the coalition of environmentalists and the Haida were seeking the same outcome (an end to logging), their understanding of the natural environment with which they were concerned (wilderness versus cultural hearth) diverged greatly once the campaign veered into national and international space, with the former capturing political discourse. In the end, the tale of environmental politics and of the Haida blockade on Lyell Island points to one of the foundational challenges that face Aboriginal and non-Aboriginal Canadians in foregoing the "two-row wampum" model for the "citizens plus" option: the vastly different concepts that Aboriginal and non-Aboriginal peoples have of the relationship between nature and culture. However, given the tentatively positive response by all parties to the comprehensive land use agreement signed for British Columbia's mid-coast in January 2006,[88] this may well be a challenge worth tackling.

NOTES

1 In December 2009 the archipelago's name was officially changed to Haida Gwaii in response to Haida claims.

2 Miles Richardson, in "B.C. Haida Block Road," *Globe and Mail*, 31 October 1985, A5.

3 John Cruickshank, "Leave Us More Than Stumps, Haida Tell Vancouver Judge," *Globe and Mail*, 7 November 1985, A10; Elizabeth May, *Paradise Won: The Struggle for South Moresby* (Toronto: McClelland and Stewart, 1990), 113.

4 Frank Beban, in "B.C. Haida Block Road."

5 "B.C. Judge Forbids Haida Indians from Obstructing Island Logging," *Globe and Mail*, 9 November 1985, A5.

6 John Cruickshank, "3 Haidas Charged with Defying Order on Island Logging," *Globe and Mail*, 18 November 1985, A5.

7 "28 Haida Are Arrested in B.C. Logging Protest," *Globe and Mail*, 26 November 1985, A5.

8 May, *Paradise Won*, 127.

9 W.R. Derrick Sewell, Phillip Dearden, and John Dumbrell, "Wilderness Decision Making and the Role of Environmental Interest Groups: A Comparison of the Franklin Dam, Tasmania and South Moresby, British Columbia Cases," *Natural Resources Journal* 29, no. 1 (1989): 147–69 at 161.

10 "South Moresby Logging Plan Sparks Ire," *Globe and Mail*, 21 October 1985, A5.

11 John Cruickshank, "B.C. Indians Vow to Halt Island Logging," *Globe and Mail*, 24 October 1985, A10.

12 May, *Paradise Won*, 113.

13 Ibid., 127–9; Moira Johnston, "Canada's Queen Charlotte Islands: Home of the Haida," *National Geographic*, July 1987, 102–27; Robert Keller, "Haida Indian Land Claims and South Moresby National Park," *American Review of Canadian Studies* 20, no. 1 (Spring 1990): 7–30.

14 Suzanne Hawkes, "Gwaii Haanas Agreement: From Conflict to Cooperation," *Environments* 23, no. 2 (1996): 87–100.

15 David A. Rossiter, "Negotiating Nature: Colonial Geographies and Environmental Politics in the Pacific Northwest," *Ethics, Place and Environment* 11, no. 2 (2008): 113–28.

16 Bill Reid, "The Shining Islands," in Islands Protection Society, ed., *Islands at the Edge: Preserving the Queen Charlotte Islands Wilderness*, 23–32 (Vancouver: Douglas and McIntyre, 1984), 27.

17 Daryl Fedje and Rolf W. Mathewes, *Haida Gwaii: Human History and Environment from the Time of Loon to the Time of the Iron People* (Vancouver: UBC Press, 2005).

18 Jean Barman, *The West beyond the West: A History of British Columbia* (Toronto: University of Toronto Press, 1996), 166–75.

19 Ethel Jones, in "Haidas Face Action in Blocking Loggers," *Globe and Mail*, 15 November 1985, A4.

20 Miles Richardson, in Cruickshank, "Leave Us More Than Stumps."

21 Jason Grek-Martin, "Vanishing the Haida: George Dawson's Ethnographic Vision and the Making of Settler Space on the Queen Charlotte Islands in

the Late Nineteenth Century," *Canadian Geographer* 51, no. 3 (2007): 393–4.

22  Daniel Clayton, *Islands of Truth: The Imperial Fashioning of Vancouver Island* (Vancouver: UBC Press, 1999).

23  Bruce Braun, "Producing Vertical Territory: Geology and Governmentality in Late Victorian Canada," *Cultural Geographies* 7, no. 1 (2000): 7–46; Grek-Martin, "Vanishing the Haida."

24  Nicholas Blomley, "'Shut the Province Down': First Nations Blockades in British Columbia, 1984–1995," *BC Studies* 111 (Autumn 1996): 5–35 at 8–9. For a good overview of the emergence of a powerful Aboriginal political movement in British Columbia up to the 1990s, see Paul Tennant, *Aboriginal Peoples and Politics: The Indian Land Question in British Columbia, 1849–1989* (Vancouver: UBC Press, 1990); for a treatment of the same for all of Canada, see Alan Cairns, *Citizens Plus: Aboriginal Peoples and the Canadian State* (Vancouver: UBC Press, 2000).

25  R. Cole Harris, *Making Native Space: Colonialism, Resistance, and Reserves in British Columbia* (Vancouver: UBC Press, 2002), ch. 8.

26  Barman, *West beyond the West*, 265.

27  Blomley, "'Shut the Province Down,'" 9.

28  Garde Gardon, in Jack Danylchuk and Brian Gory, "2 BC Ministers Meet Haida, Discuss Logging, Land Claims," *Globe and Mail*, 11 December 1985, A8.

29  Cairns, *Citizens Plus*, 170–5.

30  May, *Paradise Won*, ch. 4.

31  For a foundational essay on the construction of wilderness in this sense, see William Cronon, "The Trouble with Wilderness, or Getting Back to the Wrong Nature," in *Uncommon Ground: Toward Reinventing Nature*, ed. William Cronon, 69–90 (New York: Norton, 1995).

32  Keller, "Haida Indian Land Claims," 14–15.

33  May, *Paradise Won*; Keller, "Haida Indian Land Claims"; "Island in the Storm," *Globe and Mail*, 26 November 1985, A6; John Cruickshank, "US Panel Opposes Lyell Logging," *Globe and Mail*, 4 December 1985, A3.

34  Islands Protection Society, ed., *Islands at the Edge*.

35  See "Part 1 – The Legacy of Change," in ibid., 23–32.

36  See "Part 2 – The Natural History" and "Part 3 – The Movement," in ibid., 33–118, 119–55.

37  See "Part 3 – The Movement," in ibid., 119–55.

38  May, *Paradise Won*, 77.

39  Chief Sealth, in John Broadhead, "Islands at the Edge," in Islands Protection Society, ed., *Islands at the Edge*, 142.

40 Bruce Braun, *The Intemperate Rainforest: Nature, Culture, and Power on Canada's West Coast* (Minneapolis: University of Minnesota Press, 2002); David A. Rossiter, "The Nature of Protest: Constructing the Spaces of British Columbia's Rainforests," *Cultural Geographies* 11, no. 2 (2004): 139–64.

41 "McMillan Says Ottawa Willing to Pay for Park," *Globe and Mail*, 7 November 1985, A10.

42 May, *Paradise Won*, 108–9.

43 May's account in *Paradise One* provides myriad details of the interactions and negotiations between key campaigners and politicians and bureaucrats. Much of it is drawn from her observations as federal environment minister Tom McMillan's assistant during the South Moresby negotiations.

44 Miles Richardson, in Cruickshank, "B.C. Indians Vow."

45 Blomley, "'Shut the Province Down,'" 7.

46 "BC Haida Block Road."

47 Both the Nisga'a claim, particularly as addressed in the Calder decision of 1973, and the action on Meares Island by the Ahousaht in 1984 had significant media profiles in their time. See respectively Cairns, *Citizens Plus*, 170–5; and Rima Wilkes and Danielle Ricard, "How Does Newspaper Coverage of Collective Action Vary? Protest by Indigenous People in Canada," *Social Science Journal* 44, no. 2 (2007): 231–51.

48 "BC Haida Block Road"; "Logging Ruined Hunting Areas, BC Court Hears," *Globe and Mail*, 8 November 1985, A10.

49 Cruickshank, "Leave Us More Than Stumps."

50 "B.C. Judge Forbids Haida Indians."

51 Harry McKay, in ibid.

52 Clayton, *Islands of Truth*; Braun, "Producing Vertical Territory"; Grek-Martin, "Vanishing the Haida"; David A. Rossiter, "Lessons in Possession: Colonial Resource Geographies in Practice on Vancouver Island, 1859–65," *Journal of Historical Geography* 33, no. 4 (2007): 770–90; David A. Rossiter, "Producing Provincial Space: Crown Forests, the State, and Territorial Control in British Columbia," *Space and Polity* 12, no. 2 (2008): 215–30.

53 Harry McKay, in "Logging Ruined Hunting Areas."

54 Miles Richardson, in "B.C. Judge Forbids Haida Indians."

55 "Indians Let Loggers Visit Camp," *Globe and Mail*, 14 November 1985, A11; "Logging Companies to Open New Road after BC Court Gives Access to Island," *Globe and Mail*, 12 November 1985, A5; "RCMP Hopes to Avert Logging Confrontation," *Globe and Mail*, 13 November 1985, A8.

56 Ada Yovanvic, in "Haidas Face Action."

57 Cruickshank, "3 Haidas Charged with Defying Order."

58 Frank Collison, in "Haida Preparing for Long Struggle," *Globe and Mail*, 19 November 1985, A3.

59 John Cruickshank, "10 Haida Convicted in Logging Case," *Globe and Mail*, 30 November 1985, A12.

60 Allan McEachern, in John Cruickshank, "Haida Not Criminals, Judge Tells BC Court," *Globe and Mail*, 29 November 1985, A8.

61 "Burnaby MP Refuses to Apologize for Taking Part in Haida Blockade," *Globe and Mail*, 6 December 1985, A9.

62 May, *Paradise Won*, 128. May references a *Vancouver Sun* poll from November 1985 showing 60 per cent approval for opening land claims talks with the Haida.

63 John Cruickshank, "Haida Promised Aid in Lyell Island Standoff," *Globe and Mail*, 22 November 1985, A8.

64 Christie McLaren, "Churches Back Haida in Forestry Feud," *Globe and Mail*, 27 November 1985, A1.

65 John Cruickshank, "BC Rejects Federal Mediation in Lyell Island Logging Dispute," *Globe and Mail*, 25 November 1985, A1.

66 May, *Paradise Won*, 128.

67 "Haida Reopen Lyell Island Camp," *Globe and Mail*, 6 January 1986, A8.

68 John Cruickshank and Jack Danylchuk, "Holds Investment in Forest Company, BC Minister Quits," *Globe and Mail*, 18 January 1986, A1.

69 This summary relies on May, *Paradise Won*, ch. 20.

70 Matthew Sparke, "A Map That Roared and an Original Atlas: Canada, Cartography, and the Narration of Nation," *Annals of the Association of American Geographers* 88, no. 3 (1998): 463–95.

71 Braun, *Intemperate Rainforest*.

72 Rossiter, "Nature of Protest."

73 Rossiter, "Negotiating Nature."

74 "A Special Place," editorial, *Vancouver Sun*, 16 October 1985, A4.

75 "Island in the Storm," editorial, *Globe and Mail*, 26 November 1985, A6.

76 For a sample, see "Letters," *Vancouver Sun*, 19 October 1985, A5; "Letters to the Editor," *Globe and Mail*, 17 January 1986, A7; and "Letters to the Editor," *Globe and Mail*, 29 January 1986, A6.

77 John Turner, in May, *Paradise Won*, 126.

78 Christie McLaren, "Environmentalists Ask UN to Help Save BC Islands," *Globe and Mail*, 14 January 1986, A3.

79 Cruickshank, "US Panel Opposes Lyell Logging."

80 "Letters to the Editor," *Globe and Mail*, 17 December 1985, A7.

81 "Letters," *Vancouver Sun*, 19 October 1985.

82 McLaren, "Environmentalists Ask UN."

83 For a rare exception, see Johnston, "Canada's Queen Charlotte Islands."

84 Hawkes, "Gwaii Haanas Agreement."

85 David A. Rossiter and Patricia K. Wood, "Fantastic Topographies: Neo-liberal Responses to Aboriginal Land Claims in British Columbia," *Canadian Geographer* 49, no. 4 (2005): 352–66.

86 For an extended discussion of the "two-row wampum" versus "citizens plus," see Peter J. Usher, "Making Native Space: Separate or Shared Futures?" *Canadian Geographer* 47, no. 1 (2003): 81–3; Peter J. Usher, "Environment, Race and Nation Reconsidered: Reflections on Aboriginal Land Claims in Canada," *Canadian Geographer* 47, no. 4 (2003): 365–82; and Cairns, *Citizens Plus*.

87 Hawkes, "Gwaii Haanas Agreement."

88 Rossiter, "Negotiating Nature."

# 3

# Lubicon Lake:
# The Success and Failure of Radical Activism

## TOM FLANAGAN

On 15 October 1988 the Lubicon Lake Cree erected barriers on the four main roads leading to the oil fields on their "traditional territory." It wasn't the biggest, or the longest-lasting, or the bloodiest blockade in Indian history. The Royal Canadian Mounted Police (RCMP) dismantled the barriers five days later, no one was hurt, and only twenty-seven people were arrested. But it had an unprecedented amount of media support because the Lubicon, advised by political organizer Fred Lennarson and lawyer James O'Reilly, had worked for years to build up a network of supporters across Canada and around the world – other Native organizations, anthropologists, museums, church groups, labour unions, media personalities, and ordinary people with sympathy for Aboriginal causes.

This unprecedented support network and favourable media coverage initially seemed to succeed. The blockade led to a meeting with Alberta premier Don Getty, who agreed to some of the demands of the Lubicon and became an advocate for their cause. Yet a subsequent meeting between the Lubicon and federal negotiators ended in a stalemate. Twenty-five years later, the Lubicon still have no agreement, no reserve, and no accompanying benefits, while oil companies continue to pump out the oil and gas. Meanwhile, several nearby Native communities have settled their claims with Alberta and Ottawa. The Lubicon began their campaign as part of the "isolated communities" coalition in north-central Alberta; ironically, the Lubicon are now *the* isolated community, as the others have settled without them. This chapter asks whether the Lubicon Nation snatched defeat from the jaws of victory.

I became interested in the Lubicon situation in 1988, when Ivan Whitehall of the federal Department of Justice asked me to research the early history of the dispute. My report put together the story up to 1933, when Indians living near Lubicon Lake first made a formal request for a reserve.[1] I concluded that, although some ancestors of the Lubicon people may have been missed in the original negotiations in 1899–1900, they had had opportunities since then to adhere to Treaty 8. That ended my involvement with the Department of Justice on this issue, but my curiosity was so piqued that I carried my research forward and published my interpretation of events in several articles in the early 1990s.[2] Meanwhile, journalist John Goddard was preparing his book *Last Stand of the Lubicon Cree*, which appeared in print after I had written my own contributions.[3]

Goddard's book, based on extensive use of primary documents as well as close personal contact with the Lubicon starting in 1984,[4] contains a great deal of information not available anywhere else. It cannot, however, be used as straightforward history. Although Goddard describes his sources in an appendix, he did not equip his book with any references. Sometimes the reader can infer the source of a statement, but in other cases there is no indication. Moreover, his narrative is a morality play in which protagonists such as Lennarson, O'Reilly, and Chief Bernard Ominayak are morally pure and selfless defenders of the Lubicon Nation, whereas government actors such as Minister of Indian Affairs Bill McKnight, Department of Justice lawyer Ivan Whitehall, and federal negotiator Brian Malone are hardhearted manipulators who care nothing about the Lubicon and even actively desire to destroy them. In writing this chapter, I have checked my earlier research against Goddard's account and taken advantage of his wealth of detail without adopting his partisan view.

Needless to say, no one is truly impartial in such disputes. Those who sympathize with the Lubicon will doubtless find my own account as one-sided as I find Goddard's. Fortunately, the world of scholarship allows researchers with different views to publish their findings so that readers may compare accounts and come to their own conclusions.

## BACKGROUND

Lubicon Lake lies in a vast wilderness of woods and water north of Lesser Slave Lake between the Peace and Athabasca Rivers. When the two Treaty 8 commissions passed through northern Alberta in 1899 and 1900, there were no trails to accommodate a large party of white men and their supplies. They had to travel by water, making a circle around the area now claimed by the Lubicon Lake Band and stopping at fur trading posts and missions that the Indians sometimes visited.

After the initial negotiations at Lesser Slave Lake, each band adhered separately to Treaty 8. The text required the Indian signatories to "cede, release, surrender and yield up ... all their rights, title and privileges whatsoever" to the lands described in the treaty (all of northern Alberta plus neighbouring parts of British Columbia, Saskatchewan, and the Northwest Territories).[5] When a band adhered to the treaty, it surrendered its share of Aboriginal title to the entire region; it did not cede a specific parcel of land within the treaty area. The meaning of treaty language is always subject to whatever the courts say; but unless some new judicial interpretation emerges, the official view is still that Treaty 8 extinguished the Aboriginal title to all of northern Alberta.

The commissioners received 2,217 Indians into treaty in 1899 and 1,219 in 1900. Although the government admitted that perhaps as many as 500 Indians had not taken treaty,[6] it decided that the Indian title could be considered extinguished and that it was not necessary to send out further treaty parties. (Goddard claims 2,500 people in the Lubicon area were overlooked but gives no source for this estimate.)[7] The Indian Affairs inspectors were authorized to add individuals to treaty lists when they made their annual rounds, and many Indians came into Treaty 8 in this way.

Some, however, remained outside of the treaty for decades. There was little pressure to enter because the traditional life of hunting and trapping remained viable. Another factor inducing some to stay out was the desire to receive half-breed scrip. A half-breed scrip commission had accompanied the treaty commission of 1899 and had issued certificates for 1,195 money scrips ($240 redeemable in Dominion lands) and 48 land scrips (240 acres). Commissioner J.A. Macrae took 383 additional applications in 1900, and more Natives continued to apply for scrip in subsequent years.

Many Natives had some white ancestry and could plausibly claim to be either Indians or Métis, depending on which appeared more advantageous. Although the treaty conferred greater long-term benefits, it paid only an initial gratuity of $7 and an annuity of $5, whereas a certificate for $240 scrip could be sold immediately to speculators for about $75. A standoff ensued in which some Natives living in the area around Lubicon Lake would not enter the treaty because they wished to take scrip, whereas government officials would not grant them scrip because they wanted them to enter the treaty, believing that to be in their long-term interest.

Over the years, many Indians added their names to the band list at Whitefish Lake, about forty miles southeast of Lubicon Lake. In 1933 fourteen men petitioned the government to create a separate reserve for them at Lubicon Lake, pleading that Whitefish Lake was too far away and that they did not wish to live there.[8] In 1940 the Indian Affairs Branch gave the Lubicon permission to elect their own chief and treated them afterward more or less as a separate band,[9] but it was too late for them to obtain a reserve directly from the federal government. The Natural Resources Transfer Act of 1930 had transferred public lands from Canada to Alberta, conferring an obligation upon Alberta to "set aside out of the unoccupied Crown lands hereby transferred to its administration, such further areas as the said Superintendent General may, in agreement with the appropriate Minister of the Province, select as necessary to enable Canada to fulfill its obligations under the treaties with the Indians of the Province."[10]

Local officials urged that a reserve be approved and surveyed at Lubicon Lake as quickly as possible. Officials in Ottawa seemed sympathetic but said it could not be done in 1940 due to lack of money and the late season.[11] The Indian agent, however, visited Lubicon Lake with a federal surveyor and selected an approximate location for the reserve at the west end of the lake.[12] Under the Treaty 8 formula of one section per family of five, or 128 acres per person, about 25 square miles would have been required for the 127 Indians counted at that time.[13]

The surveyor general claimed he could not afford to do the survey in 1941 because the Second World War had reduced his budget;[14] but on 17 February 1942 the Indian Affairs Branch requested that the Province of Alberta designate 25 square miles west of Lubicon Lake as a probable Indian reserve.[15] The same year, the Department of Mines and Resources applied for a supplementary appropriation of $5,000 to pay for surveying several reserves in northern Alberta, including the one at Lubicon Lake.[16] But the surveyor general did not want to be bothered with this work until after the war was over.[17]

In the meantime, other factors caused Indian Affairs to become less enthusiastic about establishing a reserve at Lubicon Lake. The branch believed that local officials had registered many persons on Treaty 8 lists in contravention of the strict definitions of the Indian Act. In 1942, in an action that continues to be controversial, an Indian Affairs accountant, Malcolm McCrimmon, removed 663 persons from Treaty 8 band lists for reasons such as illegitimacy, adoption, reception of half-breed scrip, and marriage of females to non-Indians.[18] His recommendations reduced the Lubicon Lake Band to fewer than half of its former numbers.[19] McCrimmon then advised that a reserve at Lubicon Lake was not necessary because of the band's small size.[20]

McCrimmon's purge of band lists caused such a political uproar that the minister appointed Justice W.A. Macdonald of the Alberta Court of Queen's Bench to investigate. Macdonald reported in 1944 that 294 of McCrimmon's recommendations should be overturned, but Indian Affairs reinstated only 129 names out of this group.[21]

After the war ended, the surveyor general turned to the task of surveying the proposed reserves in northern Alberta. Lubicon Lake was the last on a list to be done in the summer of 1946; but the surveyor, who went first to Hay Lake in the far north, did not get to Lubicon Lake.[22] For reasons unknown, the survey at Lubicon Lake was not carried out the following year and was apparently "forgotten."[23]

In 1950 the Lubicon Indians asked again for their reserve,[24] touching off several confusing years. Indian Affairs officials were uncertain whether a reserve had ever been promised or whether Lubicon Lake was the best place for it.[25] In the early 1950s the ideology of the welfare state was becoming increasingly important in Canada. It was now thought that Natives should not be left unsupervised in the bush but should be moved closer to towns and roads so that they could receive medical and social benefits and their children could attend school regularly. This was also the period when the federal government began to settle the Inuit in villages and to bring the inhabitants of Newfoundland outports into more accessible towns.

Local officials were instructed to ask the Lubicon whether they really wanted a reserve at Lubicon Lake or whether they might prefer some other location. These consultations proved unsatisfactory because the Lubicon were still actively trapping and hunting. Only a handful might show up for any particular meeting, and opinion about the location of the reserve varied, depending on who was present.[26] Local officials were opposed to locating the reserve at Lubicon Lake because the site was remote and, they claimed, not suitable for farming, logging, or fishing.[27]

While these inquiries and discussions were proceeding, the Province of Alberta, which had been carrying a provisional reserve on its books, began to exert pressure for a final decision.[28] The search for petroleum was getting under way in the north, and the province wanted to allow exploration near Lubicon Lake if the land was not to become an Indian reserve. After repeated inquiries, the province issued an ultimatum on 22 October 1953: if the federal government did not commit itself within thirty days, the province would take the Lubicon reserve off its books and open the area to exploration.[29] Indian Affairs, being advised by its officials that Lubicon Lake was an unsuitable location and that some other solution could eventually be found,[30] made no effort to block Alberta's action, and the Lubicon reserve disappeared.

## THE ISOLATED COMMUNITIES

There was little immediate consequence of the failure to agree upon a reserve. The Lubicon continued to live as they always had – hunting, fishing, and trapping on otherwise unused Crown land. There was only minor petroleum exploration around Lubicon Lake – eleven wells drilled in the 1950s, twenty-three in the 1960s – and little production. But the province began constructing an all-weather road from Grande Prairie to Little Buffalo in 1971 and completed it in 1979. Eighty-two wells were drilled around Lubicon Lake in the 1970s.[31] Rising world oil prices also pointed to the development of Alberta's oil sands, so Premier Peter Lougheed officially announced on 18 September 1973 that the Syncrude project would go ahead.[32]

Harold Cardinal, a Treaty 8 Cree, was elected president of the Indian Association of Alberta in 1968. In 1969 the federal government released its famous White Paper, proposing the gradual integration of Indians into the Canadian mainstream. In reaction, Cardinal's "Red Paper" of June 1970 vigorously reasserted the separate identity of Indians. The Indian Association of Alberta commissioned an oral history program to capture the elders' understanding of treaties, which seemed to reinforce the importance of treaties by going beyond the written terms.[33]

This new activism of the Alberta First Nations was related to efforts in the neighbouring Northwest Territories to repudiate Treaties 8 and 11 in favour of a new land claims settlement with the federal government.[34] On 2 April 1973 the Indian Brotherhood of the Northwest Territories attempted to register a caveat on the land of the territories, based on the assertion that Aboriginal title had never been extinguished. The registrar of land titles referred this request to the courts, leading to the long legal battle of the Paulette case.[35] After an initial success in 1973 before Justice W.G. Morrow of the Supreme Court of the Northwest Territories, the Indian Brotherhood ultimately lost when the Supreme Court of Canada held that the Northwest Territories Act did not allow a caveat to be filed on unpatented land; but the brotherhood gained much useful publicity for its cause and did finally succeed in getting the federal government to appoint the Berger Commission of inquiry and to negotiate its claims, resulting in the suspension of Treaties 8 and 11 and the conclusion of modern land claims agreements in the Northwest Territories and Yukon.

The Indian Association of Alberta borrowed the caveat tactic at a time when it appeared to be working. On 27 October 1975 the association tried to enter a caveat on about 25,000 square miles lying north of Lesser Slave Lake between the Peace and Athabasca Rivers. This was on behalf of the "isolated communities" – Lubicon Lake and half a dozen other groups of Indians in the area – who claimed to be entitled to reserves under Treaty 8. The normal way to seek a reserve would have been to file a claim with Indian Affairs. By attempting to register a caveat, the isolated communities were asserting an unextinguished Aboriginal title to a large part of northern Alberta. They were propounding the legal doctrine that Treaty 8 had not extinguished Aboriginal title even though the text purported to do so. As a matter of political strategy, they were trying to block Syncrude and other northern oil projects and thereby wring concessions from the provincial government.[36]

The caveat tactic had some success in 1976 in bringing about an agreement with Syncrude and the federal government to create a Native employment program,[37] but its larger legal and political aims failed. When the Supreme Court of Canada rejected the Paulette appeal on 20 December 1976, it noted that one could probably register a similar caveat in Alberta because of the wording of the province's Land Titles Act.[38] Fearing that it might lose the impending court battle,[39] the Government of Alberta led the legislature to retroactively insert a new section into the act: "No caveat may be registered which affects land for which no certificate of title has been issued."[40]

Alberta announced at this time what has been called a "minimal policy." The province would not negotiate directly with First Nations but only with the federal government. Upon receiving a documented federal request, it would fulfil its responsibilities under the Natural Resources Transfer Act by transferring a land quantum based upon the Indian population at the time of the treaty (1899). All mineral rights would be retained for the province.[41] The province saw no unextinguished Aboriginal rights in Alberta, only "unfulfilled land entitlements."[42] The attorney general challenged Indian groups to go to court if they thought they could prove the existence of unextinguished Aboriginal title. "But the government," he said, "cannot be seen to be negotiating settlements to alleged legal rights when there is doubt as to the existence of those rights."[43]

## LITIGATION

The province's unyielding position caused the isolated communities coalition to fall apart, and the Lubicon band emerged as a political actor in its own right. After the young and relatively well-educated Bernard Ominayak was elected chief in 1978,[44] he made two decisions that had a profound effect on subsequent Lubicon strategy. First, he hired Fred Lennarson as the band's political adviser. Lennarson, originally from Chicago, was a product of the legendary Saul Alinsky's school of community organization. Alinsky described his unique approach as "mass jujitsu, utilizing the power of one part of the power structure against another part."[45] "*Wherever possible go outside of the experience of the enemy*. Here you want to cause confusion, fear, and retreat."[46]

Lennarson had worked for Indian groups in eastern Canada before being brought to the Indian Association of Alberta by Harold Cardinal; he also worked as an assistant to Cardinal after the latter left the association in early 1977 to become the Alberta regional director of Indian affairs.[47] Under Lennarson's guidance, Lubicon political tactics have borne the Alinsky stamp of "mass jujitsu," pitting parts of government and public opinion against each other with unexpected moves such as appealing to the United Nations and boycotting the Winter Olympics.

Ominayak's second fateful decision was to entrust the Lubicon legal strategy to a Montreal lawyer, James O'Reilly, who had been instrumental in bringing about the James Bay Agreement. In early 1980 Billy Diamond, chief of the James Bay Cree, flew in to meet Ominayak. Offering to guarantee a bank loan of $400,000 for the Lubicon plus another $300,000 if necessary, he told Ominayak to hire O'Reilly.[48]

On 15 November 1973 O'Reilly had persuaded Justice Albert Malouf of the Quebec Superior Court to issue an injunction stopping the construction of the giant Hydro-Québec project at James Bay on grounds of the unextinguished Aboriginal title of the Cree and Inuit. The Quebec Court of Appeal quickly stayed Malouf's injunction, but the Quebec government was so shaken that it entered into negotiations with the Natives, leading to the James Bay Agreement.[49] O'Reilly played a key role in negotiating the agreement and selling it to the Cree.

The political-legal strategy that had worked for the James Bay Cree in the 1970s – claiming unextinguished Aboriginal title, seeking an injunction to hold up natural resource development, entering into negotiations to achieve a settlement – must have seemed an ideal model for the

Lubicon Cree in the 1980s. But there was a difference between the two situations. Before 1975 there had been no land surrenders of any kind in northern Quebec, so the Native claim to possess unextinguished Aboriginal title had *prima facie* validity. By contrast, Treaty 8 had purported to extinguish the Indian title to all of northern Alberta, so the Lubicon had to make out the more difficult proposition that the absence of an adhesion to the treaty by what may or may not have been a Lubicon band in 1899–1900 had created an unsurrendered region of Aboriginal title in the middle of the Treaty 8 area, like a hole in the middle of a doughnut.

The Lubicon theory is a departure from the official understanding and administration of treaties in Canada. There have been eighty-one adhesions to the eleven numbered treaties in western Canada.[50] In only three of these cases has the written formula signed by the parties indicated that unceded land was being added to the treaty area: the Green Lake adhesion to Treaty 6 in 1889, the northern Manitoba adhesion to Treaty 5 in 1908–10, and the northern Ontario adhesion to Treaty 9 in 1929–30.[51] In each of these cases, the Indians signing the adhesion lived in an area that the original treaty commission had not visited and that was not contained in the land description of the original treaty document. It was clearly an addition to, or extension of, the treaty. In all other adhesions – for example, Big Bear's adhesion to Treaty 6 in 1882[52] – the chief signed a document surrendering his band's "right, title and interest" in the lands described in the original treaty; no new territory was added to the ceded area. In these cases, the Indians making the adhesion were living within the area described by the treaty.

There is little North American case law to clarify the meaning of adhesion. The closest parallel is a 1976 decision by the Supreme Court of Idaho upholding the validity of the Hellgate Treaty of 1855, even though one group of Kootenai Indians did not sign it.[53] The court held that ratification of the treaty by the Senate and proclamation by the president expressed the sovereign's intent to extinguish Aboriginal title in the area described by the treaty. Although this decision was cited favourably by the Ontario Court of Appeal in the Bear Island case,[54] its applicability to the interpretation of Canadian treaties has yet to be demonstrated.

The Bear Island case resembled the Lubicon dispute inasmuch as the Temagami Band, although living within the land described by the Robinson Huron Treaty of 1850, claimed that it still possessed unextinguished Aboriginal title because it had not not signed the treaty. There is a difference, however, because the Ontario Supreme Court, the

Ontario Court of Appeal, and the Supreme Court of Canada all agreed that a chief representing the Temagami had in fact signed the Robinson Treaty in 1850.[55] On the other hand, Osgoode Hall law professor Kent McNeil has argued that the Lubicon theory has merit.[56] It is ultimately an issue for the courts; here I can note only that the question still remains legally unresolved.

Perhaps the Lubicon were too early. In the Taku River and Haida Nation cases, the Supreme Court of Canada held that First Nations in British Columbia have a right to be consulted about resource development that might affect their land claims, even if their claim to Aboriginal title has not yet been proved. The Mikisew decision extended the same principle to the Treaty 8 area in Alberta.[57] The factual context was different from that of Lubicon Lake, but it remains possible that a new attempt at litigation might work better for the Lubicon now than it would have in the 1980s because resource development arguably affects the lands on which they may someday settle a claim and obtain a reserve.

In any case, O'Reilly, although he spent much of the 1980s in court on behalf of the Lubicon, never tackled the issue directly. His strategy was to seek an interlocutory injunction against further resource development, on the grounds that Lubicon Aboriginal rights were threatened with irreparable damage. He tried to hold up resource development first, without actually proving the continuing existence of Lubicon Aboriginal title. It was straight out of Alinsky: "*No one can negotiate without the power to compel negotiation.*"[58] Take hostages first, then talk.

O'Reilly went to work immediately, commencing an action in the Federal Court of Canada on 25 April 1980 against Canada, Alberta, and a number of oil companies. He asked for a declaratory judgment affirming Lubicon land rights, without requesting a specific remedy such as damages or an injunction. But the court held in November that the jurisdiction given to it by the Federal Court Act extended only to suits against the Crown in right of Canada. It had no power to try claims against the Province of Alberta or private oil companies, not even against Petro-Canada, which, although federally owned, was not an "officer" or "servant" of the federal Crown.[59] An appeal was quickly dismissed by the Federal Court of Appeal.[60]

From a purely legal standpoint, this seems like an odd case. O'Reilly had almost no time to prepare, and his decision to go to the Federal Court of Canada seemed predestined to fail. But the motives may have been as much political as legal: to show the Lubicon some immediate action, to attract publicity for their cause, and to build up a sense of moral outrage at yet another Indian loss in the white man's courts. Interestingly, O'Reilly had launched a similar throwaway action in Quebec before bringing his main request for an injunction to halt the James Bay project.[61]

However, these initial efforts did bring some results. John Munro, minister of Indian affairs, accepted the Lubicon claim for negotiation as a treaty entitlement,[62] and in January 1982 there was a federal-provincial meeting to consider the issue.[63] But to negotiate for a reserve within Treaty 8 would undercut the Lubicon position that they still possessed Aboriginal title because they had never adhered to Treaty 8. The potential payoff would be much higher if they could make this latter position prevail.

O'Reilly, therefore, turned to the Alberta Court of Queen's Bench. On 19 February 1982 he filed a statement of claim requesting an injunction against resource development. He asked for a complete cessation of activity in a "reserve area" of 900 square miles around Lubicon Lake and for a reduced level of activity in a surrounding area of 8,500 square miles called the "hunting and trapping territory." The theory behind the claim was that unrestricted resource development posed an imminent danger to Lubicon land rights, which were said to be of three types: (1) Aboriginal title that still existed because the Lubicon had never formally adhered to Treaty 8; (2) "in the alternative," as lawyers like to say when they espouse contradictory theories simultaneously, the reserve that had been granted but never implemented by government officials; (3) the Indians' right to hunt, fish, and trap on unoccupied Crown land protected by the Natural Resources Act of 1930.[64]

*Ominayak v. Norcen* became a complicated case. Numerous procedural arguments took up many days of hearings and resulted in two reported rulings, both of which favoured the Lubicon.[65] The case also generated a massive amount of evidence, filling thirty-two bound volumes on the history of the Cree people, the genealogy of the Lubicon band members, and the reasons for the decline in the moose population. Indeed, Justice Gregory Forsyth remarked in his second procedural ruling that since much of the evidence required to decide about the injunction was similar to what would be required to determine whether the Lubicon had any land rights, "such time and preparation might better be spent in preparation for the trial itself with the trial going forward at the earliest possible date."[66]

In the end, Justice Forsyth declined to grant the injunction. On 17 November 1983 he held that "damages would be an adequate remedy to the applicants in the event they were ultimately successful in establishing any of their positions advanced."[67] That decision might be different today if the question were relitigated in the light of the Taku River, Haida Nation, and Mikisew cases, but that's what he decided then. The Lubicon, he said, would first have to prove that their Aboriginal title still existed and then seek damages if they could show they had suffered loss. Justice Forsyth did not agree that interference with "their traditional way of life" threatened them with immediate "irreparable injury." He wrote that "the twentieth century, for better or for worse, has been part of the applicants' lives for a considerable period of time."[68] Moreover, an injunction would inflict immediate economic harm on the oil companies, for which the Lubicon would not be able to compensate them if their legal claims proved unfounded.

On 11 January 1985 the Alberta Court of Appeal upheld the lower court's decision. Writing for a 4-1 majority, Justice Roger P. Kerans said: "We think that the courts should not forget that an interim injunction is emergent relief. The claimant seeks a remedy without proof of his claim. This inversion should only be considered in cases where the harm is of such seriousness and of such a nature that any redress available after trial would not be fair or reasonable."[69]

Without judging the merit of the Lubicon theory of Aboriginal title, the court held that there was ample time to try the claim and assess damages if any. In March 1985 the Supreme Court of Canada refused leave to appeal. Two weeks later, after the British Columbia Court of Appeal granted an injunction against logging on Meares Island in circumstances that bore some similarity to the Lubicon case, O'Reilly again sought leave to appeal but was refused a second time.[70]

This defeat marked the end of attempts by the Lubicon to use the courts to achieve their objectives. Having failed to obtain an interim injunction against resource development, they chose not to further litigate their claim of Aboriginal title in the Alberta courts, just as they decided not to press their claim for a declaratory judgment in the Federal Court of Canada. The band did unsuccessfully seek an injunction in the Federal Court of Canada to compel the Department of Indian Affairs to pay its legal fees (more than $2 million),[71] but this was a sideshow. The Lubicon would now rely increasingly on Alinsky-Lennarson tactics of political guerrilla warfare.

## THE POLITICAL ARENA

During *Ominayak v. Norcen* the Lubicon had already turned to the churches, resulting in a letter dated 23 October 1983 from the World Council of Churches to Prime Minister Pierre Elliott Trudeau that

accused the Alberta government of genocide.[72] Other churchmen
quickly took up the cause. The Task Force of Churches on Corporate
Responsibility upbraided Petro-Canada for its role in oil exploration.[73]
A delegation of clergymen headed by Ted Scott, the Anglican primate
of Canada, visited Lubicon Lake in the spring of 1984.[74] The Alberta
government referred the World Council of Churches letter to the
Alberta ombudsman, who reported in August 1984 that he had found
"no factual basis" for charges of genocide.[75] Bernard Ominayak then
released a sixty-one-page statement attacking the ombudsman's report.[76]
It was indoor-outdoor political theatre, with members of the New Democratic Party in the Alberta Legislature and the House of Commons
recycling the news stories created by ecclesiastical denunciations of
the government.

Meanwhile, an important change was taking place in Alberta's position. The provincial government announced in the spring of 1984 that it
was willing to transfer mineral rights on Crown lands that might become part of Indian reserves, although it would retain the right to 50 per
cent of royalties.[77] This policy change had actually been made in 1982
in the context of negotiations over the Fort Chipewyan claim,[78] but the
public announcement at this time was clearly motivated by bad publicity
over the Lubicon dispute.

The political situation changed markedly with the election of a
Progressive Conservative majority in Parliament in September 1984. The
new prime minister, Brian Mulroney, had campaigned on a theme of
reconciliation with the provinces and with ethnic groups (e.g., payment
of compensation to Japanese Canadians interned during the Second
World War). The new minister of Indian affairs, David Crombie, had
been mayor of Toronto and was an accomplished practitioner of ethnic
politics. He met personally with Ominayak in November and agreed to
appoint a federal fact-finder to examine the Lubicon case.[79] In January
1985 he announced that the investigator would be E. Davie Fulton, one-
time federal minister of justice and former member of the Supreme Court
of British Columbia. Fulton's alcoholism had forced him to resign from
the bench, but he was now rehabilitated and able to work.

Starting in April, Fulton spent a great deal of time with the Lubicon
and ended up virtually as their advocate. On his recommendation, the
federal government made an *ex gratia* payment of $1.5 million to the
band on 8 January 1986;[80] much of this money was used to repay
the loans guaranteed by the James Bay Cree. On 7 February 1986 Fulton
submitted a long "Discussion Paper" that identified contentious issues

and highlighted points of common ground among the province, the federal government, and the Lubicon.[81] Suggesting concessions by all parties, it was meant to be the starting point of genuine negotiations.

Perhaps spooked by the prospect that Fulton's report would be relatively favourable to the Lubicon, Alberta offered in December 1985 to make an immediate transfer of 25 square miles to the band if they would drop all litigation (although their attempt to gain an injunction had been defeated, their main suit was still theoretically alive).[82] But the Lubicon rejected this offer because a reserve of 25 square miles corresponded to their band size of 127 members in 1940 and they had grown much larger in the meantime and wanted a correspondingly larger reserve. The size of the band was itself a topic of hot dispute. The band list maintained by federal authorities had 182 names in 1985, but the Lubicon claimed at least 347 members in the same year.[83] The numerical divergence had many causes, including the McCrimmon inquiry of 1940 and other disagreements about who was entitled to membership. Parliament also amended the Indian Act in 1985 to allow women disenfranchised for marrying outside the band to regain Indian status and to bring their children back with them. No one could say exactly what effect this would have on the Lubicon band, but the leadership estimated that a reserve for over 400 people would be necessary. Under the Treaty 8 formula of 128 acres per person, this meant at least 80 square miles.

This was a matter of principle for the Lubicon. Their theory of Aboriginal title asserted that they were not yet bound by Treaty 8 because they had never adhered to it. When they finally entered the treaty, it would be as a group with all of their members. They had to have the power to determine the size and membership of their band, as Indian bands had always done when they entered a treaty. To accept any external definition of their size would undercut their claim to continued possession of Aboriginal title.

The federal government was not happy with Fulton's report, and Crombie was moved to another portfolio.[84] The prime minister then appointed a new negotiator, Roger Tassé, a retired deputy minister of justice and a main architect of the Canadian Charter of Rights and Freedoms. When bilateral discussions between Tassé and the Lubicon began on 16 June 1986, the Lubicon refused to allow Alberta to join, thus rejecting the trilateral approach used for other Treaty 8 claims in the 1980s.[85] The Lubicon broke off the talks on 8 July when the federal government disputed the band size claimed by the Lubicon and denied their theory of continuing Aboriginal title.[86]

With the failure of negotiations, the Lubicon began to put more emphasis on their attempts to influence public opinion. On 14 February 1984 they had filed a complaint before the United Nations Human Rights Committee.[87] They had also established contact with European Green parties; and even as negotiations began with Tassé, a Dutch Green member of the European Parliament was touring Canada in support of the Lubicon.[88] The Lubicon had also spoken of disrupting the 1988 Calgary Winter Olympics, particularly by asking museums around the world not to participate in the Glenbow Museum's Indian exhibition, *The Spirit Sings*. In August 1986 Ominayak, Lennarson, and some Lubicon elders went on a tour of seven European countries to generate support for the boycott.[89]

Such actions continued unabated during 1986 and 1987. The boycott had some success, as a number of museums declined to loan artifacts to *The Spirit Sings*, but it did not prevent the Glenbow from mounting the exhibit. Lubicon supporters also picketed the cross-country Olympic torch relay sponsored by Petro-Canada.[90] Again, they got some media attention but did not seriously interfere with the relay or with Petro-Canada's publicity bonanza.[91]

Although not immediately successful, these efforts did indirectly lead to results. In October 1987 the federal government appointed a new negotiator, Calgary lawyer Brian Malone.[92] A meeting involving two Cabinet ministers, Bill McKnight and Joe Clark, was set up in Ottawa for 21 January 1988, in an attempt to get movement before the Winter Olympics opened in February. But the meeting got nowhere, and the minister of Indian affairs, Bill McKnight, gave the Lubicon an ultimatum. If they did not return to the table within eight days, the federal government would take further steps toward a legal resolution.[93] In response to Lubicon guerrilla tactics, the federal government now embarked on its own version of political warfare.

The Lubicon strategy at this time was to demand a prominent role for Davie Fulton as a mediator. Anglican archbishop Ted Scott telexed the prime minister, asking him to appoint Fulton, and Fulton told the *Globe and Mail* on 9 February that he could settle the Lubicon dispute in three to six months.[94] He appeared the same day before the House of Commons Standing Committee on Aboriginal Affairs, which then voted to ask the government to appoint him as mediator for bilateral negotiations.[95]

McKnight, however, pushed ahead with his own strategy. On 3 February 1988 he wrote to Jim Horsman, the Alberta attorney general and minister of federal and intergovernmental affairs, to request that Alberta provide a land quantum for a reserve according to what became known as the "McKnight formula," and he made scarcely veiled threats to sue the province if it did not quickly comply. The McKnight formula accepted the full band size and kept it open to allow for natural increase until the reserve was actually surveyed and for the return of disenfranchised Indian women and their children under the Indian Act amendments of 1985. However, it did not include the many nonstatus Indians and members of other bands whom the Lubicon had on their own list. It also would have made deductions for persons whose ancestors had received half-breed scrip in the past as well as for those who in the future might choose to take land in severalty, as allowed by Treaty 8.[96] The McKnight formula would have produced a reserve larger than Alberta had previously been willing to grant but smaller than the Lubicon demanded.

The provincial Cabinet did not like being threatened, and it was increasingly exasperated by the federal government's inability to come to terms with the Lubicon. It also embarrassed itself by announcing the Daishowa pulp mill and then having to admit that the timber-cutting licences for this project would overlap with the Lubicon "hunting and trapping territory."[97] Around this time, the Cabinet decided that Premier Don Getty should approach Bernard Ominayak personally and try to work something out.[98] Ominayak proved receptive to the overture, and the two men met for the first time on 4 March 1988.[99]

McKnight's initiative had led to an unexpected realignment of forces. Up to this point, the Lubicon, while denouncing both governments, had saved their worst rhetoric for the province and insisted on talking only with the federal government, under the constitutional principle of federal responsibility for Indians. But Getty and Ominayak got on well personally, and Getty became an advocate for the Lubicon in the spring of 1988. He tried to get the federal government to accept a proposal for arbitration in which there would be a three-person tribunal. The Lubicon would name Davie Fulton, the two governments would agree on another choice, and the two arbitrators would agree on a neutral chairperson.[100] But the federal government would not accept the proposal, perhaps because the Lubicon did not want the arbitration to be binding,[101] perhaps for other reasons not made public. McKnight, therefore, made good on his threat to litigate. On 17 May 1988 federal lawyers filed a statement of claim in the Calgary District of the Alberta Court of Queen's Bench demanding that the province make available a land quantum for a reserve according to the McKnight formula. In a strange reversal of the litigation of the early 1980s, Alberta and the Lubicon band were now joined as defendants.[102]

It quickly became evident that the Lubicon wanted to avoid proving their claim in court. In early June, Bernard Ominayak began to say openly that they were ready to "assert jurisdiction" by assuming governmental control over their traditional territory in validation of their claim that they had never relinquished their Aboriginal title.[103] On 21 September, Ominayak announced that his band would assert jurisdiction on 15 October if an agreement was not reached; this would mean a blockade of roads into oil-producing lands.[104] On 6 October, O'Reilly read a statement in court that the Lubicon were asserting jurisdiction and would not participate in any further judicial proceedings. They had no hope of obtaining justice in Canadian courts, he said, and they rejected the jurisdiction of Canadian authorities over them.[105]

Although the province declared that it would enforce the law, the Lubicon set up their blockade on 15 October. The province secured an injunction against it on 19 October; and early on the morning of 20 October, heavily armed RCMP officers took down the blockade and arrested twenty-seven people.[106] Getty and Ominayak then met on 22 October in the little town of Grimshaw. The same day, Getty agreed to sell the federal government 79 square miles with mineral rights and another 16 square miles without mineral rights for a reserve.[107] The total of 95 square miles conformed to the Lubicon band's own count of its membership.

In the trilateral treaty-entitlement negotiations with the Whitefish Lake Band and the federal government, Alberta had already decided to depart from its "minimal policy" that reserves should be determined by band size at time of treaty. It was now willing to accept the federal "date of first survey" (DOFS) position.[108] The Whitefish Lake settlement was announced on 21 December 1988.[109] Getty, however, went even farther in the Lubicon case. In approving a 95 square mile reserve, he was accepting not only the DOFS principle but also the band's own count of its membership in preference to the federal count – an issue that had not arisen in the Whitefish negotiations.

But no settlement was possible without the agreement of the federal government. Negotiations began well when Ottawa accepted a 95 square mile reserve but broke down on 24 January 1989. Many minor disagreements, such as whether Canada should pay for a hockey rink on the reserve, contributed to the stalemate, but the biggest single issue was compensation. Maintaining that they had a "comprehensive" claim based on Aboriginal title, the Lubicon demanded compensation from the federal government for failure to extinguish their Aboriginal title in 1899. The amount owed – $167 million according to one calculation – would compensate the Lubicon for various federal benefits that they had not received since 1899 because they had no reserve. The Lubicon were willing to negotiate the amount of compensation but not the principle that something had to be paid. The federal government, in contrast, viewed this as only a "specific" claim based on treaty entitlement. It recognized the Lubicon right to a reserve and was willing to pay to set up the reserve – $45 million according to its calculations. But it refused to pay a general amount for extinguishment of Aboriginal title because in its view Aboriginal title had been extinguished all over northern Alberta with the signing of Treaty 8. It was not so much the amount of money that was at stake, although that was certainly important. The federal government could not accede to the Lubicon claim for compensation without undercutting the validity of the treaties, on which it had always insisted. If it deviated from this principle in the Lubicon case, it might be forced to regard other current and potential claims across Canada as "comprehensive" (Aboriginal rights) rather than "specific" (treaty entitlement) claims.[110]

The actual collapse of the negotiations was little short of bizarre. When the federal representatives delivered a formal offer on 24 January, Fred Lennarson reacted by evoking a "Jonestown scenario." The Lubicon, he said, were "not afraid to die if they must." After lunch, he gave Ken Colby, the federal publicist, a photocopy of the chapter entitled "Of Voluntary Death" from Friedrich Nietzsche's *Thus Spake Zarathustra*. The chapter begins: "Many die too late and some die too early. Still the doctrine sounds strange: 'Die at the right time.' Die at the right time: thus Zarathustra teaches." Talks broke off in the afternoon after only twenty minutes.[111]

Days after the failure of negotiations, some Lubicon band members contacted Brian Malone to complain that they had been dropped from the band because of their opposition to Ominayak's tactics. They said they now wanted land in severalty, an option provided by Treaty 8. After repeated discussions with these dissidents, it emerged that, whereas some wanted severalty, others favoured forming another band and negotiating

a separate settlement. Talks with federal officials were well underway by
the spring of 1989 as the federal government switched to a divide-and-
conquer strategy.

Calling a snap band election for 31 May to dispel rumours of opposition to his leadership, Ominayak was re-elected chief by a unanimous
show of hands,[112] but this did not stop the defectors. On 28 August the
Department of Indian Affairs recognized a new Woodland band of about
350 members, including 117 names previously on the Lubicon list.
About 30 of these had been expelled by the Lubicon; the rest seem to
have left voluntarily.[113] Goddard claims they were led to defect by promises of cash, which was later deducted from welfare payments.[114] The
new band was an amalgamation of Lubicon dissenters and Indians from
nearby "isolated communities," such as Cadotte Lake, that had not previously been recognized as bands. The Woodland leaders immediately
began to negotiate a specific claim, resulting in an agreement in principle
on 26 March 1990. Its terms were similar to the final offer that the
Lubicon had rejected.[115] There was to be a reserve at Cadotte Lake
and a financial package to build homes and other facilities. The completed deal was signed in December 1990, with an announced value of
$56 million.[116]

On 26 March 1990 the United Nations Human Rights Committee
handed down a ruling on the complaint the Lubicon had made six years
earlier, but the rather inconclusive nature of the judgment lessened its
political impact. The committee found that, although the Lubicon had a
right to protection of their culture and identity under international
agreements, Canada "proposes to rectify the situation by a remedy that
the committee deems appropriate."[117] The committee also rejected
Lubicon charges that Ottawa had conspired to form the Woodland Cree
Band in order to undermine the Lubicon claim.

Subsequently, the federal government continued to negotiate with other isolated communities in the area on a specific claims basis. This strategy finally bore fruit in October 2007 with an agreement in principle for
the Bigstone Cree claim. As described by Indian and Northern Affairs
Canada, "The proposed settlement includes $299.5 million and no less
than 56,658 hectares (140,000 acres) of land. Also part of the agreement
was the establishment of several new reserves and a new Band for the
communities of Peerless and Trout Lakes."[118]

Ever since the breakdown of their own negotiations in 1989, the
Lubicon have been able to do little except try to slow down resource
extraction from their traditional territory. They particularly concentrated

on blocking woodcutting for Daishowa's Peace River pulp mill. In November 1990 there was an attack upon a Daishowa contractor's camp. Thirteen Lubicon members were subsequently charged with arson, but no convictions were ever obtained and the charges were eventually stayed.[119] The 1990s were also taken up with a prolonged legal struggle with Daishowa, in which the Lubicon and their support groups organized an international boycott of Daishowa paper products and Daishowa sought injunctive relief from the boycott in the courts. The Lubicon won some legal battles in the struggle, but it produced no progress toward getting a land claims settlement. Desultory negotiations did resume after the Liberals won control of the federal government in the 1993 election, but no compromise has ever been reached, and the Lubicon continue in their status of a recognized Indian band without any reserve land or the benefits that accompany having a reserve.[120]

## ANALYSIS AND CONCLUSION

The Lubicon and their supporters attribute their failure to get an agreement to the bad faith of those with whom they are dealing. They accuse governments and corporations of a desire to steal their land, to take their oil and gas without compensation, and to destroy them as a people. In 1995 Chief Bernard Ominayak described corporate outsiders:

> Over time we learned more about these outsiders and their ways. We learned how their governments operate, interact and overlap with large resource exploitation companies. We learned about their great wealth and power and how they use that wealth and power to deny the rights of other people. We learned about their cynical use and manipulation of their laws, courts and police to achieve their political and economic objectives. We learned about their lack of principle and their basic dishonesty in dealing with other people. And we learned about their lack of concern for conserving the plants and animals upon which the Lubicon people have historically depended for survival.[121]

The Friends of the Lubicon describe government actors in similar terms:

> The feds were in the middle of the 1988 election campaign and the Lubicons were becoming a thorny issue. Prime Minister Mulroney met with Ominayak and promised to negotiate, raising

Lubicon hopes and getting the Lubicon issue out of his way for the remainder of the election campaign. But Mulroney's re-elected government deliberately sabotaged these negotiations on January 24, 1989, when the feds tabled a take-it-or-leave-it offer which they knew in advance was unacceptable. The deal allows for the construction of new housing and roads, but leaves the Lubicons dependent on welfare rather than providing the compensation necessary for developing a meaningful economy. Within hours of the breakdown of negotiations, the feds had a propaganda campaign in full swing accusing the Lubicons of "greed not need."[122]

However, since 1975, during the period of the Lubicon struggle, the Government of Canada, with which the Lubicon have been unable to come to terms, has committed billions of dollars in comprehensive land claim agreements with Inuit, Indian, and Métis groups in Labrador, Quebec, Nunavut, the Northwest Territories, Yukon, and British Columbia.[123] Canada is also involved in a modern-day treaty negotiation process in British Columbia that will cost many more billions before it is concluded, and it has appropriated $2 billion in compensation for Indians who attended residential schools. Is it plausible that a country willing to spend such amounts of money to alleviate Native grievances everywhere else would refuse to deal with 500 people in northern Alberta in a genocidal attempt to steal their land and resources?

So the riddle remains: why have the Lubicon been unable to get an agreement when so many other Native groups have been able to settle their claims? To answer the question, we must focus on the protest and negotiation strategies that the Lubicon have pursued. As Christopher Alcantara has pointed out, both governments and Native organizations are actors in land claims disputes, and the actions of both sides have consequences:

In general, governments are more interested in negotiations because the costs (money, reputation and political capital) of the alternatives (i.e., litigation, protests and international lobbying) are perceived as being much higher. As such, governments are more likely to work towards an agreement with those First Nations that show a commitment to negotiations. Conversely, governments are less likely to work towards a Final Agreement with those First Nations that are confrontational.[124]

From the beginning, the Lubicon have been confrontational in both the legal and political spheres. Below is a list of their major strategic moves, more or less in chronological order:

- asserting a legally novel claim of Aboriginal title rather than a treaty-entitlement claim, which would have fitted into a well-established model of settlement;
- as part of the isolated communities coalition, attempting to register a caveat to block development of the oil sands;
- seeking an injunction in the early 1980s to block resource development in the Lubicon "reserve area" and "hunting and trapping territory";
- seeking national and international forums, such as the United Nations Human Rights Commission, to denounce Alberta and Canada for genocide;
- calling for a boycott of the Glenbow Museum's exhibition in connection with the 1988 Winter Olympics;
- blockading roads in October 1988;
- boycotting Daishowa paper products in the 1990s to prevent Daishowa from using its provincial timber leases in areas surrounding Lubicon Lake.

These radical tactics may have delayed rather than accelerated the onset of meaningful negotiations. Politicians and government officials are wary of dealing with adversaries who accuse them of genocide and organize media campaigns against them. Nonetheless, meaningful negotiations did occur in October 1988 when Premier Don Getty flipped to the side of the Lubicon after they allowed the RCMP to take down their barricades without offering violent resistance. By giving Getty a win – the restoration of law and order – the Lubicon opened the way for him to accede to their demand for 95 square miles of land for their reserve.

At that point, it seemed that the Lubicon were close to the settlement that they had sought for so long. It fell apart, however, in subsequent negotiating sessions with the federal government in late 1988 and early 1989. The Lubicon quickly got the federal negotiators to agree to their demands on land quantum and membership numbers and obtained partial acquiescence on development assistance. The government, however, rejected the Lubicon demands for financial compensation because they were based on the theory of Lubicon Aboriginal title. Confronted with Lubicon insistence on this point, the federal negotiators made a take-it-or-leave-it offer, the Lubicon and the advisers walked out, negotiations collapsed, no settlement was achieved, and the matter remains unresolved to this day.

Although the Lubicon were guided by Fred Lennarson channelling the ideas of Saul Alinsky, they seem to have overlooked Alinsky's stress on the importance of compromise:

> But to the organizer, compromise is a key and beautiful word ...
> It is making the deal, getting that vital breather, usually the victory.
> If you start with nothing, demand 100 per cent, then compromise
> for 30 per cent, you're 30 per cent ahead.
>
> A free and open society is an ongoing conflict, interrupted
> periodically by compromises – which then become the start for the
> continuation of conflict, compromise, and on ad infinitum.[125]

The Lubicon had gone far beyond Alinsky's 30 per cent; indeed, with the federal capitulation on territory and membership, and partial concessions on economic development, they had achieved at least 60 or 70 per cent of what they had been seeking. Yet they seemed to think they could get 100 per cent if they made no concessions of their own. They did get 100 per cent in the end, but it was 100 per cent of nothing.

In the real world of negotiations, you get 100 per cent of what you want only if you have achieved a position of overwhelming dominance that leaves your opponent with no viable alternatives except to concede all your demands. That's what the Allies did at the end of the Second World War when they crushed the Axis Powers and dictated the terms of unconditional surrender. But the Lubicon were far from achieving such a position of strength. With the help of Alberta, they had embarrassed the federal government into entering negotiations and making concessions, but they had never established their legal theory that they still possessed unextinguished Aboriginal title. By declining to litigate on that issue, they had left in place the legal status quo, according to which they had a treaty entitlement to a reserve and other benefits but no longer possessed Aboriginal title because it had been extinguished in northern Alberta by Treaty 8.

Without legal confirmation of their theory, the Lubicon could push only so far because the federal government had to worry about the repercussions. Recognition of the Lubicon claim to Aboriginal title could open the door to new claims in areas of Canada where it had been assumed that treaties had already extinguished Aboriginal title. In fixating on their own demands, the Lubicon failed to appreciate the position of their negotiating partner and hence missed the chance for a compromise agreement.

Yet nothing is ever really finished in the realm of Aboriginal affairs. The Lubicon people are still there, and the Government of Canada would surely like to clear up this situation. Since the 1980s the legal framework, with its new emphasis on consultations over resource development whether or not Aboriginal title has been clearly defined and proven, has evolved to the potential advantage of the Lubicon Nation. In a future iteration, the Lubicon may one day find a winning legal strategy; and if they do, they may then regard the failures of their political strategy as merely temporary setbacks. Success and failure are always relative to timeframe. As Zhou Enlai is reputed to have said when asked to assess the success of the French Revolution, "It is too soon to say."[126]

NOTES

1 Tom Flanagan, "Extinguishment of Aboriginal Title in Canada with Reference to the Lubicon Lake Case: A Report Prepared for the Federal Department of Justice," 5 January 1989.

2 Tom Flanagan, "Some Factors Bearing on the Origin of the Lubicon Lake Dispute, 1899–1940," *Alberta: Studies in the Arts and Sciences* 2, no. 2 (1990): 47–62; Tom Flanagan, "The Lubicon Lake Dispute," in *Government and Politics in Alberta*, ed. Allan Tupper and Roger Gibbins, 269–303 (Edmonton: University of Alberta Press, 1992); Tom Flanagan, "Aboriginal Land Claims in the Prairie Provinces," in *Aboriginal Land Claims in Canada: A Regional Perspective*, ed. Ken Coates, 45–72 (Mississauga, ON: Copp Clark Pitman, 1992); Tom Flanagan, "Adhesion to Canadian Indian Treaties and the Lubicon Lake Dispute," *Canadian Journal of Law and Society* 7, no. 2 (1992): 185–205.

3 John Goddard, *Last Stand of the Lubicon Cree* (Vancouver: Douglas and McIntyre, 1991).

4 Ibid., ix.

5 Treaty 8, reprinted in Dennis F.K. Madill, *Treaty Research Report: Treaty Eight* (Ottawa: Treaties and Historical Research Centre, Indian and Northern Affairs Canada, 1986), 127–35.

6 J.A. Macrae to Superintendent General of Indian Affairs, 11 December 1900, in Madill, *Treaty Eight*, 136–7.

7 Goddard, *Last Stand*, 12.

8 Alex Adams to "Dear Sirs," 25 August 1933, Archives of the Department of Indian Affairs and Northern Development, folder 777/30-12.

9  Their band status was reconfirmed on 13 November 1973 by federal
   Order in Council P.C. 1973–2571.

10 Memorandum of Agreement, 14 December 1929, s. 10, enacted by the
   Alberta Natural Resources Act, SC, 1930, c. 3.

11 H.W. McGill to C.P. Schmidt, 14 August 1940. This and following correspondence is found in exhibit B attached to affidavit 2 of Chief Bernard
   Ominayak, filed 23 September 1982, in *Ominayak v. Norcen*. Contained
   in Judge N.D. McDermid Papers, Glenbow-Alberta Institute (GAI), 6992,
   appeal book 3.

12 N.-P. L'Heureux to Secretary, Indian Affairs Branch, 1 October 1940, ibid.

13 F.H. Peters to D.J. Allan, 19 October 1940, ibid.

14 T.R.L. MacInness to N.-P. L'Heureux, 9 September 1941, ibid.

15 H.W. McGill to N.E. Tanner, 17 February 1942, ibid.

16 Minister's Chief Executive Assistant to H.W. McGill, 18 April 1942, ibid.

17 F.H. Peters to H.W. McGill, 20 August 1942, ibid.

18 A.G. Leslie to T.R.L. MacInness, 11 January 1951, ibid.

19 Malcom McCrimmon, "Report," 14 July 1942, ibid., wrote that he deleted
   58 names from the Lubicon Lake band list. Goddard, *Last Stand*, 25,
   claims he removed 90 of 154 Lubicon members.

20 Malcom McCrimmon to D.J. Allan, 11 August 1943, ibid; Malcom
   McCrimmon to Acting Director, Indian Affairs Branch, 4 July 1945, ibid.

21 A.G. Leslie to T.R.L. MacInnes, 11 January 1951, ibid.

22 C.D. Brown to R.A. Hoey, 29 October 1946, ibid.

23 D.J. Allan to G.H. Gooderham, 15 March 1952, ibid.

24 G.S. Lapp to G.H. Gooderham, 21 July 1950, ibid.

25 D.J. Allan to G.H. Gooderham, 15 March 1952, ibid.

26 Compare G.S. Lapp to G.H. Gooderham, 13 June 1952, ibid., with Lapp
   to Gooderham, 17 June 1953, ibid.

27 G.H. Gooderham to Acting Superintendent, Reserves and Trusts,
   28 November 1952, ibid.

28 T.W. Dalkin to D.J. Allan, 11 February 1952, ibid.

29 T.W. Dalkin to G.H. Gooderham, 22 October 1953, ibid.

30 G.S. Lapp to E.A. Robertson, 5 May 1954, ibid.

31 I have compiled the figures on petroleum exploration from the Map Book,
   13–16, in Justice N.D. McDermid Papers, GAI, 6992, appeal book 3.

32 Larry Pratt, *The Tar Sands: Syncrude and the Politics of Oil* (Edmonton:
   Hurtig, 1976), 18.

33 Richard T. Price, ed., *The Spirit of the Alberta Indian Treaties*
   (Montreal: Institute for Research on Public Policy and Indian Association
   of Alberta, 1979).

34 René Fumoleau, *As Long as This Land Shall Last: A History of Treaty 8 and Treaty 11, 1870–1939* (Toronto: McClelland and Stewart, 1975); Mel Watkins, ed., *The Dene Nation: The Colony Within* (Toronto: University of Toronto Press, 1977).

35 *Chief Francois Paulette v. R.*, 1974, 39 DLR (3d) 81; 1974, 42 DLR (3d) 8; 1976, 63 DLR (3d) 1; [1977] 2 SCR 628.

36 Richard Charles Daniel, *Indian Rights and Hinterland Resources: The Case of Northern Alberta* (MA thesis, University of Alberta, 1977), 195–203.

37 Ibid., 202.

38 *Paulette v. R.*, [1977] 2 SCR 628 at 638, 645.

39 *Alberta Report*, 21 March 1977, 14.

40 Bill 29, or the Land Titles Amendment Act, SA, 1977, c. 27, s. 10, amending s. 141 of the Land Titles Act (royal assent 18 May 1977).

41 Richard T. Price, "Indian Treaty Land Entitlement Claims in Alberta: Tripartite Negotiations and Settlements (1971–1988)," paper presented at the Canadian Historical Association Annual Meeting, June 1989, 18.

42 Bob Bogle, in *Alberta Hansard*, 17 March 1978, 262.

43 Jim Foster, in *Alberta Hansard*, 6 April 1977, 672–3.

44 Goddard, *Last Stand*, 60.

45 Saul D. Alinsky, *Rules for Radicals: A Practical Primer for Realistic Radicals* (New York: Vintage, 1972), 148.

46 Ibid., 127, emphasis in original.

47 *Alberta Report*, 18 April 1977, 16.

48 Roy MacGregor, *Chief: The Fearless Vision of Billy Diamond* (Markham, ON: Viking, 1989), 257–8.

49 Billy Diamond, "Aboriginal Rights: The James Bay Experience," in *The Quest for Justice: Aboriginal Peoples and Aboriginal Rights*, ed. Menno Boldt and J. Anthony Long, 265–91 (Toronto: University of Toronto Press, 1985).

50 Flanagan, "Adhesion to Canadian Indian Treaties," 188–9.

51 See the synopsis published in May 1979 by the Treaties and Historical Research Centre, entitled "Treaty Agreements between the Indian People and the Sovereign in Right of Canada," as well as the map.

52 Treaty 6, reprinted in John Leonard Taylor, *Treaty Research Report: Treaty Six* (Ottawa: Treaties and Historical Research Centre, Indian and Northern Affairs Canada, 1985), 74.

53 *State v. Coffee*, 556 P. 2d 1185 (1976).

54 *A.G. Ontario v. Bear Island Foundation et al.*, 68 OR (2d) 394 (1989) at 413.

55  A.G. *Ontario v. Bear Island Foundation*, 49 OR (2d) 353 (1985); 68 OR (2d) 394 (1989) at 408; [1991] 2 SCR 570.

56  Kent McNeil, "Commentary on 'Adhesion to Canadian Indian Treaties and the Lubicon Lake Dispute,'" *Canadian Journal of Law and Society* 7, no. 2 (1992): 207–12.

57  Tom Flanagan, *First Nations? Second Thoughts*, 2nd ed. (Montreal and Kingston: McGill-Queen's University Press, 2008), 216–18.

58  Alinsky, *Rules for Radicals*, 119, emphasis in original.

59  *Lubicon Lake Band v. the Queen*, [1981] 2 FC 317.

60  Decided 5 May 1981, 13 DLR (4th) 159.

61  MacGregor, *Chief*, 74.

62  John Munro, in *Alberta Hansard*, 12 May 1983, 953–4.

63  Boyce Richardson, "The Lubicon of Northern Alberta," in *Drumbeat: Anger and Renewal in Indian Country*, ed. Boyce Richardson, 229–64 (Toronto: Summerhill Press for the Assembly of First Nations, 1989), 242–3.

64  The theory of the case is best summarized in the appellants' factum, Justice N.D. McDermid Papers, GAI, 6992, appeal book 3.

65  *Ominayak v. Norcen*, 23 Alta. LR (2d) 284 (1983); 24 Alta. LR (2d) 394 (1983).

66  *Ominayak v. Norcen*, 24 Alta. LR (2d) 394 (1983) at 400.

67  *Ominayak v. Norcen*, 29 Alta. LR (2d) 153 (1984) at 157.

68  Ibid., 157–8.

69  *Ominayak v. Norcen*, 36 Alta, LR (2d) 138 (1985) at 145.

70  Richardson, "Lubicon of Northern Alberta," 246; *Ominayak v. Norcen*, [1985] 1 SCR xi.

71  *Ominayak v. Canada (Minister of Indian Affairs and Northern Development)*, [1987] 3 FC 174.

72  World Council of Churches, in *Alberta Hansard*, 20 March 1984, 233–5.

73  House of Commons, *Debates*, 8 May 1984, 3512–13. The letter was sent in December 1983.

74  House of Commons, *Debates*, 6 April 1984.

75  *Alberta Hansard*, 13 November 1984, 1494–5; Goddard, *Last Stand*, 96–9.

76  Bernard Ominayak, *Aboriginal Multi-Media Society of Alberta* (AMMSA), weekly Aboriginal newspaper, 14 September 1984, 3.

77  Peter Lougheed, in *Alberta Hansard*, 16 April 1984, 507–10; Milt Pahl, in *Alberta Hansard*, 25 May 1984, 2.

78  Price, "Indian Treaty Land Entitlement Claims," 16.

79  *AMMSA*, 30 November 1984, 3.

80 United Nations Human Rights Committee (UNHRC), decision of 26 March 1990, CCPR/C/38/D/167/1984, 8.

81 E. Davie Fulton, "Lubicon Lake Indian Band – Inquiry: Discussion Paper," 7 February 1986, photocopy in Thomas Flanagan Papers, University of Calgary Archives.

82 *AMMSA*, 13 December 1985, 1, 3.

83 Fulton, "Lubicon Lake Indian Band."

84 Richardson, "Lubicon of Northern Alberta," 252.

85 *Alberta Hansard*, 13 August 1986, 1055–6.

86 *Windspeaker* (successor to *AMMSA*), 12 December 1986, 3, 5; Richardson, "Lubicon of Northern Alberta," 254.

87 UNHRC, decision of 26 March 1990, 1.

88 *Windspeaker*, 27 June 1986, 1, 3.

89 *Windspeaker*, 12 December 1986, 3, 5.

90 *Windspeaker*, 20 November 1987, 3.

91 Goddard, *Last Stand*, 156–7.

92 Richardson, "Lubicon of Northern Alberta," 254. Malone was later appointed to the Federal Court of Canada.

93 Ibid., 256; *Windspeaker*, 22 January 1988, 2; House of Commons, *Debates*, 21 January 1988, 12151–3.

94 House of Commons, *Debates*, 28 April 1988, 14911.

95 House of Commons, *Debates*, 9 February 1988, 12786–7.

96 The letter of 3 February 1988, containing the McKnight formula, is quoted in the federal statement of claim, *A.G. Canada v. A.G. Alberta and the Lubicon Lake Band*, Alberta Court of Queen's Bench, 17 May 1988, 7–9.

97 House of Commons, *Debates*, 10 February 1988, 12822–3.

98 Dave Russell, interview by author, post-1989.

99 *Windspeaker*, 11 March 1988, 1.

100 Don Getty, in *Alberta Hansard*, 6 May 1988, 876–7.

101 Bill McKnight, in House of Commons, *Debates*, 18 May 1988, 15577–8.

102 *A.G. Canada v. A.G. Alberta and the Lubicon Lake Band*, Alberta Court of Queen's Bench, 17 May 1988.

103 *Windspeaker*, 3 June 1988, 3.

104 Richardson, "Lubicon of Northern Alberta," 258.

105 *Windspeaker*, 7 October 1988, 1.

106 Richardson, "Lubicon of Northern Alberta," 260; *Windspeaker*, 21 October 1988, 1.

107 *Windspeaker*, 26 October 1988; Richardson, "Lubicon of Northern Alberta," 261.

108 Price, "Indian Treaty Land Entitlement Claims," 15–19.

109  Government of Canada, untitled press release, 21 December 1988,
     included as appendix 2 in Price, "Lubicon of Northern Alberta."

110  *Calgary Herald*, 7–8 February 1989, A5.

111  From notes prepared by Brian Malone, Robert Coulter, Fred Jobin, and
     Ken Colby, 9 February 1990, in Thomas Flanagan Papers, University of
     Calgary Archives.

112  *Windspeaker*, 2 June 1989, 1.

113  *Windspeaker*, 28 July 1989, 1–2; 15 October 1990, 1, 3; UNHRC,
     decision of 26 March 1990, 20–1, 25.

114  Goddard, *Last Stand*, 212.

115  Lubicon Lake Indian Nation, "More on the Creation of the Woodland
     Cree Band," 23 December 1990, http://nisto.com/cree/lubicon/1990/
     19901223.html.

116  *Calgary Herald*, 20 December 1990.

117  UNHRC, decision of 26 March 1990, 29; *Calgary Herald*, 4 May 1990,
     B6.

118  Indian and Northern Affairs Canada, "Canada's New Government
     and Bigstone Cree Celebrate Key Milestone in Negotiations,"
     12 October 2007, http://www.aadnc-aandc.gc.ca/aiarch/mr/nr/s-d2007/
     2-2945-eng.asp.

119  *Alberta Report*, 28 January 1991, 10–11; Friends of the Lubicon,
     "Background on the Lubicon Lake Indian Nation's Struggles,"
     http://www.lubicon.ca/pa/luback.htm.

120  Friends of the Lubicon, "Background."

121  Bernard Ominayak to Friends of the Lubicon Legal Team, 1 November
     1995, http://tao.ca/~fol/pa/abofol.htm.

122  Friends of the Lubicon, "Background."

123  Aboriginal Affairs and Northern Development Canada, "General Briefing
     Note on Canada's Self-Government and Comprehensive Land Claims
     Policies and the Status of Negotiations," April 2013, https://www.aadnc-
     aandc.gc.ca/eng/1373385502190/1373385561540.

124  Christopher Alcantara, "Explaining Aboriginal Treaty Negotiation
     Outcomes in Canada: The Cases of the Inuit and the Innu in Labrador,"
     *Canadian Journal of Political Science* 40 no. 1 (2007): 185–207 at 196.

125  Alinsky, *Rules for Radicals*, 59.

126  Some think Zhou was actually referring to the French students'
     uprising of 1968, but this apocryphal quotation is too good to give up.
     http://en.wikiquote.org/wiki/Zhou_Enlai.

4

# "The War Will Be Won When the Last Low-Level Flying Happens Here in Our Home": Innu Opposition to Low-Level Flying in Labrador

P. WHITNEY LACKENBAUER

I have seen our children robbed of everything that makes us Innu in a school system which makes them look down on their own people and culture. Our people have been deeply wounded by what has happened in the past 25 years. The one thing that has stopped our total breakdown as a people has been the months we still live away from villages in our tents in the country. For the families who now have houses in Sheshatshit we find ourselves right alongside what Canada wants to make into a NATO base. Even without a base, each year military activities grow there and the number of low-level flights increases. There is now a bombing range. Most of these activities take place over or near lakes where the Innu go in the spring and fall. We have been shoved to the edge of a cliff in the last 25 years. Now they want to push us over it.

Nitassinan is our land. We never gave it to them. How can they come in and take it and treat us as if we were not human beings, as if we were invisible? There is only one Nitassinan and one Innu people ... We are fighting for our land and our identity as a distinct hunting people. We are not going to jail, becoming separated from our children just to get rich land claims. Our fight is not about land claims which is only another thing being used against us to get us to surrender what we will never, ever give up – our ownership of Nitassinan and our identity as Innu.

... In the 40 years that the military has been in Goose Bay, the Innu's culture has collapsed. The use of our lands by others, without our being consulted, has caused stress in our family relationships and links to our family violence. The Innu did not welcome foreign domination. It happened against their will. Now

we are just starting to fight back because we realize that only we can and
should decide our fate.

Elizabeth (Tshaukuesh) Penashue[1]


Elizabeth (Tshaukuesh) Penashue, born into an Innu hunting and trapping family in Labrador, moved to the community of Sheshatshit in the
1960s. Disillusioned with the plight of her people and convinced of the
need for the Innu to return to the land, she (alongside other women)
took a leadership role in initiating direct action to oppose low-level flying out of Goose Bay. Defence planners and pilots saw Labrador and
eastern Quebec as a useful *space* in which to simulate tactical air strikes,
and many non-Innu Labradorians saw the air force base as the backbone
of regional economic stability. By contrast, the Innu viewed low-level
flight training as an infringement on their unceded territory – Nitassinan –
and an existential threat to their culture.

A series of Innu occupations of the Minipi Lake bombing range and
the Goose Bay airfield between 1988 and 1990 stymied air operations
temporarily and led to the arrest of more than a hundred Innu protestors
and their supporters. Most important, from the Innu standpoint, they
provided a dramatic stage upon which to draw national and international
attention to their cause. The Innu enjoyed a high level of support from
non-Aboriginal interest groups that helped to connect their messages of
sovereignty, environmental threat, and cultural genocide to broader anti-
defence, human rights, and environmental agendas. In a concerted campaign predicated on the "politics of embarrassment," the Innu manipulated
ethnic symbols to establish "colour of right" and generate public sympathy. Although the Innu's direct action tactics did not contribute to the
Canadian government's failed bid for a NATO training centre, stop low-
level flying, or secure official acknowledgment of their sovereignty over
Nitassinan, Innu spoke about how they gained dignity and self-respect
from the experience.[2] In this sense, the failure to achieve the direct political goals was offset by internal empowerment and a sense that the Innu
could stand up to government and generate support for their plight.

## BACKGROUND

The Innu (known as Montagnais and Naskapi in Quebec) have occupied northeastern Quebec and Labrador since time immemorial.[3] As a

hunter-gatherer society, they followed a seasonal cycle based upon small family units living in camps in the interior and at river mouths along the coast. When Europeans arrived, there was little pressure to expand development into the interior of what Jacques Cartier called "the land God gave to Cain." Sustained contact came at a few fishing settlements along the Labrador coast and then through relationships with fur traders and missionaries. The larger bands that hunted and trapped for animal furs began to acquire European goods, but until the mid-twentieth century the impacts of non-Native settlement on Innu life were modest compared to the impacts on other Aboriginal groups living in areas where economic development interests had drawn extensive state attention and control.[4] This lack of pressure meant that no treaty was signed between the Crown and the Innu.

Euro-Canadian developments began to disrupt the Innu's nomadic hunter-gatherer lifestyle during the Second World War, when Labrador's strategic importance drew attention and Canadian and American soldiers, airmen, and seamen arrived in a "friendly invasion." By 1943 Goose Bay was touted as the "world's largest airport." For non-Aboriginal civilians, the air presence was a boon. Its creation, however, displaced a settlement of about thirty Native families and provided few jobs for Native peoples once construction finished. The Cold War reaffirmed Goose Bay's strategic importance and allowed Canada to make alliance contributions on the cheap. US Strategic Air Command stationed nuclear strike forces at the base in the early 1950s, and Royal Canadian Air Force and US Air Force units had begun intensive training at an air-to-air firing range by mid-decade.[5] British Royal Air Force Vulcan bombers began low-level flight training in 1967, but this training was infrequent, and the altitudes flown did not disrupt local residents or regional land use patterns. The presence of NATO allies made the base a pillar of stability in an otherwise uncertain economic geography, and despite various economic development initiatives, Goose Bay's dependence on the military made it a "single-industry town."

For the Innu, the postwar period was marked by profound changes. After Confederation in 1949, the federal and provincial governments negotiated arrangements to provide health, welfare, and education services to the Native inhabitants of Labrador. These services, coupled with declining caribou populations, low fur prices, and coercion from religious and state authorities, promoted permanent settlement in fixed communities like Sheshatshit and Davis Inlet in the 1950s and 1960s.[6]

Two Innu women noted the breakdown in Innu culture and in the relationship between the people and the land that resulted:

> In the 1950s Europeans began to move into Nitassinan in large numbers. They built a railroad and a mining town, Schefferville. At the same time, a foreign government moved into Nitassinan. They tried to stop the Innu from moving and began to build the first houses to keep us in one place.
>
> In a few short years, we have been completely robbed of our land and freedom. We have seen control of our country, the land that gave us birth as people thousands of years ago, taken from us. Now we are treated as though we are invisible. We are a hunting people. To keep us in one place, in a village, they have tried to separate us from everything that gives our life as a people meaning; it has also meant that we have been changed in only a few years from one of the most self-reliant, independent peoples in the world to one of the most dependent.
>
> The organizations that play by the European rules of the game, are supposed to help us, but they were introduced among us in the 1970s to try and control us by making it impossible for us to fight back. If we did something they didn't like, they threatened to cut off money and sometimes did so. Even here, in expressing our anger and resistance, we were dependent.[7]

Mega-projects like the Churchill Falls hydro-electric facility (which flooded Innu lands) did little to brighten their socio-economic picture. Caught in the vortex of welfare dependence and alienated from their traditional life, Innu succumbed to drug and alcohol abuse, high rates of domestic violence and suicide, low standards of living, and poor health conditions.[8]

The prospect of heightened military activity at Goose Bay, where few Innu had jobs, met with little enthusiasm in nearby Sheshatshit but did appeal to non-Innu Labradorians who faced growing economic uncertainty after the American air force drastically reduced its presence at Goose Bay in 1976. By 1979, however, Canada and its European allies had begun to discuss possible expansion to accommodate low-level flight training. Compared to population-dense western Europe, where such activities were disruptive and dangerous, Canada seemed blessed with a wealth of space.[9] The federal government allocated two expansive training areas in Labrador and eastern Quebec, representing roughly

100,000 square kilometres, and allowed aircraft to train at altitudes as low as 30 metres. From a military perspective, this contributed to Canada's NATO commitments using abundant "natural" rather than scarce financial resources.[10] As one West German air force officer told a reporter, "You've got a lot more empty space over there – except for a few caribou – than we do."[11] There was no consultation with the Innu, given that the government considered these Crown lands to be without any permanent settlements.[12]

For the Innu, these operations were intrusive and threatening. Although life in permanent settlements meant that they were not full-time hunter-gatherers, many Innu still spent parts of the year out on the land. "We are a hunting people," Ben Michel declared before a judge in Goose Bay. "It is this form of living which lies at the core of our identity as a people, which gives expression to our language, which animates our social relationships, and which for thousands of years breathed life into our people."[13] The band councils of two villages – seeking to deal with tragic rates of alcoholism, violence, and suicide – allocated government financial assistance to outpost programs that would fly Innu families to camps where they would set up tents, trap, hunt, and gather. They saw bush life as pivotal to physical and mental health. "Country life for the Innu gives great meaning to their self-worth," Chief Daniel Ashini explained. "The land is a spiritual place for us, and is normally free of the problems and stresses of the community. I should say that it was relatively stress free and peaceful until the military jets started to disturb us so much."[14] The Innu out on the land encountered low-flying aircraft swooping over or near their camps, and as early as 1978 the Naskapi Montagnais Innu Association (NMIA – formed in 1977) registered informal complaints with the base authorities at Goose Bay.[15] Although defence officials responded that the military was monitoring the training program and instituted measures to avoid negative impacts on human health and wildlife, the Innu were unconvinced and took their opposition to new forums. In the fall of 1983, amid media fanfare, an Innu delegation travelled to West Germany to contest the activities, securing the support of the German Green Party and Survival International.[16] More relationships soon followed.

A salient change in context – the renewed Cold War in the mid-1980s – increased military and political attention on Labrador and heightened Innu anxieties. In 1984 NATO proposed a new Tactical Fighter Centre in Turkey, but the Canadian government lobbied to upgrade the Goose Bay facility instead. One hundred Allied aircraft could fly up to 40,000 sorties annually, practising over eleven land and sea ranges. One of the key advantages was the low population density: central Labrador was practically uninhabited, the logic went, and was much more secure than Turkey. The provincial government and local non-Aboriginal communities believed it would bring a windfall of jobs and money into an economically depressed region.[17]

The Innu rose to the challenge. If the Innu lacked the organizational capacity and resources to protest previous development projects in their homeland,[18] they attempted to transnationalize the low-level flying dispute and leverage advocacy networks by forging alliances with international partners in the peace and Indigenous rights movements. In the fall of 1984 they announced their Campaign Against the Militarization of Nitassinan at well-publicized news conferences in Toronto, Ottawa, Montreal, and St John's. Supported by Aboriginal and human rights organizations, Peter Penashue organized a campaign against low-level flying that carried the Innu message to government officials in Canada and Europe.[19] Innu delegations repeated these tours in the years ahead, and non-Aboriginal supporters "did most of the hard work in writing pamphlets and fact sheets, organizing demonstrations and vigils, scheduling news conferences and speaking tours, circulating petitions, starting letter-writing campaigns, and lobbying the government, its NATO allies, and the media."[20] The academic community generally sympathized with the Innu,[21] and representatives of several legal and medical associations lent their support. Christian churches passed resolutions in support of the Innu cause. The environmental movement, which Aboriginal groups had previously fought over the ethics of the seal hunt and had accused of promoting "cultural genocide," now became strange bedfellows with the Innu to protect the flora and fauna of Labrador.[22] No outside group opposed low-level flying more stridently than the peace movement. After all, the image of the Innu as pacifists being "crushed by a huge and impersonal war machine" dovetailed with their criticism of military activities generally and revealed the perceived horrors of militarism close to home.[23]

The Innu also consolidated their internal support through regional assemblies that generated national media attention and allowed them to disseminate a unified message. In May 1985, for example, the Sheshatshit Innu hosted Innu leaders from across Labrador and Quebec who signed a declaration insisting that the federal government and NATO end their military training activities immediately (see figure 4.1). They also met with the Assembly of First Nations to strengthen their ties with other

We wish to make public our firm opposition to the use of our territory (Quebec-Labrador), of which a large part constitutes the migration grounds of the caribou, for military purposes, specifically the low-level flight training over our outpost camps. There are several reasons for this unconditionnal [*sic*] opposition:

1. The territory used for the low-level flying exercises has four hundreds of years been our people's territory. Many families still live on this land for a major part of the year.

2. We are firmly convinced that these low-level flights have seriously affected the wildlife in our territory – the caribou herds, fur-bearing animals, fish and fowl. Certain consequences of the flights can be clearly identified:
   – general disruption of the caribou's migration patterns,
   – abandonment of the calving grounds of the caribou,
   – severe reduction of live births of the wildlife,
   – a significant decrease in the trapping income of our people residing in the territory

3. The Innu and biologist[s] have identified the negative effects of the flights on various species of animals – the geese, the beaver, the porcupine, the partridge, all the species which the Innu depend upon for their subsistence.

4. The Innu families, in particular the elders and the children, have been traumatized by repeated overflights on their camps. It is important to emphasize that Innu children learn the traditional hunting way of life from their parents while they are in the country. But for a number of years, it has been increasingly difficult for our children to learn this way of life because they are traumatized by the military jets. It is important to emphasize that the military knows the location of our camps, and yet [they] continue to fly over at low altitudes.

5. We, the Innu people, the legitimate rightful owners of this territory, have never ceded through any treaties, land claim agreements or consultation, our collective rights to self-determination and permanent sovereignty over the territory and its natural resources.

6. The collective rights of the Innu are guaranteed by international conventions which have been signed by Canada. The use of our territory for military low-level flights training against our will constitutes a flagrant violation of these conventions.

Innu hunters are unable to leave their camps as they once did for 2 or 3 weeks at a time to hunt and trap. They can no longer leave the elders, women and children behind at the main camps because of possible accidents and other problems which may arise when the planes fly over. Problems, for example, such as: children fleeing into the forest in fear of the flights, people in canoes panicking from the sudden noise and low altitudes of the jets.

Figure 4.1
Innu letter of protest, 31 May 1985. Acquired through Government of Canada, Access to Information and Privacy (ATIP)

Canadian Native groups and received the support of National Chief George Erasmus.[24] By building internal consensus on the core issues, the Innu were able to present a united face to the national and international media, which proved receptive to their message.

NATO and government officials, however, ignored the Innu delegations, and the Canadian government seemed prepared to proceed regardless of the Innu's political lobby and indirect "tactics of embarrassment." Since 1979 foreign flight training had been governed by separate bilateral agreements between the Canadian Department of National Defence (DND) and the individual air forces. None of these agreements were significant enough to warrant a major environmental impact assessment. In 1986, however, Canada signed a Multilateral Memorandum of Understanding that allowed Britain, the United States, West Germany, and the Netherlands to practise low-level flying out of Goose Bay for the next decade. This would allow 94 aircraft at a time to conduct low-level flying out of Goose Bay – an increase in flights to up to 18,000 per year. Accordingly, the DND asked the minister of the environment to form an independent environmental assessment review panel to publicly appraise existing and potential military activities at Goose Bay.[25]

The assessment process represented an institutional venue for cooperation with the Canadian state, but the Innu were already gaining confidence by openly defying Canadian laws and asserting their sovereignty over lands that they had never surrendered to the Crown. In early 1987 Innu hunters openly defied provincial wildlife regulations and were charged with illegally hunting caribou in the Mealy Mountains. This challenge to "the foreigners' laws" was launched after consensus had been reached at community meetings. The Innu asserted that provincial laws did not apply to the Innu, who claimed the right to more than 300,00 square miles of land – a land claim that they alleged the provincial government was unwilling to settle. In the months ahead, the Sheshatshit Innu focus shifted from protesting hunting laws to resisting low-level flying.[26] On 16 April, as the court date drew near, about twenty Innu men, women, and children pitched five tents outside the fence at the southwest corner of the airbase. They expected eighty more Innu to join them, including twelve chiefs from Naskapi-Montagnais communities in Quebec, in order to protest the "interlocking issues of low level flying ... land claims and their perceived right to their traditional lifestyle."[27] Military spokesman Lieutenant Colonel John David noted ironically that the Innu chose to set up camp near the base, where the jet noise was loudest. Nevertheless, the military and the Department of

Transport (whose property the Innu occupied) did not intervene because the demonstration was peaceful and did not interfere with air personnel or operations.[28]

The transition to direct action tactics came at a time when the low-level flying debate was exacerbating local divisions. "While the provincial government, the Innu and pro-NATO groups in Labrador go on with their battle about the possible benefits and possible damage wrought by the establishment of a major NATO base at Goose Bay, all three have lost track of a very real and very obvious threat," the editor of the *St John's Sunday Express* opined on 26 April 1987. It was not the environment, alleged communist infiltration, or jobs. It was a threat to the community itself: "Regardless of the outcome of Goose Bay's attempt to land the base, people in the town are becoming more and more polarized. The issue of the expanded base is dividing the community in a dangerous way – Innu spokesmen have raised the spectre of racism, and their opponents say that the native people are trying to cash in on the base and turn it into a political football to benefit themselves ... With two clearly defined, negative and mutually antagonistic sides, there will be a winner and, obviously, a very bitter loser."[29]

### JUSTIFYING DIRECT ACTION

The low-level flying issue politicized community members and stimulated a sense of pride and courage. In the public presentation of issues and events, Innu spokespersons and their supporters manipulated ethnic symbols and rhetorical devices to forward their agenda. The subheadings in Daniel Ashini's "David Confronts Goliath: The Innu of Ungava versus the NATO Alliance" characterize the Innu framework:

The Innu: A Classically Colonized People
The Terrifying Militarization of Nitassinan
Canadian Government Committed to Our Destruction
Innu Land to Be Bombed
Our Security Threatened by Defence Policies
Gain for Others – Suffering for Us[30]

The Innu's argument suggested that the government was threatening their identity, their way of life, the physical health of their communities, and their traditional territory. Scholar-activists Peter Armitage and John Kennedy observed that the Innu had engaged in "ethnic dichotomization" by using Aboriginal symbols and stereotypes to polarize Aboriginal and non-Aboriginal interests and to create an "ethnodrama" that would mobilize public support for the Innu cause.[31]

The Innu's opposition to low-level flying was predicated on several main lines of argument. First, they claimed that jet noise endangered human health and threatened to deafen community members. When planes flew over camps, the "startle effect" traumatized children, made elders "clutch their chests," and caused widespread panic.[32] Armitage, a tireless supporter of the Innu, noted, "The unexpected, and extremely loud, jet noise induces psychological and physiological reactions typical of human responses to adverse environmental stimuli." His Innu informants were particularly upset about the negative effects of jet noise on their children. Innu hunters described the jet noise from the low-flying aircraft as sounding like a "blowtorch," "something exploding or ripping apart," a "12-gauge shotgun," and "a loud, screeching noise." Another hunter said the noise felt "like a big smack right in the ears."[33] Air training obstructed their traditional practices, the argument went, and stymied Indigenous people's attempts to nurture their communities back to health in their peaceful "country space."[34]

This tied into a second theme related to Aboriginal sovereignty, culture, and spirituality. So long as rampant militarization threatened the lands and animals, it posed an existential threat to the Innu way of life. Accordingly, military activities were inhumane, and the Innu claimed a veto to protect their inalienable Aboriginal rights. "It is as if someone comes into your home, helps themselves to your biscuits and now they are heading for the fridge," Sheshatshit Band Council member Peter Penashue told a reporter. "The war will be won when the last low-level flying happens here in our home."[35]

Third, the Innu asserted that low-level flying had negative environmental effects that only they could see on the ground. Innu hunters believed that caribou, beaver, fish, mink, ducks, and geese were adversely affected by overflights.[36] Because they claimed a more intimate connection to nature than non-Aboriginal people, they challenged the scientific data cited by government officials with their own personal observations. Furthermore, because they believed that the federal environmental assessment review would simply "rubber stamp" the military's proposal, they refused to contribute directly to the process. In this sense, having allies who were willing to disseminate their viewpoints – without the Innu actually having to directly participate in an institutionalized process that might undermine their sovereignty claim – was a particular benefit.

Fourth, social dangers posed by transient airmen brought a local, human face to the broader critique of militarism promoted by the peace movement. In particular, Innu women worried about the predatory sexual inclinations of transitory airmen stationed at the base. Elizabeth Penashue and Rose Gregoire anticipated that "Military development as a means will lead to our destruction by social ills: prostitution, disease, overcrowding. Military men are violating our women in other ways: deserted pregnant women, disgraced women who are labelled by their own community members, children growing up who will never know their fathers, women abandoning their culture by marrying men of another culture. Young women frequent military bars, becoming hopeless alcoholics. Their frustration shows up as anger against their own family members or their children."[37] Any regional economic benefits that would flow from increased military activities would not outweigh the safety issues and social trauma. Jobs would not last forever. "We Labradorians, settlers, Inuit and Innu, have survived without military development," one Innu elder explained. The "land, if you look after it, it will last forever."[38]

The protest against low-level flying was also tied to liberation from structural oppression more generally, and women played a central role. Penashue and Gregoire asserted,

> Organizations such as the Band Councils were imposed upon us. They are not Innu and do not work in the way our society works. In Innu society all people, men and women, are involved in deciding things, but in these foreign institutions which have been placed on our lives, it seems to become only the men. So in our new resistance it has been almost easier for Innu women to fight back because we were never really part of that system which has been imposed on us, and which was paid for and controlled by our foreign rulers.
>
> Our fight for our people is not a fight just for women, but for all our People. It is not a women's issue, but an Innu issue and we have welcomed any Innu person who will fight alongside us to create a free and healthy world for our children and grandchildren.

It was time for the Innu to "take over the agencies that control us. We have been masters of this land for over 9000 years. A once proud and independent people have become slaves in their own land." Elders had advised the Innu to fight for their land, which was their source of physical,

cultural, and spiritual sustenance. "We will do this by keeping up our protests against military development," Penashue and Gregoire explained.[39]

## OFFICIAL RESPONSES

The military, federal and provincial government officials, and local pro-
base supporters developed their case along several predictable lines,
seeking to undermine the factual basis of the Innu arguments. First, they
stressed that Canada was committed to upholding democratic values
through collective defence. "Canada is a member of NATO because we
believe our democratic traditions and values are worth preserving and
protecting. Collective defence is the most effective and efficient way of
doing this," a 1989 statement by the Department of External Affairs asserted. Successive Canadian governments "stated clearly that the cost of
the Canadian contribution to NATO is well worth the price, particularly
when compared to the alternatives which might well have brought less
security at a greater cost ... [and] achieving this degree of collective security in NATO requires an equitable sharing of the roles, risks and
responsibilities by all Alliance partners." This burden had to be shared,
and providing "land and facilities for training is just as much a contribution to the Alliance as modernization, budget allocations, weapons
testing, or commitment of military forces."[40]

Second, they stressed the economic benefits of NATO training. This
ensured the support of local non-Aboriginal community members,
whose foremost concern was regional prosperity. The mayor of Happy
Valley–Goose Bay, Harry Baikie, explained the importance of the military
to the town:

> The base is the only industry we've ever had at Goose Bay. Others
> have been tried but none of them have lasted. Goose Bay was a
> good northern location for the military in the '40s and it still is to-
> day. It's our industry. We're a single industry town ... We believe
> low level flying can be carried on in Labrador in such a way that
> the Innu and the Inuit live the way they want while we keep our
> jobs and our community. We don't believe it must be us or them.
> We think all the people in Labrador must find a way to live to-
> gether in harmony. But we have rights too and believe our situa-
> tion has to be understood and defended. Because if it isn't we'll be
> people without jobs and Happy Valley–Goose Bay will be another
> ghost town in the north.[41]

The Mokami Project Group, formed in 1986 to represent "the elected town, business, labour and the rural area at large" and supported by federal money, worked tirelessly to counteract critics of development.[42] Although accused of being racist (a common tactic to discredit citizens' groups that disagreed with Aboriginal agendas), the project group insisted that it was not anti-Innu, pushed the federal government to deal with the Innu land claims as quickly as possible, and insisted that it was trying to help the land claims process to proceed.[43]

Third, pro-base advocates advanced counterarguments to challenge the bases of the Innu claims. For example, John Crosbie, the federal minister of transportation from Newfoundland and a staunch proponent of a training centre, used scientific reports to challenge claims that low-level flights were a "great environmental menace." He suggested that the Innu exaggerated health impacts, asserting that snowmobiles and portable "walkmans" were far more threatening to hearing. The Innu were really engaged in a "major propaganda campaign," he asserted, to elicit public sympathy for their land claims. Some proponents also questioned Aboriginal claims to the land based on traditional pursuits, identity, and cultural survival. Should they really have a "veto" just because they were here first? Was the Innu claim to ongoing "traditional pursuits" open to debate? Were they not flown out to the bush in airplanes, and were they not sustaining their "traditional" lifestyle with store-bought goods purchased with welfare and unemployment cheques? How could they claim an intimate ecological awareness, given the shabby state of their homes and the garbage strewn about their villages? To what extent was the Innu opposition their own, and how much of it was the agenda of extremist peace groups, environmentalists, and other "outside agitators"? Were the Innu out to destroy the Euro-Canadian community?[44] The Innu and their supporters discredited such questions as racist, plain and simple.

The basic question boiled down to whether military programs were compatible with Aboriginal survival. The military was adamant that the low-level flight training and Aboriginal land use patterns were not mutually exclusive. The disruptions to human inhabitants were minute compared to those experienced in Europe, which is why Canada's NATO partners found Labrador and eastern Quebec so attractive. "Hopefully, a way can be found so that 140 aircraft and an aboriginal population of 1,100 people can co-exist in an area larger than the Federal Republic of Germany," a 1989 government backgrounder stated, trying to put the matter in perspective.[45] DND statements stressed a commitment to peaceful coexistence – and criticized Innu groups for refusing to cooperate and provide critical information on their camp locations. Colonel Philip Engstad, the commanding officer at CFB Goose Bay, reported that the Innu had not "co-operated with us in any way, shape or form."[46] Chief Daniel Ashini explained that the military could not deliver on its promise to avoid Innu hunting camps: they did not stay in one place, and they were not going to abandon their nomadic tradition.[47]

Cooperation by the Innu would also have undermined the argument that low-level flying and their cultural survival were absolutely incompatible. "We are engaged in a life and death struggle," NMIA president Greg Penashue proclaimed, "and we need to take every possible action to stop the genocide of the Innu people."[48] This position offered no room for compromise. Given that the Innu were also working closely with the peace movement, sharing information with the military also would have alienated their strongest supporters. Any concessions might have adversely affected their land claims, and it was safer – and more politically astute – to maintain that Aboriginal and military activities could not mix. The government was antagonistic by definition as long as it continued to propose any flying activities over Nitassinan.

### THE DECISION TO OCCUPY

In early April 1987 the military announced that it would increase the number of low-level flights by 25 to 28 per cent over previous levels. Innu supporters asserted that this undermined the credibility of the environmental assessment review process.[49] The following month, the Canadian Public Health Association concluded in a report that "based on the present frequency of low-level flights, neither the intensity nor the duration of exposure is sufficient to cause noise-induced hearing loss." It conceded, however, that overflights could be mentally and psychologically stressful (particularly to children) and that they could hinder the Innu's ability to pursue a traditional lifestyle. The association also concluded that the Innu's concerns about health effects were a manifestation of their political concerns regarding their right to self-determination and settlement of their land claims.[50] The provincial premier told the provincial legislature that the task force had exceeded its mandate by making recommendations on land claims,[51] which was a prolonged process in any case. Furthermore, Innu legal attempts to stymie NATO training through foreign court actions failed.[52] "With good reason," one sympathetic commentator noted, "the Innu feared that once the military had laid claim to their homeland, they would have little chance of reclaiming it for themselves and their traditional activities."[53]

Given the moral support provided to the Innu by the media and their non-Aboriginal allies, as well as the confidence generated by directly challenging state hunting laws, *peaceful* blockades and occupations represented the next logic step on a graduated scale of protest to challenge state authority. The transition to these forms of direct action reflected a shift not only in tactics but also in decision-making power in the communities. Elizabeth (Tshaukuesh) Penashue became actively involved because of her disillusionment with the ineffectiveness of community politicians in dealing with community problems. "She watched the elected men leave the village time and again for meetings with Canadian and Newfoundland officials, yet nothing ever changed," journalist-activist Marie Wadden explained. "Obviously, cooperating with outside government authorities was not working, so Tshaukuesh and other women sought new ways to achieve their goals."[54] Whereas elected politicians had acted as the spokespersons for the Innu in protesting low-level flying to this point, the decisions to occupy the South Practice Training Area and runways on the airbase was a grassroots response.

On 13 September 1987 seven Innu (five adults and two children) flew from Sheshatshit to the Minipi Lake bombing range about 100 kilometres southwest of Goose Bay. Father James Roche, a Catholic priest who had come to Sheshatshit in 1984 and a tireless crusader for the Innu cause, joined them as "chronicler." He explained,

> On the target site we were joined by other Innu people from
> La Romaine. Each year in the spring and fall these people hunt and
> trap in the Lake Formont area and their hunting area includes the
> land taken for the bombing range. While camped on the site the
> people erected a large cross and prayer shrine as well as a flag pole
> flying the Innu flag. The message of these actions was to state
> clearly their conviction that this is Innu land and that the provin-
> cial government has unjustly transferred this land to the federal
> government for use as a bombing range. During this period, the
> various air forces were unable to pursue their bombing practices.

By erecting tents on the range and radioing a warning to the base, the Innu stymied air force activities for ten days (until the Innu decided to go home). Proposed increases in low-level flight training and a NATO centre would "make life on the land impossible" by creating more restricted zones and bringing more overflights of Innu camps. Roche and the others were shocked to find a host of "unauthorized" bombs on the site, as well as an additional target site on the eastern end of the range. Was the military making changes to policies and exercises "without accountability to anyone"? Was the Canadian public's trust being "abused," and were the DND's actions a show of "disrespect" and "dishonesty"?[55]

The catalyst for more sustained direct action came a year later. In September 1988 a NATO survey team arrived in Goose Bay to assess the possibility of building the $555 million tactical fighter training centre. The Canadian and the Newfoundland and Labrador governments lobbied hard for the chance to compete for the facility, and politicians "wined and dined" the NATO team. Sheshatshit Innu requested meetings with the group, but these were denied. "The Innu were angry but could not reach a consensus about what should be done," Wadden recounted. Two Innu teenagers came up with their own plan to travel to the bombing range with Father Roche, explaining to the priest that they wanted "to show the Canadian government this is still our land and to show them that we will never stop fighting." They arrived the next day and set up camp, and aircraft practising over the target site reported their presence. The Innu in Sheshatshit issued a press release on 12 September explaining their occupation and demanding a return of the bombing range. Air operations ceased on the range, but the action failed to secure the Innu a face-to-face meeting with the delegation.[56]

On 14 September 1988, the day before the NATO visit, Sheshatshit Innu women held a meeting and decided to take their protest onto the airbase itself. The next day, seventy-five men, women, and children jumped into open trucks, walked onto the runway at CFB Goose Bay in the pouring rain, sat down, and told the commander that they would not leave until they met with the NATO survey team. Chief Daniel Ashini and Ben Michel were arrested and offered no resistance. The base commander, Colonel Philip Engstad, arrived and promised the protestors a meeting if they went to the Billy Bishop Social Centre on the base. After threatening to go back to the runway or to go on a hunger strike, the Innu were given a chance to speak to the head of the survey team. "The man listened in silence," Wadden noted, "then thanked the Innu for their comments and left."[57] The protestors went back to their community.

Six more occupations of the airfield followed that fall. They were all intended to prevent planes from landing or taking off, thus forcing temporary closures of the airport. On 22 September about one hundred

Innu, singing hymns and carrying placards, were apprehended by military police in riot gear and by officers of the Royal Canadian Mounted Police (RCMP), put on buses, and taken to the local arena. Sixty-three adults and fifteen youth were charged and released unconditionally until their trials. Father Roche and the Innu who had occupied the bombing range were also arrested and brought to the courthouse. Later the same day, at the behest of Tshaukuesh, more than two hundred Innu (a quarter of Sheshatshit's population) set up a twenty-three-tent camp in a black spruce forest on base property, just outside the fence surrounding the main runway. Innu supporters from Davis Inlet and Mingan, as well as chiefs from Quebec Innu communities, soon joined the protest camp at the base. In the ensuing weeks, the Innu mounted five more protests on the runway and even set up a tent on the front lawn of the commanding officers' homes. Chief Ashini said that the "runway camp" would remain in place until at least mid-December, even though the training flight season would not resume until the following April. The final tents came down just before Christmas, and the Innu vowed to return in the spring.[58]

The events during the fall of 1988 dramaticized the grassroots nature of the Sheshatshit Innu community protest. These were not actions orchestrated by non-Innu interest groups or elected band politicians; they were assertions of land ownership, often prompted by media visits or unfavourable federal political developments.[59] Youth activism inspired the bombing range camp, and the subsequent escalation of the protest onto the base runways and the establishment of the runway camp were largely initiated by women from the Sheshatshit community and supported by elders. Elizabeth (Tshaukuesh) Penashue explained,

> I was very concerned what's going to happen – my people and the children and land and animals – and I was writing on the paper or thinking "What should I do, what should we do"; and then we tried to get together the women. The women worked together and then we decided to do something about it, first stop low-level flying … I felt in my heart I got to do something. I got to do this because I can see that women are so strong. Almost every day I can see what women are doing. When I went in there, the airport runway, it was just women first. So I put my tent outside. First women put a tent. Now I'm thinking that's my own. That's Innu land. This belongs to Innu land, and I wasn't scared; I didn't afraid nothing. This is our land and then we put a tent and then just about evening – just about six o'clock – I never forget that – just before six

o'clock and then military police, RCMP, came and then he took me in jail. I just couldn't believe it when he took me.

I have a small grandson – I think just maybe four or three years old at that time. And I took in my arms my grandson and then when they took me to jail, then I felt I'm very strong. I'm thinking I'm not going to stay here all the time. I'm going to speak because I am not doing something bad. I'm doing this to help my people, to help the children, to protect the land, to protect the animals, and that's what happened.[60]

By taking action, the Innu overcame their fear of authority and developed a strong sense of individual and communal empowerment.[61] Elders had been "taught that you never stand up against white people, you never challenge them," Father Roche observed. The protests changed this, teaching them that "they can fight back."[62] Furthermore, the lack of any centralized leadership meant that when authorities apprehended the "known leaders" during the protests, "new leaders emerged until it was clear that this was a movement that everyone led."[63]

When air force officials prepared for the 1989 flying season, they acknowledged that the Innu had proven their intent to disrupt and even stop military flying activities at the base. The occupation and the seven runway incursions in 1988 had resulted in the closure of the South Practice Training Area, disruptions of airport operations, and reductions in Allied training activities, and they had also affected civil air operations. Military officials correctly anticipated that the Innu and their allies would begin "their protesting and media-seeking activities" before low-level flying started in April. Although all previous Innu protests had been peaceful, base officials saw the potential for the Innu to seek confrontational situations, particularly if peace alliance groups were involved. Although CFB Goose Bay would take security actions to ensure that the Innu and their supporters did not impede airfield and base operations, the commander insisted that "In the absence of illegal Innu activity, the overall security operations must not be reflected as a provocative measure to entice the Innu to demonstrate. In any reaction to a protest or demonstration, the actions of military personnel must be tempered and disciplined to prevent negative publicity from the use of excessive force or lack of discipline in a confrontation. The Innu and their followers will be seeking such circumstances to discredit the Canadian Forces and use the media coverage to support their cause."[64] In short, security officials were told explicitly to exercise restraint. The occupations were staged for the media, and the authorities had to be cautious. That spring, however, military police were better prepared to block entrances to the base and to dismantle camps quickly.[65]

In March 1989 Chief Daniel Ashini told reporters to anticipate more tents on runways and protests on airstrips. The previous fall, he explained, "the Innu discovered ... that there was a lot they could do in the struggle for their land if they worked together."[66] Accordingly, Innu protested six times inside the base fencing from 18 to 29 March 1989, with the police laying 97 charges, 49 of which were against adult women. The RCMP reported that the Innu protestors had been "peaceful, and no problem" for the police.[67] The events of 18 March were typical. At 4:15 PM, 34 Innu from Shetshashit (17 adults and 17 children) entered the base and began to erect two tents near Runway 8. With the ongoing Labrador Winter Games, it took hours to muster sufficient DND and RCMP personnel to react, and at 7:46 the protestors were advised that they were on DND property and were requested to leave. "With no identifiable leader emerging," a report from the base explained, "the group kept silent and continued to set up camp and clear bush for follow-on parties." The new north gate was closed to further Innu supporters, and the base commander and police representatives agreed that the protestors had to be removed. When the local RCMP contacted their inspector in St John's to obtain a clear mandate to act, they were told to wait until the next day, when an appointed inspector would arrive to handle the matter. The base commander, who was mindful of the projected visit by the minister of national defence a few days later, stated that the protestors had to be removed before nightfall and that he would use military personnel. The RCMP changed its tune, and 18 officers, working in conjunction with 11 military police, advised the protestors at 10:00 PM that they would be removed. The children were escorted off the property, whereas the adults and one young offender were arrested and charged with public mischief. Most were taken by DND bus to Sheshashit, whereas 9 adults remained in custody due to previous charges. The process was peaceful, with the Natives' tents neatly folded and their equipment and vehicles seized. "It is felt that the removal of protestors was essential to prevent an Innu territorial enclave – on DND land prior to [the minister of national defence's] visit," the base commander reported, and to ensure that the airport and base operations were unimpeded for flight and public safety reasons. "RCMP and DND cavalry are back in the saddle and in stride," he boasted.[68]

Despite the cavalier language, the military was careful not to use undue force while it built fences, sought a federal injunction against the protestors (which failed), and deployed a company of soldiers to bolster base security.[69] In the meantime, the protests continued unabated. On 21 March, 34 Innu protestors (14 women, 13 children, and 7 men) re-played their actions from three days earlier when they tried to set up tents in the wooded area just off Runway 8. They were again arrested by the RCMP, their equipment and vehicles were seized, and 14 women and 6 men were charged under the Canadian Criminal Code.[70] On the morn-ing of 23 March, 12 Innu (6 men, 5 women, and 1 youth) did it again. All but the youth were arrested.[71]

Accusations by the Innu's supporters that the military's response was "extreme"[72] had no basis in reality. "The Innu appear to be confused and a little disorganized," an aide-memoire for Minister of National Defence Bill McKnight observed on 22 March,[73] but the political pressure mount-ed. McKnight visited the region in late March 1989 to discuss the Innu's concerns, but they refused to let him speak. Fed up with one-way mili-tary dialogue, the Innu bombarded him with their own unilateral per-spectives, and Innu councillor Ben Michel accused him of being "not human." McKnight had hoped to begin discussions and negotiations but walked out of the meeting in recognition that little could be solved when the Innu refused to even submit a land claim.[74] Thirty-nine Innu from Sheshatshit, Davis Inlet, and a Quebec community responded by entering the base and setting up another camp on the main runway. All the adults were arrested, with the adults charged and the children released and tak-en back to their homes.[75] (A similar scenario occurred when Minister of Indian Affairs Pierre Cadieux visited Sheshatshit in June.)

A stunning victory in the courts, however, suggested the tide had turned in the Innu's favour. Provincial court judge James Igloliorte, an Inuk from Hopedale, agreed to hold the trial of four Innu protestors charged in September 1988 in Sheshatshit.[76] On 19 April 1989 he found the accused not guilty of "public mischief" based on their belief in an ancestral claim to the land. In delivering this verdict based upon the concept of "colour of right" ("an honest belief in a state of facts, which if it existed, would be a legal justification or excuse"), Igloliorte rejected the Crown claim that it "acquired magically (the land) by its own decla-ration of title."[77] This decision set a powerful precedent, and the Crown appealed it.[78]

At the time, Judge Igloliorte's decision lent legitimacy to the Innu cause. Seventy-five Innu – mainly "older children, toddlers and women" following Chief Dan Ashini – immediately gathered at Melville Hospital and broke into the base perimeter to deliver letters to the base com-mander and the four Allied commanders alleging that they were guilty of trespassing on Innu land (see figure 4.2). Their way was blocked by

Last fall we the Innu people of Nitassinan made known to you our opposition to Canada's illegal seizure and use of our land for low level flight training, bombing practice, and super sonic flight training. We remind you that Canada has no legal claim to these seized lands, and as countries flying out of Goose Bay you are accomplices to this illegal activity.

Our protests during the fall of 1988 have already shown that Canada is unable to guarantee the use of the practice bombing range and the security of the runways and ramps of CFB Goose Bay.

We promised you then that our protests would continue and that we would be back to greet you in the spring. During the past month Innu people returned to camp on their land which has been taken to establish the base. This resulted in the arrest and imprisonment of many Innu men and women. This has only strengthened our resolve to fight for our land.

We are keeping our promise today as we return again to remind you that this is Innu land. We have never given Canada, the US nor any other European government permission to use our land. The airspace in which you fly is Innu airspace and the land over which you fly is Innu land. You are trespassing on our land and we are telling you to leave. We are defending our life and land and we will not stop.

Figure 4.2
"The Innu People of Nitassinan to the Heads of Government of Canada, Great Britain, Netherlands, West Germany, and the United States of America, and to their Commanding Officers at CFB Goose Bay, 19 April 1989," letter. Acquired through Government of Canada, Access to Information and Privacy (ATIP).

soldiers who formed a human chain by interlocking their arms across the main road. The protestors were apprehended by military police and RCMP, ordered onto buses, taken off the base, and released without any charges.[79] Only the letter to the base commander was delivered, and Chief Ashini vowed that the others would be delivered in the same manner in the near future. At 6:30 PM he told the CBC media that the Innu would be demonstrating on the base runways within two weeks. Base authorities anticipated that the Innu would attempt to cut through the base perimeter fencing because Innu had purchased "most if not all of the wire cutters in the Happy Valley area" in the preceding two months.[80]

Despite the legal uncertainty, the military's approach to countering protests on the base and maintaining unimpeded air operations proved effective. Initially, the air force commander in Winnipeg emphasized "the importance of exercising maximum restraint and good judgment when confronting Innu protestors" and instructed security elements at CFB Goose Bay to refrain from making arrests unless absolutely necessary until the DND completed its legal assessment of the situation.[81] The base commander explained, however, that the military could not "play 'musical Innu' where for an extended period of time we escort protestors outside DND property only to have them re-enter immediately on the same or next day ... Our mission, manpower management and on site situation will dictate our course of action. As a bottom line any protestors who attempt to get into the fence support area or onto the airfield/ramp area proper will be considered for arresting/charging (children excluded) on the first offence ... Air force, army, and red coats are waiting."[82] They were there when Innu tried to storm the main runway that spring and summer. From March to June 1989 there were ten incidents of Innu protest activity at CFB Goose Bay. Only one resulted in the temporary closure of Runway 34. Otherwise, the military's detection and security response capabilities proved effective. "All attempts by the Innu to establish a foothold on defence property were promptly and effectively thwarted by the base security force," the air force commander noted. "We believe that there is a direct correlation between the lower number of reported incidents this year, and the effectiveness of the Op Unique deployment. The Innu have been essentially frustrated in their attempts to disrupt or stop NATO low level flying operations."[83]

The situation was manageable, but the threat that protests could disrupt operations (and "seriously jeopardize Canadian chances of being selected" for the NATO training centre) remained real.[84] Accordingly, the base commander maintained the existing security posture. Small-scale occupations and protests continued that fall, but the setbacks in the courts eroded the Innu optimism that had followed the earlier Igloliorte decision. Four Innu arrested for blocking a runway in September refused to sign undertakings promising to stay away from the base, and a provincial court judge sent them back to jail.[85] Although the regulations on defence-controlled areas made the National Defence Act an appropriate legal instrument to prohibit unauthorized use of CFB Goose Bay, legal uncertainty remained. "The recent court decision by the Newfoundland Court of Appeals which squashed the original trial due to procedural errors has not addressed any of the issues relating to the legality of the Innu to trespass onto DND property in Goose Bay," an October 1989 threat assessment explained. "No decision has been made by the Crown to relay the charges and until this matter is addressed by the courts we are unable to provide a proper assessment."[86] That month, the Innu launched a national fundraising campaign to seek a Federal Court injunction to halt low-level flying. The federal secretary of state contributed $146,000 to help with the claim, which also demanded $5 billion in damages.[87]

Despite setbacks, the blockades and occupations enjoyed widespread support within the Sheshatshit Innu community, which projected the image of a united front against military and non-Native interests. Unlike the Aboriginal protestors in cases such as Ipperwash and Gustafsen Lake, who could be labelled a "dissident" group, the Innu activists reflected a broad base of local community support. However, how much emphasis should be placed on direct action tactics rather than on land claims negotiations was open for debate. In the September 1989 Sheshatshit Band Council election, candidates were divided on whether to continue demonstrations at Goose Bay. Ben Pokue, who ran against Ashini for chief, believed that the Innu should focus on land claims negotiations rather than protests. "If you don't talk about your problems, you're not going to solve them," he told reporters. "That's the way negotiating is." Nonetheless, he lost the election, polling 100 votes to Ashini's 205.[88] This debate was also at play in the larger Innu community. For example, the Innu of Davis Inlet were less interested in the protests and believed that the NMIA should be dealing with the land claims rather than simply fixating on the low-level flying issue.[89]

Non-Native critics accused the Sheshatshit Innu of staging the protests to force the government to settle their land claims without going through the formal process. Ian Strachan of the Mokami Project Group suggested in a letter to the editor of the St John's Sunday Express on 4 June 1989,

> That the Innu of Labrador have never signed a treaty or a land claims agreement is correct. They did submit a statement of claim however to the federal government of Canada in 1978, surely an act of recognition of some sort of Canadian jurisdiction. They also agreed at that time to the rules of substantiating their claim through a land use and occupancy study. They further received in both grant and loan form from the Canadian government, approximately $1.2 million to prepare and substantiate their claim. They were slow off the mark, taking the route of protest, rather than claim substantiation and have been preceded to the negotiating table by the Labrador Inuit Association to the north of them, and the Conseil Attikamek Montagnais to the south.
>
> Left behind by virtue of their own tactics, they wanted to first somersault to the table to negotiate with Canada, juxtapositioned with claims that they were not Canadian, but a sovereign country willing to go direct to the League of Nations, ignoring totally the fact of their submission of a claim to the federal government, and

acceptance of the rules for the claim, and a large sum of money, presumably now termed "foreign aid."[90]

Defence officials were confused about the ultimate goal of the Innu protests. "The conventional wisdom when I came into the job was that it was a land claims issue," base commander Brigadier C.D. Young noted in 1990. However, when the minister of Indian affairs met with the Sheshatshit community to discuss possible land claims negotiations, the local leaders told him they were not interested.[91] They simply wanted the military out of the area.

The Innu position was difficult to discern. James O'Reilly, a lawyer who had represented the James Bay Cree and the Lubicon, asserted that "the main thrust of the case is that the Innu want to stop low-level flying, because they believe there will be irreparable damage caused to a particular way of life." The point of taking action against the Crown was "not to get the court to recognize an aboriginal claim, but to stop an activity which is interfering with a way of life. It can't be categorized in any way as a land claims case."[92] Statements by Innu leaders, however, did suggest that the protests related to concerns that low-level flying could prejudice their land claims. Chief Daniel Ashini told reporters, "The more military facilities that are put in place, and the more air combat that is conducted, the less land there will be available for us to negotiate over in our land claims negotiations ... Military expansion will bring more non-Innu people, values and political institutions into Nitassinan which will make it very difficult for us to achieve self-determination, that is, to regain the kind of control over our lives that will ensure the survival of our hunting culture ... We want to negotiate political rights that will give us meaningful jurisdiction over the lands under our control."[93] The Innu certainly insisted that low-level flying had to cease as a sign of "good faith" before land claims negotiations could begin.[94]

The Labrador Inuit, who also opposed low-level flying, pursued a different strategy. They wrote letters arguing that military activities should not expand until the environmental studies were completed, but they chose to negotiate rather than adopt direct action tactics. In 1989, for example, the Labrador Inuit Association asked the DND to enter into discussions with them concerning low-level flying and met with defence officials in December to try to develop an interim agreement related to low-level flying over the portion of Labrador that they claimed.[95] This was consistent with their typical approach to seeking negotiated solutions through institutional channels, including the comprehensive land claims process.[96] Accordingly, Inuit perspectives attracted little media fanfare compared to the less accommodating – and more sensational – Innu approach.

The preliminary Environmental Impact Statement released in December 1989 concluded that expanded low-level flying activities would not have significant adverse effects if they were carefully monitored and managed. To do so, the DND implemented a satellite monitoring system to track caribou, began to plot human and animal patterns of land and air use, promised to stop low-level overflights at designated thresholds, and set up toll-free lines so that hunters and fishermen could notify the military when they planned to use the land. Of course, it required the concurrence of Aboriginal land users to be effective.[97] However, the Environmental Impact Statement remained far from persuasive to the military's critics, and principal Innu organizations refused to participate in the compilation process, "fearing that their co-operation would merely legitimate the continuation of the low flying." They had little positive to say about the study's "objective" findings.[98] When the report was released, parliamentarian Dan Heap of the New Democratic Party still accused the Canadian Forces of conducting "war against the Innu," as did peace activists and other vocal supporters – particularly when experts pointed out flaws. The positivist faith in science was under siege, and although Aboriginal groups used scientific evidence to bolster their case when appropriate, they also played the "traditional ecological knowledge" card when facts fell into dispute.[99]

## MEDIA COVERAGE: LOCAL HOSTILITY AMID NATIONAL AND INTERNATIONAL SYMPATHY

The war for legitimacy between the various protagonists in the debate was waged in the local, regional, and national media. Both sides tried to falsify opposing perspectives, questioned legitimacy and self-interests, and vilified the motives of commentators who offered alternate viewpoints. The Innu community's successes in mobilizing national media support spoke to its ability to make its arguments more human and to adopt themes that best resonated with the tenor of the times. "We have also learned to use the media to our advantage," Innu Nation president Peter Penashue later explained. "We know that the general Canadian population does not want to see elders being thrown in jail, especially for protesting at the Parliament buildings. So we had elders with us. We knew that young people would go to jail much more quickly than the elders. We then agreed to be prepared to spend at least three weeks in jail so that our plight would become an issue and we wouldn't lose media coverage."[100] They intentionally set up the runway camp so that it would be overflown. "They invited the press, who took all sorts of shots of the Innu with their tents and these planes flying over them at low-altitude," the base commander noted. "Well, they're on takeoff! But it makes good footage."[101] All sides thought strategically.

The Innu and their supporters recognized that social movements need the media for mobilization, validation, and scope enlargement. Tapping into national and international media outlets was an essential and effective way to generate sympathy and support outside of their specific group and geographical area. Although several activists and academics have painted the Innu as the victims of critical media coverage subservient to the hegemonic order, the Innu won the sympathy of most national journalists. The most systematic analyst of the controversy assessed that the CBC, *Montreal Gazette*, *Toronto Star*, and *Globe and Mail* coverage was either "balanced" or supportive of the Innu perspective. The central Canadian media cast the Innu as stalwart defenders of their land and culture and portrayed non-Aboriginal Labradoreans as money-hungry racists, but the military's strategic imperatives garnered relatively little attention. The local media, preoccupied with economic spin-offs, were comparatively hostile to Aboriginal perspectives.[102] Given that the decision making would take place at the national and international levels, this was not a strategic obstacle to the Innu campaign.

All told, the Innu and their supporters won the media war. The national media in particular tended to accord the Innu the moral high ground, and even when journalists presented the military's perspective to provide "balance," they tended to sympathize with the Innu. If the Innu were presented in stereotypical ways that emphasized romantic depictions of noble Aboriginal people who were meant to live on the land in harmony with nature, this reflected the frames promoted by the Innu and their supporters themselves.

## AN INNU VICTORY?
### GOOSE BAY IN THE POST–COLD WAR WORLD

The end of the Cold War helped to defuse the confrontational atmosphere at Goose Bay in 1990. By March, journalist John Cruickshank

wrote in the *Globe and Mail*, expansion plans seemed out of step with
the dramatic events occurring in Europe:

> Canadian, Dutch, West German, British and U.S. pilots are already
> flying 7,000 low-level training missions a year from existing facili-
> ties. And at this crucial point in history, when there is finally some
> prospect that the reckless militarism of the recent past can be
> checked, the Canadian government proposes to enlarge the Goose
> Bay operation so that as many as 40,000 flights a year can be
> run there.
>
> This is hardly the sort of initiative that will boost confidence
> between East and West now. And it can only diminish Canada's
> credibility and flexibility in dealings with the rapidly collapsing
> Warsaw Pact.[103]

On 22 May, NATO delayed its decision about the need for a tactical
fighter training centre given the changing political climate in eastern
Europe. It announced that neither Turkey nor Goose Bay would receive
any more consideration.[104] The base pledged to maintain "business as
usual," and local proponents welcomed the decision as "quite welcome"
given that this meant the NATO countries would not be leaving, flights
could increase, and the community could grow with "any of that sudden
disruption that a NATO centre would have."[105]

The Innu welcomed the decision against the NATO training centre but
still sought a complete halt to low-level flying. The Naskapi Montagnais
Innu Association pursued legal actions against the Crown to halt air
operations,[106] but these actions did not succeed. In April 1990 a Federal
Court judge refused to grant an injunction, which would have resulted
in "extensive disruption, dislocation and prejudice against the community of Happy Valley–Goose Bay," and criticized the Innu for refusing to
cooperate with mitigation efforts. After all, the military had volunteered
to subject its current operations to environmental review, was spending
large sums of money on this process, and Allied training meant about
1,700 direct and indirect jobs for local residents (including Inuit and
Métis workers but few Innu, who had rejected DND job offers for fear
of being "co-opted"). Madam Justice Barbara Reed rejected the notion
that Innu would lose rights and saw ample space for peaceful coexistence given that fewer than two hundred Innu flew into the training area
annually and that military policy provided for a 3 mile radius around

Table 4.1
Innu demonstrations and low-level flying sorties from Goose Bay, 1988-94

| Year | Demonstrations | Demonstrators | Sorties |
|------|----------------|---------------|---------|
| 1988 | 10 | 25 to 120 at each | 6,807 |
| 1989 | 14 | 3 to 73 at each | 7,021 |
| 1990 | 1 | approx. 50 | 5,572 |
| 1991 | 0 | 0 | 6,659 |
| 1992 | 1 | approx. 15 | 7,355 |
| 1993 | 2 | 30 and 51 | 5,776 |
| 1994 | 1 | 4 | 5,476 |

Source: Compiled from "Land Force Atlantic Area Contingency Operation Plan UNIQUE,"
23 February 1996, 2–3, acquired through Government of Canada, Access to Information and
Privacy (ATIP); and Innu Nation/Mamit Innuat website, "Low Flying Sorties from Goose Bay,
1979–1998," c. 2000, copy on file with P. Whitney Lackenbauer.

any known Innu location. She pointed to no clear evidence that low-level flying had a deleterious environmental impact. Furthermore, she noted former Goose Bay mayor Hank Shouse's claim that the "Indians have told us ... they don't care about low-level flying. They want to settle land claims so they can get the benefits of it – either money today or money forever."[107] This verdict and other setbacks suggested that the Innu would not acquire a legal injunction to stop flying activities, nor would their creative efforts to disrupt legal proceedings change the court's increasingly consistent view that their blockades broke the law.[108]

Indeed, flight activities did not decline sharply with the end of the Cold War, but Innu demonstrations at the base did (see table 4.1). The Multilateral Memorandum of Understanding remained in effect with Allied countries, who continued to conduct training operations over Nitassinan. "Although international relations have improved over the past year and the tensions of the Cold War have eased, there continues to be a need for military training, including low level flying," the base commander noted. "The crisis in the Persian Gulf has highlighted the importance of the training being provided at CFB Goose Bay. Many of the British and US airmen currently flying in the Gulf have trained on the low level ranges in Labrador, and the successes achieved to date can be attributed in part to the efforts of the training centre at Goose Bay."[109] Although the US Air Force withdrew from the base in 1991, and the Innu claimed a "major victory," they pledged to fight as long as any level of flight training continued. This seldom included direct action. The 1991 flying season had been conducted without any major incident, and

Air Command assessed that local Goose Bay resources could now fulfil the requirements of Operation Unique.[110] Although CFB Goose Bay was the largest federal installation in Labrador and provided "for the best media coverage to enable the bands to air their protests," the military anticipated after 1992 that any further Native demonstrations would remain nonviolent and could be handled by civilian police.[111] Over time, the military considered the protests "more nuisance than disruptive to operations,"[112] and Innu direct action shifted to other parts of Labrador to express concerns over logging, hydro, and mining projects.

The military anticipated that the Innu threat to base activities would decline when the Innu pursued legal action related to their land claims in 1991,[113] and this expectation proved well founded. The cancellation of the NATO training centre, the declining political strength and interest of the peace movement following the end of the Cold War, and the Innu focus on land claims (it signed a framework agreement in 1996) made low-level flying an increasingly local issue. Innu spokespersons continued to complain that fighters were not avoiding hunting camps and that "avoidance criteria" proved incompatible with low-level flying,[114] but with little vested interest in cooperating and their antimilitary position well established, the Innu refused to participate in community hearings within the environmental impact assessment's public review process. They also challenged the legitimacy of groups that did, particularly the Labrador Métis, whom Innu leaders denied even had valid Aboriginal status.[115] Nonetheless, when the Goose Bay environmental impact assessment was finally completed in January 1994, it drew substantially less media commentary than its 1989 predecessor.[116] The Labrador Inuit and other Aboriginal groups were less hostile to military options than were the Innu and did not oppose the assessment panel's support for a new 130 square kilometre contiguous low-level flight training area to replace the previous ones. It would require substantial management to accommodate flight training while avoiding fauna and human activities, and the federal government agreed to ongoing consultation forums in order to ensure that the voices of local stakeholders would be heard.[117]

As a result, the relationships between the DND and regional Aboriginal groups became increasingly institutionalized. In 1990 the Labrador Inuit Association signed a memorandum of understanding to share information with the DND about flights, wildlife, and land use activities. In late 1995 the federal government created the Institute of Environmental Monitoring and Research to conduct "incisive, comprehensive, multidisciplinary and unbiased scientific research" on the effects of Allied flight training on the Labrador and northeastern Quebec ecosystems, as well as socio-economic impacts. It could advise the ministers of the environment and national defence accordingly, but its credibility depended a great deal on local stakeholder support. The institute's board of directors included strong Aboriginal representation and participation, as did an Aboriginal technical committee on caribou and a community liaison program designed to incorporate Aboriginal environmental knowledge. Aboriginal groups had to be partners, particularly after Canada and its NATO allies reached a ten-year agreement in 1996 to expand training at Goose Bay.[118]

Without mutual trust, the Institute of Environmental Monitoring and Research could not achieve its broad mandate. Various Aboriginal communities agreed to participate, but the Innu Nation of Labrador and the Mamit-Innuat of northeastern Quebec refused any initial involvement. Dr Louis LaPierre, a wildlife and ecology professor and the institute's newly appointed chair, worked with DND officials to persuade the Innu that they had nothing to lose by taking part. This demonstration of "good faith," a promise of tangible benefits to a community beset with social and economic problems, and an explicit assurance that cooperation would not adversely affect their land claims convinced the Innu to contribute on a "trial basis." At the first board meeting at Goose Bay, the participants mutually agreed to exclude the press so that meetings could be used for constructive dialogue rather than as a stage for political posturing.[119]

This institutionalization stabilized relations and legitimized the notion that low-level flying and Aboriginal survival were not mutually exclusive. The Innu did not support a 2002 government proposal to facilitate precision-guided munitions training on the range, but their development corporation received a substantial subcontract to carve a perimeter around the necessary "safety template." They completed the project on time, within budget, and "did a great job" according to long-serving DND official Frank Young. The institute is not always harmonious, but the parties had moved appreciably from protest, legal actions, and media posturing toward open, "meaningful dialogue … across board tables rather than across a courtroom." In 2000 the military took down the security fencing that it had put up at the height of Innu demonstrations at Goose Bay; the military said that it had "outlived its usefulness."[120]

The early twenty-first century also brought signs that CFB Goose Bay would soon "outlive its usefulness" for foreign military air training. The Royal Air Force closed its permanent detachment in 2005, and the

Multilateral Memorandum of Understanding governing Allied military training at Goose Bay, which expired on 31 March 2006, was not renewed. Allied nations verbally expressed an interest in future training at Goose Bay, but they have withdrawn their permanent detachments and have not committed to any training at Goose Bay in the near future.[121] Instead, a "pay as you go" pricing system has been adopted to send the message that 5 Wing Goose Bay is still "open for business."[122] Although a $20 million runway resurfacing project was completed in October 2007, and hopes of attracting new visitors to the base's "attractive flying area" remained,[123] rumours that the base could be "on the chopping block" continue to the present. Politics may intervene to prevent its closure, but the likelihood that low-level flying will resume is extremely low.[124]

### MAKING SENSE OF THE OUTCOMES

The Innu did not accomplish their expressed goal to stop all low-level flight training (their short-term objective) based upon the broader idea that they were a sovereign people who owned Nitassinan. Their broader social aim – to create and sustain a safe environment on the land where their people could nurture their ailing communities back to health – was indirectly advanced by a sense of pride and dignity more generally. "I always used to think that I was a useless Innu," Martha Hurley told journalist-activist Marie Wadden. "I felt that non-Natives always beat the Innu. But now everything has changed since our protest has begun. I feel we are stronger and our frustration feelings are being let out ... It feels like trying to get out of the years and years of being stamped under."[125]

The Sheshatshit Innu enjoyed a high level of group cohesiveness that allowed them to project the image of a united front in standing up for their rights against outside threats. There was a high degree of consensus within the Aboriginal community that military activities harmed the environment and threatened the Innu way of life. The "ethic of noninterference" – the idea that no one had the right to tell anyone else what to do – ensured that the protests arose organically within the community and that direct action tactics could not be dismissed as militant actions by a dissident faction. On one level, the decision by women like Elizabeth (Tshaukuesh) Penashue to take direct action against the air force base represented a challenge to the local political leadership's previous approach to critiquing government behaviour. Initial opposition to low-level flying included Innu meetings (with media present), domestic and international speaking tours, and public protests. When the federal government, supported by non-Native Labradorians and provincial officials, expanded military plans without consultation with the Innu (never mind consent), community members could argue that they had no choice but to occupy the bombing ranges and runways. The high degree of internal political unity in support of these actions prevented any deep political divisions from undermining these activities and their underlying justifications.

The Innu depicted their contest with the government and non-Native locals as a war of cultural genocide. The pivotal question was whether military alliances, "national security," and regional economic development were compatible with local human and environmental security in Nitassinan. One Innu supporter noted that "low-level flying was a cause that could be spun in a variety of ways, and by a lot of groups with a lot of agendas. The peace movement adopted it because it was anti-war. The environmental movement adopted it because it was protecting the earth. The Aboriginal rights constituencies adopted it because it was an issue of self-determination. The communists adopted it because it was anti-NATO ... It was a complex role that was played in many different ways."[126] These frames were effective tools to elicit support from non-Aboriginal interest groups, both nationally and internationally.

"If we have any power at all in Canada as colonized peoples," Chief Daniel Ashini noted, "it is through our ability to win the hearts and minds of the general non-Aboriginal public, to put pressure on government people who make the policies that affect us and to take our issues to international publics."[127] The Innu benefited from support and cooperation from non-Native allies, who adopted the Innu agenda and generated sympathy for their cause through the national media. Interest group supporters helped the Innu to connect their local plight to broader themes that resonated with the public outside of Labrador. National media coverage of the low-level flying controversy did not reflect the prevailing notion that the media are a "racist" tool of hegemonic state, military, and commercial interests. Innu viewpoints were accorded legitimacy and their land and resources issues were given ample and sympathetic coverage in the national and international media. They sought to delegitimize the federal government's position and played the "politics of embarrassment" to try to undermine the state's claim that it upheld peace, rationality, and security.

On a local and regional level, however, the Innu had difficulty building non-Native support. Labrador politician and author Bill Rompkey observes that "the divisions between those who occupied the land first and those who came later were sharpened and widened by the controversy over low-level flying. It provided a strong measure of solidarity both for the community of Happy Valley–Goose Bay and for the community of Sheshatshit – if not the Innu Nation – making it all the more difficult for the two communities to live together. Different aspirations, which had been dormant but growing since the beginning of the military presence, had flared into the open."[128] Happy Valley–Goose Bay had historically depended on the military base for its prosperity, and the local settler and non-Native populations of Labrador generally supported low-level flying. They challenged the Innu position and enjoyed the support of the municipal, provincial, and federal governments. Government officials emphasized alliance commitments and economic benefits, particularly from a NATO training centre. The Department of National Defence was unwavering in its adherence to international obligations and refused to become involved in what it considered to be a land claims issue.

The military had to engage the Innu, however, when Sheshatshit community members decided to move from government lobbying and media critiques issued by elected band leaders to direct action tactics inspired at the grassroots level, designed to obstruct military training and draw media attention to the Innu cause. Protests normally consisted of groups of 50 to 100 band members, including men, women, and children, and associated tactics of sit-ins, trespassing, blocking roadways, and causing damage to the perimeter fence around the Goose Bay airfield. Protestors did not carry guns and refrained from violence. Their goal, after all, was to expose the Canadian state as a militant actor that was interfering with their way of life, not to prove that they were stronger and could overpower it with force to protect Innu interests.

In response, state officials recognized that compromise was unlikely, and they developed appropriate plans to ensure that the Innu neither disrupted military training for long periods nor elicited an excessively aggressive state response. Military assessments of the threat noted,

> The stated aim of the Innu is to disrupt, and if possible stop, operational flying at CFB Goose Bay. NDHQ advises that demonstrators will try to overwhelm, by large numbers, any security forces deployed against them. Additionally, Innu will attempt to generate as much media attention as possible in order to draw attention to their land claims and affect the decision on the NATO Tactical Flight Centre. Although their spokesman has stated that their actions will be peaceful, the possibility of violent

confrontation(s) cannot be discounted. Major events, all of which will generate substantial press coverage, are likely to fuel Innu emotions and set the stage for much more active protests.[129]

In response, defence officials adopted a basic security plan that provided a "non confrontational and non provocative" military response using unarmed personnel.[130] Accordingly, because of the nonviolent approach adopted by the protestors and mirrored by state officials, the Goose Bay protests did not deteriorate into violence akin to that seen in the confrontations at Oka, Gustafsen Lake, and Ipperwash.

The Innu did not use blockades and occupations as part of a strategy of compromise and negotiation. Indeed, their messages, predicated on themes of sovereignty, genocidal impact, and inherent environmental incompatibility between state and Aboriginal practices, set up an existential struggle and negated the possibility of compromise. State authorities, who asserted that they wanted to find mutually beneficial arrangements to balance NATO needs with those of the local population, could not accept the Innu's position that their plans were fundamentally incompatible with their way of life. The end of the Cold War, the decision not to build a NATO facility, court decisions, effective base defences, and the community's eventual decision to proceed with a comprehensive land claim undermined the perceived need for and utility of blockades and occupations as a primary tactic. Other resource developments in Labrador also diluted the proportion of Innu attention devoted to the low-level flying issue; and institutionalized relationships (such as the Institute of Environmental Monitoring and Research) and the eventual decline in low-level flying further reduced the likelihood of sustained conflict.

Although Innu activism did not halt all low-level flying out of Goose Bay, Sheshatshit community members *believed* that runway blockades and occupations of practice areas made a difference. Equally important, direct action tactics served to bring together elders and youth, women and men, all of whom developed confidence and a sense of purpose. "The protests had an effect, we interrupted the flying, and the people found out that if they were united and if their efforts were concentrated they could do a lot of things they wouldn't be able to do by themselves," Daniel Ashini recalled. "There has been a lot of unity created by the Innu."[131] Direct action helped to restore Innu pride and dignity. "There is something that is very much therapeutic and healing in the act of resistance," Father Roche told a journalist in 1990.[132] In this sense, th Innu blockades and occupations were a breakthrough, and the Innu never lost the moral high ground in the national media by pushing their protest into displays of violence against the state.

NOTES

1 Elizabeth Penashue and Rose Gregoire, "Nitassinan: Our Land, Our Struggle," *Peace Magazine*, August–September 1989, 14.

2 James Ryan, "Towards a New Age in Innu Education: Innu Resistance and Community Activism," *Language, Culture and Curriculum* 11, no. 3 (1998): 339–53 at 349.

3 The Innu were formerly known as the Montagnais-Naskapi. For anthropological and historical overviews, see Edward S. Rogers and Eleanor Leacock, "Montagnais-Naskapi," in *Handbook of North American Indians*, vol. 6, *Subarctic*, ed. June Helm, 169–89 (Washington, DC: Smithsonian Institute, 1981); J. Mailhot, *Au Pays des Innus: Les Gens de Sheshatshit* (Montreal: Recherches amérindiennes au Québec, 1993); E. Plaice, *The Native Game: Settler Perceptions of Indian/Settler Relations in Central Labrador* (St John's, NL: Institute of Social and Economic Research, Memorial University of Newfoundland, 1990); and F.G. Speck, *Naskapi: The Savage Hunters of the Labrador Peninsula* (1935; reprint, Norman: University of Oklahoma Press, 1977).

4 For historical overviews, see G. Henriksen, *Hunters in the Barrens: The Naskapi on the Edge of the White Man's World* (St John's, NL: Institute of Social and Economic Research, 1973); José Mailhot, "Beyond Everyone's Horizon Stand the Naskapi," *Ethnohistory* 33, no. 4 (1986): 384–418.

5 J.N. Cardoulis, *A Friendly Invasion* (St John's, NL: Breakwater, 1990), 114–29; RG 25, G-1, vol. 1993, file 1056-AZ, Library and Archives Canada (LAC); "World's Largest Airport Operating in Labrador," *St John's Evening Telegram*, 18 May 1943; David Bercuson, "SAC vs Sovereignty: The Origins of the Goose Bay Lease, 1946–52," *Canadian Historical Review* 70, no. 2 (1989): 206–22; John Clearwater, *U.S. Nuclear Weapons in Canada* (Toronto: Dundurn, 1999), 123–54.

6 See Colin Samson, *A Way of Life That Does Not Exist* (St John's, NL: Institute of Social and Economic Research, 2003); Catherine Backhouse and Donald McRae, *Canadian Human Rights Commission on the Treatment of the Innu of Labrador by the Government of Canada* (Ottawa: Canadian Human Rights Commission, 26 March 2002), 13–14.

7 Penashue and Gregoire, "Nitassinan," 14.

8 See, for example, Samson, *A Way of Life*; Cathy White, "Labrador: The Worst Problems in the Canadian North," *Atlantic Insight*, October 1986,

26; Marie Wadden, "This Labrador Business ... What Do the Innu Want?" *Peace and Security*, Autumn 1988, 4–5.

9  West Germany and Labrador are comparable in terms of land mass, yet West Germany has a population over 2,000 times the size of Labrador's (63 million versus 30,000). Sean Patrick Dutton, "Flying the North: The Controversy over Low-Level Tactical Fighter Training in Labrador" (BA thesis, Acadia University, 1990), 10.

10  Department of National Defence (DND), *Summary: Goose Bay EIS: An Environmental Impact Statement on Military Flying Activities in Labrador and Quebec*, July 1989, S-3.

11  John Gray, "NATO Air Forces Looking to Canada as Bonn Curtails Low-Level Jet Flights," *Globe and Mail*, 30 September 1989, A1.

12  When it was announced that West Germany would be conducting flights at Goose Bay, the Labrador Inuit Association expressed two concerns: first, that Germany would increase its planes and flights and attract other countries to the area; second, that Environment Canada should form a panel on the possible impacts of the project. Judy Rowell, "Northern Labrador's Biggest Developer: The Department of National Defence," *Northern Perspectives* 18, no. 2 (March–April 1990): 11–15.

13  Ben Michel, in Marie Wadden, *Nitassinan: The Innu Struggle to Reclaim Their Homeland* (Vancouver: Douglas and McIntyre, 1991), 94–5.

14  Daniel Ashini, "Innu Opposition to Low-Level Flying," *Native Issues*, August 1987, 7–9 at 7–8.

15  David Murrell, "A Balanced Overall View? Media Reporting of the Labrador Low-Flying Controversy," paper for the Mackenzie Institute for the Study of Terrorism, Revolution and Propaganda, Toronto, 1990, 10–11. On bush camp life, see also Wadden, *Nitassinan*; Samson, *A Way of Life*; and Peter Armitage, *Homeland or Wasteland? Contemporary Land Use and Occupancy among the Innu of Utshimassit and Sheshatshit and the Impact of Military Expansion*, report for the Naskapi Montagnais Innu Association, Northwest River, Labrador, 31 January 1989.

16  Peter Armitage and John C. Kennedy, "Redbaiting and Racism on Our Frontier: Military Expansion in Labrador and Quebec," *Canadian Review of Anthropology and Sociology* 26, no. 5 (1989): 798–817 at 802–3.

17  Murrell, "Balanced Overall View?" 11–12; H.A. Pickering, "Foreign Policy as an Extra-territorial Extension of Public Policy: The Development of the 'Military Training Industry' at Goose Bay, Labrador" (PhD diss., Queen's University, 1992); DND, *Summary: Goose Bay EIS*, S-5-10.

18  See Bill Rompkey, *The Story of Labrador* (Montreal and Kingston: McGill-Queen's University Press, 2003), 143.

19  Peter Penashue, letter, 11 September 1984, file Low-Level Flying, Memorial
    University of Newfoundland, Centre for Newfoundland Studies (CNS). In
    October 1985 the Naskapi Montagnais Innu Association complained to
    the Quebec Civil Liberties Union that the low-level flying "violated the
    fundamental human and collective rights of the Innu." A follow-up investi-
    gation by the International Federation of Human Rights concluded that
    the "internationally recognized natural and legal rights of the Innu are
    being violated." Karmel Taylor-McCullum, "Space Invaders," *New Interna-
    tionalist* 186 (August 1988), http://newint.org/features/1988/08/05/wars.
20  Peter Armitage, "Indigenous Homelands and the Security Requirements of
    Western Nation-States: Innu Opposition to Military Flight Training in
    Eastern Quebec and Labrador," in *The Pentagon and the Cities*, ed.
    A. Kirby, 126–53 (Newbury Park, CA: Sage, 1992), 139.
21  Scholars no longer accepted the realist concept of "national security" as a
    given and identified how military activities seemed "disproportionately
    costly to northern aboriginal peoples." See Frances Abele, "Confronting
    'harsh and inescapable facts,'" in *Sovereignty and Security in the Arctic*,
    ed. E. Dosman, 176–93 (New York: Routledge, 1989), 189. See also Joni
    Seager, *Earth Follies: Coming to Feminist Terms with the Global
    Environmental Crisis* (New York: Routledge, 1994), 58–61.
22  Murrell, "Balanced Overall View?" 18–19; Armitage and Kennedy,
    "Redbaiting and Racism," 808; B. Yaffe, "Group's Concern Divides
    Labrador," *Globe and Mail*, 22 March 1986; Jennifer Barron, "In the
    Name of Solidarity: The Politics of Representation and Articulation in
    Support of the Labrador Innu," *Capitalism, Nature, Socialism* 11, no. 3
    (2000): 87–112. Anthropologist Mary Barker suggests, however, that the
    environmental movement played "a conspicuously minor role." Mary
    Barker, "Low-Level Military Flight Training in Quebec-Labrador: The
    Anatomy of a Northern Development Conflict," in *Aboriginal Autonomy
    and Development in Northern Quebec and Labrador*, ed. C.H. Scott,
    233–54 (Vancouver: UBC Press, 2001), 244.
23  B. McLeod, "Labrador Inquiry Smacks of Charade," *Toronto Star*, 25
    October 1988; P. Bradbury, "Luftwaffe over Labrador," *This Magazine* 19,
    no. 2 (August 1985): 9–10 at 9; Penashue and Gregoire, "Nitassinan,"
    14–15; G. Carre, "Goose Bay and NATO Air Strategy: Getting Offensive,"
    *Ploughshares Monitor* 10, no. 2 (1989): 1–4. For a critique of the peace
    movement, see John Best, "Peace Movement Using Innu for Own Arms-
    Reduction Ends," *London Free Press*, 24 April 1989, A-9.
24  Gerry Porter, "Innu Step Up Fight to Stop Proposed NATO Training Base,"
    *St John's Evening Telegram*, 29 November 1985, 1.

25  "Ottawa Appoints Seven to Review Low-Level Flying," *St John's Evening Telegram*, 9 July 1986, 1; Malcolm Spaven, "Environmental State, Military State, and Society: The Goose Bay Low Flying Controversy," *British Journal of Canadian Studies* 6, no. 1 (1991): 155–71 at 156–7.

26  See Wadden, *Nitassinan*, 93–6.

27  "Innu Flight Protest Simmers as Jailed Leaders Face Court," *St John's Evening Telegram*, 25 April 1987, 3.

28  "Indians Pitch Tents at NATO Base as Battle over Hunting Rights Escalates," *Montreal Gazette*, 22 April 1987; "Innu Camp Peacefully Near Airport in Protest," *St John's Evening Telegram*, 22 April 1987.

29  "A Real and Obvious Threat," *St John's Sunday Express*, 26 April 1987, 6.

30  David Ashini, "David Confronts Goliath: The Innu of Ungava versus the NATO Alliance," in *Drumbeat: Anger and Renewal in Indian Country* ed. B. Richardson, 45–70 (Toronto: Broadview, 1990). See also Armitage and Kennedy, "Redbaiting and Racism," 807; and C. Radha Jhappan, "Indian Symbolic Politics: The Double-Edged Sword of Publicity," *Canadian Ethnic Studies* 22, no. 3 (1990): 19–39.

31  Armitage and Kennedy, "Redbaiting and Racism," 807; Murrell, "Balanced Overall View?" 17–18; Barker, "Low-Level Military," 248–9; Armitage, *Homeland or Wasteland?*

32  Marie Wadden's oft-quoted experience during a hunting trip in May 1988 was reflective of the general tenor of the discourse adopted by the Innu and their supporters. See Wadden, *Nitassinan*, 36.

33  Armitage, "Indigenous Homelands," 134.

34  M.J. Niemans, "'For the Future for Every One of Us': Innu Women on Community, Country and Military Low-Level Flying in Labrador" (MA thesis, University of Amsterdam, 1995); Marie Wadden, "Screaming Jets Are Destroying Our Culture, Say the Innu of Labrador and Quebec," *Montreal Gazette*, 25 June 1988; Kevin Cox, "Pediatrician Sees Trauma among Labrador Children," *Globe and Mail*, 9 October 1989; Daniel Ashini, "Preface," in Wadden, *Nitassinan*, vii–ix at viii; Cathrin Degnen, "Country Space as Healing Place: Community Healing at Sheshatsiu," in *Aboriginal Autonomy and Development in Northern Quebec and Labrador*, ed. C.H. Scott, 357–78 (Vancouver: UBC Press, 2001); M.G. Mistenapeo, "Our Way of Life Comes from the Land," trans. George Gregoire, n.d., copy on file with P. Whitney Lackenbauer. On militarized masculinities and violence, see Cynthia Enloe, *Bananas, Beaches and Bases: Making Feminist Sense of International Politics* (Berkeley: University of California Press, 1990).

35 Peter Penashue, in Glen Allen, "At War with the Fighters," *Maclean's*, 7 November 1988, N2, N4.

36 For a thorough list of perceived effects, see Armitage, *Homeland or Wasteland?*

37 Penashue and Gregoire, "Nitassinan," 15.

38 In Alice Klein, "Labrador's Peace Guerrillas …," *Now Magazine*, 11–17 May 1989, 20–1 at 20. See also Armitage, *Homeland or Wasteland?* 216–19; and Lana Payne, "Labrador NATO Base Could Increase Crime," *St John's Evening Telegram*, 1 June 1989, 1.

39 Penashue and Gregoire, "Nitassinan," 14.

40 Department of External Affairs and International Trade, "Our NATO Commitment: Sharing the Burden," pamphlet, c. 1989.

41 Harry Baikie, in "The Message Was Clear … But No One Came to Listen," *Northern Reporter*, 1 January 1990, 3, 4.

42 Mokami Project Group, "An Investigation of Low-Level Flying and Its Effect on the People of Labrador," report, 17 March 1987, 1–2.

43 See, for example, Mokami Project Group, "Whose Land Is It Anyway?" *Mokami Monitor*, December 1988, 1.

44 This synopsis is based upon Armitage and Kennedy, "Redbaiting and Racism," 808–11. This perceptive article seems to overstate the pervasiveness of "communist conspiracy" arguments against the Innu. For Crosbie's view on the Innu land claim, see Ken Meaney, "Land Claims Deal Years Off: Crosbie," *St John's Evening Telegram*, 4 April 1989, 1.

45 Department of External Affairs and International Trade, "Our NATO Commitment," 2. See also DND, "Goose Bay, Low-Level Flying and the Environmental Impact Statement," backgrounder, September 1989; "Goose Bay: Flying in the Face of Native Protests," *Ottawa Citizen*, 17 September 1988; and D.N. Mainguy, "The Case for Low-Level Flights," *Ottawa Citizen*, 6 December 1989.

46 Philip Engstad, in Kevin Cox, "Innu Fighting Back on Challenges to Traditional Lifestyle …," *Globe and Mail*, 12 February 1990, A3.

47 Ashini, "David Confronts Goliath," 63.

48 Greg Penashue, in "Press Statement by Innu Leaders Accompanying the Commencement of Legal Action to Stop Low-Level Flying," *Northern Reporter*, 27 November 1989, 6.

49 "Plans to Increase Military Flights Reduces Credibility of Review," *St John's Evening Telegram*, 25 April 1987, 3.

50 Canadian Public Health Association (CPHA), untitled press release, 2 April 1987, file Low-Level Flying, CNS; CPHA Task Force on the Health Effects

of Increased Flying Activity in the Labrador Area, "Final Report," May 1987, 2, 4.

51  "Low-Level Flights Can Result in Health Problems," *Whitehorse Star*, 25 May 1987.

52  "Activists Lose Fight to Stop Low-Level Flights," *St John's Evening Telegram*, 11 June 1987, 1.

53  Ryan, "Towards a New Age," 349.

54  Wadden, *Nitassinan*, 109.

55  James Roche, OMI, to Hon. Perrin Beatty, 28 September 1987, file Low-Level Flying, CNS. On the trip more generally, see Wadden, *Nitassinan*, 99–100. "On that bombing range, I really felt for the first time what it meant to the Innu," Roche explained. "There were all these bomb shells and craters and it hit me that what was really happening here was preparation for war." He lamented that "Canada has offered Goose Bay – the homeland of the Innu, Nitassinan – as a place to rehearse and develop more advanced and efficient ways to kill each other. Any discussion of public safety has to be seen in that context." James Roche, in Kevin Cox, "RC Priest Local Hero to Natives," *Globe and Mail*, 12 February 1990, A2. Roche had spent twenty-one days in jail in 1987 for accompanying Innu on illegal hunting expeditions into the Mealy Mountains.

56  Wadden, *Nitassinan*, 101–2.

57  Ibid., 102–3; Wayne Ellwood, "Elizabeth Penashue: After Decades of Government Paternalism the Innu People of Labrador Are Fighting to Regain Their Land and Their Self-Respect," *New Internationalist*, July 1996, 31; Ryan, "Towards a New Age," 349.

58  Wadden, *Nitassinan*, 104–19, 125, 131; "Jet Flights Protested by Indians," *Canadian Press*, 23 September 1988; "Innu Protest Training, Expansion at Goose Bay," NATO *in Labrador/Quebec*, update no. 5, March 1989, 1; Allen, "At War with the Fighters." By 16 November 1988 the Innu had gone on the base eight times, prompting the RCMP to lay 129 charges of mischief, 4 of damage to property, and 1 of resisting arrest against 57 adult males, 60 adult females, 8 young men, and 5 young women. "More Than 220 Innu Now Face Charges after Demonstrations," *St John's Evening Telegram*, 15 April 1989, 13.

59  Wadden, *Nitassinan*, 120.

60  Memorial University of Newfoundland, "Interview of Elizabeth Penashue," 28 June 2006, in *Let's Teach About Women: The Women's Movement in Newfoundland and Labrador from 1970 to 1989*, http://www.mun.ca/virt/makingwaves/view_html.php?docID=72&type=3. On her leadership role, see also Wadden, *Nitassinan*, 108–9.

61 According to one hunter, he "couldn't understand how Innu Nation could tell people to do anything – like protesting, for example. If people wanted to protest, he thought, they would have to come to that themselves. They would have to make up their own minds as to what was right and what was wrong … it is not up to Innu Nation to tell people what to do." In Samson, *A Way of Life*, 37.

62 James Roche, in James Wilson, "Hunting for Peace and Quiet," *Weekend Guardian*, 19–20 August 1989, 4.

63 Wadden, *Nitassinan*, 112.

64 Col. P.C. Engstad, CFB Goose Bay Operation Order, 23 March 1989, DND f. 3350-1 (BComd), acquired through Government of Canada, Access to Information and Privacy (ATIP).

65 Wadden, *Nitassinan*, 133.

66 Daniel Ashini, in "RCMP Arrest Labrador Innu Protesting at Goose Bay Base," *St John's Sunday Express*, 19 March 1989, 4.

67 "More Than 220 Innu Now Face Charges after Demonstrations," *St John's Evening Telegram*, 15 April 1989, 13.

68 CFB Goose Bay to RCCBNVA/FGHQ North Bay (Comd) et al., Subj: Innu Protests – CFB Goose Bay, 19 March 89, acquired through ATIP.

69 LCol. A.R. Wells to DC Pol. 4, Amendment – MND Briefing Note, 21 March 1989, DND f. 2131-1 (D Secur Ops), acquired through ATIP. The Construction Engineering Unit personnel to construct the additional fencing were in place but did not proceed with their task until after the minister visited Goose Bay. LCol. T.G. Bruneau, Aide-Memoire for the Minister, Subj: CFB Goose Bay – Update, 22 March 1989, acquired through ATIP. The attorney general of Newfoundland rejected the injunction, referring to the conflict as a purely federal matter. A confidential DND memo also speculated that her decision might have been influenced by the potential costs to the province if it required additional RCMP forces to enforce an injunction, as well as her "environmentalist" leanings. DND, "Confidential Threat Update," c. 20 March 1989, acquired through ATIP. See also "Innu Enter Fifth Week of Protest," *Happy Valley–Goose Bay Labradorian*, 11 October 1988, 11; "Base Commander's Charge Rejected by Labrador's Innu," *St John's Evening Telegram*, 5 May 1989, 8.

70 CFB Goose Bay to RCCPJSA/NDHQ Ottawa (D Police Ops), 22 March 1989, acquired through ATIP. A British man, who was a member of Survival International, accompanied the Innu but was denied access to the base.

71 CFB Goose Bay to RCCPJSA/NDHQ Ottawa (D Police Ops), 23 March 1989, acquired through ATIP.

72 Wadden, *Nitassinan*, 120. For an official response to such charges, see Linda Strowbridge, "Ntesinan: The Innu Struggle for the Homeland," *St John's Sunday Express*, 13 November 1988, 25.

73 LCol. T.G. Bruneau, Aide-Memoire for the Minister, Subj: CFB Goose Bay – Update, 22 March 1989, acquired through ATIP.

74 "McKnight Visit 'No Help' to Improve Innu Relations," *St John's Evening Telegram*, 27 March 1989, 3.

75 CFB Goose Bay to RCCPJSA/NDHQ Ottawa (D Police Ops), 26 March 1989, acquired through ATIP.

76 "Judge Orders Innu Trial Moved to Native Village," *St John's Evening Telegram*, 5 April 1989, 1.

77 James Igloliorte, in Penny MacRae, "Innu Savor Victory," *St John's Evening Telegram*, 22 April 1989, 8.

78 The Crown subsequently appealed the decision, which was granted on the technicality that the court should not have dealt with four separate charges in one trial. Stephen Maher, "Ruling Inconclusive on 'Color of Right' Defence," *Happy Valley–Goose Bay Labradorian*, 10 October 1989, 1.

79 Winston C. White, "Delivering Letters Asking NATO to Leave, Innu Protestors Removed from Forces Base," *St John's Evening Telegram*, 20 April 1989, 1.

80 CFB Goose Bay to RCCBNVA/FGHQ North Bay (Comd), 26 April 1989, acquired through ATIP.

81 Instructions emphasized that "use of deadly force in defence of property alone is <u>not</u> authorized." "Security Plan – Op Unique," annex A to DND f. 3350-1 (BComd), 29 March 1990, emphasis in original, acquired through ATIP.

82 CFB Goose Bay to RCCBNVA/FGHQ North Bay (Comd), 26 April 1989, acquired through ATIP.

83 AIRCOM Winnipeg (COS Ops) to RCCPJSA/NDHQ Ottawa (DCDS), 26 June 1989, acquired through ATIP.

84 CFB Goose Bay to RCWBOCA/AIRCOM Winnipeg (COS Ops, SSO Secur), Re: Op Unique – Security Augmentation – Re-evaluation, 15 September 1989, acquired through ATIP.

85 A fifth Innu was not offered the undertaking because she had been arrested previously on similar charges, and charges were dropped against other Innu who agreed not to participate in any other protests. "Innu Protestors Opt to Remain in Jail," *St John's Evening Telegram*, 21 September 1989, 7. On the Innu occupation of 18 September 1989, see Wadden, *Nitassinan*, 169–70.

86 NSID/DUFF to NDHQ (Secur Ops 5), Re: Threat Assessment – CFB Goosebay, 19 October 1989, acquired through ATIP.

87  "Court Quashes Innu Not-Guilty Verdict," *Globe and Mail*, 4 October 1989.

88  Ben Pokue, in Stephen Maher, "Ben Pokue Calls for Land Claims Negotiations," *Happy Valley–Goose Bay Labradorian*, 19 September 1989, 3.

89  In 1988 the Davis Inlet Band threatened to leave the NMIA and form its own association. Rompkey, *Story of Labrador*, 145.

90  Ian Strachan, "Innu Difficult to Deal With," *St John's Sunday Express*, 4 June 1989, 4. The NMIA, representing the Innu of Sheshatshit and Davis Inlet, submitted a statement of claim in 1977 and a draft land use study the following year. The government conditionally accepted the claim for negotiation in July 1978, subject to a revised statement of claim, a completed land use study, and negotiations with the federal and provincial governments. The NMIA received interest-free loans to complete the documentation necessary in order to proceed but had not presented it to the government. Indian and Northern Affairs Canada, "Background on Comprehensive Claims as They Relate to the Environmental Assessment and Review Panel Reviewing Military Flying Activities in Labrador and Quebec," February 1990, 7–8.

91  C.D. Young, in "Northern Perspectives Interview: Brig.-Gen. (ret'd) C.D. Young, Manager, Goose Bay Management Office, Department of National Defence," *Northern Perspectives* 18, no. 2 (March–April 1990): 18–20, http://www.carc.org/pubs/v18no2/7.htm.

92  James O'Reilly, in Stephen Maher, "Courts May Decide Fate of Flights This Winter," *Happy Valley–Goose Bay Labradorian*, 6 February 1990, 30.

93  Ashini, "Innu Opposition," 15–16.

94  "A Research Paper, Presented by the Library of Parliament at the Request of William Rompkey, M.P. on the Low Level Flying and the Innu Claim," *Northern Reporter*, 26 February 1990, 4.

95  Goose Bay Management Office, NDHQ, "Goose Bay Status Report for the Week Ending 15 December 1989," 19 December 1989, DND f. 1956-14-7 (GBMO), acquired through ATIP.

96  Mary Barker and Dietrich Soyez, "Think Locally, Act Globally? The Transnationalization of Canadian Resource-Use Conflicts," *Environment: Science and Policy for Sustainable Development* 36, no. 5 (1994): 12–36 at 18. See also Christopher Alcantara, "Explaining Aboriginal Treaty Negotiation Outcomes in Canada: The Case of the Inuit and the Innu in Labrador," *Canadian Journal of Political Science* 40, no. 1 (2007): 185–207. The Conseil des Atikamekw des Montagnais of northern Quebec had also filed a formal statement of claim with the Canadian government, which substantively overlapped with that of the Labrador Inuit

Association and the traditional territory of the NMIA groups. Indian and Northern Affairs Canada, "Background on Comprehensive Claims."

97  DND, *Summary: Goose Bay EIS*; Barker, "Low-Level Military," 241; Paul Koring and Kevin Cox, "Study Sees Little Harm in Labrador NATO Base," *Globe and Mail*, 1 November 1989. Aboriginal land claims and defence policy were explicitly excluded from the criteria of the environmental impact assessment.

98  In February 1990 the Government of Canada approved an additional $200,000 so that the Naskapi Montagnais Innu Association could participate effectively in public environmental assessment hearings on military flying activities in Labrador and Quebec. The DND and the Department of Indian Affairs and Northern Development jointly provided the money to assist the Innu in their assessment of the impacts of low-level flying on their land, traditional lifestyle, and cultural heritage. Government of Canada, "Government Approves Additional Funding for Naskapi Montagnais Innu Association," press release, 13 February 1990.

99  DND, *Summary: Goose Bay EIS*; Wadden, "Screaming Jets"; Spaven, "Environmental State," 158–60; Federal Environmental Assessment and Review Office, "Environmental Assessment Panel Reviewing Military Flying Activities in Labrador and Quebec: Compilation of Comments Received from Technical Experts Concerning the EIS," December 1989; Geoffrey York and Loreen Pindera, *People of the Pines: The Warriors and the Legacy of Oka* (Toronto: Little Brown, 1991), 280; Kevin Cox, "Innu Fighting Back on Challenges to Traditional Lifestyle," *Globe and Mail*, 12 February 1990. On Spaven's ideological bias, see "A NATO Role for Canada," *Globe and Mail*, 15 June 1989.

100  Peter Penashue, "Healing the Past, Meeting the Future," in *Aboriginal Autonomy and Development in Northern Quebec and Labrador*, ed. C.H. Scott, 21–30 (Vancouver: UBC Press, 2001), 24.

101  C.D. Young, in "Northern Perspectives Interview." See also F. Cleverley, "'Oppressed' Innu Are Masters of Propaganda," *Winnipeg Free Press*, 17 May 1990, 7.

102  See Murrell, "Balanced Overall View?" The Innu have described this as "a superficial report" from an "ultra-conservative" institute that "chastis[ed] central Canadian media for biased reporting in favour of the Innu." Innu Nation, "A Chronology of Military Flight Training over Nitassinan," c. 1995, printed copy in University of Alberta Library, file Goose Bay.

103  John Cruickshank, "No Basis for a Base for NATO," *Globe and Mail*, 9 March 1990, A7.

104  Bill McKnight to Robert R. De Cotret, 21 December 1990, acquired
     through ATIP.
105  Diana Alyward, "Mayor Disappointed with NATO Choice, but Glad
     Decision Has Finally Been Made," *St John's Evening Telegram*, 23 May
     1990, 3.
106  John Gushue, "Court Battle against Low-Level Flying May Cost Innu
     over $400,000," *St John's Sunday Express*, 11 March 1990, 31.
107  Hank Shouse, in Rompkey, *Story of Labrador*, 144–5.
108  Provincial Court judges found Innu leaders guilty of mischief for their
     blockades of runways in 1988, even though the Innu tried to disrupt
     proceedings by refusing to stand when one judge entered the room and
     by speaking only Innuaiman. "Judge Is Forced to Postpone Trial When
     Innu Refused to Speak English," *St John's Evening Telegram*, 20 February
     1990, 6; "Innu Leaders Found Guilty of Mischief as Goose Bay Protest
     Trials Continue," *St John's Evening Telegram*, 11 December 1990, 7.
109  MGen. P.J. O'Donnell to Comd FMCHQ et al., Op Unique: Operation
     Order 1 (U), 19 March 1991, DND f. 3350-1 (Comd), acquired
     through ATIP.
110  J3 Ops 3035, Re: DCDS Op Order – Secur Arrangements Op Unique,
     1992–1996, 6 February 1992, acquired through ATIP.
111  AIRCOMHQ Winnipeg (SSO Secur) to NDHQ CIS Ottawa (D Secur
     Ops 2), Re: Threat Assessment for CFB Goose Bay on Native Activism,
     28 February 1992, acquired through ATIP. In 1992 Innu women returned to
     the base to picket the continuing flights, and the following year a group of
     Sheshatshit Innu were arrested after they wrote slogans opposed to low-
     level flying on a Dutch F-16. Maggie Helwig, "Low-Level Flight Testing:
     Innu Women Fight Back," *Canadian Woman Studies* 13, no. 3 (Spring
     1993): 52–3 at 52; Mark Vaughan-Jackson, "Innu Use Dutch Plans as
     Billboard for Cause," *St John's Evening Telegram*, 9 September 1993, 7.
112  LFAAHQ Halifax to RCEKGHA/CTCHQ Gagetown (G3), 4 March 1996,
     acquired through ATIP.
113  DCDS Op O – Op Unique 91, 10 January 1991, acquired through ATIP.
114  Innu Nation, "Military Jets Not Avoiding Innu Camps," press release,
     9 August 1993, copy in file Low-Level Flying, CNS; Denise Hillier,
     "Low-Level Flight Assessments Inadequate, Innu Nation Says," *St John's
     Evening Telegram*, 18 August 1993, 8.
115  See Survival International, "Hunters and Bombers," pamphlet (1990);
     Canadian Press, "NATO Choice Won't End Fight, Innu Say," *Globe and
     Mail*, 16 March 1990; Kevin Cox, "NATO Rejects Goose Bay for Base,
     Innu Protestors Claim Victory," *Globe and Mail*, 23 May 1990; Frank

Young, Goose Bay Management Office, interview with author, 11 September 2003; and "Innu Claim No Such People as Labrador Metis," *Times Colonist*, 17 September 1996.

116 See Barker, "Low-Level Military," 245–7.

117 Frank Young, Goose Bay Management Office, interview with author, 11 September 2003. Interestingly, the Labrador Inuit Association originally *opposed* shifting the training area to the south because it would lose leverage in consultations and would not be able to observe effects as readily.

118 "Memorandum of Understanding between the Department of National Defence and the Labrador Inuit Association Concerning Military Low-Level Flying in Labrador," 3 July 1990; Institute for Environmental Monitoring and Research, *Annual Reports*, 1997, 1999, 2000; DND, "Allies Sign New Agreement to Continue Training Activities in Goose Bay," news release NR-96.012, 20 February 1996. For a critical perspective, see B. Robinson and P. Chapman, "Security for Whom? Low-Level Flight Training in Nitassinan," *Ploughshares*, briefing 95-3, n.d., http://ploughshares.ca/pl_publications/security-for-whom-low-level-flight-training-in-nitassinan; and Innu Nation, "Military Flight Training in the Innu Homeland," 15 March 1995, copy on file with P. Whitney Lackenbauer. On monitoring, see the documents in DND file A98-0138, acquired through ATIP.

119 DND, "The Government's Response to the Facilitator's Report," backgrounder BG-95.022, December 1995; DND, "Establishment of an Environmental Institute to Monitor Allied Training at Goose Bay," news release NR-95.04211, December 1995; DND, "Chairman Appointed to Environmental Institute," news release NR-96.045, 16 May 1996; "Native Groups Boycott Meeting," *Globe and Mail*, 1 November 1996; "Meeting on Low-Level Flights Delayed after Native Protests," *Globe and Mail*, 13 November 1996; Innu Nation, "Update on Innu Nation Activities Concerning Military Flight Training at 5 Wing Goose Bay," 1998, copy on file with P. Whitney Lackenbauer.

120 Frank Young, Goose Bay Management Office, interview with author, 11 September 2003; CBC Regional News, evening news broadcast, 24 August 2000; Barker, "Low-Level Military," 251–2. The military compromised when the Innu expressed concerns about proposed supersonic Allied training. See Innu Nation, "Innu Nation Launches Court Challenge to Military Plans for Supersonic Test Flights over Innu Lands," press release, 8 August 2000; and Innu Nation, "Decision on Supersonic Test Flights Deferred," press release, 17 August 2000.

121 DND, "New Investments in CFB Goose Bay," backgrounder BG-05.040, 24 November 2005.

122 Holly Bridges, "5 Wing Goose Bay Hosts German Airborne Rangers," DND press release, 31 January 2007, copy on file with P. Whitney Lackenbauer.

123 Jenn Gearey, "Paving the Way for Success at 5 Wing," c. 2007, copy on file with P. Whitney Lackenbauer. In July 2007 the DND transferred ownership of the air terminal building and the civil aviation area at the airport to the Goose Bay Airport Corporation.

124 See David Pugliese, "Will CFB Goose Bay's Goose Be Cooked Part Deux?" *Ottawa Citizen*, 12 January 2010. On cancelled plans, see also David Pugliese, "NATO Forward Air Controller Exercise Slated for Goose Bay to Be Moved Down to U.S.," *Ottawa Citizen*, 20 April 2010. In 2009 the minister of national defence and the minister of transport, responsible for the Atlantic Gateway, announced $300 million to fund ongoing remediation efforts and to generate economic opportunities. DND/CF News, "5 Wing Goose Bay Remediation Project Announcement," 12 July 2009, http://www.forces.gc.ca/en/news/article.page?doc=5-wing-goose-bay-remediation-project-announcement/hnps1ukk.

125 Martha Hurley, in Wadden, *Nitassinan*, 169–70. Also in Rompkey, *Story of Labrador*, 145.

126 In Barron, "In the Name of Solidarity," 103.

127 Daniel Ashini, in ibid., 92.

128 Rompkey, *Story of Labrador*, 146.

129 Annex A (Security Plan) to Operation Order No. 1 (PA), 8 March 1990, acquired through ATIP.

130 DCDS Op O – Op Unique 91, 10 January 1991, acquired through ATIP. The passive nature of the occupations and blockades, and the "effective reaction drills" developed by the Wing Auxiliary Security Force at the base, allowed the military to execute Operation Unique with unarmed personnel. "Land Force Atlantic Area Contingency Operation Plan UNIQUE," August 1995, 5, acquired through ATIP.

131 Daniel Ashini, in Rompkey, *Story of Labrador*, 145.

132 James Roche, in Penny MacRae, "Priest Wages Lonely Fight against Low-Level Flying from Goose Bay Jail Cell," *St John's Evening Telegram*, 24 February 1990, 24.

# A Bridge Too Far? The Oka Crisis

P. WHITNEY LACKENBAUER

The "Indian Summer" of 1990[1] profoundly changed the perception of Aboriginal-government relations in Canada. Elijah Harper defeated the Meech Lake Accord in the Manitoba Legislature, his eagle feather becoming a symbol for peaceful Native resistance and the unwillingness of Aboriginal people to tolerate their concerns being relegated to the political margins. The complex and prolonged confrontation at Oka, Quebec, proved even more destabilizing, suggesting that Aboriginal communities were volatile powder kegs that could erupt into open violence. The Mohawks had long asserted title over a parcel of land known as "the Pines," but their failure to secure a favourable resolution through the official land claims process during the 1970s and 1980s made a bad situation worse. When impatient members of the local Euro-Canadian community initiated plans to expand a private golf course on the disputed property, Mohawks peacefully occupied the Pines to stymie development. The conflict, however, soon escalated into an eleven-week armed standoff between Mohawk Warriors, the Quebec provincial police, and the Canadian Forces (CF) and drew unprecedented political and media attention.[2]

The politics of the Oka Crisis were both internal and external for the Mohawk Nation. The Mohawks, despite projecting a united front to the media, covered a spectrum of opinion from those who encouraged a moderate, peaceful approach to reclaiming disputed lands to militant Warriors who sought formal recognition of Mohawk sovereignty and the creation of an independent state. Although the immediate catalyst for direct action by the local community related to the Pines, the political objectives of the Mohawk Warriors – particularly outsiders whom local critics accused of hijacking the agenda – escalated to include sweeping sovereignty claims. "For the Kanien'kehaka (Mohawks) from Kahnawà:ke and Akwesasne ... this really had nothing to do with Oka, a bridge or a golf course," Kiera Ladner and Leanne Simpson suggest. "This was about 400 years of resistance."[3]

This image of armed freedom fighters standing up to four centuries of colonial injustice was, in some government officials' and local Mohawks' views, a veiled cover to protect illicit activities that disempowered Kanesatake residents. On the other side of the barricades, the federal and provincial governments were caught in a jurisdictional quagmire that highlighted the political problems inherent in dealing with Aboriginal issues. Federal minister of Indian affairs Tom Siddon tried to avoid being implicated in the situation, suggesting that the Quebec government was responsible for what was essentially a policing issue. Provincial premier Robert Bourassa and his minister of Native affairs, John Ciaccia, asserted that land claims and title issues were a federal domain and that their negotiating options were limited. "By August it seemed that the entire affair was being run by the military and the Warriors," policy scholars Robert Campbell and Leslie Pal note. "The terms of debate and the way that the issues were framed had been appropriated by men in arms, not by political leaders."[4]

If the Rotiskenhrakete (Mohawk Warriors) claimed to "carry the burden of peace," so too did the members of the Canadian Forces who were called upon to stabilize the situation in an "aid to the civil power" capacity. After the provincial police botched their raid on the Kanesatake barricades on 11 July, the Mohawks had little trust in civil authorities, and the Warriors' escalating (and confused) demands for state recognition that the Mohawks were sovereign – coupled with weak government leadership – precluded a negotiated solution to the confrontation. Canadians, accustomed to seeing their soldiers serve as proud peacekeepers abroad, instead watched the CF perform "a traditional form of peace-restoration at home" from August to October 1990.[5] The armed forces and Aboriginal people were visibly on opposite sides of the proverbial fence, an image etched into the Canadian psyche by the provocative photograph of Private Patrick Cloutier caught in the fiery glare of Mohawk Warrior Bradley Larocque (alias Freddy Krueger).[6] Although the CF performed admirably during the Oka Crisis and moderated a volatile situation without resorting to bloodshed, the political outcomes were less decisive. Core issues over land claims processes and sovereignty remain unsettled. Nevertheless, the crisis served as a catalyst for promises of Aboriginal self-government and the reform of Indian Affairs policy at the federal level, as well as the largest royal commission in Canadian history. Oka also served as the quintessential example of Aboriginal resistance in the late twentieth century, and its influence continues to reverberate in direct actions that emulate the Warrior rhetoric and tactics at Kanesatake and Kahnawake.

### BACKGROUND TO THE OKA CRISIS

Historian Jim Miller notes that a fixation on specific, immediate factors leading to the Oka Crisis provides limited explanation of this complex affair. Indeed, commentary during and immediately following the crisis was largely superficial:

> The Mohawk Warrior Society is portrayed either as a collection of righteous militants pursuing a sacred constitutional principle or as a band of goons. The local residents of Oka and Chateauguay are long-suffering neighbours or red-necked hooligans. The Sûreté du Québec are uniformed thugs or inexperienced law enforcement officers trying to mediate in a hopelessly polarized situation. Quebec is either the most tolerant and generous of provinces in its treatment of Aboriginal peoples or the home of a nationality becoming increasingly unwilling to permit dissent by distinctive ethnic and racial minorities. Ottawa is to blame either for mollycoddling the Mohawk with promises of accommodation after their claims were rejected, or for failing to act decisively ... Where in this welter of charges and counter-charges do the roots of the exceptional and lamentable eleven-week stand-off at Kanesatake lie?[7]

In March 1990 provincial courts gave the the Town of Oka the "go-ahead" to extend a nine-hole golf course into an eighteen-hole course through a disputed piece of land known locally as "the Pines." The Mohawks of the Kanesatake settlement adjacent to the town[8] claimed the land as their own, maintaining that it was both part of their traditional hunting grounds and a sacred burial ground. Armed with this belief, the Mohawks rejected the decision of the court, and on 9 March 1990 they dragged a fishing shack onto the Pines to observe when the workers came to cut down trees. A banner asked, "Are you aware that this is Mohawk land?"[9]

The question of why the Mohawk of Kanesatake and the Town of Oka both claimed ownership of the same piece of land can be answered only by looking at the historical antecedents of the conflict. Historians generally agree that the trouble began in 1717 when the land, then referred to as the Lake of Two Mountains, or Kanesatake, was granted to the Seminary of St Sulpice to be used as a refuge for the largely Mohawk population within its mission.[10] These Mohawks were relocated from the area of Sault-au-Récollet because of the Sulpicians' concern that their involvement in the fur trade – particularly their exposure to alcohol – would be morally dangerous to them. The Mohawks themselves readily agreed to the move because the land to which they were relocating was part of their traditional hunting grounds and the Sulpicians promised that they would be given the land and would no longer be "molested in [their] habitation." The Mohawks accepted this promise and recorded the transaction in a wampum belt; however, there was no written record of the agreement. This omission later became a problem when the Sulpicians claimed that they owned the land in trust for the Native peoples and could provide written documentation for their position. The Mohawks' belief that they legitimately owned the land was based on historical use and on the Sulpicians' verbal promises.[11]

Over the course of the eighteenth century, the relationship between the Sulpicians and the Mohawks soured. Following the Conquest of New France, Mohawks presented their land claims to the British authorities in 1781, 1787, and 1795. Although their claims were rejected, the Mohawks continued to press the issue, and disputes continued throughout the nineteenth century when denominational differences exacerbated an already tense situation. By 1869 the majority of the Mohawk population in the area had converted to Protestantism – a "symbolic act of rejection and defiance," according to Miller.[12] Other disputes over matters like the sale of timber from the area were amplified accordingly. In 1877 the Catholic Church at Oka burned to the ground, and the Sulpicians blamed the Mohawks. Over fifty Mohawks were arrested for the crime, but no one was convicted. Predictably, the prosecutions did little to alleviate the distrust between the two groups. The Natives at Kanesatake were offered alternative land at Maniwaki and Doncaster in 1853, and the Algonquins and Nipissing departed, as did twenty-two Mohawk families who left for a reserve at Gibson, Ontario, in the 1880s. The majority stayed at Kanesatake, insisting that the land belonged to them.[13]

Tensions between the remaining Mohawks and the Sulpicians at Kanesatake persisted into the twentieth century. The Judicial Committee of Privy Council in London (the highest appellate court in the empire) reaffirmed that the land rightfully belonged to the Seminary of St Sulpice in 1909. In the 1930s the seminary began selling off parcels of the land to pay various debts.[14] In 1945, in an attempt to settle the problem once and for all, Ottawa negotiated an agreement with the Sulpicians to purchase land for the remaining Mohawks at Oka. This appeared, on the surface, to represent an effective means of settling the issue, but disagreement and misunderstanding prevailed. Non-Mohawks assumed that the Native population would confine themselves to a 1,556 acre parcel set aside by the government. For their part, the Mohawks did not believe that this sale resolved the original question of ownership of the Pines. Moreover, it relegated them to an area of 2.5 square miles – they had once occupied over 64 square miles – which was not set aside as a legal reserve, so the settlement was vulnerable to future non-Native encroachment. Regardless, the federal government considered the case to be closed. When the municipality of Oka decided in 1958 to build a nine-hole golf course on land it had purchased from the Sulpicians, the Mohawks (who were not consulted) protested to the minister of Indian affairs to prevent the development. The Department of Justice decided in the town's favour, and the golf course went ahead, located immediately adjacent to the Pines.[15]

By this time, the Mohawk community had become divided into two factions: those who supported the band council government and favoured cooperation with the Canadian authorities and those "traditionalists" who advocated increased autonomy rooted in traditional Iroquois-style governance and a confrontationist strategy.[16] These currents surfaced during a time of changing official policies. Native groups' hostile response to the ill-fated White Paper of 1969, coupled with court decisions recognizing Aboriginal title in the early 1970s, led the federal government to reconsider its stance on land claims.[17] In August 1973 it announced a new policy that confirmed the government's responsibility to meet its lawful treaty obligations (specific claims) and to negotiate settlements with Native groups in areas where Canada had not extinguished rights based on traditional use and occupancy of the land (comprehensive claims). The new land claims policy emphasized provincial and territorial cooperation. In 1975 the Mohawks of Kanesatake, in conjunction with the communities at Kahnawake and Akwesasne, submitted a comprehensive claim[18] asserting Aboriginal title to lands along the St Lawrence and Ottawa rivers. It was rejected for two main reasons. First, the Mohawks had not maintained possession of these lands since time immemorial and therefore could not claim Aboriginal title. Second, Indian Affairs and Northern Development concluded that any Aboriginal title that might have existed had been extinguished by the king of France, who had granted the land to the Seminary of St Sulpice, and later by the British Crown. When this claim was rejected, the Mohawks tried another course of action. In June 1977 they submitted a specific claim to the lands at Oka. In 1986 they received notice from the federal government that it recognized no outstanding lawful obligation. The minister of Indian affairs did note, however, that he would consider alternative means to address the Kanesatake Band's grievances, outside of the formal claims process.[19]

The following year, the matter came to a head when the Kanesatake Band Council learned through the media that the Town of Oka planned to allow an expansion of the golf course into the Pines. The council protested to municipal and provincial officials to no avail. Even the appointment of a federal mediator to work with the Mohawks and the municipality failed to break the impasse. Legal scholar Jane Dickson-Gilmore concluded that the conflict was "always about the land" – centuries of crisis over the status of the land culminated in "78 days of conflict."[20] Linda Pertusati drew a different conclusion, suggesting that the crisis was really an expression of ethnopolitics – an assertion of Mohawk sovereignty and independence.[21] This echoes Gerald (Taiaiake) Alfred, whose studies about the assertion of Mohawk nationalism reveal that, by the 1990s, Mohawk ethnonationalist politics had evolved from localized goals aimed at stability to reformative and sovereigntist goals. The purpose of Mohawk activism was to expose the contradictions of colonialism and secure autonomy from the state. Although Gerald Reid has demonstrated that Alfred paints his picture "with strokes too broad to reveal the fine grain of the community's internal political and cultural dynamics," the divided community was home to a sizable faction inclined to a confrontational stance toward the Canadian government.[22] The issue was not confined to the land title issue itself but extended to the broader issue of Aboriginal self-government and to the eventual resumption of Mohawk sovereignty. The members of the Warrior Society who manned the barricades asserted that they embodied traditional Mohawk values and offered a viable political alternative to an unfavourable status quo.

## THE WARRIORS

Mohawk scholar Taiaiake Alfred insists that the Mohawk Warrior Society is an "authentic" and "organic" expression of "timeless indigenous values" and that its membership, strategy, and tactics are "bound to the territory and community ... they exist to protect." As a "security force," a warrior society will adopt any offensive or defensive positions that the situation warrants either to repossess and reassert jurisdiction or to defend the territory from external encroachments. "The ultimate goal of the warrior society is to defend indigenous lands and people from external threats, particularly state authorities, in order to achieve justice and eventually peace," Alfred explains. "To achieve this goal, the warrior society's objectives are three: 1) organize a group of indigenous people who are ready, willing and able to physically defend the land and the people at all times, 2) maintain a presence in the community representative of a warrior ethic, and 3) develop a political, cultural and ideological consciousness that is rooted in the territory and traditions of the community/nation in which it originates." Alfred asserts that the responsibilities of warriors to defend their people against external violence are rooted in "an ethical framework rooted in traditional cultural values and always considered within the context of self-defence in response to immediate threats of violence to communities or persons." As "a loosely knit fraternity" based in a community, the Mohawk Warrior Society does not need to organize extensively but can "galvanize and mobilize a larger, peripheral membership if necessary. The core group maintains the organization and acts as central command during times of crisis."[23]

The Rotiskenhrakete, or Mohawk Warrior Society, emerged at Akwesasne and Kahnawake in the late 1960s, during a time of rekindled Aboriginal activism in North America. The Red Power movement was raising awareness about oppression and discrimination against Aboriginal peoples in general through "civil rights" tactics (such as sit-ins, rallies, and marches). The American Indian Movement (AIM), founded in 1968, adopted more militant strategies and embraced the term "warrior society" to promote the fight against non-Native authorities. That same year, Mohawks blockaded the St Lawrence Seaway bridge at Akwesasne, near Cornwall, Ontario, and the Kahnawake Singing Society adopted the term "warrior society" to describe themselves. Alfred suggests that the Mohawk Warrior Society's "overall strategy was to repossess and protect Kanien'kehaka territories according to the *Kaienerekoawa*, the Great Law of Peace" – a code of conduct handed down orally that provides detailed instructions on when and how to go to war against foreign nations. Armed with a highly idealistic desire to protect cultural values and assert Mohawk claims to sovereignty, and trained by war veterans, the Warriors began to take action. Following the example of the Red Power activists who occupied Alcatraz in 1969, Warriors "reclaimed" Stanley and Loon Islands in the St Lawrence River. They also clashed with the elected Mohawk band councils, adopted aggressive tactics, including barricades and roadblocks, to prevent Canadian and American authorities from entering their territories, and occupied/repossessed lands within Kanien'kehaka territory.[24] The Kahnawake Warriors allied with AIM and clashed with Quebec provincial police in 1973 during the "siege at the Longhouse," where both men and women brandished guns for the first time and flipped over police cars. The Warriors' confidence grew. The Kahnawake Longhouse sanctioned the Mohawk Warrior Society and, backed by AIM, began to evict non-Native "trespassers" living on the reserve. The local and national media began to take note.[25]

During the 1970s and 1980s, the Warrior Society expanded into neighbouring Mohawk communities and engaged in the lucrative cigarette trade to generate revenues. "After hours sales of alcohol, high stakes bingo, and slot machines have operated in defiance of the efforts of both traditional and elected Mohawk governments," one reporter observed. "Canadian and American governments, while occasionally invading and assaulting such activities in a blundering way, have generally frustrated the regulatory efforts of Mohawk governments. By-laws regulating arms have been repealed in the name of Mohawk sovereignty, thus strengthening the Warriors' Society's armed protection of gambling casinos."[26] These activities, clearly illegal in the eyes of outside authorities, prompted government action. In 1988, 200 officers of the Royal Canadian Mounted Police (RCMP) raided cigarette stores at Kahnawake, prompting Warriors to seize the Mercier Bridge for twenty-nine hours. New York State Troopers raided gaming and cigarette establishments on the other side of the international border the following year. The Warriors established the Mohawk Sovereign Security Force – an armed patrol – to prevent further government incursions on their lands.

The Mohawk Security Force did not prevent further internal violence. Rick Hornung describes in *One Nation under the Gun* how factional conflicts over the control of gaming and the cigarette trade (and those residents who opposed both activities) led to heavy fighting with automatic weapons and even grenades.[27] Historian Timothy Winegard suggests that Akwesasne was "undergoing a gradual metamorphosis into a narco-parasitic state" – an unrecognized "nation" that survives on the trafficking of drugs and other illicit materials to further political independence.[28] The small fifteen-member Akwesasne Mohawk Police Service was overwhelmed following the murder of two Mohawks at Akwesasne and significant property damage. The challenge of policing a diverse First Nation, which harboured "highly sophisticated and powerful organized criminal elements," became starkly apparent.[29] Order on the reserve was temporarily restored by sizable numbers of Ontario Provincial Police and RCMP officers, supported by CF armoured vehicles, secure communications, and engineer services such as rafts and high-speed inflatable boats. Still the violence continued. In early 1990 a Canadian mechanized battalion moved to Cornwall in preparation for an "aid to the civil power" mission and was eventually deployed to Akwesasne.[30]

The Warriors did not enjoy the easy support of all Mohawks, and their tactics and approach divided the community. "The anger on the reserve between those opposed to gambling, drug-running and smuggling, and those who feel the natives should be a law unto themselves, will not easily be overcome," Captain Tony Keene noted in early 1990.[31] The Warriors were fiercely opposed by other traditional Mohawks, such as the followers of Handsome Lake – "pacifists who believe the Peacemaker long ago instructed them to bury all their weapons and cease all warfare."[32] Accordingly, some commentators questioned the legitimacy of the self-proclaimed defenders of traditional Mohawk society, suggesting that the Warriors represented contemporary militant ideals with no historical precedent. Dissenters faced the Warriors' wrath. Kahnawake radio host Joe Delaronde, an outspoken critic of the Warriors, recalled getting death threats and finding a skinned cat on his lawn.[33]

Political divisions within the Mohawk community further challenged Warrior supremacy. "The warrior society usually has an adversarial or tense relationship with the elected Band Councils," Alfred explains, "seeing them as an illegitimate form of governance imposed by state authorities that serves to undermine traditional political structures."[34] The Warriors rejected (and continue to reject) the band council structure of governance, seeing it as a creature of the Indian Act and thus as an artifact of colonial control, and cast themselves as freedom fighters. Journalist Ann Charney observed just before the Oka Crisis in 1990, "These days, militant Mohawks see themselves as engaged in a struggle for survival – the last great Indian war. They are aiming at nothing less than economic, cultural, and territorial sovereignty. While Canada remains transfixed by ... Quebec nationalists, the Kahnawake Indians, invoking the force of ancestral tradition and combining it with contemporary Western know-how, are going about the business of building an independent Mohawk republic, capable of defending itself, in the very shadow of Montreal's skyscrapers and superhighways."[35]

## THE SQ RAID AND POLITICAL FALLOUT

In the early spring of 1990, Mohawks from Kanesatake blockaded a road just north of Montreal to stop the expansion of the golf course. On 8 March, Kanesatake band administrator Dan Gaspé co-chaired a meeting where "about ten people decided that there would be an occupation of the territory."[36] It was originally a "peaceful" action, undertaken in consultation with the Alliance for Non-Violent Action, and the protestors remained unarmed for several weeks. Mohawk families "sauntered through it, there was no inconvenience to the local Oka residents, and it soon became a fixture of town life." Developers and the town mayor, Jean-Guy Ouellette, grew increasingly impatient with what effectively prevented progress on the golf course. After four months of waiting, the municipality of Oka obtained an injunction from the Quebec Superior Court on 30 June affirming that the Mohawk demonstration was illegal. The Mohawks ignored the injunction and continued to bar access to the disputed lands. The provincial minister of Native affairs, John Ciaccia, urged the mayor to indefinitely suspend development plans so that the government could negotiate the removal of the barricades. Ouellette, however, decided to appeal to the provincial police, the Sûreté du Québec (SQ), to enforce the injunction.[37]

The threat of police intervention brought salient changes to the composition of the barricade. In April the demonstrators at Kanesatake – who did not have a Warrior Society of their own – sought advice from Kahnawake and Akwesasne Warriors on how to patrol, construct barricades, and watch over the Pines.[38] Early the following month, the Kanesatake Mohawks received a tip that the SQ was planning a raid and issued a "distress call" to the other Mohawk reserves. In response, more Warrior Society members from other Mohawk communities arrived on the scene with advice and with weapons. For example, Francis Boots (the "War Chief" from Akwesasne) made three trips to Kanesatake in May and June, insisting that "he was there at the invitation of the people in the Pines to advise, not to take over the fight." The disorganized group at the barricades, who had access to few resources, received truckloads of food, tents, sleeping bags, and other equipment from several Aboriginal communities in Canada and the United States. The Warriors and their supporters began to dig trenches and fortifications to prepare for a raid.[39]

Internally, however, the Kanesatake Mohawks were divided about what course of action should be taken to protect the Pines and the Mohawk cemetery. The Six Nations Traditional Hereditary Chiefs supported the picketing of the Pines, but distrusted elected Kanesatake band chief George Martin and his non-Native lawyer. The Longhouse was also divided. Chief Samson Gabriel had asked Allen Gabriel, Curtis Nelson, and Marshall Nicholas to represent the Longhouse, in conjunction with Linda Cree, Ellen Gabriel, and Debbie Etienne, but the women publicly severed their ties with the others on 14 June because they were not consulted on key decisions and meetings. The key division within the Longhouse was over whether the occupiers of the Pines should use arms, which Ellen Gabriel and others opposed. "We really felt like we were set up by people from our community, who knows maybe Kahnawake," she later explained. "We said we don't want weapons here, take them out, take them out," but three Mohawk men insisted on walking around with their guns. "They had already created in the public sense that there were people there with weapons, when the perspective of the group was no weapons." By this point, more than one hundred people were involved in the protest in the Pines, including American and Ontario residents, and the mood grew increasingly militant. Longhouse chief Samson Gabriel left the Pines, insisting that his institution did not support the extremists' concept of "stand and fight." Ellen Gabriel explained the confusing politics behind the barricades:

> Allan, Samson Gabriel and his son David, Curtis Nelson and some women who followed Samson, came to us in early July to say that we should bring the blockade down and that they disagreed with what was going on even though it was they who officially invited the "Warriors" and it was Marshall Nicolas, Curtis and Allan who encouraged and carried guns early on in the movement. The "People of the Pines" were a group of people in the community of Kanesatake who decided that all members made up of Longhouse and Christian members would put away our differences and that we would unite to fight the expansion of the golf course. I include myself in this group.

The federal government, for its part, refused to negotiate with the Longhouse Council or the self-declared "Longhouse People of the Pines" (as the occupiers called themselves) because this would have undermined the elected band council and the Indian Act, as well as implicitly recognized a sovereign Mohawk Nation.[40]

The SQ's disastrous dawn raid on 11 July 1990, a day after Chief Martin had met Quebec Cabinet ministers and received assurances there would be no attacks, changed the situation in fundamental ways. One hundred tactical force officers arrived in trucks, police cruisers, and a front-end loader. Twice the SQ tried to clear the road with the loader but was rebuffed. Then officers in riot gear stormed the barricades, armed with assault rifles and concussion grenades. In the confusion and chaos, shrouded by tear gas, each side claimed the other shot first. When the dust settled a few minutes later, the implications of the confrontation were clear: SQ police corporal Marcel Lemay lay dead from a bullet. Two political scientists later recounted: .

> In its confused retreat, the SQ had abandoned the front-end loader and some cars, and the Mohawks used them to good effect to buttress the barricade. Police cars were overturned and pushed around as needed with the front-end loader. The Warriors also captured police radios, rifles, and ammunition. They then commandeered golf carts from the nearby club to manoeuvre in and around the barricade. It was a strange sight: men dressed in military fatigues, masked in ways vaguely reminiscent of PLO fighters, triumphantly waving rifles that they obviously knew how to use, whooping atop overturned police cruisers. The vision of these big, serious, and lethal men on golf carts was just incongruous enough to be frightening.[41]

The assault broadened and deepened the crisis, and the SQ's ill-executed offensive galvanized the Mohawk community in its need to resist government aggression. The Warriors, who had enjoyed limited support at Kanesatake until that time, could now justify their claim that the state would use excessive force to end the Mohawk resistance. The moderate voices within the Mohawk community were quickly marginalized, and the Warriors consolidated their self-proclaimed right to speak for the Mohawk community by issuing ultimatums and courting media attention. Following the raid, the Kanesatake Band Council's leaders left the community and attempted to continue their consultation with government officials from nearby St Eustache. Bereft of community support, and beyond the gaze of television cameras, the elected band council was politically marginal for the remainder of the crisis.[42] The failed police raid had altered the local power dynamic. "There was a lot of resistance to the Warriors within the Mohawk Nation, and they needed some kind of catalyst to get the support they did get and were able to hold on to for a certain period," a military intelligence report noted. "11 July was that catalyst. We had found evidence that the closure of the [Mercier] bridge was already planned and 11 July hastened it or was the perfect excuse."[43]

According to the usual narrative offered by the Mohawks, the confrontation at Kanesatake immediately prompted Warriors on the Kahnawake Reserve, across the St Lawrence southwest of Montreal, to show their support by barricading vehicle access to the Mercier Bridge – a vital link between Montreal and Chateauguay for 60,000 commuters each day. Other Warriors barricaded three other highways that ran through the reserve. Anecdotal evidence suggests that this was a spontaneous effort by individual Warriors, not an action sponsored by the Kahnawake Warrior Society or the band. However, this version is problematic, as historian Timothy Winegard demonstrates in his careful analysis of events. The first blockade of the Mercier Bridge actually went up *before* the SQ assault at Kanesatake. "The seizure of the bridge was not a reaction to the events of 11 July," he explains. "Rather, it was a stratagem and an action designed to support Kanesatake, while providing more negotiation leverage through the importance of the bridge itself."[44] This strategic decision by Warriors led to the deployment of the CF in an "aid to the civil power" role, as well as a dramatic shift in Quebecois public support away from the Mohawks.[45]

What had started as a relatively peaceful barricade over a rather confined parcel of disputed land had morphed into a political nightmare. Quebec's minister of Native affairs, John Ciaccia, met with Mohawk negotiators but recognized that any resolution of the land claims issue required federal participation. On 15 July, Ciaccia proposed a package that would recognize the contested land around the golf course as Mohawk land (but the transfer of title was unclear), withdraw the SQ from Oka under the monitoring of a Catholic religious order, work to secure "nation-to-nation" talks between the Mohawks and Ottawa, conduct public inquiries and investigations into the confrontation and Lemay's death, and refer all civil and criminal prosecutions to the World Court in the Hague. However, the federal minister of Indian affairs, Tom Siddon, refused to intervene, and the municipal government expressed dismay that it had been cut out of the negotiations. For her part, Ellen

Gabriel, the principal Mohawk negotiator to that point, insisted that if the SQ took any direction action against the blockades, the Warriors would blow up the Mercier Bridge. Furthermore, any negotiations would be complicated. Gabriel explained that there would have to be more than twenty Mohawk "resource persons" at the bargaining table – a reflection of traditional decision-making practices, as well as the lack of consensus within the Mohawk community. Although the vast majority of Kanesatake residents fled their community, those who stayed remained divided in their support for the band council or the Warriors. Ciaccia detected radical changes in the atmosphere behind the barricades – where people like Kenneth Deer, Joe Deom, and Loran Thompson were displacing Ellen Gabriel as the principal spokespersons. The presence of nonresident Warriors certainly complicated the situation and raised perplexing questions about voice and legitimacy.[46]

Contextual stresses confused matters even further. In response to the Mohawk barricades at Kahnawake, the SQ shut down access to the reserve and dispatched hundreds more officers in Oka. This provoked strong reactions locally and nationally. Canadian human rights groups and Opposition politicians like Audrey McLaughlin expressed concern with attempts to starve the Mohawk community into submission. On 18 July, 150 First Nations chiefs from across the country gathered at Kahnawake to demand federal intervention, threatened roadblocks, and appealed to the international community and the United Nations to impose sanctions on Canada similar to those imposed on South Africa.[47] Eventually, representatives from the Canadian Labour Congress, the National Action Committee on the Status of Women, and the Canadian Ethnocultural Council joined in local marches to support the Mohawks. On the other side, furious Chateauguay residents tried to prevent reserve residents from buying anything at a local supermarket, and mobs vented their anger by burning effigies of Natives and later politicians at the barricades and by launching insults at the SQ for failing to open the bridge. On the nights of 17 and 18 July, thousands of local residents broke down police fencing and advanced on the police lines, only to be repelled by 300 RCMP officers.[48]

The political fallout was intense. Premier Bourassa issued a statement anticipating a long standoff, and Tom Siddon finally held a conference to explain the federal position. "We cannot engage in negotiations at gunpoint," he suggested. Policing was provincial jurisdiction, and the Quebec authorities had to resolve the armed standoff before federal land negotiators would intervene. At Ciaccia's request, Siddon agreed to accede to three of the Mohawks' main conditions, but Ellen Gabriel insisted that the Mohawks had every right to defend themselves and insisted on immunity from criminal and civil prosecutions – including for Mohawks involved in the unrelated conflict at Akwesasne.[49] The deputy minister of Indian affairs in Ottawa, Harry Swain, insisted that this was an "armed insurrection" led by a "criminal organization," predicated on "a potent combination of guns, cash, and ideology," that was cloaking itself "in the guise of Indian Rights"[50] and had taken control of Kahnawake and Kanesatake. The Quebec government offered to transfer the parcel of land that lay at the heart of the original dispute to the Mohawks (after Ottawa purchased part of it in late July), but divisions remained within the Mohawk ranks. "Moderates" allied with the elected band council supported an agreement, whereas Warriors insisted on amnesty and emphasized that since they already owned the land, the government offer was baseless.[51] The dominant Mohawk voices at the barricades were explicitly sovereigntist, and the Kanesatake land settlement issue seemed to recede to secondary importance, overshadowed by broader efforts to extract official recognition for the Mohawks' distinct political and legal status.

In their succinct analysis of the Oka Crisis, Robert Campbell and Leslie Pal explain that by late July the situation had spun out of control owing to the array of competing actors and interests. The Mohawk communities of Kanesatake and Kahnawake were split between band councils, moderates, traditionalists who opposed the Warriors, and the Warriors themselves. The Warriors chased Chief George Martin (who called the Warriors outsiders and ordered them to "get the hell off" the reserve) and the elected band council out of the community on 2 August, claiming that 500 Kanesatake community members had petitioned them to depose Martin from his leadership position. The dubious veracity of this pretext notwithstanding, the sound of gunfire from within the reserve certainly compounded existing tensions. Governments were also divided. Quebec sought federal intervention to settle the underlying land dispute, to which the federal government was intrinsically a party. Ottawa was willing to purchase and transfer the land, but the barricades were a provincial policing and legal issue. Furthermore, as the situation escalated, the Mohawks secured broader national and international support. "The confrontation at Oka had generated unprecedented levels of native solidarity and commitment" despite the Warriors' methods, Campbell and Pal observe, and had generated sympathy blockades of bridges, roads, and rail lines across Canada. The Mohawks also reached out to international bodies (including the United Nations) to solicit support for their cause and enjoyed sympathetic international media coverage. This dimension was also critical in that the Mohawks sought external recognition of the sovereignty of the Kanien'kehaka, the Mohawk Nation. By contrast, the Mohawks did not enjoy support from the local non-Native community. Furious local residents threatened to escalate the violence if legal authorities were unprepared to act, and the Oka Town Council refused to sell its stake in the disputed land.[52] In the context of this complicated morass of actors and competing interests, the Canadian Forces were now called upon to carry the burden of peace.

## MILITARY INTERVENTION

After the failed assault of 11 July and the death of Lemay, as well as the erection of sympathy barriers on Mercier Bridge, the Province of Quebec officially requested the assistance of the Canadian Forces in an "aid to the civil power" capacity. The SQ required armoured vehicles and equipment loans at both Oka and Kahnawake, and the chief of the Defence Staff directed the commander of the Mobile Force to provide support. In mid-July the first combat units were deployed to the military base at Longue Pointe. So began the first phase of Operation Salon. At this stage, military support was not publicized in hopes that the ongoing negotiations between the Mohawks and provincial government would not be jeopardized. Accordingly, armoured vehicles and soldiers moved discreetly from Valcartier to Montreal, and strict limits were imposed on any visible CF presence or overflights near the Mohawk reserves. Nevertheless, a small battalion headquarters liaised with the SQ and provided on-site technical aid.[53]

Hope for a quick settlement dissipated on the negotiating front as the issue grew beyond municipal golf course expansion. Quebec's minister of Native affairs, John Ciaccia, who had been sympathetic to the Native position, broke off talks in early August, accusing the Mohawks of purposely sabotaging a deal to end the standoff. The federal government refused to negotiate as long as armed Warriors manned the barricades, but the Mohawks would not relinquish their positions until negotiations took place. On the evening of 5 August, Premier Bourassa announced a forty-eight-hour ultimatum for an agreement to bring down the barricades, but Ellen Gabriel replied that the Mohawks "will not be bullied by the power and arrogance of Quebec." All attempts to negotiate failed, and on 6 August 1990 the Quebec attorney general forwarded a second request for armed assistance. It was no longer a local crisis – it was now a national one. "Le Gouvernment du Québec, face à une situation qui prenait des allures de guérilla, n'a eu d'autre alternative que de se préva-loir de son droit de faire appel aux Forces armées canadiennes," Brigadier General J.A. Roy later reflected.[54] Lieutenant General Kent R. Foster, the commander of the Mobile Force, concurred. "The Sûreté du Québec was not capable of facing the kind of weaponry in the Warriors' arsenal," he explained. "My view was that the army would eventually have to con-front the natives. No police force in the country could be expected to deal with the circumstances that faced the Sûreté du Québec on July 11."[55]

The second phase of Operation Salon required a military plan to re-lieve the SQ at Oka and Kahnawake, to deploy CF resources in order to remove the barricades and Warrior strongpoints, and to restore freedom of movement on all roads and bridges, as well as normal law and order. On 13 August troops were deployed to forward bivouac areas, and on 18 August the first military units took over the SQ perimeters around the Kahnawake and Oka (Kanesatake) communities.[56] Salon was a typical internal security (IS) operation in several respects. First, the military was subject to political direction at all times. Second, section 11 of the National Defence Act explains that the Queen's Regulations and Orders govern military behaviour in an "aid to the civil power" role and explic-itly stipulate "the law, that no more force may be used than is necessary, applies at all time; lethal weapons must not be used to prevent or sup-press minor disorders or offenses which are not serious, and in no case shall firearms be discharged if less extreme measures will suffice."[57] In short, the military's role was to help restore law and order with a mini-mum of force. The rules of engagement, explained to the media, stipu-lated that CF personnel at all levels were legally bound to a policy of "no first use of lethal force."[58]

Political considerations complicated the clear and timely transmission of orders from the onset, and military commanders ended up taking a lead role in planning and conducting operations beyond mere support to police operations.[59] This situation reflected political confusion and lead-ership shortcomings at both the federal and provincial levels. "Indian Affairs minister Tom Siddon was a cipher throughout the affair," Campbell and Pal observe. "The Prime Minister [still reeling from the defeat of the Meech Lake Accord] studiously avoided dealing with the crisis. Premier Bourassa and his cabinet addressed the problem in almost purely technical terms: the bridge was closed and the bridge must be opened." In this political vacuum, CF personnel and the Warriors framed the issues and dominated the debate.[60]

The CF strategy during the crisis emphasized restraint and professionalism. "My aim from the beginning was to resolve the crisis without further loss of life," Foster explained. "A Quebec policeman had already been killed trying to resolve the problem and it was evident to everybody that no one else should die over this. For my soldiers, this meant intensive discipline, following orders, dealing with uncomfortable situations such as receiving abuse, and so on. It also meant they could not respond in kind."[61] Given the high political stakes involved – pronounced by the fact that Aboriginal groups across Canada had erected sympathy blockades of road and rail lines in support of the Mohawks – and the possibility of bloodshed, the military's strategy had to be measured, adaptable, and humane. Accordingly, all ranks needed to display skill, discipline, and incredible patience during the operation.

The chief of the Defence Staff, General John de Chastelain, was in Europe when National Defence Headquarters received Quebec's request to send troops to Oka. "The CDS was confident that an infantry battalion could quickly overwhelm them," policy scholar Douglas Bland later recorded, but he knew that the immediate, direct attack that Quebec politicians were demanding "would be unpleasant for everyone." Both sides would sustain casualties, "the CF would subsequently be accused of acting rashly and de Chastelain suspected that politicians would be quick to shift blame for the incident onto him and his officers." De Chastelain knew that this was "a no-win situation for the CF and had the potential to stain our reputation and our relations with the native people for years into the future." He immediately decided that two fundamental principles would guide military actions: first, the CF would use only minimum force to contain the Mohawks and facilitate a "cooling-out period"; and second, the military would not use weapons or attack the Mohawk barricades unless the Warriors took the first shots. He also informed the media – and therefore the Warriors and the Canadian public – that the military was there to relieve the SQ and help maintain "an atmosphere of calm" while negotiators settled the dispute. In short, his approach was the "traditional peacekeeping concept learned in dozens of UN missions around the world."[62]

Bland astutely observes that the chief of the Defence Staff's directives to the CF at Oka "also provided a very pragmatic example of how responsibility for national defence is shared between politicians and the

CDS" in the National Defence Act. De Chastelain decided the military's course of action, "and no amount of prodding by politicians to end the crisis earlier than he thought prudent ... changed his plan." Indeed, his concept of operations was vindicated by the success of the operation,[63] but during the crisis, he faced considerable pressure from the Quebec government to assault the barricades. One Native spokesperson later testified that army officials explained, in an off-the-record discussion, that intense provincial pressure almost brought about the resignation of Foster and several other "key officers."[64] The prime minister's conflicted policy was to balance Quebec's calls for decisive action against the Warriors with the rest of Canada's comparative sympathy for the Mohawk cause. These competing political agendas adversely influenced field commanders, whose command decisions were second-guessed by members of the Prime Minister's Office and the Privy Council Office. Indeed, National Defence Headquarters insisted on controlling CF operations down to "the most trivial actions in the field," and the deputy minister eventually demanded that Foster clear all of his speeches through his Ottawa office before speaking to the press.[65]

The potential battlefield was situated in a highly populated urban area that demanded particular attention and intricate planning.[66] The presence of civilians would complicate any military assault on the barricades, and the Mohawks regularly called in elderly community members, women, and children to the barricades when they anticipated a CF assault. Reflecting a classic "guerrilla" style, there were no clear lines between "military" and "civilians" in the Mohawk ranks – a deliberate tactic employed to offset the CF's preponderance of military assets. The Mohawk Warriors also possessed impressive military capabilities. A lawyer for the Kanesatake Band Council confirmed that many of the militant Warriors spearheading the Oka barricade were Vietnam veterans from the American side of the Akwesasne reserve. Their combat training and experience were reflected in the Mohawk positions: their barricades were well sited and well positioned to maximize cover and concealment, and they laid out an effective network of trenches and military obstacles. For example, Kahnawake was divided into nine or ten sectors with three squad leaders per sector who rotated on eight-hour shifts.[67] Furthermore, the Warriors established a sophisticated communications network between Akwasasne, Kanesatake, and Kahnawake, making use of air raid sirens and fire hall bells, hand-held radios, cellular telephones, local radio stations, and human patrols. They also possessed a large number of automatic weapons, supplemented by an array of hunting rifles, and had ample stockpiles of rations and ammunition. Overall, they were well organized and well disciplined, with various calibre combat weapons of very high quality, Chief Warrant Officer Réginald Gagnon said. "Certains d'entre eux, non seulement portaient un fusil, mais également un revolver et un couteau de combat de type Rambo."[68]

Military officers also had to be aware that the English Canadian and international media were sympathetic to the Mohawks' position.[69] The federal government sent an envoy to Geneva to represent its interests before the United Nations Working Group on Indigenous Peoples after that body asked Canada to explain its actions and treatment of the Mohawks. Furthermore, on 12 August the federal and provincial governments signed an agreement with the Mohawks allowing the Paris-based International Federation of Human Rights to monitor events.[70] Finally, the European Parliament passed a resolution expressing its concern about Canadian treatment of Aboriginal peoples and sympathized with the Mohawk perspective. The Canadian government, and by extension the Canadian Forces, recognized that the Mohawks' publicity-seeking agenda was designed to embarrass the government and tarnish its reputation as a staunch defender of human rights.[71] The military had to carefully adopt discourse and practices that would not legitimize the Mohawks' claims or erode public support for CF actions. Indeed, adopting a successful strategy would "turn the tables" and allow the CF to project itself as the legitimate, moderate actor in the situation.

### OPERATION SALON

Operation Salon was conducted using normal army planning and deployment procedures.[72] Major Alain Tremblay, a company commander with the 3rd Battalion of the Royal 22nd Regiment, led his troops on their initial advance to make contact with the Mohawks. "The soldiers were not aware of the extent of that action," he explained afterwards. "They operated under the control of their officers and NCOs [noncommissioned officers], and their only concern was to carry out the orders they were given. The NCOs and officers were more aware of the seriousness of the situation. We knew that we were trained to deal with this sort of situation but, until it actually occurred, we didn't know how we would react. It was only after the fact that we realized that our military training prepared us well for it."[73]

The different situations in Kahnawake and Oka (Kanesatake) required adaptability and considerable restraint. Lieutenant Colonel Robin Gagnon, commanding officer of the 3rd Battalion, recalled that "when we arrived in the Kahnawake area, tension was running high. At my first meeting, I attempted to defuse the situation. I explained my mission [to the Warriors] and told them that my men would not aim their weapons at them provided that the Warriors did likewise." The ensuing atmosphere of trust and mutual understanding, which reflected Gagnon's "personal commitment, calm and attentive approach to native reality," avoided bloodshed. He regretted, however, that he had learned about Mohawk culture only during the crisis. "It would have helped beforehand to be familiar, not only with the underlying reasons for their demands, but also with their culture and traditions. Their outlook is altogether different from ours. Moreover, the chiefs have no decision-making power whatsoever. They must constantly consult their people and reach a consensus."[74]

Chief Warrant Officer Réginald Gagnon, the sergeant major of "C" Company of the 2nd Battalion, notes that between 23 and 31 August not a day passed without members of his company coming face-to-face with Warriors. It became obvious to the soldiers that "chaque occasion de provoquer un accrochage coïncidait avec la presence des medias d'informations demeurant sur leur côté des barricades." Despite the high-stress atmosphere, the soldiers of his company displayed discipline and appropriate reactions to provocations from the outset. "À chaque fois, ils gardaient leur calme et leur sang-froid," Gagnon explained, "meme si la pression était forte et que les menaces à leur égard provoquaient souvent des frissons glacés dans le dos."[75] Gagnon concludes that the adaptability of the officers, noncommissioned officers, and soldiers allowed them to assess the evolving situation, build momentum, and not succumb to the taunts of the Mohawks. The soldiers had to evoke an aura of strength and control and had to intimate to the Warriors that they could carry out an armed assault if needed; this consideration was essential to maintaining credibility in the field. The military's rules of engagement, however, emphasized that the soldiers would not fire the first shot and would even take the first casualty. From the CF's standpoint, this requirement had the unfortunate impact of lessening the perceived threat to the Warriors and preserving their will to resist.[76]

Developments at Oka (Kanesatake) required a different approach than at Kahnawake. The ongoing discussions with the military reflected the decentred and disjointed Mohawk leadership. Every Mohawk claimed decision-making authority, which helped to explain the Warriors' ever-changing demands. In mid-August, for example, federal and provincial negotiating teams (each consisting of three representatives) were shocked when fifty-four Mohawks representing various segments of the community showed up to talk.[77] This factionalism rendered negotiations untenable. On a deeper level, however, the situation embodied the Warriors' overarching agenda, which could not accommodate any government or military interests without an explicit recognition of Mohawk sovereignty. Of course, the government could not concede on a point that could jeopardize the integrity of the entire Canadian state, and Lieutenant Colonel Pierre Daigle's battalion was called upon to bring pressure to bear in the field. Daigle adamantly denied, however, that the military was provocative toward the Warriors, reassuring reporters that "There are no sparks. We are not here to attack. We are here to contribute to a swift and peaceful resolution of the crisis."[78]

Company commander Major Alain Tremblay explained that, when he faced the Warriors in the pine woods on 1 September, he "took a calculated risk during that operation. I was not supposed to push our advance so far, but the CO had authorized me to exploit the terrain. We met resistance at the first barricades. I evaluated the situation and, despite the Warrior's threats, I decided to continue the advance. The Warriors seemed surprised and fell back." Major Tremblay urged his men to remain calm when the Warriors, isolated within a limited perimeter, loaded their weapons and aimed at the soldiers. "The soldiers had to have a lot of confidence in their superiors not to fire when a loaded weapon was aimed at them," Tremblay later noted, explaining that the noncommissioned officers were instrumental in reassuring the infantry and allowing them to maintain their composure when faced with the taunts of nervous Warriors, including one who screamed at the soldiers to open fire if they dared. At this juncture, Private Patrick Cloutier had his famous encounter with a masked Warrior that was captured by a photographer and broadcast around the world. Cloutier claimed that anyone in the company would have demonstrated the same poise and self-control. "I told myself to be calm and not let anyone see that I was not completely confident," he later described. "Besides, I felt that I was protected by my buddies and I knew that the Warriors would take advantage of the cameras to put on a show."[79]

The military also had to grapple with rising intolerance among the local non-Native population. Chateauguay residents, furious that the barricades continued to cut off their access to Montreal, continued to burn effigies at the Mercier Bridge, hurled stones at fleeing cars filled with Mohawk women and children, and yelled at authorities whom they believed should be taking direct action to repulse the Mohawk dissidents. A decade later, an article in the *First Nations Drum* recalled that, "during those torrid nights in the summer of 1990, mobs of enraged vigilantes roamed the outskirts of the reserve, waving baseball bats. They roughed up anyone who looked native, they roughed up white people who tried to drive through their road blocks, they roughed up reporters. And then they turned their ire on the police, who tear-gassed them during several nights of wild rioting."[80] The military was expected to act as the sober interlocutor between various hostile factions of society, but not everyone was convinced that it was accomplishing this mission. When members of the International Federation of Human Rights tried to enter Kahnawake in late August in order to determine whether food and medical supplies were reaching the community, non-Native protestors wielding baseball bats attacked their car while nearby soldiers and police did nothing. The observers fled, prompting one to note, "The only persons who have treated me in a civilized way in this matter here in Canada are the Mohawks. The Army and the police do nothing. It's very degrading ... degrading to us, and perhaps more degrading to the government who can't give us access."[81]

By mid-August public statements from all parties suggested that a resolution was in sight, but government officials expressed dismay at the Mohawks' tendency to continuously extend their bargaining demands when a deal was near completion. For her part, Ellen Gabriel remained convinced that someone within the Mohawk ranks was trying to sabotage negotiations and force Canada to legitimate the Warriors.[82] In this context, unrealistic demands were strategically useful to buy time. On 21 August, Tioteroken, a spokesman for the Mohawk Nation Office, told reporters that the barricades would come down when the federal and provincial governments agreed to turn over the disputed lands to the Mohawks of Kanesatake, stop prosecutions related to the operation of the high-stakes Mohawk Super Bingo Hall on the Kahnawake Reserve, and commit to the creation of Kanien'kehaka – a unified Mohawk Nation spanning six reserves in Ontario, Quebec, and New York State – within three years.[83] The Mohawk negotiators soon added the right to their own armed forces, a Native justice system, and submission of their sovereignty claim to the World Court in the Hague. Politicians found the talks "arduous, laborious, and difficult" and complained about the Mohawks' lack of focus. Sam Elkas, the provincial minister of public security, was dismayed that although they were supposed to be discussing the dismantling of the barricades, the Mohawks were "always coming back with other subjects of discussion."[84]

The Mohawks' negotiating strategy was no longer about localized demands but about larger issues of sovereignty and immunity from criminal law. "Land claims and certainly sovereignty were, from the government perspective, issues that could be addressed later," Campbell and Pal note. "For the Mohawks, however, the barricade was their only bargaining chip. Without it, they were merely a ragged band of protesters; with it, they could attract attention and extract concessions."[85] Although the Warriors tried to project the image of a common Mohawk front, public fractures began to appear. "Condoled chiefs" (elders) of the Six Nations held a meeting at the Onandaga Reserve in New York on 24 August to seek a peaceful resolution to the crisis, and Chief Jake Thomas, the traditional Cayuga chief and faithkeeper of the Onondaga Longhouse, dismissed the Warriors as fakes who hid behind the Mohawk tradition to protect their illegal cigarette and gambling interests.[86] In his bold assessment of the situation, Winegard agrees:

> Obviously those trying to protect the Pines were no longer formulating the Mohawk agenda and were relegated to the background. The Oka Crisis was now about sovereignty whereby outside police forces could not disrupt the lucrative smuggling and gaming operations. The Oka Crisis was now about securing the right to operate bingo parlours and casinos without any form of government reprisal. The Oka Crisis was now about power and money and a struggle for those in possession to maintain and increase their shares. The crisis was no longer about saving a small patch of White Pines on the western edge of a tiny golf club at Oka, Quebec. The Warriors felled 155 of these sacred trees to build barricades and bunkers. The Pines were being used to protect profit.[87]

For its part, Minister of Indian Affairs Tom Siddon insisted that the federal government would never concede to the "balkanization of Canada which would see first nations become independent sovereign states." Neither he nor the prime minister was prepared to continue negotiations geared toward this outcome.[88]

When political discussions between Mohawk dissidents and government authorities broke off in late August, all practical negotiations devolved to the soldiers on the ground. On 28 August, Generals Foster and

Roy announced on national television that the military would "not cease our overall or local operations until Mohawks and the Warriors lay down their weapons and surrender in front of the barricades." Foster reinforced that military operations "could involve the use of 2,500 combat troops and armoured personnel carriers," that three Leopard tanks with bulldozer blades were being held in reserve, and that surveillance would increase. "We are now entering a new phase in this crisis," he explained. "We are going into a military operation." The next day, local military commanders and Kahnawakeronon successfully negotiated a "gentleman's agreement" to remove the barricades at Kahnawake and the Mercier Bridge. Over the next six days, the Mohawks dismantled their outer barricades, and the military effectively occupied the outer half of the Kahnawake Reserve. The Mohawks retained a defensive barricade guarding the entrances to the heart of the community, but the Mercier Bridge opened for general traffic on 6 September.[89] In Réginald Gagnon's assessment, "le démantèlement des barricades de Châteauguay le 30 août, eut un effect dévastateur sur le moral et la determination des Warriors de la region de Oka."[90]

Although the military had restored freedom of movement at Kahnawake, the situation at Kanesatake remained dangerous. About twenty armed Warriors withdrew into a final barricade around a Drug and Alcohol Treatment Centre, and the military established a perimeter securing the surrounding area.[91] Logistically, containing these Warriors was far easier than had been the case at Kahnawake, given that it was a confined area. Douglas George-Kanentiio explains,

> Strands of barbed wire kept the warriors in while preventing them from either interfering with regional traffic or threatening their opponents within Kanehsatake or nearby Oka. When the Kahnawake roadblocks were taken down on August 29, the warrior group at the treatment center was left without any significant bargaining chip. All the Canadian officials had to do was to wait and allow the internal pressures within the warrior group to break it apart as a natural consequence of sleep deprivation, restricted diets, weak command structure, and a complete lack of formal training in sustaining a long-term siege against superior numbers. Also working against the warriors was the fact that they were never a cohesive group and had considerable mistrust among their ranks.[92]

The Warriors were told that they were free to leave the area without their weapons (a safe passage was promised to the rear of the centre), but they refused in fear of arrest by the s q once they were outside of the military cordon. Tensions continued to mount as the Warriors became increasingly concerned and frustrated with military actions, including aggressive nighttime reconnaissance patrols undertaken to gather intelligence on Warrior dispositions, to make noise intended to intimidate them, and on one occasion to steal a Warrior flag.[93] Other psychological warfare techniques further destabilized the remaining Warriors, from low-level flights to well-aimed spotlights. In *Entering the War Zone*, Donna Goodleaf explains that the Mohawks behind the barricades recognized the military intimidation tactics: low-level surveillance sweeps by military helicopters, continuous military encroachments on what the Mohawks called "the demilitarized zone," and references to potential "collateral damage" (which she interpreted as civilian casualties). The military presented the press with aerial, land, and marine reconnaissance photographs and diagrams, revealing their knowledge of the Mohawk defensive positions, and described the military weapons they could use.[94]

These tactics were designed to intimidate the Warriors into capitulating, and they worked. Goodleaf quotes Oneida subchief Bob Antone's comment about deliberations in the treatment centre:

> We had several discussions in the midst of all the turmoil that was going on. There was constant pressure put on us by the military and psychological war games were played to ensure that we did not have time really to deliberate on these issues. We spent a lot of our time arguing with the military to back off a little bit and to keep the helicopters maybe 30 feet away. It is very hard to hear yourself talking when a helicopter is hovering over your head ... Those were the kind of things that were going on inside when we were attempting to look for a solution.[95]

Carefully coordinated, measured advances on Mohawk positions and psychological operations pushed the Warriors back on their heels and "unhinge[d] the occupants psychologically."[96] With momentum clearly working against them, the Warriors subjected the soldiers to a constant barrage of racial insults, particularly toward French Canadians.[97] c f personnel maintained their composure. Troops took video recordings at key moments, which helped to "calm the situation, and had a certain restraining effect on dissidents that might have been contemplating violent actions." Orders were carefully documented and records preserved in acknowledgment that they could be subject to legal proceedings and would have to be defensible in court.[98]

The reopening of the Mercier Bridge allowed state authorities to focus on the last group of Mohawk Warriors holding out at Kanesatake, without the same level of intense political pressure to negotiate a solution. Neither federal nor provincial politicians were willing to negotiate while armed Warriors remained, and the governments would accept nothing less than unconditional surrender at this point. The Warriors, for their part, put together a "peace proposal" in which a joint commission with government, Mohawk, and human rights agency representatives would determine their fate. The provincial government rejected any immunity for the dissidents and any recognition of Mohawk sovereignty. "In the name of fundamental principles of democracy and of our justice system, the proposal is unacceptable to the Quebec government," Premier Bourassa explained on 11 September. "There would be no question of allowing a certain group of citizens to be treated differently than other Quebec citizens." Although Bob Antone, who was negotiating for the Warriors in the treatment centre, insisted that the Mohawks were offering "a very flexible position" and were "willing to sit down and proceed with talks to fine-tune the details," the problem was hardly one of fine print.[99] The Mohawks insisted that they were sovereign and deserved some form of amnesty, whereas government officials were unwilling to compromise on applying Canadian laws to the Warriors. The time for government conciliation had passed.

The barricades had come down at Kahnawake, but tensions remained high and the situation remained volatile. Soldiers conducted cordon and search operations in hopes that they would ferret out arms dumps in the community. As a result, troops of the 2nd Battalion faced angry Mohawks in the Kahnawake sector on 18 September. Hundreds of Mohawk residents taunted and then assaulted CF and SQ personnel who were searching for weapons on Tékakwita Island, resulting in injuries to about forty members of the Royal Canadian Regiment who were not equipped for riot control but managed to repel the mob with teargas grenades. Lieutenant Colonel Greg Mitchell, the commanding officer of the 2nd Battalion, reflected that his unit was "shocked and surprised at what happened." They had already conducted five previous searches without any significant confrontation, advised Kahnawake officials in advance of the search, and estimated that they would need about 30 men to block access to the bridge to the island. In the end, they needed 140 men to complete the six and a half hour operation. He was appalled by the physical abuse of his soldiers, who thought that they were not allowed to hit back because of the principle of the minimal use of force that guided CF operations.[100] About 75 Mohawks were treated at the Kateri Hospital, mainly for the effects of tear gas, including children, women, and elders who had been on the scene.[101] No one seemed satisfied with the status quo.

By mid-September the situation at Kanesatake had entered a new phase. "At this stage the confrontation had been reduced entirely to a military engagement," Campbell and Pal explain, "a play of force and physical threat where negotiations, when they occurred at all, were about the terms of surrender."[102] The army erected light towers to better observe the Mohawk side of the razor wire at night and cut off all external communication lines to the treatment centre (except their own "Hot Line" straight to the army negotiations office). Journalists' cell phones were also jammed, and Major George Rousseau strongly urged the remaining reporters to leave the building before nightfall. They chose to stay.[103] The main barricades were down, and the SQ arrived in Oka to patrol the territory, indicating that the army would not remain longer than a week. American civil rights activist Jesse Jackson arrived to try to broker a peaceful settlement, but the military did lot let him cross its lines. "It was very clear in the army's mind that the Standoff would end," the Kanesatake community website recalls, "With or Without the Warriors consent."[104] Although media depictions cast the army as more belligerent and uncompromising by this point, Geoffrey York and Loreen Pindera suggest that the CF created a hidden "back door" in hopes that the Warriors would simply "disappear," as they had done at Kahnawake. Razor wire barriers suggested that the settlement was tightly encircled, but the army told the remaining Warriors that it had left a safe corridor through the woods and mountains north of the community and encouraged them to use it.[105] They remained barricaded in the treatment centre rather than surrendering, debated how to end the crisis, and put together a final offer for the provincial government to negotiate a settlement. Premier Bourassa rejected it on 25 September, and most of the Warriors holed up in the treatment centre acknowledged the futility of continuing the standoff any longer. "The leaders of Kanehsatake wanted them out," Douglas George-Kanentiio explains, "while many of the key Kahnawake-based warriors, those who had accelerated the crisis by blocking the Mercier Bridge, had fled the province, fearing arrest." The Warriors' leaders at Akwesasne were "more concerned with getting the casinos up and going while resuming their highly lucrative smuggling operations" than with supporting the last holdouts at Kanesatake.[106]

The following day, the remaining Warriors decided to surrender in a confused exit from the treatment centre.[107] Although some commentators later blamed the military for the ensuing chaos, the withdrawal was carefully orchestrated by the Warriors to allow some of the main protagonists to escape. It caught the military off guard. "We could have made all sorts of contingency plans," Lieutenant Colonel Daigle explained, "but we were busy negotiating the details of the Warriors' surrender." The military had stationed buses near an exit so that "everything would be handled with respect to human rights," but the remaining Warriors and their supporters "chose to surprise us by coming out where the reporters were waiting, with women and children preceding them so their companions most wanted by the police could escape."[108] Journalist Jack Todd described the scenes broadcast across the country: "A Canadian soldier pushing a Mohawk child to the pavement and then kicking her mother down on top of her ... crying children being dragged back and forth after their screaming mothers ... It ends in chaos and confusion, with soldiers and Warriors and journalists and children running back and forth in the semi-darkness, and army helicopters overhead illuminating the nightmarish scene with their powerful searchlights." Minor skirmishes broke out between the soldiers and the individuals fleeing the treatment centre. "What have we allowed to happen here?" Todd asked. "Is this a country where women and children can be shoved and kicked by armed troops?"[109] Given the discipline and reserve displayed by the soldiers throughout the preceding weeks, it was an unfortunate end to a tumultuous situation.

The crisis was over. Twenty-six men, sixteen women, six children, and ten journalists were transported to the Farnham military custody area at the Mohawks' request, where they remained until 5 October when they were turned over to civilian authorities. The s Q had resumed patrolling at Kahnawake by the middle of the month, and the military's phased withdrawal had been completed by 31 October 1990.[110]

THE MEDIA WAR

Let's face it, in strict military sense, this standoff could be ended in less than two minutes, but the real battle is being fought on TV news and in the living rooms of Canada. The army is winning because they have mounted a brilliant public relations campaign.

Christopher Cushing, 22 September 1990.[111]

Various scholarly studies have assessed the media coverage of the Oka Crisis, typically concluding that the Canadian newspaper and television industry was biased against the Mohawks (and by extension, Aboriginal peoples more generally) during the crisis. Although hegemonic and discourse theories may help us to understand the media's framing of the crisis and its main protagonists, the scholarly fixation on demonstrating anti-Native racism has tended to downplay the *effectiveness* of the CF's communication strategy.[112] Armed forces are traditionally suspicious of journalists (believing, in the words of General de Chastelain, that they "will seek to over-dramatize the events they cover" or will jeopardize military security and surprise),[113] but the military leadership at Oka understood the role of the media and dealt with them effectively. The army's successful application of a consistent, coherent, and "peaceful" message during the crisis contrasted with the SQ's more hostile message. Furthermore, the Mohawks' multicentric and dispersed voice, with attendant problems of incoherence and inconsistency, contrasted with the military's aura of discipline, confidence, and strength, which was amplified through its press relations.[114]

Claude Beauregard's exceptional short study of the army's communication strategy reveals how and why Canadians' perceptions of the military "changed completely in the whirlwind of events at Oka." The military's proactive engagement of the media to inform the public of developments and win credibility also influenced the operational situation.[115] Its effectiveness was tied directly to the military's leadership. The operational commander, Brigadier General Roy, controlled the flow of information to the press and thus to the Canadian public. Rather than viewing journalists as an enemy, he recognized that they served as a critical conduit to Canadians for communicating the military's message with minimal ambiguity and distortion:

> Strategically, certain aspects of the intervention went beyond the responsibility of tactical commanders and influenced the conflict in its entirety. The approach taken by the media, for example, when effectively developed, increased the operational benefits expected in the strategic plan. The presence of reporters served not only to

inform the people but also to influence them to a certain point. In fact, announcing all troop and equipment movements via the press contributed to a reduction of tensions in the field and even went as far as to spark dialogue. Also, the omnipresence of cameras encouraged opposing groups to remain calm and not commit themselves to an escalation of violence. When first looking for the support of the people, the Warriors did not know how to effectively exploit the support given them by Canadians at the beginning of hostilities. Their violent and unjustified actions, once broadcast, had the effect of turning opinion against the Mohawks.[116]

By stressing transparency and openness (insofar as this did not compromise the security of operations or personnel), and by reiterating the principle of minimum force (for example, the chief of the Defence Staff announced during a televised press conference on 17 August that the public would be kept informed of all the army's moves against the barricades), the CF was able to convince Canadians that it had no hidden agendas and was committed to a peaceful resolution.

The CF's proactive media program began immediately upon deployment.[117] Federal and provincial authorities announced each major military initiative to journalists, and the military elaborated upon its actions and plans at press conferences, in follow-up press releases, and in on-site media briefings by Public Affairs officers. Whenever events transpired that might have raised public or media controversy, the CF took prompt, coordinated action to convey the facts to the press.[118] "During the Oka crisis," a postoperation communications report noted, "not until the military was on site with ... regular daily briefings for media did key messages begin to get out and misinformation corrected." Although much of the misinformation about military activities would not have warranted ministerial comment, it was still essential "to public understanding of the crisis (ie: food access, Warrior criminality, role of [the Assembly of First Nations])."[119] Journalists who attended military news conferences received background papers, news releases, photos, and video tapes intended for publication. This strategy allowed the military to counter the Mohawks' spin on developments in a systematic and coherent manner.

From the outset, the Warriors employed symbolism to heighten their media profile. Their camouflage fatigues and concealed faces, for example, played upon images of the Palestinian Intifada, which had enjoyed favourable media attention earlier in the year. "Identification with the

Palestinian cause was an identification with a well known national-determination movement," Martin Morris notes in an insightful article on the crisis as a form of political communication. "The garb identified them as outside the official and legitimate political sphere: they viewed themselves as freedom fighters for their nation, while from the government's perspective they appeared as 'terrorists.'"[120] Citing a July 1990 poll, *Montreal Gazette* editor Norman Webster was perplexed at how "Canadians have reacted in a remarkably positive manner to the Mohawk cause" and to their land claims.[121] When the military became directly engaged, senior officials recognized that if the CF did not take a proactive role, it would face public criticism for perpetuating centuries of injustice toward the Mohawks.

Morris explains that "the central communicative action of the crisis consisted of power and influence communications, since the breakdown of authority necessarily brought these types into play."[122] The threat of violence, on both sides, precipitated a battle for legitimacy over who had the right to wield force for self-defence. The Mohawk Warriors enjoyed early legitimacy in media portrayals, but the military managed to at least partially reverse the symbolic representation of who was "carrying the burden of peace." Alfred has summarized the competing images of the warrior as follows:

> Since the warrior society first pierced Canadian consciousness in the 1970s, the indigenous warrior has been characterized as both the Noble Savage – "a heroic champion of native rights ready to die for the cause" – and the bloodthirsty renegade – a "testosterone-driven gun junkie out to die in a blaze of glory." Falling back on hackneyed stereotypes and one-dimensional portrayals of indigenous existence, the Canadian media, governments and citizenry invariably cast indigenous warriors, whether heroes or tyrants, as misguided and irrational malcontents who have taken Canadian law into their own hands. Today's Noble Savage is the masked, camouflaged superhero of indigenous nationhood, glorified and romanticized during the Oka standoff. As the imagery changed in 1990, from braided, Red Power rebels to authentic indigenous freedom fighters, armed and ready for battle, the Noble Savage myth grew even stronger in Canadian consciousness. The bloodthirsty renegade, meanwhile, is cast as a terrorist, a thug, a tyrant and a fascist, whose gun-wielding posturing instils fear and engenders condemnation in indigenous communities.[123]

Whereas the Mohawks justified their actions on the basis of national self-determination and systematic injustice, the military framed its representations with themes of law and order that legitimized state action. It was consistent throughout the crisis in asserting that there could be no exceptions to Canadian law.[124] This message was matched by strong leadership and measured actions that seemed to legitimize this rationale in practice, and it played upon Canadians' imagined virtues of dialogue, harmony, and tolerance.[125]

Sociologist J. Rick Ponting has aptly summarized the competing discourses during the crisis. Indian rhetoric characterized the federal government as "an oppressive, untrustworthy, interfering, aggressive, and uncivilized opponent." Mohawk spokespersons complained that the dominant society's legal system oppressed them and that Mohawk sovereignty placed them beyond Canadian law. On the other hand, to draw a sharp delineation between protagonists and to place Indians above the Quebecois, they depicted Native peoples as "sovereign, spiritual and peace-loving people who are at one with nature and with each other, while simultaneously under siege from the state and police." The federal government's rhetoric rationalized its actions as "restrained, committed to the rule of law, generously responsive, and liberal." It portrayed the Mohawks as "atypical, factionally divided, and violent and criminally deviant." The competition for legitimacy permeated the entire crisis:

> One can observe that for almost every theme projected by the Indians, an opposing theme could be found in the federal government's discourse. For instance, Indians' emphasis on peace was countered in government rhetoric by the emphasis on the Warriors' violence. Indians' emphasis on government aggressiveness is juxtaposed with government's emphasis on its restraint and on Mohawks' "ambush" behaviour. Indians' characterization of government as dishonourable faces government's claims to moral rectitude and its characterization of Mohawks as criminal. Indians' professed solidarity with the Mohawks is implicitly contested by the government's claim of the atypicality of the Mohawks. Indians' complaints that the federal government fails to heed the rulings of its own Supreme Court can be contrasted with government's definition of the events of summer 1990 as revolving around the upholding of the rule of law … Indians decry government interference, while government decries Indian

factionalism. Indians' demands for sovereignty meet categorical rejection from government.[126]

The military could not ignore this symbolic competition. If Canadians seriously questioned the CF's legitimacy during the crisis, it would erode political support and trust. Indeed, the ensuing battle for the "hearts and minds" of Canadians and the world reflected the dichotomy played out daily in the press.

The CF recognized that the Mohawk strategy was to discredit it and undermine its mission, and it knew that sympathetic journalists who remained behind the blockades had adopted the Warriors' mindset. "Playing the press had become a daily occupation," the Kanesatake website later noted about the crisis. "The Mohawks on their side were putting out press releases by the dozens. They also knew how to win the hearts and minds of the world by influencing press coverage." The Mohawks saw this as a "new era in journalism ... The media was present from day 1 and 10 journalists stayed inside the Treatment center until the very last day. A mutual friendship also emerged with the Mohawks, even though weapons were always present, and tensions were often very high."[127] The military had to counter the pro Mohawk sentiments that these journalists expressed in their behind-the-barricade depictions with images that depicted the CF as humane and sensible actors up against irrational aggressors threatening social order. For example, General de Chastelain offered the following "throw-away line (literally)" in response to media accusations that the CF was denying food to journalists behind the perimeter: "We have been sending in food daily, based on a ration scale of 60 people, and it is our understanding that only 54 are in there. The other day we sent in four eggs per person (ie 240) which were used by the Warriors to throw at the soldiers across the wire!"[128] Although the "Communications Lessons" document produced after the crisis remains largely classified, a few sections have been released under the Access to Information Act. It observed that the media was "becoming more and more a part of its own stories" and offered several examples, including:

- the media presence behind the barricades;
- media ignoring military advice to leave the area;
- reporters holding their own news conferences after exiting from behind the barricades; and
- the issue of reporters having access to supplies.[129]

In short, some journalists eschewed the risks involved in remaining behind the barricades and flanked the military's controlled media environment, posing new dilemmas for Public Affairs officials seeking to fix the boundaries of public engagement.

Nevertheless, the CF succeeded in setting the discursive agenda. For example, when federal ministers repeated the same message about the need to uphold "the rule of law" over a four-day period, both the media and Indian leaders took note "and even began to repeat it themselves in their defence for their positions."[130] The image of the Warriors "as a beleaguered band of freedom fighters was never really consolidated, partly because the greatly superior fire-power of the army was never used and the steadfast discipline of the soldiers (portrayed in the media most markedly in the face of heated obscenities hurled at them by enraged Warriors) was an essential part of the army's strategy to avoid such an image and to win over public sympathy." Morris observes that "the struggle – or 'war of manoeuvre' – between the Mohawks and the governing forces occurred in the sphere of strategic power communications" and that popular perceptions factored heavily into all attempts by both sides to influence the other. As Peter Desbarats, the dean of the graduate School of Journalism at the University of Western Ontario, suggested at the time, the confrontation was "more of a media war than a true battle for territory," a "war of words," and a "war of images," where "play-acting in front of the cameras did seem to present an alternative to shooting."[131]

The army's communication strategy created a public image that, coupled with the military discipline displayed on the ground, engendered sufficient public support to undermine the Warriors' counterclaims for Canadian sympathy. National polls suggested that Canadian support for the Mohawks declined precipitously as the crisis dragged on, whereas support for the federal government – particularly the CF – improved accordingly.[132] A 26 September 1990 article in *Le Devoir* applauded the military's performance: "In regards to Quebec public opinion, the Army will have been the big discovery of the native crisis. So while the soldiers have begun returning to their bases, the public can't stop praising these young men whose behaviour deeply impressed all during these days which could have, any one, turned to tragedy: Self control, restraint, discipline, and even a surprising coolness in communication ... All of this, under an unfailing lucky star, almost faultlessly. The Army ends the affair with all honour, the honour of peace."[133] In short, what could have been a disaster for the military, being deployed against Aboriginal protestors in a volatile domestic situation that could easily have deteriorated into large-scale violence and loss of life, exemplified their professionalism.

## CONCLUSIONS

Many an Aboriginal person recognizes the irony that the "crisis" is referenced to the white town and not some Kanien'kehaka point of reference. The word "crisis" is also interesting to me as it infers that the situation occurred at a moment in time. But the dispute that underlies the stand the people made at the Pines has gone on for hundreds of years.

Patricia Monture, 2010[134]

The Oka Crisis was the culmination of a long and tortured history of competing ownership claims, legal battles between the Mohawks and the Canadian state, and rising militancy among certain Mohawk factions. Although the immediate goal of the initial peaceful protests was to protect the white pine forest, it quickly became engulfed in larger political issues of Mohawk sovereignty, the Warriors and their illicit enterprises, and land claims more generally. The Warriors and the Native groups across the country who supported them "succeeded in broadening the issues surrounding the crisis to include fundamental grievances over land claims and self-determination," political scientist Martin Morris observes. "Whether they thought that these issues and demands really would be dealt with within the context of the crisis negotiations is beside the point. The Oka crisis created a communicative context much broader than the one-on-one negotiations: it enabled Native peoples to speak louder or, rather, to speak *as* Native peoples and to be *heard*."[135]

Gauging the success of the blockades depends upon the goal that one seeks to assess. Ellen Gabriel has since written that "the issue that sparked the Crisis of 1990 was the blatant theft of our homelands, the Mohawk peoples' sovereignty over those lands and the continued efforts by governments to undermine and defraud us of our international human rights to our homelands."[136] Depending on how far one expands the idea of homeland theft and sovereignty, and whose interests the observer prioritizes, the standoff could represent a partial victory or a failure. On a local level, Prime Minister Brian Mulroney noted that "once the guns are down, we will be in a position to hand the disputed land over to the people of Kanesatake."[137] If this had been the key objective of the Mohawks, they probably could have secured a land transfer through negotiations in mid-July 1990. Owing to the prolonged standoff, discussions about a land transfer had to wait until the crisis was over. In 1991 the Kanesatake Mohawks and the federal government agreed on a framework for negotiations, and three years later they signed a memorandum of understanding for land purchases. In 1997 the federal government purchased land in the name of the community, and in December 2000 the Mohawks and Ottawa signed a new land governance agreement. Nevertheless, the status of the burial ground and golf course remains unresolved, and some residents continue to criticize the Kanesatake Interim Land Base Governance Act for adversely affecting Kanien'kehaka rights.[138]

The Oka Crisis has left a mixed legacy, at best, on community-level politics. "Above all, and despite much internal stress and conflict," political scientist Peter Russell asserts, "the Mohawks' resistance at Kanehsatà:ke and Kahnawà:ke strengthened those societies' sense of being responsible for their own future. They had held off the Canadian army and provincial police force. By showing their determination and ability to defend their vital interests they asserted their own sense of sovereignty." In turn, Russell notes that the Kahnawake community has secured control of education, social welfare, and security on its territory "through pragmatic agreements with Ottawa and Québec City – agreements in which none of the parties concede an ounce of sovereignty."[139]

By contrast, Kanesatake residents and the elected band leadership were clearly disempowered by the Warriors who moved into their community and used intimidation to take control of the blockade. Mohawk Douglas George-Kanentiio, in his damning indictment of the violence that engulfed Iroquois communities in 1990, observed how the "quiet, respectful" residents of Kanesatake had taken modest action to prevent the destruction of the Pines. "In March of 1990 they had, as was their way, erected a small roadblock to protest the planned destruction of a wood lot near one of their cemeteries." This action attracted little attention compared to the concurrent violence at Akwesasne, and "there were no weapons – no one brandished clubs for the press." This changed on 11 July, when "a band of Akwesasne warriors descended upon Oka with the trunks of their cars full of the same assault rifles they had used at Akwesasne." Only one resident had invited the Warriors, who did not enjoy widespread community support. Their presence convinced the Quebec authorities to take decisive action so that they could not be "accused of another act of cowardice" like their unwillingness to intervene at Akwesasne.[140]

The disastrous SQ raid, which left Corporal Lemay dead, not only changed the nature of Aboriginal politics in Canada but also thrust the local community into chaos as rival Mohawk factions vied for control. "Without a stable, centralized government with effective law enforcement powers, there was no way to control the more extreme elements who used warrior intimidation tactics to create a climate of fear and intimidation," George-Kanentiio explains. "The resulting anarchy meant Kanehsatake became a haven for warriors who served the drug trade as traffickers, distributing cocaine and marijuana to dealers in the Montreal area, or who profited from the harvests of their own hydroponics farms." Police could not intervene without being "confronted by masked men waving the blood red death's head banner of the warrior society that had become quite popular across Canada whenever Aboriginal people elected to challenge the state." Kanesatake has never recovered from the Oka Crisis, as violent developments in 2004 demonstrated.[141]

For the Warriors, however, the Oka Crisis was a partial success. "Once the Quebec officials sent in the Surete," George-Kanentiio observes, "the same warriors who had been defeated at Akwesasne hijacked control over both Kahnawake and Kanehsatake."[142] The expansion of the resistance against provincial authorities to the Kahnawake Reserve, and the blockade of the Mercier Bridge, inspired a fiery public response from irate non-Native residents, who were readily derided as racists by the national media. By contrast, the Warriors (whether cast as militant rebels or freedom fighters) were elevated in status to worthy combatants facing off against the Canadian Forces. Reporters conferred legitimacy on the Warriors as spokespersons for the Mohawks and failed to critically interrogate their connection to criminal activities at Akwesasne. Instead, by establishing stark "we"-"they" lines between the Mohawks, their non-Native neighbours, and the provincial and federal governments, the confrontation concealed deep internal divisions within the Mohawk communities. This heightened the power of the Warriors vis-à-vis other groups, undermined internal Iroquois political structures that may have helped to diffuse the situation from within, and allowed the Warriors to cast themselves as the defenders of the Mohawk Nation against outside aggression. In the end, George-Kanentiio laments, the crisis "empowered the warriors by making them powerful symbols of Native activism, while obscuring their involvement in the undermining of the very Mohawk nationalism they publicly espoused."[143]

Given the national and international attention that the Oka Crisis generated for the Warriors and for the broader idea of Mohawk sovereignty, it was clearly a watershed for the Warrior movement. Mohawk scholar Taiaiake Alfred observes that "many of the people who became involved in the warrior society movements on the east and west coast have cited the 1990 Oka crisis as a turning point in their lives." This form of "militant assertion of indigenous nationhood" inspired young Indigenous people by "awakening ... indigenous consciousness and radicalization of the agenda." After Oka, "indigenous resistance came to be virtually defined in terms of the approach, technique, vocabulary and style of the Mohawk Warrior Society's actions during that summer."[144] Indeed, Oka changed the way that Aboriginal people across Canada thought about Native-state relations and the place of militant action in protecting Native rights. "The summer of 1990 was the summer that we stopped playing Cowboys and Indians and started being warriors," writes Anishinabek hip-hop artist and CBC host Wab Kinew. The games that Aboriginal children now played were "teaching us to become warriors who would stand up for our people, our land and our rights. I have heard some activists talk about having an 'Oka' on every Rez and how that would be a 'revolution.'"[145]

Although journalists, documentary filmmakers, and activist-scholars would later vilify the military for being aggressive and provocative during the confrontation, the Canadian Forces succeeded where the Sûreté du Québec had failed. Whereas the provincial police had blundered in their 11 July raid, CF operations were well planned and well orchestrated. In typically turgid military language, the regional army commander concluded in his Oka after-action report,

> Operation SALON was a large, complex, and drawn-out IS operation. It centered around a potentially explosive situation that could have deteriorated into armed violence between the police and military on one side, and the Warriors and their sympathizers on the other. While acknowledging the forbearance and restraint of the native factions and civil authorities, tragedy was averted and Canadian principles of law enforcement upheld in large measure because of the manner in which disciplined and well-trained units were able to conduct a wide range of military operations. The utility of a general purpose, combat capable army at an adequate level of readiness was amply demonstrated on Operation SALON. A less capable force would have failed in its task.[146]

Although some localized confrontations during the crisis have been overemphasized in popular accounts to undermine the army's positive image, the military played an essential role in the management and eventual diffusion of the crisis, projecting an image of professionalism, respectability, and discipline.[147] "We reflected positively on the way Canada will go into the next decade," Lieutenant Colonel Greg Mitchell explained after the crisis had ended. "If we had blown it – if people had been killed or if we had lost control of the situation – we would have spent the next 10 years crisscrossing the country putting out fires. I hope this can now be avoided."[148]

The military also won the decisive battle at Oka: media spin. At the time, popular opinion polls confirmed that two-thirds of Canadians supported the military's presence and held a positive impression of its actions, particularly in Quebec, where 78 per cent of the population viewed the military favourably.[149] At Oka the Warriors pushed direct action against the state beyond most Canadians' comfort level. The Warriors mobilized strong ethnic symbols to appeal to society's sense of justice and fairness and challenged the credibility of the state. "From the strategic point of view," sociologist C. Radha Jhappan observes, "Oka showed that, once the imaginary line of legitimacy was crossed, the government was able to reverse the terms of discourse and itself invoke the symbols of law and order, justice and fairness."[150] The CF's carefully measured escalation of pressure and projection of power, under intensive media and political scrutiny, remained consistent with perceived Canadian values during the crisis.

Hindsight can distort public memory, and advocacy literature (sometimes disguised as objective research)[151] and documentaries have romanticized the Mohawk Warriors and demonized the Canadian Forces. Reflective of the typical storyline that casts all Native-government relations in a tragic "David versus Goliath" emplotment, most narratives characterize the CF as aggressors to support their depiction of a coercive Canadian state. The CF's operational successes at Oka, however, need not be overlooked or downplayed because of intrinsic problems in the broader structures of Aboriginal-government relations. Strong and effective leadership allowed the army to defuse a dangerous situation. When the last of the Mohawk Warriors and their supporters gave themselves up in late September 1990, and the standoff ended without further bloodshed, the underlying issues remained unresolved. From the military's standpoint, however, it had ensured that these issues would be negotiated in the political realm, not fought out at the barricades.

The Oka Crisis did not resolve the underlying conflict between the Mohawks and the Canadian state about sovereignty, but it did provoke official promises that Ottawa would re-examine its relationships with Aboriginal people. The governments in Ottawa and Quebec continue to reject the Mohawks' position that they are a sovereign nation, and after Oka the Quebec government became even more resolute in resisting Mohawk self-government.[152] Nonetheless, Oka was the catalyst for constitutional change and greater self-government. "I look at Oka as a victory, a victory for native rights," Kenneth Deer, editor of the Mohawk newspaper the *Eastern Door*, reminisces. "In the end, the governments had to listen to us." He mentions Native gains such as the unprecedented powers provided in the Nisga'a Treaty and creation of the northern territory of Nunavut. Without Oka, he insists, these advances would never have been made.[153]

On 25 September 1990 Prime Minister Mulroney announced a new agenda for dealing with Native issues in Canada. The federal government was prepared to deal with broad issues facing Native people across Canada, from accelerating land claims resolution processes to improving economic and social conditions on reserves, bettering Aboriginal-government relations, and addressing "the concerns of Canada's aboriginal peoples in contemporary Canadian life." Mulroney commented that "Canada's aboriginal peoples deserve a special place in this country as our first citizens, based on the aboriginal and treaty rights recognized in the constitution." The Mohawks' demands for national independence struck at the heart of Canada, and the Warriors were subject to the Criminal Code like every other Canadian, but the government could entrench self-government within the Constitution to include community development, social and education systems, and economic controls.[154] These themes factored into Native participation in the constitutional talks that produced the ill-fated Charlottetown Accord. Concerns about the land claims process led to the creation of the Indian Specific Claims Commission in 1991. That same year, the federal government established the Royal Commission on Aboriginal Peoples to investigate the evolution of the relationship between Aboriginal peoples, the Government of Canada, and Canadian society. By the time it produced its massive final report five years later, it had proved to be the largest and most expensive royal commission in Canadian history. Its "two-row wampum" approach to self-government – viewing Native and non-Native peoples as coexisting parallel sovereignties – echoed the Assembly of First Nations and many First Nations leaders, but the national debate over Aboriginal rights, land claims, self-government, and sovereignty provoked by the Oka Crisis remains.[155]

Despite the mixed legacy of the crisis for the Mohawk communities of Kanesatake and Kahnawake, Oka changed the trajectory of Canadian-Aboriginal relations more generally. "What began as a dispute over a small parcel of land escalated into demands for Mohawk sovereignty and self-determination," policy scholars Leslie Pal and Robert Campbell observe. "Although the Mohawk community was internally divided over the Warriors' role, issues of land title and sovereignty were now inextricably linked."[156] A few years after the crisis, Assembly of First Nations national chief Ovide Mercredi summarized,

> During the summer of 1990 we in Canada saw events and scenes that, depending on one's personality or politics, either raised consciousness or triggered the most primary emotions. Whether or not you are for or against the Mohawk Nation, the warriors, the Sûreté du Québec, the Canadian army, the Québec government, the Department of Indian Affairs or its Minister, the federal government, Premier Bourassa or Brian Mulroney, one thing is certain: none of us can escape the impact, the implications or the consequences of the imbalance in the relationship between Canada and the First Nations. We must live with that show of force against Mohawk people.

Oka had led to a clear realization, Mercredi concluded, namely "that ignoring the rights and aspirations of the First Nations in this country will imperil the unity and stability of Canada."[157]

NOTES

Thanks to Jennifer Arthur, Yale Belanger, J.R. Miller, Scott Sheffield, and Timothy Winegard for their comments on drafts of this chapter. An earlier version appeared as "Carrying the Burden of Peace: The Mohawks, the Canadian Forces, and the Oka Crisis," *Journal of Military and Strategic Studies* 10, no. 2 (Winter 2008): 1–71.

1 J.R. Miller, *Skyscrapers Hide the Heavens: A History of Indian-White Relations in Canada*, rev. ed. (Toronto: University of Toronto Press, 1991), 289.
2 The vast literature on Oka in English includes Craig Maclaine, Michael Baxendale, and Robert Galbraith, *This Land Is Our Land: The Mohawk Revolt at Oka* (Montreal: Optimum, 1990); Canada, House of Commons, Standing Committee on Aboriginal Affairs, *The Summer of 1990: Fifth Report of the Standing Committee on Aboriginal Affairs* (Ottawa: Supply and Services Canada, 1991); John Ciaccia, *The Oka Crisis: A Mirror of the Soul* (Dorval, QC: Maren, 2000); Donna Goodleaf, *Entering the War*

*Zone: A Mohawk Perspective on Resisting Invasions* (Penticton, BC: Theytus Books, 1995); Rick Hornung, *One Nation under the Gun: Inside the Mohawk Civil War* (Toronto: Stoddart, 1991); Linda Pertusati, *In Defense of Mohawk Land: Ethnopolitical Conflict in Native North America* (Albany: State University of New York Press, 1997); Geoffrey York and Loreen Pindera, *People of the Pines: The Warriors and the Legacy of Oka* (Toronto: Little, Brown, 1991); Timothy C. Winegard, *Oka: A Convergence of Cultures and the Canadian Forces* (Kingston: Canadian Defence Academy Press, 2008); Kiera Ladner and Leanne Simpson, eds, *This Is an Honour Song: Twenty Years since the Blockades* (Winnipeg: Arbeiter Ring, 2010); and Harry Swain, *Oka: A Political Crisis and Its Legacy* (Vancouver: Douglas and McIntyre, 2010).

Books on Oka in French include Gilles Boileau, *Silience des messieurs: Oka, terre indienne* (Montreal: Méridien, 1991); John Ciaccia, *Crise d'Oka: Miroir de notre ame* (Montreal: Leméac, 2000); Francois Dallaire, *Oka: La hache de guerre* (Ste-Foy, QC: Éditions de la Liberté, 1991); Jacques-A. Lamarche, *L'été des Mohawks: Bilan des 78 jours* (Montreal: Stanké, 1990); Robin Philpot, *Oka: Dérnier alibi du Canada anglais* (Montreal: VLB, 1991); and Hélène Sévigny, *Lasagne: L'homme derrière le masque* (Saint-Lambert, QC: Éditions Sedes, 1993).

Documentary films on Oka include *Acts of defiance* (Montreal: National Film Board of Canada, 1992); *Kanehsatake: 270 ans de résistance / Kanehsatake: 270 Years of Resistance* (Montreal: National Film Board of Canada, 1993); *Spudwrench: Kahnawake Man* (Montreal: National Film Board of Canada, c. 1997); and *My Name Is Kahentiiosta* (Montreal: National Film Board of Canada, 1995).

3 Kiera Ladner and Leanne Simpson, "This Is an Honour Song," in *This Is an Honour Song*, ed. Simpson and Ladner, 1–9 at 1.

4 Robert Campbell and Leslie Pal, "Feather and Gun: Confrontation at Oka/ Kanesatake," in *Real Worlds of Canadian Politics: Cases in Process and Policy*, ed. Robert Campbell and Leslie Pal, 267–333 (Toronto: Broadview, 1991), 329.

5 J.D. Harries, "Peacekeeping Futures," *Canadian Defence Quarterly*, October 1991, 25–31 at 27.

6 When it was over, journalists, documentary filmmakers, poets, and Aboriginal spokespersons seemed to ignore the reserve displayed by the CF and remembered the confrontation as a quintessential example of perpetual governmental injustice. See, for example, Alanis Obomsawin, *Kanesatake: 270 years of Resistance* (Ottawa: National Film Board of Canada, 1993); and Goodleaf, *Entering the Warzone.*

7  J.R. Miller, "Great White Father Knows Best: Oka and the Land Claims Process," *Native Studies Review* 7, no. 1 (1991): 23–51 at 24–5.

8  The Mohawk community of Kanesatake is located on the north shore of Lake of Two Mountains, where it meets the Ottawa River, 53 kilometres west of Montreal. The lands set aside for the Mohawks do not constitute a reserve and are interwoven with lands belonging to non-Aboriginal people of the village and parish of Oka. The surface area of Kanesatake is 958.05 hectares. The community also includes the Doncaster Reserve, an uninhabited territory of 7,896.2 hectares located 14 kilometres north of Sainte-Agathe-des-Monts, northwest of Lac-des-Îles, which is shared with the Mohawks of Kahnawake. Indian and Northern Affairs Canada, "Fact Sheet: Kanesatake," 2000.

9  Winegard, *Oka*, 69.

10  See Jane Dickson-Gilmore, "Always about the Land: The Oka Crisis of 1990," in *Canada: Confederation to Present*, ed. Bob Hesketh and Chris Hackett, CD-ROM (Edmonton: Chinook Multimedia, 2001); and Miller, "Great White Father."

11  Dickson-Gilmore, "Always about the Land," 5–6.

12  Miller, "Great White Father," 27, 30.

13  Dickson-Gilmore, "Always about the Land," 7; Miller, "Great White Father," 32; Serge Laurin, "Les 'troubles d'oka' ou l'histoire d'une résistance (1760–1945)," *Recherches amérindiennes au Québec* 21, nos 1–2 (1991): 87–92; Winegard, *Oka*, 34–6.

14  In 1933, for example, the Sulpicians transferred over one hundred lots to repay a debt of $1,025,000 to the Province of Quebec. This land was later sold to the Municipality of Oka for one dollar. The province also sold land to a Belgian company that refused to negotiate amiably with the resident Aboriginal population. Dickson-Gilmore, "Always about the Land," 7; Miller, "Great White Father," 36.

15  Miller, "Great White Father," 36; Winegard, *Oka*, 44.

16  Gerald F. Reid, *Kahnawà:ke: Factionalism, Traditionalism, and Nationalism in a Mohawk Community* (Lincoln: University of Nebraska Press, 2004).

17  In the Calder case of 1973, the Supreme Court of Canada split in recognizing the Aboriginal land title of the Nisga'a in northwestern British Columbia, and in the same year, the Yukon Indian Brotherhood presented a formal claim to the federal government, Justice William Morrow of the Northwest Territories recognized the Aboriginal title of the Dene of the Mackenzie River Valley, and Justice Albert Malouf of Quebec recognized the title of the Cree and Inuit of Quebec. Although these

decisions were later overturned, they gave important weight to the Aboriginal rights lobby.

18  Comprehensive land claims agreements are based on the concept of continuing Aboriginal rights and title that have not been dealt with by treaty or any other legal means and thus can be seen as the modern "treaty-making process." The negotiations and settlements deal with land ownership, management of lands and underground resources, harvest of and management rights for wildlife, fish, and forests, economic development, access rights, and financial compensations.

19  Indian and Northern Affairs Canada, "Backgrounder: Oka Land Claim," July 1990.

20  Dickson-Gilmore, "Always about the Land."

21  Pertusati, *In Defense of Mohawk Land.*

22  Gerald R. (Taiaiake) Alfred, *Heeding the Voice of Our Ancestors: Kahnawake Mohawk Politics and the Rise of Native Nationalism* (Toronto: Oxford University Press, 1995), 187–9; Reid, *Kahnawà:ke,* 186.

23  Taiaiake Alfred and Lana Lowe, "Warrior Societies in Contemporary Indigenous Communities," paper prepared for the Ipperwash Inquiry, May 2005, http://www.attorneygeneral.jus.gov.on.ca/inquiries/ipperwash/policy_part/research/index.html, 13, 36.

24  For a laudatory introduction to the Mohawk Warriors, which describes them as ethically grounded actors, see Alfred and Lowe, "Warrior Societies." For a critical introduction, see John C. Thompson, "The Long Fall of the Mohawk Warriors," paper for the Mackenzie Institute for the Study of Terrorism, Revolution and Propaganda, Toronto, 2006, http://www.numberswatchdog.com/THE%20LONG%20FALL%20OF%20THE%20MOHAW%20WARRIORS.htm.

25  York and Pindera, *People of the Pines,* 174; Winegard, *Oka,* 47–51. Louis Hall (Karoniaktajeh) was a major inspiration to the warrior societies of the 1970s, designing the Warrior flag and writing the *Warrior's Handbook.* See Warrior Publications, "Indigenous Resistance, from the 1960s to 2006," n.d., http://wiinimkiikaa.wordpress.com/indigenous-resistance-from-the-1960s-to-2006. The (in)famous efforts by the American Indian Movement to back a Sioux independence movement at Wounded Knee, South Dakota, in 1973 served as a tactical model for militant groups after 1974.

26  John Bacher, "Roots of the Mohawk Crisis," *Peace Magazine,* October–November 1990, 7, 29, at 7.

27 Hornung, *One Nation*. Opponents of gambling saw it as a corruption of Native culture, whereas supporters saw it as a tool for economic progress. For the c f's role in these developments, see Tony Keene, "Guns among the Mohawks," *Sentinel* 24, no. 4 (1988): 2–4.

28 Winegard, *Oka*, 55. Sean Maloney coined the term "narco-parastate" in "Domestic Operations: The Canadian Approach," *Parameters* 27, no. 3 (Autumn 1997): 135–52 at 135.

29 John Borrows, "Crown and Aboriginal Occupations of Land: A History and Comparison," paper prepared for the Ipperwash Inquiry, 15 October 2005, 71, http://www.attorneygeneral.jus.gov.on.ca/inquiries/ipperwash/policy_part/research/index.html.

30 Maloney, "Domestic Operations"; Hornung, *One Nation*, 15–20; Canada, House of Commons, *Minutes of the Proceedings and Evidence of the Standing Committee on Aboriginal Affairs*, 19 March 1991, 55:92. For a critical look at the Warriors and Mohawk community relations, see Thompson, "Long Fall." See also Timothy C. Winegard, "The Forgotten Front of the Oka Crisis: Operation Feather/Akwesasne," *Journal of Military and Strategic Studies* 11, nos 1–2 (2009): 1–50.

31 Keene, "Guns among the Mohawks."

32 Loreen Pindera, "The Making of a Warrior," *Saturday Night*, April 1991, 30–9 at 34.

33 "Crisis Inspired Many Native People," *First Nations Drum*, 26 December 2000, http://www.firstnationsdrum.com/2000/12/crisis-inspired-many-native-people.

34 Alfred and Lowe, "Warrior Societies," 44.

35 Ann Charney, "The Last Indian War: A War of Independence Built on Cut-Rate Cigarettes," *Idler Magazine*, no. 29 (1990): 14–22 at 16.

36 On this decision, see Winegard, *Oka*, 97.

37 Campbell and Pal, "Feather and Gun," 276. Ironically, acting Kanesatake band chief Clarence Simon had called in the s q in April to forcibly remove supporters of dehorned Chief George Martin, who had occupied the band council office. See Hornung, *One Nation*, 182.

38 On this decision, see Winegard, *Oka*, 97.

39 Francis Boots, in Pindera, "Making of a Warrior," 36.

40 This section, including the Gabriel quotation, is dervied from Winegard, *Oka*, 102–3. Thanks to Dr Timothy Winegard for his help in clarifying these issues. See also York and Pindera, *People of the Pines*, 65–74; Guy Gilbert, *Rapport d'enquête du coroner Guy Gilbert sur les causes et circonstances du deces de Monsieur Marcel Lemay*, report for the

Coroner's Bureau, Government of Quebec, Quebec City, 1995, 155–7; and Ciaccia, *Oka Crisis*, 45.

41  Campbell and Pal, "Feather and Gun," 276–7. See also Winegard, *Oka*, 107–11; and Gilbert, *Rapport d'enquête du coroner*. The Mohawk Warriors claimed publicly that the police fired first and that Lemay had been a victim of fratricide (killed by a police bullet). Five years after the standoff, a coroner's report concluded that the shot was fired by a Mohawk warrior, but the report did not identify the killer and no one was charged with Lemay's murder. Gilbert, *Rapport d'enquête du coroner*.

42  Peter Williamson, "So I Can Hold My Head High: History and Representations of the Oka Crisis" (MA thesis, Carleton University, 1997), 93.

43  In Winegard, *Oka*, 110–11.

44  Ibid., 109–10.

45  Douglas M. George-Kanentiio, *Iroquois on Fire: A Voice from the Mohawk Nation* (Lincoln: University of Nebraska Press, 2006), 122–3.

46  Campbell and Pal, "Feather and Gun," 280, passim; Ciaccia, *Oka Crisis*, 80–97; André Picard and Patricia Poirier, "Peaceful End to Oka Standoff Possible," *Globe and Mail*, 16 July 1990, A1.

47  André Picard, "Chiefs to Hold Summit on Kanhawake Reserve," *Globe and Mail*, 18 July 1990, A1; Geoffrey York, "Natives Denounce Ottawa for Failing to Defuse Oka," *Globe and Mail*, 18 July 1990, A4.

48  "RCMP Repel Angry Châteauguay Mob," *Globe and Mail*, 19 July 1990, A1; Ciaccia, *Oka Crisis*, 84–5.

49  Tom Siddon and Ellen Gabriel, both in Ciaccia, *Oka Crisis*, 127. The federal government would buy the disputed land near the golf course, help to provide additional land for the Kanesatake Mohawks, and help to improve social and economic conditions in the community. Ciaccia had also wanted Ottawa to suspend its normal land claims process, but Siddon was non-committal. Campbell and Pal, "Feather and Gun," 281. The Mohawks eventually included the negotiation of land claims at Akwesasne in their list of demands.

50  Harry Swain, in York and Pindera, *People of the Pines*, 219; Hornung, *One Nation*, 222. Harry Swain's *Oka: A Political Crisis and Its Legacy* appeared in 2010, after this chapter was written, and provides insight into his views on the crisis.

51  Campbell and Pal, "Feather and Gun," 283.

52  Ibid., 284. On sympathy blockades, see Winegard, *Oka*, 149–50. On 12 August, Siddon, Ciaccia, and representatives from five Mohawk communities signed an agreement permitting the Mohawks access to

"necessities" and "legal advisors," as well as authorizing twenty-four
representatives of the Paris-based International Federation of Human
Rights to monitor the standoff. Ottawa was concerned with the last provision and wanted observers from the Quebec and Canadian Human Rights
Commissions to reaffirm that it was a domestic affair. "The reliance on
international observers to the exclusion of domestic ones was an important
symbolic victory for the Mohawks" because "it implied that they were
a nation equal in status to Canada." Campbell and Pal, "Feather and
Gun," 286.

53  Mobile Command, "Eastern Region after Action Report: Operation Salon"
("ERAAR"), January 1991, 3, sections released under the Access to
Information Act (AIA).

54  J.A. Roy, "Opération Salon," *Revue canadienne de défense* 20, no. 5
(1991): 15–19 at 16. See also Campbell and Pal, "Feather and Gun," 285.

55  Kent Foster, in Gerald Baril, "Mission Accomplished," *Sentinel* 26, no. 6
(1990) 2–8 at 4.

56  Mobile Command, "ERAAR," 4. This major internal security operation
was officially described as "a brigade sized force in a confrontation with a
well-armed dissident group whose potential military capabilities exceeded
the capacity of civilian law enforcement agencies." Mobile Command,
"ERAAR," 1.

57  Queen's Regulations and Orders (1968), ch. 23, s. 5, art. 23.15, note D,
quoted in Claude Beauregard, "The Military Intervention in Oka: Strategy,
Communication and Press Coverage," trans. Graham Timms, *Canadian
Military History* 2, no. 1 (Spring 1993): 23–47 at 27.

58  Winegard, *Oka*, 128.

59  Mobile Command, "ERAAR," 5.

60  Campbell and Pal, "Feather and Gun," 329. Accordingly, it is not
surprising that misunderstandings and ambiguity plagued civil-military
liaison, particularly given that Operation Salon was the first major IS
operation conducted in several decades. Mobile Command's "Eastern
Region after Action Report," 8, noted that the "lack of military knowledge
in the general population, the absence of recent IS operations, and the tendency for police forces to broaden their capabilities and self-sufficiency,
and a decline in military-police liaison and training have resulted in poor
mutual understanding between the military and civil authorities." Without
a solid understanding of military capabilities and procedures, politicians
and government officials were ill-prepared to provide feasible guidance.
"As a result, great care and considerable time and discussion were required
to arrive at an appropriate, mutually agreed and fully understood

allocation of tasks to military and civilian agencies. The Judge Advocate General noted in his after action report that the CF should 'consider "educating" all provincial authorities on our roles, responsibilities and their responsibilities.'" Excerpts from this section of the "ERAAR" were removed under the AIA, so the assessment of limited political and government understanding of military practices is speculative but seems grounded in available evidence. See, for example, Kent Foster, in Baril, "Mission Accomplished," 6. On the Judge Advocate General, see Deputy Chief of the Defence Staff (DCDS), Annex A: Lessons Learned, 22 March 1991, Department of National Defence file 1000-1 (DCDS), acquired under the AIA.

61  Kent Foster, in Baril, "Mission Accomplished," 6.
62  Douglas Bland, *Chiefs of Defence: Government and the Unified Command of the Canadian Armed Forces* (Toronto: Canadian Institute of Strategic Studies, 1995), 198–9.
63  Ibid., 199–200.
64  Mike Myers, testimony in Canada, House of Commons, *Minutes of the Proceedings and Evidence of the Standing Committee on Aboriginal Affairs*, 12 March 1991, 53:39.
65  Bland, *Chiefs of Defence*, 199–200.
66  On the CF weapons, see Réginald Gagnon, *Fait d'Armes à Oka* (Ottawa: Arion, 1994), 53.
67  Debrief 002 – SIU Informant, 12 September 1990; and SIU/Source Meeting, PM 21 September 1990, to Coys, both released under the AIA. Original CF estimates placed Warrior and supporter strengths between 150 and 250 at Kanesatake, with another 300 to 500 at Kahnawake. At least 20 had seen combat action in Vietnam, and another 6 were ex-members of the CF. In addition, there were between 10 and 20 Mohawks who had more recently received military training with American forces, most significantly the United States Marines, and many Warriors with no professional experience had been pseudo-trained in basic military skills at Ganienkeh. The Mohawks relied on those with military background to design the extensive defensive fortifications and positions in both territories. According to Geoffrey York and Loreen Pindera, active Mohawk members of American military forces took their annual leave to return to Kahnawake and help man the barricades, as did 12 Mohawks who quit their CF Reserve training in Longue-Pointe to return home. Furthermore, 100 Oneida Warriors arrived in Kahnawake in the middle of July after a "request for assistance" was sent to Oneidas in Ontario, New York, and Wisconsin by the Kahnawake Longhouse. Winegard, *Oka*, 131, based

upon CF intelligence reports, 15–26 August 1990; York and Pindera,
*People of* the Pines, 241.

68 Réginald Gagnon, in Roy, "Opération Salon," 16; Campbell and Pal,
   "Feather and Gun," 280; Gagnon, *Fait d'Armes*, 64, 66. On communica-
   tions, see Sgt D.D. Campbell, Senior Night Analyst, 1 Cdn Int Coy,
   "Mohawk Alert System for Kahnawake in the Event of Military Searches/
   Movements," n.d., released under the AIA. On the Warriors' arsenal, see
   Winegard, *Oka*, 138–9, passim.

69 There was also sympathy for the Mohawks in Montreal. On 15 July 1990
   the *Montreal Gazette* released the results of a CROP–*La Presse* poll of
   446 Montreal adults, of whom 53 per cent supported the Mohawk claim
   to the disputed land, only 18 per cent supported the municipality's claim,
   and the rest were ambivalent. The poll indicated that 69 per cent supported Native peoples' pressure tactics to back their land claims and that
   19 per cent did not. "Most Disapprove of Police Tactics: Poll," *Montreal
   Gazette*, 15 July 1990, A1.

70 This group eventually left because it was frustrated with the tight security
   that inhibited its work.

71 On these themes, see C. Radha Jhappan, "Indian Symbolic Politics: The
   Double-Edged Sword of Publicity," *Canadian Ethnic Studies* 22, no. 3
   (1990): 19–39; J. Rick Ponting, "Internationalization: Perspectives on an
   Emerging Direction in Aboriginal Affairs," *Canadian Ethnic Studies* 22,
   no. 3 (1990): 85–109; Winegard, *Oka*, 152–4; and P. Whitney
   Lackenbauer and Andrew F. Cooper, "The Achilles Heel of Canadian Good
   International Citizenship: Indigenous Diplomacies and State Responses in
   the Twentieth Century," *Canadian Foreign Policy Journal* 13, no. 3 (2007):
   99–119.

72 Operation Salon involved a considerable military force, at one point
   reaching 3,300 officers and men, twenty helicopters, two fighter planes,
   three high-tech Leopard tanks, and numerous artillery and specialized
   elements. MacLaine, Baxendale, and Galbraith, *This Land Is Our Land*,
   52–3. At the brigade level, a coordination cell (consisting of the army, the
   SQ, the RCMP, and the local police) reported to the commander of the
   Mobile Force, who chaired a larger coordination cell that included representatives from the Communications Security Establishment and the
   Canadian Security Intelligence Service. The chief of the Defence Staff participated in federal Cabinet meetings, and the commander of the Mobile
   Force sat in on provincial Cabinet meetings related to the crisis. Arrière-
   garde 12e RBC, Opération Salon, Rapport intérimaire post-opération,
   5 octobre 1990, released under the AIA.

73  Alain Tremblay, in Baril, "Mission Accomplished," 4.

74  Robin Gagnon, in ibid., 5. One informant explained in mid-September that "moderate" residents continued to listen to the band council (which did not support the Warriors), whereas those involved in the sale of cigarettes and the running of bingos listened to the "Nation Office" (the administrative arm of the Longhouse). Indeed, he had reported earlier that the Nation Office, Tribal Council, and Warrior Society seemed to have "merged into a single entity" that made decisions on the basis of consensus and then passed them on to the barricades through the tactical command post situated at the Legion Hall. Debrief 002 – SIU Informant, 12 September 1990; and SIU/Source Meeting, PM 21 September 1990, to Coys, both released under the AIA.

75  Gagnon, Fait d'Armes, 66.

76  According to Winegard, Oka, 128–9, insufficient rules of engagement hindered military operations by prolonging the crisis, preventing the soldiers from defending themselves when physically abused by the Warriors, and necessitating backward tactics.

77  "The Mohawks eventually reduced their team to five, with a large number of observers." Campbell and Pal, "Feather and Gun," 297. On the different tactical situations at Kanesatake and Kahnawake (Chateauguay), see Alain Tremblay, quoted in Winegard, Oka, 183.

78  Pierre Daigle, in André Picard, "Soldiers Advance, Halt Talks at Oka," Globe and Mail, 24 August 1990, A6.

79  Alain Tremblay and Patrick Cloutier, both in Baril, "Mission Accomplished," 7. In an interview with Winegard, Oka, 161, Tremblay recalled that Robert "Mad Jap" Skidder "was basically commanding their troops [on 1 September], he was the one calling the shots. There were a lot of youngsters in the armed Mohawks at Oka and it was very difficult for them to maintain control. By using some of the elder women which were very well placed, and they are key from the Mohawk point of view, they always managed to diffuse the situation before it reached the point of no return."

80  "Crisis Inspired Many Native People." On the racial hatred, see also Winegard, Oka, 175–6.

81  Judge Finn Lynghjem, in York and Pindera, People of the Pines, 321.

82  Winegard, Oka, 126.

83  André Picard, "Mohawks Demand Amnesty for Bingo," Globe and Mail, 22 August 1990, A1. The communities were Kanesatake, Kahnawake, Akwesasne, Ohsweken, Tyendinaga, and Ganienkeh.

84 Rhéal Séguin and André Picard, "Mohawks Tricked Quebec, Minister Says," *Globe and Mail*, 23 August 1990, A1.

85 Campbell and Pal, "Feather and Gun," 298.

86 Ibid., 300.

87 Winegard, *Oka*, 142.

88 Tom Siddon, in R. Howard and Patricia Poirier, "Army Sent to Remove Mohawk Barricades," *Globe and Mail*, 28 August 1990, A1.

89 Goodleaf, *Entering the War Zone*, 91–3.

90 Gagnon, *l'uit d'Armes*, 68.

91 On these developments, see Winegard, *Oka*, 167–73.

92 George-Kanentiio, *Iroquois on Fire*, 124–5. George-Kanentiio also mentions substance abuse problems that plagued the Warriors. "At Akwesasne the warriors were free and open in their use of drugs and alcohol, habits they brought to Kanehsatake, yet never curtailed," he notes. "Those more extreme in their abuse were told to leave, but to remove all mind-altering substances would have decimated the warriors almost to a man."

93 See, for example, York and Pindera, *People of the Pines*, 317–18, 340; and MacLaine, Baxendale, and Galbraith, *This Land Is Our Land*, 67, 70.

94 Goodleaf, *Entering the War Zone*, 70–1.

95 Bob Antone, in ibid.

96 Maloney, "Domestic Operations," 147.

97 This verbal abuse was captured by journalists and certainly did not generate Mohawk support among francophone Quebecois. See, for example, Martin J. Morris, "Overcoming the Barricades: The Crisis at Oka as a Case Study in Political Communication," *Journal of Canadian Studies* 30, no. 2 (Summer 1995): 74–90 at 81.

98 Mobile Command, "ERAAR," 13.

99 Rhéal Séguin, Geoffrey York, and André Picard, "Quebec Rejects Mohawk Peace Plan," *Globe and Mail*, 12 September 1990, A1.

100 Greg Mitchell, in Baril, "Mission Accomplished," 7–8. On previous notification, see Kent Foster, "Army Details New Measures to Be Taken to Resolve the Crisis," press statement, 20 September 1990, annex E to CDS War Diary, 17–23 September 1990, released under the AIA.

101 André Picard, "Shots Fired during Raid on Reserve," *Globe and Mail*, 19 September 1990, A1.

102 Campbell and Pal, "Feather and Gun," 302. See also Geoffrey York and André Picard, "Warrior Surrender Sole Topic for Army," *Globe and Mail*, 20 September 1990, A1.

103  "The Army Closes In," Kanesatake.com, Our Heritage, Summer of 1990, n.d., copy on file with P. Whitney Lackenbauer. "The last resisting Mohawks had no independent way of communicating with the outside world," Morris notes in "Overcoming the Barricades," 84, "yet even then, they could still receive media communications via television and conventional radio." In fact, the Warriors managed to find a place where cellular phones were not affected by the blackout and called it the "Phone booth," thus managing to contact outside advisers prior to surrendering.

104  "The Final Days," Kanesatake.com, Our Heritage, Summer of 1990, n.d., copy on file with P. Whitney Lackenbauer.

105  York and Pindera, *People of the Pines*, 341–2.

106  George-Kanentiio, *Iroquois on Fire*, 125.

107  They referred to their abandonment of an armed confrontation as a "unilateral cessation of hostilities," not a surrender, but the reality was unambiguous to military officials. Ibid.

108  Pierre Daigle, in Baril, "Mission Accomplished," 8.

109  Jack Todd, "A Last Nightmare: Army Allowed Surrender to Denigrate into Chaos," *Montreal Gazette*, 27 September 1990.

110  Mobile Command, "ERAAR," 4.

111  Christopher Cushing, in André Picard, "Army-Mohawk Strife a Public Relations War," *Globe and Mail*, 22 September 1990.

112  See, for example, Morris, "Overcoming the Barricades"; Warren H. Skea, "The Canadian Newspaper Industry's Portrayal of the Oka Crisis," *Native Studies Review* 9, no. 1 (1993–94): 15–31; Williamson, "So I Can Hold My Head High"; Marc Grenier, "Native Indians in the English-Canadian Press: The Case of the 'Oka Crisis,'" *Media, Culture and Society* 16, no. 2 (1994): 313–36; and Roger Larose, "La crise d'Oka à la télévision: L'éloge du barbare" (PhD diss., Concordia University, 2000).

113  John de Chastelain, "A Personal Perspective on Command," in *Warrior Chiefs: Perspectives on Senior Canadian Military Leaders*, ed. Bernd Horn and Stephen Harris, 347–60 (Toronto: Dundurn, 2001), 355–6.

114  Beauregard, "Military Intervention," 33; Morris, "Overcoming the Barricades."

115  Beauregard, "Military Intervention," 31–3, provides a detailed overview of the development of the communication strategy at Mobile Force headquarters in St Hubert.

116  Roy, "Opération Salon," 18.

117  This "proved to be a key factor. Spokespersons were designated, media lines were prepared, media scrums were organized and a spokesperson

was available to respond to media queries, regardless of whether the news
was good or bad. The military side was reported and the respect for, and
confidence in the military continued because of this." Op Salon, POR
Comment, *Dispatches*, September 1990, cited in Department of National
Defence, "Civil-Military Cooperation in Peace, Emergencies, Crisis and
War," B-GG-005-004/AF-023, in *Lessons Learned Information
Warehouse*, CD-ROM, version 9.0 (Kingston: Army Lessons Learned
Centre, April 1999).

118 S.J. Kelly, "Public Affairs: The Eleventh Principle of War," Exercise New
Horizons paper for the Canadian Forces Command and Staff College,
Toronto, 1994.

119 "Secret, Communications Lessons from Oka," n.d., annex A to CDS War
Diary, 5–11 November 1990, acquired under the AIA.

120 Morris, "Overcoming the Barricades," 84.

121 Norman Webster, untitled editorials, *Montreal Gazette*, 15 July 1990,
28 July 1990.

122 Morris, "Overcoming the Barricades," 80. See also Williamson, "So I Can
Hold My Head High."

123 Alfred and Lowe, "Warrior Societies," 31. On 25 July 1990 the *Montreal
Gazette* quoted Jean Parizeau calling the Warriors "terrorists who should
not be tolerated." The following day, it quoted the Kahnawake band chief
stating that "Parizeau should recall how the terrorist FLQ sparked the
separatist movement he now leads." In Elizabeth Thompson, "Police
Should Have Attacked Mercier Barricades," *Montreal Gazette*, 25 July
1990; and in Elizabeth Thompson, "1000 Show Support for Mohawks
outside Bourassa's Office," 26 July 1990.

124 On the law and order theme as hegemonic discourse, see Charles Stuart,
"The Mohawk Crisis: A Crisis of Hegemony" (MA thesis, University of
Ottawa, 1993), 37–40.

125 Amelia Kalant, *National Identity and the Conflict at Oka: Native
Belonging and Myths of Postcolonial Nationhood in Canada* (New York:
Routledge, 2004), 123.

126 Ponting, "Internationalization," 100.

127 "Media," Kanesatake.com, Our Heritage, Summer of 1990, n.d., copy on
file with P. Whitney Lackenbauer. See, for example, J. Heinrich, "News
Media Leave Warrior Territory in Protest," *Montreal Gazette*, 2 August
1990.

128 De Chastelain to Paul Tellier et al., "Update on Operation SALON
Activity, Thursday 20 Sep 90," annex E to CDS War Diary, 17–
23 September 1990, released under the AIA.

129 "Secret, Communications Lessons from Oka," n.d., annex A to CDS War Diary, 5–11 November 1990, released under the AIA.

130 Ibid.

131 Morris, "Overcoming the Barricades," 83; Peter Desbarats, in Rudy Platiel, "Oka Battle Fought in Living Rooms," *Globe and Mail*, 15 September 1990, A3.

132 See Winegard, *Oka*, 154.

133 Jean Francoeur, "Avec les honneurs de la paix," *Le Devoir*, 9 October 1990, 14, translated and cited in Beauregard, "Military Intervention," 41. Contrast this perspective with Canadian Association of Journalists, "The Truth Was Left to Suffer on Its Own: Covering the Mohawk-Government Crisis," brief to the Parliamentary Committee on Aboriginal Affairs, 21 February 1991.

134 Patricia Monture, "The Human Right to Celebrate: Achieving Justice for Aboriginal Peoples," in *This Is an Honour Song*, ed. Simpson and Ladner, 289–98 at 291.

135 Morris, "Overcoming the Barricades," 86, emphasis in original.

136 Ellen Gabriel, "Epilogue: Fradulent Theft of Mohawk Land by the Municipality of Oka," in *This Is an Honour Song*, ed. Simpson and Ladner, 345–7 at 345.

137 Graham Fraser, "PM Unveils Indian Agenda," *Globe and Mail*, 26 September 1990, A1-2.

138 Borrows, "Crown and Aboriginal Occupations," 37; Gabriel, "Epilogue," 345.

139 Peter H. Russell, "Oka to Ipperwash: The Necessity of Flashpoint Events," in *This Is an Honour Song*, ed. Simpson and Ladner, 29–46 at 39–40.

140 George-Kanentiio, *Iroquois on Fire*, 121, 125–6.

141 Ibid.

142 Ibid., 122.

143 Ibid., 123.

144 Alfred and Lowe, "Warrior Societies," 21-2.

145 Wab Kinew, "Cowboys and Indians," in *This Is an Honour Song*, ed. Simpson and Ladner, 47–52 at 47, 50.

146 Mobile Command, "ERAAR," 23.

147 J.A. Roy, in Baril, "Mission Accomplished," 8.

148 Greg Mitchell, in ibid.

149 Claude Beauregard, "The Army and Public Affairs from 1990 to 1998," *Army Doctrine and Training Bulletin* 2, no. 1 (February 1999): 56–62. See also Steve Flemming, *Public Opinion Toward Defence and the*

*Canadian Forces, 1978–1994: An Overview of Post–Cold War Trends* (Ottawa: Directorate of Social and Economic Analysis, Department of National Defence, 14 September 1994).

150  Jhappan, "Indian Symbolic Politics," 35.

151  My own work has been criticized for demonstrating a neoliberal bias that is "favourable to the maintenance of the status quo with regard to indigenous people's claims to varying degrees of independence from Canadian law." See Alexa Conradi, "Uprising at Oka: A Place of Non-identification," *Journal of Communication Studies* 34, no. 4 (2009): 547–66 at 548.

152  Russell, "Oka to Ipperwash," 38–9, notes that Cabinet minister John Ciaccia, who had the most sympathy of any government official for the Mohawk position, was "completely sidelined" in the latter stages of the Oka Crisis.

153  "Crisis Inspired Many Native People." This is an excessive (but revealing) claim considering Nunavut's creation was on the cusp of being formally negotiated.

154  Brian Mulroney, in Fraser, "PM unveils Indian Agenda."

155  See J.R. Miller, *Lethal Legacies: Current Native Controversies in Canada* (Toronto: McClelland and Stewart, 2004), 277–83.

156  Campbell and Pal, "Feather and Gun," 302.

157  Ovide Mercredi and Mary Ellen Turpel, *In the Rapids: Navigating the Future of First Nations* (Toronto: Viking, 1993), 49.

## 6

# The Oldman River Dam and the Lonefighters' Response to Environmental Incursion

YALE D. BELANGER

Overshadowed by the more sensational events that occurred at Oka in 1990, a small group modelling themselves after a traditional clan known as the Lone Fighters worked at diverting the Oldman River traversing the Peigan Reserve of the Piikani Nation of southern Alberta late that summer.[1] Incensed at the provincial government's refusal to halt dam reservoir construction occurring on what they considered sacred, albeit surrendered, Piikani lands located 13 kilometres north of the reserve, the new Lonefighters rented an earth mover to divert the river's course around an irrigation inflow located on the reserve that served several downstream communities. On 7 September, as the Lonefighters prepared to expand the diversion project in direct violation of a recently approved court order, the Royal Canadian Mounted Police (RCMP), escorting provincial employees assigned to repair the damaged riverbed, entered the reserve. A confrontation ensued, punctuated by the Lonefighters' spokesperson, Milton Born With A Tooth, firing two "warning" shots into the air. No one was hurt and the RCMP soon withdrew from the reserve as calmer heads prevailed. The tense situation then slowly petered out over the next two weeks, even though provincial officials outwardly appeared to succeed: dam construction was quickly completed, and Born With A Tooth was arrested and later convicted of his crimes. Despite the month-long standoff and the potential for violence, it appeared that the blockade did not harm the chief and band council's reputation or their relationships with either the premier's office or local officials from nearby communities, all of whom quickly put the summer's events behind them.

At the heart of the dispute was the province's desire to ensure that thousands of southern Alberta farmers and ranchers had water for irrigation. This policy orientation conflicted with Piikani desires to manage the river according to traditional values, as well as conservationist demands for an environmental impact assessment. The conflict involved farmers and ranchers, provincial and federal politicians, First Nations political leaders, and environmental activists, each citing the river's central importance to their chosen strategies. The Piikani, for instance, considered the Oldman River running through traditional lands their cultural lifeblood, which, if properly managed, could house a dam and reservoir that would improve their political and economic capital. Provincial officials held fast to the belief in the river's importance to ensuring regional economic progress and future prosperity. Environmentalists portrayed the Oldman River as the region's ecological lifeblood. The stakes of the impending struggle were noteworthy to all parties involved, even if there was far more to the story than the print or electronic media presented. Few commentators realized at the time that provincial concerns over regional irrigation problems, and hopes for dam construction, dated to 1958 or that the burgeoning and seemingly ubiquitous environmental alliances were little more than loose coalitions guided primarily by one driven individual. What did not escape the media's gaze was the Piikani's social and political intricacy and how various community members guided what at times appeared to be a disjointed response to environmental incursion.

Notably, provincial officials did not anticipate Piikani resistance to the Oldman River Dam Project, and understandably so. Prior to the 1970s, the Piikani had remained largely confined to their reserve, policy artifacts with limited political input due to a federal policy orientation that anticipated "Indian" disappearance or cultural assimilation. Although neither occurred, the Piikani and their relations at the Kainai and Siksika First Nations remained outside the political imaginary.[2] Culturally, the Piikani were considered what environmentalists coined the first ecologists, and although their well-timed political re-emergence may have surprised some, the Piikani's resistance also appeared to make perfect sense. The complexity of the response was nevertheless unexpected and involved suing the federal government for illegal placement of waterworks dating to the 1920s and a submission seeking dam placement on the reserve following the province's announced project approval. On the surface, the Piikani Band Council's response evolved into a concerted resistance to ongoing colonization of their traditional land base that resurfaced with the dam announcement. Fearing that burial and ceremonial sites would be flooded, community leaders were distressed that provincial politicians did not consult with them to determine the project's potential impact. The combined concern for ensuring territorial integrity and a lack of political agency drove this response.

Although the dam and reservoir were parts of a crucial provincial conservation project of vast economic development potential, the project and its related procedures replicated colonization processes that had led to the Piikani's sequester on the reserve and a loss of traditional homelands. Uneven social relations had emerged as normative values, leading to exploitation of the reserve that was justified by provincial officials seeking to maintain mainstream political and economic success. Although the Piikani were largely left alone, local town and municipal growth had led to increased demand for local resources, suggesting that colonization's ubiquity operated within a "constantly shifting dialectic between society and land-based resources, and also within classes and groups within society itself."[3] This indicates that the nature of colonization is apt to change as social structures evolve. Nonetheless, as will be demonstrated, the southern Alberta environment, which had historically excluded First Nations interests, continued to advocate political separation. Hence to appreciate the nature of the Piikani resistance to the proposed dam and reservoir demands, we must understand the historical contexts bearing these values.

The resistance of First Nations is often as much about cultural survival as it is about challenging societally accepted normative values grounded in a colonial history that has resulted in their political and ecological exclusion.[4] In its various formats, it contests hegemonic power brokers such as provincial officials who have access to state resources with which to ward off challenges. At times, as Jack Glenn demonstrates in his important study on the Oldman River Dam conflict, the response to this resistance has entailed government agents discounting the rule of law.[5] This chapter specifically assesses the strategies utilized by the Piikani Band Council, the Peigan Lonefighters Society, and the Friends of the Oldman River Society, from which a brief and unlikely alliance developed, as well as the counterstrategies employed by the Province of Alberta in response to all attempts to halt dam construction. It demonstrate three things: (1) how the various opponents understood the stakes of the struggle and the strategic options available to them; (2) how the resources available to these parties guided their responses to institutional opportunities and constraints; and (3) how institutional rules shaped their strategies or determined outcomes. Finally, this chapter examines the two specific frames to emerge during this period, which continue to animate public policy debates: (1) the inherent tensions associated with the convergence of multiple cultural, political, and corporate perspectives; and (2) how these frames challenge multiple conceptualizations of economic progress and ecological preservation.

## THE POLITICS OF EXCLUSION

Piikani leaders signed Treaty 7 in September 1877 with commissioners representing the British Crown and the Canadian government.[6] In return for annuities, promises that the last buffalo herds would be protected, and the creation of sheltered reserves, the three member nations agreed to cede virtually 40,000 square kilometres of land to facilitate settler migration. Piikani leaders considered the treaties nation-to-nation agreements establishing the rules of conduct that guided cultural interaction, including territory-sharing provisions,[7] a position substantiated by the treaty's primary negotiator, Treaty Commissioner Alexander Morris.[8] The treaty's main provision reveals the Crown's intent to establish working relationships with First Nations leaders in order to promote cultural interaction for the purposes of opening tribal lands to settlers wishing to *share* the territory.[9]

As an aspect of the treaty, the Piikani chief Sitting On Eagle Tail Feathers could select the site for his reserve, and in 1882 he chose the traditional Old Man River, Crowlodge, and Porcupine Hills territories. The selected reserve is important, for the Piikani had occupied the Oldman River region, which runs through this territory, for at least 5,000 years.[10] The Piikani regard the river valley as both provider and a site of spiritual significance, leading elder Joe Crowshoe to proclaim that the Piikani would cease to exist as a people if they failed to retain an aspect of their sacred geography.[11] As the elder Percy Bullchild explains in *The Making of the Oldman River*, the story represents an assertion of sovereignty that demarcates Piikani territory while guiding individuals to an important point about Creation.[12]

The reserve site remained physically isolated from nearby communities, its economic production tied to limited farming and ranching enterprises. It also served a more heinous function by segregating "Indians" from Canadian society while paradoxically promoting their societal incorporation.[13] In 1885 a prairie pass system was established to confine Native leaders to reserves in order to neutralize political gatherings. Federal Indian agents specifically were granted substantial powers that forced individuals to obtain permission to leave the reserve to visit friends or family members located on another reserve.[14] In 1889 they were granted powers as justices of the peace for the purposes of the Vagrancy Act, which were applied strictly to Indians.[15] The primary goal was assimilation, and urban relocation was championed. Once reserves were empty of their former tenants, the reserve system was slated for decommission. Provincial officials embraced these and like federal policies of exclusion, which trickled down to southern Alberta municipal politics, as evidenced by the emergence of local norms that ensured municipal prohibitions resulting in a limited Aboriginal presence.[16]

The Piikani's complex land tenure system was obliterated by the imposition of the reserve model, which effectively compelled reserve residents to adopt land utilization norms that shoehorned private property regimes into historic land use models.[17] Reserve economic development was effectively constrained, which to residents located in communities peripheral to the reserve reflected a First Nations failure to properly utilize coveted farmland. Southern Alberta entrepreneurs did exploit their one available resource – First Nations labour – to grow a regional economy that by the 1920s had outstripped and destabilized regional reserve economic development.[18] All the while, the Piikani demonstrated great restraint by not challenging the Canadian government for failing to adhere to the spirit and intent of Treaty 7. The Department of Indian Affairs nevertheless continued to exert tremendous pressure on Piikani leaders to surrender portions of their reserve, a move that promoted western settlement while ridding the federal bureaucracy of the dreaded "Indian problem."[19] By the 1920s the Piikani were surrounded by Mormon immigrants from Utah and by other settlers seeking to capitalize on the regional farming and coal mining economies.[20]

### IRRIGATION AND PROVINCIAL POLITICS

The Piikani First Nation is located on the southwestern boundary of Palliser's Triangle. In the mid-nineteenth century, British explorer John Palliser described this region as an extension of the Great American Desert that lacked the necessary rainfall for permanent agricultural development.[21] Farmers quickly occupied much of the arable land in turn-of-the-century southern Alberta, particularly Utah Mormons who established the community of Cardston on the southeast boundary of the Blood Reserve just north of the Canada–United States border. This small group of settlers exploited generous federal land grants to excavate more than 150 kilometres of irrigation canals linking Lethbridge and the St Mary's River between 1898 and 1900.[22] Coupled with newly constructed regional railways, these initiatives encouraged agricultural expansion. European homesteaders flooded the region in the early twentieth century, finding work in the burgeoning local sugar beet industry.[23] This amalgam of settlers to the southern Alberta territory embraced a common belief:[24] that community development should be guided by the Protestant work ethic.[25] They established a community of locally developed and operated businesses whose economy was augmented by trade with neighbouring communities, thus achieving an accumulation of personal wealth that directly influenced social progress.[26] Aboriginal issues did periodically arise, followed by local officials citing popular attitudes that anticipated "Indians'" disappearance, or cultural absorption.[27]

First Nations leaders were immediately confronted by administrators demanding access to reserve lands for irrigation projects, and the Piikani were among the first to succumb. The Northwest Irrigation Act of 1894 assigned all water to federal control. Southern Alberta residents and western entrepreneurs soon recognized that water was a vital resource, but it was not until 1930 that the provinces assumed administrative control. Irrigation projects in southern Alberta flourished unabated for three decades, and what began as make-work projects during the Depression years evolved into three large irrigation projects in the 1940s. In the mid-1960s the Social Credit government proposed the Prairie Rivers Improvement Management and Evaluation Program (PRIME). Formulated to catalogue all canals, tunnels, dams, and reservoirs needed to deliver these waters to southern farming regions, PRIME fitted with several proposed American engineering projects to transfer Canadian waters to American dry spots. In particular, the $500 billion North American Water and Power Alliance proposed an artificial waterway constructed through the Canadian Rockies to divert Arctic waters to southern California. Public response in Alberta was overwhelmingly negative, something aspiring premier and leader of the Progressive Conservative Party Peter Lougheed successfully capitalized on during the 1971 elections. Determined to capture greater control over provincial resources, the newly elected Progressive Conservative government quickly established the Department of Agriculture's Water Resources Division and implemented various water management regimes to support Tory-advocated irrigation expansion projects reminiscent of PRIME. In 1973 the federal government devolved to Alberta responsibility for the extensive network of provincial irrigation works.

Public resistance did not stop the Lougheed government from forging ahead with the construction of the Bighorn Dam on the North Saskatchewan River and the Dickson Dam on the Red Deer River.

Similar actions were needed in areas like the Lethbridge Northern Irrigation District (LNID) that were unable to meet farmer and rancher demands during dry years. One proposed strategy for southern Alberta
was to locate a dam at the confluence of the Oldman, the Crowsnest,
and the Castle Rivers. The political fallout associated with PRIME halted this project until 1975; however, the provincial Water Management
for Irrigation Policy was implemented, granting irrigators access to
South Saskatchewan River water and reviving what was now being labelled the Oldman River Dam Project (ORDP). Sensing that the ORDP
was still (internally) considered a viable strategy, the Environmental
Council of Alberta ruled in 1979 "that a dam on the Oldman River
is not required now or in the foreseeable future" to support the suggested level of irrigation expansion, adding that a dam at "the Three
Rivers site would be the worst possible location from environmental and
social perspectives."[28]

## RESISTANCE STRATEGIES

The Piikani Nation remained economically marginalized into the 1980s.
Limited farming and a scattering of wage labour, a locally operated construction company, and a few small businesses provided insufficient opportunities in a community with a 95 per cent unemployment rate. Most
individual income came from social assistance.[29] Nonetheless, the Piikani
seemed poised to emerge from a protracted community-based economic
depression for various reasons. The nascent nationalism discourse borne
of the United States' Red Power movement and impressive constitutional leaps made by Canadian First Nations led Piikani leaders to pursue a
successful land claim against the provincial government, which was later
determined to have unlawfully diverted water from the Oldman River in
1922. A second claim settlement related to a 1909 surrender due to
Indian agent duplicity that had resulted in an illegal land transaction.
Finally, the United Nations announced the construction of the Head-
Smashed-In Buffalo Jump and Interpretive Centre, a historic site where
the Piikani had stampeded buffalo to death over a large cliff.[30]

These federal claims were being negotiated as the province moved toward dam creation in the early 1980s. Piikani interest in the dam project
hastened negotiations with Alberta, and on 30 April 1981 the Piikani
Band Council and the provincial government announced a final agreement that was ratified in June. In exchange for permitting unfettered
provincial access to the irrigation headway, the band council received a

one-time $4 million payment and $300,000 annually, as well as provincial training programs and new fences to contain livestock.[31] The province also committed to partner with the Canadian government to fund research into locating the dam on the reserve, despite Piikani declarations "that the province would not have sole ownership and control of the dam."[32] As newly elected chief Peter Yellowhorn awaited word on negotiations, Premier Lougheed (against recommendations to the contrary) announced the $353 million ORDP in 1984, shocking Piikani leaders and environmentalists alike. He also indicated that the project would move forward without a second environmental review. Alberta officials asserted that, because the ORDP was occurring on provincial land, the province was not bound by federal environmental impact assessment laws guiding large-scale industrial projects. Lougheed anticipated that an Oldman River Dam would be operational by the early 1990s.

The Alberta minister of the environment, Fred Bradley, wrote Chief Yellowhorn to explain that placing the dam on the reserve would cost an estimated $72.5 million more than the three rivers site. Reservoir storage capacity was also an issue. The minister's response to Piikani jurisdictional claims and desires for dam ownership was most revealing. Specifically, Bradley replied that "the position outlined in your letter that the Peigan Band claims historical and legal jurisdiction over the waters of the Oldman River are not accepted by the Government. The Alberta Government maintains it has sole jurisdiction over all waters in the province."[33] Chief Yellowhorn responded in January 1986 that "the Peigan Nation is engaged in a battle for its survival," and he immediately sought legal advice to formally oppose the ORDP.[34] The band council also crafted a six-page response entitled "Proclamation, Peigan Indian Nation: Respecting Title to Water and Water Rights in the Oldman River," which asserted the band council's certainty of Piikani riparian and treaty rights to water and the need to protect the quality of the water flowing through the reserve.[35] Individuals unwilling to await legal proceedings also issued veiled threats of militant action.

On 11 April 1986 the band filed a statement of claim against the Alberta government seeking an injunction to halt the ORDP, citing continued Piikani water and riverbed ownership rights to the Oldman River running through the reserve, as well as construction and operations damage anticipated from the ORDP (including the destruction of Piikani spiritual values). The band filed a similar claim against the federal government in June, which was altered to claim Piikani ownership of and exclusive right to the use of river waters in their present quantity and quality running through the reserve. The claim again cited potential construction damage to the river and concluded that a constitutionally accepted fiduciary obligation required the federal government to protect the Piikani's rights and interests by preventing construction and operation of the dam.[36] These two injunctions were unsuccessful. Next the Piikani focused on claiming sovereign rights to water in order to ensure that the ORDP would not negatively affect reserve water quality levels or band access to sufficient quantities. The Alberta government's certainty of authority over provincial waters was as much a jurisdictional claim (in response to recent federal attempts to compel an environmental assessment on the ORDP) as an attempt to undermine Piikani political strategies. Indian Affairs officials in Ottawa failed to acknowledge Canada's fiduciary relationship with First Nations and to protect Piikani reserve interests in the process.

The Friends of the Oldman River Society (FOR) joined forces with the Piikani Band Council in an effort to halt dam construction. Formed in September 1987 and led by the late Martha Kostuch, whose previous experience guiding various environmental causes would provide an alternative perspective that was initially media-friendly, the FOR had been actively involved in the development of the Canadian Environmental Assessment Act and engaged in environmental protection activities, particularly the safeguarding of rivers and fish habitats.[37] In 1987 the FOR initiated a lawsuit against Alberta for failing to obtain the required clearances. The Federal Court of Appeal agreed, ruling that provincial transport and fisheries departments had ignored federally established criteria by failing to carry out the proper environmental assessments. The provincial licence was ultimately quashed, although a new one was issued that the FOR was unable to overturn. In September the federal minister of transport approved dam construction under the Navigable Waters Protection Act.

Unsuccessful with its two injunctions, the band council sought out renowned lawyer and Native rights advocate Thomas Berger for advice in 1988 about the efficacy of applying for an interlocutory injunction on the basis that the dam infringed upon Piikani religion. "I think that an application by the band for an injunction on the ground that the construction of a dam infringes the freedom of religion of the Peigan Indians, is likely to fail," Berger replied, due in part to the ambiguous nature of spirituality in the courts. He added, "Do not think that whatever the Peigans and the experts say about Peigan religious belief and practice would go unchallenged." He also challenged the argument that the dam would adversely damage Piikani water quantity because he did not believe that the dam would "infringe [on] the band's reserved water rights."[38] This echoed the legal position in the Piikani's 1986 federal statement of claim, which intentionally avoided mentioning religious or spiritual values or the dam's anticipated negative impact upon Piikani spirituality. Regardless, the Lonefighters, who had recently entered the fray, adopted a two-pronged resistance strategy. On the one hand, their upstream strategy focused on nonreserve lands and the legally nebulous category of spirituality in an attempt to decommission the ORDP. On the other hand, the Piikani Band Council's downstream strategy focused on reserve lands in an attempt to ensure that present and future generations of Piikani had an adequate water supply.

## THE POLITICAL ENVIRONMENT

As the band council awaited word on the lawsuits and injunctions filed against the Alberta and Canadian governments, cultivating dissent was a small group of men living on the reserve who were livid at the provincial government's response to Piikani demands. After several years of legal battles against Alberta that were slowly being resolved in the Piikani's favour, the group led by Milton Born With A Tooth – which now called itself the Lonefighters Society – faxed southern Alberta media outlets a six-page press release on 9 May 1990 demanding an immediate halt to dam construction. The statement described the Lonefighters Society as the protector of the Piikani way of life, indicating also that it would respond immediately and aggressively to perceived community threats. The Lonefighters charged the minister of the environment (later Alberta premier), Ralph Klein, with genocide against the Piikani Nation under section 260(A)(11) of the United Nations Convention on the Non-applicability of Statutory Limitations to War Crimes against Humanity. The upstart Lonefighters also took aim at the chief and council's response to the affair. "The chief, Leonard Bastien and his colleagues have been conquered to a point where they have forgotten how to protect the future of the Peigan Tribe," the press release asserted, adding that the surrounding environment's destruction showed the leadership's incompetence and inability to make proper "life decisions especially when it comes to the environment." According to the Lonefighters, the actions resulted in the popular misconception that the Piikani no longer needed the Oldman River "because we are conquered to live the white man's way of life" of consumption based on environmental destruction.

In sum, they charged that the band leaders had "failed as overseer's [*sic*] of the Peigan's destiny."[39]

The Lonefighters took aim at two distinct political entities: the Piikani Band Council and the Alberta government. Interestingly, at this point there was no mention of Indian Affairs ineptitude or any demands for federal intervention. The primary target of the Lonefighters' antipathy was the chief and council, who were identified as collaborators in Piikani genocide perpetrated by Alberta, the latter considered a secondary menace as a result of its support for the ORDP. These harsh words contrasted with how the chief and band council had handled the situation: through negotiations and the courts.

Who exactly were the Lonefighters? The media identified Born With A Tooth and his followers as members of an ancient, albeit dormant, clan recently resurrected.[40] According to Piikani elders Dr Reg Crowshoe and Geoff Crow Eagle and historian Hugh Dempsey, the Lone Fighters Clan was a distinctive and still operational political entity. Crow Eagle explains, "When people had family disputes, they would not take their problems off to different clans – they tried to solve their problems right in that clan, amongst themselves."[41] Dempsey identifies Calf Shirt as a leader of the Lone Fighters Band, which originated with the Bloods. Calf Shirt's death at the hands of whiskey trader Joseph Kipp in 1874 led the Lone Fighters to merge with the Many Fat Horses Band, with both bands agreeing to keep the Lone Fighters' name since they were the larger of the two groups.[42] As of 1990, however, the traditional Lone Fighters were located within the larger Piikani community and did not appear to support Born With A Tooth and his small group of followers who adopted the name "Lonefighters" for their movement.

Three men at this stage comprised the self-proclaimed Lonefighters Society: Born With A Tooth and his two closest supporters, Devalon Small Legs, son of former chief Nelson Small Legs Sr, and Glenn North Peigan. Little has been written about North Peigan other than to highlight his participation in the events of August 1990. Small Legs was the brother of Nelson Small Legs Jr, leader of the American Indian Movement's (AIM) southern Alberta chapter, who in 1976 killed himself "to show the conditions Indians live in. I give my life in protest to the Canadian government for its treatment of Indian people for the past 100 years."[43] Small Legs Jr disagreed with AIM's hardline tactics at Wounded Knee in 1973 and promoted university degrees as opposed to guns as the most effective weapons available in the Piikani's fight against the federal and provincial governments. His actions motivated

his father's 1978 blockade of the water intake, thereby compelling the
1981 Piikani-Alberta agreement. Small Legs Sr also adopted his son's
moderate stance, although he recognized that "all I had to do was raise
my hand, and AIM was ready across Canada."[44] Born With A Tooth was
by far the most militant and experienced of the three. When he returned
to Canada after travelling around the self-described "wino routes" of
southern California, he led a road blockade and brief standoff in
Cardston in 1980, claiming that the Mormons were illegally occupying
the southeastern portion of the Blood Reserve.[45] Conspicuously present
was AIM, and following the RCMP's deployment, a physical altercation
resulted in the arrest of more than thirty Natives, including Born With A
Tooth.[46] These three men came together in the summer of 1990, claiming they had the support of the most venerable of elders and the chief,
and attempted to mobilize community support for decommissioning the
ORDP. From May to the end of July, the Lonefighters grew in number
from three to ten.

The Lonefighters were not heard from again until 3 August 1990,
when ten men blockaded a portion of the reserve. They also rented a
bulldozer from a local construction firm and attempted to divert water
from the Oldman River by redirecting it into an abandoned oxbow
channel, effectively bypassing the LNID weir and thereby cutting off
water to hundreds of irrigation farms and some small towns north of the
Oldman River.[47] In so doing, the Lonefighters adopted a political strategy
previously dismissed by Chief Peter Yellowhorn. That is, they espoused
a discourse identifying Alberta as advocating Piikani cultural genocide
that could be thwarted only by securing the safety of off-reserve sacred
sites destined for destruction through reservoir flooding.[48] Whereas the
band council sought to protect downstream water quality and to ensure
water rights needed for irrigation, the Lonefighters demanded that the
ORDP be decommissioned. Dam construction was by now nearly three-
quarters complete, suggesting that this was a naive strategy, and enraged
outsiders condemned the diversion project. Lethbridge farmer Bill Arsene
and the mayor of Picture Butte (Lethbridge member of Parliament,
1997–2011), Rick Casson, were critical of what they described as aggressive acts, leading Arsene to conclude that "when they start getting
militant, then it's time to put your foot down. There are 48 little towns
that need the water." Alluding to recent events at Oka, where federal officials had discussed sending in a military occupation force to restore
order, he added, "they should bring in the army with rifles and I don't
have to tell you the rest of it." Casson also warned of the potential for

violence against the "radical element within the Peigan band," explaining that the arduous four-year fight to guarantee dam construction had produced a tinderbox and that the Lonefighters' threats to the project could be "the straw that broke the camel's back."[49]

Early on it appeared that the Piikani community embraced Born With A Tooth and his followers, even though their press releases indicated that they lacked band council support for the diversion project. Chief Bastien indicated that although he did not endorse the excavation, he did support the action.[50] The same could be said for the FOR, who donated $5,000 so that the Lonefighters could purchase food and rent a bulldozer.[51] Four days following the start of the blockade, however, the *Edmonton Journal* reported that both the traditional Lone Fighters Clan and delegates of the Piikani Women collective denounced Born With A Tooth, his followers, and the diversion project. Describing the Lonefighters as a splinter group that was improperly using the Lone Fighters' name, the report stated that Piikani Women demanded an immediate halt to a project that they claimed lacked community support.[52] Within days, the Piikani Band Council met and officially censured the Lonefighters. In particular, Chief Bastien, who had previously supported the blockade, was now openly critical of the diversion activities.[53] Born With A Tooth responded, "To me, whether chief and council say yes or no to our action, the Lonefighters Society is going to continue. This is an action of the people going to be affected the most."[54]

Despite claims to have secured the chief's support and the confidence of venerable elders, Born With A Tooth appeared to callously disregard the traditional Lone Fighters and the Piikani Women. Given that the Lonefighters Society operated in a community where elders played an important and prominent political role, this indifference was problematic, especially when these highly respected groups were consequently able to influence band council decisions and sway public opinion. Disregarding their opinions was considered disrespectful and a sign that the Lonefighters did not have the community's best interests at heart.

However, the Lonefighters' cause still enjoyed minimal support. Two weeks after riverbed excavation had begun, approximately seventy-five people were camped at the diversion site, a largely youthful contingent made up of the three leaders' families. After air reconnaissance showed no signs of firearms, explosives, or ammunition, the RCMP announced that they did not consider the small group of Lonefighters dangerous. Superintendent Owen Maguire also informed the media that no legal action was warranted since no laws had been broken. In short, the police and provincial officials alike demonstrated an increasingly aloof attitude about the situation. RCMP sergeant Gary Mills, for instance, described the Lonefighters as campers "fooling around with a bulldozer," comments echoed by the member of the Legislative Assembly (MLA) for Calgary-Millican, Gordon Shrake, who suggested that the blockade was simply the action of "a few young bucks who have seen all the excitement of the Oka Indians and they want to get in on the act."[55] This view seems to have encouraged several small groups of non-Native protestors (described by North Peigan as "vigilantes") to enter the reserve and challenge the Lonefighters from across the Oldman River.[56] The nature of officialdom's stance and an increasingly hostile attitude by non-Native observers toward the Lonefighters (and all Piikani by association) served to gradually inflame an already tense situation. It did not help that the Lonefighters were suffering from a highly publicized and embarrassing lack of progress. In particular, the bulldozer broke down several times, leading Alberta's attorney general, Ken Rostad, to conclude that "the project is going nowhere."[57] Officials with the provincial Department of the Environment estimated at the time that based on the Lonefighters' current pace, it would be weeks before any water was potentially diverted.[58] Nonetheless, each day the Lonefighters arose to conduct ceremonies that included regular sweats prior to their firing up the bulldozer for the day's work.

During the first three weeks of August, the Lonefighters extended invitations to various groups and individuals to discuss the issues, particularly to provincial officials, who initially did not respond. Increasingly described in the media as a faction and splinter group, the Lonefighters were forced to unsuccessfully compete with Chief Bastien and the Piikani Band Council for legitimacy. For example, on 12 August the Southern Alberta Water Management Committee insisted that Chief Bastien and the band council adhere to the 1981 agreement.[59] The next day, the Lonefighters demanded a meeting with the federal minister of Indian and northern affairs, Tom Siddon, promising only at that point to halt the diversion project. Twenty-four hours later the Alberta government tersely responded, indicating that it would not tolerate any diversion of the Oldman River. All the while, Chief Bastien and the band council were jockeying for position with the Lonefighters, exploiting the blockade to pursue their previous agenda to secure Piikani water rights and water quality. On 16 August the Canadian Press reported that a newly established committee, including Rostad, Minister of the Environment Klein, Minister of Lands LeRoy Fjordbotten, and Pincher Creek MLA

Fred Bradley, would meet with Bastien and the band council.[60] Although the Lonefighters were excluded from the dialogue, spokesperson Lydia Scott indicated that "if something good comes out of it," the diversion project would likely cease.[61] When additional meeting requests were ignored, Born With A Tooth reached out to various farmer groups to reveal that "we are not their enemy. Our enemy is the people upstream."[62] Their expressed desire for an alliance with farmers reveals that the Lonefighters had misread the political lay of the land by anticipating shared hostility to the ORDP outside of the reserve. Given that farming and irrigation interests had initiated the ORDP process in the mid-1970s, nothing could have been further from the truth. Within days, Unifarm president Ralph Jesperson was openly criticizing Chief Bastien in the media for violating the 1981 agreement and thereby threatening irrigation-dependent southern Alberta farmers and ranchers, thus conflating Piikani administration and the renegade Lonefighters.[63]

Chief Bastien's sustained pressure to meet with provincial officials was eventually successful when Klein agreed in mid-August to a 31 August meeting. When the Lonefighters made progress on their diversion project, provincial officials pressured the Piikani Band Council to accept responsibility for its citizens' actions. Within days of Klein agreeing to a meeting, Rostad issued a warning letter to Bastien indicating that no negotiations would occur unless diversion work stopped. Rostad then cleverly pitted the Lonefighters against the band council by describing the former as a "group of malcontents that want to have the Oldman River dam construction stopped" and the latter as a moderate political agent with legitimate concerns. Once the diversion was abandoned, provincial officials professed that they would be pleased to converse with the band council about its concerns.[64] In early September the Lonefighters brought in additional heavy equipment, including a backhoe and several dump trucks, and hastened their pace of excavation. The media identified a more orderly work pattern, and for the first time since early August, it appeared that their threats to divert the Oldman could come to fruition.[65] Several well-known international environmental organizations and Native groups donated money to keep the estimated $50,000 project on track.[66]

On 29 August, twenty-six days after excavation began, the Lonefighters succeeded in diverting water away from the irrigation duct. Downstream communities began storing water in anticipation of the worst. In one case, the leaders of a small community, Nobleford, were developing plans to construct a 13 kilometre direct-access pipeline to the river.[67]

But reports from the camp (which at times numbered as many as 120 people) spoke of a sense of prevailing optimism, despite the RCMP's promises of protestor arrests. Through their lawyer, the Lonefighters also proclaimed that they wanted to gain the chief and council's support prior to continuing work on the diversion, explaining that they did not want to "split the Peigan nation. They want to make a united front if they can."[78] But this did not stop various Lonefighters from intermittently firing up the tractors and roaring the engines, threatening to defy the injunction.

In Edmonton politicians under increasing pressure to respond sent a team of equipment operators and engineers onto the reserve on 7 September to restore both the riverbed and the Oldman flow. Shortly after midnight, an RCMP Emergency Response Team covertly took up position on the Oldman River opposite the Lonefighters' camp, followed the next morning by the RCMP and the provincial Department of the Environment entering the reserve, their eyes set on the weir. The previous evening, RCMP superintendent Owen Maguire had unsuccessfully attempted to contact Chief Bastien in order to inform him of the action, and efforts to contact the chief the following day also proved fruitless. A fleet of vehicles, including ambulances, RCMP escorts, and Department of the Environment transports, arrived at the weir at 8:20 AM, taking the Lonefighters by surprise. Forty minutes later, six provincial employees and six RCMP officers arrived at the diversion dike to observe the damage. At this point, Born With A Tooth warned the men to leave the reserve. He then fired two shots into the air, sending officers scrambling and provincial employees scurrying for safety. The Department of the Environment quickly removed all employees and equipment, followed by the police twelve hours later. After securing a twenty-four-hour truce, Maguire later testified that removing the police and provincial employees was needed due to the increasingly volatile situation and fears that "somebody was going to get hurt." He claimed that the officers on site were carrying only their police-issue handguns and were under strict orders to keep them holstered.[79] Born With A Tooth responded, "we are under siege and our main concern right now is to protect," and "we want the RCMP to move out of this area. It is our area. They do not have a right to be here."[80] In addition to denouncing the chief and council for failing to remove the RCMP from Piikani land, he added, "I'm going to leave a free man or I'm going to leave a dead person."[81]

Although Born With A Tooth was immediately charged with the unlawful use of a firearm and unlawful discharge of a firearm, helicopter searches failed to disclose his whereabouts. He had simply and quickly disappeared. The Lonefighters celebrated the RCMP's departure from the reserve with dancing, songs, and prayer. Devalon Small Legs proclaimed, "I do believe that the tide has turned and the truth has prevailed. The real criminals have left and this will never happen again on Peigan soil." At the request of Court of Queen's Bench justice William Egbert, who was assigned the responsibility of deciding whether to lift the injunction halting the diversion project, both sides agreed to act in a calm and dispassionate manner.[82] During the thirty-three-hour standoff, however, Born With A Tooth gave several interviews indicating that the diversion work would continue and that "no court, no policeman, no provincial government is going to stop us."[83] Several media outlets, including the *Edmonton Journal*, were critical of the Alberta government's response, criticizing its ad hoc approach to an escalating conflict. An editorial entitled "Preventing an Oka Here" identified provincial officials as the culprits: "The environment minister sent in staff members to watch helplessly as the Lonefighters meddled with the river. The solicitor general asked the RCMP to monitor the situation to guard the peace. And the attorney general, the minister responsible for native affairs, made it clear he isn't interested in talking."[84] This was followed by the Piikani Band Council's announcement that it had voted nine to one to endorse the Lonefighters and by Chief Bastien's statement to the gathered media that "we now support the Lonefighters in their attempt to fight the dam" based "on our traditional, cultural and religious beliefs."[85] This show of support was short-lived, and by year's end the band council and the Lonefighters were once again at odds.

The next day, Born With A Tooth was arrested in Calgary. Three days later, Justice Egbert upheld the injunction, prohibiting further diversion work while also concluding that Alberta owned the Oldman River and its riverbanks. Just hours before, the RCMP had covertly entered the reserve with provincial work crews to repair the damaged riverbed, leading the remaining Lonefighters to threaten an armed resistance in response to any attempt by the officers to occupy the reserve. Small Legs suggested the Lonefighters would consult with the band council when formulating their response.[86] Acting premier Jim Horsman told a conference of the Alberta Weekly Newspaper Association that the Lonefighters were criminals – the strongest denunciation to date by a provincial politician. He stated that "what the Lonefighters are doing would be intolerable in any democracy, but especially in a country whose very basis is peace and order." He equated the Lonefighters to a special-interest group, which legitimized the Piikani Nation's political status and authority: "We cannot allow any interest group to break the law of Canada. And we certainly cannot allow any interest group to use violence as a tool."[87] These conclusions were eloquently countered by Ojibwa columnist Richard Wagamese, who described the Lonefighters' camp as anything but a militant environment. "Tribal elders visit regularly for traditional pipe ceremonies and prayers. The people talk of problems other groups around the world are facing and what they can learn from them," he observed. "Visitors are encouraged and welcomed and each day someone makes the long drive into Brocket for the four newspapers each of the clan members will read and discuss. *These are informed people.*"[88]

Over the next several months, the Lonefighters' camp was characterized by intermittent activity, punctuated by repeated threats to restore the diversion project. Small Legs and North Peigan asked for a six-month armistice that would have prohibited them and the provincial government from working at the diversion site. Rostad dealt the final blow by once again publicly refusing to meet with the Lonefighters' representatives. "I don't recognize the Lonefighters as having any authority as a group," he insisted. "That's why we deal with the chief and council and not the Lonefighters."[89] Born With A Tooth did his best to spark protest from jail, pronouncing his martial actions legal in the wake of an aggressive invasion force. Little came of this verbal barrage.[90] On 1 December the RCMP again escorted provincial workers onto the reserve to begin work on $500,000 of repairs to the riverbed diversion. They were unopposed, likely owing to the fact that an incarcerated Born With A Tooth was not on hand to motivate the protestors, who simply watched from a distance as repairs were effected. The combination of Born With A Tooth's loss and the now very real threat of jail seemed to counter activist resolve. Born With A Tooth was released from jail on 20 December. The Lonefighters' blockade of the Oldman River was over.

## AFTER THE BLOCKADE

In the wake of the Lonefighters' resistance, southern Alberta media agencies limited their coverage of ORDP-related issues: the dam and reservoir project were to most a fait accompli. The FOR, however, maintained its presence and in November filed notice in the Federal Court of Canada to order the minister of the environment to appoint an environmental review panel for the Oldman River Dam, as was required by an Environmental Assessment and Review Process Guidelines Order (EARPGO).

On 16 November, four days before the court heard the FOR's notice, an Environmental Assessment Review Panel (EARP) was struck to review the relevant studies and consider further information needed "to fully understand the project and its potential impacts." Since the panel was authorized to initiate its own studies and conduct public hearings, its chair, Dr W.A. Ross, indicated that although the dam was now 80 per cent constructed, its completion "will not make any material difference in the nature of the enquiry being undertaken by the panel, nor to the recommendations expected to flow from its work."[91] Stating earlier that it was unwilling to cooperate with the federal review panel, Alberta unsuccessfully sought the EARP's suspension. After reviewing the findings of various reports, the EARP concluded that the wildlife studies submitted were deficient in most regards and that no wildlife impact assessment had been conducted. The Oldman River's cultural significance was identified, followed by an order for additional studies and an independent archaeological review of the flood zone. Finally, the EARP criticized the federal government for not conducting studies that may have contra-·dicted those produced by dam proponents.[92]

Almost one year after it was struck, the EARP noted, "it was a challenge for the contributors ... to base their response ... on information provided by the proponent." Alberta failed to deliver the information requested, and it limited and in certain cases restricted EARP access to employees or consultants.[93] Alberta also refused to participate in the public hearing stage from November to December, while once again denying the EARP access to employees and consultants, many of whom had initially presented their findings advocating dam development.[94] In May 1992 the EARP report submitted to the federal government concluded that "the environmental, social and economic costs of the project are not balanced by corresponding benefits and finds that, as presently configured, the project is unacceptable." Only one panel member took exception to decommissioning the dam, where it was recommended that "the low level diversion tunnels to allow unimpeded flow of the river" be opened. Recognizing the dams nearly complete status, an additional twenty-two recommendations were developed, including the stipulation that the Piikani and the proponents of the dam would have to reach an agreement and make a long-term commitment to mitigating "the many environmental impacts of the project."[95]

The report's release followed two significant events. The first was the Supreme Court of Canada's January decision that under the terms of the EARPGO "the federal Minister of Transport was required to conduct an environmental impact assessment with respect to Alberta's Oldman River dam project." The court found that the EARPGO was not "mere administrative directives, but that they had the force of law, and consequently, had to be complied with in all cases to which they applied."[96] The decision legitimized the EARP's mandate, although this did not stop the Alberta government from transferring ownership from the Department of Public Works, Supply, and Services to the Department of the Environment. Alberta also disregarded the EARP report, which was released after the dam became fully operational.[97]

The FOR remained diligent and was increasingly disturbed by several events. For example, in December, prior to the EARP report's release and the Supreme Court's pronouncement, the provincial Department of Water Management Services had issued itself a licence to operate the dam and licences to seven irrigation districts in the Oldman Basin to divert water.[98] Spurred by recent events and a year of federal inaction, the FOR petitioned the Federal Court to compel the federal minister of transport to implement the EARP's recommendations. In May 1993 the court ruled that the minister was required to take action but "only on those panel recommendations that the federal government agreed should be implemented."[99] Frustrated by the court's slow pace and the lack of provincial concern, the FOR's vice president, Dr Martha Kostuch, initiated legal action against Alberta for the destruction of fish habitat. After the attorney general stayed the charges, and an appeal was denied in the Court of Queen's Bench, Kostuch unsuccessfully petitioned to have her case heard by the Supreme Court of Canada.[100] In July, still in need of a cogent operating policy, the Department of Water Management Services appointed the Oldman River Dam Environmental Advisory Committee. As the committee started meeting, the Canada-Alberta Agreement for Environmental Assessment Cooperation, negotiated without public consultation, was signed. The agreement was slated to promote the development of other water projects while avoiding similar public protests.[101] Finally, the federal Ministry of Transport issued approval for the Oldman River Dam under the Navigable Waters Protection Act, disregarding an EARP proviso that federal approval of the dam be withheld until an agreement between the Piikani and Alberta was reached.[102] Several years of unsuccessful FOR petitions and appeals followed, and as of the early 2000s, irrigation came to represent nearly 90 per cent of all water use on the Oldman.

The Piikani similarly discovered the lingering effect of working through government channels. The band council in particular remained a mitigating influence during the heated dispute between the Lonefighters and the Alberta government. Yet councillors were also concerned about territorial integrity and their influence over decisions about regional land use. In November 1990, for example, the band council voted for a six-month cessation of work at the disputed site. Premier Don Getty acknowledged receipt of the resolution but vowed to see repairs to the LNID site affected, ignoring the band council's proclamation. Despite the bad feelings, Alberta and the Piikani Band Council proceeded to negotiate the EARP-mandated agreement over damages resulting from dam construction. In November 2001 the band received a $64.3 million payment, annual payments of $500,000, and a payment of $1,000 to each of its 2,600 members. The agreement was ratified in October 2002 by 58 per cent of Piikani voters. Four additional agreements were negotiated, including an environmental impact assessment of the Oldman River Valley, guaranteed Piikani Nation participation in the Oldman Dam Hydro Project, the establishment of a joint provincial-Piikani committee on economic development initiatives, and the use of Piikani labour and resources in LNID canal maintenance.[103]

## CONCLUSION

The Lonefighters initial occupation of the Oldman River in August 1990 catapulted a small group of activists from the Piikani First Nation into the national media spotlight. They managed also to capture southern Alberta's attention during that fateful "Indian summer." Already aware of events occurring at Oka, the media promptly sided with the Lonefighters and published their manifesto highlighting band council culpability in promoting a Piikani genocide initiated by the Alberta government's plans to construct a dam and reservoir on traditional Piikani lands. Before most parties had an opportunity to publicly respond, a good-versus-evil narrative had unfolded that pitted a small group of activists against the state and, to a minor degree, against their own people at Piikani. Accordingly, the media identified provincial ignorance of Piikani environmental concerns as the catalyst driving the Lonefighters' response, which was ostensibly intended to protect what the media portrayed as an increasingly vulnerable community. It took a while, but journalists shifted their investigative lens toward the Lonefighters, soon discovering that it was little more than a core of three men who had appropriated the name of the Lone Fighters Clan for their nonviolent agitation. Announcing to the media that their goal was to halt dam construction, the Lonefighters were unable to capitalize on this publicity. By late summer, the once media-friendly Lonefighters had lost the public's support by advocating violence to stem dam and reservoir construction. In September they aggressively confronted the RCMP's community incursion, leading to the arrest of their self-appointed leader, Milton Born With A Tooth; and by December the occupation had petered out, as Born With A Tooth watched events unfold from a jail cell while awaiting a court appearance.

Not unlike the majority of the case studies in this book, the Oldman River standoff reflected a complex interplay of history, politics, economics, culture, and personalities. It was poorly planned, a visceral reaction of relatively young men who felt violated by a system ignorant of their and their families' living conditions. Yet interestingly, it had an opportunity to become a larger movement, perhaps powerful enough to compel band council support. The Lonefighters attracted as many as 129 individuals out of a community of 2,500 to a handful of protests. Support was also forthcoming from the Friends of the Oldman River, a promising environmental organization that donated $5,000 to support the Lonefighters' cause, as well as from several local environmental groups. This outside help, however, was not sufficient to secure the support of the Piikani Band Council, which expressed concern that the occupation could potentially undermine several lawsuits being waged against the provincial government and further alienate the Piikani from provincial politicians and local farmer and rancher groups. The band council would win these cases, leading to a $64 million award from the Alberta government for failure to ensure Piikani interests, something the Lonefighters did not anticipate – and a strategy they did not approve of at the time. The resulting conflict drove a wedge through the heart of the community, ultimately pitting family members, clans, and societies against one another to the point that even today the events of 1990 are rarely discussed, especially with outsiders. It permitted provincial officials to undermine the Lonefighters' actions by publicly dismissing them as those of impudent children lacking political legitimacy.

Notably, the Canadian government was absent during the entire event, which was not surprising considering the time and effort being directed at resolving the Oka dispute. It is troubling to suggest that the Indian Affairs bureaucracy is susceptible to complete shutdown in the wake of one or even two major protests simultaneously occurring at opposite ends of the country. Also disturbing was the Canadian government's opportunism: by directing resources to resolve the Oka affair, federal

14 Laurie, F. Barron, "The Indian Pass System in the Canadian West, 1882–1935," *Prairie Forum* 13, no. 1 (1988): 25–42; Sarah Carter, "Controlling Indian Movement: The Pass System," *NeWest Review* 10, no. 9 (May 1985): 8–9.

15 John Leslie and Ron Maguire, *The Historical Development of the Indian Act*, 2nd ed. (Ottawa: Indian and Northern Affairs Canada, 1978).

16 Sheila McManus, *The Line Which Separates: Race, Gender, and the Making of the Alberta-Montana Borderlands* (Edmonton: University of Alberta Press, 2005).

17 Treaty 7 Elders and Tribal Council, *True Spirit and Intent*; Betty Bastien, *Blackfoot Ways of Knowing: The World View of the Siksikaitsitapi* (Calgary: University of Calgary Press, 2004).

18 Keith W. Regular, *Neighbours and Networks: The Blood Tribe and the Southern Alberta Economy* (Calgary: University of Calgary Press, 2009).

19 Peggy Martin-McGuire, *First Nations Land Surrenders on the Prairies, 1896–1911* (Ottawa: Indian Claims Commission, 1998); Canada, *Annual Report of the Department of Indian Affairs for the Year Ended March 31, 1910* (Ottawa: Department of Indian Affairs, 1910); Noel Dyck, '*What Is the Indian Problem': Tutelage and Resistance in Canadian Indian Administration* (St John's, NL: Institute of Social and Economic Research, 1991).

20 James G. MacGregor, *A History of Alberta* (Edmonton: Hurtig, 1972).

21 Barry Potyondi, *In Palliser's Triangle: Living in the Grasslands, 1850–1930* (Saskatoon: Purich, 1995); Irene M. Spry, *The Palliser Expedition: The Dramatic Story of Western Canadian Exploration, 1857–1860* (Calgary: Fifth House, 1995).

22 Tom R. Johnston and Marvin Sundstrom, "Irrigation Agriculture and Local Economic Development," in *The Sustainability of Rural Systems*, ed. Christopher Bryant and Claude Marois, 290–303 (Montreal: Department of Geography, University of Montreal, 1995).

23 John Campbell Lehr, "Mormon Settlements in Southern Alberta" (MA thesis, University of Alberta, 1971); Archie G. Wilcox, "Founding of the Mormon Community in Alberta" (MA thesis, University of Alberta, 1950).

24 On this aspect of community formation, see Benedict Anderson, *Imagined Communities: Reflections on the Origin and Spread of Nationalism*, 4th ed. (London: Verso, 2006).

25 Max Weber, *The Protestant Ethic and the Spirit of Capitalism*, trans. Talcott Parsons (New York: Dover, 2003).

26 William M. Baker, "Lethbridge: Founding the Community to 1914: A Visual History," Occasional Paper No. 27, Lethbridge Historical Society, Alberta, 1992.

27 John MacLean, *Canadian Savage Folk: The Native Tribes of Canada* (Toronto: W. Briggs, 1896).

28 Cy Gonick, "Save the Oldman River," *Canadian Dimension* 25, no. 8 (December 1991): 6–8 at 7.

29 Brant and Brant Native Development Consultants, *Indian Band Economic Development Potential and Its Implications for Indian Self-Government: A report to Indian and Northern Affairs Canada* (Deseronto, ON: Brant and Brant Native Development Consultants, 1985).

30 Helen Buckley, *From Wooden Ploughs to Welfare: Why Indian Policy Failed in the Prairie Provinces* (Vancouver: UBC Press, 1992).

31 Brant and Brant Native Development Consultants, *Indian Band*, appendix 2.

32 Glenn, *Once Upon an Oldman*, 40.

33 Fred D. Bradley to Chief Peter Yellowhorn, 9 August 1984, copy in possession of Yale D. Belanger.

34 Peter Yellowhorn, in Glenn, *Once Upon an Oldman*, 45.

35 Peigan Band Council, "Proclamation, Peigan Indian Nation: Respecting Title to Water and Water Rights in the Oldman River," January 1986.

36 Thomas R. Berger to Chief Peter Yellowhorn, 15 August 1988, copy in possession of Yale D. Belanger.

37 Martha Kostuch, submission to Victor Lichtinger, Executive Director, Commission for Environmental Cooperation, 4 October 1997, http://www.cec.org/Storage/68/6226_97-6-SUB-E.pdf.

38 Thomas R. Berger to Chief Peter Yellowhorn.

39 Lonefighters, untitled press release, 9 May 1990, copy in possession of Yale D. Belanger.

40 Gonick, "Save the Oldman River."

41 Four Directions Teachings.com, "Piikani Blackfoot Elders: Dr. Reg Crowshoe and Geoff Crow Eagle," n.d., http://www.fourdirectionsteachings.com/blackfoot_bio.html.

42 Hugh A. Dempsey, "Onistah-Sokaksin," in *Dictionary of Canadian Biography*, vol. 10, *1871–1880* (Toronto: University of Toronto Press; Quebec City: Presses de l'Université Laval, 2003), http://www.biographi.ca/en/bio/onistah_sokaksin_10E.html.

43 Nelson Small Legs Jr, in Joan Ryan, *Wall of Words: The Betrayal of Urban Indians* (Toronto: Peter Martin Associates, 1978), 40.

44 Nelson Small Legs Sr, in Brian Brennan, "Son's Death Spurred Father to Action," *Calgary Herald*, 12 February 1994, B2.

45 Jackie Red Crow, *The Blood Land Dispute: Collector's Edition* (Blood Reserve, AB: Blood Band Council, 1980).

46 Peter Verburg, "The Price of Irresolution," *Alberta Report* 22, no. 41 (25 September 1995): 17.

47 Glenn, *Once Upon an Oldman*, 77.

48 It was anticipated that the reservoir would result in the destruction of 300 archaeological sites, 46 historic sites, and as mentioned, graves and other Piikani sacred sites.

49 Bill Arsene and Rick Casson, both in Lorraine Locherty, "Farmers Call for Army as Peigans Threaten River," *Calgary Herald*, 5 August 1990, A1.

50 "Alberta Ignoring Dam Protest," *Vancouver Sun*, 7 August 1990, D10.

51 Jan MacDonald, "Indian Guards Harassed at Water-Diversion Site; Whites Drive to Reserve to Hurl Racial Insults," *Edmonton Journal*, 16 August 1990, A7.

52 Ibid.

53 Ibid.

54 Milton Born With A Tooth, in "Faction Intends to Divert River with or without Band's Approval," *Ottawa Citizen*, 17 August 1990, A3.

55 Gordon Shrake, in MacDonald, "Indian Guards Harassed," A7.

56 Glenn North Peigan, in "Faction Intends to Divert River," A3.

57 Ken Rostad, in "Attempt to Divert River Has Failed, Minister Says," *Montreal Gazette*, 21 August 1990, F8.

58 In ibid.

59 MacDonald, "Indian Guards Harassed," A7.

60 Mike Lamb, "Peigans Want Quick Meeting on Dam," *Calgary Herald*, 14 August 1990, A3.

61 Lydia Scott, in ibid.

62 Milton Born With A Tooth, in "Faction Intends to Divert River," A3.

63 Ralph Jesperson, in "Attempt to Divert River Has Failed, Minister Says," *Montreal Gazette*, 21 August 1990, F8.

64 Ken Rostad, in Lynda Shorten, "Gov't Refuses Peigan Talks 'til Diversion Bid Stopped," *Edmonton Journal*, 23 August 1990, D13.

65 "Peigans Beef Up Oldman Diversion," *Edmonton Journal*, 27 August 1990, A8.

66 Jim Morris, "Alberta Native Band Says Breakdowns Have Delayed Its Diversion of Disputed River," *Ottawa Citizen*, 28 August 1990, A4.

67 Susan Mate, Ashley Geddes, and Phillip Jang, "Militant Peigans Say They'll Die for Cause," *Calgary Herald*, 30 August 1990, A1.

68 "Alberta Band Restricts Water to Farms, Towns," *Toronto Star*, 30 August 1990, A10.

69  Milton Born With A Tooth to Martha Kostuch, Friends of the Oldman River Society, n.d., copy in possession of Yale D. Belanger.

70  "Alberta Band Restricts Water," A10.

71  "Court Injunction Halts Peigans' River Diversion," *Windsor Star*, 31 August 1990, A10.

72  Devalon Small Legs and Leonard Bastien, in "Injunction Halts Bid to Divert River; Lonefighters' Leaders Defiant in Fight against Oldman Dam," *Globe and Mail*, 31 August 1990, A5; Devalon Small Legs, Glenn North Peigan, and Leonard Bastien, in Jim Morris, "Peigans Ordered to Halt Diversion; Indians Debating Whether to Obey Alberta Court," *Montreal Gazette*, 31 August 1990, B1.

73  Alberta, *Métis Settlements Act: Métis Settlements Land Registry Regulation*, Alberta Regulation 361/91, 1990.

74  "Prospect of Bloodshed Won't Stop Diversion of Dam, Indian Says," *Ottawa Citizen*, 1 September 1990, F7.

75  "Siddon to Meet Alberta Natives," *Montreal Gazette*, 5 September 1990, B1.

76  Leonard Bastien, in Mike Lamb, "Peigan Band Backs Lonefighters' Battle against Dam," *Calgary Herald*, 11 September 1990, B4.

77  Willie Littlechild, in Lynda Shorten, "Use of Troops 'Hurts' Native MP; But Tory Won't Resign," *Edmonton Journal*, 5 September 1990, A3.

78  Susan Mate, "Siddon Cancels Trip to Alberta," *Calgary Herald*, 6 September 1990, A8.

79  Owen Maguire, in "Police Retreated to Avoid Conflict with Lonefighters, Trial Told," *Edmonton Journal*, 25 February 1994, A8.

80  Milton Born With A Tooth, in "Shots Fired as Indians Protest Dam," *Toronto Star*, 8 September 1990, A12.

81  Milton Born With A Tooth, in Susan Mate, Rick Mofina, and Ashley Geddes, "Dam Standoff: Lonefighter Vows He Won't Give Up," *Calgary Herald*, 8 September 1990, A1.

82  Devalon Small Legs, in Jennifer Bain and Bob Bergen, "RCMP Withdraw from Reserve; Lonefighters Celebrate but Police May Be Back Today," *Edmonton Journal*, 9 September 1990, A2.

83  Milton Born With A Tooth, in "Militant Lonefighters Leader Vows to Defy Court on Oldman Diversion," *Ottawa Citizen*, 10 September 1990, A3.

84  "Preventing an Oka Here," *Edmonton Journal*, 11 September 1990, A12.

85  Leonard Bastien, in Lamb, "Peigan Band," B4.

86  Devalon Small Legs, in Susan Mate and Anthony Johnson, "Angry Peigans Fight On," *Calgary Herald*, 14 September 1990, A1.

87  Jim Horsman, in Ross Henderson, "Lonefighters' Actions 'Intolerable,'" *Edmonton Journal*, 14 September 1990, A7.

88  Richard Wagamese, "Lonefighters Call Dam 'Desecration,'" *Calgary Herald*, 26 September 1990, A5, emphasis in original.

89  Ken Rostad, in Katherine Bell, "Lonefighters Group Shut Out of Talks on Dispute over Oldman River Dam," *Montreal Gazette*, 15 November 1990, B4. Eventually, Born With A Tooth also utilized the courts, filing a statement of claim in 1992 that cited the adverse effects of mercury poisoning in a last ditch attempt to halt filling the reservoir.

90  "Oldman River Update," *Canadian Dimension* 26, no. 2 (March 1992): 41.

91  W.A. Ross, in Glenn, *Once Upon an Oldman*, 103–4.

92  Ibid., 104–7.

93  Ibid., 110.

94  Ibid.

95  Canada, *Federal Environmental Assessment and Review Process 42: Oldman River Dam, Report of the Environmental Assessment Panel, May 1992* (Hull, QC: Federal Environmental Assessment Review Office, 1992).

96  Monique Hébert, "The Oldman River Decision of the Supreme Court of Canada," background paper BP-287E, Research Branch, Library of Parliament, Ottawa, 1992.

97  Glenn, *Once Upon an Oldman*, 110–13.

98  Ibid., 117.

99  Ibid., 117–19.

100  Ibid., 121–2.

101  Ibid., 127.

102  Ibid., 235–6.

103  Wendy-Anne Thompson, "Band Says No to $64M Offer: Peigan Nation's Vote Results In," *Calgary Herald*, 13 December 2001, B8; Shari Narine, "$64.3 Million Settlement Gets Thumbs Up from Community," *Alberta Sweetgrass* 9, no. 11 (October 2002): 4.

# The Tragedy of Ipperwash

P. WHITNEY LACKENBAUER
with VICTOR GULEWITSCH

The death of Native protestor Anthony O'Brien (Dudley) George on 6 September 1995 after a confrontation with the Ontario Provincial Police (OPP) at Ipperwash Provincial Park has become a quintessential example of government perfidy and aggression over Native land claims. The decision by members of the self-proclaimed "Stoney Point First Nation" to occupy the park reflected a tortured history of dispossession, divisions within the local Native community, and political frustration. After decades of failed attempts to secure a return of the former Stony Point Reserve[1] – which the military had appropriated from the Kettle and Stony Point Band in 1942 to create Camp Ipperwash – a faction of the local Aboriginal community decided to occupy the military ranges in May 1993. This decision divided the local Native community and complicated relationships with the federal government, which faced competing interests and conflicting demands for the return of the camp. Although the military announced the following year that the land would be returned to the Kettle and Stony Point First Nation, frustrated Stoney Pointers decided to unilaterally "reclaim" the army barracks and administrative quarters in July 1995. The military's decision to withdraw rather than physically confront the occupiers emboldened the Stoney Pointers and outside supporters who came to the army camp. Their decision to occupy neighbouring Ipperwash Provincial Park led to the fateful confrontation with police that culminated in George's death and provoked a massive public inquiry into government and police behaviour during confrontations with Aboriginal people.

The Ipperwash Inquiry's extensive final report, published in 2007, provides a detailed narrative of the political and bureaucratic developments that culminated in confrontation in the fall of 1995.[2] This chapter does not replicate the detailed analysis of decision making within the OPP and the Ontario government that the inquiry undertook to allocate responsibility for the tragic outcome. Instead, it focuses on the complex history of the Kettle and Stony Point First Nation and its land base, relationships between the elected band council and the dissident group that decided to occupy Camp Ipperwash and Ipperwash Provincial Park, the strategies and tactics used by the various stakeholders during the occupations, and the media and political fallout from the crisis. The inquiry report (particularly the executive summary) uses vague terms like "First Nations people" to conceal or downplay divisions within the Kettle and Stony Point community, the competing struggles for legitimacy between rival groups, and the dilemmas that these power contests posed for band leaders and government officials. This case study highlights the internal competition between Aboriginal claimants and suggests that the internal situation plays a central role in how land claims are pursued and resolved. The media and the inquiry's simplistic juxtaposition of "First Nations," "warriors," and "government" interests do not adequately convey the social and historical subtleties at play.

## NATIONS, BANDS, LAND, AND FAMILIES: THE CHIPPEWAS OF KETTLE AND STONY POINT

A detailed knowledge of community history is essential to understanding the local social divisions and political factionalism within First Nations that often underlie disputes over land, identity, and leadership such as the Ipperwash Crisis. Although the "dissident" group of Stoney Pointers may be characterized as the disgruntled descendants of residents evicted from their reserve in 1942, their history of dispossession extends to the early nineteenth century. Perhaps even more fundamental is the issue of the ethnic, "tribal," or geographic origins of the populations who occupy the Kettle and Stony Point Reserves. Today most community members are status Canadian Indians as defined by the Indian Act. After the American Revolution, however, the distinction between Chippewas (British Indians) and Potawatomis (American Indians) divided them into groups receiving differential rights and status. The British colonial administration failed to distinguish who was who throughout the treaty negotiations after the War of 1812 and did not fully understand the seasonally migratory subsistence patterns of the Anishinabek. The national border created by British and American colonial governments became a barrier to the normal operation of Indigenous social, political, and subsistence systems.

The ancestors of the Georges of Stony Point became displaced persons under the American forced removal policies beginning in 1830. After finding a place of refuge at Stony Point in 1837, members of the family were forced to give up their homes and leave Canada in 1900 after the Sarnia Band Council determined that they had no right of membership or land ownership. By 1942 some had regained their land only to lose it to the state with the creation of Camp Ipperwash. In 1995, 165 years after the family's first dispossession, Dudley George's life abruptly ended because of his dedication to reclaiming his family's place in the world.

The Ojibwa (Chippewas) ceded over 2 million acres to the Crown in Treaties 25 and 29, which created four reserves totalling 17,951 acres. The treaty did not identify the 440 Chippewas by band designation, but discussions as early as 1818 mentioned the need to create reserves for specific kin-based patrilineal bands. The treaty also contains the signatures of eighteen "Chiefs and principal men" with unspecified connections to local populations. Nevertheless, Native groups that utilized the southern Lake Huron shoreline and the Aux Sable River system were encouraged to settle in permanent communities on the Kettle and Stony Point Reserves.[3]

Chippewa power structures were complicated. Chief Wahpagas of Stony Point, a signatory to the 1825 provisional treaty, was descended from a line of chiefs who had controlled the Aux Sable River Valley prior to European contact. (This lineage was distinct from that of the band at Sarnia, where the traditional leadership claimed origins from Michigan.) Local petitions and sworn declarations from Kettle and Stony Point elders traced their lineage back to the earliest known ancestor of Wahpagas – Chief Mamahwegezhego, born around 1700.[4] The descendants of Wahpagas, namely the Johnstons, were recognized as the hereditary chiefs of Stony Point. Oshawawanoo, or John Big Knife,[5] a Shawnee or possibly of mixed Chippewa-Shawnee ancestry, was reputed to be Tecumseh's nephew and had settled at Kettle Point with his half-brother, Shegwahnahbik, or Grindstone, in 1815. The descendants of Big Knife include the Shawnoos, Sapahs, Davids, Pewashs, and Shawkences. Elders of the family were considered to be the legitimate hereditary leaders of Kettle Point until the imposition of Indian Act elections in the 1870s.[6]

The entry into Upper Canada of dispossessed British-allied Natives from the United States further complicated the situation. The majority of these families were Potawatomi from Wisconsin, who had resided for a time in Michigan and are frequently referred to as the "Saginaw Indians."[7] The British encouraged these Potawatomi migrants to settle on established reserves, but they were not signatories to the treaties, and both the British and Canadian administrations failed to clarify their legal status or their rights to land and treaty annuity payments. By 1839 five Potawatomi families had settled in with the few Chippewa families residing at Stony Point. Their descendants eventually came to be known by the surnames George, Henry, Wahndahsega, Thomas, and Wolf. The leader of the Potawatomi group was Manidoka, or Spirit Maker, eventually known as George Manidoka – missionaries christened his sons with the surname George in the 1850s. (By the twentieth century many Stony Point residents were Manidoka's descendants, who had intermarried with the local population of Kettle and Stony Point.) Although the Potawatomi families were generally welcomed by their hosts, some were treated as foreign Indians or squatters well into the twentieth century, and their ambiguous legal status with regard to lands and annuities remained a point of contention. This complex history is essential to understanding the underlying tensions that defined local political factionalism in the early 1990s, when the "Stoney Pointers" sought to be recognized as members of an independent First Nation.

Efforts to remove "foreign Indians" from the Sarnia Band's reserves in the 1870s sparked a major debate about the Potawatomis' rights to land and treaty annuity payments, which eventually culminated in efforts by Kettle and Stony Point leaders to form their own band.[8] Chippewa residents of Kettle and Stony Point jointly resolved to adopt the Stony Point Potawatomis in 1873, and E.A. Meredith, the deputy minister of the interior, supported this recommendation. However, the Sarnia Band Council refused the adoption and renewed its efforts to displace the Potawatomis six years later. In response, the Kettle and Stony Point leaders petitioned Indian Affairs to disregard the council, to grant status to the Potawatomis, to allow them to retain their land and resources, not to survey or subdivide the reserves, and to grant them distinct band status.[9] They emphasized their desire to retain a traditional collective land use pattern, and chiefs of both reserves resolved never to allow a survey that involved subdivision and individual allotment of lands. Their reasons were clearly stated: their ancestors had strictly forbidden it, and prominent local whites had advised them that it could ultimately be the means through which they would lose their lands.[10]

The Pottawatomi families continued to face persecution from the Sarnia Band Council and Indian Affairs, despite local efforts to support their claims to the lands and status. Council pushed through resolutions to survey and subdivide the Kettle and Stony Point lands without any representation from those reserves, whose councillors either boycotted or were excluded from meetings.[11] Despite clear objections from the Chippewas living at Kettle and Stony Point, a survey and subdivision were carried out in 1901. Sarnia chief Wahwanosh's council had resolved the year before that seven families at Stony Point had to vacate their residences and move to a single 50 acre lot in the southeast corner of the reserve – without compensation. If they refused, they would have to "return" to the United States – a strange phrase given that all of the original migrants from the United States were deceased.[12] The heads of these families appealed to Indian Affairs through a lawyer, who learned that officials considered the 1873 adoption to be invalid. When the Chippewa leaders at Kettle and Stony Point appealed on behalf of these "oppressed families" – including the Georges – who "felt deeply attached" to the land and "adored" the country, the department remained unsympathetic to "people and their ancestors [who] have always been regarded by this Department as Non-British Indians and trespassers." The government had recently taken steps "to dispossess them of the lands upon which they have been squatting" and encourage them to return to the United States. The following autumn, the Sarnia Band Council allowed recognized band members to purchase the farms of the Potawatomis. Local oral tradition indicates that after losing their land at Stony Point, the Potawatomi families left for the United States. Some of them returned several years later and eventually received membership and location tickets to unclaimed parcels of land at Stony Point after the Kettle and Stony Point Band (KSPB) was created as a separate entity in 1919.[13]

The band members living on the Kettle and Stony Point Reserves, furious that the larger Sarnia community overwhelmed their interests, continued to petition the Department of Indian Affairs to form a distinct band in the early twentieth century. Although some commentators have deliberately distorted the evidence to assert that the Kettle Point and Stony Point "bands" undertook this campaign as separate entities, leading to a distinct band on each reserve,[14] the archival record clearly indicates that chiefs and councillors lobbied to form a separate band spanning the two reserves. They succeeded in May 1919. Indian Affairs administered the Kettle and Stony Point residents and lands as a single entity with a common band list, a shared trust fund account, and a common chief and council. Residents adopted practices that reaffirmed some internal cultural distinction between the two communities: members from both reserves elected a common band chief, but it was customary for residents of each reserve to elect councillors to represent their particular local interests in band decision making. Some members held location tickets on both reserves, maintaining a residence at Kettle Point and a farm or a wood lot at Stony Point, for example. Furthermore, residents of both reserves voted together on land surrenders, and all shared in the proceeds, irrespective of whether they lived on the affected reserve.[15]

## BEACHFRONT SURRENDERS AND THE ESTABLISHMENT OF IPPERWASH PROVINCIAL PARK

It took less than ten years for the territorial sanctity of the Kettle and Stony Point Band's land base to break down. Band members saw the potential for tourist income and proposed that the band lease cottage lots in 1923. Accordingly, the band council decided to neither sell nor lease its valuable waterfront property. Three years later, however, local non-Native real estate speculators and investors convinced the federal government's local Indian agent that, since the lands had no agricultural value, the Indians should surrender 83 acres of beach at Kettle Point. The local member of Parliament, Ross Gray, intervened on behalf of the investors to facilitate the surrender. The 1927 surrender vote was divisive and was tainted by allegations of bribes paid to counsellors for voting in favour of the sale. (Furthermore, Chippewa traditional leaders whose ancestors had signed the treaty objected to the Potowatomi-descendant males having a vote.) Nevertheless, twenty-seven of thirty-nine individuals on the KSPB voter's list favoured the surrender. In 1929 the band voted under similar circumstances to surrender the entire 377 acre waterfront at Stony Point to the Crown. Sarnia real estate agent W.J. Scott purchased the land for $13,500 cash. Some band members again expressed clear disfavour, arguing that the surrender was tainted with bribes and coercion. Several elders again contested the right to vote of the nontreaty Indians. In the end, twenty-five of twenty-eight KSPB voters endorsed the surrender.[16] The Stony Point beachfront thus passed into private hands.

A few years after the surrender of the beach lands at Stony Point, several hundred local non-Native residents signed a petition requesting that part of the tract be made into a public park. Following discussions between municipal, provincial, and federal departments, the Province of Ontario paid $10,000 to acquire 109 acres from W.J. Scott to establish Ipperwash Provincial Park in December 1936.[17] During the construction of the park the following summer, two points of conflict emerged with the KSPB. The first concerned the province's practice of freely removing shale for fill from the lake bed along the shoreline of Kettle Point to build the park.[18] The second concerned the discovery of a Native cemetery within the park boundaries. Kettle and Stony Point residents worked on park construction through 1937, and some expressed concern about the desecration of their "old Burial Grounds" within the park boundaries. The KSPB council passed a resolution requesting that Indian Affairs ask the provincial government to mark and fence off the old cemetery so that it would be protected. The local Indian agent, J C. Tremouth, supported this "entirely reasonable" resolution and forwarded it to his superiors, who submitted it to the provincial Department of Lands and Forests. Apart from a favourable reply, no further correspondence regarding the cemetery issue has been found. The matter was overlooked in the rush to complete the works on the new park, officially named Ipperwash Beach Provincial Park on 24 June 1938.[19] As a result, the old cemetery remained unmarked under a parking lot.

## THE CREATION OF CAMP IPPERWASH

The military's appropriation of the Stony Point Reserve to create Camp Ipperwash has been depicted as a national crime, a brazen example of the federal government's draconian tendencies during the Second World War. The story has been narrated in detail elsewhere,[20] but the general outline is essential to understanding the frustration felt by the KSPB and the Stony Point residents in particular.

In early 1942 military officials approached Indian Affairs about establishing an army training centre on the Stony Point Reserve. When the matter was put before the KSPB on 1 April, it voted resoundingly against surrendering the land to the military for the sum of $50,000. Nevertheless, the government got its way (despite Toronto lawyer B.J. Spencer-Pitt's attempts to advocate for the band), forcing the removal of the Stony Point residents to the Kettle Point Reserve. Indian Affairs was placed in the awkward position of helping the Department of National Defence (DND) to acquire Stony Point while it was also the legal guardian of the band's resources. Using the War Measures Act, Cabinet could take over properties with or without landholder consent. On 14 April 1942 it appropriated the reserve for "military purposes." The order-in-council noted that "if, subsequent to the termination of the war, the property was not required by DND negotiations would then be entered into to transfer the same back to the Indians at a reasonable price to be determined by mutual agreement." Was this a promise to return the land? A simple pledge to entertain negotiations? An affirmation that the military could occupy the land as long as required? These questions would cause confusion in evolving historical contexts and would plague discussions of the appropriation a half-century later.[21]

Once the war ended, the band lobbied the Indian policy community to secure the return of Stony Point to its rightful owners. Although the DND and Indian Affairs seemed poised to reach an agreement in early 1948, the return of the reserve was left in abeyance for undisclosed reasons. In the ensuing decades, Camp Ipperwash served as a training area for the Royal Canadian Regiment and for militia and cadet units in southwestern Ontario. A few Kettle Point residents worked at the camp as caretakers and cooks, and band members cut timber and visited the Stony Point graveyard by special arrangement. These few concessions to the band hardly offset the psychological and economic costs of the army's presence. In 1991 Ronald George, a local lawyer, testified on behalf of the Stony Point locatees (former residents) to parliamentarians: "As Kettle Point veterans returned and the population underwent a baby boom, demand for housing exacerbated the resentment at Kettle Point toward the former residents of the Stoney Point reserve. Because the Stoney Point natives occupied the available house sites, young Kettle Point natives were also being forced off the Kettle Point reserve. By the 1950's the realization that the Stoney Point reserve would not be returned in the foreseeable future began to sink into everyone's consciousness. To Kettle Point, the temporary 'refugees' had become a permanent irritation."[22]

When Camp Ipperwash was not returned after the war, the continued alienation of Stony Point continued to unravel the political fabric of a band that had existed on two reserves. The displaced residents of Stony Point lost any distinctive community voice in the postwar Kettle Point community, and some locatee spokespersons alleged that they were systematically marginalized in internal band politics. Good land at Kettle Point was at a premium with little room to accommodate either the growing families of Kettle Point or those displaced from Stony Point. Some relocated houses were severely damaged in the move, and others were placed in swampy locations. Several families were apparently forced to live off-reserve, with little prospect of returning home, contrary to what they believed had been promised once the war was over.[23] Because the locatees were bereft of political power under the new band regime, their frustrations would simmer for decades and have a dramatic impact on developments in the late 1980s and 1990s.

## EARLY EFFORTS TO RECLAIM CAMP IPPERWASH

During the 1960s and 1970s, the fate of Camp Ipperwash, and the plight of local Indians, attracted political and media attention. A 1968 resolution of the Kettle and Stony Point Band Council encapsulated its continuing claim to the land. First and foremost, the band's members understood that the land was taken from them for wartime use and would be returned when the war ended. Second, Chief Charles Shawkence and band officials were "dedicated to becoming independent in the management of our affairs but are seriously handicapped through a shortage of revenue." Developing the former Stony Point Reserve could generate "the required funds to enable us to reach our goals." Officials of the Department of Indian Affairs and Northern Development (DIAND) now suggested that the military was being unreasonable, not the Indians. Minister Jean Chrétien signed a letter stressing the band's need for socio-economic development and its longstanding "dissatisfaction" with the government's handling of Ipperwash. Recent cuts to Canadian Forces bases made it appropriate for the DND to reconsider its requirements.[24]

DIAND officials insisted that the band and the DND should negotiate a solution, wanting as little to do with the issue as possible.[25] However, the military wanted to retain the land because it was the only regional centre for regular force, militia, and cadet training. Furthermore, it was heavily contaminated with unexploded ordnance and would cost millions to clean up. The Kettle and Stony Point Band's "tactics of embarrassment" placed the DND in a precarious political situation, and the negotiation process revealed the array of interests involved. The band's lawyer advised the chief and council not to accept a lump sum payment and explained to military officials that he spoke for the band, not for the locatees – the families living at Stony Point who had been displaced in 1942. However, the DND refused to settle with multiple parties and insisted that the band and the DIAND would have to take responsibility for all of the locatees' claims. The conspicuous absence of the DIAND at the negotiating meetings forced the military to deal with the liability issues alone. The DIAND, as both a branch of government and the band's trustee, seemed reluctant to support either party.[26]

The negotiation logjam was broken in 1979. The DND and the KSPB agreed that Camp Ipperwash would be returned at no cost – including the lucrative beachfront properties – when it was no longer needed and that the DND would reconsider its ongoing need for the property at "regular intervals." Furthermore, the band would receive about $2.5 million in compensation, interest, and expenses. In a 6 September 1980 referendum, band members voted 211 to 54 to accept the settlement.[27] Despite the resounding majority of support at the ballot box, the Kettle and Stony Point Band remained divided. The settlement package made no reference to individual claims, and about fifty descendants of the original Stony Point locatees picketed the entrance to Camp Ipperwash to protest the agreement immediately after the votes were cast. They objected to the cash settlement and demanded that the land be returned specifically to them – not to the band at large. The following month, a Stony Point Defence Committee was formed whose lawyer informed the DND that "Under the law there exist three (3) separate and distinct legal entities which make up an Indian Band. These are the individual members, the Band as a collectivity of its members and the Band Council. Each entity has specific rights and authority afforded them respectively pursuant to the Indian Act (Canada). In this connection, there is a very real question as to whether the Camp Ipperwash proposal was negotiated and/or included all proper parties. The Band Council may not have been authorized by the Band nor its individual members to act on their behalf."[28] Questioning the validity of the vote and alleging that the band council had breached its legal obligations, the committee declared the settlement agreement null and void, despite Cabinet approval in early 1981.[29]

Nonetheless, the compensation monies were paid to the KSPB that year in a manner that elicited allegations of unfairness from the locatees. Four years later, the band reached a further agreement with the DND to access the camp's natural resources, to hunt and fish, and for spiritual purposes. However, local frustrations simmered, and the band's lawyer complained that community members had not secured employment at the camp as promised. A vocal minority also complained that they had not received adequate compensation money – or that it should have flowed only to the original Stony Point descendants. A Stony Point

Association undertook independent action to pursue locatee land interests.[30] Obviously, the band was not speaking with a single voice.

An institutionalized land claims process created opportunities for Aboriginal communities to pursue their grievances with the Crown, but it also channelled and limited the discourse. The elected Kettle and Stony Point First Nation (KSPFN) Band Council maintained during negotiations that it represented a common band with legitimate rights to Camp Ipperwash. A dissident faction of Stony Point locatees and descendants, who perceived internal discrimination by the Kettle Point leadership, began to meet in the late 1980s, wrote letters to federal politicians, handed out pamphlets, and staged protests in front of the army camp. They wanted the land returned to them and compensation so that they could re-establish their community at Stony Point.[31] By 1992 they had declared themselves a separate "Stoney Point First Nation" or "band," accused Ottawa of negotiating with the wrong "band," questioned the legitimacy of the elected council at Kettle Point, and asserted that they were legally entitled to the camp lands and additional compensation – it had to be returned exclusively to them.[32]

The assertion of independent status was strategic. The land claims process did not accommodate negotiations with Aboriginal groups that were not recognized as bands. The "Stoney Pointers," by self-constructing themselves as a band with a land base, thus declared their legal right to consultation. History, their spokesperson Maynard T. George argued, demonstrated that the Stony Point "band" had existed as a distinct social and political entity at the time of the appropriation. Although the Stoney Pointers claimed that this assertion was substantiated in oral tradition and archival records, the preponderance of historical paperwork confirmed that Ottawa had dealt only with a single Kettle and Stony Point band since 1919.[33] Nevertheless, in a new political and social climate, the Stoney Point "band" found ready outlets for its perspective. The local and national media were attracted to the plight of this small group doubly oppressed by the government and the Kettle and Stony Point First Nation Band Council. Their grievances and conspiracy theories appeared in articles and on the evening news. Even the House of Commons Standing Committee on Aboriginal Affairs, still recoiling from its Oka inquiries, sympathized with a Stoney Point delegation in December 1991. It casually dismissed government testimonies that the Stoney Pointers had no legal, independent status; these parliamentarians displayed little faith in senior military perspectives and mistrusted government behaviour. "The government [must] rectify a serious injustice done to the Stoney Point First Nation," the committee recommended in 1992, "by returning the land at Stoney Point to its original inhabitants and their descendants from whom the land was seized."[34] In short, the committee repudiated the official government position and offered legitimacy to the Stoney Pointers' claim.

For their part, federal politicians were anxious to see the camp's return to the KSPFN. In 1990 former minister of Indian affairs Doug Frith went on record in support of the elected band's reclamation efforts, citing the government's "legal and a moral duty." The next year, Minister of Indian Affairs Tom Siddon also sided with the band. "The return of the base will greatly benefit the community both socially and economically," he explained. "The band needs land for hunting purposes and the area fronting on Lake Huron has excellent potential for summer cottage development. The return of this land will not only resolve a long-ongoing sense of grievance in the community but will also allow the Indian community to build a better future for themselves."[35] The military, however, maintained that it still needed the camp. Its justifications now seemed even more tenuous. Aboriginal representatives spoke of intimate spiritual and economic ties and stressed their vision of community building. Media reports made frequent mention of an old Stony Point burial ground as well as utopian images of a vibrant reserve community prior to 1942.[36] The DND's narrower, legalistic position was less in tune with the public mood: the military's continued presence seemed immoral. After half a century, the Indians and their supporters argued, it was time to return Ipperwash to its rightful owners.

The media were overwhelmingly sympathetic to the Native cause and served as the primary outlet for public history battles. Journalists scrutinized developments and pushed the military to right a wrongful situation. "We don't blame Ottawa for expropriating the land in the first place," a *Sarnia Observer* editorial carefully explained in early 1991. "Canada faced a grave crisis in 1942 and the government had the right to do whatever it felt was necessary for the war effort. But the war has been over for more than 45 years." The injustice and the imperative were clear. Things became more confusing when journalists suggested to whom the land should be returned. Almost two years later, the *Observer* still supported the camp's return to the local Natives but recognized that unless the competing Kettle Point and Stoney Point groups "buried the hatchet," the military could not return it. "As it stands, division in the two groups is playing directly into the hands of Ottawa, which is seldom inclined to hand over prime real estate or pay out compensation packages needlessly," the editor opined. "It's an old adage but one equally true today: winners divide and conquer, losers divide and fall."[37] The triangle of intrigue, which pitted the elected Kettle and Stony Point Band Council against a self-proclaimed Stoney Point "band," created a muddle that defied easy solutions.[38]

## THE OCCUPATION OF CAMP IPPERWASH

In the growing history war, militant and romantic rhetoric seemed more compelling than voices encouraging patience, due process, and any sort of compromise. Indeed, conflicting identities and internal divisions within the Native community made any resolution improbable. In early May 1993 "Chief" Carl George of the "Chippewas of Stoney Point First Nation #43" told military and OPP officials that his people were planning to occupy Camp Ipperwash peacefully. A notice drafted by Stoney Point historian Maynard T. George explained,

> We have come home in the name of our people, tradition and custom.
>    We are not claiming that Stoney Point Reserve No. 43 in the name of only those uprooted, but also in right of the (1st) first and (2nd) second and third generation children, who's [sic] parents and grandparents have been victimized by the taking of their lands (farms) in 1942 ...
>    We request all outside First Nations, to stay away from our legal takeover, that misrepresentation, or civil disobedience may not occur.
>    We are not hindering the elected Kettle Point Council or people from joining us but, they do not represent us, in any way, shape or form.[39]

On 6 May 1993 "Chief" George and at least fifteen other people entered the army camp off Highway 21, far from the built-up camp area, with tents and an old trailer. They served eviction notices to the military, explained that the occupation was peaceful and that they did not have weapons, and immediately told the media that they would not be leaving the camp and that they wanted it returned. A few weeks later, Carl George and Maynard T. George led about fifty occupiers (including the Manning family and the family of Glenn George) to cut the lock on a gate at the east end of the camp. They did so under the watchful eye of an OPP staff sergeant, who did not intervene, and the media. Some members of the group took up residence indefinitely on the Ipperwash grenade range and refused to leave.[40] The "Stoney Point First Nation," as the occupiers called themselves, soon swelled to more than one hundred – far outnumbering the military caretakers.

This dramatic action, which rejected the negotiated land claims approach advocated by the elected band council, deeply divided the KSPFN. The elected band council condemned the move and distanced itself from what it considered a rogue element. Although it supported elders such as veteran Clifford George, who wanted to return to their homeland, the chief and council believed that the actions of the Stoney Pointers would impede further progress in their negotiations with the federal government. In May 1993 Chief Tom Bressette met with a representative of the Ministry of Natural Resources and explained that the KSPFN did not recognize the Stoney Pointers as a First Nation, nor did it condone the actions of the occupiers. The following month, he indicated that he and his council were prepared to officially negotiate with the DND to secure a return of the camp and asked the occupiers to come forth with copies of the location tickets upon which they were basing their claims to the land. However, attempts that summer to synchronize the efforts of the band with those of the Stoney Point group failed because the elected band council rejected the assertion that the Kettle Point and Stoney Point groups had been autonomous First Nations in the past.[41]

The DND, for its part, was nonconfrontational. When the Stoney Pointers served the military with an eviction notice on 18 May and gave the soldiers thirty days to withdraw, the army decided not to pull out – but it allowed the occupants to remain. Their occupation of the southeast corner of the camp did not have a major effect on the use of the training area, and the military believed that it could continue "business as usual." For the time being, the dissident faction focused on community building: they held a celebratory powwow, began fundraising, erected a small church at the site, elected their own chief and councillors to legitimize their assertion of independent status, and purported that their band was returning to its pre-1942 state. Friends and family offered support, as did Christian coalitions, the Mennonites, and the Canadian Auto Workers. Soon the occupiers' shacks and trailers claimed more ground, and they removed the DND's signs from the beach area.[42]

The Stoney Pointers' activities escalated in tempo and in tenor. They staged a walk from Stony Point to Ottawa to draw attention to their cause (which attracted little media coverage), and minor confrontations with camp personnel "slowly escalated."[43] The most extreme occupiers intimidated non-Native neighbours with bonfires and chanting and set up roadblocks to charge public visitors who wanted access to the adjoining public beach. Military policemen began to complain about random gunfire and sandbagged their detachment headquarters.[44] During the summer training season, journalists began to question whether the standoff would become another Oka. Occupiers felt "harassed" by low-flying surveillance helicopters, and in late August one of them (Abraham George) took action. When an aircrew found a bullet lodged in a helicopter fuselage after a routine patrol over Camp Ipperwash on 23 August 1993, occupant Clifford George told journalists that "people can only stand so much." He told reporters that the residents were peaceful and did not have any arms (a claim later belied by testimonies at the Ipperwash Inquiry), but other local inhabitants began to worry about the threat posed by camp "criminals" and "terrorists" who made the area increasingly dangerous. The KSPFN council tried to resolve issues with the "splinter group," but Chief Tom Bressette eventually asked the premier to cut off welfare assistance to the dissident faction, arguing that the occupation would otherwise continue in perpetuity.[45]

The February 1994 federal budget announced that Camp Ipperwash would be closed and turned over to the KSPFN. "This day will be celebrated as a landmark victory for all members of the Kettle and Stony Point First Nation ... for all those who fought for the return of the land since 1942, and for our generations yet to come," Chief Bressette announced to local band members. "We have persevered and we have won!" Outstanding issues remained unresolved, however, including more compensation for loss of economic use, locatee claims, new infrastructure, and clean-up costs.[46] The military wanted out, and it adopted a nonconfrontational approach while it removed recoverable assets from the camp in anticipation of its transfer to the band. Before the land could be relinquished, however, it had to be cleaned of contamination and unexploded ordnance. Negotiations between the DND and the elected council took place in 1995 but soon broke down over issues of who controlled the proposed environmental assessment.

The First Nation no longer considered the land "safe" for occupancy and now acknowledged that extensive contamination required intensive remediation. Its members wanted the DND to pay them to engage their own independent consultants to assess the unexploded ordnance and wanted international lawyer Charles Lipton of New York (whom they had hired in late 1993) to threaten court action. The DND refused to fund "duplicate" third-party consultant reports and disavowed any responsibility for further damages. This delayed the land's return to reserve status, as did persistent cleavages between the KSPFN and the Stoney Pointers (who demanded recognition as a separate band and the return of the camp to them directly).[47] Deadlock seemed inevitable.

Salient changes had taken place among the increasingly impatient occupiers, who sought to break an unfavourable status quo. Glenn George was elected leader of the group in May 1995 (now described by one critic as "a small group of youngsters and misfits" uninterested in "replicating the orderliness managed by Carl George" to that point), which welcomed militant "warrior" outsiders like Oneida arms dealer Isaac ("Buck") Doxtator and brothers Les and Russ Jewel from Michigan. The rhetoric was sharper, with Glenn George mentioning an "Intifada-style Pontiac Rebellion" and declaring Ipperwash a "sacred healing place" for all Natives.[48] At the same time, other KSPFN members worried that the occupation was turning into a separatist movement.[49] Dudley George, a fun-loving protestor who "delighted in irritating the soldiers and police" and regularly dropped his pants to "moon" them, drove a car around the camp with "Pig Fucker" painted on the side. The Stoney Pointers launched a $25 million lawsuit against the "Chippewas of Kettle Point," alleging that the elected council had no authority to negotiate for them, and escalated their direct action campaign in the summer of 1995. Journalists reported a litany of activities: a camp building was "fire-bombed, weapons have been fired, military police and a commissionaire have been assaulted, two vehicles have been rammed and civilians have been accosted and assaulted."[50] Furthermore, the occupiers now walked around the camp at night with rifles.[51] The military caretakers reacted very cautiously to these intimidation tactics,[52] which the occupiers likely saw as a sign of weakness.

On 29 July 1995 the Stoney Pointers decided to take over the "built-up" area of Camp Ipperwash. That day, up to thirty occupiers met on the beach to craft their plans. The federal government would negotiate only with the KSPFN, thus precluding dialogue on an autonomous basis that could secure the lands for the occupiers themselves. Seizing control of the barracks and administrative buildings would also secure warmer accommodations for the winter months. Several occupiers had already appealed to Native people from other Ontario reserves to support the takeover of the barracks, and "Glenn and a few other guys" asked Buck Doxtator whether he knew where they "could get some guys to come down and support them." Doxtator advised them, "you don't need all those men and you just need the people that are here that live here, and the women and children. Go back, it's your homeland." He nevertheless complied with their request, and soon "people just showed up at the camp from everywhere ... Even the States, they were there."[53]

Early that afternoon, without any advance notice to the police or military, the Native occupiers executed their multipronged plan. In a diversionary action, fifteen-year-old Harley George was instructed to drive a bus full of male teenagers into the northern side of the built-up area where the military patrolled. When the military went to investigate the bus, the men, women, and elders entered through other routes. Harley George backed through the gate that obstructed his path, drove up to the door of the drill hall, and tried to push it open with the bus. When a military jeep parked behind him, he threw the gears into reverse and slammed into it, driving it more than forty feet. "I didn't want to be contained by that vehicle," Harley told the inquiry later. "I didn't want to deal with them. I didn't want to talk with them." He also testified that it was an "act of retaliation" for past military actions against his people. As a military policeman struggled with Harley (who initially tried to kick him), eventually using pepper spray, the other teenagers exited through the rear door, and one drove a forklift through the drill hall doors. Soon the other occupiers arrived on the scene, "swarmed" the military commissionaires who were trying to maintain order, and told the military to leave the barracks, even serving an eviction notice to the guard shack.[54]

Captain Doug Smith, who took over as the tactical commander of the security forces at Camp Ipperwash, recognized that the military's position was untenable: the situation was "chaotic" and "mini-confrontations" were taking place "all over" the camp. He instructed the other military personnel not to engage in altercations with the occupiers. He then reached an agreement with the Stoney Pointers' leaders about which buildings they might occupy and which ones were off-limits, but soon they confessed to Smith that they had little to no control over the young men in the group. He brought in two Oneida negotiators to help resolve the conflict. When the occupiers informed them that they had no intention of leaving, the military had two options: use force to eject them or simply evacuate the property itself. (Co-habitation was dismissed as unsafe.) Captain Smith, who wanted to avoid physical confrontation, received authorization that night to pull the remaining thirty or forty army personnel from Camp Ipperwash. He turned over the keys to the occupiers. In the days ahead, the army showed the occupiers how to operate camp equipment and eventually entered into maintenance contracts with some of them.[55] The military did not need another violent standoff like the concurrent one unfolding at Gustafsen Lake in British Columbia (see chapter 8) and simply walked away.

The military decision to vacate the camp heightened local anxieties in the non-Native and Kettle Point communities, who reframed the occupation as a law enforcement issue. Local residents complained about thefts, harassments, and threats by Natives living at the camp, but the OPP refused to enter it.[56] They investigated the takeover of the built-up area and considered the occupiers' aggressive use of the school bus to be "an overt criminal act,"[57] but they did not lay any charges. Inspector John Carson described how the situation had changed:

> This was the first time that, in conjunction with the aggressive behaviour involving a drill hall, there had been altercations with vehicles on the rifle ranges and other roadways within the Base where they had been playing this cat and mouse game. And there had been several near misses involving vehicles as far as near collisions. But this was the first time that the altercation became such that, quite frankly, people's safety was in jeopardy. It was more good luck than good fortune that no one was injured in this incident with the bus and the drill hall. And it was clear as a result of that altercation that, you know, some ... very aggressive demands were being made on the Military. And it wasn't a matter of just verbal rhetoric. This time it had certainly come to explicit behaviour. And ... that was certainly the issue that caused concern and in and amongst this event, comments are ... overheard by persons there that the Ipperwash Park is next. So quite frankly, the – this had gone on. There had ... been a very modest tolerance of the military and the occupiers on the base, but clearly, at this point in time, the tolerance level was no longer appearing to be the norm.[58]

The OPP assigned twelve Emergency Response Team officers to the Ipperwash area, and Inspector Carson deployed four OPP officers disguised as campers to Ipperwash Provincial Park.

The police shared KSPFN concerns that Aboriginal people with no ancestral ties to Stony Point were in the army camp. An Iroquois Nation flag flew at the camp entrance, and elders at Kettle Point were upset that "outsiders" were telling them that they could not enter Stony Point land.

"If you're from Kettle Point you weren't welcome," Chief Tom Bressette explained. "If you were from anywhere else, the door was wide open." On 2 August the KSPFN issued a press release asking nonband members to leave Camp Ipperwash and stressing that negotiations could proceed only if the occupiers worked in conjunction with the KSPFN. Chief Bressette and several councillors tried to deliver the message to the occupiers, but they were "told there were no spokespersons, and that their presence was not welcome." Flyers from the council appealing for unity and cooperation were returned immediately after delivery. That same day, the acting legal director of the Ontario Native Affairs Secretariat in Toronto convened an interministerial committee meeting on Aboriginal emergencies to discuss the camp occupation and the possibility of the Stoney Pointers taking over the adjacent provincial park. The consensus was that the federal government's "dithering" explained the problems at the camp and that the occupation of lands already promised to be returned to "the Native community in the area" did not concern the provincial government. As long as federal officials perceived the situation as "low risk," provincial authorities were not prepared to "really do anything" about what Premier Mike Harris "viewed primarily as a federal issue."[59]

The military's willingness to accommodate the occupants' demands elicited mixed responses. Journalist Diane Francis chastised the military for its "cowardly evacuation" of the camp "after a few native rowdies broke the law," citing this as "simply the latest example of Ottawa's cowardice when it comes to dealing with aboriginal problems."[60] Local non-Native residents were appalled at the absence of law enforcement when they faced threats and physical abuse, and KSPFN chief Tom Bressette also deplored the military's quick surrender and abandonment: it showed the sorry state of the government. He also criticized the occupants' resistance to environmental clean-up and their assertion that the land would "heal itself."[61] On 30 August, KSPFN councillor Gerald George denounced the Stoney Pointers in a letter to the editor of the local newspaper:

When I read your article last week about the natives that harassed the family on the Camp Ipperwash Beach it made me very angry. I am a councillor for the Kettle & Stony Point First Nation. I am glad these Army Camp Indians call themselves separate from my First Nation because I would not want any of my fellow band members to act like animals and give my home a bad name.

I do not refer to these jerks as Stony Pointers either because my grandparents were Stony Pointers, also my mother and uncles are as well and I am sure that they never acted this way ... When the army pulled out of Camp Ipperwash, the actions that followed reminded me of the L.A. Riots.

The army camp Indians have strained relations between Kettle & Stony Point and the surrounding communities. We all do not act like the army camp Indians, so please do not think that all Chippewas act this way.[62]

Divisions within the Kettle and Stony Point community ran deep, as did frustrations with the lack of government resolve to deal with what was perceived as illegal behaviour by a dissident faction.

### THE OCCUPATION OF IPPERWASH PROVINCIAL PARK

The Stoney Pointers' confidence, buoyed by their successful takeover of Camp Ipperwash, led them in August to begin planning to expand their occupation into neighbouring Ipperwash Provincial Park. They had indicated to the OPP as early as May 1993 that they intended to take it over (and had served an eviction notice on park personnel),[63] but no occupation had taken place at that time. Unlike Camp Ipperwash, there were no public protests, letters, or marches arguing for the return of the park prior to the takeover in September 1995.[64] Witnesses appearing before the Ipperwash Inquiry justified this move on several grounds. First, they considered it part of traditional Aazhoodena (Stoney Point) territory, which had been dispossessed through government perfidy and never returned. Second, they asserted that they had an obligation to protect sacred gravesites in the park. Third, the formal reclamation process being pursued by the KSPFN was proceeding too slowly, and this faction was unprepared to wait. (Indeed, the KSPFN had never submitted a land claim for the provincial park and Stony Point beach lands.)[65] This was not a simple protest to kick-start negotiations with the government. The occupiers intended to take over the park permanently, and they were prepared to use force to take possession of it if necessary.[66]

In late August senior OPP officials met to discuss possible tactics if Ipperwash Park was occupied, and on 1 September Inspector Carson convened a meeting with about twenty officers to develop Project Maple. The police objective was "to contain and negotiate a peaceful resolution."

In short, Ministry of Natural Resources representatives and the OPP would tell any Native occupiers that they were trespassing and that, if they refused to leave, the ministry would prepare a court injunction. There was no expectation that the occupants would use firearms, but four Emergency Response Teams (a total of sixty officers) would wear their grey uniforms and have semi-automatic rifles in the trunks of their vehicles. Inspector Carson, the incident commander, intended for the police officers to "always stay in their face," interacting and communicating with the occupants to try to keep the situation calm. He also recognized the potential for violence, given some of the outsiders who were at the camp, the aggressive actions by the occupiers there in July, and the 29 July school bus incident.[67]

On 4 September the Stoney Pointers made their move to occupy the park. At about 4:00 PM two OPP constables were moving debris off of Matheson Drive on the east side of the park when brothers Roderick "Judas" George and Stewart George drove up close to the police cruiser. Both men had been drinking, as had some of the other Natives (the evidence varies from three to fifteen people) who soon arrived on the scene. The Georges told the police that it was their land and that they should leave. One of the constables testified that Stewart George had threatened him with the question "how many rifle sights do you think you're in?" The OPP, worried that the situation was escalating and that violence was possible, called for backup. One of the officers testified that, when he arrived, he saw a First Nation male at the trunk of another car start to pull out a firearm but that the individual did not finish when another First Nation male motioned for him to leave it. The OPP decided to withdraw, but the officers passed along their concerns to Inspector Carson.[68]

That evening after 7:30, as Labour Day weekend drew to a close, Glenn George and fifteen to seventeen people in other cars drove up to the east gate, yelled and swore at the police officers there, used bolt cutters to sever the chain and lock, and moved into Ipperwash Provincial Park.[69] The OPP did not resist (as per their operational plan) but asked the occupiers to allow them to evacuate the non-Native campers still in the park. At nightfall, however, officers remained in the park despite repeated Native demands that they leave. One of the occupiers threw a flare at the officers, and Roderick "Judas" George – brandishing a three-foot stick – cursed at the police and ordered them out of the park. When they did not leave, he smashed the rear window of a police cruiser. Occupiers also threw fluorescent phosphorous flares (which could burn clothing or skin) and strobe light firecrackers at the officers. Sergeant Stan Korosec testified,

> Now I'm really concerned. We have flares being thrown at us, we got the windshield, we got women and children in the Park, our officers in the Park; it was not a good spot to be and I'm the one in charge. So I had some real concerns ... A lot of things were running through my mind at the time. I didn't want to escalate things any more or get anyone hurt on either side. If we were going to take some action against Judas, there probably would have been a fight. To effect a proper arrest would require several officers and I'm thinking, well, what if some of the women and children get involved in this too, or innocent bystanders, and whatever would have occurred.[70]

To de-escalate the situation and avoid bloodshed, the OPP left the park. A few hours later, officers tried to serve the issue of trespass notice and the injunction on the occupiers, who told them, "We don't do business at night" and to "get off their land."[71]

The next day, it was clear that the occupation had heightened fears among local residents, including the elected band council, who wanted the police to take action. Chief Bressette of the KSPFN explained to the OPP that the elected council did not support the occupation and had filed no land claim to the park. Inspector Carson and the OPP considered it a "trespassing issue," and Chief Bressette replied that there was "a bunch of wackos running around" and that the police would "continue to have problems with our group until somebody ... enforces a law against them." Bressette was frustrated with the endless barrage of calls his band council was receiving to address actions that it was not taking and claimed that the occupiers would not respond to OPP demands if the authorities persisted in "treating them with kid gloves."[72] Meanwhile, more occupiers flooded into the park from the adjoining army camp, Kettle Point, and outside communities like Oneida, Walpole Island, and the Chippewas of the Thames. The "quite irate" Conservative member of the Legislative Assembly of Ontario Marcel Beaubien contacted a police staff sergeant to express his concerns about the occupation, as did the Town of Bosanquet. Mayor Fred Thomas issued a press release, entitled "Reign of Terror Continues," which accused the occupiers of rampant "terrorist" and illegal activities. They had kicked the army out of the camp and the province out of the park. "What's next?" Thomas asked. "The Federal Government assured me that all these terrorist activities would be confined within the perimeter of the Army Camp, but this hasn't happened." Members of the Bosanquet Town Council reported that local residents were "terrified." No arrests had been made for sexual and physical assaults on the beach, shots fired at municipal workers, and arson, sending out the message that illegal activities were "rewarded rather than punished." The mayor repeated rumours that residents were "buying guns to protect themselves and their families." This reflected a breakdown in trust that government authorities were able to manage the situation. "The laws of Canada and Ontario must be enforced equally for all Canadians," Thomas pleaded. "This reign of terror must stop."[73]

While such public statements continued to inflame the local situation, there was a meeting in Toronto of the interministerial committee, consisting of political staff and bureaucrats from various provincial ministries, such as the Attorney General' Office, Natural Resources, the Solicitor General's Office, and the Premier's Office. "Several IMC [interministerial committee] participants subscribed to a patient, measured, careful, and slow response to the Ipperwash Park occupation," the Ipperwash Inquiry discovered, "while others, such as the Premier's Executive Assistant Deb Hutton, had a 'sense of urgency' and thought the government 'should be doing more and doing it faster.'" Adopting a "one law for all" philosophy, Hutton insisted on immediate action. "It was clear to the participants at the meeting that this government was focused on quickly ending the occupation," the inquiry report noted. "Sworn in about ten weeks earlier, the new government wanted to focus their efforts on their 1995 campaign promises and did not want to be diverted by such issues as a First Nations park occupation. The government also wanted to convey to the public the message that it was addressing the occupation in a quick, strong manner." This "law and order approach" did not leave time to appoint a facilitator or negotiator to try to deal with the occupiers. Instead, the Premier's Office directed the minister of natural resources to issue a public statement reaffirming that the province had valid title to the park, that the occupants were trespassing and had been told to leave, and that the province would remove the occupiers as soon as possible.[74]

In the meantime, the OPP focused its energies on preparing for any eventuality. The police arranged for armoured vehicles, helicopters, weapons, and other equipment, and more OPP cruisers arrived on the scene. The police set up checkpoints and stepped up their surveillance activities using boats and helicopters. Concurrently, Inspector Carson tried to engage the occupiers in a dialogue. Unlike the military, which had turned to Aboriginal negotiators from outside the community to defuse volatile situations at Camp Ipperwash, the OPP turned to one of its own experts in crisis negotiation. He failed. "The conduct of both the OPP and the Aboriginal occupiers created misconceptions," the inquiry concluded. When two officers and the park superintendent arrived to speak with the occupiers and serve them a notice of trespass, the occupiers refused to talk. They were worried that anyone who spoke would be labelled as a leader or spokesperson and would be arrested. Furthermore, it was not in their interests to talk with the police because doing so would not secure the land for them.[75] In short, despite the inquiry's decision to place the blame for the lack of dialogue on the OPP, the Stoney Pointers repeatedly refused to talk with any government representatives or to consider participating in any hearings through a "white man's court." Furthermore, the lack of clear leadership among the occupiers made it impossible for the police to identify someone through whom they could effectively communicate.[76]

On the evening of 5 September, the occupiers erected a "blockade" of picnic tables in the sandy parking lot outside of the park fence, barring access to the beach from the paved road. An OPP vehicle deliberately pushed into one of the tables while some of the occupiers sat at it, prompting them to flip it onto the hood and windshield of the cruiser. Insults were hurled back and forth, and the occupiers threw rocks at the officers and at their cruisers, damaging three vehicles. In a regrettable foreshadowing of what was to come, one of the officers pointed at Dudley George and taunted, "Come on out, Dudley. You're going to be first." One of the occupiers promptly threw sand in the officer's face, and he responded with pepper spray. With tensions escalating, internal dialogue among OPP authorities in the area revealed a growing sense of frustration and aggression. (Their racist comments, captured on tape, later undermined OPP claims to impartiality and cultural sensitivity.) Later that evening, when an OPP constable reported "large amounts of automatic gunfire way back in the army base," this information was passed along to park officials. Civil servants and political staff in Toronto received this intelligence the following day and attached significant importance to it, which increased the anxiety surrounding the situation.[77]

The following morning, the OPP continued their efforts to contain the occupation to the provincial park. Two Emergency Response Teams carrying shields and scanning the area with firearms approached picnic tables where Dudley George and a teenaged occupier were sitting in a sandy parking lot outside of the park boundaries. Rather than confronting the police, who loaded the picnic tables onto a flatbed truck while a helicopter patrolled overhead, the two ran into the park. Although the OPP intended the removal of the barricade as a signal to the occupiers that they should stay out of the parking lot – and that the police had no intentions of entering the park – this message was unclearly conveyed to the occupiers, who saw this incident as another act of aggression. The occupiers refused to talk with OPP negotiators that day, but Inspector Carson was "optimistic" when he left his command post around 7:00 PM that the "status quo" would continue overnight. There was no clear plan to take action that evening, particularly because the police were waiting for an injunction that would give them the authority to remove the protestors the next day.[78]

The report of the Ipperwash Inquiry reconstructs the meetings between provincial officials and politicians on 6 September in great detail. The acting legal director of the Ontario Native Affairs Secretariat recommended to the attorney general that the province should seek a regular injunction with notice to remove the occupiers – an approach that emphasized the lack of risk to public safety and thus caution and reserve. Deb Hutton, however, insisted that the main goal was "ending the occupation [and] remov[ing] the occupiers" as quickly as possible. Unverified reports of automatic gunfire heightened the atmosphere of tension and urgency. "Premier is firm that at no time should anybody but OPP, MNR [Ministry of Natural Resources] be involved in discussions, despite any offers that might be made by third parties (Chief, etc.) because you get into negotiations and we don't want that," Hutton explained. In Premier Mike Harris's view, it was an illegal occupation and thus a simple law enforcement issue. The fact that the occupiers were Aboriginal was irrelevant. The message coming out of the meeting of the interministerial committee was that the government would seek an injunction as soon as possible, that the police had been asked to remove the occupiers from the park within twenty-four hours, and that public safety was paramount. The so-called "dining room" meeting between the premier, ministers, and their staff after the formal Cabinet meeting that morning made it clear that Harris sought quick, decisive action.[79]

Ipperwash Inquiry commissioner Sidney Linden later noted that the premier's determination to end the occupation quickly "unduly narrowed the scope of the government's response to the Aboriginal occupation ... [and] closed off many options endorsed by civil servants in the

Ontario government, including process negotiations, the appointment of mediators, and opening up communication with the First Nations people." Ron Fox, a police officer seconded to the Solicitor General's Office, called the OPP command post in Forest to share his frustrations with Inspector Carson. "John, we're dealing with a real redneck government," Fox asserted. "They are fucking barrel suckers, they just are in love with guns ... There's no question they couldn't give a shit less about Indians." Carson replied that the OPP had no intention of going into the park until they "had received the appropriate injunction." This conversation revealed a breach of chain of command but also suggested that the OPP inspector was not allowing political considerations to influence his tactical decisions.[80] Nevertheless, local developments conspired to undermine his goal of negotiating a peaceful solution.

On the early evening of 6 September, OPP sergeant Mark Wright met up with a gathering of more than thirty local residents and cottagers – including Mayor Fred Thomas – who held a rally and were preparing to march to the park to express their frustration. After dissuading them from doing so, Wright headed down the road and encountered a group of the occupiers standing in the sandy parking lot outside of the park boundaries, several of whom held clubs, sticks, bats, or axe handles. They told him to leave, tapping their weapons in their open palms in an obvious attempt at intimidation. He reported the encounter to the command post. Soon after, KSPFN councillor Gerald George (who had criticized the "army camp Indians" in the newspaper in August) also reported an altercation that suggested belligerence on the part of the occupiers. When Gerald drove up to the sandy parking lot in his sister's car, Stewart "Worm" George slapped his face. "Worm, you're going to get it," Gerald hollered. In response, Stewart threw a rock and dented the car. Gerald promptly went to an OPP checkpoint and told officers that the occupiers possessed an impressive arsenal of weapons: "AK-47s with a 30 round mags duct taped to the back," "Mini Ruger 14s," hunting rifles, and Molotov cocktails.[81]

Although the police were later criticized for faulty intelligence work in not recognizing that Gerald George was an insider and a biased source who might have been presenting unreliable information, one of the common problems in uncertain situations is difficulty developing a "clear" picture of events and the other side's intentions. Although subsequent commentators and conspiracy theorists based their analysis on hindsight, and expected that OPP and political actors must have or should have known better, this is ahistorical. (For some reason, these commentators never place similar expectations on the occupiers.) Part of the "chess game" of confrontations is the control of information. In a tense standoff without open communication across the lines, the likelihood that both sides would misread signals was amplified. When women and children left the park out of fear that the police were planning to confront the occupiers that night, the OPP saw this as an indication that the occupiers had planned aggressive activities.[82] Both readings of the situation were plausible given the context. The Ipperwash Inquiry report paints a dramatic picture of the scene that warrants quoting at length:

> Before sunset, First Nations people in Ipperwash Park became increasingly anxious about the OPP's plans for that evening. The occupiers decided it would be good to have walkie-talkies and scanners to listen to police communications at the park that evening. Cecil Bernard George retrieved some of these supplies from Kettle Point. Other occupiers returned to the barracks to get a spotlight to illuminate police officers in the vicinity of the park. The occupiers built bonfires and collected rocks and sticks, placing them inside the park at the fence line in order to defend themselves from the police if this became necessary ... The occupiers believed the heavily armed OPP would confront them that night ...
>
> The OPP observed much of this activity and it increased their concern that the occupiers were planning "offensive" activities for that night. The large bonfires, the activity in the kiosk, the movement of the cars and dump truck between the park and the camp, and other actions by the Aboriginal people reinforced their belief. The Aboriginal people were deliberately trying to create the illusion that there were many more occupiers in the park than there actually were. These actions caused the police to believe the Aboriginal people intended to engage in "offensive" activities when, in fact, they were simply making "defensive" preparations for a move by the OPP on the First Nations occupiers.[83]

Trying to differentiate between "offensive" and "defensive" preparations is difficult, particularly when faced with incomplete and imperfect information, and the lack of communication between the police and the occupiers made it difficult to manage escalation on all sides.

The OPP's operational plan was to contain the occupation to the park itself, and allegations that they deliberately provoked a confrontation are unfair. Instead, the more plausible explanation is that the police expected to engage in a crowd control exercise, but events spiraled out of control. Just before 8:00 PM, Inspector Carson decided to mobilize the

Crowd Management Team (CMU) to clear the parking lot, with the Tactical Response Unit (TRU) providing "the visuals" and "cover" in the belief that the occupiers possessed assault weapons and (erroneously) that eight Native males had destroyed a woman's car with baseball bats. Just after 9:00 PM, the police closed the roads leading to the park, and the CMU – dressed in body armour and helmets with visors – marched toward the park "in box formation" ninety minutes later. Their objective was to move the demonstrators back into the park, arresting anyone who refused. This was not communicated to the occupiers, and the miscommunication proved fatal:

> It was Inspector Carson's hope and expectation that when the
> CMU marched down the road to the sandy parking lot, the
> occupiers would move back into the park. However, the Aboriginal
> occupiers did not understand the OPP's intentions. They believed
> the OPP was preparing for a confrontation and would enter the
> park and arrest them. They themselves were preparing that night
> for the heavily armed police officers in grey uniforms. They collect-
> ed rocks, sticks, and stones, they carried baseball bats, they put gas
> in the school bus and drove it and other vehicles to the park, they
> assigned occupiers to particular areas as "look-outs," and the
> Aboriginal people listened on the scanner for the approach of the
> police to Ipperwash Park.[84]

Although the twenty to twenty-five occupiers retreated behind the park fence as the police formed a cordon, they began to throw burning sticks, rocks, and bricks at the police. The inquiry report exhorted that even at this point the Aboriginal people intended this to be "a peaceful occupation," but this belligerence signalled otherwise. (Nonetheless, the occupiers' behaviour did not represent a dramatic change from their previous provocations, which had usually led to the military or police backing down.) The protestors told the police to get off of their "sacred ground" and to "get back on the Mayflower." The voice order "pun-chout" signalled to the police to run into the parking lot, beating on their shields in hopes that this would intimate the occupiers to retreat back into the park.

The tactic backfired, with tragic consequences. Sergeant George Hebblethwaite later described the scene:

> When we arrived at the sandy parking lot and the occupiers went
> back into the Park, I believed that we had completed our task.

I thought it was done. Having reached our objective, we were in the process of leaving. Within moments, a finished event turned into a hailstorm. We were withdrawing to the pavement. All of a sudden people were coming over the fence at us. There was dust everywhere, almost like a smoke or a haze. Figures were advancing. I could see their silhouettes ... more than I could see who they were, due to the bonfires behind them, backlighting them, along with the two vehicles that were in the Park. It was like they were not real. I could see the outlines of weapons in their hands. It was like being in a horror movie. To this day I find it difficult to believe that this happened. It did not make any sense.[85]

The occupiers were unnerved by the police actions, became angry, and attacked the officers. Band councillor Cecil Bernard (Slippery) George, who was outside of the fence, picked up a steel pipe, swung it at an officer, and heard the officer's shield break on impact.[86] With his baton, Staff Sergeant Wade Lacroix, the leader of the CMU, knocked George to the ground, where other officers promptly kicked and hit him. More than a dozen occupiers brandishing sticks, clubs, and poles ran out of the park to rescue him. The police officers, bombarded with rocks and pieces of wood or hit with baseball bats, engaged them in hand-to-hand combat.[87]

The situation continued to escalate when Judas George called for someone to get the school bus:

Sixteen year old Nicholas Cottrelle [his son] ran to the school bus and climbed into the driver's seat. Fourteen-year-old Leland White was panicked by the OPP's approach in riot gear and had sought refuge in the bus with his dog because he "felt safer there." Nicholas Cottrelle drove through the sandy parking lot in the direction of East Parkway Drive and toward the officers, trying to find Cecil Bernard George ... Staff Sergeant Lacroix and the other officers watched the bus move forward through the sandy parking lot toward the road. They watched the bus push the dumpster across the sandy parking lot in the direction of the officers. Staff Sergeant Lacroix yelled, "[S]plit formation," to move his officers off the road to enable the bus to drive through. But the bus drove near the fence where CMU officers were standing. Some officers tried to climb the fence, while others "tried to dive ... back towards the pavement." Sergeant Hebblethwaite was convinced "someone was going to be killed as the bus neared [their] men."[88]

When Warren George jumped into his car and swerved to hit a group of officers, Staff Sergeant Lacroix and an OPP constable fired at the driver. His car took several bullets but he was not hit. Other TRU and CMU members fired at the bus, and Cottrelle suffered minor injuries when bullets hit his seat and sent fragments into his back. A younger boy, Leland White, was on the floor protecting his dog (which was hit but not killed). Although the inquiry report emphasized that there were no firearms, the drivers were certainly intending to use the vehicles as weapons.

Both drivers survived the confrontation, but Dudley George did not. Acting Sergeant Ken Deane, walking toward the park on the north side of East Parkway Drive, later claimed that he saw two muzzle flashes coming from the bush area and that one of the occupiers walked onto the roadway with a long rifle, shouldered it, and pointed it at OPP officers. Deane later testified that he believed Dudley George was "a millisecond away from shooting one of [the] officers." The officer fired three shots in rapid succession and watched "Dudley George falter, fall on one knee, spin to his right, and then spin to his left." Deane later concocted a story that George threw his rifle into the bushes before several occupiers carried his body into the park, but this was a *post facto* fabrication.[89] Deane called for an ambulance, but George's siblings and a friend drove him to Strathroy Hospital, where he was pronounced dead.

The confrontation ended soon after George was shot. Staff Sergeant Wade Lacroix ordered a cease fire and pulled the CMU back to the police post. No one pursued the occupiers into the park.[90] OPP officers later testified that they were shocked by the intensity of violence that had erupted and that they had not anticipated this "worst case scenario."[91] Lacroix later testified: "The whole situation was a bad situation ... It was very tragic, the fact that any man died. I did not expect it to end this way going down the road. I thought it was going to be a disturbance, there might be some sticks and stones. I certainly did not expect it to break into gunfire. I certainly didn't expect to see my men get run over by cars, and we especially did not expect to be taking human life."[92] When the park occupiers learned that Dudley was dead, they torched the park restaurant and burned it to the ground. About two hundred non-Native cottagers living nearby were evacuated to the town of Forest. Within hours, the entire Kettle and Stony Point First Nation "was galvanized into action," blocking Highway 21 at Kettle Point, and the following day "they marched in numbers to the army camp, then down to the park and then to the TAC [tactical] centre where, again, OPP officers were forced to withdraw. Their mobile command centre was trashed, they lost vehicles and other equipment, and, as it turned out, they lost the park as well."[93] The occupiers defied a court injunction to leave the park, and Ontario solicitor general Bob Runciman announced on 8 September that the OPP would not forcibly remove them. Native representatives met with the provincial government, the OPP pulled back from the barricades around Camp Ipperwash, and local Native people put out several of their protest fires. Government officials maintained that they would not negotiate with Native leaders until the occupiers left the park.[94] The occupiers, however, never ceded physical control of it.

## MEDIA AND POLITICAL FALLOUT

The media took modest interest in the occupations prior to the confrontation of 6 September 1995, but they became a major media issue following Dudley George's death at the hands of the OPP. The confusing nature of the relationship between the Kettle and Stony Point First Nation, the self-proclaimed "Stoney Point First Nation," the military, and the federal and provincial governments made it a complex story to cover. Journalists could chose from various frames, all of which fitted the situation: Aboriginal people as troublemakers, Aboriginal people with a legitimate dispute with the government, Aboriginal people disputing one another, law and order versus anarchy, and/or militancy versus moderation.[95] "The crisis lacked a defining image in the public mind," journalist Peter Edwards notes. "It was just so many words, and many of those were confusing."[96] This changed with the death of Dudley George.

Scholars Allan McDougall and Lisa Phillips Valentine suggest that the presentation of the Ipperwash occupations in the *London Free Press* represented a "selective marginalization of Aboriginal voices" that was tantamount to censorship of the Stoney Pointers in their community's struggle "to regain control of its land and to acquire band status within the First Nations of Canada." By refusing to entitle the Stoney Pointers to full First Nation status, they argue, the media's coverage of the occupations adhered to a "hierarchy of liberal democratic values." The Stoney Pointers' occupations generated media attention, but McDougall and Valentine suggest that the media chose to confer greater legitimacy on negotiations between the elected band council and the federal government. By presupposing that the Stoney Pointers *should have* First Nation status, and by asserting that they had it prior to the 1990s (based upon a deliberately selective reading of the archival record), these authors try to portray them as victims of hegemonic state control. Furthermore, they observe that Native leaders who condemned "lawlessness," "militancy," and "criminality" were legitimized, whereas those who promoted direct action were cast as renegades. The Stoney Pointers existed "outside both the native and state hierarchies," the authors note, and thus their community was "invisible to the system and the system reacted by denying it entitlement, explicitly and implicitly."[97]

Although McDougall and Valentine's assessment is appropriate on one level, it misses the extensive coverage that the Stoney Pointers' perspectives did receive. Their views were hardly "censored out" in newspapers. Furthermore, many journalists who were not attuned to the nuances of Aboriginal governance or the Stoney Pointers' complicated relationship with the elected Kettle and Stony Point First Nation accorded them the status of a separate band. Others cast them as doubly victimized by both the federal and provincial governments as well as the Kettle Point community. This perception was certainly the intent of the Stoney Pointers, who attempted to demonstrate that their *residency* on the *reserve lands* that they *reclaimed* was not a violent occupation against the wishes of the majority of Kettle and Stony Point First Nation members but the normal resumption of community life stolen away earlier in the twentieth century. Furthermore, journalists questioned the military's continuing claims that it needed to retain the camp prior to February 1994, as well as the slow pace of returning the land. The media were understandably confused about who the rightful owners were.

Given the competing interests in the land and the complex web of relationships that underpinned them, simply championing the Stoney Pointers' perspective (as scholars have typically done) would not have allowed journalists to fulfil the principles of factual accuracy, balance, sensitivity, and context. As regional journalists became more educated on the complexity of the situation over time, they did not assume the claims of the Stoney Pointers as readily and uncritically as they had early on. They accorded space and legitimacy to the Kettle and Stony Point First Nation chief and council's perspectives and questioned the motives and tactics of the more militant occupiers who claimed entitlement to the land. Although journalists tended to criticize the military's continued retention of Camp Ipperwash, they also acknowledged the government's predicament: to whom could it return the land when faced with competing claims, one by a group occupying the land, the other by an elected chief of a federally recognized band who did not enjoy the support of the occupants?

The group most underrepresented in media coverage was local non-Native landowners. They believed that the media were not presenting a balanced view that incorporated their experiences. "From the original illegal take-over of the military camp and then the occupation of the park grounds, the news media, for the most part, talked only to native people and presented their side," a local resident noted in early 1996. "The media ignored the problems and effect this situation was having on permanent residents. Our government also ignored these people and showed a lack of care for their safety or protection of their homes."[98] Their message fitted with a broader current of opinion that chastised the government for failing to apply the law consistently to all Canadian citizens.[99]

No media were present at the deadly confrontation on 6 September, and "the public was left with widely conflicting accounts of what happened, without independent verification by a media witness."[100] In the month before the shooting, the occupations of the built-up area of Camp Ipperwash and the provincial park received little national media attention. In the month following, however, the story was front-page news. "As the story went on, the roots of the dispute seemed to get lost," journalism professor John Miller observes. "It became less and less a story about a land dispute between the Chippewa people and the federal government, and more and more about a police investigation into troublesome events caused by First Nation people." Because journalists had not been "behind the barricades" as they had been at Goose Bay and Oka, they did not have a trust relationship with the Stoney Pointers who occupied the camp and the provincial park. Accordingly, most reporters relied on interviews with "official sources" (Chief Bressette, Assembly of First Nations chief Ovide Mercredi, police, and politicians). Editorials and opinion columns tended to associate the Ipperwash tragedy with the confrontations at Oka and Gustafsen Lake (where occupiers did use weapons), and the OPP version of events (which claimed that the Stoney Pointers were armed and shot first on 6 September) was usually placed before the Stoney Pointers' claim that they were unarmed. Although most journalists lamented Dudley George's death, they did not tend to sympathize with the Stoney Pointers' perspective. Instead, commentators often adopted a "law and order" framework that vilified Native violence and militancy.[101] Journalists were also critical of the federal and provincial governments, which, in their view, displayed cowardice and a "double standard" toward Aboriginal people who committed illegal acts. "Ipperwash is fast becoming a symbol of the failure of various government agencies," an *Ottawa Citizen* editorial offered on 25 July 1996, adding that in land claims "accountability ... starts at the top."[102]

Further investigations confirmed the Stoney Pointers' claim that they did not possess any guns during their confrontation with police and indicated that events on the ground had spiralled out of control. After a special investigation unit review, Acting Sergeant Kenneth Deane, the OPP officer who shot Dudley George, was charged with criminal negligence causing death. Deane insisted that he believed George was carrying a rifle when he was shot, but his testimony did not convince the judge. In April 1997 the OPP officer was convicted and handed a conditional sentence of two years less a day to be served in the community. The revelation that the OPP had used excessive force against unarmed Native people influenced subsequent media coverage. Although reporters had questioned the legitimacy of the Stoney Pointer occupiers around the time of Dudley George's death, this began to change after the 1997 court ruling (coupled with external reports like that of Amnesty International, which labelled the death an "extrajudicial execution"). Journalists again reshaped history to "accentuat[e] George's legitimacy to land (property ownership) and his victim status (human life)." By extension, the Stoney Pointers' human rights were championed over state power, and the history was now reframed as the Stoney Pointers protecting their ancestral ground against state force.[103]

In the late 1990s journalists and opposition politicians supported the George family's calls for a public inquiry into the events at Ipperwash with increasing strength. Dudley George's siblings launched a lawsuit against Premier Harris and several of his key advisors for "personally directing the OPP to get tough with Natives in the park."[104] Allegations made in the provincial legislature and the media echoed this idea that the premier and other government officials had decided to "order action that was bound to bring bloodshed," had basically assumed tactical command of the police operation, and had even given "shoot to kill orders."[105] Peter Edwards of the *Toronto Star*, one of the first reporters on the scene after Dudley George was killed, reconstructed events from the Stoney Pointers' view in a series of articles that culminated with the publication of *One Dead Indian: The Premier, the Police, and the Ipperwash Crisis* in 2001. He became a tireless advocate for a public inquiry, and other journalists echoed his message, as did human rights organizations. The Coalition for Public Inquiry into Ipperwash brought the issue before the United Nations Human Rights Committee in 1998 and the Committee on the Elimination of All Forms of Racial Discrimination in 2002. Both international bodies called for a public inquiry.[106] A *Toronto Star* editorial noted on 20 January 2002, "Deane's dismissal, while welcome, doesn't cast any more light on the truth of what really happened in Ipperwash. Who, for example, demanded that the cops muscle their way into the Park against the advice of OPP commanders who were pushing for a peaceful resolution to the Indian occupation? The damning memos and briefing notes that trace a path right to the Premier's door hint at the answer."[107]

Concurrently, non-Aboriginal residents and cottagers in the Ipperwash area voiced their frustration at the unwillingness of the OPP to deal with rampant criminal activities emanating from the occupied camp and provincial park. For years, local landowners had threatened legal action when the local Natives had engaged in destructive activities or denied non-Natives access to the beach. After 1995 rapid decline in their property values and a litany of "break and enters, vandalism, theft, assaults and death threats" prompted furious local residents to protest what they saw as rampant lawlessness perpetrated by the Ipperwash occupants. "The Native Agenda here has been exercised with militancy and violence that no one in Canada will address or rectify," Ontario Federation for Individual Rights and Equality president Mary Lou LaPratte complained. This locally formed protest group questioned the special rights claimed by the Stoney Pointers and criticized the military and police for inaction. The federation's political incorrectness made its members' perspectives easy to dismiss, but the group also supported the camp's return to the KSPFN. Everyone was a victim amid the uncertainty, and government legitimacy eroded on all sides.[108]

## OUTCOMES

The spilling of blood did not heal factional wounds. Within a week of the 6 September 1995 confrontation, the minister of Indian affairs and federal officials met with the national chief of the Assembly of First Nations and the KSPFN chief and council. They signed a memorandum of understanding promising to clean up the land with community participation, transfer the camp to the First Nation as a reserve, support community healing, and appoint a federal negotiator acceptable to the community. For its part, the DND had no interest in retaining the lands longer than was required. As long as the Stoney Pointer faction occupied the reserve and challenged the KSPFN council's title claims, however, liability issues were omnipresent. Furthermore, how could the military clean the land if government contractors were denied access?[109]

In 1998 the federal government and the KSPFN reached an agreement-in-principle to transfer the Camp Ipperwash land back to reserve status and to pay $26 million in compensation. Many Stoney Pointers (even the most militant) were included on the various community committees, but they eventually denounced the process, insisting that that they were marginalized in negotiations, and refused to participate in the agreement. Even after the deal was signed, the elected KSPFN council wrangled with Ottawa over environmental clean-up plans, resulting in sporadic negotiations and little progress. Until the land was decontaminated, Indian Affairs refused to return it to reserve status. Environmental investigation and clean-up could not take place, however, without a working relationship between the camp occupants and the KSPFN. The continuing local anarchy pushed 120 Bosanquet residents to file class action lawsuits against the federal and provincial governments in 2000, seeking $2 billion for turmoil, lost property values, and fear.[110] By then, the Stoney Pointer community was well established on the former military camp, which in functional terms was again Aazhoodenaáng – their home. In legal terms, however, the lands remained in limbo.

On 12 November 2003 the newly elected Liberal government of Dalton McGuinty took office in Ontario and appointed an independent Ipperwash Inquiry. Throughout his campaign, McGuinty had promised to call a public inquiry to examine the events surrounding the death of Dudley George and to recommend how to avoid violence in similar circumstances. "This particular Inquiry was borne out of a sense of anger and a feeling of frustration regarding unanswered questions as to what occurred at Ipperwash Provincial Park in September 1995," Commissioner Sidney Linden noted in his opening remarks. Indeed, anger and frustration had been brewing in the community since the Second World War. The public inquiry could not address all the questions, but it provided a forum for the Aazhoodena and George family, as well as the Chippewas of Kettle and Stony Point First Nation, to share their perspectives. Evidentiary hearings stretched from July 2004 to June 2006, and the inquiry heard from 140 witnesses.[111] Aboriginal witnesses could swear an oath on an eagle feather rather than a bible and could take a break during proceedings to perform rituals if they felt stressed. There were no strict rules of evidence, and witnesses could answer questions in a "non-linear," discursive fashion. In these respects, the inquiry certainly tried to be culturally respectful.[112]

The inquiry's final report was released in May 2007, and Commissioner Linden came down heavily against state authorities. He determined that the OPP, the government of then Ontario premier Mike Harris, and the federal government all bore responsibility for the events that led to Dudley George's death. In his assessment, the OPP, supported by the provincial government, had been confrontational and had mishandled the occupation. Operational commanders should not have deployed the crowd control unit to force the Natives out of the parking lot and back inside the park. The federal government had not returned Camp Ipperwash to the local Native community after the Second World War. The provincial government was too "impatient" to resolve the occupation. Most media (given their previous incrimination of Premier Harris) chose to downplay Linden's conclusion that although the premier had been "critical of the police," he had not "interfered with or [given] inappropriate directions to the police at Ipperwash."[113] The overall message sharply criticized government and police behaviour and offered extensive recommendations on how situations like this could be better handled in the future.

All of these conclusions seem appropriate given the evidence, but the report is overly one-sided. The lack of criticism directed toward the Native occupiers is striking, given that their direct action tactics certainly contributed to escalating tensions. Although the inquiry's decision to absolve the Stoney Pointers and the Kettle and Stony Point First Nation of any responsibility might have fitted with its focus on political behaviour, policy, and police practices, it also deliberately avoided discussing core identity issues that lay at the heart of the occupations. In its final submission to the inquiry, the KSPFN explained, "Only recently has there been a degree of cooperation between the First Nation and the camp residents to facilitate an investigation of environmental, cultural and unexploded ordnance concerns at Camp Ipperwash. Even so, the tensions of the past two decades are not completely dissipated and the First Nation wishes to register its concern that the Inquiry [did] not address these matters in any way," which "will make them more difficult to resolve."[114] Downplaying divisions between the KSPFN and the Stoney Pointers who occupied the camp and park might be conducive to a political healing process. Casting the Aboriginal occupiers as peaceful protestors also required a heavily sanitized version of history, which the inquiry provided.

Although the final report of the Ipperwash Inquiry struck all the right chords of political correctness, it also provoked some critical responses. For example, National Post columnist Andrew Coyne explained that the report made Native violence "blameless" and "effectively legitimize[d] illegal protests." The inquiry rightly blamed governments, the military, and the police, but was "there no part that should be apportioned to the native occupiers themselves?" The occupations were illegal, regardless of whether the Natives' grievances were justified, and they were not supported by the local band council. Indeed, other band members actively opposed the occupiers' tactics, and "many of those who participated were not even from the area, but had travelled from as far away as the United States to show their support." Whereas the inquiry report chose to blame only the provincial government and the police for failing to communicate their intentions, Coyne noted that the Natives had offered

> no formal warning … that the park was about to be occupied. No grievance was clearly articulated beforehand, other than a vague, disputed and intermittently advocated claim that the park contained a native burial ground. Even after the occupation began, the protesters refused to communicate in any way with the police. And in almost every case where police and natives clashed, the violence was initiated by the natives. While the beating of Cecil Bernard George at the hands of several OPP officers, the proximate cause of the events leading to the other Mr. George's death, was clearly deplorable, it came only after the first Mr. George had whacked an officer with a six-foot length of pipe. The fatal shooting – again, as wholly unjustified as it was – came after natives drove a bus at police.
>
> So the police badly mishandled the occupation, yes. But had this particular group of natives not taken it into their heads to break the law, defy their band council, and seize the provincial park, they would never have come into conflict with the police. Yet throughout his report, Judge Linden takes the existence of this and other such native occupations as a given.
>
> They simply "occur," as if by acts of God, rather than being the result of conscious decisions by morally responsible adults. At no time does he call into question the advisability of such a strategy, let alone its acceptability in a democratic and law-abiding state.

Linden's refusal to criticize the occupiers implicitly supported their behaviour, Coyne argued. This stance constituted "nothing less than the normalization of lawlessness, the legitimization of violence as a means of political protest. And by a judge! Native radicals elsewhere can only take the appropriate cues, and be emboldened."[115]

In contrast to the ample opportunities that the Stoney Pointers, the KSPFN, the OPP, and the provincial government had to testify before the inquiry, neighbouring non-Native residents complained that their story had been marginalized and that justice had not been served. The final report downplayed the long history of violence and lawlessness prior to the death of Dudley George, did not call upon any full-time non-Native residents to testify (even though some had filed sworn statements alleging to have seen Native men with rifles prior to the confrontation with police), and misrepresented a community consultation session where residents emphasized the fear in which they lived. Local activist Mary Lou Lapratte explained in a speech at the March for Freedom event at Caledonia in October 2006,

> When the native land disputes erupted at Ipperwash in 1992, 1993 and 1995, the OPP took the position the lands would be treated as reserves. This is without benefit of the land claims process, be it negotiation or through the courts. The OPP refused to enter the disputed land simply because the natives did not want them there. We have no policing at two occupied areas of Ipperwash, or authority of any kind over those on the land.
>
> As soon as the occupations and land claim on the West [Ipperwash] Beach started we [local residents] noticed a disturbing OPP policy evolving. Natives coming off the occupied lands into surrounding areas to harass, threaten, intimidate, steal from or assault innocent homeowners and tourists, were exempt from criminal charges upon reaching the safe haven of the disputed land ... Our lives became a daily nightmare of threats, intimidation, and harassment tactics which, over the years, became home invasions and physical assaults. We became a community with no policing, no province and no country. No one in the OPP, the Provincial Government, or the Federal Government would give us any relief or help with the aggression. At one point after the death of ... Dudley George, the police totally deserted our community because they and their families became targets. Our community was in chaos. We were so terrified we asked the OPP what they would do if one of us was taken against our will onto the occupied land. The reply, "We will negotiate the return of your body." The families of two victims at Ipperwash deserve closure to bury the remains of their loved ones.[116]

This perspective on the occupations, conspicuously absent in the Ipperwash Inquiry report, suggested that selective policing and weak political leadership had ruined the lives of the non-Native residents trapped in the local anarchy that continued after George's death.

## FINAL REFLECTIONS

The Stoney Pointers' decision to occupy Camp Ipperwash in 1993 grew out of frustration with the federal government's refusal to return lands that had been appropriated fifty years earlier. It also reflected a sharp divergence from the expressed desires of the elected Kettle and Stony Point First Nation chief and council, who sought to negotiate a return of the former reserve and publicly denounced the occupation. Indeed, the entire situation was complicated by divisions within the KSPFN. The criteria for membership in the self-proclaimed "Stoney Point First Nation" was never articulated, and public statements by KSPFN leaders suggest that the majority of band members did not support the idea of a separate Stoney Point "band" or the use of physical force to takeover Camp Ipperwash.[117] Both groups battled with each other for legitimacy. The elected KSPFN chief (who, along with a majority of elected band councillors at the time, was related to people from Stony Point) repeatedly told government officials that the Stoney Pointers who occupied Camp Ipperwash and then the provincial park were a splinter group.[118] The elected band council insisted that it was the moderate and rational voice of the broader Kettle and Stony Point community. Furthermore, the occupiers eventually included outsiders who did not have any historical connection to the land and did not enjoy the support of the majority of Kettle Point residents or the chief and council. In response, the Stoney Pointers portrayed the KSPFN council as oppressive, corrupt, and a historical anachronism. They presented their case before parliamentary committees and reinvented historical evidence to claim distinct band status before 1942, but their adoption of direct action tactics in 1993 was not pre-empted by a significant amount of "lower-level" protest actions such as lobbying and court action.

The goal of the Stoney Pointers who took direct action tactics was to reclaim land that some descendants of the original Stony Point Reserve believed was rightfully theirs and to attain First Nation status separate from the KSPFN. By mid-1995 the elected band leadership had no influence over the Stoney Pointers, who adopted increasingly aggressive tactics to intimate military caretakers and to eventually take over the camp. This was not simply a "protest," as later media coverage tended to describe it. In its final submission to the Ipperwash Inquiry, the KSPFN recalled,

> Going into the summer months of 1995, the small group of
> "Stoney Pointers" had enjoyed considerable success in occupying

the ranges at Camp Ipperwash, then occupying the built-up area of the camp and even displacing the army from the camp. They had also enjoyed the public support of several prominent and other lesser-known groups and attracted generally sympathetic coverage of their quest. They were, to this point, dealing largely with a vapid and ineffectual federal bureaucracy no longer interested in the camp for its own purposes and having only a tepid commitment to restore the camp lands to the First Nation as reserve lands. The military at all times seemed more interested in "managing" the occupation rather than ending it.[119]

The federal government refused to seek an injunction to remove the occupiers and instead withdrew from the camp to avoid further confrontation. This signalled a lack of state resolve and weakness. Chief Bressette observed that the occupiers were allowed to "overstep their boundaries in many ways," indicating that their tactics appeared to be effective. This led to further escalation and confrontations.

Federal government inaction placed the elected KSPFN council in an increasingly difficult position. The DND's delay in closing Camp Ipperwash and returning it to the KSPB exacerbated internal tensions, and the lack of unity within the band made negotiations with the federal government difficult and inhibited progress toward having the land returned. As long as the Stoney Pointers were unwilling to compromise or negotiate through the KSPFN, governments also found themselves in an impossible legal position. Although the histories of Camp Ipperwash and Ipperwash Provincial Park were distinct from a government standpoint (the former appropriated without consent and the latter acquired through a band surrender), they converged in the minds of the increasingly confident Stoney Pointers in the summer of 1995.

The Kettle and Stony Point First Nation had never filed a claim against Ipperwash Provincial Park prior to September 1995 and thus did not support the Stoney Pointers' decision to "reclaim" a property that they claimed was rightfully "theirs." The evidence suggests that the Stoney Pointers simply decided to repeat a tactic that had worked at the military camp. Officials of the Ministry of Natural Resources and OPP officers withdrew from the park during the initial confrontation to avoid further escalation and violence, allowing the Stoney Pointers to physically occupy the property. Premier Harris insisted that the occupation was an illegal, criminal act, which fell under police jurisdiction and would be dealt with through the courts. The police adopted an unstated but consistent strategy to contain the occupation to the park itself, and the provincial government was seeking a court injunction against the occupiers when the situation on the ground boiled over.[120] The confrontation that led to the death of Dudley George was not the result of an orchestrated political and OPP plot to forcibly remove the occupiers from the park but the product of a volatile situation that spiralled out of control.

Despite repeated exhortations from the Stoney Pointers and their supporters that the occupations were peaceful, the takeovers of the military camp and the park were marked by violence and the threat of violence. The occupiers did not have guns on the fateful night of 6 September 1995, but they had previously shot at helicopters, had hunted on the camp property with rifles, and had sent clear signals that they were prepared to fight for their land. For example, David George's sawed-off shotgun, which he carried around the camp, contained the words "BASTARD BLASTER," "KILL THEM," and "DESTROY." Obviously, these words were not directed at deer.[121] Judges later deemed that the police were unjustified in firing on unarmed protestors, which is consistent with the evidence of the threat posed on the night of Dudley George's death. This does not mean, however, that the situation was peaceful, stable, or lacking in danger to safety or security. The weapons that the Stoney Pointers typically used varied from rocks to pipes to motor vehicles. Furthermore, some occupiers believed that acts of violence and destruction of property – such as smashing police car windows with clubs – were justified and consistent with a peaceful occupation.[122]

After Kenneth Deane was convicted of criminal negligence causing death, the popular image of the Ipperwash Crisis shifted from state authorities upholding law and order to government malfeasance. This latter framework for understanding the dispute was reflected in the final report of the Ipperwash Inquiry, which blamed federal and provincial officials, as well as the OPP, for the tragic outcome. Did this deny that the provincial government, as the owner of the park, had an obligation on behalf of the citizens of the province to respond to the forcible occupation of the property? Should it have entered into substantive negotiations while any occupation was ongoing, or would this simply have encouraged other groups to engage in illegal activities in order to force the government's hand?[123] These questions were conveniently pushed aside. In his final submission to the inquiry, Premier Harris and his lawyers suggested, "The real question arising from Ipperwash is how government may restore and maintain the rule of law and civil order where it is disregarded by persons who have experienced historical injustice. There are no civil rights without civil obligations to respect the law and civil order. No civil society can tolerate the taking of public lands by force. No civil society can do so and continue to *be* a civil society." Harris accused the Liberal government and its "media allies" of avoiding the policy issues that arose at Ipperwash in favour of "smear tactics for short term political gain." Their approach had two main consequences for public policy in his view. First, it "discredited the obligation of government to maintain the rule of law and civil order in cases of direct action." Second, it disabled the McGuinty government "from standing in support of principles of law and civil order in opposition to the unilateral taking of land by First Nations persons."[124] In the end, the tragedy for the George family became a political tragedy as well.

All told, did the Stoney Pointers achieve their aims by occupying Camp Ipperwash and the provincial park? If the primary goal was to obtain physical control of the properties for the Stoney Pointers, and thus *de facto* ownership, the tactics worked. If the goal was also to secure distinct legal status as a "Stoney Point First Nation" with legal ownership to the former Stony Point Reserve, then it was a failure. The occupations did break an unfavourable status quo from the standpoint of the occupiers, but the chaotic state of local Kettle and Stony Point politics posed a major problem. Critics accused government officials of delay tactics but did not address the intractable problem of how to transfer land claimed by rival Aboriginal groups.

In the final report of the Ipperwash Inquiry, Linden recommended that "the federal government should immediately return the former army camp to the peoples of the Kettle and Stony Point First Nation and guarantee that it will assume complete responsibility for an appropriate environmental cleanup of the site."[125] Despite the 1998 agreement between the federal government and the KSPFN on a land transfer, the process remains incomplete. The federal government and KSPFN continue to negotiate a full and final settlement regarding the former Camp Ipperwash, and investigative fieldwork on a survey of unexploded ordnance began in October 2007. As of spring 2010, the survey was 45 per cent complete. In due course, this will lead to a clean-up and to restoration of reserve status. "The overall goal of the negotiations is to resolve the outstanding issues surrounding Camp Ipperwash once and for all," a government background statement notes. "A final settlement will assist the First Nation in rebuilding a strong and economically viable community and in continuing the process of healing and reconciliation."[126]

On 28 May 2009 the province formally signed over control of Ipperwash Provincial Park to the Kettle and Stony Point First Nation.[127] Brad Duguid, the Ontario minister of Aboriginal affairs, proclaimed that "this agreement will lead to further healing and reconciliation across Ontario as we work together with Aboriginal partners to implement the recommendations of the Report of the Ipperwash Inquiry." KSPFN chief Elizabeth Cloud expressed her gratitude that the inquiry's recommendation was fulfilled and thanked "the many people and especially Dudley for his personal sacrifice."[128] Critics held this up as another indication that Premier McGuinty was playing politics with Ipperwash. Linden had never suggested returning the park, and it seemed ironic that the elected KSPFN chief and council had never laid claim to the park prior to the Stoney Pointers' occupation of it. "In transferring Ipperwash park and tolerating absolute terrorism in Caledonia, McGuinty is clearly signalling that in Ontario, the right way to claim land is to occupy it with an armed force," former Conservative Cabinet minister John Snobelen asserted.[129] The tragedy of Ipperwash, it seemed, had left a lasting legacy that continued to perpetuate government and police mismanagement of blockades and occupations.

NOTES

1   Variations in the names used to identify the Aboriginal communities are both confusing and illuminating. "Stony Point" and "Stoney Point" refer to the same reserve, the former being used in most government correspondence. In recent years, the use of the term "Stony" has been linked to the Kettle and Stony Point First Nation (KSPFN), the band officially recognized by the federal and provincial governments. "Stoney" has been linked to the Stoney Pointers occupying the former Camp Ipperwash and neighbouring provincial park, who claim distinct band status from the KSPFN. To add to the confusion, the KSPFN often refers to the land as "Stoney Point" but retains the spelling "Stony Point" in its name. In early-nineteenth-century records, the Stony Point Reserve was commonly known as Aux Sable, Ausable, or Sable. During the early post-treaty period, most documents referred to the "Aux Sable Indians," the "Sable Indians," the "Indians at Kettle Point," or the "Bosanquet Indians" to describe the communities on the Kettle and Stony Point Reserves.

2   Sidney B. Linden, *Report of the Ipperwash Inquiry*, 4 vols, Attorney General of Ontario, Toronto, 2007, http://www.attorneygeneral.jus.gov. on.ca/inquiries/ipperwash/index.html. See also Peter Edwards, *One Dead*

*Indian: The Premier, the Police, and the Ipperwash Crisis* (Toronto: Stoddart, 2001), which offers a compelling journalist's perspective but is limited by the absence of any references to source material.

3 Although it is difficult to substantiate the precise range of any particular band prior to contact, these Native groups likely observed a seasonal migratory pattern that centred on the general coastal area between Blue Point and Goderich and inland along the creeks and river systems that drain into Lake Huron. Neal Ferris, "Continuity within Change: Settlement-Subsistence Strategies and Artifact Patterns of the Southwestern Ontario Ojibwa, A.D. 1780–1861" (MA thesis, York University, 1989).

4 RG 10, vol. 2022, file 8520, Library and Archives Canada (LAC). See also Memorial of the Chippewa, RG 10, vol. 2568, file 115,678, LAC. The position of chief descended through Pewash (possibly the source of the name Ipperwash) to his son Mahwajewong. He in turn had three sons: Takishma, Wahpahgas, and "King George." Wahpahgas became chief and later became known as Johnston Wahpahgas. Eventually, his sons adopted the surname Johnston. Wahpagas's line intermarried with one of the prominent families residing at Kettle Point. The daughter (or granddaughter) of Chief Pewash married Oshawawanoo, friend and co-warrior of Wahpagas.

5 He was variously referred to as Ashkebahgahneguod, Chemokomon (Big Knife), Oshawawanoo, Shahwahwahnoo, or John Big Knife. Census data from 1861 indicate that he and Shegwahnahbik were both born in Indiana and were still "pagans" at 102 and 98 years of age. Family testimony indicates that as a reward for their role in the 1812–14 conflict, these brothers were recognized as having the right to occupy land at Kettle Point long before the conclusion of the treaty. The Shawnee connection is said to be a maternal tie that has not been substantiated from the literature on Tecumseh and his family. The legitimacy of their status as Kettle Point's first family was never questioned, and they seem to have been considered part of the original Chippewa Nation at the time of the treaty. Shegwahnahbik apparently had no wife or descendants.

6 RG 10, vol. 2022, file 8520, LAC. A chief known as Jacob Quakeegwon (originally of Walpole Island) was also, for a time, associated with the Stony Point area. Quakeegwon's band moved to a lot in Bosanquet near Stony Point in 1839 after a dispute with Wawanosh at Sarnia. Between the years 1839 and 1851, his small band lived near Stony Point on a small parcel purchased from a white settler. Most of Quakeegwon's band had returned to Walpole Island by 1851. The Indians living on the three parcels of land were generally referred to collectively as the Aux Sable Band from the 1830s to the 1850s. During that time, most documents concerning the

"Aux Sable Indians" were signed by Wahpagas, Quakeegwon, Shahwawanoo, and other "principal men." The identification of a band with the river they lived near was common practice in the early nineteenth century, and in other cases a band was sometimes identified by the name of the recognized chief. Following the return of Quakeegwon's group to Walpole Island after 1850, Shahwawanoo, Wahpagas, their supporters, and their descendants were the only leaders of the Aux Sable Indians.

7   William Jones reported the arrival of about three hundred Indians in 1837 who sought to settle on the Chippewa reserves. "They say that they have never swerved from their allegiance to the British Government," Jones recounted, "and wish to remain under the protection of their great father the King and that about as many more of their tribe wish to follow these if they can get leave to settle, they further promise to leave off their roving habits and become permanent residents." William Jones Papers, 7 July 1837, Archives of Ontario, MS 296.

8   Investigations into every person's pedigree were conducted during the 1870s in a fiasco of claims and counterclaims. By 1872, according to the records compiled in Robert Mackenzie's investigative report, the Chippewa population was primarily located at Kettle Point (fifty-six persons), with only two Chippewa families (ten persons) residing at Stony Point. About thirty-eight Potawatomis lived on the latter reserve. RG 10, vol. 1863, file 322, LAC. Mackenzie, a believer in assimilation as the road to progress, recommended the survey and subdivision of both reserves and the allotment of land parcels to the individual families.

9   RG 10, vol. 2022, file 8520; vol. 1916, file 2752; vol. 1884, file 1260; vol. 2568, file 115,678; vol. 2763, file 151,900; and vol. 1863, file 322, LAC.

10  RG 10, vol. 2763, file 151,900, LAC.

11  See RG 10, vol. 2763, file 151,900; and vol. 1916, file 2752, LAC.

12  The MacKenzie report of 1872 noted, "They have almost all been born there ... and are not oppressed in any way by the Chippewas, on the contrary they are getting more and more connected with them by intermarriage; but they are naturally anxious that a title of occupation of the only home they now know should be guaranteed to them ... [T]hey seem to cherish an expectation that the badge of inferiority will by and by be removed altogether by their incorporation into the Chippewa Band." RG 10, vol. 1863, file 322, LAC.

13  RG 10, vol. 1916, file 2752, LAC. Between 1892 and 1918, repeated requests that they be recognized and set apart as a *separate band from Sarnia* did not contain any request that the *Kettle and Stony Point communities* be divided into two separate bands.

14  On the "two bands" idea, see, for example, Maynard T. George, "Factum:
    The History of the Chippewa of Stoney Point First Nation # 43," 1 June
    1993, 2–7, in Department of National Defence (DND), Director General of
    Aboriginal Affairs (DGAA), file 1003-Ipperwash; Helen Roos, "It
    Happened as If Overnight: The Expropriation and Relocation of Stoney
    Point Reserve #43, 1942" (MA thesis, University of Western Ontario,
    1998); Helen Roos, "'My Parents, They Became Poor': The Socio-economic
    Effects of the Expropriation and Relocation of Stoney Point Reserve #43,
    1942," *Past Imperfect* 7 (1998): 155–75 at 159–60; Helen Roos, "Ready,
    Aim, Fire! The Appropriation of Stony Point Reserve #43, 1942," *Western
    Journal of Graduate Research* 6, no. 1 (1997): 28–40 at 29–30; Timothy
    Bisha, "Seeds of Conflict on a Southwestern Ontario Reserve" (MA thesis,
    University of Western Ontario, 1996), 21; Stoney Point Band, "The Case
    of the Stoney Point Reserve No. 43: A Brief of Fact and Argument," paper
    submitted to the Standing Committee on Aboriginal Affairs, 11 December
    1991, 2; Lisa Phillips Valentine and Alan McDougall, "A Separation
    Agreement Forty Years in the Making," in *Papers of the Thirty-Third
    Algonquian Conference*, ed. H.C. Wolfart, 392–413 (Winnipeg: University
    of Manitoba, 2002), 394–5, 398. If the terms "band" and "village" or
    "community" are employed as synonymous, nonlegal descriptors for a
    group of people with shared experiences, the current author has no objec-
    tion to use of the term "band" to describe the residents of the Stony Point
    Reserve from 1919 to 1942. However, because the term also contains a le-
    gal definition within the Indian Act and hence is inextricably linked to cur-
    rent legal land claims, it can be used to project distinct legal status on a
    group that has not, historically, been recognized as having such status.
    Several commentators on the Ipperwash case have used this word to fur-
    ther the claims of the locatees displaced by the camp's creation. To be more
    faithful to the documentary record – which forms the basis for recent land
    claims by descendants of the Stony Point locatees – the term "band" will
    refer to the legal construct as defined by the Indian Act and Indian Affairs
    administrators, and "community" will be used to describe a group living at
    a particular location with a shared culture and experiences that may or
    may not have legal "band" status. On the confusion in this particular case,
    see also J. Holmes, testimony to Ipperwash Inquiry, 17 August 2004, 35–8.
    Transcripts of testimonies before the Ipperwash Inquiry are available
    through the official website at http://www.attorneygeneral.jus.gov.on.ca/
    inquiries/ipperwash/transcripts/index.html.

15  The archival record provides a preponderance of evidence on this explicit
    intent. See voluminous correspondence in RG 10, vol. 2297, file 59,207;
    vol. 2568, file 115,678, parts 1–2; vol. 2648, file 130,893; vol. 2740,

file 145,267; and vol. 2763, file 151,900, LAC. See also Aboriginal Affairs and Northern Development Canada (AANDC), Indian Land Registry instrument X014790; Valentine and McDougall, "Separation Agreement," 395–412; and submissions of the Chippewas of Kettle and Stony Point First Nation to Ipperwash Inquiry, 31 July 2006, 16–19. Transcripts of written closing submissions to the Ipperwash Inquiry are available through the official website at http://www.attorneygeneral.jus.gov.on.ca/inquiries/ ipperwash/closing_submissions/index.html.

16  See Indian Claims Commission, *Inquiry into the 1927 Surrender Claim of the Chippewas of Kettle and Stony Point First Nation*, report, Indian Claims Commission, Ottawa, March 1997, 3, 9–93.

17  Ibid. Gray once again acted as solicitor for Scott and his partner, J.A. White. The other lots remained in private hands until the federal government appropriated them in 1942 to create Camp Ipperwash. Ipperwash Provincial Park was never part of Camp Ipperwash.

18  When the council learned about shale removal, it appealed to the Royal Canadian Mounted Police for help. Guided by their interpretation of the Indian Act, the police intervened to protect the rights of the band. Discussions revealed that the province and the Department of Indian Affairs disagreed over the ownership of the offshore shale, with the province insisting that it owned the lakebed and Indian Affairs arguing that the reserve's boundaries extended below the high-water mark and well into the lake. Negotiators settled on a payment to the band of 25 cents a load for "the use of the road" to access the shale, thus avoiding the legal question of who owned the actual lakebed.

19  Records that document the progress of the works, the plans, and maps of the construction do not show the burial ground location. The survey conducted by W.G. McGeorge that summer did not indicate the burial ground location in written reports or maps. Through a study of the burial grounds issue conducted jointly in 1996 by the First Nation and Canada, evidence came to light of the discovery of human remains in the park in 1950. Archaeological opinion is inconclusive about whether these remains represented postcontact "Christian" burials or were precontact burials. The area is known to be rich in archaeological sites, some going as far back as the earliest Aboriginal settlements 8,000 to 10,000 years ago.

20  See P. Whitney Lackenbauer, *Battle Grounds: The Canadian Military and Aboriginal Lands* (Vancouver: UBC Press, 2007), 115–43; and P. Whitney Lackenbauer, "Combined Operation: The Appropriation of Stoney Point Reserve and the Creation of Camp Ipperwash," *Journal of Military and Strategic Studies* 2, no. 1 (Fall 1999): 1–31.

21 For more on this process and ensuing effects on the band, see Lackenbauer, *Battle Grounds*; and Roos, "'My Parents, They Became Poor.'" Member of Parliament Ross Gray again lobbied politically and used his legal skills to advocate for the government's position. In 1941 he indicated to the government that the village of Thedford would provide lands known as Pine Hill Camp (formerly used for military training) to the military without charge for the duration of the war. The DND rejected the proposal because of the excessive cost of providing an adequate water supply to what would be a base only for the duration of the war.

22 Ronald George, in House of Commons Standing Committee on Aboriginal Affairs (HCSCAA), *Minutes of Proceedings and Evidence*, 12 December 1991, 8, 30.

23 See, for example, ibid.; and George, "Factum," 14, 18. Contrast the views of Ronald George and Maynard T. George with Councillor Bonnie Bressette's statements in D. Collins, "The Struggle for Camp Ipperwash," *London Free Press*, 26 October 1991. The band ceased to have multiple "electoral sections" for councillors after 1951, whereas previously the Stony Point locatees had elected a councillor. See P.C. 6016, 12 November 1951, in RG 10, vol. 7117, file 471/3-5, part 1, LAC; and Indian Act, SC 1951, c. 29, s. 73(4).

24 Kettle Point BCR 1968/69-25, 5 December 1968, and Kettle and Stony Point BCR, 15 September 1970, University of Western Ontario (UWO) Library, microfiche F9; Churchman to Bergevin, 16 December 1968, Faulkner to Acting Regional Director-Ontario, DIAND, 17 March 1970, and Knapp to Verrette, 24 March 1970 and marginalia, all in AANDC, file 471/30-8-43, vol. 1; Chretien to Cadieux, 4 June 1970, AANDC, file 471/30-8-43, vol. 2; "The Indian Claim to the 2500-Acre Ipperwash Base," *Globe and Mail*, 17 September 1970; "Indians Confirm Land Demands," *Sarnia Observer*, 22 September 1970.

25 DND, file 7800-J34, vol. 1; R. Banting, "Ipperwash," research report, February 1976; "Camp Ipperwash Belongs to Indians," *Windsor Star*, 12 June 1972.

26 Reg Wild, minutes of meeting, 12 March 1979, DND, file 7800-J34, vol. 3.

27 Chippewas of Kettle and Stony Point BCR, 2 May 1980, UWO Library, microfiche F27; Milner to Ryan, 21 October 1980, AANDC, file 471/30-171–44, vol. 9; D. Pattenaude, "Chippewas Approve Compensation Plan," *Sarnia Observer*, 8 September 1980; "$2.4 Million Offer Accepted by Sarnia-Area Indian Band," *Globe and Mail*, 8 September 1980; "Indians Accept Millions for Land," *London Free Press*, 8 September 1980. Out of an eligible 489 band members, 266 voted. "Band Members Vote in Favour

of Settlement," *Forest Standard*, 10 September 1980. Federal norms governing the return of expropriated lands provided individuals with the right to buy back their former land when it was no longer required for its intended purpose. In this case, the band received full market value, plus it would get the land back for free.

28 Laforme to Minister of National Defence, 23 September 1980, DND, DGAA, file 1003-Ipperwash; Hill to Rowcliffe, January 1980, and Crutchlow to Minister of National Defence, 4 September 1980, DND, file 7800-J34, vol. 5; various documents in AANDC, file 471/30-171-44, vol. 9; George, "Factum," 18–19, 21, 26–30; "Dissenters Picket," *Forest Standard*, 10 September 1980.

29 Milner to Ryan, 21 October 1980, AANDC, file 471/30-171-44, vol. 9; P.C. 1981-499, 26 February 1981, copy on file with P. Whitney Lackenbauer.

30 Agreement between KSPB Council and Minister of National Defence, 14 March 1985, DND, DGAA, file 1003-Ipperwash; Chippewas of Kettle and Stony Point BCR 1278, UWO Library, microfiche F27; Roos, "It Happened as If Overnight," 121; Gilby to Minister of Indian Affairs and Northern Development, 16 May 1985, AANDC, file E5643-06193, vol. 3. Descendants of individual location ticket holders had already sued the Crown and elected band officials. See *Angeline Shawkence v. The Attorney General of Canada, Earl Bressette, et al.*, Supreme Court of Ontario Action 1480/83; and *Shawkence v. The Queen*, Federal Court of Canada Trial Division, T-702-85.

31 Testimonies to Ipperwash Inquiry of Ron George, 28 February 2005, 47–51, 80–1; Warren George, 8 December 2004, 78–9; Gerald George, 12 January 2005, 195–6; Rose Manning, 6 April 2005, 216–17; Vince George, 5 April 2006, 22–4; and David George, 19 October 2004, 19–23.

32 This group first organized as a "Stoney Point Steering Committee" but soon began to refer to themselves as the "Stoney Point Community Association." Helen Roos, "Broken Promises and Deadly Bullets: The Stoney Point Native Land Claim," in *Canada: Confederation to Present*, ed. Bob Hesketh and Chris Hackett, CD-ROM (Edmonton: Chinook Multimedia, 2001)"; Stoney Point First Nation #43, "A Reaffirmation of Independence," 30 September 1991; Collins, "Struggle for Camp Ipperwash."

33 See, for example, George, "Factum." On self-construction as resistance, see J. Cruikshank, "Oral Tradition and Oral History: Reviewing Some Issues," *Canadian Historical Review* 75, no. 3 (1994): 403–18 at 418.

34 HCSCAA, "Issue No. 8: Study on Claim from the Stoney Point Reserve,"
   12 December 1991," in *Minutes of Proceedings and Evidence*, 8, 9–10, 15,
   41; HCSCAA, "Third Report," 13 March 1992, 1; B. MacKenzie,
   "Commons Committee Urges Return of Camp Ipperwash," *Sarnia
   Observer*, 14 March 1992.

35 Tom Siddon, in D. Collins, "Frith Supports Land Claim," *London Free
   Press*, 18 August 1990; Siddon to Minister of National Defence, 21 June
   1991, cited in House of Commons Standing Committee on Aboriginal
   Affairs, *Minutes of Proceedings and Evidence*, 12 December 1991, 8, 34.

36 See, for example, "Burial Renews Hope for Return of Land," *London Free
   Press*, 15 October 1990; T. Hodgkinson, "The Fight for Camp Ipperwash,"
   *London Free Press*, 15 August 1992.

37 "No More Excuses," *Sarnia Observer*, 12 January 1992; "Natives Must
   Settle Dispute," *Sarnia Observer*, 20 September 1993. On disputed per-
   spectives, see Kettle and Stony Point Council, untitled press release, 7 May
   1993; N. Bowen, "Natives' Differences Stall Camp Ipperwash Talks,"
   *Sarnia Observer*, 17 September 1993; DIAND, "Camp Ipperwash," 1996;
   D. McCaffery, "Natives Dispute Booklet," *Sarnia Observer*, 18 July 1997;
   J. Carl, "Natives Plan to Sway Public to Their Cause," *London Free Press*,
   18 July 1997.

38 Maynard T. George, who was elected a KSPFN councillor in 1992 and
   received money and research support to gather evidence that the Stoney
   Pointers were a separate and distinct First Nation, never produced information for the chief and council. Submissions of the Chippewas of Kettle
   and Stony Point First Nation to Ipperwash Inquiry, 31 July 2006, 28. The
   KSPFN council hired an anthropologist in 1992 to conduct a community-
   based research program to investigate the community's genealogy, history,
   past political composition, and land surrenders. Despite years spent re-
   searching government archival material and documenting the positions of
   the local factions, the committed Stoney Pointers still rejected any evidence
   that questioned their separate First Nation position. Accordingly, although
   the work was useful in KSPFN legal and negotiating processes, it failed to
   bring about any resolution of the deep internal divisions.

39 Maynard T. George, in Linden, *Report*, vol. 1, 89–90, emphasis in original.
   See also Carl George, testimony to Ipperwash Inquiry, 9 February 2005,
   35–6, and 22 February 2005, 166–7.

40 Linden, *Report*, vol. 1, 92–3; Glenn George, testimony to Ipperwash
   Inquiry, 2 February 2005, 61–3; Carl George, testimony to Ipperwash
   Inquiry, 9 February 2005, 54–8, 61–6, 104, 182. Carl George testified

before the inquiry that he signed as "Chief" because others wanted to call him that, but he explained that he was never elected chief. Carl George, testimony to Ipperwash Inquiry, 9 February 2005, 50–2.

41  Linden, *Report*, vol. 1, 90, 95. See also KSPB Council, untitled press release, 7 May 1993. Tom Bressette was first elected chief of the KSPB in 1990 and was re-elected every two years until 1997, when he was elected Ontario regional chief and vice chief of the Assembly of First Nations.

42  DND, Annex C, Paff Plan – Op Orion, 6b, 14 May 1996, acquired through Government of Canada, Access to Information and Privacy (ATIP); J. Ivison, "Native Tents Near Grenade Range," *London Free Press*, 18 May 1993; P. Adamick, "Natives Serve Military with Eviction Notice," *Toronto Star*, 14 June 1993; P. Morden, "Stoney Point Natives Build Church at Camp Ipperwash," *Sarnia Observer*, 30 June 1993; Clifford George, testimony to Ipperwash Inquiry, 10 September 2004, 113. In March 1994 the Stoney Pointers honoured Clifford George and Dudley George as nation builders following their difficult winter on the land at the military range.

43  J.L. Steckley and B.D. Cummins, *Full Circle: Canada's First Nations* (Toronto: Pearson, Prentice-Hall, 2001) 202–3.

44  Edwards, *One Dead Indian*, 61–3; S. Rose, "Indians Celebrate Return," *London Free Press*, 7 June 1993; DND, "Camp Ipperwash," backgrounder, September 1993. For different portrayals of Dudley George, see Tim Southam, *One Dead Indian*, television movie (CTV, 2005); and John C. Thompson, "The Ipperwash Protest," *Mackenzie Institute Notes*, no. 5 (July 1996): 11.

45  P. Morden, "Kettle Point Chief Welcomes Idea of Mediation," *Sarnia Observer*, 17 July 1993; Clifford George, in C. Parsons, "Land Claim Cited after Bullet Hits Helicopter," *Globe and Mail*, 25 August 1993; Clifford George, in W. Immen, "Band Chief Denies Natives Shot at Helicopter," *Globe and Mail*, 26 August 1993; C. Ganley, "Will Stoney Point Become Another Oka?" *Toronto Sun*, 30 August 1993; L.P. Valentine and A.K. McDougall, "Unveiling the Hegemon: Political Imag(in)ing of Stoney Point (Ipperwash)," in *Papers of the Thirtieth Algonquian Conference*, ed. D.H. Pentland, 397–410 (Winnipeg: University of Manitoba, 1999). See also documents in DND, file A99-1042, acquired through ATIP. Thompson, "Ipperwash Protest," 8, notes that the man who fired on the helicopter was immediately evicted from the camp. Abraham George was identified as the shooter at the Ipperwash Inquiry. See Carl George, testimony to Ipperwash Inquiry, 9 February 2005, 145–7, and 22 February 2005, 206–8.

46 Tom Bressette, in Linden, *Report*, vol. 1, 104. Bressette had met with Jean Chretien during the 1993 election campaign, and Chretien intimated that, if elected, he would make every effort to have the land returned. Tom Bressette, testimony to Ipperwash Inquiry, 2 March 2005, 42–4.

47 Kettle and Stony Point First Nation (KSPFN), "Camp Ipperwash," c. 2002, copy on file with P. Whitney Lackenbauer; documents in DND, DGAA, file 1003-Ipperwash; "Native Band Wants Cleanup of Camp Ipperwash," *Hamilton Spectator*, 23 February 1994; R.-M. Ur and D. Collonette, *Hansard*, 17 February 1995; R. Platiel, "Time Running out for Munitions Cleanup," *Globe and Mail*, 3 August 1995; I. Timberlake, "Ipperwash Transfer to Band Opposed," *Windsor Star*, 23 February 1994; "Natives Already Feuding over Camp Ipperwash," *Kitchener-Waterloo Record*, 24 February 1994. Lipton had extensive experience negotiating for the Tsuu T'ina over the clean-up of the Sarcee range at CFB Calgary. See Lackenbauer, *Battle Grounds*, 197, 217.

48 Glenn George, in Thompson, "Ipperwash Protest," 9. See also Linden, *Report*, vol. 1, 109, 166. Carl George later acknowledged his difficulties in keeping the Stoney Pointers cohesive and explained that by the spring of 1995 they seemed to have lost patience with his approach. See Carl George, testimony to Ipperwash Inquiry, 9 February 2005, 212–13, 216–17.

49 See, for example, Gerald George, testimony to Ipperwash Inquiry, 13 January 2005, 20–2; and Elizabeth Thunder (a Stony Point descendant), request to Stoney Pointers' lawyer, quoted in Deb Hutton, "Final Submission of Deb Hutton," submission to Ipperwash Inquiry, 28 July 2006, 74.

50 See, for example, "Military Transition Team Helps Renegade Natives," *Halifax Chronicle*, 5 August 1995; Edwards, *One Dead Indian*, 66; and Captain Howse, testimony to Ipperwash Inquiry, 27 June 2006, 75. Harley George and Nicholas Cottrell were involved in an incident where George, driving the bus, tried to collide with a military vehicle. He claimed that this was intended "to bully the Army around" and intimidate them because "they've been doing it to our people for years. I might as well return the favour." Harley George, testimony to Ipperwash Inquiry, 20 January 2005, 233–5.

51 Although the occupiers originally did not have hunting rifles at the camp, "after a while then it was like nobody paid much attention to it." Carl George, testimony to Ipperwash Inquiry, 9 February 2005, 182. See also George Speck, testimony to Ipperwash Inquiry, 22 March 2006, 88–93.

52 See OPP, "Operation Maple Law Enforcement Guidelines," 4 July 1995, quoted in Michael D. Harris, "Written Submission of the Hon. Michael D.

Harris to the Ipperwash Inquiry," n.d., 61; and Captain Smith, testimony to Ipperwash Inquiry, 26 June 2006, 27–39.

53  Isaac Doxtator, testimony to Ipperwash Inquiry, 25 November 2004, 107–8. Although several Stoney Pointers testified that the occupation was planned in advance, their evidence is contradictory on the number of meetings and the participation therein. Testimonies to Ipperwash Inquiry of Rose Manning, 17 April 2005, 36–40; Tina George, 9 January 2005, 96–7; Wesley George, 1 December 2004, 20–1; and Harley George, 20 January 2005, 139–40.

54  Testimonies to Ipperwash Inquiry of Marlin Simon, 12 October 2004, 214–19, and Harley George, 20 January 2005, 251; Linden, *Report*, vol. 1, 131–3.

55  Testimonies to Ipperwash Inquiry of Doug Smith, 26 June 2006, 112–20, 171–2, and Harley George, 20 January 2005, 225; J. Liebner, "Natives to Wait Another Year to Take over Ipperwash Land," *London Free Press*, 18 April 1995; LFCA HQ to Bcomd CFB Toronto, 30 June 1995, DND, file A96-0876, acquired through ATIP; E. Oziewicz, "Forces Leave Camp to Occupiers," *Globe and Mail*, 31 July 1995. The military called for OPP assistance, but Smith refused to ask the occupiers to leave and the DND was not prepared to seek an injunction, so the OPP did not respond. See John Carson, testimony to Ipperwash Inquiry, 12 May 2005, 62–9.

56  See, for example, Mary-Lou LaPratte, "Ipperwash," 23 June 2004, http://www.ipperwashpapers.com/ipperwashdocuments/A-1.pdf. In August 1995 LaPratte's husband, Roland, claimed that five Natives in a brown van had shot at a municipal work crew, before driving back to Dudley George's trailer on Camp Ipperwash, where they got out of the car armed with rifles.

57  John Carson, testimony to Ipperwash Inquiry, 12 May 2005, 65–6.

58  Ibid., 157.

59  Linden, *Report*, vol. 1, 146–50, 152–62, and vol. 4, 13; testimonies to Ipperwash Inquiry of John Carson, 12 May 2005, 67–79, and Tom Bressette, 2 March 2005, 69–80. At a band meeting on 1 August 1995, various KSPFN members complained that outsiders were treating the lands like a dumpster, denying former residents access to the camp and the beach, and causing trouble. One elder said that she had attended the camp, where Bruce Elijah had identified himself to her as a "shit disturber," and that she had heard him "telling the people to go the Oka way to settle things." See quotations in Hutton, "Final Submission," 86. On outsiders, see also Peter Moon, "Oneida Chiefs Begin Oka-like Talks to Defuse Tension at Ipperwash," *Globe and Mail*, 15 Iuly 1995; "Outsiders Won't

Quit Native Fight," *Victoria Times Colonist*, 3 August 1995; "Outsiders Say They're Staying at Ipperwash," *Sarnia Observer*, 3 August 1995; and Thompson, "Ipperwash Protest," 7–9.

60 Diane Francis, "Native Rowdies Run Amok," *Toronto Sun*, 5 August 1995.

61 Tom Bressette, in Oziewicz, "Forces Leave Camp"; "Ipperwash Army Base Covered with Live Shells, Indians Warned," *Montreal Gazette*, 1 August 1995.

62 Gerald C. George, letter to editor, *Forest Standard*, 30 August 1995, quoted in Edwards, *One Dead Indian*, 68.

63 Les Kobayashi, testimony to Ipperwash Inquiry, 24 October 2005; Hutton, "Final Submission," 33. Chief Bressette did not condone these actions and advised the Ministry of Natural Resources to have the Stoney Pointers removed from the camp for fear of encouraging other occupations by anyone else with a claim. Tom Bressette, testimony to Ipperwash Inquiry, 1 March 2005, 233–41.

64 Glen Bressette, testimony to Ipperwash Inquiry, 10 November 2004, 90–1.

65 The OPP met with Kettle Point elders, who indicated that there was no evidence of a burial ground in the park. Testimonies to Ipperwash Inquiry of Sergeant Brad Seltzer, 13 June 2006, 129–30, 134–44, and Trevor Edward Richardson, 8 June 2006, 277–9. The KSPFN considered a claim but dropped it after the band lost its civil litigation for the West Ipperwash beach lands. See, for example, Julie Carl, "Natives Lose Ipperwash Beach Claim," *London Free Press*, 20 May 1998.

66 See, for example, testimonies to the Ipperwash Inquiry of Glenn George, 1 February 2005, 19, 209–11, and 2 February 2005, 237–40; Roderick George, 23 November 2004, 79, 104, and 25 November 2004, 20–1; Marlin Simon, 28 September 2004, 214–17, and 18 October 2004, 166–7; Mike Cloud, 9 November 2004, 129–30; David George, 20 October 2004, 8–9, and 1 November 2004, 127, 190–1; and Glen Bressette, 10 November 2004, 59.

67 See Linden, *Report*, vol. 4, 15–17; John Carson, testimony to Ipperwash Inquiry, 16 May 2005, 14–17, 21–31, 175–92.

68 Testimonies to Ipperwash Inquiry of Stewart George, 2 November 2004, 121–9; Roderick George, 23 November 2004, 56–7, 105–11, and 24 November 2004, 139–41; Neil Michael John Whelan, 29 March 2006, 114–19; Wayde Ellard Jacklin, 25 April 2006, 85–90; and Trevor Edward Richardson, 8 June 2006, 105–1.

69 The first people to enter the park included adult men such as Dudley George, Marlin Simon, and David George, teenage boys such as Nicholas

Cottrelle, Wesley George, and J.T. Cousins, and women such as Tina George and Carolyn George. Linden, *Report*, vol. 1, 201–3; testimonies to Ipperwash Inquiry of Marlin Simon, 29 September 2004, 10–11, and Warren George, 8 December 2004, 121. Glenn George yelled at Korosec that they were taking the park and that he should tell all the people living between the western park boundary and Ravenswood that they would be taking their land next. Stan Korosec, testimony to Ipperwash Inquiry, 6 April 2006, 28–31. On Korosec's previous exchange with Bert Manning, which suggested that they would sit down to discuss matters, see ibid., 23–8. Glenn George refused any meeting with the police.

70 Ibid., 35–6.

71 Linden, *Report*, vol. 4, 19; testimonies to Ipperwash Inquiry of Neil Michael John Whelan, 29 March 2006, 132–4; Wayde Ellard Jacklin, 25 April 2006, 110–12; Wesley George, 30 November 2004, 189–91; and Stan Korosec, 6 April 2006, 33–5.

72 Tom Bressette, in Hutton, "Final Submission," 137–9.

73 Fred Thomas and Ken Williams, "Reign of Terror Continues," press release, 5 September 1995, quoted in Hutton, "Final Submission," 167.

74 Linden, *Report*, vol. 4, 21–4.

75 Ibid., 26.

76 Testimonies to Ipperwash Inquiry of Mark Wright, 22 February 2006, 152–4; and John Carson, 12 May 2005, 536.

77 Linden, *Report*, vol. 1, 269–84, and vol. 4, 27–30. Tina George initially testified to the inquiry that she had not heard gunshots, but later recalled that she had accompanied Russ Jewell and Marlin Simon on target practice at the camp and that each had fired shots in the bush by the inland lakes. She then retracted these comments the next day. Tina George, testimony to Ipperwash Inquiry, 19 January 2005, 171–6, and 20 January 2005, 8–14.

78 Linden, *Report*, vol. 1, 294–7, 326–9, 335.

79 Attendees included Premier Mike Harris, Attorney General Charles Harnick, Solicitor General Bob Runciman, Minister of Natural Resources Chris Hodgson, their deputy ministers, and their executive assistants. The attorney general later testified that he had heard the premier say, "I want the fucking Indians out of the park," which Harris denied. Although Harris was critical of the police for being inadequately prepared to deal with the occupation, Ipperwash Inquiry commissioner Sidney Linden found that "the Premier did not inappropriately direct the OPP on its operations at Ipperwash or enter the law enforcement domain of the police. Although one may disagree with his view, it was legitimate for the Premier to take

the position that the First Nations people were illegally occupying the park, and that he wanted them out of Ipperwash Park as soon as possible." Linden, *Report*, vol. 4, 37–50.

80 Ibid., 50–2.

81 Ibid., 54–7, 60–1; testimonies to Ipperwash Inquiry of Mark Wright, 22 February 2006, 256–62; Gerald George, 13 January 2005, 82–92; and Stewart George, 2 November 2005, 75–9. OPP officer Vince George met with a confidential source who informed him that Buck Doxtator, six men from Muncey, and a person from Oka were in the park and that Doxtator had weapons with him. Previously, the informant had told Vince George that Doxtator was very dangerous. Vince George, testimony to Ipperwash Inquiry, 5 April 2006, 70–2, 126–32, 139–43.

82 Testimonies to Ipperwash Inquiry of Mike Cloud, 8 November 2004, 137–41; Rose Manning, 7 April 2005, 91–5; and Constable Mark Dew, 4 April 2006, 75–83.

83 Linden, *Report*, vol. 4, 57–8.

84 Ibid., 62.

85 George Hebblethwaite, testimony to Ipperwash Inquiry, 11 May 2006, 291–2.

86 Cecil Bernard George, testimony to Ipperwash Inquiry, 7 December 2004, 49–50, 59–65, 115–16.

87 There was no evidence of firearms at the time. Shortly after 10:27 PM, Staff Sergeant Lacroix stated by radio that "good news they've got rocks and sticks piled up and we all know we can beat that ... rocks and sticks that's in our bailiwick. All we have to worry about is little brown stocks and black barrels. Okay we're going to [be] advancing in a moment. Advance." John Carson, testimony to Ipperwash Inquiry, 30 May 2005, 85. Cecil Bernard George later conceded, "I knew I did wrong by picking up that pipe and hitting – striking at those officers. But yet I did it to protect what I felt needed to be protected." Cecil Bernard George, testimony to Ipperwash Inquiry, 7 December 2004, 101.

88 Linden, *Report*, vol. 4, 68–9.

89 Linden, *Report*, vol. 1, 475–8.

90 Wade Lacroix, testimony to Ipperwash Inquiry, 8 May 2006, 233–47.

91 John Carson, testimony to Ipperwash Inquiry, 31 May 2005, 172.

92 Wade Lacroix, testimony to Ipperwash Inquiry, 10 May 2006, 175.

93 Submissions of the Chippewas of Kettle and Stony Point First Nation to the Ipperwash Inquiry, 31 July 2006, 67.

94 Norman De Bono, "Ipperwash Occupation: Province Won't Forcibly Remove Natives," *London Free Press*, 9 September 1995.

95 Space precludes a formal newspaper analysis, but the *Sarnia Observer*, *London Free Press*, and *Toronto Star* have been thoroughly canvassed for the period 1991–98. See also A.K. McDougall and L.P. Valentine, "Selective Marginalization of Aboriginal Voices: Censorship in Public Performance," in *Interpreting Censorship in Canada*, ed. K. Petersen and A.C. Hutchinson, 334–50 (Toronto: University of Toronto Press, 1999), 340–3; and Valentine and McDougall, "Unveiling the Hegemon," 402–8.

96 Edwards, *One Dead Indian*, 123.

97 McDougall and Valentine, "Selective Marginalization," 334–48.

98 Letter to editor, *London Free Press*, 22 February 1996, quoted in McDougall and Valentine, "Selective Marginalization," 345. For concerns regarding the deteriorating local conditions, see *The Ipperwash Papers: The Untold Story*, 14 March 2007, http://www.ipperwashpapers.com/ IW-documents.htm. See also Canadian Press, "Communities Fear They'll Be Dispute Victims," *Victoria Times Colonist*, 20 September 1995.

99 See, for example, Rory Leishman, "Fair or Not, Laws Can't Be Flouted – No Matter by Whom," *London Free Press*, 10 August 1995.

100 George Sanderson, *London Free Press*, 9 September 1995. Three reporters were at Ipperwash on the day of the shooting (Paul Morden of the *Sarnia Observer*, Don Lajoie of the *Windsor Star*, and Julie Carl of the *London Free Press*), but all had gone home prior to the confrontation. John Miller, "Ipperwash and the Media: A Critical Analysis of How the Story Was Covered," paper prepared for the Ipperwash Inquiry, October 2005, 29, http://www.attorneygeneral.jus.gov.on.ca/inquiries/ipperwash/ policy_part/projects/pdf/ALST_Ipperwash_and_media.pdf.

101 Journalism professor John Miller found that the staff reporters who were sent to Ipperwash prior to the shooting were mostly from regional papers (*Sarnia Observer*, *London Free Press*, and *Windsor Star*) and that most papers printed Canadian Press versions of the stories, "mostly written in Toronto using material filed by reporters for newspapers who were at the scene." Miller, "Ipperwash and the Media," 6–9, 38, 48.

102 For a journalist's discussion of the political fallout, see Edwards, *One Dead Indian*.

103 Valentine and McDougall, "Unveiling the Hegemon," 402, 404–5.

104 Edwards, *One Dead Indian*, 141. However, the case was divisive within the George family, and two siblings withdrew from the suit.

105 See, for example, R. Mackie, "Notes Reveal Harris's Stand on Ipperwash," *Globe and Mail*, 31 July 1997; P. Edwards and H. Levy, "Secret Talks Held on Ipperwash," *Toronto Star*, 29 May 1996; R. Howard, "Ipperwash Fallout" *Hamilton Spectator*, 14 July 2005;

and Ontario Legislature, *Hansard*, 30 May 1996, 973, and 30 April 1997, 1084.

106 Lynne Davis, Vivian O'Donnell, and Heather Shpuniarsky, "Aboriginal–Social Justice Alliances: Understanding the Landscape of Relationships through the Coalition for a Public Inquiry into Ipperwash," *International Journal of Canadian Studies*, no. 36 (2007): 95–119 at 104.

107 "Deane Deserved to Lose His Badge," editorial, *Toronto Star*, 20 January 2002, A12.

108 Edwards, *One Dead Indian*, 67; "Indians Block Access to Ipperwash Beach," *London Free Press*, 2 August 1990; "Indians Getting Ready for Court Battle," *London Free Press*, 3 August 1990; Canadian Press, "Communities Fear"; J. Sims, "A Season of Uncertainty," *Victoria Times Colonist*, 17 May 1997; "Homeowners, Aboriginals Clash over Ipperwash Dispute," *Ottawa Citizen*, 14 August 1996; G. Mathewson, "Victims of Crime Spree Want Action," *Sarnia Observer*, 12 May 2000. For a critical look at the rhetoric of the Ontario Federation for Individual Rights and Equality as liberal democratic "equality" discourse, see Valentine and McDougall, "Unveiling the Hegemon," 399–402, 408–9.

109 KSPFN, "Camp Ipperwash"; "Natives, Government Reach Ipperwash Deal," *Globe and Mail*, 14 September 1995; "Ontario Ipperwash Deal Close," *Globe and Mail*, 24 December 1997; Norman De Bono, "Ipperwash Cleanup Will Be Complex," *London Free Press*, 8 August 1995; D. Collonette, *Hansard*, 18 September 1995; DIAND, "Camp Ipperwash"; "Cleaning Up Military Base Won't Be Easy," *Montreal Gazette*, 9 August 1995. On allegedly deliberate government delays, see Roos, "It Happened as If Overnight," 156.

110 "Land Deal Rebuffed by Band Members: Agreement Signed Despite Protests," *Victoria Times Colonist*, 18 June 1998; E. Anderssen, "Ottawa to Return Ipperwash Land," *Globe and Mail*, 18 June 1998; B. Wickens, "Blood and Land," *Maclean's*, 12 March 2001, 32–6; KSPFN, "Negotiations Update: Summer 2003," 2003, 1–3; Mathewson, "Victims of Crime Spree."

111 See Canada NewsWire, "Experts on Aboriginal Culture and History to Testify at Start of Ipperwash Inquiry Next Week," 7 July 2004; "Commissioner Linden's Opening Remarks at the Hearings for Standing and Funding for the Ipperwash Inquiry," 20 April 2004, http://www.attorneygeneral.jus.gov.on.ca/inquiries/ipperwash/li/pdf/CommissionerOpeningRemarks.pdf; and transcripts of testimony to the Ipperwash Inquiry.

112 On the other hand, there "was no manner of accountability involved in the hearings format." S.J.C. Cooper, "Analysis of the Inquiry as a Conflict Management System: Case Study – The Ipperwash Inquiry (MA thesis, Royal Roads University, 2006), 52–3.

113 Linden, *Report*, vol. 4, 47.

114 Submissions of the Chippewas of Kettle and Stony Point First Nation to the Ipperwash Inquiry, 31 July 2006, 32.

115 Andrew Coyne, "Native Violence Becomes Blameless – Ipperwash Report Effectively Legitimizes Illegal Protests," *National Post*, 2 June 2007.

116 Mary-Lou LaPratte, untitled speech presented at March for Freedom event, Caledonia, 15 October 2006, http://www.ipperwashpapers.com/ipperwashdocuments/D-14.pdf.

117 See, for example, submissions of the Chippewas of Kettle and Stony Point First Nation to the Ipperwash Inquiry, 31 July 2006, 25; Hutton, "Final Submission," 53; and testimonies to Ipperwash Inquiry of Carl George, 22 February 2005, 166; Tom Bressette, 3 March 1995, 224–5; and Gerald George, 21 February 2005, 134–8, and 17 January 2005, 174–5. Even Stoney Pointer Carl George acknowledged that he never had a mandate to occupy Camp Ipperwash from the majority of the people who had an interest in the lands. Carl George, testimony to Ipperwash Inquiry, 22 February 2005, 167–70. He testified that approximately three-quarters of the Kettle and Stony Point population (about 1,900 members) had a connection to the Stony Point Reserve as a result of intermarriage or direct descent and, therefore, had an interest in the lands. Carl George, testimony to Ipperwash Inquiry, 21 February 2005, 134–8, and 22 February 2005, 166.

118 See, for example, Tom Bressette, testimony to Ipperwash Inquiry, 2 March 2005, 72–6.

119 Submissions of the Chippewas of Kettle and Stony Point First Nation to the Ipperwash Inquiry, 31 July 2006, 37.

120 McDougall and Valentine, "Selective Marginalization," 342.

121 David George, testimony to Ipperwash Inquiry, 19 October 2004, 113–29, and 1 November 2004, 45–9, 53–7, 60–1.

122 See, for example, Clayton George, testimony to Ipperwash Inquiry, 8 November 2004, 62–3.

123 Hutton, "Final Submission," 8.

124 Harris, "Written Submission," 14, emphasis in original.

125 Linden, *Report*, vol. 4, 97.

126 Aboriginal Affairs and Northern Development Canada, "Fact Sheet – Camp Ipperwash Negotiations," August 2008, http://www.ainc-inac.gc.ca/ai/mr/is/cin-eng.asp.

127 When the provincial government first announced its intention to return the park to the KSPFN in December 2007, Lambton Shores mayor Gord Minielly was not consulted. He noted that the Ipperwash Inquiry report had called for better cooperation and that he had been in co-management discussions with Chief Bressette. Gord Minielly, in Anthony Reinhart, "Ontario to Return Ipperwash to Natives," *Globe and Mail*, 21 December 2007.

128 Brad Duguid and Elizabeth Cloud, both in Ontario, Ministry of Aboriginal Affairs, "Healing and Reconciliation Continue at Ipperwash Park," press release, *28 May 2009, http://www.news.ontario.ca/maa/ en/2009/05/healing-and-reconciliation-continues-at-ipperwash-park.html.*

129 John Snobelen, "Park Transfer Legitimizes Armed Takeover," *London Free Press*, 6 March 2010.

# 8

# The Gustafsen Lake Standoff

NICK SHRUBSOLE and P. WHITNEY LACKENBAUER

It's not like a war, it is a war. Where they're going to kill us, or we're going to kill them. I mean, good God man, and this is Canada. We're not prepared for this.

RCMP constable Ray Wilby, September 1995[1]

In the summer of 1995, while Native peoples at Ipperwash Provincial Park in Ontario were engaged in a confrontation with the Ontario Provincial Police, a small group of Aboriginal people and non-Native supporters were involved in an armed standoff with the Royal Canadian Mounted Police (RCMP) over a small portion of privately owned cattle ranch land in south-central British Columbia. They had been using this site at Gustafsen Lake for a sun dance and insisted that they needed to protect and control the neotraditional sacred space. This justification was quickly superseded by the more general claims of Aboriginal sovereignty over unceded lands in British Columbia.

The one-month standoff ended on 17 September 1995, after tensions had boiled over into violence. Firefights left one occupier wounded, two Emergency Response Team officers shot, another occupier dodging sniper fire, and the discharge of thousands of rounds of ammunition.[2] Each party perceived the other to be criminals. Provincial politicians, the RCMP, and the elected Shuswap leadership branded the occupiers as "terrorists" for taking up arms against the Crown and illegally occupying private lands. The occupiers, who inherently opposed the institutional land claims process pursued by the elected band councils (which they dismissed as collaborators in state-sponsored genocide), grounded their claims in Aboriginal sovereignty. Alongside legal-historical arguments for sovereignty, the occupiers found strength and justification for their claims through their spiritual convictions. The self-proclaimed "Defenders of the Shuswap Nation," who came from across North America, saw themselves as the rightful heirs of sovereignty over a sun dance site that they argued had never been ceded by Native peoples.

This chapter critically examines the underlying justification that the Defenders of the Shuswap Nation articulated during the standoff, their relationships with the local elected band councils and national Aboriginal community, escalating violence, and the respective roles and responses of state authorities and the media. Although many of the occupiers were "outsiders" who did not belong to the Shuswap Nation, they asserted sovereignty over the land, declared the sun dance site sacred space, and denounced the elected leaders of the local Shuswap bands as sellouts to colonial authority. The defenders declared their willingness to die for their beliefs, and authorities emphasized that this was a "law and order" issue in which the state would not concede to armed militants asserting a dubious land claim. The media were an important battleground on which both the RCMP and the occupiers sought to manipulate the situation in their favour. However, the defenders did not convince the media that they or their violent tactics were legitimate, and the media disseminated RCMP information that depicted the occupiers in a negative light. This "smear campaign" was effective and ensured that, by the time the occupiers began to garner support from BC Native leaders, the standoff had drawn to a close. No lives were lost, but the Gustafsen Lake confrontation further entrenched the popular notion that Aboriginal "militants" refused to work through the official land claims process, rejected elected First Nations leadership, and were willing to take violent action against the state.

## BACKGROUND

First Nations have occupied the arid Interior Plateau between the Rocky Mountains and the Coastal Mountains since time immemorial. The Interior Salish peoples were strongly influenced by their Plains and Northwest Coast neighbours but developed a distinct culture typified by pacifistic and egalitarian societies, grouped in autonomous villages or clusters. The Secwepemc (formerly known as the Shuswap) are the northernmost group, occupying the largest territory, which stretches from the Fraser River in the west to the Rockies in the east. Although warfare was "far from unknown" between the Shuswap and their Chilcotin and Lillooet neighbours, the Interior Plateau groups enjoyed peaceful trading relationships.[3] In the nineteenth century, the influx of fur traders, missionaries, gold miners, and settlers transformed Secwepemc culture. Smallpox and other diseases wiped out thirty-two Shuswap villages, and the remaining people were relegated to small, scattered Indian reserves. No treaties were signed with the government to cede traditional lands, but non-Native ranches and settlements drove away game, destroyed berry patches and root-digging sites, and closed access to fishing grounds.[4]

Scholars like Robin Fisher, Paul Tennant, and Cole Harris have documented the long history of the Crown and Native peoples in British Columbia and have explained how Interior Plateau groups formed political organizations and tribal councils to fight for their land claims and other issues.[5] Petitions protesting the poor size and quality of the Shuswap reserves in the 1870s eventually led to the creation of a short-lived Secwepemc confederacy. In the end, however, Cole Harris notes that "two months of skilful colonial diplomacy ... undermined a confederacy, stayed the threat of war, and turned some Secwepemc chiefs into allies" with the Joint Indian Reserve Commission.[6] Secwepemc representatives signed and presented a memorial to Sir Wilfrid Laurier in 1910, organized the Allied Tribes of British Columbia in 1915 (which lasted until 1927), and were active in the founding of the Union of British Columbia Indian Chiefs in 1969 (which was eventually led by Secwepemc president George Manuel) to improve intertribal relations and protect Aboriginal title.[7] When the federal government retreated from its ill-fated 1969 White Paper, the Secwepemc began to manage their community administrations. Protest marches and rallies against the poor quality of federal services to Secwepemc communities prompted the closure of the Department of Indian Affairs office in Kamloops in 1975. Land title issues remained unsettled, but the split decision in the Calder case of 1973 launched a new treaty-making era. The federal government agreed to settle comprehensive land claims based on the assertion of continuing Aboriginal rights and title that had not been dealt with by treaty or other legal means.[8]

The British Columbia Treaty Commission (BCTC) implemented the modern land claims process in the province in 1993. The product of a taskforce established by BC premier Bill Vander Zahn, the BCTC included representatives from the federal and provincial governments and three representatives elected at a First Nations summit (two of whom were hereditary chiefs). This change in provincial policy was preceded by a recommendation on the part of the newly appointed minister of

Indian affairs that land claims negotiations would be "the best course of action for the government to pursue."⁹ The BCTC was established to be an impartial, tripartite body that would monitor treaty talks, provide funding for Aboriginal groups, suggest solutions when needed, and provide reports on ongoing processes to both federal and provincial governments. The commission also created a six-stage process for treaty negotiations. By 1995 only a few groups had reached stage three of the process: the establishment of a framework to negotiate.¹⁰

The Cariboo Tribal Council (CTC, now known as the Northern Shuswap Tribal Council), representing the interests of four northern Secwepemc te Qelmucw bands,¹¹ first submitted its statement of intent (the first stage of the treaty process) on 15 December 1993. The statement lists the "People of Canim Lake, Canoe Creek, Soda Creek, [and] Williams Lake First Nations" as the represented parties, comprising 1,644 people.¹² At the time of the standoff, the CTC had yet to begin stage two of the process; however, ten days after the standoff ended, a "Tripartite Procedural Agreement" between Canada, British Columbia, and the tribal council was ratified, effectively beginning stage two of the process, which is "readiness to negotiate."¹³ The initial claim to traditional territory included the space at Gustafsen Lake.¹⁴

Gustafsen Lake (Ts'peten) is located 35 kilometres southwest of 100 Mile House in the interior of British Columbia on the James Cattle Ranch, between the Canim Lake and Dog Creek Reserves.¹⁵ Lyle James moved from Montana to British Columbia in 1972, purchasing a ranch for $1.1 million that, with lease extensions and grazing permits, consisted of 182,000 hectares. He and his wife, Mary, an elderly couple, lived next to the Dog Creek and Canoe Creek Reserves. They had hired people from the local reserve, and his son-in-law, Keray Camille, was a councillor of the Canoe Creek and Dog Creek Band.¹⁶

In 1989 Percy Rosette, who lived on Alkali Lake Reserve No. 1 south of Gustafsen Lake, informed James that spiritual leaders and elders had seen visions of a sun dance site at Ts'peten. Accordingly, they reached a verbal agreement allowing Rosette to hold a sun dance ceremony there. Practitioners of the sun dance, which was not traditional to the Shuswap in British Columbia, adopted the practice as a form of "spiritual renewal," a modern redemptive tool for its nontraditional practitioners in the face of social, political, and economic hardships.¹⁷ Joseph Jorgensen explains that the modern form of the sun dance originates in the postreserve period in the United States, where the meaning of the ritual changed from securing good hunts to strengthening community in the face of misery and oppression. In the case of the Utes, who Jorgensen studied, sun dance leaders had become politically engaged in internal band politics and treaty negotiations by the 1960s. Jorgensen even noted in a *Vancouver Sun* article during the standoff that it was not surprising to see the ritual emerging in places where it had not traditionally been practised.[18] According to this logic, the fusion of sovereignty and neotraditional spiritual elements in the emerging dispute at Gustafsen Lake (Ts'peten) was not surprising, even though the site could hardly be considered a "traditional" sacred space.[19]

Despite simmering concerns about the violent proclivities of some sun dancers, the situation was managed locally until 1995. After fishers and campers complained about threats from sun dance participants (including a 1992 incident in which shots were fired through a tent), Rosette and James signed a formal agreement (witnessed by a Native RCMP officer) specifying that the sun dancers would not erect any permanent structures on the site. The agreement expired the following year, but the sun dance continued, and James worried about threats issued by "outsiders" who attended the sun dance. He discovered that Percy Rosette and his partner, Mary ("Toby") Pena (from Adams Lake), had built a shelter on the sun dance site for cooking and then had begun living there in 1994. James considered this occupation to be a private civil matter, contacted the RCMP about an eviction, and consulted with a lawyer.[20] The occupiers, however, refused to back down. Pena requested the assistance of the warriors in late 1994, and automatic weapons began arriving at the cabin.[21]

## THE DEFENDERS OF THE SHUSWAP NATION

In January 1995 "Faith Keeper" Percy Rosette and sun dance "spiritual leader" John Stevens requested the aid of lawyer and Aboriginal rights activist Bruce Clark to defend their claim to the site on "sovereignty" grounds.[22] Rosette claimed that research he had conducted proved that Gustafsen Lake had been set aside for a reserve during the Douglas Treaty negotiations but that the Alkali Lake Band had intentionally destroyed the evidence because its members were government collaborators.[23] Recognized authorities – both Aboriginal and non-Aboriginal – could not be trusted, and the activists opposed state authority and all institutions and decisions derived from it. For the occupiers, spirituality and the sun dance itself were connected to sovereignty, justice, culture, and survival.

Although the occupiers called themselves the "Defenders of the Shuswap Nation," their notion of sovereignty was not confined to the local Shuswap population, with whom the occupiers had strained relations. Instead, the presence of many outsiders within their ranks broadened their scope to a general Aboriginal sovereignty – suggesting a pan-Indian identity rooted in the collective experience of oppression under the state. At a coffee house benefit in the summer of 1996, Mary Pena spoke about the reason they had occupied the lake area: "Why we were there at the lake – it was not for ourselves, not for glory, not for money, not for any kind of recognition. We were doing this for our children and our grandchildren and our future generations to come. We figured that this would help our people along in waking up and starting to realize what the government is doing to our people, what they've asked the chief and band council to do to the people, because the chief and band council were put there to cause our people to suffer."[24] In their view, the sun dance provided the emotional and psychological tools needed to combat perceived oppression.[25]

The sun dance was not simply a vehicle for sovereignty claims. More generally, the close relationship between sovereignty and spirituality for Aboriginal peoples in the BC interior has a long history dating back to the 1877 Okanagan-Shuswap Declaration, where the protection of land bestowed upon them by a Creator was cited as one of the foundational principles for Indigenous sovereignty. The occupiers at the lake reiterated this point.[26] More specifically, the continuation of the sun dance at Gustafsen Lake presented an opportunity, in Percy Rosette's view, to "revive a culture" that is integral to just self-government.[27] James ("OJ") Pitawanakwat (an Anishinabe from Ontario) felt that it was his duty, as it was his ancestors, to ensure that "ceremonies and religions survived" so that they could "continue to provide life and security."[28]

The spiritual basis for direct action was bolstered by a legal justification provided by activist lawyer Bruce Clark, who had become one of the most strident advocates for Indigenous sovereignty in Canada. Rosette insisted that he had proof the land belonged to the Shuswap people, and he accused the local leadership of a cover-up by alleging that they "lost" the information he had gathered. This was an attractive case for the renegade lawyer who on 3 January 1995 had unsuccessfully petitioned the queen of England to hold the Canadian government accountable for "treason and fraud and complicity in crimes related to genocide due to usurpation of jurisdiction in relation to the [Natives'] Hunting Grounds."[29] Clark's sovereigntist claims were echoed in statements by the Defenders of the Shuswap Nation throughout the standoff, which asserted that the sun dance site (and most of British Columbia) was unceded land that the Canadian government had no right to sell and over which the state had no jurisdiction. He drew in supporters like William Ignace, known as "Wolverine" (a name granted to him by the spiritual leader of the sun dance, John Stevens, during the 1994 ceremony),[30] who had been travelling with Clark after they met in support of the Lil'Wat at the Mount Currie blockade in 1990. Wolverine travelled with Clark to rally support for Canada's Aboriginal communities as sovereign peoples[31] and was actively involved in supporting Native blockades across the country. He entered the camp at Rosette's request on 13 June to help protect the site.[32]

Although the two primary leaders of the occupation (Rosette and Ignace) were from the territory on which the standoff took place, many of the participants involved in the direct action were from outside the local area, and critics suggested that they were generally drifters who sought out confrontations with state authorities.[33] Splitting the Sky (also known as John Boncore Hill, John Pasquale Boncore, and "Doc"), a Mohawk Cree originally from New York but residing in Canada since February 1993,[34] had been actively involved in direct actions across Canada, travelling to various blockades with Wolverine and Clark in support of Aboriginal sovereignty.[35] Although Splitting the Sky was not in the camp during the standoff with police, he played a pivotal role in the early stages of the confrontation and tried to secure international support for the occupiers. Gustafsen Lake was, for occupiers like Wolverine and Splitting the Sky, one more battle site in an ongoing war against an oppressive state. This included the elected chiefs, who they accused of being "civil servants" collaborating with the government and operating in complicity with the Indian Act.[36]

Because the self-proclaimed "Defenders of the Shuswap Nation" rejected official Aboriginal government structures and the authority of the Canadian state over the campsite, they did not enjoy the support of the elected chiefs and councils comprising the Cariboo Tribal Council. The CTC tried to distance itself and the entire Shuswap Nation from the Gustafsen Lake occupiers while denouncing their actions as illegitimate and unrepresentative of the Aboriginal community. It insisted that all members of the Northern Shuswap Nation condemned the actions at Gustafsen Lake. "We don't know for sure who these people are," the CTC explained in August, "but we do know many are from outside this area, from outside B.C. and possibly outside Canada." The elected leaders claimed that they had legitimate authority to speak for the Shuswap people and that the *actual* members of the Shuswap community did not share the views of the occupiers at Gustafsen Lake.[37]

The council also asserted their authority on subjects concerning the Shuswap people and their lands. Canoe Creek chief Agnes Snow said that "no one can and no one will speak about our territory but ourselves."[38] Even at the first meeting between Lyle James, the occupiers at Gustafsen Lake, the RCMP, and the CTC, the council attempted to control the meeting despite Wolverine's objections.[39] Elected representatives denounced the occupiers as simple criminals who had "not asked for the permission of the Canoe Creek band or the current land owner. They have rejected all governments and all laws, including our own first nations governments."[40] Furthermore, the council dismissed Percy Rosette's spiritual claims as invalid, asserting their own authority in authenticating religious practices. Chief Antoine Archie, who had met with the sun dancers in 1992, suggested that they "were mixing politics" and deviated from "traditional" sun dances in other places. The sun dance is not a ritual native to the BC interior, Archie explained. "We challenged them out there. And we told them – the Sundance was supposed to only occur for four years, and you've got to give the land a rest, according to the *real* sundancers."[41] Archie questioned the legitimacy of the so-called "spiritual leaders" occupying Gustafsen Lake and denied that there was anything special about the site beyond its general inclusion in the large land claim that they had submitted.[42]

In contrast to the occupiers, the Cariboo Tribal Council openly supported the land claims process. Agnes Snow and the rest of the council acknowledged that Lyle James had legal ownership of the property and that they would "give these negotiations a chance" out of respect for the BCTC process.[43] There was noticeable reluctance on the part of Chief Snow to offer unwavering support for the land claims system, but affirming the new process was an assertion of authority and legitimacy in direct response to the occupiers' claims. The council did not condone illegal occupation as a method of enacting political change.

## EARLY CONFRONTATIONS

On 13 June 1995 James's ranch hands presented an eviction notice to the sun dancers. The sun dancers considered this a racist and aggressive act,[44] whereas James and his crew saw this formal and witnessed serving of an eviction notice as necessary to prevent the sun dancers from staking out territory.[45] Rosette and other sun dancers simply ignored it, erecting a fence to protect the site from grazing cattle, which would defecate on the "sacred grounds," and posting signs to discourage "trespassing." In response, ranch hands complicated the situation by bringing a bullwhip and allegedly proclaimed that it would "be a good day to string up some red niggers." The occupiers claimed that James's men "desecrated the Council Lodge, photographed Sacred Sites and violated the purification ritual fast of a Sundancer," in addition to sticking a "hand-made 'Final Eviction Notice' addressed to Shuswap Faith Keeper and Pipe Carrier Percy Rosette ... on a Sacred Staff."[46] Although James denied that this confrontation took place,[47] lawyer Donald Campbell (representing Wolverine) contended at trial that this incident presented imminent danger to the occupiers. Campbell also presented evidence that police had advised James to pursue a civil injunction to remove the occupiers – advice that he apparently chose to ignore.[48] In response, "sundance chief" Splitting the Sky asked Wolverine to bring men with weapons up from the Shuswap Reserve at Adams Lake to mount "an armed defensive stance."[49]

The initial role of the RCMP at Gustafsen Lake was that of mediator. The police considered the matter a civil one in the early summer, and the occupiers invited them into the camp on several occasions to explain their position.[50] Throughout June and July the RCMP also sought to avoid inflaming the issue by awaiting permission before entering the site.[51] Escalating violence, however, drew them into a more direct role. On 14 June 1995 the RCMP received reports that forestry workers had been shot at while trying to do some work near the occupiers' campsite. The police instructed James to refrain from visiting the sun dance site. Two days later, the occupiers at Gustafsen Lake reported that "a lone ranch hand came into the Sundance grounds, yelling and whooping in a drunken stupor." When confronted by the camp occupants about "what he was doing in Shuswap territory," he boasted that "the ranchers intended to burn the council lodge and that the RCMP were planning an invasion of the camp." In response, the sun dancers expanded their "security force" and declared that "given the prevailing mood of violence against the Defenders of the Land and Sacred Sundance ceremonies ... force will be met with resistant force."[52] This prompted Bruce Clark to announce publicly that the occupiers had every right to defend themselves against an impending police "invasion."[53]

The sun dancers' claims transcended those surrounding the "sacred site" at Gustafsen Lake and sought to address government perfidy more generally. Couched in language that revealed the influence of lawyer Bruce Clark, the occupiers issued a press release on 17 June with four demands:

1 That an investigation of the Governor General's Office in Ottawa be undertaken to expose the illegal leasing and/or selling of Native lands on unceded territory.

2  That an investigation into the DIA [Department of Indian Affairs] and all cohorts in the various band councils be undertaken to expose illegal leasing and/or selling of Native lands, specifically within the Shuswap Nation. The immediate and long term impact of these fraudulent deals on the traditional people must be addressed and acted upon.

3  That an audience with the Queen of England and the Privy Council be convened to renew the treaty obligations of the Royal Proclamation of 1763, which states that all unceded territories will remain unmolested and undisturbed.

4  That every individual reading this urgent press release is asked to call the RCMP at (604) 395–2456 and express their concern over the potential for violence against the occupiers of the Sundance grounds in Shuswap territory. We invite all sundancers to come to Gustafson Lake and ensure that this Sundance will be held as planned to sustain our inheritance and religious freedom.[54]

These were sweeping aspirations that far exceeded the RCMP's mandate, but the police held out hopes that local discussions would yield a peaceful outcome. Chief Agnes Snow arranged a meeting with Lyle James and the chiefs of the Cariboo Tribal Council, which was held on 17 June just inside the main entrance to the sun dance site. Two band council chiefs, seven band members, five employees of the James Cattle Company, and the RCMP (who attended as observers) were greeted by three males dressed in army fatigues with covered faces. Wolverine and Splitting the Sky, representing the Defenders of the Shuswap Nation, did not recognize the elected chiefs or "any white man's deed to the property."[55] During the meeting, James's daughter said, "I guess you guys know what we're here for. The law's been broken. We want to have something done about it." Wolverine agreed, asserting, "The law has been broken but by you people because we don't have a treaty, there's no purchase."[56] Both sides understood each other to be criminals and refused to back down. No simple resolution was possible.

The RCMP tried to reassure the sun dancers that they would "do their best to keep aggravators away from the grounds during the Sundance," but anxieties continued to grow. Officers met with the Cariboo Tribal Council to discuss a purchase of the sun dance site. "Percy [Rosette] would have taken that piece of cheese," Splitting the Sky later recounted, "but Wolverine and I made it clear that the issue was much bigger than a few people's vision of a sacred piece of earth. The issue belonged to all Original Peoples' [sic] in the Western Hemisphere."[57] The occupiers rejected the proposal. Furthermore, local chiefs emphasized to the RCMP that they and their counterparts in the Kamloops area did not support direct action. Reports of "radicals" en route from Penticton, Merritt, and Adams Lake pointed to escalation. So did information from Gil Bremner, an Aboriginal man from Lac La Hache, suggesting that warrior society militants from across Canada had arrived – even though the local Natives did not want them there. Bremner described Rosette as a "radical with no home base" who harboured visions of an "armed underground storage facility" at Gustafsen Lake. (In the days ahead, Bremner's house was shot up with automatic weapons, but no charges were laid.) Splitting the Sky reiterated to an RCMP constable that they would not leave until their lawyer, Bruce Clark, had resolved the matter in court. If they were left alone, it would remain peaceful, but he warned that any aggression would be reciprocated. RCMP constable G. Findley reassured him that the RCMP would do "nothing, unless something happens that forces us to act. We are only involved to keep the peace. We are peacekeepers!" The sun dance was held from 6 to 9 July, under RCMP protection, without incident. A spirit dance followed from 10 to 13 July.[58]

When the sun dancers remained at the site at the conclusion of the ceremonies, the RCMP tried to avoid a confrontation. On 12 July, Constable Findley recommended against any police action to remove the occupiers because "public support from local native bands would or could shift in a hurry." Findley noted that he had "established a good rapport with the Sundancers and I believe some trust." They had given him berries and coffee and had shaken hands with him when he left. "Four eagles were seen to circle the Arbor area and the Sundancers believed this was a good omen," he observed.[59] The Cariboo Tribal Council also continued to seek a negotiated solution. It invited the occupiers to attend a meeting at the Canoe Creek and Dog Creek Reserve on 18 July. They agreed to attend but indicated that they were not prepared to abandon their beliefs and would defend the sun dance site. When the CTC informed them that the local Natives did not support their cause and that they should vacate the site, the occupiers emphasized that they were taking a stand and were willing to die if necessary. No resolution was reached. Afterward, a council member reported to the RCMP that the Gustafsen Lake protestors had acquired automatic weapons, rifles, crossbows, and high-powered sling shots.[60]

Developments on the ground indicated that the probability of a bloody confrontation was growing. On 20 July the RCMP received reports from Lyle James and Chief Agnes Snow that Ron Tenale, an Aboriginal wrangler who worked for James, had been shot at when he visited the sun dance grounds the night before. Information was sketchy, but Tenale told police that he went to complain that several of his horses had been let out of their stalls. He was told to leave because he was not welcome at the site, and as he rode toward the main gate, he saw an unidentified male running with a rifle in his hand. As Tenale rode away, he heard six shots fired from behind him.[61] Chief Snow encouraged the police to look into the matter and worried "that the people at Gustafsen Lake are heading for a confrontation and will do anything to start the confrontation at any cost."[62] The occupiers had a different story. Tenale had charged through the gate, confronted them about an alleged theft of horse hobbles, and called elder Percy Rosette an "asshole." They told him to leave because he had disrespected an elder. As he wheeled around to leave, Splitting the Sky alleged that two shots were fired into the camp that narrowly missed some "women and children near the cookhouse." The occupiers "immediately scrambled for our concealed weapons and returned a volley of bullets. We fired warning shots over the bush area where we had heard the first two shots." Splitting the Sky later justified these "warning shots" as compliant with both law and human decency.[63]

Although the ranch hands suggested that the gunfire might have come from semi-automatic weapons, the RCMP initially concluded that it likely came from rifles. This changed after officers of the federal Department of Fisheries and Oceans arrested two men who had been involved in the sun dance – David Pena and Ernie Archie – for illegal fishing in the Fraser River on 11 August. The officers pulled out their guns when they thought that one of the men, who was clearly agitated, reached for a weapon. When the police searched the truck, the *Vancouver Sun* reported, they found "a loaded AK-47, a Glock 9-mm semi-automatic pistol loaded with Black Talon [hollow point] bullets designed to inflict maximum damage on human tissue, knives, machetes, camouflage clothing and a garrotte made of piano wire." The men were taken into custody.[64] This arsenal of combat weapons raised suspicions about the intentions of the occupiers. Accordingly, the RCMP made plans to conduct reconnaissance patrols of the Gustafsen Lake site in the days ahead.

The RCMP's decision to "recce" the campsite brought simmering tensions to a head and precipitated the formal armed "standoff" at Gustafsen Lake. On 17 August the RCMP dropped off five Emergency Response Team members in camouflage and armed with handguns, M-16 rifles, and a sniper rifle near the sun dance site.[65] The occupiers described what transpired the next day in a press release entitled "Deep Red Alert":

On Saturday, 18 August 1995, at about 6:00 a.m., eight camouflaged, fully armed and unidentified men were happened upon by a member of the Sundance camp in the bush outside the fence. Thinking they might be red-neck vigilantes bent upon killing Indians, the Sundancers phoned the RCMP at about 7:00 a.m. regarding these men. It was also later rumored these men might be a SWAT team from Kamloops. A red, white and blue helicopter flew over camp about 8:25 a.m. and about 9:00 a.m. a shot was heard from down by the Lake. At 10:00 a.m. a man in camouflage was seen up a tree and about 12:00 p.m. another man, similarly dressed, was seen crossing the road from camp. There was also a man in a boat on the lake with binoculars and a walkie-talkie. Calls to the RCMP on Saturday, from outside allies across the country, elicited denials of any of the above events although by Sunday they admitted that was their men in the area, there had been a helicopter, and a shot had been fired allegedly at one of their men. No Sundancer fired any shot at one of their men.[66]

Splitting the Sky later alleged that Percy Rosette had fired on Constable Ray Wilby, but Joseph ("Jo-Jo") Ignace, the son of Wolverine, was charged with the offence. At the time, however, the occupiers proclaimed that it was all a police conspiracy to justify killing the occupiers. From the site, Rosette reported to Splitting the Sky – who had left for Hinton, Alberta, eight days earlier and continued to maintain communications with lawyers and Native activists from there – that "they're coming to kill us" and that "the army is invading." Splitting the Sky promptly passed on the information to Kahn-tineta Horn, who mobilized the Canadian Alliance in Solidarity with Native Peoples to send faxes around the world.[67] The occupiers braced for another "invasion" of the sun dance site.

The situation had changed, and the RCMP were no longer a mediator in the dispute. The next day, the police held a press conference and explained that they would take action to remove the "terrorists" at the sun dance site. "We won't just sit back and do nothing," Superintendent Len Olfert told reporters. "We have all the residents to consider, and the area has to be secured. There has been an escalation; the threat is serious. We see this as an act of terrorism." The occupiers did not "seem interested in talking to us," the RCMP spokesperson explained, "so now we have to consider our options."[68]

In the same newspaper article, Rosette was quoted as asking, "If someone came into your house with a SWAT team what would you do?" Like Clark and Splitting the Sky, Rosette implied that violence was a legitimate response to RCMP encroachment on unceded lands. The occupiers asserted that the RCMP had acknowledged that the police had no jurisdiction in their previously "cordial" visits to the camp. They parked outside the fence, entered the camp unarmed, and even asked for permission so that the rancher could transfer his cattle from one pasture to another.[69] On 21 August 1995 the Defenders of the Shuswap Nation issued a press release describing the occupation of unceded lands as an act of genocide over which the RCMP had no jurisdiction and asserting their right to defend "the Indians' yet unsurrendered territories" against "illegal invasion."[70] Rosette situated the protest historically:

> The Shuswap people, who remain true to the Creator and the Land of our Ancestors, seek a peaceful resolution to a crisis which has been going on for 139 years. Domestic laws, which we have had no hand in signing, do not apply here. Tribal councils of so-called "chiefs" paid by the Government of Canada do not speak for us. We have never ceded or sold our territory. Anyone claiming title to our stolen lands should be compensated by the government of British Columbia and our lands returned to us. The legal precedence protecting our rights as Indigenous Peoples have never been heard.[71]

In response to media concerns that lives might be lost, lawyer Bruce Clark insisted that thousands of "Indian lives have been, and are being lost" because Aboriginal peoples had been "invaded and terrorized treasonably, fraudulently, and genocidally. The high mortality rates of natives in our country are a consequence of the legal establishment's crimes. My clients' intent at Gustafsen Lake is to save many lives at the risk of their own. That is heroism not terrorism."[72]

The escalating tensions and violence had, in the opinion of the RCMP and government officials, transformed the Gustafsen Lake occupation into a serious crime. BC attorney general Ujjal Dosanjh refused to concede that the matter related to land claims, insisting that it was about weapons and violence. On 30 August 1995 he told reporters, "this is not a political issue ... I speak as the chief law-enforcement officer of the province."[73] Two days later, RCMP sergeant Peter Montague noted that "before the Force makes any physical move the public should be made aware that our actions are being precipitated by the criminal actions of proven criminals."[74] The following day, he told reporters that the RCMP were "still pursuing very serious criminal acts."[75] For his part, Premier Mike Harcourt had no sympathy for the occupiers. He explained on 5 September, "There is no place in British Columbia where threats of violence, and acts of violence will be tolerated." He asserted,

- there is only one law in British Columbia and the police have a responsibility to apply the law equally and fairly to all;
- the police enforce the law in a manner that minimizes the danger to the public and themselves;
- the use of weapons to resolve differences is intolerable and a challenge to the very fabric of our society;
- we will not negotiate or make deals with people who use or threaten violence;
- and, the armed occupation of Gustafsen Lake is the action of a handful of violent extremists, without the participation or support of a single band or tribal council.[76]

Harcourt publicly dismissed the sun dancers as being seized by a "cult mentality" and refused to accept their claims. When Bruce Clark failed in his attempt to lay charges of criminal trespass, criminal settlement, fraud, high treason, extortion, and genocide against Supreme Court of Canada chief justice Antonio Lamer for "stonewalling" his legal challenge regarding unceded traditional territories, he hardly helped to legitimize their case.[77]

Although Clark's ostentatious claims and political grandstanding may have reflected poor legal practice and did little to resolve the standoff, they helped to generate a national profile. The Cariboo Tribal Council called on Ovide Mercredi, the national chief of the Assembly of First Nations, to counter Clark's "bad legal advice" and to help resolve the situation. He arrived to meet with the occupiers at the camp on 25 August, but they did not accept his authority and legitimacy any more than they did those of the locally elected Aboriginal leadership. "All Indian leaders are sell-outs; you included," Mercredi heard from the occupiers. "You are nothing but a waterboy for the white man." They told him that if he wanted to be a "great Indian leader," he had to "pick up a gun and stand with us."[78] They also solicited his endorsement of Clark's petition of 3 January 1995 to Queen Elizabeth II. Their lawyer now suggested that the sun dancer's only demand to end the standoff was that this petition be addressed publicly by an independent party. Mercredi, however, refused to support Clark's claims, which essentially dismissed his authority as national chief.[79]

Mercredi, when facing such direct challenges to his own authority, tried to deflect the blame onto "White politicians" whose failure to address the concerns of Aboriginal people necessitated their use of force. Although he did not condone violence, he asserted that the problem at barricades like Gustafsen Lake and Ipperwash was not Native protestors but politicians who refused to get involved in what were political disputes – not criminal ones.[80] He also accused the RCMP of aggressive tactics, harkening back to the "bad experience at Oka," which elicited accusations in the provincial media that he was actually "aggravating the situation." If the public was looking to National Chief Ovide Mercredi to resolve the situation at Gustafsen Lake, he failed. Indeed, the shot fired into the air as he left camp symbolized the ongoing resistance. The occupiers did not leave the camp, and more violence ensued after Mercredi's visit. However, he insisted that he had succeeded, and he criticized the provincial leadership and their use of local and national law enforcement to settle political disputes – similar to his criticisms of Ontario premier Mike Harris and the Ontario Provincial Police over Ipperwash.[81]

Mercredi called on BC premier Mike Harcourt to intervene at Gustafsen Lake, but the provincial government refused to negotiate at gunpoint. Attorney General Ujjal Dosanjh continued to remind the public that Gustafsen Lake was not a political matter but a criminal action.[82] On 25 August, Sergeant Montague informed the media that the RCMP were interested in discussing only the "unconditional surrender" of the occupiers and their weapons.[83] The RCMP cut the phone line to the camp, hoping that this would stop the influence of their renegade lawyer, Bruce Clark. It also choked off media access to the occupiers. RCMP superintendent Len Olfert was officially in charge at the site, but Montague took centre stage as media liaison. He admitted after the trial that he and the RCMP had conducted a "smear campaign" to discredit the occupiers in public discourse by manipulating and controlling the media coverage (discussed later).[84]

The occupiers also sought to manipulate the media to attract wider attention and use their presence to dissuade the authorities – which now included military armoured personnel carriers (or Bisons) and crews to support the RCMP – from assaulting their positions. When Splitting the Sky anticipated that the RCMP would storm the camp on 25 August 1995, he employed tactics to draw the media to Gustafsen Lake and render any secret plans of the RCMP and military unfeasible. He explained,

I told Trond [Halle], "Look, Trond, I want you to edit the footage of the videotaped guerilla theatre and take the piece out which

shows me on the hill advantage, saying that if they come up from
the rear flank, BAM BAM." I then said to him, "Once CBC gets
this clip it will make them salivate with sensationalism, they will
air it immediately as they will think they have another Oka crisis."
I know Canadians have never gotten over the Oka Standoff and
the press would converge at Gustafsen Lake with a feeding frenzy
to sell news and boost ratings.

Splitting the Sky's carefully staged guerrilla training video deliberately
presented the occupiers as ready for battle. Previously, he had reminded
his camp mates to conceal their weapons at all times;[85] now he brandished a weapon on national television. Although later commentators
were quick to chastise government officials and journalists for painting
the occupiers as violent people preparing for war, it is telling that this
was exactly the image that the occupiers themselves sought to project.

Even those within the camp admitted to contributing to the rise in violence at the site. Non-Native occupier Suniva Bronson supplied most of
the weapons to the site and instigated some of the early confrontations
with local residents and campers. Splitting the Sky recounted that
Bronson thought of herself as the "War Chief of the standoff." Her self-
appointed leadership became so confrontational at one point that
Splitting the Sky had to pull her aside and tell her that if she was not
going to listen to Wolverine or himself, she should "hit the road." He
recalled, "Suniva was overstepping her bounds. She was an observer not
a defender. Just because she read a few books on war did not entitle her
to lead a revolution, particularly a revolution of the Original Peoples. It
didn't surprise Sandra [Bruderer] and I that she would be the only person to get shot by the E.R.T. [Emergency Response Team] forces during
the escalation. Her disrespect, stupidity and romanticism would catch
up with her."[86] Complicated power dynamics between non-Native and
Native occupiers at the site certainly contributed to rising tensions
between those inside and outside of the camp.

On 27 August two RCMP officers were supervising forestry workers
removing trees felled by the occupiers to block the road near the campsite when occupiers allegedly opened fire on their police truck. According
to police and media reports, the officers were shot in the back, but neither was fatally injured thanks to their flak jackets.[87] However, the occupiers denied that this incident took place, and no charges were laid
against them. Skeptical journalist William Johnson questioned whether
the "ambush" and the "hail of bullets" were a police fabrication,[88] but

most of his counterparts accepted the police reports and contended that the potentially fatal shooting of two officers "changed the whole situation." Because the media did not have access to the camp, they could not access alternate perspectives for several days. When Bruce Clark was finally allowed access to the camp on 31 August, he produced bullets and alleged that the police had instigated the shooting incident, not the occupiers. He quickly became a "media celebrity," despite journalists' wariness about his volatility and propensity to exaggerate accusations of harm against the camp occupants.[89]

The Aboriginal politics surrounding the standoff were also increasingly complicated, as some provincial chiefs indicated their support for the occupiers, whereas the Cariboo Tribal Council continued to reject the camp members' legitimacy. On 28 August, Chief Saul Terry, the president of the Union of British Columbia Indian Chiefs, released a statement that accused the RCMP, the BC attorney general, and the media of having gone

> to great lengths to discredit the Shuswap sundancers and their supporters at Gustafsen Lake as dangerous fanatics in order to justify the use of armed force to remove them from the Sundance grounds ... In trying to discredit and isolate the sundancers, the RCMP and the Attorney General are laying the groundwork for bloodshed – needless bloodshed. I condemn the RCMP and the Attorney General for the dangerous provocative course they have embarked upon ... The positions expressed by the sundancers on their nations' sovereignty and aboriginal title and rights are not "extremist." They are shared by many Indian peoples across this province. British Columbia is unceded Indian land ... Our peoples demand JUSTICE and RECOGNITION but whenever they stand up for their rights, they are subjected to the RULE OF LAW and POLICE STATE TACTICS!"[90]

This view suggested that the people at the camp had legitimate grievances and sovereign rights to the land. The Cariboo Tribal Council, however, continued to assert its authority over the land claim by negotiating directly with Lyle James. On 30 August, James and the elected leaders of the Canoe Creek Band reached an agreement to guarantee that the sun dancers could continue to use the site until 1997, "subject to conditions and time limits," at which point the two parties would discuss a contract extension. The CTC and the cattle company would also decide what would happen with existing structures at the site. However, the occupiers of Gustafsen Lake were not consulted, and they opposed the agreement.[91] For his part, Bruce Clark told the RCMP that the occupiers would leave the camp if the federal attorney general and minister of justice did not oppose his January petition to the queen. Predictably, the provincial attorney general, Dosanjh, vetoed the proposition before it reached Ottawa, and Clark promptly accused the police of "complicity in genocide."[92]

From this point onward, the police and government officials delivered a consistent law and order message designed to deny the occupiers any legitimacy or room to manoeuvre. "I can tell you that the position of the province is very clear," Dosanjh told reporters. "There shall be no participation in what amounts to criminal and political extortion of the administration of justice in this province at the hands of a few people holed up at this camp who use AK-47s to shoot police officers in their backs."[93] In early September the RCMP announced an expansive "no-go zone" around the camp. Although the police admitted that they could not enforce it, they hoped to keep hunters out of the area while the standoff continued. Armoured personnel carriers were deployed into the "buffer zone" between the RCMP checkpoint and the encampment to transport and protect RCMP patrols. Such protection was needed, according to police reports that RCMP officers had come under fire on 5 September "by persons believed to be from the armed encampment at Gustafsen Lake." Two days later, the RCMP reported that a red truck heading away from the camp had shot at a police helicopter.[94] After a meeting at Alkali Lake in which the Native community insisted that the conflict was "a Native problem for which a Native solution would be found," a delegation of Secwepemc elders and chiefs entered the camp to try to settle the dispute peacefully.[95] Their efforts proved futile, and the RCMP reiterated that a "criminal element" among the occupiers had "usurped any legitimate goal and objectives of the local people with their own self-serving criminal agenda." On 10 September, Dosanjh lamented that "the chances of a peaceful solution are dimming day by day."[96]

The following afternoon, a red truck with two camp occupiers and a dog was disabled and partially destroyed when an "early warning device" (a type of landmine)[97] was detonated beneath the truck on a logging road where it was driving. After the blast, the vehicle's occupants ran toward the river. An armoured personnel carrier rolled toward the disabled truck, eventually ramming it.[98] Wolverine arrived at the scene in support of his comrades and fired a rifle at the carrier (allegedly with no intention to kill).[99] Other than the dog, which was killed during the firefight, the only injury was a gunshot wound to the arm suffered by Suniva Bronson. The incident was complicated in that the occupants of the vehicle said that they had been travelling to get food and water for elders who were scheduled to enter the camp later that evening for negotiations.[100] The RCMP, however, confiscated an AK-47 rifle from the disabled vehicle after the firefight ended.[101]

The following day, four RCMP officers set up a .308 sniper rifle on a perch near the lake and spotted a "Native male in camo and gilly suit, and carrying an AK-47 walking across the field from the camp to shoreline where the small dock was located." Inspector Roger Kembel authorized the sniper to take the shot.[102] However, the Native male was in a designated "no shoot zone" established by the RCMP and communicated to the occupiers, which eventually led to a police inquiry. The shooters later admitted to this mistake. Another issue with the situation was that the aerial footage of the incident does not support RCMP claims that the man was wearing camouflage and in possession of an automatic rifle. The video shows a man in a red shirt casually walking across a field. "Black," a man from the camp, later recounted that he had been shot at while attempting to wash up in the lake that morning and was saved by spiritual intervention.[103]

After the standoff ended, the events of 11 to 12 September 1995 served as the quintessential examples of police aggression at Gustafsen Lake. The RCMP recognized the potential repercussions at the time. Psychologist Mike Webster communicated to the RCMP at their general meeting in the command centre at 100 Mile House on 12 September that "in the final analysis, the perception may be that [we] were working against ourselves yesterday." The incident had precipitated a "fire fight," which in turn had reinforced the Natives' "belief about the *white man*" as violent oppressors of Aboriginal peoples. Superintendent Rick Hall concurred with Webster's foresight.[104] Nevertheless, after the gunfight the RCMP ordered five more armoured personnel carriers (four new ones and one to replace a disabled vehicle) and two more Emergency Response Team divisions, as well as 20,000 more rounds of bullets to replace the ones that had been used during the shootout.[105]

The increased ammunition, weaponry, and troops increased anxieties in the occupiers' camp. So did the police's selection of an elected chief to try to convince them to end the standoff. On 13 September the RCMP arranged with CBC Radio to broadcast assurances from Canim Lake

Band chief Antoine Archie (in English and Shuswap) that the occupiers would be treated fairly if they came out of the camp. However, the protestors never trusted Archie, which heightened uncertainty about police motives and intentions. They continued to insist that they would not leave unless the government acceded to their original demands and also demanded that United Nations observers guarantee their safety.[106] After Lakota Sioux spiritual leader Arval Looking Horse failed to convince the occupiers to leave on 13 September, and after Bruce Clark was jailed for a tirade in the 100 Mile House courtroom (which included kicking police officers and insulting the judge),[107] the police allowed "spiritual leader" John Stevens to enter the camp on 16 September. He carried a message from Splitting the Sky that assured the Defenders of the Shuswap Nation that their work was done, and he succeeded where others had failed. The twelve remaining occupiers left the camp the following day.[108] The Cariboo Tribal Council released a press release expressing its relief that the "volatile situation at Ts'peten (or Gustafsen Lake)" had ended and thanking Ovide Mercredi, provincial chiefs, their communities, and "the RCMP for their patience and restraint in the face of considerable provocation from both inside and outside of the camp."[109]

## THE ROLE OF THE MEDIA

Sandra Lambertus's 2004 book *Wartime Images, Peacetime Wounds* furnishes a detailed analysis of the media and the Gustafsen Lake standoff. Her most important contribution is her discussion of how various relationships – between the media and the RCMP, the media and Aboriginals, the RCMP and Aboriginals, the media and the public, the RCMP and the public, and Aboriginals and non-Aboriginals – were damaged. This chapter does not intend to replicate her efforts and focuses briefly on the RCMP's control of the media and corresponding depictions of the occupiers. Both the police and the occupiers recognized the importance of the media in generating support for their positions and actions. In the end, the RCMP succeeded in promoting an image of the occupiers that diminished their credibility in the eyes of the Canadian public. Only after the standoff was over did journalists recognize that they had been manipulated and had disseminated skewed information because of the police's management of the flow of information.

Lambertus argues that, by September 1995, the RCMP had launched a "smear campaign" to discredit the occupiers. After the 11 September 1995 firefight, the police released the criminal records of various occupiers (and, erroneously, background information on some Aboriginal people who were not at the site) to convince the public that these militants were dangerous and violent. In an interview years later, Sergeant Peter Montague defended the actions of the RCMP:

> But I don't mention "smear campaign" in my media plan – but you can interpret it – by putting out criminal records we were smearing these people's reputations – you can say that, and you'd be justified in saying it. But – we're not running a smear campaign, we're running a truth campaign – the brutal truth – it's never been done before – and we know that people are going to be some ticked off …
>
> Now we realized that, you know – if this thing gets out of control – the public have to know what we're dealing with here. We're not dealing with a bunch of innocent people in there, and this is no Sunday school picnic.[110]

The RCMP also restricted media access to the site and effectively disrupted the ability of those in the camp to communicate their position to the Canadian public. On the 23 August the police confiscated the *Defenders of the Land* documentary from the CBC, recorded by Trond Halle in the camp, and on 6 September they confiscated footage the network had recorded within the camp. The footage was taken as evidence of the criminal activity in the camp, depicting occupiers shooting at police helicopters and walking around the camp with what appear to be AK-47s. The seizure of these tapes not only provided evidence against the occupiers at trial but also provided information on their weaponry, positioning, and size. It also breached the trust between the camp and the media.[111]

After the standoff ended, several reporters expressed dissatisfaction with how they had been treated by the RCMP. In an "off the record" press conference, the RCMP admitted that they had adopted media-control strategies first employed in the 1991 Persian Gulf War. One journalist told Lambertus, "we knew we were getting a controlled version of reality – but no other reality was legally possible."[112] Gary Mason, editor of the *Vancouver Sun*, expressed similar discontent over the way the media had been treated:

> Basically, the more this thing dragged on, the more we really felt – it was – almost like the B.C. version of the Kuwait War. Where the … Pentagon and the U.S. government did such an unbelievable job

of controlling the message. And the RCMP – it was a mini-version of that – that they were doing exactly the same thing, employing exactly the same strategy, in terms of controlling where the media could go, exactly the information that they were going to get on a daily basis, making sure that they didn't have access to the opposing forces.[113]

Some commentators argued that, rather than being manipulated, journalists had been overly compliant and even complicit with the police strategy. Joey Thompson argued in the *Vancouver Province* that the media should apologize for their gullibility:

We bought the Mounties' take on what was going down during that tense month-long summer siege. A lot of what we got – and dutifully reported – was crock. It's time we conceded that and apologized to the natives and citizens of B.C. The fact is camp members weren't the terrorists RCMP made them out to be. Nor did they invite the shootouts the police press releases claimed. Officers were ordered to back off the "terrorist" label three days into the mudslinging and name-calling. But the damage was done. By then we were sold on the RCMP's script of good vs. evil: Our men in red blazers against trigger-crazed Indian thugs. And that's what stung the most. "To be called terrorists in their own country; they're still hurting over that," natives' defence lawyer George Wool told me yesterday. "It's set relations between them and the police back 100 years. All the good work RCMP have done with native youth is lost. The trust is gone." Ditto for members of the media.[114]

The presentation of the occupiers as "proven criminals" was, Superintendent Len Olfert asserted, a statement of fact. Media restrictions, however, left several journalists frustrated with the RCMP and its actions, which precluded the media from presenting several sides to the story.

The idea that the media were a powerless victim of police information management was not universal. Local media were less affected by the tactics of the RCMP for a number of logistical reasons: they had been covering the story since 1993, they knew of whom to inquire when investigating the story, and those who had information were more willing to speak with local media. Steven Frasher, the editor of the *100 Mile House Free Press*, told Lambertus that the local media "had the ability to stand back and refuse to be spoon fed."[115] Furthermore, media outlets ultimately decided what information to disseminate to the public. Ted

Byfield, writing in the *Edmonton Sun* on 17 September 1995, was appalled by the CBC's supposedly "objective" coverage, which he felt gave
the occupiers too much credibility:

> One the one hand, we are shown the RCMP, even-handed,
> dutifully trying to enforce the law. On the other hand we have
> the idealistic natives, committed to their cause, environmentally
> sensitive, asserting the prerogatives of their culture, appealing to
> Queen Elizabeth. Night by night, we hear the CBC intoning: The
> Mounties say this ... But the natives say that ... the one as credible
> as the other.
>
> Except in one case. When the Mounties disclosed the identities
> of some of the committed crusaders on the other side of the barri-
> cade, the CBC didn't manage to put this on the national airwaves.
> So the TV audience never did find out just who these crusaders for
> justice, culture and spirituality actually are ... There is something
> of a gulf between all this high-sounding spirituality and the actual
> records of the people who are portrayed as espousing it, and the
> CBC has deliberately denied that information to the public. More-
> over, what it has been, in fact, covering is the deliberate defiance
> of the law by a gang of obvious hoodlums and a squad of police
> officers who are very feebly directed by an irresolute provincial
> government that isn't prepared to enforce its own laws.[116]

In seeking to "balance" the stories and offer "objectivity," media outlets
could also confer legitimacy on actors whom some commentators
believed did not deserve it.

From the police standpoint, the control of information prevented the
occupiers from generating outside sympathy or securing popular legitimacy for their armed protest. In this sense, shutting off media access to
the occupiers may have established the futility of violent struggle, short-
ened the standoff, and prevented further injury or death. A friend of
Percy Rosette conceded after the standoff ended that the police had been
provocative during the dispute, "but I suppose the fact that everyone
walked out of there more or less in one piece then they probably did a
pretty good job."[117] On balance, however, the RCMP's information
strategy precluded the media from doing its job. An editorial in the
*Vancouver Sun* on 22 September 1995 noted,

> In one sense, Gustafsen Lake has been a justly-celebrated triumph
> for the RCMP, a demonstration that the force is worthy of its

reputation for restraint, decency and common sense. But in another sense it represents a failure for the media. We were prevented, always for the best of reasons, from providing that independent scrutiny by which the official version can and should be tested against the unofficial version. If Gustafsen Lake is a harbinger of the future, it should bring a chill of foreboding to everyone concerned about democracy and the right of every citizen to be as fully informed as is reasonably possible.[118]

## CONCLUSIONS: THE LESSONS OF GUSTAFSEN LAKE

The Canadian taxpayer spent over ten million dollars for the RCMP chicanery; so you might as well get your money's worth in the lessons of Gustafsen Lake.

Splitting the Sky[119]

In the end, the Defenders of the Shuswap Nation did not succeed either in establishing their sovereignty over Gustafsen Lake (Ts'peten) or in protecting the sun dance site. John Stevens, the spiritual leader of the sun dance in previous years, decided to host the 1996 ceremony in Alberta and gave permission to elected chiefs Antoine Archie and Agnes Snow to ritually destroy the arbor at Ts'peten. Elders had advised the Cariboo Tribal Council that this was a necessary act to put the standoff behind them and to rebuild respect among the local community. Percy Rosette was dismayed at this action, given RCMP and CTC promises at the time of the occupiers' surrender that they would preserve the site, which he saw as a violation of spiritual freedom.[120] There was little he or the others could do about it.

Eighteen people were charged in the Gustafsen Lake standoff, including four non-Native supporters. The trial in Surrey, British Columbia – conducted under high security given the nature of the "event under review"[121] – began in July 1996. On 20 May 1997 the jury returned with its verdicts on the sixty charges laid against the defendants. Wolverine and his son JoJo were acquitted of the most serious charges of attempted murder, but Wolverine, James ("OJ") Pitawanakwat (an Anishinabe from Ontario),[122] Edward Dick (from nearby Chase),[123] and non-Native supporter Suniva Bronson were all convicted of "mischief causing danger to life."[124] Wolverine received the stiffest sentence of four and a half years.[125] Lesser convictions of mischief and mischief to property were given to Wolverine's wife, Flora Sampson, to his daughter Sheila Ignace, to Percy Rosette, Mary Pena, Glenn Deneault (from Chase),[126] and Ron

Dionne (a Mohawk from St Catharine's, Ontario, who had been involved at Oka),[127] and to the three non-Native supporters.[128]

The trial proceedings revealed that the occupiers had not represented a united front, despite the strong rhetoric expressed during the standoff. After it was over, Mary Pena accused Splitting the Sky and Bruce Clark of hijacking the occupation to further their broader sovereigntist claims. "They could have had us massacred in there for their own agendas," she asserted. "They walked away while the faithkeeper [Percy Rosette] is imprisoned."[129] Defence lawyer Sheldon Tate divided the camp between the violent and peaceful occupiers, whom he called the "hawks" and the "doves."[130] He alleged that the religious contingent was peaceful, whereas the sovereigntist group, led by Wolverine and Clark, was not.[131] Splitting the Sky accuses Rosette of being the "hawk" in the camp, not Wolverine or himself, and he claims that Rosette fired the shot at RCMP officer Ray Wilby on 18 August. Furthermore, he alleges that Mary Pena asked for warrior assistance.[132] Strong accusations of subterfuge and perfidy were no longer directed only at the elected politicians, the police, Lyle James, and his ranch handlers. The occupiers now turned on one another.

The issues of sovereignty raised during the standoff also elicited mixed responses during the trial and afterward. "Like Judas, who betrayed Christ before the Romans crucified him, Percy would deny he ever supported Clark's treatises on the rule of law," Splitting the Sky bitterly notes about Rosette after the latter rejected the sovereigntist claims that once defined the standoff. "He stated that Gustafsen Lake had nothing to do with unceded land but was only a spiritual ceremony." Typically, Splitting the Sky dismisses Rosette's change of heart as evidence of government coercion and a corrupt defence council.[133] Sheldon Tate and the Shuswap Liaison Committee also abandoned their sovereigntist claims.[134] The lines between spiritual beliefs and Aboriginal sovereignty were increasingly stark and now suggested different agendas. Accordingly, the occupiers were unable "to form a united circle" at the trial,[135] and fractures within the group undermined its claims to ownership of unceded lands.

Gustafsen Lake exemplified a complex set of relationships between Aboriginal protestors, elected band leadership, and national Aboriginal organizations. The occupiers' assertions directly challenged the authority of elected Aboriginal leaders, which they rejected, even though the Cariboo Tribal Council was deeply invested in the situation at Gustafsen Lake given that the land was included in a larger comprehensive land claim. Chiefs Agnes Snow and Antoine Archie became involved in the negotiations that took place between Lyle James and the occupiers and consistently differentiated themselves and the local Aboriginal communities from the militant protestors. Whereas some of the occupiers considered the sun dance site to be sacred space, which tied their neotraditional spirituality to their sovereigntist political agenda and to the standoff against the RCMP, Chief Antoine Archie and the CTC rejected their claims. They asserted that the allegedly "traditional" spiritual practices of the occupiers were incorrect and that the land was not a specifically sacred site. They also stridently objected to the militancy and violence that marked efforts by the Defenders of the Shuswap Nation to hold onto the sun dance site and supported the law and order framework that provincial politicians and the RCMP adopted to justify their actions against protestors with a "criminal agenda."

Although several occupiers and their supporters called for a public inquiry into the events at Gustafsen Lake, none was held. Even activist member of Parliament Svend Robinson, who had participated in blockades in Gwaii Hanas and Clayoquot Sound in support of Aboriginal rights, did not believe that one was warranted. "At Gustafsen Lake, both the hereditary and the elected first nations leadership in that area condemned the use of arms by protestors," Robinson wrote on 10 November 1998. "As well, the First Nations Summit leadership and B.C., and Assembly of First Nations Grand Chief Ovid Mercredi joined in this condemnation of the taking up of arms, including AK 47 automatic rifles and other guns. They voiced gratitude for the fact that there was no loss of life, and thanked the Cariboo tribal council leaders for the peacemaking role they played." Although Robinson would denounce violations of Aboriginal peoples' human rights in Canada and abroad, he supported the treaty-making process. "While often painstakingly slow and difficult," he explained, the process was "certainly preferable to taking up guns and violence, as occurred in the summer of 1995 at Gustafsen Lake."[136]

The standoff publicly challenged the legitimacy and authority of federally supported Aboriginal leadership both locally and nationally. Assembly of First Nations national chief Ovide Mercredi intervened unsuccessfully to try to stop the escalating violence, but the occupiers never wavered in their dismissal of nonhereditary leadership and derided him for being a "puppet Indian."[137] Mercredi claimed that he had done his job – he emphasized that governments needed to start paying attention to Aboriginal peoples' concerns and that Gustafsen Lake and Ipperwash provided visible examples of the problems he was identifying. When

Hana Gartner of the *National Magazine* asked Mercredi why Aboriginal people at the barricades were ignoring him, "hijacking the process and undermining your credibility and your authority," he replied,

> I think what they're saying – and that's what I'm saying – that this is a wake-up call for Canada. I think in fact what they are saying is that the process is too slow; that the results are not there; that young people are still dying; that unemployment in our communities is still too high; that the housing conditions are too deplorable; that our issues with respect to treaty rights are not being respected; and our land issues are being ignored. And I think what in fact they're saying is … get on with the issues and find the resolutions. But what I'm trying to suggest to you is this: that the Indian leadership has been very determined to find the resolutions but we're only one part of the equation. The other part is your politicians. They're the ones who have the power to decide whether or not something will be settled and ultimately they have the supreme responsibility of acting in the interest of everybody, not just for their population but for our people as well.[138]

In short, Mercredi intimated that militant protestors shared the same frustrations as he did, and he tried to promote the image of a unified Aboriginal community seeking meaningful political change – despite the very public division apparent at the local level. Mercredi also aligned himself with the occupiers at Gustafsen Lake even though they clearly would not align with him – implying that what *they* were saying was what *he* was saying. In this sense, the standoff became a powerful platform from which Mercredi could proclaim the ineffectiveness of the current system and the necessity of consultation with Aboriginal leadership – a position inconsistent with the occupiers' rejection of the legitimacy of elected chiefs.

An interesting shift took place among some Aboriginal leaders who reconstructed the Gustafsen Lake standoff as an understandable manifestation of Aboriginal frustrations once it had ended. Chief Arthur Manuel, a member of the Shuswap Nation Tribal Council, which had castigated the occupiers earlier, told reporters, "If there's a lesson for the public (from Gustafsen) it's that Indian people in general feel these deep feelings of injustice. We can't look at it as actions of our own … but the feelings are there."[139] Manuel did not condone the violence, but his acknowledgment of the injustice that lay at the core of the Aboriginal experience brought a sort of legitimacy to the standoff. Chief Ko'waintco Linda Shackelly of the Assembly of First Nations also shared Manuel's sentiments. Appearing before the provincial Standing Committee on Aboriginal Affairs in November 1996, she held up Gustafsen Lake as an example of "the frustration of no respect being shown ... to the one law for all."[140] Gustafsen Lake had become a symbol of resistance to injustice and the need for political change.

Mercredi made this interpretation clear before a Senate committee in Ottawa just months after the standoff had ended, suggesting that Gustafsen Lake – alongside Ipperwash and Oka – represented "an alternative which we do not want, but an alternative which we cannot avoid if the nation continues to treat us as if we do not exist." As long as the federal Liberals kept First Nations out of discussions on national unity and constitutional change, he argued, the prospect of violence would grow:

> I have travelled a lot across this country. I have seen army fatigues in virtually every community. I am saying to you that there is a real danger here. While you may have a united country with Quebec in place, if you do not address our needs there will not be any peace. It will not be because of me; I will not be around. I will be replaced. Whoever replaces people like myself will not be gentle or kind. They will not believe in the constitutional process. They will believe in direct, violent confrontation. That is the option I am trying to avoid.[141]

The local context of what had transpired at Gustafsen Lake now seemed less important than the simple warning that shared Aboriginal frustration with the state could precipitate more violence. Mercredi held himself up as the moderate. Despite the fact that occupiers of Gustafsen Lake had rejected him, they had unintentionally provided him with a powerful political tool, an example of what unaddressed concerns and frustrations of Aboriginal peoples can trigger.

There is no conclusive evidence that the Gustafsen Lake standoff produced any explicit gains for the Aboriginal protestors. If they had wanted to provoke a bloody fight to generate publicity and support for their cause, as Chief Antoine Archie suggested, they did not succeed. Despite *post facto* critiques of the RCMP and the media by activists and sympathetic scholars, the occupiers were unable to overcome their image as "trigger-crazed Indian thugs."[142] They did not undermine the local elected leadership or generate significant support for militant action among the Secwepemc population. The BCTC process remains unchanged, the Cariboo Tribal Council claim remains in progress, sovereignty has not been granted to those who sought it, and the queen never made a ruling on Bruce Clark's petition of 3 January 1995.[143] The standoff at Gustafsen Lake was a failure by any political measure, even though it reinforced the neotraditional spiritual convictions and increased the public profile of some occupiers.

NOTES

This chapter draws heavily from John Boncore Hill (Splitting the Sky), with Sandra Bruderer (She Keeps the Door), *The Autobiography of Dacajeweiah, Splitting the Sky: From Attica to Gustafsen Lake, Unmasking the Secrets of the Psycho-sexual Energy and the Struggle for Original Peoples' Title* (Chase, BC: John Pasquale Boncore, 2001), which provides insight into the sovereigntist claims and reproduces occupier, police, media, and court documents. Lawyer Janice G.A.E. Switlo's uneven book *Gustafsen Lake: Under Siege* (Peachland, BC: TIAC Communications, 1997) was published while the trial was in progress and contains a chronology that is useful when cross-referenced with other sources, as some dates and descriptions are erroneous. Sandra Lambertus's study of media coverage, *Wartime Images, Peacetime Wounds: The Media and the Gustafsen Lake Standoff* (Toronto: University of Toronto Press, 2004), offers a more reliable but equally critical overview of developments within the framework of media constructions. The Settlers in Support of Indigenous Sovereignty (SISIS) have compiled an archive of legal documents and material produced by the Ts'peten Defenders, or Defenders of the Shuswap Nation, at http://sisis.nativeweb.org/gustmain.html. All of their press releases are available at this site unless otherwise noted.

1 Ray Wilby, in Boncore Hill, *Autobiography*, 364.
2 Sergeant Mike Schleuter was also maimed by a faulty RCMP stun grenade that exploded in his hand during the operation.
3 Alan D. MacMillan, *Native Peoples and Cultures of Canada* (Vancouver: Douglas and McIntyre, 1988), 150, 158–9. MacMillan notes that "war parties were led by a war chief and accompanied by a shaman, who used his supernatural powers to weaken the enemy" (159).
4 Secwepemculecw, "History of the Secwepemc People," http://landoftheshuswap.com/history.html.
5 Robin Fisher, *Contact and Conflict: Indian-European Relations in British Columbia, 1774–1890* (Vancouver: UBC Press, 1977); Paul Tennant, *Aboriginal Peoples and Politics: The Indian Land Question in B.C.*

(Vancouver: U B C Press, 1990); Cole Harris, *Making Native Space: Colonialism, Resistance, and Reserves in British Columbia* (Vancouver: U B C Press, 2002); John Lutz, *Makúk: A New History of Aboriginal White Relations* (Vancouver: U B C Press, 2008).

6  Harris, *Making Native Space*, 120–2.

7  See Union of British Columbia Indian Chiefs, "Who We Are," http://www.ubcic.bc.ca/about.

8  Christopher McKee, *Treaty Talks in British Columbia* (Vancouver: U B C Press, 2000), 27–8; Secwepemculecw, "History of the Secwepemc People"; "Secwepemc History of Resistance," *Wii'nimkiikaa*, no. 2 (2005), http://wiinimkiikaa.wordpress.com/secwepemc-history-of-resistance.

9  Vander Zahn, prior to creating the taskforce that would result in the creation of the B C T C, also met with protestors involved in "spillover" blockades in British Columbia during the Oka crisis. McKee, *Treaty Talks*, 29–35.

10  Quite simply, the framework includes a list of important issues to be discussed and a timeline for the fourth stage of the treaty process. Aside from the historical retractions of Aboriginal title and federally sanctioned laws effectively stopping land claim discussions, the ruling handed down in the Delgamuukw case was a limited victory for Aboriginal peoples in Canada. The B C Supreme Court's ruling in 1991 initially concluded that Aboriginal title had been extinguished in British Columbia. The 1993 Court of Appeals decision overturned the conclusion that Aboriginal title had been extinguished, but the appellate court did apply some limitations to this reversal. "[T]he majority [of appellate judges] were careful to make it clear that those Aboriginal rights that do remain do not entail the unfettered right to use, occupy, and control the lands and their resources," Christopher McKee explains. "On the question of jurisdiction, which amounted to a claim to a right to self-government, the court's majority held that such authority would constitute legislative powers that could encroach upon those of the federal and provincial governments." In short, the Aboriginal title that was confirmed in 1993 was limited in scope. The ruling still asserted federal and provincial authority over the land and stipulated that Aboriginal title did not mean Aboriginal groups could use and occupy lands based on pre-existing rights. McKee, *Treaty Talks*, 30–1.

11  See the Northern Shuswap Tribal Council website at http://northernshuswaptribalcouncil.com. The four First Nations members are Tsq'escen' (Canim Lake Band), Xat'sūll and Cm'etem (Soda Creek and Deep Creek Band), T'exelc (Williams Lake Band), and Stswecem'c and Xgat'tem (Canoe Creek and Dog Creek Band). The Cariboo Tribal Council

(CTC) was formed in the early 1970s to represent the interests of fifteen bands from the Cariboo Chilcotin region. In the 1980s the Chilcotin and Carrier tribal groups formed their own tribal councils. The CTC changed its name to the Northern Shuswap Tribal Council in 2006.

12  Cariboo Tribal Council, *Statement of Intent*, submission to British Columbia Treaty Commission, 15 December 1993, http://www.bctreaty.net/soi/soicariboo.php.

13  The status of this claim by the Northern Shuswap Tribal Council can be monitored through the British Columbia Treaty Commission website at http://www.bctreaty.net/nations/cariboo.php. The Cariboo Tribal Council (now called the Northern Shuswap Tribal Council) continues to negotiate its land claim. The last progress came in 2004, when the council completed some aspects of stage four of the treaty process – "creating an agreement in principle" – but this stage still remains open. Treaty discussions have continued within the various groups involved in the claim. See Northern Shuswap Tribal Council Treaty Department, http://www.nstqtreaty.ca.

14  As of July 2010, the boundaries of the claim remained under review by the First Nation.

15  Four Native reserves are located in the region. Canirn Lake is about 30 kilometres northeast of 100 Mile House, Dog Creek is about 50 kilometres west, Canoe Creek is about 60 kilometres west, and Alkali Lake is about 130 kilometres west and easier to access from Williams Lake. The three reserves to the west are located off Highway 97, accessible only by forestry roads. Lambertus, *Wartime Images*, 28.

16  Switlo, *Gustafsen Lake*, 105.

17  Stephen Hume, "The Lure of the Sacred Sun Dance," *Vancouver Sun*, 30 August 1995, A19. Joseph Jorgensen approaches the sun dance ritual not in terms of a validation based on tradition or historical legitimacy but through its meaning and usefulness to its practitioners. The adoption and adaptation of traditional religious practices (neotraditional practices) did not comply with conceptions of religion held by CTC leaders like Chief Antoine Archie. Although this does not mean that the conception supported by the social and political elites (whether that be local Aboriginal leadership or the Canadian state) should be authenticated and the other demarcated, it is salient that the sun dancers assumed that their spiritual practices were legitimate enough to warrant direct action against the state. On this theme, see also Lori G. Beaman, "Aboriginal Spirituality and the Legal Construction of Freedom of Religion," in *Religion and Canadian Society: Contexts, Identities, and Strategies*, ed. Lori G. Beaman, 229–47 (Toronto: Canadian Scholars' Press, 2006).

18 He cited the cases of Black Mountain on the Navajo Reservation and the Pajutes of Nevada and Northern Oregon. Joseph Jorgensen, in Hume, "Lure of the Sacred Sundance."

19 For a more detailed examination of religion and the Gustafsen Lake standoff, see Nicholas Shrubsole, "The Sun Dance and the Gustafsen Lake Standoff: Healing through Resistance and the Danger of Dismissing Religion," *International Indigenous Policy Journal* 2, no. 4 (2011): 1–17; and Nicholas Shrubsole, "The Colonial Discourse of Indigenous Religions and the Challenge of Diversity," ch. 5 in "Religion, Land and Democracy in Canadian Indigenous-State Relations," 115–44 (PhD diss., University of Waterloo, 2013).

20 Switlo, *Gustafsen Lake*, 94; Lambertus, *Wartime Images*, 29–30.

21 Boncore Hill, *Autobiography*, 80.

22 Lambertus, *Wartime Images*, 28–30.

23 Rosette claimed to have buried paper evidence somewhere, but he could not recall which rock it was under. Boncore Hill, *Autobiography*, 71.

24 Mary Pena, untitled speech presented at La Quena Coffeehouse, Vancouver, 1996, http://sisis.nativeweb.org/gustlake/mary.html.

25 Several occupiers testified after the standoff that it was their spirituality that protected them on the battlefield, shielding them from bullets. See Boncore Hill, *Autobiography*; and Switlo, *Gustafsen Lake*.

26 Tommy Gregoire et al., *Confederated Traditional Okanagan-Shuswap Nations Declaration*, 8 December 1986, http://www.landoftheshuswap.com/declare.html.

27 Percy Rosette, interview of 20 August 1995, quoted in Michael D. Smith, "Unsettling British Columbia: Interventions in a Neocolonial Politics" (MA thesis, University of British Columbia, 1997), 143–4.

28 OJ Pitawanakwat, "I Release Another Arrow," in *Statements by Ts'peten Political Prisoners*, ed. Free the Wolverince Campaign – Seattle Office, December 1997, http://sisis.nativeweb.org/gustlake/dec97fwc.html.

29 Boncore Hill, *Autobiography*, 71, 81–3; Ben Mahony, "'Disinformation and Smear': The Use of State Propaganda and Mulitary Force to Suppress Aboriginal Title at the 1995 Gustafsen Lake Standoff" (MA thesis, University of Lethbridge, 2001), 78–9. Clark has also raised the jurisdiction argument in the United Kingdom, in the United States of America, and in international bodies such as the United Nations. Bruce Clark, *Justice in Paradise* (Montreal and Kingston: McGill-Queen's University Press, 1999), 162–3.

30 Boncore Hill, *Autobiography*, 76.

31 Ben Mahony and Wolverine, "Whose Land Is It? An Interview with Wolverine," in *The Gustafsen Lake Crisis: Statements from the Ts'Petsen Defenders*, ed. Montreal Anarchist Black Cross Federation, 17–29 (Montreal: Solidarity, 2001), 18. This interview was originally published in Vancouver's *Terminal City*, 21–7 March 1997.

32 Ibid., 26.

33 Of those involved in the standoff, the three men recognized as the leaders were significantly older than the other occupiers: Splitting the Sky was in his early forties, Rosette in his mid-fifties, and Wolverine in his mid-sixties. The majority of occupiers (seven Native people and one non-Native person) were in their twenties.

34 Boncore Hill, *Autobiography*, 61.

35 In February 1994 Splitting the Sky responded to a "warriors red alert" regarding the potential invasion of Mohawk and Oneida territory; Wolverine asked Splitting the Sky to "pull a few boys together and back our play in the bunkers." Splitting the Sky agreed. During the Adams Lake blockade near Gustafsen Lake – a blockade erected to stop condominium development on known burial grounds – Wolverine, Splitting the Sky, and Stewart Dick had travelled the short distance in support. Stewart Dick had assaulted a construction worker, and Wolverine had thrown someone into the lake and smashed the window of a tugboat that was hauling supplies to the shore. Boncore Hill, *Autobiography*, 71–2, 89.

36 After one Cariboo Tribal Council chief tried to control a meeting with Lyle James, Wolverine told him, "you are a civil servant therefore I don't want to hear from you." Mahony and Wolverine, "Whose Land Is It?" 26. Bruce Clark echoed this critique in Sherryl Yeager and Justine Hunter, "Indian Rebels Plan to Leave in Body Bags," *Vancouver Sun*, 22 August 1995, A1.

37 Rudy Platiel, "Significant Differences Seen between Native Standoffs," *Globe and Mail*, 29 August 1995, A4.

38 Agnes Snow, in Mark Hume and Sherryl Yeager, "Hopes Rise for Ending Armed Standoff," *Vancouver Sun*, 31 August 1995, A1.

39 Mahony and Wolverine, "Whose Land Is It?" 26.

40 Platiel, "Significant Differences."

41 Antoine Archie, in Lambertus, *Wartime Images*, 30–1, emphasis added.

42 Platiel, "Significant Differences."

43 Hume and Yeager, "Hopes Rise"; Platiel, "Significant Differences."

44 Boncore Hill, *Autobiography*, 93–4.

45 Lambertus, *Wartime Images*, 32–3; Defenders of the Shuswap Nation, untitled press release, 17 June 1995, http://sisis.nativeweb.org/gustlake/chronap1.html.

46 Ts'peten, "Defenders of Sacred Shuswap Sundance Grounds Preparing for RCMP Assault," press release, 19 July 1995.

47 Lyle James, in Mark Hume, "Standoff at Gustafsen Lake Preceded by a Vision," *Vancouver Sun*, 12 September 1995, A3.

48 Greg Joyce, "B.C. Standoff 'Self-Created' Crisis of RCMP," *Globe and Mail*, 26 April 1997, A7.

49 Boncore Hill, *Autobiography*, 94–6.

50 Ibid., 94, 113. On RCMP meetings, see also Switlo, *Gustafsen Lake*, 94–6.

51 Defenders of the Shuswap Nation, "Deep Red Alert – Action and Support Urgently Requested by Shuswap Traditionalists Threatened at Sacred Sundance Grounds, Gustafsen Lake, B.C.," press release, 21 August 1995, http://sisis.nativeweb.org/gustlake/aug2195.html.

52 Defenders of the Shuswap Nation, untitled press release, 17 June 1995; Ts'peten, "Defenders of Sacred Shuswap."

53 Bruce Clark, in Hume, "Standoff at Gustafsen Lake."

54 Defenders of the Shuswap Nation, untitled press release, 17 June 1995.

55 Defenders of the Shuswap Nation, untitled press release, 18 June 1995; Switlo, *Gustafsen Lake*, 95–6.

56 Mahony and Wolverine, "Whose Land Is It?" 26.

57 Boncore Hill, *Autobiography*, 113.

58 Switlo, *Gustafsen Lake*, 96–9, 102, 111–12; SISIS, "A Chronology of the Gustafsen Lake Standoff," October 1996, http://sisis.nativeweb.org/gustlake/chrono.html; G. Findley, in Boncore Hill, *Autobiography*, 114, 122.

59 G. Findley, in Switlo, *Gustafsen Lake*, 104.

60 Ibid., 104–5, 109.

61 RCMP Report to Crown Counsel Kamloops Sub-division, file 95KL-334, reproduced in Boncore Hill, *Autobiography*, 117.

62 Agnes Snow, in Switlo, *Gustafsen Lake*, 107.

63 Boncore Hill, *Autobiography*, 117.

64 Hume, "Standoff at Gustafsen Lake"; Carolyn Lewis, "RCMP Ready to Move on Armed Native Squatters," *Edmonton Journal*, 20 August 1995, A3; Lambertus, *Wartime Images*, 40–1.

65 Switlo, *Gustafsen Lake*, 113.

66 Defenders of the Shuswap Nation, "Deep Red Alert"; Mike Crawley and Sherryl Yeager, "Mounties Duck Rebels' Bullets," *Edmonton Journal*, 28 August 1995, A1. See also Switlo, *Gustafsen Lake*, 113–14.

67  Boncore Hill, *Autobiography*, 132–3. Splitting the Sky insists that the RCMP knew that Percy Rosette had fired the shot because he had admitted it over a tapped phone line and that the knowledge that Jo-Jo had ended up being charged "caused [Percy] to go completely insane for the rest of his life." Boncore Hill, *Autobiography*, 137.

68  Len Olfert, in Paul Chapman, "RCMP on Warpath," *Vancouver Province*, 20 August 1995, A5.

69  Ibid.

70  Defenders of the Shuswap Nation, "Deep Red Alert."

71  Percy Rosette, untitled press release, 24 August 1995, quoted in Switlo, *Gustafsen Lake*, 117.

72  Bruce Clark, untitled letter to editor, *Vancouver Sun* and *Vancouver Province*, 20 August 1995, quoted in Switlo, *Gustafsen Lake*, 116–17.

73  Ujjal Dosanjh, in Brian Kieran, "Dosanjh Passes His First Test," *Vancouver Province*, 30 August 1995, A6.

74  Peter Montague, in excerpt from unclassified RCMP memo, 1 September 1995, quoted in Lambertus, *Wartime Images*, 217. Contributing to these comments were the reports that two RCMP officers had been shot while doing surveillance of the camp. The officers were not injured but were reportedly saved by their flak jackets, which stopped the bullets.

75  Peter Montague, in Hume and Yeager, "Hopes Rise."

76  Mike Harcourt, "Premier's Statement – Gustafsen Lake," 5 September 1995, http://sisis.nativeweb.org/gustlake/sep0595b.html.

77  SISIS, "Chronology."

78  Parliament of Canada, *Proceedings of the Special Senate Committee on Bill C-110: Issue 3 – Evidence*, 24 January 1996, http://www.parl.gc.ca/35/1/parlbus/commbus/senate/Com-e/c110-c/03ev-e.htm?Language=E&Parl=35&Ses=1&comm_id=25.

79  Bruce Clark, "Demands of the Ts'Peten Defenders," 25 August 1995, http://sisis.nativeweb.org/gustlake/aug2595d.html.

80  Hana Gartner and Ovide Mercredi, "Aboriginal Rights: How Do We Resolve Indian Land Claims?" *National Magazine*, CBC broadcast, 11 September 1995, http://www.cbc.ca/archives/categories/society/native-issues/the-battle-for-aboriginal-treaty-rights/how-do-we-resolve-land-claims.html.

81  Ovide Mercredi, in Kieran, "Dosanjh Passes."

82  Crawley and Yeager, "Mounties Duck Rebels' Bullets."

83  Peter Montague, in Sherryl Yeager, "The Gustafsen Lake Dispute," *Vancouver Sun*, 28 August 1995, A3.

84  Peter Montague, in Gary Bellett, "RCMP Say Talk of Smear Campaign in Jest: Testimony in the Gustafsen Lake Standoff Trial Centres on a Video That Captures Officer's Comments on Media Strategy," *Vancouver Sun*, 23 January 1997, B2; Lambertus, *Wartime Images*, 60–74. When Clark flew to Williams Lake on 28 August to meet with his clients inside the camp, the RCMP refused to grant him access.

85  Boncore Hill, *Autobiography*, 95.

86  Ibid., 96. Splitting the Sky also accused Bronson of trying to usurp his authority by buying off sun dancers and sleeping with young men.

87  Crawley and Yeager, "Mounties Duck Rebels' Bullets." Did this event actually occur? Splitting the Sky conducts his own trial within the pages of his autobiography, analyzing forensic reports, matching bullets to guns, and even discussing the manufacturer's report on the flak jackets worn by the members of the Emergency Response Team. He finds that only one Native man was witnessed by the officers and that he was unarmed and wearing a yellow shirt; the police were either firing at themselves or concocting evidence to support a seizure of the camp. The helicopter responsible for aerial footage was not active when the alleged incident took place, so there was no video footage with which to sort out the facts. Boncore Hill, *Autobiography*, 168–70.

88  William Johnson, "RCMP Should Avoid Waco-Style Shootout in BC," *Montreal Gazette*, 29 August 1995, B3.

89  Lambertus, *Wartime Images*, 74–6, 81; SISIS, "Chronology."

90  Union of British Columbia Indian Chiefs, untitled press release, 28 August 1995, emphasis in original, quoted in SISIS, "Chronology."

91  Hume and Yeager, "Hopes Rise"; Agnes Snow, "The Talking Stick," *KAHTOU*, October 1995, 15.

92  SISIS, "Chronology," provides a more detailed discussion of Clark's demands.

93  Ujjal Dosanjh, in Switlo, *Gustafsen Lake*, 120.

94  CBC Radio, 5 September 1995, cited in SISIS, "Chronology."

95  Lambertus, *Wartime Images*, 97.

96  Ujjal Dosanjh, in Justine Hunter, "A-G Fears Peaceful End Dimming," *Vancouver Sun*, 10 September 1995, A3; and in Switlo, *Gustafsen Lake*, 126.

97  On 2 January 1996 Splitting the Sky appeared on a Rogers Community Television program in Vancouver called *Nitewatch* and played police aerial footage of the two major incidents that occurred on these days. Although Rogers Community Television no longer exists in Vancouver, excerpts from the show remain readily available to the public on YouTube. The "early

warning device" explosion that began the events on 11 September 1995 can be found at http://www.youtube.com/watch?v=rQH9MAPdqws and http://www.youtube.com/watch?v=aWWRKBsWwXQ. The segments are entitled "Ts'Peten Defenders – Nitewatch Part 5" and "Ts'Peten Defenders – Nitewatch Part 6." Excerpts from the sniper incident on 12 September 1995, with commentary from Splitting the Sky, can be found at http://www.youtube.com/watch?v=yblZMMGqV48 and http://www.youtube.com/watch?v=SxkopDjouFA. The segments are entitled "Ts'Peten Defenders – Nitewatch Part 7" and "Ts'Peten Defenders – Nitewatch Part 8."

98 Boncore Hill, *Autobiography*, 295; Youtube, "Ts'peten Defenders – Nitewatch Part 5." Splitting the Sky notes that the occupants of the truck did not step out of the disabled vehicle and start firing, as was initially reported.

99 Boncore Hill, *Autobiography*, 295. Although Wolverine later claimed this was self-defence and a diversion to save his friends, the incident led to a charge of attempted murder. He did not disable the armoured personnel carrier; a Department of National Defence report read at the general meeting at the command centre at 100 Mile House on 12 September 1995, the day following the firefight, reported that the carrier was disabled after running over three fallen trees and that 95 per cent of its damage was caused by the other carrier when it towed the first one out of the zone of engagement. RCMP, "Minutes of the General Meeting Held on 95.09.12 at 0830 Hrs 100 Mile House Command Center Conference Room," cited in ibid., 302.

100 Defenders of the Shuswap Nation, untitled press release, 14 September 1995, cited in ibid., 336.

101 RCMP command would commend the actions of those involved in the shootout, stating that they went "above and beyond the call of duty" in facing heavy-weapons fire in the retrieval of the disabled armoured personnel carrier. Quoted in ibid., 301.

102 Facsimile message from M.T. Callander, Williams Lake Detachment, to Kamloops Sub-division Major Crime Unit, 16 October 1995, quoted in ibid., 313. The RCMP conducted an inquiry into the shooting.

103 RCMP, audiotape 14, side B, 12 September 1995, cited in ibid., 303. The man identified as "Black" said, "the main thing is, there's somebody out there right now who could be bleeding to death. People left to go for a swim this morning and got shot at, and you guarantee their safety." Sergeant Dennis Ryan told the occupiers that he could guarantee their safety only if they were unarmed. The conversation continued as the

camp representative again expressed concerns regarding the ability of occupiers who needed water to get it; he also said, "We will engage them if they keep it up." RCMP, audiotape 14, side B, 12 September 1995, cited in ibid., 305. For an interesting analysis of the violence that erupted at Gustafsen Lake, see Erin Runions, *How Hysterical: Identification and Resistance in the Bible and Film* (New York: Palgrave-Macmillan, 2003). Utilizing Slavoj Žižek's Lacanian psychoanalytic approach, she contends that "aggressive responses to resistance" are firmly embedded with Western ideology (rooted in the Hebrew Bible). She examines the subject through the "theory of interpellation (a theory of how individuals come to act in accordance with dominant ideology)" and tries to understand why the law reacts in the violent manner it does when people refuse to be "interpellated." Runions, *How Hysterical*, 15–17. For suggestions that Black was shot in the forehead but was "protected from death by spiritual intervention," see Switlo, *Gustafsen Lake*, 128–9.

104 Mike Webster and Rick Hall, in RCMP, "Minutes of the General Meeting," emphasis in original, quoted in Boncore Hill, *Autobiography*, 302.

105 Ibid., 301–3, quoted in Boncore Hill, *Autobiography*, 314.

106 SISIS, "Chronology."

107 Jeff Lee, "Lawyer Jailed for Tirade in Court," *Vancouver Sun*, 16 September 1995. See also Peter MacFarlane and Wayne Haimea, "The Strange Sojourn of Bruce Clark," *Globe and Mail*, 16 September 1995.

108 For a list of occupiers at the camp, see Switlo, *Gustafsen Lake*, 129–30. Splitting the Sky suggests that Stevens passed along his messages to the camp members, which explained their decision to withdraw. Boncore Hill, *Autobiography*, 360–2, 370.

109 Cariboo Tribal Council, untitled press release, September 1995, reprinted in ibid., 370–1.

110 Peter Montague, interview of 27 May 1997, quoted in Lambertus, *Wartime Images*, 121.

111 Lambertus, *Wartime Images*, 95–6.

112 In ibid., 53.

113 Gary Mason, in ibid., 192.

114 Joey Thompson, "Media Should Apologize for Gullibility on Gustafsen Lake," *Vancouver Province*, 29 September 1997, A12.

115 Steven Frasher, interview of 23 July 1997, quoted in Lambertus, *Wartime Images*, 174.

116 Ted Byfield, "Native Crimes Whitewashed," *Edmonton Sun*, 17 September 1995.

117 Rob Diether, in David Hogben and Mike Crawley, "RCMP Restraint Praised," *Vancouver Sun*, 18 September 1995.

118 "All the News That's Fit to ... Be Manipulated," editorial, *Vancouver Sun*, 22 September 1995.

119 Boncore Hill, *Autobiography*, 120.

120 Steven Frasher and Jonathan Green, "Chiefs Raze Sacred Arbor," *100 Mile House Free Press*, 19 April 1996; Boncore Hill, *Autobiography*, 400; Steve Mertl, "Rebel Standoff Ends Peacefully," *Ottawa Citizen*, 18 September 1995, A1.

121 Scott Steele, "Legal Marathon," *Maclean's*, 2 June 1997, 74–5.

122 Boncore Hill, *Autobiography*, 95. When he was released on parole in 1998, James Pitawanakwat fled to the United States and sought to avoid extradition back to Canada through the "political offence exception" included in the extradition agreement between Canada and the United States. On 15 November 2000 Judge Janice M. Stewart in an Oregon District Court ruled that Pitawanakwat would not be returned to Canada to serve his sentence, recognizing the political nature of his actions against the Canadian state. The "political offence exception" stems from the American and French revolutions and has, as Stewart explains, become a staple of international extradition law. The exemption preserves the right of individuals to rebel against unjust and oppressive governments. Furthermore, the charged offence must occur during an "uprising or other violent political occurrence" and must be "incidental to" the uprising or occurrence. The perception of the Oregon District Court was that the occupation at Gustafsen Lake was a political action akin to those of the Tamils of Sri Lanka or, at its outset, the sit-ins of the Vietnam War protests in the United States. Stewart acknowledged that both sides were responsible for the violence that occurred, deemed the act political (not criminal), and criticized the reductionist interpretation of the motives of the occupiers, stating that to regard the standoff as "a mere land dispute or disagreement with government policy is to trivialize the nature of the controversy." *United States of America v. James Allen Scott Pitawanakwat*, 00-M-489-ST, United States District Court for the District of Oregon, 120 F., Supp. 2d, 921, 2000 US Dist., 15 November 2000. This case was the first time in US-Canada relations that a judge had enacted the political exemption clause embedded within extradition law. Anthony J. Hall, *The American Empire and the Fourth World: The Bowl With One Spoon*, vol. 1 (Montreal and Kingston: McGill-Queen's University Press, 2003), 207. See also Rick Mofina and Glenn Bohn, "U.S. Judge Backs Gustafsen Lake Rebellion in '95," *Vancouver Sun*, 24 November 2000, A3.

123  Steve Mertl, "Gustafsen Lake: Natives Propose UN-Style Peacekeeping at B.C. Standoff," *Ottawa Citizen*, 13 September 1995, A3.

124  "Gustafsen Lake Accused: The Verdicts," *Vancouver Sun*, 21 May 1997, A6.

125  Gail Johnson, "Jail Terms Infuriate Natives," *Vancouver Province*, 31 July 1997, A3.

126  Mertl, "Gustafsen Lake."

127  Trond Halle, "Monday, November 4, 1996 – Day 68," in *Week 15 of the Gustafsen Lake Trial*, ed. Roz Royce and Trond Halle, n.d., http://sisis.nativeweb.org/court/wk15sum1.html.

128  "Gustafsen Lake Accused." Other defendants who were convicted of this charge included non-Native supporters Shelagh Franklin and Robert Flemming, who represented themselves at trial. The additional Native occupiers convicted of these lesser charges included Brent Potulicki and Grant Archie. Three defendants, among them Joseph Ignace, were acquitted of all charges.

129  Mary Pena, in Sherryl Yeager, "Divided They Stand," *Monday Magazine* (Victoria), 27 November 1997, http://sisis.nativeweb.org/gustlake/nov24mon.html. For responses to Yeager's article from the Settlers in Support of Indigenous Sovereignty, see this webpage and http://sisis.nativeweb.org/gustlake/mar2398mon.html.

130  Gerry Bellett, "Lawyer Blamed for Gustafsen Standoff," *Vancouver Sun*, 25 April 2007, B2.

131  Trond Halle rebutted this characterization: "I understand that the rumour still persists that there was a split in the camp between the hawks and the doves … Certainly most people have a bit of both in their personal make ups and the Defenders were no different, but to suggest that some people followed the spiritual strength of Percy, while others followed the warrior strength of Wolverine is an insult to the brave spirits of each and every Defender … We were a family and we took care of each other. There was a strong and enduring bond of love, greater than anything I'd ever felt before … Without a doubt, the only divisions that existed and continue to exist were the ones outside of the camp." Trond Halle, "Life Inside the Ts'peten Camp," September 1995, http://sisis.nativeweb.org/gustlake/sep95tro.html. This portrait of internal unity is not supported by the other protagonists.

132  Boncore Hill, *Autobiography*, 126, 425.

133  Splitting the Sky believes that Rosette, Pena, and others were threatened with longer jail sentences if they did not reject Bruce Clark as their council and the jurisdictional arguments included within the sovereigntist

claims. Ibid., 137, 341. Rosette's untitled press release of 14–15 September 1995, which asks for the protection and preservation of the sun dance site, makes no mention of the jurisdiction arguments that dominated early press releases by the occupiers. Cited in ibid., 336–7.

134 Ibid., 484. After Bruce Clark testified on the jurisdiction argument, Judge Ian Josephson reminded the jury that the jurisdiction argument had already been dismissed as an issue for the jury and that it was not to consider the matter. The legal problems did not end there. Wolverine's first lawyer was fired by his client after describing Wolverine's position as "believing you could jump off a mountain and fall upwards." Ibid., 305, quotation at 411.

135 Ibid., 398.

136 Svend Robinson, in Joshua Goldberg, for Settlers In Support of Indigenous Sovereignty, "Open Letter to Canadian MP Svend Robinson," 18 November 1998, http://sisis.nativeweb.org/gustlake/nov1898.html.

137 Boncore Hill, Autobiography, 428.

138 Gartner and Mercredi, "Aboriginal Rights."

139 Arthur Manuel, in Holly Horwood, "'Fast-Track Land Claims,'" Vancouver Province, 23 May 1997, A20. Manuel also openly criticized the British Columbia land claims process, which was "not the solution" unless it was sped up and socio-economic issues were addressed alongside land settlements.

140 Ko'waintco Linda Shackelly, in British Columbia Select Standing Committee on Aboriginal Affairs, Transcripts of Proceedings, no. 17, 14 November 1996, http://www.leg.bc.ca/cmt/36thParl/CMT01/1997/hansard/ab1114a.htm.

141 Ovide Mercredi, in Parliament of Canada, Proceedings.

142 Boncore Hill, Autobiography, 558; quotation in Thompson, "Media Should Apologize."

143 Boncore Hill, Autobiography, 320. Splitting the Sky claims that Gustafsen Lake was the catalyst for the overturning of the Delgamuukw case. And US judge Janice M. Stewart concluded in her ruling that Gustafsen Lake was responsible for prompting the "intense negotiations" over land between Canada and British Columbia and forty Indigenous groups in 1996 (see note 120). These are dubious assertions.

# 9

## Seeking Relief: The Dispute in Burnt Church (Esgenoôpetitj)

### SARAH J. KING

The fishing dispute in Burnt Church, New Brunswick, began in September 1999 and continued until August 2002. At its conclusion, a bureaucrat for the federal Department of Fisheries and Oceans was heard to comment, "Perhaps it never really was about fish."[1] Indeed. The prolonged violence in Burnt Church has complex origins. Many scholars have focused on the importance of the Supreme Court of Canada's 1999 Marshall decision as the event that triggered a Mi'kmaw fishery and hence the violence at Burnt Church.[2] Ken Coates suggests that the violence occurred because the "federal government was caught unaware" by the court's decision and because non-Native people in the region had failed to acknowledge the depth of the rupture between them and their Native neighbours.[3] This chapter demonstrates that attending to the values and experiences of the Mi'kmaq of Burnt Church (Esgenoôpetitj) is critical to understanding the dispute and its importance both as a blockade and as a breakthrough.

To learn what motivated people to risk their lives in the dispute, I moved to Burnt Church in July 2004 and conducted twelve months of ethnographic fieldwork. There are actually two Burnt Churches – the Burnt Church First Nation, known in Mi'kmaq as Esgenoôpetitj, and the settler village of Burnt Church. The communities are built side by side on Miramichi Bay in northeastern New Brunswick (see figure 9.1). My research focused on the social, political, and religious dimensions of people's lives in the Mi'kmaw and English communities at Burnt Church, the attitudes and understandings of those who involved themselves in the conflict, and the historical and political construction of these communities and of the conflict. In both communities, this research included participant observation, conducting interviews, keeping a journal, and collecting ephemera, augmented by the collected personal archives shared with me by two locals.[4]

In Esgenoôpetitj, people engaged in the dispute for a variety of reasons: to create livelihoods, to maintain their rights, to enact Mi'kmaw sovereignty, to seek relief for injustice. There were differing opinions about what tactics would best achieve these goals. The agreement that was signed to end the dispute did not meet the goals of all involved, and many traditionalists and sovereigntists lament its signing. The dispute itself is seen as a success, as a time when the Mi'kmaq of Burnt Church worked together across community divisions to advance a common purpose. Individual actions are celebrated as times when justice was momentarily achieved. Although the dispute did not achieve everyone's goals, it did provide moments of great hope and relief.

## THE DISPUTE

In 1998 the Supreme Court of Canada heard an appeal in the case of Donald Marshall Jr, a Mi'kmaw man from Nova Scotia, who was charged under federal fishery regulations with fishing eels illegally. At trial, Marshall admitted that he had been fishing eels and argued that this was not illegal. His position was that Mi'kmaw people held the right to fish according to treaties signed with the British in 1760–61 and that the regulations of the Canadian government did not apply to Mi'kmaw fishers. In a decision handed down on 17 September 1999, the court recognized Marshall's treaty right to fish and gather wildlife, saying that "nothing less would uphold the honour and integrity of the Crown in its dealings with the Mi'kmaq people to secure their peace and friendship, as best the content of those treaty promises can now be ascertained."[5] Within days, Mi'kmaw people began to enter the lobster fishery across Atlantic Canada.

In Esgenoôpetitj, the court's decision was greeted with great celebration. Previous rulings in favour of Native rights to harvest and sell natural resources, such as timber, had resulted in little new employment under the terms of agreements that elected chiefs had signed with the federal government. In 1999 the community had just held an election in which longstanding chief Wilbur Dedam and his allies had lost their controlling power on the band council. In this shifting political landscape, the Marshall decision was seen as an opportunity for people to exercise their rights on their own terms in order to make a living. As one couple told me, *When the Marshall decision came down, everybody just said, "All right! We have fishery rights now!" And they didn't even consult with the council or anything, they just started putting their traps in – bang bang bang bang ... It was pretty exciting, really. People were happy* (Dalton and Cindy).[6] The sense of celebration in the community continued as more and more people began to fish. People worked cooperatively in small fishing dories, purchased refurbished traps, and hauled in their catch by hand. *You could see, down the far flung reaches of our community, our people were so excited about the possibility of permanent employment* (Miigam'agan).

The non-Native communities neighbouring Esgenoôpetitj rely heavily on the lobster fishery. In the English village of Burnt Church, every resident either fishes lobster or has family members who do. The growing Native fishery caused increasing concern in the English village: *Almost within a week we had Indians from Big Cove, from Millbrook, and from the Burnt Church Reserve all converged on the wharf over here with their fishing boats, and they started fishing lobster in September. There has never been a fishery out here in September; it has always been a spring fishery. So all of a sudden there were a tremendous amount of people fishing here. And that raised a great deal of concern from the people living here, that fished here for years ... If they're out there destroying the stock, then they're gonna ruin the fishery* (Paul).[7] The Mi'kmaw fishery did not conform to the federal government's regulated season.[8] Native fishers across the region were fishing without licences and tags, which is also against government regulation. This situation rapidly escalated concerns about the stock and about the unfairness of some people apparently acting outside the law.

In the Burnt Church First Nation, any attempt to tell the story of the dispute to outsiders begins by taking them to see the places where the dispute happened. In the English village of Burnt Church, people say, "You have to live here to understand what the dispute was like." Burnt Church itself is a contested place, where each community's ties to its home are threatened by the presence of the other and have been shaped by the larger forces of colonization and globalization. The English and Mi'kmaw communities of Burnt Church and Esgenoôpetitj live side by side, but their social and cultural lives are almost entirely separate. Neighbours from the two communities know one another and each other's family histories but rarely socialize or work together. Acadian villages surround them, the largest being Néguac, which lies to the north. The distinctions between these three communities are strong and fast and have held for generations. In these communities, simply by knowing people's last names, you also know their language and culture (English, French, or Mi'kmaw), their religion (Protestant, Catholic, or traditional Aboriginal), their political affiliation (Liberal, Conservative, or sovereigntist), as political opinion usually runs in the family, and perhaps even the lands on which their family lives.

"Esgenoôpetitj" means "look out place where one waits for the others"[9] or "the People watching for those to come."[10] Esgenoôpetitj has been a traditional summer camp and gathering place for Mi'kmaw people since before contact with Europeans. The people of the Burnt Church First Nation have survived much since the arrival of the first colonists: conflicts with the federal government, disease, residential schools, and loss of land and traditional ways of life. These experiences have contributed to housing shortages, lack of employment, addiction, despair, and depression in more recent times. At the turn of the twentieth century, the community had shrunk to about 200 people.[11] By the time of the dispute, it had grown to about 1,300 people, many of them children. Housing and employment are huge issues for the members of this community, where the only local infrastructure is that supported by the elected band council.

Esgenoôpetitj is a contested place and a colonized one. The identity of the people and their ties to their home have been under threat since contact. The Mi'kmaq's alliances with the French, first cemented by missionaries, and their later treaties with the British did not alleviate the conflict that came with the arrival of the Europeans in Mi'kmaw territories. Many in Esgenoôpetitj, especially those engaged in the traditionalist and sovereigntist movements, saw the fishery as an important opportunity to reassert a Mi'kmaw government and way of life in this contested place.

The Mi'kmaq of Esgenoôpetitj thrived for centuries, fishing and hunting in communities of great numbers, before the epidemics associated with European contact of the sixteenth and seventeenth centuries. The first contact that Mi'kmaq of the Miramichi region had with European colonists was likely with European fishers in the mid-sixteenth century. In the 1620s French traders built a post on the Island of Miscou, an easy trading distance from Miramichi Bay, and about a decade later Jesuit missionaries began to make visits to the area, some of which are documented in the *Jesuit Relations*.[12] By the end of the seventeenth century, Christian missionaries had built relationships and a mission in Esgenoôpetitj, including a church. This church gave Esgenoôpetitj its first colonial name, Pointe-à-l'Église, or Church Point.

In 1755 the British expelled the Acadians from Port Royal and the surrounding settlements,[13] one stage in the ongoing violence between the French and British over the colonies of New France. Some moved north into the coastal woods of present-day New Brunswick, seeking shelter from which to resist the British. By the winter of 1756–57, some of these Acadian resisters had arrived along the Miramichi, taking shelter in the woods, building alliances, and planning raids on the British with the Mi'kmaw people who lived there.[14] The first winter that the Acadians spent in northern New Brunswick was brutal. They lived on the very edge of survival, and those who made it through only did so with the help and aid of the Mi'kmaq, who showed them how to survive in the frozen forest. Yet the Acadians continued their attacks on British ships in the Gulf of St Lawrence. In the fall of 1758, frustrated by ongoing losses, British general James Wolfe ordered soldier James Murray to remove the final pockets of Acadian resisters who had taken refuge on the Miramichi. Murray targeted the settlement at Esgenoôpetitj (Pointe-à-l'Église): "I therefore in the evening of the 17th in Obedience to your instructions embarked the Troops, having two Days hunted all around all around Us for the Indians and Acadians to no purpose, we however destroyed their Provisions, Wigwams, and Houses, the Church which was a very handsome one built with stone, did not escape ... and I am persuaded that there is not now a French Man in the River Miramichi, and it will be our fault if they are ever allowed to settle there again."[15] In fact, the Acadians, the Mi'kmaq, and a missionary had all taken to the woods, where they hid successfully until the departure of the British. They returned to find their homes destroyed. The Acadian settlers eventually moved north and built the new settlement of Néguac. In 1760 and 1761 Mi'kmaw leaders signed treaties of peace and friendship with the British, treaties that became the basis of the Marshall decision in 1999.

After a period of about thirty years, British settlers arrived, and a colony developed west of the Mi'kmaw community at the old Church Point site, now known as Burnt Church.[16] These people were mostly Scottish Presbyterians, many of whom came from other communities along the

Miramichi River. They were given king's grants to settle and clear lands that had been traditional Mi'kmaw territory. Most people who live in the English village today can trace their ancestry to those original grantees or to two or three other English families who arrived at the same time. Some families still have the original grant papers that awarded them their land.

In the fall of 1999, as the post-Marshall Mi'kmaw fishery continued, the non-Native residents of Burnt Church decided to make a public statement against the Native fishery. They organized a protest to take place on the afternoon of Sunday, 3 October, after church, and invited people from other local (non-Native) fishing communities to join them. The fishers organized a flotilla of boats from many villages, scheduled to arrive at the wharf in Burnt Church at the same time as other locals marched there. On the wharf, this group of about twenty non-Native people carried a Canadian flag, along with signs that said things like "Do we not have rights too?" While protesters were gathering on the wharf, some of the fishers on the water began to cut Native lobster traps,[17] destroying them and other fishing equipment. To this day, the white residents of Burnt Church insist that they didn't cut the traps; fishers from other villages did. *But everything came back on us, because everyone knew we organized it* (Mark).[18]

As word reached the reserve that their equipment was being destroyed, people started to come down to the wharf to investigate. *When we heard the news, we went to the wharf and waited for our folks to come ashore and discovered that everyone's traps were destroyed. At the same time, the families of the Burnt Church white fishermen came marching on the wharf to protest against the Indian fishing. They already knew ... while the wives were coming to worship, the husbands had already gone out and destroyed all of our equipment* (Miigam'agan). Native people were also shocked to see that some of the men in the boats had dressed up in Indian costumes, with wigs and fake war paint, and were waving tomahawks in the air, dancing, and yelling racist taunts.

The tension in the two communities erupted. On the wharf and along the shore road, people were yelling and fighting with one another. Fistfights broke out; people threatened one another's lives and properties. Natives yelled, "Go back where you came from!" Non-Natives screamed, "No special treatment!" Each side felt victimized by the other. Eventually, the Royal Canadian Mounted Police (RCMP) escorted the white protesters off of the wharf, suggesting that this was for their own protection. *We [Mi'kmaw people] stayed back and decided to take over the wharf. Because of what we had just witnessed from the* R C M P *'s reaction and the comments against our people, we knew there was not going to be justice for us. We needed to respond to what happened to us, but how? We organized ourselves and had a community meeting at the wharf. The people started to feel a little relief after talking about their experience and knowing we were going to stick together* (Miigam'agan). The Natives occupied the wharf.

Violence spread quickly that night. Groups of non-Native fishers stormed three area fish plants accused of processing Native-caught lobster. On the Burnt Church wharf, some Native people sought additional "relief" for their anger by burning trucks left by non-Native fishers. Others sought to protect the property of their neighbours and drove a non-Native boat to another wharf for safekeeping. In an effort to replace their destroyed fishing equipment, Native youths attempted to raid the equipment shed of one local fisher, ramming the doors with their truck. In the ensuing altercation, a young Native man was beaten with a baseball bat and hurt seriously. By dawn on Monday morning, the smouldering wrecks of trucks were being towed from the wharf, people were visiting their family members in hospital, those arrested were calling their lawyers and trying to get bail, and the people of Esgenoôpetitj were looking for a way to replace their destroyed equipment. The threat of further violence in Burnt Church was the lead story in the national news; the media descended.

Tensions around the fishery continued throughout the fall. While the fishery continued, so did the Native occupation of the Burnt Church wharf, the concerns of the non-Native fishers, and the anger on both sides. The threat of violence was ongoing, but direct altercations were few. By the onset of winter, most Mi'kmaw communities had agreed to a moratorium on fishing – although most of these communities were landlocked and had not entered the post-Marshall fishery. The Burnt Church First Nation remained a significant holdout. As commercial fishers looked toward the first post-Marshall fishery in spring 2001, the federal government and the First Nation were at the negotiating table. Negotiations were troubled. The people of Esgenoôpetitj were interested in negotiating in a context that recognized their rights and sovereignty; the Department of Fisheries and Oceans (D F O), negotiating on behalf of the federal government, wanted to talk about fisheries management.[19]

Since the 1980s some Mi'kmaw activists had been working to revive traditional Mi'kmaw religion and culture. These traditionalists felt that the survival and well-being of the community depended on the revitalization of Mi'kmaw ways of life and Mi'kmaw spiritual traditions. At the same time, sovereigntist politics grew stronger as people began to articulate the importance of Mi'kmaw government over Mi'kmaw territory and refused to recognize the legitimacy of Canadian governmental structures or the legitimacy of Canada's existence. The community chooses the elected chief and council, but the election process and form of government are regulated by the Indian Act. Although some traditionalists and sovereigntists participated in the politics of the elected council, others rejected it as a structure that was under Canada's control. According to the processes and traditions of the Grand Council, the community appoints the traditional chief, or keptin. During and after the dispute, the elected chief was Wilbur Dedam, and the keptin was Lloyd Augustine (Kwegsi). When Dedam lost his council majority in 1999, just prior to the dispute, the traditionalist and sovereigntist movements in the community gained strength.

A community-wide consultation process led by Lloyd Augustine and Sakej (James Ward) resulted in the decision to develop a Mi'kmaw plan and infrastructure to manage the fishery, based in part upon Mi'kmaw worldviews.[20] On 15 March, six weeks before the start of the spring commercial season, the negotiators for the Burnt Church First Nation walked away from the table. By the end of April, Augustine and Ward had co-authored *Draft for the Esgenoôpetitj First Nation (EFN) Fishery Act*, the plan under which the community would issue its own tags and regulate its own fishery.[21]

Once the spring 2000 fishing season began, the government's ongoing raids of the Native fishery became a major additional challenge to a negotiated settlement. Violence escalated on the waters of Miramichi Bay. As Mi'kmaw fishers began to set traps with the community's own tags, the DFO began to raid their fishery, hauling out any traps with Native tags. Mi'kmaw fishers persisted in asserting their rights to fish under the management plan according to their understanding of the Marshall decision. A coalition of regional and national environmental and social justice groups issued a public statement exhorting the federal government to recognize the legitimacy of the Native tags. Instead, the government escalated its enforcement, often removing traps in early morning hours, before daylight.[22]

   The Burnt Church First Nation created its own fisheries enforcement program, the Rangers, with the support of other bands in the region. Warriors arrived from communities across North America and worked under the leadership of local men. Together, the Rangers and Warriors met the government boats in boats of their own in attempts to protect their traps. Leo Bartibogue, who led the Rangers, describes early efforts to stop the raids:

> *The Department of Fisheries started coming around [taking our traps], and it started happening every day. They keep taking and we keep putting, taking and putting. It got to the point where we're not only intercepting them, but we're trying to make it difficult for them to be taking our traps. So we used different tactics, like putting little letters and toys in Ziploc bags in the traps, just to try and let them know that they are taking food away from our tables and a livelihood from our children. But it got to a point where they got more and more intense ... The women stopped going in the waters because now it was getting more dangerous because they were coming with a different kind of aggression, and it intensified every time they came.*

People in Esgenoôpetitj began to feel that the greatest threat they experienced was not from their neighbours or from commercial fishers, as had been the case the previous year. Now they were most frightened of the government, represented by the DFO, the RCMP, and the Coast Guard agents present in their community.

   Women had begun the post-Marshall fishery in Burnt Church. Although women stopped fishing as the dispute became more violent, they continued to provide significant leadership within the community. Karen Somerville, who had been a part of the traditionalist movement, became the community spokesperson. Although the media focused on Somerville and the events on the waters, women in Burnt Church took on a variety of other critical roles: facilitating community decision making, supporting and consulting elders, ensuring the safety and well-being of children, managing money, households, and community events, feeding and housing the people who had arrived to support the fishery, as well as continuing to be involved in direct actions on land. The fishery was not simply the men in boats: it involved the mobilization of men and women from many families, political positions, and social locations within the First

Nation. This experience of common purpose across division was tremendously important to those involved and in itself gave people hope.

When the fall fishery began in August 2001, both the First Nation and the Canadian government issued threatening statements through the media. The CBC reported,

> The Department of Fisheries has said it has as many as 600 officers on standby, ready to enforce the law if anyone tries fishing without licences and federally issued tags.
>
> The band, meanwhile, has said its own reinforcements are only a phone call away, including warriors who are not easily intimidated.
>
> "We have a lot of young men who are more than willing to get together and protect our traps," Ward told CBC News on Thursday.[23]

By 14 August the confrontations on the waters between the DFO and Native fishers had escalated. SWAT teams and police dressed in riot gear patrolled Miramichi Bay and the reserve boundaries. Violent altercations began to break out between these officers and Mi'kmaw activists. Community members kept careful tabs on encounters that Rangers and Warriors had with the government:

> *When my sister's husband was taken by the DFO, they maced him. And they couldn't knock him down – they were trying to knock him down so that they could get him on the boat. James Ward [the head of the Warriors] was the number one enemy. They were saying over the radio, "We caught James Ward! We caught James Ward!" And my sister's husband could hear them. It was him they were battling with, not James Ward!*
>
> *They were hitting him with billy clubs and whatever they had, and he said, "I just reached back, and the first thing I could grab was a 2x4." He started swinging away at them. And he got a couple of them real good I guess. When they took him to court, they charged him for assaulting nine officers. They were the ones that were beating him up! And they charged him with assault! (Barb)[24]*

Stories of people's experiences on the waters galvanized the community. By mid-August people had erected barricades at the edges of the community, blockades marked by bonfires and patrolled by Warriors.

DFO officers continued to remove Native traps and arrest Native fishers. Native fishers told reporters that DFO officers confronting them on the waters had pointed guns at them, which the DFO denied. The public credibility of the DFO was compromised, however, as the violence escalated. On 29 August a government boat chased a Native dory across the waters of Miramichi Bay directly in front of the community. This had happened before; when Rangers and Warriors attempted to confront government officials and prevent the seizure of their traps, they would often be chased off. Local people gathered on the shore, and television networks set up their cameras there, to observe the ongoing conflict. This day, with cameras rolling, the larger DFO boat rammed and sank the Native dory. As people scrambled to rescue the Mi'kmaw men, the DFO officers on the boat drove their boat over the dory and those in the water underneath it. These events were broadcast internationally and drew tremendous public attention to the ongoing dispute in Burnt Church.

The dispute in Burnt Church (Esgenoôpetitj) was drawn out over four fishing seasons, beginning with the Marshall decision in the fall of 1999. The events of these years were not centred on a single blockade or occupation. The fishery itself was the main location of action and resistance for the Mi'kmaq. Events on the waters would spark community responses on land; there was a rolling series of actions, including blockades of roads and occupations of the fishing wharf, that community members and Warriors undertook to support those who were engaging the DFO, the RCMP, and the Coast Guard on the bay. The Mi'kmaw community had many allies in those years:

- Warriors came to Burnt Church from across North America and worked under the leadership of two local men.
- The neighbouring Mi'kmaw communities of Big Cove (Elsipogtog) and Restigouche (Listiguj) sent boats, fisheries officers, and resources.
- Resources, including money and supplies, were sent by many First Nations communities and individuals.
- Former Assembly of First Nations chief Ovide Mercredi visited the community. He provided significant leadership and encouragement to the people in Esgenoôpetitj.
- Non-Native allies were invited by the community to monitor its fishery and the government's response. Christian Peacemaker Teams and the Aboriginal Rights Coalition–Atlantic had an ongoing presence in Esgenoôpetitj, recording events as they unfolded.

After the high-profile violence of the 1999 and 2000 fishing seasons, things seemed to simmer down in 2001. This was due, in part, to a change in strategy on the part of the federal government. The government's direct actions against the Mi'kmaw fishers, particularly the chasing and ramming of fishing dories, had raised public outcry when broadcast in the media. In an effort to change its profile, and the situation, the Department of Fisheries and Oceans changed its tactics. One day after Native fishers entered the fall fishery, the DFO announced that it was granting them a licence to fish for traditional and ceremonial purposes, largely to catch lobster for the annual powwow. Native fishers and activists argued publicly that the presence or absence of the federal licence made no difference in their ability to fish. The difference it made was to the DFO; since the Native fishery was happening under a federal licence (even one the fishers had not applied for and did not recognize), the DFO could argue that the fishery was legal and that aggressive and violent enforcement action was unnecessary.[25]

In August 2001 previously longstanding elected chief Wilbur Dedam was returned political control over the band council. Dedam, who was heavily involved in community leadership during the fishery dispute, was also seen as a moderate with ties to the federal government. His main opponent in the election, Leo Bartibogue, was the leader of the Rangers and more closely allied with the sovereigntists and traditionalists in Esgenoôpetitj. Although some argue that the election itself was tainted by interference from the federal government, all agree that by this time people in the community were getting tired. The challenge of sustaining everyday life in the context of the ongoing dispute was becoming too great. In September 2001, after the attacks of 9/11, the federal government's approach to policing and protest changed, and its powers of arrest and seizure increased. Some in the Mi'kmaw community began to feel far more vulnerable, especially as they began to be publicly labelled terrorists.

On 1 August 2002 Canada's new minister of fisheries and oceans, Robert Thibault, and Chief Wilbur Dedam announced that they had reached an agreement-in-principle that would govern the fishery in Burnt Church.[26] Native leaders agreed that the fishers in their community would participate in the spring commercial fishery and in a fall fishery for food and ceremonial purposes, both under the regulation of the DFO. In return, the government provided the community with commercial licences, boats to fish, training for fishers, and funding for fisheries officers from within the community, as well as money to fund studies of the lobster populations. The primary concerns addressed by this agreement were access to, and governance of, the regulated commercial fishery and the traditional and ceremonial fishery; responsibility for the management of lobster populations was placed in the hands of the Canadian government for the duration of the agreement.

## BLOCKADE OR BREAKTHROUGH?

Were the events in Esgenoôpetitj a blockade or breakthrough for the Mi'kmaq? Did the direct action undertaken by the Mi'kmaq achieve their goals? The answer depends on who is asked and on whose experiences are seen as the most important. Evaluating the outcome of the action requires a fair understanding of Mi'kmaw goals. Since it was the Mi'kmaq of Esgenoôpetitj (Burnt Church) who initiated the disputed fishery, and who supported and protected it with a variety of tactics, any study of the dispute must begin with the Mi'kmaw community itself. What were their goals and aspirations in the fishery? This remains a complicated question; the Mi'kmaw community at Burnt Church is not a monolith. People took action in the dispute with a variety of goals in mind: creating livelihoods within their community, having their rights recognized, re-establishing Mi'kmaw sovereignty over Mi'kmaw territory. Even community members who agreed on underlying goals often disagreed on tactics. Understanding the outcomes of the dispute begins with understanding the experiences and motivations of those most closely involved.[27]

Framing this dispute as either a blockade or a breakthrough also focuses attention on violent activism, when really a broad variety of strategies and tactics were employed. Across Esgenoôpetitj, people had diverse opinions about how best to get the government to recognize their fishery. Some placed toys and letters in their traps in an attempt to send a message directly to the DFO, some spoke directly to the media, and others stopped speaking or writing publicly, as they felt they were misrepresented. Some met in traditional ceremony, some in Christian prayer. Non-Native allies from Christian Peacemaker Teams and the Aboriginal Rights Coalition–Atlantic were invited to come to Burnt Church and work as monitors in the hope that their testimony about events on the waters would be taken more seriously by government and the media. People worked to learn about the government's monitoring and surveillance techniques and tried to stymie them as best they could.[28]

Questions of violence and nonviolence were constantly under negotiation both during the dispute and in the ways that the dispute was spoken about in its aftermath. Throughout the community there were ongoing tensions, with some elders fearful of the repercussions of violence, including possible government invasion of the community, and many youth and sovereigntists pressing for direct action. Sakej (James Ward) was an outspoken and articulate proponent of the necessity of using violent tactics. He is now well known across the continent as a leader in the Warrior Society, and in his home community of Burnt Church, he was one of two men who led groups of Warriors throughout the dispute. Ward discusses his view of the dispute at length in Taiaiake Alfred's book *Wasáse*. He argues that the only way that self-determination and nationhood will be realized for Indigenous people is if they fight for it. "You know, there was a plea from some of our people that we should just pursue the politics of pity and try to get Canadian society to somehow identify with our issues so much that they would put a stop to their government's actions against us," he explains. "Obviously, it didn't work."[29] Ward argues that the most important things that were accomplished in Burnt Church were accomplished through violence and that a willingness to do violence is required in order to create the conditions for decolonization.

Others within the community suggest that their emphasis was on finding less violent strategies to get their message across to the Canadian people – throwing stones instead of firing guns at government vessels, for example. Leo Bartibogue illustrates the complexity of struggles over tactics as they were negotiated within his own family:

My brother got beat up on the waters, and it became personal. He's been hurt, and somebody whispers in your ear he's in the hospital ... And you know they're still in the water, the very same people that just put a beating on him.

So you look at this group of boys that's looking at you and you say, "All right, let's go finish it."

And when I said "Let's go finish it," that didn't mean let's go throw rocks over there. It meant let's go finish it. And so they were all jumping with joy, these boys that were ready to go ... They wanted that word ... All we gotta do is just let 'er rip, just start spraying, shooting. That'll be it.

All the army would have come in, and everything. That didn't dawn on me because my anger was taking over.

*But I remember that one word my sister told me was, "What kind of a leader will [you] be to our people when they're dead, or they're in jail? What can you do for the people then?" So ... those are the things that I had in my mind.*
*When we were going down, I changed my mind.*

For Bartibogue, *this* is a story of breakthrough, a moment when he understood that there was more to be accomplished than he could do through violence. But he should not be misread as a pacifist; rather, his account illustrates the challenges of discerning the best tactic in each moment.

There are related stories where violence is precisely the thing that is credited with changing unjust behaviour. Many Mi'kmaw activists tell the story of the destruction of an Acadian fishing vessel off of the shores of Esgenoôpetitj. Non-Native commercial fishers were chasing Native fishers on the waters, taunting them with caricatured enactments of Native culture – like face paint, made-up chants, and tomahawk dancing – and threatening to harm them and their fishing gear. Eventually, one boat ran aground – the men aboard had been drinking – and Warriors and Rangers captured the men and their boat. Although the fishers were turned safely over to the RCMP, their boat was burned and destroyed. One Native fisher characterized this as sovereign action – the people enacting their own justice: *And the thing with that was when [the community] did it, you know, it was a great relief in their hearts, because when we did that, they [Acadian fishers] never came in our waters again. Because sometimes you have to have your own justice. Because the justice that we were gettin' here wasn't too good* (Anonymous). The creation of justice for and by the people is an important dimension of sovereignty for many in Esgenoôpetitj. Their anger is channelled, and the government challenged, by the creation of Mi'kmaw justice. Ward argues that undertaking fights such as this one, although illegal, is necessary in the face of a Canadian government that he considers illegitimate. For him, "the demonstration of our ability to defend our traps, our people and our rights was a real victory."[30] In similar situations, other community members argue that violence against property, although undesirable, allows the community to seek relief for its anger in a way that is far preferable to violence against persons.

Some suggest that the fact that no lives were lost in the course of the dispute was itself a breakthrough. The community's tactics in specific situations led to victories in those moments, even though success could not be sustained in the long term. These actions are understood as honourable and necessary and the Canadian government as violent and intransigent. Some say, *If only we'd held out a little longer, the Canadian government would not have been able to stand in the face of what they did to us.* The implication here is that the Mi'kmaq experienced success precisely because they were using tactics more publicly acceptable than those of the government and its agents. In this context, the success of the dispute is measured in terms of the nature of the actions that were taken, not only in terms of their outcome.

## Livelihood

Unemployment levels in Esgenoôpetitj were very high at the time of the dispute. In 2000 the on-reserve unemployment rate was 85 per cent.[31] The only stable local employment was with the band council, or programs funded by the band council, and all such appointments were political in nature. Those who were seen as critics of the elected chief were much less likely to find employment than those who were supporters. Prior to the dispute, because the entry costs for licences and gear were prohibitive to most Mi'kmaq, there was only one commercial fisher in the community. A lobster licence, for example, was listed for sale at between $300,000 and $450,000 in August 2007, although the prices change over time and according to the zone in which the licence is held.[32] When there are large government buybacks of licences, such as the one that took place to secure licences for distribution to Natives at the end of the dispute, the price goes up. Since credit is largely not available to residents of the reserve, as they have little collateral (all property is held communally, according to the Indian Act), these costs are a barrier to independent entry into the fishery.

The opportunity to fish lobster following the Marshall decision presented a chance for people to make a little extra income to support their families. The lobster fishery is a relatively lucrative one, and because it is an in-shore fishery, it can be fished with small dories in shallow water. Esgenoôpetitj lies on the shores of Miramichi Bay, so people were essentially fishing in their own front yards, using small boats and refurbished equipment. In principle, the people of Burnt Church could also have begun to fish oysters, or herring, or snow crab.[33] In practice, the lobster fishery allowed individuals to earn money by fishing on a small scale, without the need of large equipment or permission of the band council. The dispute was a conflict about livelihood: Mi'kmaw people were trying to reclaim a livelihood for themselves in their waters, and their non-Native neighbours were trying to protect their existing livelihoods from overfishing.

Livelihood is not simply an individual or familial concern in Esgenoôpetitj. The establishment of reliable incomes for people in the community is crucial to the life of the community itself. The disputed lobster fishery gave people hope that the community, on its own terms, could pull itself out of the cycle of poverty and violence in which it was living. There was hope that the young people of the community would see a future for themselves beyond the welfare cycle, that the addictions and abuse borne of despair would be curtailed. Renewed livelihood would be the foundation of a revitalized and self-reliant community.

So was the agreement-in-principle signed at the end of the dispute a breakthrough, creating jobs and income for people across the reserve? Its terms certainly seem to indicate that this is possible: twenty-one commercial licences to be divided among the community, along with upgraded equipment; millions of dollars for training, infrastructure, and research; snow crab quotas and equipment; tuna quotas; and continuation of the fall fishery for food and ceremonial purposes. In 2004 and 2005 people interviewed in the English village of Burnt Church observed that their neighbours seemed better off than they had before the dispute; some felt that they could see the positive benefits of increased employment, at least for some. The distribution of boats and licences to members of the Mi'kmaw community was handled by the elected chief and council, as was the allocation of the quotas and dollars that came into the community from the federal government. The boats and licences certainly created jobs for those within the community who were given them. These people are now able to work during the fishing season and to claim employment insurance in the off-season, just as their non-Native neighbours do.

The benefits of the agreement are not felt across the community as a whole: poverty, violence, and addictions remain serious problems. Roger Augustine, a chief involved in mediation efforts during the dispute, commented, "I fail to see how this money is going to be able to stabilize a whole community, when it's only a small portion of what all communities want and need at this time."[34] Four years after the dispute subsided, the poorest postal code in Canada according to census data from Statistics Canada was that of the Burnt Church First Nation. The money that was given to the community was soon spent to hire non-Native people to provide training and conduct research, and some within the First Nation have privately protested the swiftness with which those dollars left their community. The chief controls the snow crab and tuna quotas. Every member of the community gets a small payment each year, their "share" of the band's fishery earnings. By 2009 the fisheries officers had been moved from their new, purpose-built fisheries centre to the old fire hall, and the fisheries building had been converted into a gambling hall. Livelihood remains a critical issue for the people of Burnt Church.[35]

### Rights and Sovereignty

People engaged in the dispute believed in the importance of their rights as Aboriginal peoples, rights that they understood the Marshall decision to uphold, rights that they attempted to exercise through their fishery. *This is what the fishery was all about. To take a stand against our rights ... getting smaller and smaller and smaller, and [soon] they'll be worthless* (Cindy). Concerns about Mi'kmaw rights, and about the Canadian government's responsibility to honour rights and to uphold rightful relationship, were articulated in literally every interview and conversation that I had in Esgenoôpetitj about the dispute. The Marshall decision affirmed the community's own understanding of its history and motivated members to act upon it, using rights as a tool to point to the gap in their relationship with the federal government.

Many people in Esgenoôpetitj understand rights within the context of an Indigenous view of the world, which is embedded in the relationships of community, family, and nation and is enshrined in their agreements with the Canadian government through the treaties. For some, "rights" is not in itself an Aboriginal concept but a Western idea encountered through colonization: "We never had to fight our Clan Mothers and Sachems for our inherent right to be and to exist."[36] In this sense, "rights" talk in the Mi'kmaw community also represents an effort by some Indigenous people to express their concerns in the framework of a non-Native language and culture. "Like much of the english language usage in NDN [Indian] Country, the way and understanding of this usage [rights] is quite a bit different than the standard mainstream, because the usage for NDN People is culturally based."[37] In the context of the dispute, rights became a critical idea with which Mi'kmaw people expressed their concerns and priorities, negotiating the gulf between Indigenous understandings and Western frameworks. Indigenous "rights," then, are not understood to reside primarily in individuals (as they might in a non-Native view) but are a part of the responsibilities and obligations embedded in communal relationship, belonging both to the community and to individual Aboriginal persons.[38]

In the Burnt Church First Nation, many people's actions for Native rights were motivated by this concern for the rights "of the people," and they understand rights themselves as residing with the community as well as with its individual members. These people also argue that Native rights are enshrined in the treaties made between their ancestors and the early British colonists (treaties that were the basis of the Marshall decision). These treaties outline relationships between the Mi'kmaw and British nations, on the collective level, and are understood by Mi'kmaw people to characterize what is rightfully theirs as members of their nation (not simply as individual Native persons). For many Mi'kmaq of Burnt Church, their activism during the dispute was intended to uphold these communal rights guaranteed by the treaties.

A smaller group within the community, including most who provided leadership during the dispute, believed the fishery was an important opportunity to enact Mi'kmaw sovereignty over Mi'kmaw territory. Sovereigntists in Esgenoôpetitj see themselves as members of the Mi'kmaw Nation, not as Canadians at all. This more radical position is also grounded in the treaties. For sovereigntists, it is precisely because the Mi'kmaq never ceded any of their lands or voluntarily extinguished any of their rights that the legitimacy of traditional Mi'kmaw government over Mi'kma'ki (Mi'kmaw territory) must be recognized. For them, the dispute is not about fish or only about fishing rights but about the right of the Mi'kmaw people to govern themselves and about Canada's systematic and historic denial of this right. Sovereigntist resistance was directed not only against the Canadian government but also against the structures it imposes upon the community, including the elected chief and council.

Lloyd Augustine, the traditional chief in Esgenoôpetitj, articulates a strong sovereigntist position. Lloyd argues that the land on which Canada is built is not rightfully Canadian but Mi'kmaw and has never been ceded:

*Whatever I keep from taxes and resource revenues from the
Canadian government, it's actually a pittance of what rightfully
belongs to me. There's no paperwork that's there where we have
handed over to them the deed to what is there ... We have always
believed that what is there belongs to the Creator and cannot be
sold or given up.*

*White people's anger stems from the idea that they are dealing in
stolen goods. They tried to terminate or exterminate or assimilate
the Indian ... but their own guilt makes them realize that no
matter what they do ... it'll always be to their own shame. Even if
they wiped us all out, the children looking at history books will
always question, "Who are these people? Why did they die?"*

*"Because they thought this was their land."*

*"Why did they think that?"*

*"Because they were here first."*

For Lloyd, Mi'kmaw sovereignty over Mi'kma'ki is at the heart of the
conflict between First Nations people and Canadian settlers, between his
people and their neighbours. The lands and waters, in his understanding,
are not things that can be owned and parcelled out. "What is there" is a
sacred trust given to the people by the Creator, something that cannot be
given up. For Lloyd, this is part of what must be understood if one is
to fully appreciate what was at stake in the dispute. Sovereignty is not
simply a political position but also a cultural and religious one.

During the dispute, sovereigntist community leaders were important
figures in the work of the community. With the signing of the agreement-
in-principle, the traditional and community-based leaders who had
eclipsed the Indian Act chief during the dispute lost political power.
Although the sovereigntist activists feel good about the stand that they
took, the agreement that was made with the federal government does
not recognize their goals of sovereignty, justice, and Mi'kmaw management of Mi'kmaw resources.

Under the agreement-in-principle, more people in the community are
now fishing and have proper gear, yet they are not doing so according to
the terms of the treaties. The Mi'kmaq have temporarily signed away
their right to self-regulation and have agreed to participate in the federally regulated fishery.[39] Not all community members feel that the chief
and council had a clear mandate to sign this agreement with the federal
government. The agreement is seen as a mixed victory since it allows for

a Native commercial fishery but not under Native regulation and governance. Some feel that their ability to continue to agitate for self-regulated
fishing rights is undermined by the presence of fisheries officers from
their own community, who work in cooperation with the federal government: *We've just been put in a really good situation where we would
be fighting each other* (Miigam'agan). Many argue that the benefits that
were supposed to come to the community with the signing of the agreement were not distributed fairly to all, accruing instead to a few people
aligned with the chief and council and to the non-Native fishers in surrounding communities who were paid to carry out training for Natives
entering the fishery. There are also situations where the distribution of
fishing boats to families in the community has made a difference to
incomes and well-being. For many, criticism of the chief and council,
and of the agreement, and strong feelings of despair and discourage-
ment dominate the aftermath of the dispute. For others, slim hopes exist
that the boats that are in the community now will continue to make
some kind of small difference to the lives and incomes of people who
can fish, even if this is not accompanied by a change in government or
government relationships.

The "loss" of the dispute was profoundly challenging for those most
radically committed to sovereignty. As the Indian Act chief and council
reconsolidated their power in the community, those who gave leadership during the years of the dispute were shut out of the economic life
of the community in many ways. *Most of the people that were involved, were basically used and then dropped ... People that had jobs
at that time, still have jobs now. But the people that didn't have jobs,
and they were in the forefront of the dispute, they have [no hope]*
(Dalton). People who worked full time during the dispute for the needs
of the community often found themselves without work or support in
the years after it subsided. At the same time, as people in the forefront
of the dispute, they had to cope with the aftermath of the tremendous
stress and trauma both from the conflict and from the public scrutiny
and vulnerability that they experienced. Relationships between some
dispute leaders cracked and broke. Many sovereigntist and traditionalist leaders left the community to find work and support their families,
or to heal, or to continue their commitment to Indigenous activism.
And for most of these activists, the "end" of the dispute was a profound challenge to their hopes for their community and for the future
of their people. They believe in the importance of what they did and

in its significance for future generations but have little hope that they will see change in their lifetimes. For these people, the signing of the agreement-in-principle reinforced their experience of Esgenoôpetitj as a colonized place and again marginalized those within the community, moderates and sovereigntists alike, concerned with larger questions of rights and sovereignty.

## BLOCKADE *AND* BREAKTHROUGH

Evaluating the results of the actions taken in Burnt Church is not a simple or clear task, and for the people of Esgenoôpetitj it was not an all-or-nothing experience. Looking back, people talk about the dispute with regret and anger at their inability to effect the wholesale changes that were their goals, with pride in the way the community came together and in what was accomplished, and with hope that more change can be made in the future. Although the specific goal of a self-governed fishery was not realized, the emergence of a mobilized unified community was of tremendous importance for the time that it lasted. In the aftermath of the dispute, with the community once again divided, people continued their work in other ways.

Among traditionalists and sovereigntists, the struggle still continues on the spiritual plane, even though it is not a part of political life at this moment. The goals of the dispute remain the goals of the community's spiritual struggle, which is a pervasive reality that traditionalists understand to be guided by the prophecies of the ancestors and by a connection to their nonhuman relations. Although the dispute itself did not create the new reality for which they had hoped, one woman described what she experienced as a spiritual liberation, which she believed would be the foundation of ongoing change for her children and grandchildren: *Maybe it's not being practised or remembered every day, but the kids are going to even make it more of a legend, you know what I mean? It's gonna be bigger than, even what we know of today ... It's a balance always, it's a lot of deep wounds, deep hurt, [but] the other side to that is liberation and spirituality, spiritual liberation – something you can't hold [on to] but you know* (Miigam'agan). The hurt of the dispute has refocused hopes on spirituality and has affirmed the importance of the traditional ways for people who no longer expect change in their lifetimes. They believe that future generations will have the visions and the tools they need to make change when the time comes.

Concern for sovereignty and traditional practice was certainly not unanimous in Burnt Church during the dispute. Most people became involved because they believed that the ability to exercise their economic and resource rights under the Marshall decision would improve the lives of the people in the community. In the view of many, fishing rights provided an opportunity for people to solve these problems on their own terms, allowing them to improve life for their families and their communities without waiting for government bureaucracies to do it for them. After the signing of the agreement-in-principle, incomes increased for the families who got fishing boats, but things returned to the status quo for everyone else. The critical problems that people attempted to address through the dispute remain. Those who have energy for change focus on raising and educating the next generation by getting their children and grandchildren through high school and university. They do this in the belief that it is the best thing for their children and also for the long-term hopes of the community. Those working at the community level focus on healing the community's ills by addressing issues of addiction and despair. They have not stopped believing in their rights and in the importance of them, but when the dispute subsided they began to focus instead on family and healing.

The events in Esgenoôpetitj (Burnt Church) have regional, national, and international significance. Yet to understand what was really at stake in this conflict, and how and why it happened, we must attend first to the local community itself. The complexity of the community's goals was not clearly reflected in media reports, which focused instead on incidents of violence and confrontation. In the dispute, the Mi'kmaq employed diverse and shifting strategies to move their community's interests forward, and the community came together across a variety of political positions. This complicated reality must be understood as the first step in examining such conflicts. When looking across the Canadian landscape at the complicated terrain of Indigenous-settler relationship action, the first question must remain "what is happening here, and why?" In Burnt Church the complicated answer tells of success and failure, breakthrough and blockade, hope and despair.

NOTES

1  Bob Allain, in "Panel Aims for Peace in Burnt Church Dispute,"
   CBC News, 9 April 2002, http://www.cbc.ca/news/story/2002/04/08/
   burntchurch020408.html.

2 *R. v. Marshall (No. 1)* [1999] 3 SCR 456. For a discussion of the
Marshall case and related court decisions (e.g., in the Sparrow and
Van der Peet cases) and their implications for Burnt Church, see Sarah
J. King, "Conservation Controversy: Sparrow, Marshall, and the
Mi'kmaq of Esgenoôpetitj," *International Indigenous Policy Journal* 2,
no.4 (October 2011), http://ir.lib.uwo.ca/iipj/vol2/iss4/5. There were ac-
tually two decisions in the Marshall case, the second *in R. v. Marshall
(No. 2)* [1999] 3 SCR 533. For discussion of the Marshall decisions in
legal, political, and historical perspective, see William C. Wicken,
*Mi'kmaq Treaties on Trial: History, Land, and Donald Marshall Junior*
(Toronto: University of Toronto Press, 2002); Alex M. Cameron, *Power
without Law: The Supreme Court of Canada, the Marshall Decisions,
and the Failure of Judicial Activism* (Montreal and Kingston: McGill-
Queen's University Press, 2009); Thomas Isaac, *Aborignal and Treaty
Rights in the Maritimes: The Marshall Decision and Beyond* (Saskatoon:
Purich, 2001); and James (Sakej) Youngblood Henderson, "Aboriginal
Jurisprudence and Rights," in *Advancing Aboriginal Claims: Visions/
Strategies/Directions*, ed. Kerry Wilkins, 67–90 (Saskatoon: Purich,
2004).

3 Ken Coates, *The Marshall Decision and Native Rights* (Montreal and
Kingston: McGill-Queen's University Press, 2000).

4 Those who are interested in reading further about the events in Burnt
Church, and their relationship to life in both the Indigenous and settler
communities, may refer to Sarah J. King, *Fishing in Contested Waters:
Place and Community in Burnt Church/Esgenoôpetitj* (Toronto: University
of Toronto Press, 2014). Much of the material in this chapter is drawn
from that larger work.

5 *R. v. Marshall (No. 1)* [1999] 3 SCR 456, file 26,014, 17 September 1999,
2, http://scc-csc.lexum.com/scc-csc/scc-csc/en/item/1739/index.do.

6 These italicized quotations are all taken directly from interviews carried
out by the author in 2004 and 2005. The names Dalton and Cindy are
pseudonyms; all pseudonyms are indicated upon first use.

7 This is a pseudonym.

8 The official lobster season in Burnt Church opens in spring and finishes in
early summer. Since the Supreme Court's earlier Sparrow decision, there
has been a small Native fishery in the fall for "traditional and ceremonial
purposes." *R. v. Sparrow* [1990] 1 SCR 1075.

9 Barb Martin, "History of the Mi'kmaq and the Burnt Church First
Nation," unpublished paper, n.d.

10 gkisedtanamoogk, email message to author, 2007.

11 Martin, "History of the Mi'kmaq."

12 Maurice Basque, *Entre Baie et Péninsule: Histoire de Néguac* (Neguac, NB: Village de Néguac, 1991), 27.

13 Port Royal is located in present-day Nova Scotia, also Mi'kmaw territory.

14 For a detailed account of the settlement of Néguac, see Basque, *Entre Baie et Péninsule*.

15 James Murray, in W.F. Ganong, "The Official Account of the Destruction of Burnt Church," *New Brunswick Historical Society Collections* 3, no. 9 (1914): 301–7, cited in ibid., 55.

16 This account of the settlement of the English village of Burnt Church is based on interviews and on a history compiled by local residents Manford Wasson and Lottie Murdoch for the anniversary of St David's United Church, Burnt Church. See St David's United Church, "St. David's United Church History," 1999. Their sources included Ganong, "Official Account"; W.F. Ganong, "History of Neguac and Burnt Church," *Acadiensis* 8, no. 4 (October 1908): 267–86; as well as local archives and popular knowledge.

17 "Cutting traps" means either cutting the traps from their buoys so that they cannot be retrieved or hauling up the traps and cutting their nets out before throwing them back in so that they can't catch anything. The first method is ecologically damaging, as it creates "ghost traps" that sit on the bottom and catch lobster that can never be retrieved. Local fishers insist that any traps cut need to be done "properly" in order not to create more ghost traps.

18 This is a pseudonym.

19 King, *Fishing in Contested Waters*.

20 Sakej (James Ward) was also one of the leaders of the Warrior Society at Burnt Church.

21 Lloyd Augustine and James Ward, *Draft for the Esgenoôpetitj First Nation (EFN) Fishery Act*, May 2000, http://www.cifas.us/page/draft-esgenoopotitj-first-nation-efn-fishery-act-fisheries-policy-may-2000. See also Lloyd Augustine and James Ward, *Draft for EFN Management Plan*, May 2000, http://www.cifas.us/page/draft-efn-management-plan-may-2000.

22 King, *Fishing in Contested Waters*.

23 "N.B. Natives and DFO Face Off over Lobster," *CBC News*, 12 August 2000, http://www.cbc.ca/news/canada/n-b-natives-and-dfo-face-off-over-lobster-1.238527.

24 The story continues: *We went down to the court with him, and the judge said, "You mean to tell me this one man beat up nine officers?"*
     *The nine officers stand up – they're all big guys, eh? "This one man beat all of you?" And they said, "Yes." He [the judge] said, "This is ridiculous!"* (Barb).

25 King, *Fishing in Contested Waters.*

26 Canada, Department of Fisheries and Oceans, "Key Elements of an Agreement-in-Principle for a Comprehensive Fisheries Agreement with Burnt Church," 1 August 2002.

27 King, *Fishing in Contested Waters.*

28 Ibid.

29 Sakej (James Ward), in Taiaiake Alfred, *Wasáse: Indigenous Pathways of Action and Freedom* (Peterborough, ON: Broadview, 2005), 69, 73.

30 Sakej (James Ward), in ibid., 73.

31 Titch Dharamsi, "No Retreat from Burnt Church," *National Post,* 20 September 2000.

32 These prices are as found on 9 August 2007 at TriNav Marine Brokerage, which hosts an online listing service for licences and boats across Atlantic Canada at http://www.trinav.com.

33 The treaties upheld in the Marshall decision dealt with the continuing ability of the Mi'kmaq to fish in general terms. Donald Marshall Jr was actually fishing eels when he was arrested in Cape Breton.

34 Roger Augustine, in Bob Klager, "A Nation Divided: Despite Outward Signs of Peace, Burnt Church Still Facing Internal Turmoil," *Saint John Telegraph Journal,* 24 August 2002, https://groups.yahoo.com/neo/groups/GrandMananIsland/conversations/topics/2183.

35 King, *Fishing in Contested Waters.*

36 gkisedtanamoogk, email message to author, 2007.

37 Ibid.

38 Vine Deloria Jr argues that there is a great gulf between Western thinking about religion and culture, on the one hand, and Native cultural and religious practice, on the other. This difference is, at its core, "the difference between individual conscience and commitment (Western) and communal tradition (Indian)." He suggests that the foundation of Native social order is the sanctity of the individual *and* the group and that Aboriginal religious and cultural meaning and identity emerge from the fundamental relationships of family, community, and nation. Vine Deloria Jr, *God Is Red: A Native View of Religion* (New York: Putnam,

1973), excerpted in Richard C. Foltz, ed., *Worldviews, Religion and Environment: A Global Anthology* (Toronto: Thomson Wadsworth, 2003), 83.

39  The agreement-in-principle is temporary insofar as the Mi'kmaq must agree to its renewal every four years.

# Blockades, Occupations, and the Bay of Quinte Mohawks' Fight for Sovereignty

YALE D. BELANGER

On 28 February 2006 several protestors from the Six Nations of Grand River occupied a housing development in the tiny community of Caledonia located approximately 20 kilometres southwest of Hamilton, Ontario. The media descended on the low-key protest, only to witness it flare into periodic confrontations that would soon subsume Six Nations residents, Caledonia's populace, the Ontario Provincial Police (OPP), and provincial politicians. To this point, Six Nations leaders had rarely engaged in civic disorder, choosing instead to rely on a historic self-determination discourse in order to press their territorial claims both in Canada and on the international stage.[1] It was interestingly not the only Aboriginal protest activity occurring in Ontario, as protestors from the Mohawks of the Bay of Quinte (MBQ) were involved in six major events over a nineteen-month period beginning in April 2006. Some blockades ended calmly, whereas state authorities forcibly terminated others. Some protested what participants would have described as the state's genocidal policies aimed at Aboriginal annihilation, whereas others protested the chief and band council's failure to acknowledge their demands. The media's obsession with the Caledonia occupation all but eclipsed several tense and potentially violent blockades that divided MBQ residents. Moreover, it overshadowed the economically debilitating effects of Aboriginal blockades that temporarily grounded both rail and highway traffic along the Toronto-Montreal corridor in lieu of presenting sensational images from Caledonia. The MBQ blockades nevertheless offer a fascinating series of events and relationships that illustrate the dynamic nature of Aboriginal blockades specifically and activism more generally, which in this case involved a First Nation that was traditionally tolerant of internal factions but by the 2000s had become divided on the utility of aggressive strategies.

## HISTORICAL SETTING

During the Revolutionary War (1775–83), scores of Mohawks from Fort Hunter in central New York fled to Quebec and Ontario, abandoning their lands that happened to be located in strategic military zones.[2] Mindful that this development was due to Mohawk loyalty to the British Crown, the governor of Quebec, Sir Guy Carleton, promised the Six Nations members that following the conflict's resolution, he would restore their land base, a guarantee reaffirmed in April 1779 by Sir Frederick Haldimand, commander-in-chief of Quebec and His Majesty's Forces.[3] The Treaty of Paris, signed in 1783, formally ended the conflict, after which the remaining British-allied Mohawks in New York immigrated to Ontario. Among them was John Deserontyon, a Fort Hunter chief who fought for the British in the Seven Years' War (1755–63) and was an English supporter during the American Revolution. With Joseph Brant and his followers, Deserontyon relocated to Grand River (Six Nations) in 1783, a tract of Mississauga land located along the Grand River north of Lake Erie obtained by the Crown specifically to assist with Mohawk resettlement.[4] Internal political disagreements led Deserontyon and 100 followers to establish the Tyendinaga Mohawk Reserve on the east shores of the Bay of Quinte on 22 May 1784.[5] This region was popular with Loyalist settlers, who in their desire to acquire local lands began to chip away at the newly established Tyendinaga's social and economic base. Lieutenant Governor John Graves Simcoe acknowledged these difficulties and in 1794 set aside 92,700 acres of land in an agreement later known as Treaty 3½.[6] The land was "to be held and enjoyed by [the Mohawks] in the most free and ample manner and according to the several Customs and usages by them the said Chiefs, Warriors, Women and People of the Six Nations," with the added purpose of securing "the free and undisturbed possession and enjoyment of the same."[7]

Influenced by nearly a century of Anglicanism and European capitalism, the Mohawks of the Bay of Quinte during the nineteenth century would evolve into what Deborah Doxtator describes as "a single nation community with few internal cultural divisions."[8] Community members fashioned an economy emphasizing cultivation and localized trade and remained Loyalist allies keen on instituting economic and political structures that replicated those of nearby non-Native communities. With relative economic stability came a permanent settlement of small cabins scattered along the Bay of Quinte waterfront whose owners experienced external pressure to surrender their lands for construction of a road connecting Kingston and York. By 1820 the Mohawks had lost nearly half of their territory. Settlers seeking access to Mohawk-held lands became a common trend. In 1835, for instance, the 999 year Turton Penn Lease promised each family in the community an annual bag of flour for colonial use of 200 acres of reserve land. In 1836 and 1837 the MBQ lost an additional 827 acres of the reserve land located within the original Mohawk Tract of which they were illegally disposed. But since the land was not formally surrendered, Mohawk complaints fell silent among Canadian politicians.[9] Moreover, the Canadian government asserted its own outright claims of land ownership, and by the end of the century, the MBQ land base had been reduced to nearly one-fifth of its original allocation. A lack of available farmland compelled local residents to seek out and accept extra-community wage labour in order to complement their meager farming incomes.[10] Government pressure to surrender reserve lands did not ease. Interestingly, it also did not deter the MBQ from establishing institutions paralleling those of the Canadian government, and the community became the first, and perhaps only, First Nation in Canada to apply for an elected council under the terms of the 1869 Gradual Enfranchisement Act.[11] For this reason alone, the MBQ have never been accepted as part of the Grand River Iroquois Council.

Economically, things evolved at a leisurely pace until the First World War, when increased off-reserve employment, combined with reserve out-migration, upset the mixed farming economy. It briefly bounced back in the 1930s when several Depression-burdened members returned to the community to resume subsistence farming, but an inability to secure development capital marred attempts to expand community-farming operations.[12] In addition to the added pressure of regional development surrounding the community, this economic strife meant that by the 1960s Doxtator's professed "single nation community with few internal cultural divisions" had fractured into two restrained but visible factions: one emphasized past treaties and agreements to guide political interface with Canadian officials; the other was intent on integrating mainstream political processes into the band's administration.[13] A blend of wage labour and government assistance formed the basis of the reserve economy well into the 1980s, which led Rona Rustige to comment, "the way of life and culture of Tyendinaga's 1,300 residents differs little from the North American norm of their neighbours. The nuclear family is the most common type of household, forms of Christianity predominate, intermarriage with non-Mohawks is common, and the primary language is English." She added, "The physical appearance of homes and buildings at Tyendinaga, which is basically a rural settlement, is virtually indistinguishable from the surrounding community. The band council is the local elected government."[14]

Nearly two centuries earlier, Deserontyon expressed his disappointment with the land allocated by Treaty 3½, which he considered too small to guarantee economic development or community growth.[15] His concerns proved prophetic; combined with a shrinking land base (the original 92,700 acre Simcoe land allotment had shrunk to 17,050 acres by 1980, representing 18.3 per cent the original grant), the lack of economic development was a widespread source of frustration that would influence the post-1980 response of the MBQ Band Council and community activists to outside pressures. These emergent factions had specific ideas about how to both protect the local land base and politically engage federal officials, thus setting the stage for conflict as the two sides established dissimilar methods based on the common objective of securing a larger land base and thus superior economic opportunities.

## EARLY PROTESTS AND COMMUNITY FACTIONALISM

Prior to 1998 a number of smaller protests against the federal and provincial governments occurred at the Tyendinaga Mohawk Reserve. In 1990, for example, 300 Tyendinaga protestors marched through downtown Kingston in support of both Mohawk nationalism and their Oka brethren, followed by a smaller march a few days later in Belleville. At the time, band councillor Will Brant informed the media that his neighbours "get along well with the surrounding communities" and that the MBQ are "normally a passive community." He added that "this is the first time we have ever staged this kind of demonstration" but said that it was necessary to "make our fellow Canadians aware of the seriousness of the [Oka] situation." Chief Earl Hill claimed that regardless of his aversion to violence, "the response of our native people all across this land is hardening. Our land claims will not be denied any longer. The Canadian people know that we do not want all of the land in Canada ... just enough land to support the needs of our people today and the unborn generations of tomorrow." The potential for violence was not to be ignored, traditional firekeeper James Maracle warned. Referring to a half-dozen young men on the reserve who were demanding a more radical response, Maracle said that he and others "convinced them, for now, let's do it this way. The peace people like myself, we say to our people now, let's put those arms down ... but when we have to, people understand, they will pick up their arms."[16] As evidenced by both protest's speeches, the MBQ asserted political and territorial sovereignty over their community's land base and expressed unease at their youth's frustration.

A common goal of securing territorial control drove the band council and the protestors' actions, as each side promoted a universal desire to secure territorial sovereignty. Each, however, formulated distinctive definitions of sovereignty and thus developed unique strategies intended to safeguard it. The MBQ Band Council, for one, relied on the Gus Wen Tah, or two-row wampum, thus emphasizing Indigenous political sovereignty and economic agency characterized by the principles of sharing, mutual recognition, respect, and partnership. The wampum consists of three parallel rows of white beads separated by two rows of purple that symbolize two paths, or two vessels travelling down the same river of life together, which in turn represent each group's laws, customs, and beliefs. The two rows are symbolic of the nation-to-nation relationship between Native people and the Crown, autonomous parties simultaneously interconnected within the same environment (the bed of white beads).[17] Iris Marion Young's relational autonomy model similarly illustrates how national sovereignty is established through relations of interdependency typified by economic exchange and political and legal agreements.[18] Jessica Cattelino further maintains that Indigenous sovereignty is enacted "in part through relations of interdependence" – a sovereign interdependency "that deeply conditions and structures political distinctiveness."[19] In this context, the MBQ Band Council reflected the spirit of sovereignty embraced by the Gus Wen Tah in advocating sovereign interdependency, what I describe as the *sovereignty-nationalist* discourse.

In contrast, the protestors' established a *sovereignty-resistance* discourse. An analysis of the associated speeches reveals elements of the MBQ Band Council's sovereignty-nationalist approach. The key difference is that they portrayed the state, its agents, and Canadian citizens more generally as overt threats to Indigenous territorial and cultural integrity. Given cultural identity's inextricable link with the land, threats against territorial integrity in such cases are considered grave threats to cultural survival, which demand a response sanctioning physical retaliation in the wake of genocidal forces. Interestingly, the reserve itself is both symbolic of this threat and a contested site in need of protection.

Since formal negotiations failed to resolve the outstanding issues, protestors were increasingly disinclined to consider cultural interaction or face-to-face consultation as viable options for resolving difference. Rather, a common response slowly evolved that was dependent on an escalating series of threats of violent reprisals for any perceived aggression. On the surface, each model promotes cultural and territorial protection, and political independence and cultural survival exemplified each discourse. How both sides operationalized their respective ideologies in resisting outside threats portrays their respective ideological differences.

For example, in April 1992 the MBQ camped alongside the Salmon River, demanding that their historic pickerel-spearing right be acknowledged during spawning season. Here a sovereignty-nationalist trope was employed to pronounce the recent Sparrow decision as proof of an Aboriginal right to fish.[20] Accepting the court's conferral of Aboriginal rights resonated with the band council's desire to resolve conflicts based on their belief in the Gus Wen Tah, or reliance on the historic existence of Aboriginal rights and ongoing territorial sovereignty. The sovereignty-resistance trope was later utilized in December during a protest at the Revenue Canada office in downtown Toronto. Upset at the prospect that new tax guidelines would lead to the taxation of Native people working for off-reserve Native firms, thirty-six protestors threatened a violent response to any attempt at removal. "If we get hit on, they'll be hell to pay eternally," threatened the protestors' leader, Shawn Brant, who further claimed that for the youth who "kill themselves [because] they think no one cares," his actions offered "hope, resistance [and a] commitment that shows you [do] care."[21] Brant's speech reflects the central tenet of the sovereignty-resistance trope: the need to consider or actively engage in an extreme physical response to potentially deadly or economically debilitating threats to the community.

Activism was not confined to agitating against the federal and provincial governments, and it was during this period that the relationship between the protestors and the band council endured its first test when, on 30 May, thirteen protestors led by Mario Baptiste occupied the band offices while threatening to shut down the "whole damn territory" over alleged band council mismanagement, specifically band councillor spending on fancy lunches and gifts for one another.[22] Rather than working collectively with political leaders, the protestors portrayed the MBQ Band Council as an additional threat to community stability. Chief Maracle identified sloppy bookkeeping as the key issue and noted that an investigation by the provincial police antiracket squad had not resulted in charges being filed.[23] The extended occupation forced the band council to request OPP assistance, which led to a police raid that quickly penetrated a makeshift barricade of trees and brush and ended with the protestors' removal. Baptiste complained that the band council had "turned the riot squad on us," adding, "It's pretty sad when your own chief and council turn non-native armed forces on people."[24] Angry residents criticized the protestors, and many screamed, "It's a shame you had to go against your own people." They also pressured the band councillors to "throw those idiots off the territory."[25] Several additional protests closed out the 1990s, setting the stage for increased advocacy the like of which the community had previously not experienced.

Protest leaders left their imprint on means of local Mohawk activism all the same. A self-proclaimed member of the Fundamental Indian Rights Movement, Baptiste remained a leading community figure of most protests. Arrested in 1995 while protesting the dumping of waste materials on the reserve, he was later charged for illegally occupying the Ottawa office of Assembly of First Nations national chief Ovide Mercredi.[26] Angered at the high national Aboriginal youth suicide rates and Mercredi's seeming complicity in interpreting the Indian Act for federal policymakers, Baptiste travelled to Ottawa to inform the national chief "that he [Mercredi] doesn't speak for all Indian peoples."[27] Perhaps more important for this narrative, Baptiste's measured withdrawal from public life led to Shawn Brant's emergence in the late 1990s, an individual who would catalyze many in the community to heretofore unseen levels of political advocacy.

## TWO SIDES EMERGE

Born and raised on the Tyendinaga Mohawk Reserve 1 kilometre from the rails he would one day blockade, Brant briefly worked for the federal Auditor General's Office and Department of Employment and Immigration until 1989, the year his wife miscarried twins while fetching well water.[28] He started a short-lived cabinet-making business in 1992, after which he and his business partners failed to repay $430,000 in loans to an Aboriginal financing company and Industry Canada.[29] The band council, led by newly elected (and current) chief Don Maracle, proceeded to sue them for $588,000 in damages and costs over a section of land to which Brant claimed personal ownership that he had never formally purchased. Afterward, he briefly moved to downtown Toronto to fight skinheads as a member of Anti-Racist Action, and it was during the next

decade that Brant grew his public persona by participating in and leading a number of smaller protests, actions that included briefly visiting
Oka in 1990, travelling to Ipperwash and the site of the Dudley George
shooting in 1995, and organizing several busloads of MBQ citizens to
join a march of homeless people in Ottawa in 1999.[30] The one-time civil
servant and business owner had during this period morphed into a
professional activist.

Brant's actions signalled a period of augmented and increasingly
aggressive forms of activism, and they amplified community factionalism among the MBQ, highlighted by the emergence of two key groups:
band supporters and activists. This outcome in many ways was not surprising, for historically Mohawk factionalism was "a common aspect of
Iroquoian politics from as far back as the era of the League's inception,"
historian Scott Trevithick explains. "The original league in fact seldom
formulated a unified policy as Europeans understood it, each nation often following its own self-interested external policy." This factionalism
persisted into the contemporary reserve period[31] but was never considered inherently divisive. Debate among the Haudenosaunee was integral
for achieving a good mind, and in turn factions ensured political and
social balance. As the various communities grew and became increasingly diverse during the late nineteenth century, social balance became
more difficult to effect in the wake of political upheaval fraught with
economic crises, land disputes, and the constant reminder of the British
Crown's failure to adhere to past policies and political agreements.
Political complexity among the MBQ flowered in the early twentieth
century following the introduction of Christianity, a capitalist economy
that led individuals to abandon the reserve for urban employment, and
a Department of Indian Affairs presence.

Notably, the MBQ Band Council never forswore the spirit of the
Gus Wen Tah and chose negotiations to pursue its political claims.
Unconventional strategies such as blockades were periodically considered, but the chief and council preferred to pursue the band's land claims
through government-fashioned processes. A case in point is the aforementioned Turton Penn Lease, a 999 year charter that in 1835 assigned
200 acres of reserve land for colonial use, which would become the village of Shannonville's home. In 1991 the MBQ signed a memorandum of
understanding with Indian and Northern Affairs Canada to initiate historical research into the construction of Highway 2, first built in the
1920s and widened during the 1960s. The sanctioned research identified
legal uncertainty about the portion of highway running through the

leasehold area, leading to an eight-year period of negotiations (1997–2004) between the MBQ and the governments of Ontario and Canada. In 2005 they reached an agreement entitling the MBQ to title over 1.8 kilometres of King's Highway 2 running through Shannonville. The band was also awarded ownership of the 1.8 kilometres with a bare right of passage assigned the public, $1.2 million for past and future use of the highway, and return of the Turton Penn lease area.[32] Although time consuming, the final outcome appeared acceptable to all involved.

The Culberston Tract claim submitted in 1995 did not proceed as smoothly. The MBQ stated that a 923.4 acre parcel of reserve land had been illegally acquired in 1873. Canada even conceded that the MBQ "did not consent by way of surrender to the alienation of the Culbertson Tract lands."[33] Chief Maracle was pleased by federal officials' conciliatory tone and pleased that negotiations were underway for return of nearly 360 acres of the Culbertson Tract. MBQ leaders soon learned, however, that Canada would consider only a financial settlement, as third parties owned the claimed lands (Canada would not consider any settlement leading to their dispossession). A disappointed Chief Maracle did acknowledge that this may be an acceptable outcome, but Brant and several of his followers were not as accommodating, and they refused to formally acknowledge this decision. The resultant challenge to what Brant and his followers publicly portrayed as the band council's complicity in Canada's genocidal policies against the MBQ foreshadowed how these two community factions would frame their respective responses to federal officials and one another over the next several years.

## WHO MADE THE DECISION TO CONFRONT?

Brant and his followers refused to acknowledge the federal land claims process because they believed that it failed to provide adequate redress of historic injustices. Simply put, it was antithetical to securing Mohawk sovereignty over historic territories. Only when Canada returned these lands to their rightful owners, Brant reasoned, would the outstanding issues be resolved.[34] This situation was aggravated by two separate challenges to MBQ sovereignty: the expansion of a nearby landfill and the construction of a housing development in the disputed Culbertson Tract territory operated by two non-MBQ companies. These projects were moving ahead quickly as the land claim wound itself through time-intensive and procedurally complex stages. Moreover, the immediate threat – the Richmond Landfill expansion – was projected to grow considerably over a twenty-five-year period, leading many to question whether the introduction of 750,000 tonnes of garbage from Toronto and other outlying areas annually would lead to property and water well contamination.[35] Chief Maracle uncharacteristically challenged Napanee City Council members in October 2005, stating that "the Mohawk nation will never allow anyone sitting in this room or any water management officials with their greed of profit to poison the people of our nation. As part of your risk assessment, you better take into account civil unrest."[36]

Tensions simmered for the next five and a half months, until 22 April 2006, when, just after midnight, 100 Mohawk protestors led by Brant blocked a small section of VIA Rail track 20 kilometres east of Belleville, disrupting freight trains and stranding 3,500 rail passengers.[37] Chief Larry Hay of the Tyendinaga Police Service telephoned Chief Maracle at 3:00 AM at home to notify him that protestors dressed in military fatigues and carrying clubs were blockading the rails.[38] Acknowledging that the protestors possessed a right to demonstrate, Maracle nevertheless declined to offer his endorsement and suggested that the event supported the Caledonia protestors who had been occupying a construction site since late February. He did concede, however, that the protest signalled local frustration at the slow pace of land claims negotiations.[39] Within a week, Caledonia protestors and Ontario officials had negotiated a temporary end to the dispute, and Brant dismantled the blockade upon being informed by the traditional confederacy council of the agreement.[40]

It appeared that the brief Brant-led blockade achieved several goals. On 11 January 2007 Minister of Indian and Northern Affairs Jim Prentice appointed Sean Kennedy to negotiate a settlement for the Culbertson Tract. Less than two weeks later, the housing developer Intergroup Financing AG suspended construction plans until federal officials met with Mohawk leaders.[41] Brant boasted of the protest's success and suggested that such peaceful demonstrations were but one aspect of an overall strategy, hinting at the use of violence. "I think that if they took an aggressive action against us before the outcome of the talks was revealed," he asserted, "we'll be ready to defend ourselves and respond in kind."[42] Notably, this was the first time violence was mentioned as a means to repel territorial encroachment, and Brant was not simply posing as a radical militant. Rather, he acknowledged the economic impact of temporarily halting the transport of millions of dollars in product and disrupting personal travel. For instance, in 2007 it was estimated that each day upward of thirty freight trains shipped $102 million worth of cargo and that twenty-two Via Rail trains traversed the Montreal-Windsor corridor.[43] In March, Brant followed this brief blockade with a seventy-strong occupation of a gravel quarry located on disputed land, threatening to remain on-site until the operator's licence was revoked. Chief Maracle responded, "The Mohawk council certainly understands the frustration young people have in achieving a resolution that's in the best interest of future generations." Brant replied, "it's very difficult to carry out meaningful negotiations at the table while they're taking out 10,000 truckloads a year of our land."[44]

While Chief Maracle and the band council pursued a negotiations strategy, two notable shifts occurred in Brant's discourse in the aftermath of these inaugural protests. First, he again highlighted the possibility of armed conflict, this time in more tangible and aggressive terms. Second, he started referring to himself as a community representative by subtly alluding to his role in MBQ-Canada negotiations. This was not the first time this contentious issue had emerged. In 2001, after announcing a protest planned during the Summit of the Americas meeting in Quebec City, Akwesasne leaders fearful of a repeat of the civil unrest that had threatened community stability in 1990 summoned Brant in an effort to determine how his planned action would represent "the honour and integrity of Mohawk people."[45] The majority of people in attendance opposed Brant's planned protest, claiming it was inciting fear among the residents. One individual in particular warned of the potential violence, suggesting that even though Brant believed he was in control of the situation, "there's not going to be any control." Akwesasne chiefs from Canada and the US portion of the reserve, the St Regis Mohawk Tribe, were united in their opposition. Former grand chief Russell Roundpoint summed it up nicely: "The overwhelming voice here is we don't support it. I think the message has come out loud and clear. Don't do it. Take it somewhere else. Akwesasne is at the biggest risk here, not you. You're going to go home (after the protest)."[46] Ignoring these pleas, Brant carried through with the protest while taking the opportunity to criticize Chief Mike Mitchell and others for refusing to champion traditional Mohawk ways of life and governance.[47]

Things changed drastically on 20 April 2007, when Brant and thirty-five supporters again blocked the VIA Rail tracks between Kingston and Belleville. Citing the illegal use of quarry materials for a condominium development located on disputed Culbertson Tract lands, and the slow pace of land claims negotiations, Brant claimed that "this is one of the targets on the list for disruption for the fact the quarry license still hasn't been revoked." He further indicated that the rails would be blockaded "as part of the ongoing rotational economic disruption campaign we promised." Chief Maracle decried the activists' use of blockades and vigorously distanced the band council from the protestors' actions. Maracle claimed that community politicians "were never consulted on the blockade of the railway," adding that Brant's actions "could have the potential of jeopardizing the negotiation table."[48] He similarly denounced subsequent protests. Following National Day of Action activities in June 2007, the MBQ Band Council openly remonstrated protestors in the community newsletter while indicating, "We do not agree with blockades."[49] An April 2008 rail blockade and a simultaneous barricade of the Highway 401 traffic corridor at Kingston elicited the following response: "We do not support or condone the blockages of public roads as appropriate measures to resolve the Culbertson Tract land claim. It's unfortunate that a group have taken actions into their own hands. People need to remain calm and allow for peaceful negotiations to continue in a climate not hampered by protests and blockades."[50]

It is evident that what began in the 1980s as limited community participation in regional protests had by the early 2000s evolved into what could best be described in certain circles as a community-based activist consciousness, even though the MBQ writ large remained divided. The majority of community members sided with Chief Maracle's land claims strategy, although a smaller, albeit increasingly vocal and potentially violent, contingent favoured Brant's more aggressive tactics. Either way, the antagonists deemed their competing interests irreconcilable despite the parallel aspiration to repatriate the community's alienated lands. The difference was how each side approached securing territorial sovereignty: by negotiating or by resisting outside agents in an attempt to foster a sense of domestic nationhood vis-à-vis blockades and occupations.

## ASPECTS OF THE CONFRONTATIONS

During this rich period of activity, the print and electronic media focused primarily on four events: (1) the first rail blockade on 22 April 2006; (2) a second rail blockade on 20 April 2007; (3) a rail and highway blockade during the National Day of Action on 29 June 2007; and (4) a final rail blockade on 20 April 2008. Without notifying the chief and band council, or seeking their support, Brant forged ahead in April 2006 with a plan that included revolving and escalating protests directed at strategically identified targets. Key blockade sites included the rail line near Kingston and Belleville and Highway 401. In April the first barricade was constructed, which consisted of 100 Mohawk protestors blocking a small section of track 20 kilometres east of Belleville with two old school buses and lighting a bonfire of old railway ties. This disrupted freight trains and forced Via Rail to halt bookings for weekend travel.[51] Brant's support of the roughly two-dozen Six Nations protestors preventing construction workers from entering the Douglas Creek Estates building site at Caledonia became the media's primary focus. This minor occupation, which began in February, slowly developed and eventually led to several skirmishes between the police, Caledonia residents, and Six Nations protestors. These conflicts culminated in an OPP raid that led to the arrest of sixteen protestors on 20 April.

Irritated with the slow pace of land claims negotiations, Brant sought to educate the media and the public about his community's plight. Reflecting on recent events at Caldeonia and regional attempts to force what he deemed to be foreign occupants from Tyendinaga lands, Brant opined, "The situation in Caledonia has been repeated numerous times around here ... on lands that are specifically ours." He said that "most of the time, these claims – there's no land that's ever returned. We want the land back and not money ... The land is forever; money is temporary."[52] But a closer reading of Brant's language, as previously suggested, indicates that the option of a violent response informed his activism. It is also essential to note that Caledonia catalyzed Brant by providing him with an arena needed to foster support. Yet Brant remained regionally isolated, and he refused to reach out beyond his tiny circle of supporters. For example, it does not appear that allying with Six Nations protestors was ever considered despite parallel concerns and an awareness of each community's resistance strategies. On 30 April 2006 Six Nations protestors blocked Caledonia's Highway 6 bypass as a show of support for Tyendinaga protestors.[53] The potential for partnership was never more evident, and it was something Brant publicly supported, but the two communities' representatives never met.[54] That MBQ and Six Nations protestors did not discuss establishing a concerted model of civic disruption is startling, considering their strategic geographic placement in relation to the central Ontario travel networks essential to regional economic stability. Upsetting these networks for protracted time periods would have negatively impacted the millions of people living in Quebec, upstate New York, northern Michigan, and their surrounding communities, which would have provided protestors and their respective communities with significant political leverage.

A preference soon developed for smaller, localized, and isolated events. On 23 March 2007 seventy protestors dressed in army fatigues and carrying Mohawk flags occupied the quarry in an attempt to stem the housing development. A limited police response prompted Deseronto mayor Norm Clark to state, "I would hope the police would take care of that situation."[55] Tensions slowly dissipated until 20 April, when thirty-five Mohawks protesting the use of quarry materials and the housing development used three school buses to block train tracks between Kingston and Belleville. Claiming his actions were a response to the failure to resolve ongoing quarry issues, Brant intended to shut down a specific section of tracks indentified as "one of the targets on the list for disruption" for forty-eight hours. "We shut (the rail lines) down as part of the ongoing rotational economic disruption campaign we promised."[56] Brant then hinted at future actions: "We said that we would develop a plan and we would target each level of government, either through the rail lines, the provincial highways, the town of Deseronto itself. The next [action] coming will be one of the latter two."[57] Unlike in the previous year's blockade, Brant was charged by the police, and Via Rail obtained an injunction against future blockades.[58]

Despite the chief and band council's determined opposition of Brant and his followers, the Canadian National Railway chose to pursue legal action against the MBQ. Soon after the lawsuit was initiated, the railway dropped its legal action against the MBQ when it was determined that political leaders did not sanction the blockade. Of course, this did not occur before the band council had used a portion of its limited financial resources to respond to the charges. Brant and his followers ignored the potential ramifications and maintained their course of action, which received Assembly of First Nations national chief Phil Fontaine's implicit support. Fontaine also warned railway officials to be "very careful" with rail lines running over expropriated lands: "I urge caution on CN before it once again threatens anyone with lawsuits."[59] Another blockade occurred during the National Day of Action on 29 June 2007 in direct response to Fontaine's call for actions that potentially included interfering with road, rail, and port service across the country.[60]

Whether Brant influenced Fontaine in not known, but the latter's appeal for national Aboriginal civic disruption forced the hand of the federal minister of Indian Affairs. Jim Prentice published an open letter in the *Winnipeg Free Press* on 29 March indicating his willingness to reprimand participant First Nations and Aboriginal organizations, thus threatening their financial viability.[61] Mohawk protestors seized the opportunity. Claiming to be armed with shotguns, they lit bonfires and blockaded the rails and Highway 401 for eleven hours. Interestingly, despite advocating like actions, Fontaine retracted his support for rail blockades, fearing that poor publicity could lead Canadians to "criminalize First Nations with respect to the actions they plan to take on 29 June and beyond. Our people do have a right to protest, as do all Canadians."[62] He indicated that these and similar actions undermined future agreements reached in a peaceful and honourable manner. The blockade immediately assumed an ominous tone following Brant's proclamation that his followers had taken to possessing firearms in anticipation of future Highway 401 actions. Prentice remained optimistic of a nonviolent outcome, indicating, "with the exception of what we experienced with illegal blockades in eastern Ontario, I think it has been a good day. It's been a good day for democracy and for the articulation of a peaceful point of view by First Nation Canadians."[63]

Reflecting on what was by now three years of agitation, the media began evaluating the success of Native blockades, given the police unwillingness to engage what were portrayed as Aboriginal lawbreakers. The *Ottawa Citizen* denounced Brant's actions as little more than bully tactics. Its editor, however, highlighted the success of such campaigns, while concluding that it was not surprising to see other First Nations adopting similar strategies. For example, the chief of Roseau River First Nation in southern Manitoba, Terence Nelson, threatened to block rail lines, sending "a signal that the federal government is susceptible to intimidation; even if the timing was coincidence, it didn't look that way."[64] Back in Ontario, OPP commissioner Julian Fantino spoke with Brant and discovered that the protestors were armed and would remain so to ensure "a safe day," as "previous incidents have shown that aggressive tactics by the police need to be met by equal resistance by the people that they're bringing those against." This is a curious comment, seeing as the police to that point had never aggressively challenged the Brant-led group of protestors. Brant all the same agreed to dismantle the blockade, although he did not turn himself into the police immediately. Instead, he humorously insisted that "you don't go to jail on the long weekend."[65] In a fascinating twist, several of the protestors' supporters posted a YouTube video entitled "When Justice Fails, Stop the Rails," providing instructions on how to sabotage train tracks. The instructional video's preamble read, "At a time when money is more powerful than justice governments need financial (dis)incentives to live up to their own laws. The Mohawks have shown the vulnerability of a major trade corridor for people and material. While few other communities would hold off a frontal assault by the OPP, there are other ways to close the rail lines. Consider some discreet non-traceable way of expressing your solidarity with indigenous struggles at the wire's location."[66]

Brant eventually gave himself up and was subsequently jailed. He was eventually charged with nine offences, including six for mischief, and faced a potential twelve years in prison. Protests subsided during the summer of 2007. Whereas Brant publicly downplayed the impact of the charges and potential jail time, his wife, Sue Collis, was clearly concerned. Speaking at McGill University in October about her husband's difficulties, she claimed that the authorities "want to make an example of him ... Shawn acted as a spokesperson for the community of Tyendinaga, and not only did he give a voice to the suffering that exists [in Native communities], but he compelled Canadians to look with new clarity ... at the legacy of the Canadian government." In her view, the railway blockades were borne "of poverty and suicides on reserves, poisoned drinking water, and the mess that is the land claims [process]." Brant's lawyer, Peter Rosenthal, stated, "If you have an honest belief in a factual situation, it would legally and criminally justify your actions. We will argue that Shawn Brant had an honest belief that it was Mohawk land, and so he had a right to put a bus on the train tracks. We will be alleging that given the history of CN's treatment of native peoples, and the federal and provincial government's treatment of indigenous peoples, such as the licensing of the quarry, those historical facts justify, criminally and socially, the actions [of Shawn Brant]."[67] Canadian National Railway spokesperson Mark Hallman stated that the protest affected the entire Ontario-Quebec rail corridor, even though the dispute had nothing to do with the railway.[68]

Three points arise from these dialogues. First, Brant was not a community spokesperson but the leader of a small group of individuals that numbered no more than 100 during the course of several separate events. Although he raised the spectre of community suffering for the media, the various railway operators had not been singled out as targets until this point. Rather, it was Collis who identified the Canadian National Railway as a colonial agent now implicated in increased suicides, poor health, and general impoverishment. Lastly, Brant's lawyer stated that since he was acting on Mohawk land, he should be immune from prosecution. Referring to what is also known as the "colour of right" defence, legal analyst W. Wesley Pue argues, "In many cases what would otherwise seem to be merely a matter of political protest takes on a different character because Aboriginal peoples are uniquely able to claim interest in or ownership of land that to all external appearances seems to belong to public authorities or (possibly) others."[69] In Brant's case, he "had an honest belief that it was Mohawk land, and so he had a right to put a bus on the train tracks."[70] Accordingly, the Crown could not charge him with trespassing, for he faithfully believed that it was not possible to trespass on one's own lands.

Rosenthal also stated that the actions of OPP commissioner Fantino expanded the blockades into the realm of civil liberties. Specifically, Fantino threatened Brant's civil rights, something apparently confirmed by the release of transcripts drawn from a legally questionable wire-tapped cell phone discussion between the two.[71] Particularly revealing were Fantino's remarks suggesting that Brant's "whole world's going to come crashing down" and his warning that he would "do everything I can within your community and everywhere to destroy your reputation."[72] He also criticized Brant for using children to help with the blockade despite his claims of being a children's rights advocate.[73] As Rosenthal anticipated, provocative comments such as this did little more than fan the flames of an already volatile situation. And more important, they conflicted with the Police Preparedness for Aboriginal Critical Incidents protocols developed in the wake of the Ipperwash Inquiry's final report. When the report was released the previous May, the inquiry's commissioner concluded that blockades and occupations were neither "inevitable, nor are they inevitably violent," and that the "police must exercise restraint and use force only as a last resort."[74] Notably, Fantino admitted that there were plans to forcibly remove protestors in June 2007. Responding to questions from Brant's lawyer, he said, "There comes a time when the balance of the greater public good shifts, and the feeling was that under the circumstances, this situation could no longer continue, and we were, in fact, preparing to move on the blockades."[75]

Undeterred, Brant regularly employed the threat of violence in an attempt to solidify his leadership among the protestors and to deter law enforcement officials from overtly challenging his and his followers' actions. Unlike at Caledonia, however, Tyendinaga protestors and police rarely physically engaged one other. The *threat* of violence nevertheless forced Chief Maracle to regularly remind the media that the band council intended to pursue peaceful negotiations and that he and his council "were never consulted on the blockade of the railway." He expressed his disappointment with actions that "have the potential of jeopardizing the negotiation table."[76] Federal negotiators nevertheless pursued negotiations, apparently unfazed by the protests and intent on resolving the outstanding Culbertson Tract claim. On 27 April 2008, for the third straight year, a roadblock was raised in protest – this time a large trench was dug across a busy highway leading into Deseronto – something the band council once again did not support, and the OPP cleared it the next day.[77] Now out of jail and cleared of all charges associated with the 2006 blockade, Brant kept a low profile during this protest. Tyendinaga resident Dan Doreen escalated activity in response to Nibourg Development's announcement that it was initiating construction by blocking a main street running through Deseronto with an old motorhome. Echoing Brant's "colour of right" defence, he told the media, "this is Mohawk land and developers, you better stay the hell away," while adding, "I want every developer … that plans to develop in Deseronto to stay the hell out or we're going to go through this again, and again, and again, and again until it's done. It's not a fight with the OPP … We're sick and tired of having to come down to Deseronto every week and protect our land. We're sick of it."[78] Upward of fifty Mohawk protestors confronted workers arriving to clear brush, and over the next few days the protestors grew in number to seventy-five. Two hundred OPP officers were dispatched to dismantle the blockade.

Land developer Theo Nibourg issued a statement indicating that he would not challenge the issue until a government resolution was proposed.[79] "The OPP will continue to uphold the right to lawful, peaceful protest," Commissioner Fantino informed the media; "however, we do not condone illegal activity and will not tolerate conduct intended to disrupt public peace and threaten public safety." The blockade was just one of several protests to occur during a brief two-day period, and each resulted in property damage. "Fires were lit on the highway, damage done to property," the OPP observed. "Those responsible for criminal wrongdoing will be held accountable to the full extent provided by the law."[80] Theo Nibourg and Emile Nibourg stated, "The inaction of the government is leading to unrest between the natives and non-natives and putting all people at great risk. The federal government cannot accept the validity of the land claim and at the same time, not deal with private land owners."[81] These events seemed to resonate with various factions. A group of non-Aboriginal supporters carrying placards reading "Solidarity with Tyendinaga" rallied on behalf of the Mohawks, blocking the Hanlon Expressway for a brief time.[82] On 30 April, Six Nations protestors blocked Caledonia's Highway 6 bypass in support of Tyendinaga protestors.[83] This was nevertheless a short-lived campaign.

The protests continued to undermine the MBQ Band Council's attempts to establish business relationships with regional business owners. Mortified that outsiders associated the MBQ with the protests, community spokesperson Brant Bardy informed the media, "That's the kind of support we don't need. If that's our support we're in trouble. We feel there is no need to block roads and heighten tensions ... because it's already pretty tense." The protests "actually have the potential to stall negotiations."[84] Violence had occurred the previous day after police attempted to arrest Brant for his involvement in the previous year's National Day of Action. Two officers were injured and a cruiser's windshield smashed.[85] A tense standoff followed after police claimed that a protestor had pointed a rifle at them. In response to the arrests, protestor Jason Maracle proclaimed, "They're going to have to kill every God damn one of us to get us off our land. We're not moving ... I guess if they want another 1990 scene [Oka], then OK, I guess we'll have one." Following this protest, Indian Affairs spokesperson Margo Geduld reported that the MBQ had broken off negotiations with the federal government when they learned that purchasing non-Native property in Deseronto was not an option. In what could be described loosely as a day late and a dollar short, Chief Maracle reversed his position in the wake of Indian Affairs' unwillingness to negotiate for land, threatening future litigation and alternative political strategies. Doreen said that he and his people would never give up their claims and protests: "Our land is not open for business. And the mayor of Deseronto needs to figure out how they're going to move Deseronto because we're going to get it back."[86] By now, however, the two sides were hopelessly divided.

Activist momentum waned following Brant's incarceration, and protests at and near the Tyendinaga Mohawk Reserve subsided. Not surprisingly, two protests occurred following Brant's release in 2008. The first transpired at the reserve in October and involved a small group of protestors preventing the delivery of a prefabricated, $1.9 million police station. Endorsed by the band council following a positive community referendum, the police station's construction was opposed by protestors who claimed that the money should be spent improving the public school's water system. Tyendinaga police chief Ron Maracle, brother of Chief Don Maracle, promised that charges would be laid against protestors and those participating in future events, and the Tyendinaga police issued twelve warrants for fellow Tyendinaga Mohawks. All of these individuals were eventually arrested and charged for their part in the protests. On 7 June 2009 Brant helped to organize a protest of forty individuals who blocked access to both sides of the Skyway Bridge, which spans the Bay of Quinte and links the MBQ territory and Prince Edward County. Claiming the support of the Akwesasne clan mothers, the protestors demanded meaningful discussions between the Canadian government and the Mohawks of Akwesasne in response to the Canada Border Services Agency's announcement that it intended to arm guards assigned to posts on Cornwall Island, the heart of Akwesasne territory, which straddles Quebec, Ontario, and New York.[87]

Channelling the spirit of previous protests, the group's leaders declared state violations of Mohawk territorial sovereignty and proceeded to halt traffic despite a heavy police presence. Chief Maracle denounced the participants and requested that the OPP assist the Tyendinaga Mohawk Police with the protestors' removal. At Rooseveltown, New York, the Longhouse of the Mohawk Nation Council of Chiefs, representing the Six Nations, formally asked Brant to remove the roadblock, and Tyendinaga police chief Ron Maracle delivered the message. Several Akwesasne Band Council members voiced their displeasure with Brant's approach, claiming it could negatively impact their community. As many as one hundred Mohawks opposing Brant's actions travelled to the bridge to confront him and his followers, demanding he dismantle the blockade and leave the site.[88] The OPP moved in to shut down the protest, after which upward of eighty Mohawks and police engaged in a violent struggle, resulting in thirteen arrests and an OPP officer's hospitalization. This was the last and most violent protest to date involving MBQ members. Of note, while police chief Maracle was dealing with Skyway Bridge protestors, an individual pumped six shots into Maracle's personal vehicle parked at the police station, resulting in three of the windows being blown out and the passenger seat riddled with bullets.[89] Community divisions had by 2009 developed to the point where the potential for internecine violence had indeed become a reality – all in the name of Mohawk sovereignty.

## FINAL THOUGHTS

The six protests that occurred over nineteen months beginning in April 2006 illustrate how two local factions – one a group of protestors, the other the elected band council – with overlapping demands for territorial sovereignty threatened to politically unravel a community already burdened by poor economic development and expensive, time-consuming land claims negotiations. What is so remarkable is how the two factions constructed different definitions of sovereignty from a common desire to repatriate their community's lands lost through colonial duplicity and to have territorial sovereignty recognized. Furthermore, both factions considered Canada the key antagonist. Whereas the chief and council were frustrated by the slow pace of a federal land claim to resolve outstanding issues, Brant and his followers were upset with federal policies that they believed had overwhelmed the band council into blind adherence. Accordingly, they used the MBQ government as the foil to justify actions that they deemed community-based and intended to improve local socio-economic and socio-political conditions. In the end, Brant and the protestors' actions did little more than upset community stability, never generating the community support needed to pursue their vision of sovereignty, and Maracle's unbroken tenure as elected chief dating to 1992 indicates that he maintained majority support during this tenuous period. The media latched onto this division and consistently portrayed the MBQ Band Council and citizens as progressives battling an uncontrollable splinter group of protestors, who were simultaneously portrayed as a poor man's militia clad in camouflaged fatigues, as speaking in military terms about repelling the enemy, and as consistently threatening violence if not taken seriously. The media also shrewdly captured the internal battle for political legitimacy that regularly favoured Maracle.

From the outside looking in, the various Brant-led protests appear triumphant. In addition to slowing the housing development's progress, they helped to restrict the removal of quarry materials while educating the public about the Haldimand Agreement, the Culbertson Tract, and the Simcoe Deed. Assembly of First Nations national chief Phil Fontaine briefly capitalized on the protests' popularity to propose similar strategies if Canada insisted on ignoring First Nations. Chief Terence Nelson of the Rouseau River First Nation in Manitoba publicly spoke of the importance of rail blockades as a way to ensure that officials took his community's land claims seriously. From an MBQ community-based perspective, however, these nonsanctioned blockades hurt local relationships; to that point, band investments totalling more than $15 million in regional businesses and projects dependent on local patronage were threatened. That the media connected the MBQ Band Council and community residents with a small group of dissidents was a public relations disaster. Adding insult to injury, the Canadian National Railway named the MBQ as a defendant in a multimillion dollar lawsuit seeking to recoup lost revenues resulting from the blockades, and land claims negotiations also lingered. The latter could have been anticipated. What could not was the tremendous amount of time and money directed toward repairing public opinion. Furthermore, the media's constant reminder of community factionalism reinforced popular stereotypes portraying First Nations as poorly governed and prone to destructive, internally divisive behaviour.[90] The media frequently exploited this theme, despite exposing an inherently complex MBQ kinship network and set of political relationships. Not predisposed to regularly providing in-depth analyses, the media frequently resorted to simply associating MBQ protests with events such as Oka and Ipperwash, both of which were offered as sites of conflict and violent deaths.

The clear division between protestor and band council desires notwithstanding, further analysis suggests that the rail and Highway 401 blockades had the potential to inflict significant economic damage, suggesting that their utility as direct action tools was underexploited. For instance, it is estimated that a ten-day rail blockade could ultimately halt the movement of more than $1 billion in freight, whereas a similar highway blockade could potentially halt $13 billion in freight. Brant's failure to partner with Six Nations protestors, whose home community is also located near strategic transportation routes (Highways 6, 24 and 403), was noteworthy. If the two groups engaging in direct action had organized a common blockade, they could have indefinitely immobilized southern Ontario transportation. Such is the nature of political leverage. Similarly, the MBQ blockades impacted local businesses. One reporter estimated that, from November 2006 to mid-2008, Deseronto businesses suffered a 75 per cent drop in revenue. This financial loss heightened tensions between the MBQ and local non-Native residents. Fears of blockades drove away tourist traffic and harmed businesses that depended on summer tourism, leading to several businesses closing and one physically relocating to another town. In 2008 tourists spent an average of $113 for day visits and $133 for overnight visits. From 2006 to 2008, as protests grew in number and intensity, hotel occupancy rates dropped from 60.1 per cent to 49.9 per cent, the lowest rate in more than a decade.[91]

A brief conversation with an anonymous Deseronto official suggested that each blockade set back tourism and local development by three to six months. This conversation and the abovementioned news reports suggest that the protests did have an impact on local tourism; however, more empirical work is sorely needed that examines the impact of Aboriginal activism on the tourism industries of neighbouring non-Native communities. Larger projects such as plans to renovate a Hasting County senior's home were also suspended when project bidders could not be secured; and all development plans on the Culbertson Tract have been frozen, thus impacting local development plans.

In recent years, the number of protests has subsided, even though the memory of their disruptive nature lingers at the Tyendinaga Mohawk Reserve and in the surrounding communities. This divisive chapter pitted protestors confident in their vision of sovereignty against a chief and band council that they deemed to be little more than complicit colonial agents. The chief and council's pursuit of sovereignty demanded that they in turn frame the protestors as a reactionary splinter group that lacked community legitimacy and political voice. The two sides conveyed the centrality of territorial sovereignty to their respective agendas, yet they were never able to reconcile their political beliefs and develop a unified front. This undermined any hopes of establishing an allied MBQ community pursuing a collective belief in nationhood.

NOTES

1 See, for example, Yale D. Belanger, "The Six Nations of Grand River Territory's Attempts at Renewing International Political Relationships, 1921–1925," *Canadian Foreign Policy* 13, no. 3 (2007): 29–43.

2 James J. Talman, ed., *Loyalist Narratives from Upper Canada* (Toronto: Champlain Society, 1946), 341.

3 Michael P.P. Simon, "The Haldimand Agreement: A Continuing Covenant," *American Indian Culture and Research Journal* 7, no. 2 (1983): 27–50.

4 Rona Rustige, *Tyendinaga Tales* (Montreal and Kingston: McGill-Queen's University Press, 1988), xi.

5 Charles Hamori-Torok, "The Tyendinaga Mohawks: The Village as a Basic Factor in Mohawk Social Structures," *Ontario History* 57, no. 2 (1965): 69–77.

6 Beth Brant, *I'll Sing the Day Idle: Conversations with Tyendinaga Elders* (Toronto: McGilligan Books, 1995), 15.

7 Canada, *Indian Treaties and Surrenders: From 1680–1902: Treaty Numbers 1–138* (Ottawa: Printed by Brown Chamberlain, Printer to the Queen's Most Excellent Majesty, 1891), 7–8.

8 Deborah Doxtator, "What Happened to the Iroquois Clans? A Study of Clans in Three Nineteenth Century Rotinonhsyonni Communities" (PhD diss., University of Western Ontario, 1996), 95.

9 Canada, *Indian Claims Commission: Annual Report, 2004–05* (Ottawa: Minister of Public Works and Government Services Canada, 2005), 50.

10 See generally Robin Jarvis Brownlie, "'Living the Same as the White People': Mohawk and Anishinabe Women's Labour in Southern Ontario, 1920–1940," *Labour/Le Travail* 61 (Spring 2008): 41–68.

11  See Doxtator, "What Happened to the Iroquois Clans?"

12  Charles Hamori-Torok, "The Iroquois of Akwesasne (St. Regis), Mohawks of the Bay of Quinte (Tyendinaga), Onyota'a:ka (the Onieda of the Thames), and Wahta Mohawk (Gibson)," in *Aboriginal Ontario: Historical Perspectives on the First Nations*, ed. Edward S. Rogers and Donald B. Smith, 258–72 (Toronto: Oxford University Press, 1994), 262–63.

13  Charles Hamori-Torok, "Structures and Factions in Tyendinaga Politics," *Anthropologica* 14, no. 1 (1972): 31–41.

14  Rustige, *Tyendinaga Tales*, xii.

15  Doxtator, "What Happened to the Iroquois Clans?" 165.

16  Earl Hill and James Maracle, both in "Native Violence Could Explode, Chief Tells Rally," *Kingston Whig-Standard*, 29 July 1990, 1.

17  For this discussion, see John Borrows, *Recovering Canada: The Resurgence of Indigenous Law* (Toronto: University of Toronto Press, 2002), 148–50, 159–60. See also Kathryn V. Muller, "Holding Hands with Wampum: Haudenosaunee Council Fires from the Great Law of Peace to Contemporary Relationships with the Canadian State" (PhD diss., Queen's University, 2008).

18  Iris Marion Young, "Two Concepts of Self-Determination," in *Human Rights: Concepts, Contests, Contingencies*, ed. Austin Sarat and Thomas R. Kearns, 25–44 (Ann Arbor: University of Michigan Press, 2001).

19  Jessica Cattelino, *High Stakes: Florida Seminole Gaming and Sovereignty* (Durham, NC: Duke University Press, 2008), 190.

20  *R. v. Sparrow* [1990] 1 SCR 1075; "Natives Fear Reprisals for Spearing Pickerel: Anglers Protest as Mohawks Cite Rights," *Hamilton Spectator*, 20 April 1992, A5.

21  Shawn Brant, in Peter Edwards, "Federal Offices Occupied: Indian Activists 'Standing Up' to Federal Tax Rules," *Toronto Star*, 16 December 1994, A4.

22  Bruce E. Johansen and Barbara A. Mann, eds, *Encyclopedia of the Haudenosaunee (Iroquois Confederacy)* (Westport, CT: Greenwood, 2000), 320–1.

23  James Maracle, in "Mohawks Vow Shutdown as Riot Police End Sitin," *Victoria Times-Colonist*, 5 June 1994, 1.

24  Mario Baptiste, in "'We'll Shut 'Whole Damn Territory'; Ontario Police Arrest 13 in Mohawk vs. Mohawk Clash," *Montreal Gazette*, 5 June 1994, A6.

25  Ibid.

26  Harry Killfoyle, "Occupation to Draw Attention to Problems Facing Natives: Group," *Kingston Whig-Standard*, 16 September 1995, 12.

27 Mario Baptiste, in ibid.

28 Colin Freeze, "Mohawk Activist Resigned to Time Behind Bars," *Globe and Mail*, 2 July 2007, A3.

29 "Native Rights Crusader, Two Others Ordered to Pay $600,000 to Mohawk Band," *National Post*, 19 September 2008, A12.

30 Catherine Dunphy, "Homeless Head to Ottawa to Protest Housing Policy," *Toronto Star*, 10 February 1999, 1. See also Freeze, "Mohawk Activist."

31 Scott Trevethick, "Conflicting Outlooks: The Background to the 1924 Deposing of the Six Nations Hereditary Council" (MA thesis, University of Calgary, 1998), 17–18.

32 Mohawks of the Bay of Quinte, *Tyendinaga Newsletter*, no. 2 (2005).

33 Ibid.

34 Shawn Brant, in "Protest Hits the Road: Mohawks from Tyendinaga Join Natives in Caledonia," *Kingston Whig-Standard*, 24 April 2006, 3.

35 Ian Elliot, "Design Expert, Lawyer to Speak at Landfill Meeting," *Kingston Whig Standard*, 5 January 2006, 7.

36 Don Maracle, in Derek Baldwin, "HELL NO! Tyendinaga Chief Hints at Civil Unrest If Dump Expansion Goes Through," *Belleville Intelligencer*, 28 October 2005, A1.

37 "Native Land Protest Spreads: CN Gets Injunction to Remove Protestors," *Sarnia Observer*, 22 April 2006, A9.

38 Katie Rook, "Train Blockade Strands Passengers as Natives Rally in Support of Caledonia Standoff," *Cornwall Standard-Freeholder*, 22 April 2006, 1.

39 Michelle Thompson and Henry Bury, "Blockade Reflects Native Frustration," *Belleville Intelligencer*, 22 April 2006, A1.

40 "Protest Hits the Road."

41 "Developer Hires Lawyer in Deseronto Land Dispute," CBC *News*, 24 January 2007.

42 Shawn Brant, in Joel Korn, "Mohawk Protesters Show Solidarity: Barricade Halts Rail Traffic near Belleville," *Ottawa Citizen*, 22 April 2006, A5.

43 Leah Keller, "Mohawks Remove Blockade," *Belleville Intelligencer*, 22 April 2006, A1; Joel Korn and Peter Brieger, "Native Protest Strands 3,500 Travellers, Freight," *National Post*, 22 April 2006, A1.

44 Don Maracle, in "Mohawk Protesters Take Over Deseronto," CBC *News*, 23 March 2007; Shawn Brant, in "Ticker," *Toronto Star*, 25 March 2007, A3.

45 Jennifer Ditchburn, "International Link Is Venue for Protest against Summit: Traditional Mohawks Are Helping to Organize April 19 Demonstration," *St Catharines Standard*, 23 March 2001, D6.

46 Russell Roundpoint, in Bryan Parker, "An Emotional Meeting," *Cornwall Standard-Freeholder*, 6 April 2001, 3.

47 Ditchburn, "International Link."

48 Don Maracle, in Allison Jones, "Aboriginal Blockade Shuts Down Train Service," *Whitehorse Star*, 20 April 2007, 16.

49 "First Nations Gathered across the Country – Rallies, Marches," *Turtle Island Native Network's Forums*, 28 June 2007, http://www.turtleisland. org/discussion/viewtopic.php?t=5456.

50 "Native Blockade of Ont. Highway Not Backed by Band: Council," *Canwest News Service*, 21 April 2008. Highway 401 is North America's busiest thoroughfare: 400,000 drivers and 35,000 trucks travel some part of the route daily carrying upward of 460,000 tonnes of goods valued at $1.3 billion. "Transportation Turmoil: There's Hope for Toronto's Traffic Troubles," *OnBoard*, February 2006, 6.

51 "Native Land Protest Spreads: CN Gets Injunction to Remove Protestors," *Sarnia Observer*, 22 April 2006, A9.

52 Shawn Brant, in "Protest Hits the Road."

53 Rachel De Lazzer, "Protest Dissolves, Bypass Reopened: Natives Say Goal Achieved," *Hamilton Spectator*, 30 April 2008, A1.

54 Keller, "Mohawks Remove Blockade."

55 Norm Clark, in "Mohawk Protesters Take Over Deseronto."

56 Shawn Brant, in Jones, "Aboriginal Blockade."

57 Shawn Brant, in Andrew Thomson, "Rail Traffic Resumes as Blockade Lifted: Mohawks Promise More Action over Land-Claims Conflict in Eastern Ontario," *Victoria Times-Colonist*, 22 April 2007, A4.

58 Maria Kubacki and Andrew Thomson, "Mohawk Blockade Disrupts Weekend VIA Travel: Natives Protest Developer's Bid to Build Condos," *Ottawa Citizen*, 21 April 2007, A1.

59 Phil Fontaine, in "CN Rail Drops Part of Suit against Indian Band over Blockade," *National Post*, 17 May 2007, FP6.

60 Paul Barnsley, "Native Leaders Ask: Where's Our Canada?" *Windspeaker* 25, no. 1 (April 2007): 8.

61 Jim Prentice, "Budget Generous to Aboriginals, Minister Says," *Winnipeg Free Press*, 29 March 2007, A12.

62 Phil Fontaine, in "Fontaine Tried to Play Down Threats of Native Blockades," *National Post*, 28 June 2007, A4.

63 Jim Prentice, in "Protests Block 401, Rail Lines: Mohawk Protester Says He'll Turn Himself In to Police Next Week," *Toronto Star*, 29 June 2007.

64 "Beware of Blockades," *Ottawa Citizen*, 28 June 2007, A16.

65 Shawn Brant, in "Protests Block 401."

66 Allison Hanes, "'When Justice Fails, Stop the Rails,' Video Instructs: Primer on Sabotage," *National Post*, 16 May 2007, A5.

67 Sue Collis and Peter Rosenthal, both in Martin Lukacs, "Mohawk Faces 12 Years in Jail for CN Protest: Sue Collis, Wife of Mohawk Activist Shawn Brant, Brings Facts and Context to McGill Students," *McGill Daily* 87, no. 14 (22 October 2007).

68 Mark Hallman, in Joanne Smith, "Police Inaction over Native Blockade Irks CN Rail," *Globe and Mail*, 30 June 2007, A4.

69 W. Wesley Pue, "Trespass and Expressive Rights," paper prepared for the Ipperwash Inquiry, 4 February 2005, 45, http://www.attorneygeneral.jus. gov.on.ca/inquiries/ipperwash/policy_part/research/pdf/Pue.pdf.

70 Lukacs, "Mohawk Faces 12 Years."

71 The wiretap was obtained according to section 184.4 of the Criminal Code of Canada, which allows for "Interception in exceptional circumstances." Notably, in April 2012 the Supreme Court of Canada struck down the law allowing police to tap telephones without a warrant in an emergency, as section 184.4 does not provide an appropriate oversight framework for police actions. See "Supreme Court Tells Parliament to Rewrite Wiretap Law," CBC *News*, 13 April 2012, http://www.cbc.ca/news/canada/story /2012/04/13/supreme-court-wire-tapping.html.

72 Julian Fantino, in "NDP Call for Fantino 'to Resign or Be Fired' over Brant Wiretaps," CBC *News*, 21 July 2008, http://www.cbc.ca/news/canada/ story/2008/07/21/fantino-ndp.html.

73 Julian Fantino, in Ontario Coalition against Poverty, "Brant/Fantino Transcripts," 29 June 2007, http://www.ocap.ca/supporttmt/files/ brant-transcript-24.pdf.

74 Sidney B. Linden, *Report of the Ipperwash Inquiry*, 4 vols, Attorney General of Ontario, Toronto, 2007, vol. 4, 79, 86, http://knet.ca/ documents/Ipperwash-Executive-Summary-Vol4.pdf.

75 Julian Fantino, in "Ontario Police Almost Moved in on 2007 Mohawk Blockades," CBC *News*, 18 July 2008, http://www.cbc.ca/news/canada/ story/2008/07/18/fantino-blockade.html.

76 Don Maracle, in Jones, "Aboriginal Blockade."

77 Tiffany Crawford, "Cops Dismantle Native Blockade," *Windsor Star*, 29 April 2008, C5.

78 Dan Doreen, in "Mohawk Protesters Set Up Blockade in Eastern Ont. Town," CBC *News*, 21 April 2008.

79 Ibid.

80 Julian Fantino, in Linda Nguyen, "Charges Possible for Road Blockage," *Windsor Star*, 23 April 2008, C11.

81 Theo Nibourg and Emile Nibourg, in Linda Nguyen, "Charges Eyed in Native Highway Blockade: Anyone Guilty of Criminal Acts 'Will Be Held Accountable,'" *National Post*, 23 April 2008, A10.

82 Lisa Varano, "Protesters Close Hanlon: Group Says Half-Hour Protest Was to Show Solidarity with Natives in Deseronto," *Guelph Mercury*, 29 April 2008, A1.

83 De Lazzer, "Protest Dissolves."

84 Brant Bardy, in Tracey Scott, "No Thanks: Ontario Native Leaders Have a Message for Guelph Protesters," *Guelph Mercury*, 30 April 2008, A1.

85 "Protesters Arrested at Occupied Quarry," *Kamloops Daily News*, 26 April 2008, A10.

86 Jason Maracle, Margo Geduld, Don Maracle, and Dan Doreen, all in "Mohawks Halt Talks with Feds over Deseronto Land Claim," CBC *News*, 18 June 2008.

87 "Mohawk Protesters Block Ontario Bridge over Arming of Border Guards," CBC *News*, 8 June 2009, http://www.cbc.ca/news/canada/mohawk-protesters-block-ontario-bridge-over-arming-of-border-guards-1.851640.

88 Jeremy Ashley and W. Brice McVicar, "Blockade Dismantled Early Friday Evening," *Belleville Intelligencer*, 12 June 2009.

89 "Mohawk Police Chief's Vehicle Shot Up," *Belleville Intelligencer*, 13 June 2009.

90 This evident factionalism within First Nations recalls the Pine Ridge conflict of the early 1970s, which developed into a civil war that resulted in more than sixty-one homicides from 1973 to 1976. See Ward Churchill and Jim Vander Wall, "AIM Casualties on Pine Ridge, 1973–1976," in *Indians Are Us? Culture and Genocide in Native North America*, ed. Ward Churchill, 197–205 (Monroe, ME: Common Courage, 1994).

91 Ministry of Tourism, *Regional Tourism Profiles, 2008: Hastings County* (Ontario: Ministry of Tourism, 2009).

# Your Home on Native Land?
# Conflict and Controversy at Caledonia and the Six Nations of the Grand River

TIMOTHY C. WINEGARD

The record of Aboriginal barricades since Oka in 1990 – from Ipperwash and Gustafsen Lake to the Mohawks of the Bay of Quinte and Akwesasne – demonstrates that direct confrontation has increased. Certain elements of the Aboriginal population erect barricades or (re)occupy lands as a means to promote legitimate grievances and bring governments to the negotiating table. For a minority of others, however, these actions represent an opportune avenue to safeguard lucrative commercial enterprises – such as gambling, the tobacco trade, and a sophisticated smuggling network – with a view to intimidating domestic residents, usurping authority, and establishing "no-go zones" for internal and external security forces. To the detriment of those engaged in justifiable protest, this minority often usurps control of the original political action to promote their own interests under the guise of historical grievance. Like the Oka Crisis, subsequent blockades and barricades, including those by the Six Nations, have been exercises of power on intertwined political, social, and economic frontiers – not only between First Nations and governments but internally within First Nations themselves. Understanding the historical roots, the agendas of multiple, webbed actors or factions, and the divisive atmosphere surrounding Aboriginal barricades is a challenge in its own right. This understanding, however, is made all the more complex by the inevitable, often sensationalized, media exposure and disinformation campaigns that accompany Aboriginal actions.[1] Comparing Aboriginal barricades is specious in that each bears a unique history and must be researched, mediated, and resolved within its individual context.

Nevertheless, comparisons are useful to highlight the differences between what appear to be analogous elements of Aboriginal blockades.

The Government of Canada assessed future Aboriginal "hot-spots" during the Oka Crisis. In response to other First Nations communities' support for the Mohawks in 1990, the Canadian Forces and other security agencies completed a threat assessment of reserves to determine where potential violence was most likely. The final document was called "The Next Oka." Heading the list of 118 locations was Stony Point at Ipperwash.[2] In 1995 this prediction became reality. The confrontation culminated in the death of Anthony O'Brien (Dudley) George and a drawn-out inquiry into the actions of the Ontario Provincial Police, the Ontario government, and Premier Mike Harris.

The Six Nations of the Grand River, boasting the largest Aboriginal population in Canada (23,289 as of 31 December 2008), were not included in the 1990 threat assessment. Although its population delivered food, clothes, and other provisions to the Mohawks at Kanesatake and Kahnawake during the Oka Crisis, the Six Nations of the Grand River remained relatively detached from the militant posture and political demands of the Warriors and their supporters.[3] Nevertheless, on 28 February 2006, barricades were erected along Highway 6 near the Six Nations Reserve south of Caledonia, Ontario. Residents from the reserve, mostly Mohawks, were joined by others from Akwesasne and New York State to protest the construction of a new subdivision with seventy-two homes (of which only ten were in various stages of production) called Douglas Creek Estates by the local firm of Henco Industries Limited. To the public and media, these actions outwardly mirrored the beginnings of the Oka Crisis sixteen years earlier.[4]

## TITLE, TREATIES, AND THE LAND CLAIMS PROCESS FOR THE GRAND RIVER TRACT

Although commonly known as the Six Nations, the band has a membership list that formally incorporates thirteen distinct bands, and marriage has led to the adoption of Aboriginal people from other nations and of non-Aboriginal people from across southern Ontario. Furthermore, the original migrants from the United States in 1784, following the American Revolution (1775–83), were not solely representative of the Six Nations (Iroquois, or Haudenosaunee) Confederacy (from east to west: Mohawk, Oneida, Onondaga, Cayuga, Seneca, and as of 1722, Tuscarora).[5]

From the time of its consolidation in what is now New York State in the mid-fifteenth century, the Iroquois Confederacy was the most proficient political and military Aboriginal coalition east of the Mississippi River and north of what became the Mason-Dixon Line. The Iroquois used a combination of military might and skilled diplomacy to attain an empire (albeit short-lived) that served the British as a protective buffer between British North America and the French and later the Americans. The confederacy, which reached its zenith of power in the seventeenth century, was a powerful British ally in colonial warfare, so much so that during the American Revolution a lengthy report was submitted to the colonial secretary, Thomas Townshend (Lord Sydney), detailing "Means Suggested as the Most Probable to Retain the Six Nations ... in the King's Interest." In return, Joseph Brant (Thayendengea) sought assurance from the Crown that his Mohawk, and Iroquoian, brethren were still regarded and treated "as His Majesty's faithful allies, and have that support and countenance such as old and true friends expect."[6] This allegiance, however, was maintained through the confederacy's adherence to the belief that its nations, as a collective, were a sovereign political entity and imperial military ally. Robert S. Allen argues that, "historically, the 'faithful Mohawks' had been loyal and active military allies of the crown since well before the days of Sir William Johnson. At Oka in the summer of 1990, with the Mohawk combating forces of the crown, the wheel had come full turn."[7]

In this atmosphere of imperial cooperation with the British, and as a result of treaties signed with the Crown, the confederacy and its member nations regarded themselves (and still do) as autonomous within the confines of North America. The Two-Row Wampum Belt and Silver Covenant Chain, originally agreed to by the confederacy and the Dutch in 1613, were extended to the British in 1664 and again via the covenant chain in 1677. In 1794 they continued with the United States through the Treaty of Canandaigua. The two parallel beaded purple rows of the wampum belt signify the mutual coexistence of two sovereign entities – the Iroquois and a European partner – in North America.[8] Accordingly, First Nations fought and allied with a European partner to promote and protect their own interests and agendas. According to J.R. Miller, "notions that one nation, or another, took up arms to advance a commercial or strategic aim of the French or British were erroneous."[9]

Following the American Revolution, Lieutenant General Sir Frederick Haldimand, the governor and military commander of the Province of

Quebec and surrounding territories, reported to Whitehall in 1784 that "the fidelity of these Indians [Six Nations] has alone preserved the Upper Country."[10] In recognition of their service to the Crown, Loyalist Iroquois and their allies, under Joseph Brant, were given lands in Ontario along the Grand River under the tenets of the Haldimand Proclamation. The previous year, other Mohawks under John Deserontyon (or Deseronto) had been granted land at the Bay of Quinte (Tyendinaga) east of Belleville. Although Brant appealed for their relocation to the Grand River, Deserontyon and his 200 Mohawk followers refused.[11]

On 25 October 1784, Haldimand signed a document now known as the Haldimand Proclamation:

> Whereas His Majesty having been pleased to direct that in
> Consideration of the early Attachment to his Cause manifested by
> the Mohawk Indians and of the loss of their Settlement, which
> they thereby sustained, that a convenient Tract of Land under his
> protection, should be chosen as a safe and Comfortable Retreat for
> them and others of the Six Nations, who have either lost their
> Settlements within the Territory of the American States, or wish to
> retire from them to the British; I have at the earnest desire of many
> of these His Majesty's faithful Allies purchased a Tract of Land
> from the Indians situated between the Lakes Ontario, Huron, and
> Erie And I do hereby in His Majesty's name Authorise and permit
> the said Mohawk Nation, and such other of the Six Nation Indians
> as wish to settle in that Quarter to take possession of and settle
> upon the Banks of the River commonly called, Ouse, or Grand
> River, running into Lake Erie; Allotting to them for that purpose
> six miles deep from each side of the River beginning at Lake Erie,
> and Extending in that proportion to the Head of the said River,
> which them and their posterity are to enjoy for ever.[12]

Given the ambiguous wording of the proclamation, the exact boundaries of the grant were unspecified. Estimations and surveys conducted between 1791 and 1821 varied, and the original allocation was between 570,000 and 675,000 acres. The 1821 survey conducted by Thomas Rideout, concluding the original grant to be 674,910 acres, was subsequently accepted and maintained by the Crown. The Six Nations argue that the original grant was upward of 950,000 acres.

The land in question, acquired legally through a quit claim deed from the Mississauga on 22 May 1784, is mentioned in no less than seventeen pre-Confederation Crown documents with conflicting views of title, lease, and ownership.[13] Like most land claims, interpretations and perspectives concerning treaties, documents, and occupation are often disparate. The claim of the Six Nations at Caledonia adheres to this paradigm. These decrees, in conjunction with occupancy, are vital to understanding the basis for the land dispute and, in turn, possible approaches to resolution.

Lawyer John Hagopian identifies five evolving legal rights that justify land claims under Canadian law:

1 *Sovereignty*: a land right belonging to the political society that has jurisdiction over the lands.
2 *Fee simple ownership*: ownership of land in the usual sense, limited only by taxation, eminent domain, police power, and escheat – short, however, of allodial title (which is free of such encumbrances).
3 *Aboriginal title*: a group of rights that, in Canada, flow from continuous, exclusive occupancy of land by an Aboriginal society or nation when not extinguished by treaty. These rights continue to be defined by courts and are usually the basis for a comprehensive land claim. The Delgamuukw case (1997) was the precedent for such rights in the aftermath of the Supreme Court decisions in the Calder case (1974) and the Guerin case (1984), both vaguely recognizing Aboriginal title.
4 *Exclusive occupancy rights*: a right to possess, but not own, land.
5 *Usufructory rights*: the right to use the resources of the land, such as game, fish, and other natural resources, as outlined in treaties or inherent Aboriginal title. The Sparrow (1990) and Marshall (1999) cases were the precedents for such rights.[14]

Since 1970 formal land claims have usually been submitted to the federal government through the Department of Indian Affairs as either comprehensive or specific. A comprehensive claim is based upon historical use and occupancy "since time immemorial" and focuses on unextinguished Aboriginal title. A specific land claim refers to claims made by an Aboriginal group or nation against the federal government, which relate to the administration of land and other assets and to the fulfilment of obligations made in treaties. Each claim must be based on evidence proving the government's failure to fulfil treaty rights or to administer lands in question.[15]

At European contact, the Grand River watershed was occupied by the Attiwanderon (Neutral) Nation, which first encountered French missionaries around 1615. These Iroquoian-speaking peoples were conquered and killed, displaced, or absorbed by the Five Nations Confederacy in 1651 during its forays into southern Ontario and Quebec to secure dominance in the lucrative trade of furs for weapons and to augment a declining population. Weakened and overstretched, the confederacy was driven out of southern Ontario in 1695–96 by a coalition of Ojibwa, Odawa, and Potawatomi and would return to traditional lands in the United States (predominantly New York State) by the early eighteenth century. The Mississauga gradually moved into southern Ontario from Manitoulin Island and surrounds, occupying the Grand River area until 1784, when they surrendered title to the Crown for the creation of the Haldimand Tract.[16]

On 19 July 1701, shortly after the Five Nations were driven back to their ancestral homelands, twenty chiefs signed the Nanfan Treaty (or "Deed from the Five Nations to the King, of Their Beaver Hunting Ground") with John Nanfan, acting colonial governor of New York. Ratified on 14 September 1726, this agreement forever ceded to the Crown a large tract of land surrounding the Great Lakes, including the land later conferred to Brant in the Haldimand Proclamation: "[A]ll that Land where the Bever [sic] hunting is w$^{ch}$ we won by the Sword 80-years ago & pray that He [the King] may be our Protector & Defendor there; And desire that our Secretary may write an Instrument w$^{ch}$ we will Sign & Seal that it may be carried by him to the King." In return, the Five Nations were guaranteed timeless hunting rights and protection under the British Crown.[17] Hagopian argues that "by the Nanfan treaty, the Five Nations and their successors forever surrendered any claim they might have had to sovereignty, aboriginal title, fee simple ownership, and exclusive occupancy to the subject lands that were 800 miles long and 400 miles wide extending from New York State to Georgian Bay to Mackinac Island to beyond Chicago and back to New York State. The treaty is best understood within its historical context."[18]

By 1701 the confederacy had been fighting wars on all fronts, had been reduced in population, and had begun to seek a means to secure its interests in the fur trade so that it could acquire weapons to stave off traditional enemies. In a strategic course of action, it signed a peace treaty with the French, declaring neutrality in any future conflict between Britain and France, while gaining access to select French trading posts. Similarly, it signed the Nanfan Treaty with the British, surrendering all rights to the land, save for hunting, which was of primary concern. However, the treaty was dubious since neither the British nor the confederacy had extensive control over the land in question and since the French did not recognize the treaty or British claims of sovereignty. Furthermore, even the British were confused about whether the confederacy had surrendered sovereignty and ownership of the lands, as the wording and content of the treaty itself are convoluted and nebulous.[19]

Following the British defeat of the French in North America during the Seven Years' War (1756–63), King George III issued the Royal Proclamation of 1763, which declared British sovereignty over a vast territory that included former French possessions and Ontario (and those lands ceded in the Nanfan Treaty). The Quebec Act of 1774 reinforced the tenets of the proclamation. At these times, the Six Nations did not occupy lands in the region; rather, they resided in New York State and in French-Catholic mission settlements along the St Lawrence River such as Kahnawake, Kanesatake, and Akwesasne (after having been relocated and renamed multiple times). According to the Royal Proclamation,

And whereas it is just and reasonable ... that the several Nations or Tribes of Indians with whom We are connected, and who live under our Protection, should not be molested or disturbed in the Possession of such Parts of Our Dominions and Territories as, not having been ceded or purchased by Us, are reserved to them, or any of them, as Hunting Grounds – We do therefore ... declare it to be our Royal Will and Pleasure, that no Governor or Commander in Chief in any of our Colonies ... do presume, upon any pretence, whatever, to grant Warrants of Survey, or pass any Patents for Lands beyond the Bounds of their respective Governments ... upon any Lands whatever, which, not having been ceded to or purchased by Us as foresaid, are reserved to the said Indians, or any of them.

The proclamation also required that persons residing on land "reserved to the said Indians as aforesaid, forthwith ... remove themselves from such Settlements." Lastly, to protect Indians from "great Frauds and Abuses," the proclamation forbade the purchase or transfer of any lands directly from Indians. This jurisdiction was vested solely in the Crown.[20] These principles were enshrined in section 35 (1) of the Constitution Act of 1982, which recognized and affirmed "the existing aboriginal and treaty rights of the aboriginal peoples of Canada." Subsequent Supreme Court decisions confirmed unextinguished Aboriginal title as an "existing" right, as section 35 (3) "includes rights that now exist by way of land claims agreements or may be so acquired."[21] Hagopian argues that the lands of the Haldimand Tract

> were provided in an occupancy permit during the pleasure of the Crown. No ownership rights could be given to the Six Nations because King George's Proclamation of 1763 clarified that Indians on British lands were not sovereign and could not own lands; the only right they could be given were occupancy rights ... Haldimand issued his proclamation in 1784 in this legal context. He authorized the Six Nations to '[take possession of and] settle upon' the lands at the Grand River. There was no mention of aboriginal sovereignty, fee simple title, or anything resembling ownership rights.[22]

In summary, the land claim of the Six Nations does not fall under the parameters of the comprehensive claim framework. First, given that the Six Nations did not occupy the lands at the time of contact, they have no claim to Aboriginal title. This right was vested in the Attiwanderon (Neutral) Nation, which was conquered by the Five Nations in 1651 and ceased to exist as a distinguishable entity. Otherwise, it might lie with the Mississauga, who relinquished title in 1784. According to J.R. Miller, "neither British officials nor the Mississauga said or did anything that indicated they thought any group but the Anicinabe had a claim to the lands to which Britain hoped to move displaced Loyalists and First Nations allies."[23] The Five Nations only briefly occupied the land between 1651 and 1696. Second, sovereignty over these specific lands cannot be asserted by way of the Nanfan Treaty and the Royal Proclamation, which specifically refer to lands not previous ceded or purchased by the Crown. The Iroquois ceded the lands in question in the 1701 Nanfan Treaty, and the Crown purchased them from the Mississauga in 1784. Third, fee simple ownership of the land is not possible under the Royal Proclamation, the Constitution Act, and the Indian Act. Therefore, the Six Nations arguably possess limited occupancy title to the land in question, excluding the boundaries of the current reserve.

Conflicting interpretations of the treaty and proclamation and issues of legitimacy concerning the sale, lease, or transfer of lands of the original Haldimand Tract, including the parcel in question, by both the government and Joseph Brant lie at the core of the Caledonia protest and claim. If validated, the grievances of the Six Nations represent a failure of the federal government to properly administer lands or revenue from lands reserved for them – justification for a specific land claim. Conversely, Hagopian asserts that the Haldimand Proclamation was not a formal treaty. Therefore, the federal government cannot be at fault for any mismanagement, and the actions of Joseph Brant, whether fair or foul, are irrelevant.[24]

When Brant, Loyalist Iroquois, and their allies occupied the Haldimand Tract in 1784–85, the Crown and Brant immediately disagreed over title and the land transaction, with lasting and unresolved implications. John Graves Simcoe, the lieutenant governor of Upper Canada, confirmed the lands of the Haldimand Tract on 14 January 1793 in a limited deed, after having reduced it to 111,000 hectares the previous year. Known as the "Simcoe Patent," it specified that the Six Nations could dispose or surrender land only directly to the Crown, that all other leases, sales, and grants to non–Six Nations people were unlawful, and that such people occupying said lands would be evicted. Although these principles followed the Royal Proclamation, Brant and the majority of chiefs rejected them.

In 1795, in the face of strong objections from the Crown, thirty-five chiefs (some self-appointed) gave Brant power of attorney to sell and lease lands of the tract and to invest the proceeds for the Six Nations community. Brant reasoned that money was needed to establish the settlement and initiate agriculture. He also viewed prosperous Euro-Canadian families and farmers (many of whom were personal acquaintances) astride Six Nations communities as a means to encourage and teach his people successful farming techniques and Euro-Canadian culture. Between 1795 and 1812 the administration of Upper Canada repeatedly tried to halt or regulate Brant and the chiefs' sale or leasing of land through orders-in-council and royal instructions. Nevertheless, from 1795 to 1797 Brant sold almost 381,500 acres (mostly in the northern half) to speculators for 85,332 pounds. The speculators, however, were unable to resell enough land to meet payments. By 1801 all were in arrears, prompting Brant to sell more lands.[25]

In 1798 the Six Nations appointed and authorized three land trustees, an arrangement that, although modified, lasted until 1839, when power was vested in Indian Affairs. Then in 1835 the Crown received legal authorization from Six Nations chiefs to lease and develop the lands along Plank Road (now Highway 6) in trust for the Six Nations. The Crown, however, began selling these lands to third parties. To complicate matters, in 1840 the government recommended creating a reserve of 8,000 hectares south of the Grand River, with the remainder of lands to

be either leased or sold. On 18 January 1841 the Crown and chiefs pur-
portedly agreed that the Crown could lease or sell lands outside of the
prescribed reserve, with the money invested for the Six Nations. On
three occasions in the ensuing two years, however, chiefs petitioned
the government over the 1841 agreement, stating that the Six Nations
had not reached consensus (traditionally customary for the Longhouse
Council under the Great Law of Peace), that too few chiefs had signed
the agreement, and that those who had acquiesced had been "intimidated" into doing so.[26] They also argued that the boundaries of the proposed reserve were too small and requested 22,000 hectares. In December
1844 the Crown and forty-seven chiefs reached an agreement authorizing the sale of lands along Plank Road. George Marlot Ryckman purchased this specific tract of land on 15 May 1848 for 57 pounds and
10 shillings, and the Crown issued him a land deed. Two years later, the
Crown passed a proclamation setting the reserve at 19,000 hectares. The
chiefs agreed, and the current reserve comprises roughly 18,800 hectares
(46,500 acres).[27]

In 1992 Henco Industries purchased a company that presumably
owned the 40 vacant hectares of what eventually became Douglas Creek
Estates. Henco Industries argued that the parcel of land was originally
granted to the Six Nations in the form of a licence to occupy but that
ownership was vested with the Crown. The Six Nations disputed this
claim and began to oppose the sale in 1995.[28]

In March the Six Nations sued the federal and provincial governments, citing fourteen specific allegations over the Douglas Creek
lands.[29] The federal government did not accept the Six Nations' specific
claim, and the issue remained unsettled following meetings between the
Six Nations and federal and provincial representatives in 1999, 2000,
and 2001. In fact, between 1976 and 1995 the Six Nations of the Grand
River submitted twenty-nine specific land claims concerning various
portions of the Haldimand Tract. All were closed or not accepted by
Indian Affairs, and no settlements were negotiated or concluded.
According to the Six Nations, these claims were submitted based on four
arguments under the framework for specific claims:

i  Were the terms of the October 25, 1784 Haldimand Proclamation
   and other treaties fulfilled and honoured;
ii  Were the alienation[s] of portions of the Six Nations tract undertaken
   lawfully;
iii  Were the terms and conditions of the alienation[s] fulfilled; and

iv Were the financial assets derived from the land alienations properly accounted for and maximized to benefit the Six Nations of the Grand River Indians?[30]

The federal government contends that the dispute over Caledonia "is not a land claims matter [and] has nothing to do with the federal government." Accordingly, it has not participated in resolving it.[31]

Like the 1990 Oka Crisis and the rejected Kanesatake Mohawk land claims in 1975 and 1977, confrontation at Caledonia followed repeated refusals to address local grievances. The admission of such claims – even if the outcome decided against the submitting First Nation – would have demonstrated the willingness of the government to consider grievances and conduct research. It also would have avoided public scrutiny, sensationalized media exposure, and civil disobedience. Nevertheless, in this case – as at Oka and Ipperwash – federal inaction led to confrontation between Aboriginal protestors, federal and provincial law enforcement personnel, and local non-Aboriginal residents.[32]

## CONTENTION AND CONFLICT

In July 2005 the blueprint for the planned Douglas Creek Estates received registered approval, and the Province of Ontario guaranteed title to the property.[33] On 26 October, Six Nations chief David General wrote a letter to Henco Industries warning the company of the probable dangers of developing the property. On 28 February 2006 roughly two dozen Aboriginal protestors began to occupy Douglas Creek Estates and prevented construction workers from entering the building zone. They brought forward a motorhome and erected tents and a small barricade (complete with Haudenosaunee and Mohawk Warrior flags) on the access road west of Highway 6. Signs reading "Canada, your home on Native Land," "Thou shall not steal, including Land," and "This country needs a true history lesson" were visible along the highway. Although the elected band council did not officially support this direct action, protestor spokesperson Dawn Smith stated that the council did not have jurisdiction over land issues and that "it doesn't matter if they support us or not." The following day, Janie Jamieson replaced her as the leading voice of the protestors, who called for a moratorium on the building of the subdivision. No moratorium was negotiated or granted by the courts.[34]

On 3 March, Ontario Superior Court Justice David Marshall issued an injunction "requiring the occupiers to clear the site by March 10,

2006 at 10:00 am." They did not leave but instead burned the court order. Two weeks later, Marshall issued a second injunction stipulating
that if the protestors did not vacate the site by 2:00 PM on 22 March,
the Ontario Provincial Police (OPP) would arrest them for contempt of
court.[35] As the deadline approached, there was no indication that the Six
Nations faction and its supporters were prepared to break camp. Shortly
before the deadline, the OPP stated that they did not intend to arrest or
remove the group by force. Instead, they parked patrol cars along the
northern and southern boundaries of the barricade and monitored
the situation. Also present was a throng of journalists and media, including the Canadian Broadcasting Corporation (CBC). The barricade at
Caledonia had gone from a local dispute to a national story.[36]

The protestors asked for negotiations with the federal government
and the Department of Indian Affairs on a nation-to-nation level, citing
the Royal Proclamation. Developer Don Henning thanked the community for its support and stressed to local residents that the "Six Nations
people are our neighbours and friends … We are being held hostage between a splinter group and the federal government, a situation over
which we have no control." He added, "We have done nothing wrong or
illegal. The real problem is with the federal government. It has nothing
to do with us. We are caught in the middle. We'd like to see a quick and
peaceful resolution to this."[37] He repeatedly appealed to the minister of
Indian affairs, Jim Prentice, to help resolve the land dispute. The only
response from Indian Affairs was to send an emissary on a "fact-finding
mission." The people at the barricade did not welcome Michael Coyle, a
law professor from the University of Western Ontario,[38] who was asked
"to investigate the nature of the grievances, identify the jurisdictional
implications and explore the possibility for mediation." According to
Indian Affairs, the dossier on Six Nations' claims already contained
some 70,000 pages of materials dating back to the seventeenth century.[39] The protestors insisted that they were "here for the long haul until
it is recognized as Six Nations territory."[40] Accordingly, after just three
days on site, Coyle was "given his walking papers," journalist Paul Legall
reported. The clan mothers "said to him to send somebody of more
importance to the table."[41]

On 29 March the OPP met with the Six Nations chiefs and the clan
mothers and hinted that they would remove the protestors by force. This
was challenged by Michael (Sahtakaientes) Laughing of Akwesasne, one
of about two dozen men behind the barricade. He repeated that his own

clan mothers of Akwesasne had ordered him to the barricade in order to protect the people and the land. "If I have to die here that's what I'm going to do," he told reporters. "They will have to kill me to take me out of here." Laughing also alluded to the Great Law of Peace, the Two-Row Wampum Belt, Oka, and the allegation that elected band councils are an oppressive appendage of the federal government. "I hope the world sees this," he noted. "We are here ready for a confrontation again."[42] Deirdre McCracken, a spokesperson for Minister of Indian Affairs Jim Prentice, reiterated that the blockade "has nothing to do with the federal government. This isn't a land-claims matter. The actual root of the problem is *not a land claim*."[43]

Up to this point, the protest remained peaceful and relations with local Caledonia residents were, for the most part, cordial. Some stopped by to chat, offer support, and deliver supplies. However, this relatively affable relationship would not last. As the protest extended into April, groups of local residents began to confront the protestors directly. The minister of community safety and correctional services at Queen's Park, Monte Kwinter, proclaimed that he was "absolutely staying out of it. All you have to do is take a look at the Ipperwash Inquiry. It's not my role to interfere with operational issues of the OPP."[44] On 5 April in an incident eerily mirroring the Oka Crisis, 300 to 400 angry Caledonians gathered in front of the OPP station to protest police and federal government inaction. The Caledonia OPP detachment released a public statement stressing that it did not intend to forcibly remove the protestors from the site, stating that the OPP had learned their lesson at Ipperwash in connection with the fatal shooting of Dudley George.[45] Numerous Caledonia residents responded by urging officials to deploy the Canadian Forces (CF). "I understand they [Six Nations] have a cause," said one unidentified man. "But as Canadian citizens they also have to abide by the law of the land. The only thing I don't understand is why the army, the police or somebody else in authority doesn't go in and put a stop to it."[46] This reflected a misunderstanding of the legal framework governing the domestic deployment of the CF, which is not intended as a "court of last resort" to end protracted, negotiable Aboriginal grievances. Furthermore, unlike the Warriors at Oka, who possessed an assortment of sophisticated weapons, including rocket-propelled grenades, antipersonnel mines, .50 calibre sniper rifles, and a wide range of automatic rifles and heavy machine guns, the protestors at Caledonia were not armed.

Although the OPP were reluctant to use force to solve the dispute, the court order compelled them to act. At roughly 4:30 AM on 20 April, OPP officers raided the protest lines using helicopters, tear gas, pepper spray, and Tasers. After violent skirmishes, the OPP retreated in the face of an unexpected and rapid response from the Six Nations community. Sixteen Aboriginal protestors were arrested, but the remainder refused to vacate the site – and the barricade remained. Maurice Pilon, the deputy commissioner of the OPP, acknowledged that the police had "no immediate plans to go in there again."[47] Similar to the repercussions of the failed Sûreté du Québec raid at Kanesatake on 11 July 1990 and of the failed OPP raid at Ipperwash on 6 September 1995, the ramifications of the OPP's actions extended beyond the Six Nations Reserve. Mohawks in Kahnawake responded by raising Warrior flags and temporarily blocking the Mercier Bridge, as they had done after 11 July 1990. Joe Delaronde, spokesperson for the Mohawk Council of Kahnawake, explained that "the message was: No one wants another 1990."[48] Mohawks from Tyendinaga lit bonfires on a Canadian National Railway line, suspending cargo and passenger rail service for two days. A railway bridge near Caledonia was set ablaze. A van was hurled over a bypass on Highway 6, and a new barricade was erected on the highway using burning tires and gravel. On Argyle Street South in Caledonia, two more barricades were erected by Aboriginal protestors using a dump truck, tires, and gravel, blocking the road to both the north and south of the original barricade on the service road leading into the subdivision.[49] The Mohawks at Tyendinaga, in a situation appearing similar to that of Caledonia, occupied a disputed potential subdivision on 15 November 2006. Suffice it to say, incidents at one location directly influenced those at the other from 2006 to 2008.[50]

In response to the growing unrest, the Grand Erie School Board and the Brant-Haldimand School Board closed their schools for the two days following the 20 April raid. This action was similar to that at Akwesasne from April to May 1990 during the zenith of the Mohawk "civil war" between factions divided over gaming and smuggling. In addition to the swelling number of OPP officers, members of the Royal Canadian Mounted Police (RCMP) also became a more regular presence at the barricades. Correspondingly, Aboriginal numbers at the multiple barricades increased, with people filtering in from parts of Ontario and the United States, including members of various Warrior Societies. Although "appreciative of the support," Six Nations chief David General publicly appealed for members of other First Nations not to come to Caledonia, "as the situation is at a crisis stage."[51] After all, the Aboriginal protestors were met by an increasingly larger and more hostile crowd of local Caledonia residents, backed by members of outside, radical, racially motivated groups.[52]

As in 1990 at Kahnawake and Chateauguay, the police found themselves in the precarious position as an intermediary force between Aboriginal and non-Aboriginal protestors. On 24 April roughly 3,000 area residents marched toward the police lines. During the ensuing violence, police vehicles were smashed, and sporadic fights erupted between Aboriginals, local residents, and police forces before order was restored and the angry crowds melted away. This ugly scene was repeated on 29 April. Non-Aboriginal protestors regularly appeared at the barricades. Caledonia businesses suffered from the blockade of the two major north-south traffic arteries (Highway 6 and Argyle Street), and residents grew increasingly restless about perceived police inaction.[53] "It's really dividing the community," Mayor Marie Trainer lamented. "It's sad because we lived beside each other for 300 years ... after this is over we want to go on being friends, neighbours and families."[54]

Following the 20 April violence, Caledonia residents (including Trainer) again urged that the CF be deployed. Local farmer Woodrow Sparks pleaded, "Bring in the army, if you can't stop it with diplomacy and dialogue." During a rally on 25 April, a woman held up a placard reading, "Invoke the War Measures Act." She told a reporter, "If these people are not Canadians, then they're bloody terrorists."[55] Although this sign illustrated public ignorance about when the CF could be legally deployed during times of civil disobedience or other internal threats, it indicated the depth of frustration with the status quo. In April 2008 Brantford City Council, tiring of frequent Six Nations protests at various construction or development sites, filed an injunction for the deployment of the CF due to the "increased frequency of, and sites affected by, the defendant's [Six Nations'] unlawful activities ... a physical confrontation and disturbance of the peace or riot is inevitable and imminent." Aware of the parameters sanctioning CF use, the council cited section 275 of the National Defence Act and requested that the Superior Court justice send notice to the attorney general of Ontario that "the services of the Canadian Forces are required in aid to the civil power because a disturbance of the peace or riot is occurring or is likely to occur." No action was ever taken by the CF.[56] Nevertheless, it was conducting intelligence assessments in unison with other federal agencies and was developing contingency plans for a possible, yet improbable, "aid to the civil power" operation at Caledonia.[57]

As tensions mounted, the Six Nations, Henco Industries, and the Province of Ontario continued political negotiations. Although federal minister of Indian affairs Jim Prentice monitored the situation and communicated with his provincial and municipal government counterparts, most notably Ontario minister of Aboriginal affairs David Ramsey and local member of Parliament Diane Finley, both he and Prime Minister Stephen Harper insisted that the dispute remained a provincial matter.[58] On 30 April the Government of Ontario responded by appointing a chief arbitrator, former Liberal Ontario premier David Peterson, who held thirteen negotiating sessions between 29 April and 5 June. Peterson stated that he was aware of the complexities of the situation. "The genius here is to find common ground," he told reporters. "The reality is this has been going on for 200 years, so we have to find something that everybody wins with ... What you fear is something like the permanent stain of an Oka." Peterson also contradicted Prime Minister Harper by insisting that Ottawa had the biggest role "by a long-shot" in solving the Six Nations standoff.[59] The leaders of the protest agreed, still upholding their argument that it was a Crown issue as set forth in the Royal Proclamation. Seeking international recognition, Clan Mother Doreen Silversmith relayed this and other grievances to the United Nations Permanent Forum on Indigenous Peoples in Geneva, Switzerland, on 1 May, mirroring a submission by the Kanesatake Mohawks in 1990.[60]

Growing frustrations over the political impasse and the barricades heightened tensions in Caledonia itself. On 16 May, Aboriginal protestors removed part of the barricade on Highway 6, allowing traffic on one lane of the road, stopping each vehicle that passed through. They also issued identification cards to those living behind the barrier. Non-Aboriginal residents responded by erecting their own barricade, preventing protestors from entering the disputed site. In what was described as a "gesture of good will," Six Nations protestors were to remove the barricade on Highway 6 at 8:00 AM on 22 May after the government announced an indefinite moratorium on construction the previous day. This promise did not mollify the non-Aboriginal protestors.

At roughly noon on the 22 May, a human barricade was formed across Highway 6, preventing Six Nations members from passing through. Shortly thereafter, Aboriginal protestors re-established their barricade using an electrical transmission tower. In addition, two backhoes were used to tear a trench across the road. Soon, Six Nations and non-Aboriginal protestors began trading punches and racial slurs. The OPP quickly formed a buffer between the hostile groups. During the violent exchanges, vandals shut down a transformer in Caledonia, cutting power to 8,000 residents in surrounding Norfolk and Haldimand Counties. The OPP Emergency Response Team arrived later that night in riot gear to shore up the police buffer zone, and calm was restored.[61]

The following day, seventeen schools were closed due to the ongoing power disruption, which was resolved on 24 May at a cost of $1.5 million. Also on 23 May the barricade on Highway 6 was removed, and the trench was filled in; however, barricades still remained on Argyle Street and at the original site. Following a week of relative calm, Ontario Superior Court Justice David Marshall ordered all parties involved in the dispute to a special court session in order to explain why his initial court order for the Aboriginal protestors to be evicted was not enforced. The session appeared futile and nothing was resolved.

The situation at the barricades escalated on 9 June with a series of violent events all occurring within the period of one hour. The first incident involved a couple in their seventies, Kathe and Guenter Golke, from Simcoe, Ontario, who pulled their car over to the side of the road near the protest site. Six Nations demonstrators quickly surrounded the car, forcibly removed the occupants, and stole the vehicle. A short time later, two news reporters from Hamilton's CHCH television station approached the couple, who were standing in front of the nearby Canadian Tire store, for an interview. The reporters were attacked by protestors, who demanded the footage and stole their cameras. Both were taken to hospital for treatment. The third incident involved an unmarked US Border Patrol car, which was studying the methods used by the OPP in dealing with the standoff. The car was swarmed, and protestors dragged out the officers. The car was stolen, and the driver proceeded to try to run down an OPP officer, who was subsequently injured. During this incident, classified police documents, including the identities of undercover agents and information from informants, were taken from the vehicle.[62]

The violence ended the ongoing negotiations between the Six Nations and the Province of Ontario. The OPP issued arrest warrants for seven people believed to be involved in the violent events. The OPP inferred that they were taking refuge on the reserve but maintained a protocol not to enter the land base of the actual reserve – a lesson learned by the CF at Kahnawake in 1990, specifically through the provocative raids at Tekakwitha Island and at the Longhouse. Ontario premier Dalton

McGuinty stated that negotiations would resume only after the barricades had been dismantled. Six Nations protestors responded by using heavy machinery to remove the Argyle Street barricade made of tires and twisted metal. However, the original barricade into the construction site remained intact. In another effort to resume the negotiations, the stolen documents were returned to the OPP but not before being photocopied.[63]

On 15 June negotiations resumed between the Six Nations group and the Province of Ontario. The following day, the province revealed that it had purchased the land in question from Henco Industries for an undisclosed amount. On 23 June, David Ramsey finally revealed the amount paid for the land – $12.3 million. The McGuinty government also offered $1 million, in addition to the already proposed $760,000, to compensate Caledonia businesses affected by the barricades.[64] Despite these events, the barricade remained at the construction site, with protestors conducting an archaeological dig of the site, claiming a burial ground. An archaeological survey conducted during Henco Industries' initial layout of the subdivision revealed Aboriginal artifacts but showed no evidence of burials.[65] On 5 July the Henco lands in question were officially transferred to the Government of Ontario, not to the Government of Canada, as Crown lands "reserved for the use of Indians" as stipulated in the Royal Proclamation. The land was privately owned before the transfer and was not, in the eyes of the government, Aboriginal land; therefore, was not transferred to the Six Nations.

Although the land was now in the possession of the Government of Ontario, neither the protestors nor elements of the Caledonia community were assuaged. Protests continued from both parties, one resulting in a violent clash on 7 August. Many citizens of Caledonia were questioning why the OPP had not enforced the injunction to remove the protestors, citing a two-tier judicial system and arguing that the rule of law should be applied equally to all Canadian citizens regardless of ethnicity. The following day, Justice Marshall stated that, "in the court's view, after much deliberation, there should be no further negotiations till the blockades are lifted and the occupation is ended … [and] these reasons be sent to the Attorney General who has the responsibility for enforcing the criminal law … in regard to the criminal contempt." He also ordered the province to have the OPP arrest and charge the protestors with contempt of court for not obeying his previous court injunctions.[66]

The following day, after another violent confrontation between residents, Aboriginal protestors, and police, Ontario attorney general

Michael Bryant stated that, although the province would comply with the ruling, all negotiations would cease and the province would appeal the decision. Tactically, the OPP continued to separate the crowds but did not make the arrests demanded by Justice Marshall. The appeal was heard on 25 August in the Court of Appeal for Ontario, which granted a stay on the injunction to ensure "the maintenance of the rule of law." Moreover, the court gave instructions to the OPP to proceed cautiously: "The uncontradicted evidence of the O.P.P. is that a stay of the injunction order will reduce the risk of harm to the community. The Province should be permitted to determine what level of occupation and what use of its own property best promote the public interest in these difficult times ... and negotiations will continue."[67]

One unique and unexpected outcome was the inclusion of the traditional Longhouse Council at the formal negotiations. During the Oka Crisis, for example, the refusal of the government to negotiate with the equivalent councils at Kanesatake and Kahnawake severely mired approaches to resolution. Kanesatake Mohawk spokesperson Ellen Gabriel indicated that this failure to include traditional leaders in negotiations to end the Oka Crisis "hindered everything."[68] The reasoning for the government's decision was the realization, given the enhanced political and military complexities of Oka, that any inclusion of the Longhouse would validate the Warriors, while tacitly recognizing the sovereignty of the Mohawk Nation and the greater Iroquois Confederacy (both of which were demands during negotiations). In relation, Six Nations spokesperson Hazel Hill exclaimed that the incorporation of the Longhouse into negotiations was "monumental ... I can't even explain the enormity of what's happening ... It's history in the making. You're living it. I'm living it." Accordingly, the Indian Act band council chief David General deferred to the Longhouse during negotiations.[69] Having both Six Nations councils at negotiations was a significant, and necessary, departure from previous stringent governmental policy. In Canada, prior to this occurrence, only elected Indian Act councils were recognized, and consulted, by Canadian governments and their ministries. An Indian Act council had not been established at the Six Nations Reserve until 1924 and had required enforcement by the RCMP, the arrest of Longhouse chiefs, and the confiscation of wampum belts.

Although negotiations continued, increased civil unrest prompted a consensus by the Six Nations and the Ontario government to form a 100 foot buffer zone on the north end of the disputed lands. This arrangement, worked out on 25 September, was "intended to facilitate a

better sense of privacy and security for both the people living in close
proximity ... and the Haudenosaunee/Six Nations." Signs and yellow
police tape were used to cordon off the area. According to the agreement, only the OPP and other authorized persons, such as the archaeological teams, were permitted in the buffer zone, with the OPP monitoring
the area "as operational requirements necessitate."[70]

The buffer zone did not bring an end to protests. On 15 October more
than 300 Caledonia residents and their supporters staged a rally headed
by Gary McHale of Richmond Hill. In response, Aboriginal protestors
and their advocates staged a "pot-luck dinner for peace." Dozens of
police officers formed a protective barrier between the two factions.
Although there were three arrests, the feared violence did not break out.
Caledonia residents continued to voice their concerns about two-tier justice while "Caledonia is held hostage." The Conservative member of the
Legislative Assembly of Ontario for Haldimand-Norfolk-Brant, Toby
Barrett, took the opportunity to criticize the McGuinty government:
"There does appear to be a double standard. People see a different application of the law depending on which side of the barricade you
stand."[71] According to an October 2006 survey conducted by a Canadian
public opinion and market research firm, 80 per centof Ontario residents
wanted to see federal intervention, 67 per cent favoured RCMP involvement, and 60 per cent supported instituting a deadline after which the
protestors would be forcibly removed.[72]

On his first day as newly appointed commissioner of the Ontario
Provincial Police, former Toronto police chief Julian Fantino stated on
30 October that the OPP's job was to "preserve the peace, deal with offences and bring those who transgress the laws of the land to justice.
Beyond that, the resolution of this is beyond the police doings, beyond
any scope that I could have." He also alluded to the fact that the drain
on his force's manpower could not continue.[73] Up to this point, sixty-
nine charges had been laid against thirty-two people, both Aboriginal
and non-Aboriginal, in the dispute at Caledonia. The following day,
however, federal Indian affairs minister Jim Prentice cancelled a scheduled meeting with his Ontario counterpart David Ramsey, his office stating that he was "disturbed [by the] political grandstanding" of both
Ramsey and McGuinty. Ramsey was planning to ask the federal government for $25 million in order to cover some of the provincial costs.
McGuinty, on the other hand, stated that the crisis and land claims at
Caledonia were, constitutionally, "solely the responsibility of the federal
government." Ramsey concurred, adding, "This is another example of

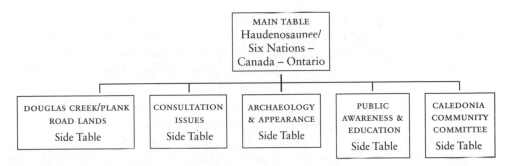

Figure 11.1
Six Nations–Caledonia negotiation structure, August 2006. Ontario Secretariat for Aboriginal Affairs, *Press Release: Structure of Negotiations*, February 2007.

the federal government failing to live up to its obligations to the people of Ontario."[74]

This political manoeuvring came on the heels of Michael Coyle's submission and presentation to the Senate Committee on 3 October detailing his investigation into the Six Nations standoff. Coyle concluded that the Governments of Canada and Ontario must cooperate. "Each takes the position that it is confident that if the Crown is liable for wrongdoing in relation to Six Nations' land claims, that it is the other government that is legally responsible," he noted. "It is difficult to see how the Crown will be able to reach a settlement of Six Nations' land claims unless Canada and Ontario can agree on a reasonable sharing between them." Among his recommendations were the following:

1 The government should significantly increase the number of personnel devoted to the historical and legal review of claims.
2 Canada should establish an independent body with the power to resolve disagreements over the validity of all Specific Claims, and where negotiations reach impasse, on the extent of Canada's liability in accordance with legal principles.
3 The same body, or a related independent body, should be established to supervise the adherence to agreed time frames in claims negotiations and to offer mediation where requested by one party.[75]

Despite these suggested reforms, the barricades remained. Negotiations continued, as did local protests.

Adding to the confusion and animosity, Gary McHale, who established a website called Caledonia Wake Up Call, dedicated to those opposing

the occupation, led a rally on 16 December. He was arrested with another man, although the OPP indicated that he and his associate would
not face criminal charges. This did not deter negotiations at the main
table from taking place on 11 January 2007, with side table meetings
sitting for the week of 15 to 19 January.[76]

During these discussions, Ontario's Department of Culture stated that
stones discarded by nomadic hunting groups dating back to 9,000 years
ago were found on the disputed land. Spokesperson Gary Lepage also
indicated that the remains of an 800-year-old Longhouse, complete with
pottery and waste refuse pits, had been unearthed. Under current federal
legislation (which protestors claim has no bearing), the evidence found
in the digs has minimal influence on the actual specific claim submitted
by the Six Nations. Such evidence, if admissible, corresponds only to a
comprehensive claim. Given that the Six Nations exclusively occupied
the land only beginning in 1784, the artifacts could belong only to another First Nation, most likely the Iroquoian-speaking Attiwanderon
(Neutral) Nation, a finding that supports the forfeiture of Six Nations
Aboriginal title. Therefore, this criterion and contention are not part of
the twenty-nine specific land claims made by the Six Nations as of 1995,
including the Douglas Creek Estates claim.[77]

### RECOMPENSE AND RELATIONSHIPS

Over the course of 2007, little was accomplished in the way of appease-
ment or negotiations, although talks continued. Elected chief David
General spoke out against the continued occupation of the land and was
blocked from attending negotiations by Longhouse supporters. As in the
Oka Crisis, the rift between traditionalists and those who supported the
elected council was omnipresent. According to Hazel Hill, "Almost 85%
of the community, probably more, don't vote [in Indian Act band council
elections]. They support the traditional government." Elected band
councillor Ava Hill identified the frustrations of partisan support and the
apparent confusion of leadership: "This has been going on for too long.
We have to start working together for future generations." Mayor Marie
Trainer agreed: "They've got to get the governance straightened out.
Who's in charge? They can't all be in charge." She added, "Many
Caledonia residents don't want their children to go on the reserve to
play baseball or hockey. It's pretty sad."[78]

Various community groups organized by residents of Caledonia reflected the diverse stance on action and reaction. The Caledonia Citizens

Alliance (Caledonia Resistance) publicly condemned the Aboriginal occupation and adopted an aggressive posture when monitoring or confronting Aboriginal protestors, similar to the Regroupement des citoyens d'Oka of 1990. Conversely, the organization Community Friends for Peace and Understanding with Six Nations, comprised of residents from both Caledonia and the Six Nations Reserve as well as members of local trade unions, sought to counter the violence and racism through discussion and mutual respect. Unfortunately, hostility and contention occurred among members of these various groups, in addition to the larger violent manifestations at the barricades.[79]

Taiaiake Alfred of Kahnawake, a professor at the University of Victoria, noted that "Oka pretty much demonstrated to me that the way to achieve change was not to negotiate it. It left a lasting impression on me."[80] This will, perhaps, be the enduring legacy of the Six Nations–Caledonia dispute. Over the prior 225 years, cordial relations had existed between residents of the Six Nations and Caledonia. Many residents of both communities believe that it will take generations to repair the damage to this relationship and to heal. This is an unfortunate by-product for the majority of residents of both Caledonia and the Six Nations who are peaceful and law-abiding members of their greater community. In relation, the situation was especially difficult for certain business owners and tourist-trade entrepreneurs in Caledonia whose sales decreased by as much as 75 per cent during the initial two years of the protest. Although the government did provide roughly $2 million in financial assistance to local enterprises, this sum did not equate to the actual lost revenue, which has been tabulated at $4.1 million.[81] No similar assistance was paid out after the Oka or Ipperwash Crises.

The government strategy of financial payout to maintain political distance was repeated throughout the proceedings and negotiations. It was used again during a 2009 court case. On 22 September 2007 Dave Brown and his partner, Dana Chatwell, launched a $7.5 million lawsuit against the OPP and the provincial government. In summary, they alleged that the OPP and Queen's Park had failed to carry out their proscribed duties to protect them, their home, and their property, which was bordered by the disputed land on two sides. The couple alleged that they were required to show "passports" to the protestors when coming to and from their home and were constantly monitored and harassed by the protestors. Three other families were in a similar situation, all obviously unable to sell their homes at a competitive price. One claimed that when she called the OPP, they refused to act or told her to call the Six

Table 11.1
Expenditures for the Six Nations standoff as of 1 February 2007

| Item | Cost ($ millions) |
|---|---|
| Purchase of Douglas Creek Estates property | 15.8 |
| Other costs paid to Henco Industries | 1.1 |
| Acquisition of interests of other builders to Douglas Creek Estates lands | 4.0 |
| Other costs paid to builders | 1.8 |
| Financial Assistance Recovery Program to businesses of Caledonia | 1.4 |
| Support for Haldimand County economic recovery activities (including charities affected by lower business contributions) | 0.56 |
| Policing operations (to date) | 21.6 |
| Total | 46.26 |

Note: On 29 March 2007 the federal government reimbursed the province $15.8 million for the actual purchase of the property. See Ontario Secretariat for Aboriginal Affairs, *Press Release: Frequent Questions and Answers*, February 2007.
Source: Ontario Secretariat for Aboriginal Affairs, *Press Release: Six Nations (Caledonia) Negotiations Costs to Date*, 1 February 2007.

Nations Police. Upon doing so, the Six Nations Police told her that "we weren't their responsibility." These allegations, among a litany of others, were heard by Ontario Superior Court Justice Thomas Bielby beginning in November 2009. After weeks of testimony, an out of court settlement was quietly reached on 29 December without the government or the OPP admitting liability. The couple signed their house over to the government and received an undisclosed monetary sum in exchange for dropping their lawsuit.[82] It appears, whether justifiable or not, that non-Aboriginals are using Aboriginal land claims to force the government into monetary recompense so that it can avoid further public and media scrutiny. With Caledonia, then, the cycle seems to have come full turn. As of February 2010 the dispute at Caledonia had cost taxpayers over $80 million.[83]

The controversy of a two-tiered policing system was also at the core of a protest directed at the Province of Ontario and the OPP by Gary McHale and his associate Mark Vandermaas, who head the organization Canadian Advocates for Charter Equality. Both men had previously founded websites dedicated to the dispute at Caledonia and its broader implications concerning equal rights for all Canadians.[84] McHale was instrumental in organizing non-Aboriginal rallies against the Six Nations protestors. Critics chastised his organization for being a radical, destabilizing force with ties to organizations advocating white supremacy and racial hatred, a claim McHale fervently denied.[85] Supporters applauded him and his organization as a way to hold the government and the OPP accountable for their actions – or lack thereof. As with most facets of Aboriginal contention, perspectives were often disparate and extreme. McHale's organization also argued that the lawlessness had led to a "no-go zone" on the contested land, bereft of any control by provincial or Six Nations security forces. In their eyes, the presence of criminal elements, smoke shops, and other by-products of the lucrative Mohawk smuggling network stemming from Akwesasne were stern evidence of the lawlessness that accompanied the barricades and protests.[86]

To draw attention to the plight of local residents, McHale laid a private information charge against OPP commissioner Julian Fantino for allegedly trying to influence Caledonia City Council and Mayor Trainer in April 2007. Although a Hamilton justice of the peace originally refused to proceed with the charge, Ontario Superior Court Justice David Crane overturned this decision on 31 December 2009. The following month, Fantino was summoned to appear in court. He maintained, however, that "every criminal occurrence that has happened in Caledonia has either resulted in a person or persons being arrested, warrants of arrest being issued or ongoing investigations being pursued. No one has gotten away with anything." As of January 2010 eighty-two people from the Six Nations Reserve had been charged with over 120 offences.[87] On 2 February the Crown withdrew the charges against Fantino, who issued a statement saying he was "content that this vexatious allegation was dealt with in a just and appropriate manner." McHale vowed to continue with legal action and to "file another judicial review."[88] Although the violence had subsided at the actual barricades, the ramifications of the drawn-out contention appeared to be ongoing.

## CONCLUSION

The conflict and confrontation at Caledonia has left scars on community-specific relations. More important, the dispute between First Nations peoples and the societies and governments of Canada are yet to be reconciled. On the one hand, clinging to an isolationist past while refusing either to accept or, more proactively, to navigate historical occurrences is counterproductive. On the other hand, denying past legal and settler-promulgated transgressions has not worked for either Aboriginal or non-Aboriginal Canadians. Nevertheless, the current national chief of

the Assembly of First Nations, Shawn Atleo, is well aware of both constraints and has been a positive mediator in Native-newcomer relations.
He expounds an approach that favours progressive negotiation over an
attitude of victimization, which is paramount to the settlement of
Aboriginal, Inuit, and Métis grievances and to a negotiated and mutually
acceptable reinvention of the Native-newcomer paradigm. Both relationships and their histories must evolve to meet contemporary issues. It
is precisely this realization that has been relatively stagnant in Indigenous-
Canadian relationships and in the policies of Indian Affairs.

Polling data cited in this chapter suggest that general Canadian society
is becoming more disillusioned with Aboriginal barricades and is losing
patience with and faith in current governmental policy and its application. It also appears that monetary solutions can no longer mollify the
various parties involved or resolve the deeper issues of historical debate.
More often than not, Aboriginal negotiators reject offers of financial
recompense from the government, maintaining that only the transfer or
protection of their lands is an acceptable conclusion. The unfortunate
manifestation of failed negotiation is the discord that now accompanies
most Aboriginal direct action. Change is undeniably necessary to avoid
further conflict and contention. This transformation must occur within
Aboriginal communities and also within the broader spheres of Canadian
society and politics.


NOTES

The author wishes to acknowledge Yale D. Belanger and Gabrielle Weaselhead
for supplying a vast collection of media-based sources.

1  In her book *Helpless: Caledonia's Nightmare of Fear and Anarchy, and
   How the Law Failed All of Us* (Toronto: Doubleday Canada, 2010),
   Christie Blatchford completely omits any investigation or mention of the
   historical context of the contention at Caledonia between 2006 and 2010.
   As a result, her book is a series of sensationalized snapshots of the more
   media-grabbing occurrences, completely removed from any historical
   framework. She bluntly states, "This book is not about Aboriginal land
   claims. It is not about the disputed one in this particular case" (vii). This is,
   indeed, the most valid statement of the book, and she remains true to her
   word. Blatchford summarily ignores the background and history of the
   twenty-nine land claims (submitted between 1976 and 1995), as well as
   the land tenure of the Haldimand Tract and the Six Nations of the Grand

River. In paradoxical logic, given the tenor of her writing, Blatchford admits that "they [the reasons] are, in one way or another, in the background of everything that occurred in Caledonia" (viii). This crucial chronological framework is something to which Blatchford should have given greater consideration before she "sat down to write this sucker" (vii).

2 Department of National Defence (DND), "Op SALON War Diary," 23 July 1990, acquired through Government of Canada, Access to Information and Privacy (ATIP); DND, "Liaison between DND and DIAND: The Next Oka," 6 September 1990, acquired through ATIP. See also chapter 7 in this volume.

3 Geoffrey York and Loreen Pindera, *People of the Pines: The Warriors and the Legacy of Oka* (Toronto: Little, Brown, 1991), 210. The population in 1990 was approximately 18,000. The population as of 31 December 2008 was composed of roughly 11,634 persons living on the reserve and 11,655 living off the reserve, with an average annual growth rate of 1.67 per cent. However, 40 per cent of the total population is under the age of thirty years. All statistics are from the Six Nations of the Grand River website, http://www.sixnations.ca.

4 According to a 1785 census, the demographics at the Grand River were 448 Mohawks, 381 Cayuga, 245 Onondaga, 162 Loyalist Oneida, 129 Tuscarora, and 78 Seneca – with smaller numbers of Delaware, Tutelo, Nanticoke, Creek, and Cherokee – for a total population of 1,843. See Timothy C. Winegard, *Oka: A Convergence of Cultures and the Canadian Forces* (Kingston: Canadian Defence Academy Press, 2008).

5 John Moses, "The Return of the Native: Six Nations Veterans and Political Change at the Grand River Reserve, 1917–1924," in *Aboriginal Peoples and the Canadian Military: Historical Perspectives*, ed. P. Whitney Lackenbauer and Craig Leslie Mantle, 117–28 (Kingston: Canadian Defence Academy Press, 2007), 117–18; Isabel Thompson Kelsay, *Joseph Brant, 1743–1807: Man of Two Worlds* (Syracuse, NY: Syracuse University Press, 1984), 370. The Oneida, and to a lesser extent the Tuscarora, predominately sided with the Americans during the revolution.

6 In Robert S. Allen, *His Majesty's Indian Allies: British Indian Policy in the Defence of Canada, 1774–1815* (Toronto: Dundurn, 1992), 60–5.

7 Ibid., 209.

8 Although exact dates for the creation of the confederacy vary, it is certain that it was established prior to European contact. Deganawitha (Peace Maker) and Hiawatha sought to end the protracted warfare and cannibalism that existed between the Five Nations. It likely began in the mid-fifteenth century and transpired over a number of years. See Daniel K.

Richter, *The Ordeal of the Longhouse: The Peoples of the Iroquois League in the Era of European Colonization* (Charlotte: University of North Carolina Press, 1993); and Bruce E. Johansen, "Dating the Iroquois Confederacy," *Akwesasne Notes* 1, nos 3–4 (1995): 62–3.

9  J.R. Miller, *Skyscrapers Hide the Heavens: A History of Indian-White Relations in Canada*, 3rd ed. (Toronto: University of Toronto Press, 2000), 76.

10  Allen, *His Majesty's Indian Allies*, 54.

11  Brant was never a traditional Iroquoian sachem (chief); rather, was vaguely appointed war chief, although even this is debated. Given his personal affiliation with Sir William Johnson, it is possible that Johnson viewed and interacted with Brant in this position despite the fact that neither the confederacy nor the Mohawks ever bestowed these powers upon Brant, who was not in a heredity clan position to attain such a title. Nonclan hierarchy titles were, and are, conferred by the Grand Council (comprising fifty sachems of the confederacy) under the title of pine tree chief, which Brant never attained.

12  Haldimand Proclamation, 25 October 1784, quoted in Barbara Graymont, *The Iroquois in the American Revolution* (Syracuse, NY: Syracuse University Press, 1972), 299.

13  Six Nations Lands and Resources, "Pre-Confederation Documents," n.d., 1–6, http://www.sixnations.ca/LandsResources/PreConfederation.pdf. The Crown did not reveal to the Mississauga that the land was allotted to their traditional Iroquoian enemies.

14  Compiled from John S. Hagopian, "The Myths of Caledonia," *Hamilton Spectator*, 24 February 2007; and John S. Hagopian, "Rebuttal: The Myths of Caledonia," *History News Network*, 2 May 2007.

15  Aboriginal Affairs and Northern Development Canada (AANDC), *General Briefing Note on Canada's Self-government and Comprehensive Land Claims Policies and the Status of Negotiations*, 31 July 2013, http://www. aadnc-aandc.gc.ca/eng/1373385502190/1373385561540.

16  The Mississauga made numerous land surrenders in southern Ontario to the British beginning in 1781.

17  Library of Congress, *A Century of Lawmaking for a New Nation: U.S. Congressional Documents and Debates, 1774–1875*, US serial set no. 4015, http://memory.loc.gov/ammem/amlaw/lawhome.html. 552–4; J.R. Miller, *Compact, Contract, Covenant: Aboriginal Treaty-Making in Canada* (Toronto: University of Toronto Press, 2009), 57. See also Richard Aquila, *The Iroquois Restoration: Iroquois Diplomacy on the Colonial Frontier, 1701–1754* (Lincoln: University of Nebraska Press, 1997).

18  Hagopian, "Myths of Caledonia." Hagopian raises a number of interesting questions: (1) Why did Brant seek assurances, before supporting the British in the revolution, that compensatory lands would be given to the Six Nations in the event that the Americans won the war if they were already the owners of the lands covered in the Nanfan Treaty? (2) Why did the British obtain a quit claim deed from the Mississauga prior to awarding these lands to the Six Nations if the Five Nations were already the legitimate owners? (3) Why was the Haldimand Proclamation necessary if the Six Nations had already secured these lands under the Nanfan Treaty? (4) Why were the Six Nations willing to receive the relatively small parcel of land in the Haldimand Tract if they believed themselves to be the rightful owners of a substantially larger land base outlined in the Nanfan Treaty?

19  Allen, *His Majesty's Indian Allies*, 19, 34–6. Nevertheless, in recent times, the court decision in *R. v. Ireland and Jamieson* [1991] 2 CNLR 120, concluded that ownership and sovereignty had been transferred to the Crown and that the Five Nations had enjoyed only hunting rights (which were also limited based on other court decisions and decrees).

20  Royal Proclamation, 7 October 1763, RG 10, vol. 660, reel C-13,4000, 89–99, Library and Archives Canada.

21  Indian and Northern Affairs Canada (INAC), *The Government of Canada's Approach to Implementation of the Inherent Right and the Negotiation of Aboriginal Self-Government* (Ottawa: Minister of Public Works and Government Services Canada, 1995).

22  Hagopian, "Myths of Caledonia." See also Hagopian, "Rebuttal."

23  Miller, *Compact, Contract, Covenant*, 79. The Anicinabe (or Anishinaabeg), meaning "the people" or "original people," loosely encompass the related nations of the Ojibwa, Odawa, Potawatomi, Nipissing, Mississauga, and Algonkin.

24  Hagopian, "Myths of Caledonia."

25  "Caledonia Land Claim, Historical Timeline," CBC *News*, 21 April 2006, http://www.cbc.ca/news2/background/caledonia-landclaim/historical-timeline.html.

26  An Indian Act (elected) band council was not established at the Six Nations Reserve until 1924, occurring under the enforcement of the Royal Canadian Mounted Police; yet a traditional council has simultaneously been maintained.

27  Ontario Reports, 82 OR (3d), *Henco Industries Ltd. v. Haudenosaunee Six Nations Confederacy Council et al. Superior Court of Justice, Marshall, J.*

(Toronto: Law Society of Upper Canada, 2007), 347–50; Six Nations
Lands and Resources, "Pre-Confederation Documents." The size of the current reserve represents roughly 4 to 5 per cent of the original Haldimand
Tract, depending on perception and opinion regarding the acreage of the
original land grant. Like the numbers on other Mohawk reserves
straddling densely populated Canadian communities, the Six Nations
population continues to grow, but the land base of the reserve does not.

28  "Caledonia Land Claim, Historical Timeline."

29  AANDC, "Background – Six Nations – Claims and Negotiations,"
    1 February 2012, http://www.aadnc-aandc.gc.ca/eng/1327936926534/
    1327936993812.

30  Six Nations Lands and Resources, "Six Nations Land Claims Summaries
    (Basis & Allegations)," n.d., http://www.sixnations.ca/LandsResources/
    ClaimSummaries.htm.

31  Graham Darling, *Land Claims and the Six Nations in Caledonia*, report
    for the Centre for Constitutional Studies, University of Calgary, September
    2006, 1–3. As of 2008, 855 specific claims had been lodged with Indian
    Affairs, with an average annual settlement of 10. Only 275 specific claims
    have been resolved since 1970. An extrapolation based on these numbers
    reveals that those already in the system will, arguably, be settled only in
    the 2090s.

32  "Harsh Response to Day of Protest Unwise Strategy," *Saskatoon Star-
    Phoenix*, 24 May 2007. When dealing with non-Aboriginal lands, the
    provinces of Canada have exclusive rights to legislate on concerns of prop-
    erty and civil rights, including land transactions, under section 91 (13) of
    the Constitution Act. Although it is law that First Nations can surrender
    their land only to the Crown, full title to the land passes to the province
    once transferred.

33  Darling, *Land Claims*, 1.

34  Dawn Smith and other protestors behind the barricade, interviews with
    author, Caledonia, Ontario, 23 March 2006.

35  Ontario Reports, 82 OR (3d), *Henco Industries Ltd.*, 351.

36  Protestors behind the barricade, interviews with author, Caledonia,
    Ontario, 22 March 2006; "Native Protesters Face Deadline to Leave
    Subdivision," CBC *News*, 22 March 2006.

37  Don Henning, in Karen Best, "Showdown Looms as Deadline
    Approaches," *Dunnville Chronicle*, 22 March 2006.

38  Paul Legall, "Six Nations Protestors Say Land 'Stolen'; Developer Says It's
    the Federal Government's Problem," *Hamilton Spectator*, 26 March 2006.

39 INAC, untitled press release, 24 March 2006.

40 Protestors behind the barricade, interviews with author, Caledonia, Ontario, 23 March 2006.

41 Paul Legall, "Ottawa Mediator Quickly Rejected; Native Protestors Give Law Professor 'His Walking Papers' in Dispute over Title to Subdivision Site," *Hamilton Spectator*, 30 March 2006.

42 Michael (Sahtakaientes) Laughing, in "Standoff – Native Protestor Prepared to Die over Rights to Land," *Hamilton Spectator*, 30 March 2006; Paul Legall, "Natives Vow to Stand Their Ground; Mood Tense as Sheriff Visits," *Hamilton Spectator*, 31 March 2006. Laughing, aged forty, a high-steel worker, assisted in the 9/11 rescue and recovery operation in New York City. He was charged in the United States with smuggling 220 pounds of marijuana on 14 March 2007.

43 Deirdre McCracken, in Carmela Fragomeni, "Native Standoff Is a Provincial Matter: Ottawa," *Hamilton Spectator*, 7 April 2006, emphasis added.

44 Monte Kwinter, in Lee Greenburg, "'The Whole Town Is Ours,' Natives Say as Standoff Drags On," *Ottawa Citizen*, 31 March 2006.

45 Signe Katz, "Caledonia Protest," CBC News, 5 April 2006.

46 In Paul Legall, "Homeowners Losing Patience as Protest Drags On," *Hamilton Spectator*, 3 April 2006.

47 Maurice Pilon, in Peter Edwards, "Standoff at Caledonia: Native Land Claims, Police Raid Sparks a Long Day of Confrontation at Housing Development Near Hamilton," *Toronto Star*, 21 April 2006.

48 Joe Delaronde, in Katie Rook, "Hundreds Flock to Protest Site: Officers Arrest 16 in Dispute over Caledonia Development," *National Post*, 21 April 2006.

49 "Quebec Mohawks Raise Banner on Bridge to Support Ontario Native Dispute," *Canadian Press*, 21 April 2006; "Natives Block Rail Line in Eastern Ontario," *Canadian Press*, 21 April 2006.

50 Samantha Craggs, "Heated Confrontation with Mohawks at Development," *Belleville Intelligencer*, 15 November 2006. On the Tyendinaga and Deseronto dispute, see chapter 10 in this volume.

51 David General, in Edwards, "Standoff at Caledonia."

52 "Caledonia Land Claim, Timeline," CBC News, 1 November 2006, http://www.cbc.ca/news2/background/caledonia-landclaim.

53 Ibid.

54 Marie Trainer, in Rachele Labreque, "Akwesasne Warriors Threaten Bridge Blockade; Action Possible If Violence Used in Dispute," *Cornwall Standard-Freeholder*, 25 April 2006.

55  In ibid.

56  Brantford City Council, in Tom Keefer, "Declaring the Exception: Direct Action, Six Nations, and the Struggle in Brantford," *Upping the Anti*, no. 7 (2008): 113, 117–18. On the CF's legislation regarding domestic operations, see Winegard, *Oka*, ch. 9.

57  Confidential source.

58  Marissa Nelson, "Harper Rapped on Caledonia Issue," *Hamilton Spectator*, 26 May 2006.

59  David Peterson, in Joan Walters, "Peterson Fears Another Oka," *Hamilton Spectator*, 23 May 2006.

60  "Message from the Onkwehonweh to the United Nations," statement delivered by Doreen Silversmith to the United Nations Permanent Forum on Indigenous Peoples, Geneva, Switzerland, 1 May 2006.

61  Bob Aaron, "Tough to Reconcile Caledonia Land Dispute," *Toronto Star*, 27 May 2006.

62  "Ontario: Police Seek Arrest Warrants after Violence at Native Blockade," *Ottawa Citizen*, 11 June 2006.

63  Ontario Reports, 82 OR (3d), *Henco Industries Ltd.*, 351–5. As of 20 June only one of the seven had been arrested. Audra Ann Taillefer of Victoria, British Columbia, was arrested in conjunction with the swarming of the elderly couple's vehicle.

64  "Government to Buy Disputed Caledonia Land," *Canadian Press*, 23 June 2006.

65  "Six Nations Protesters Dig for Caledonia Burial Ground," CBC *News*, 20 June 2006, http://www.cbc.ca/news/canada/six-nations-protesters-dig-for-caledonia-burial-ground-1.603248.

66  Ontario Reports, 82 OR (3d), *Henco Industries Ltd.*, 343–61.

67  Ibid.

68  Ellen Gabriel, interview with author, Kahnawake, Mohawk Territory, 1 September 2005.

69  Hazel Hill, in Peter Edwards, "'The Warrior Spirit Is in All of Us': Clan Mothers Play Significant Role, Mohawks Claiming Major Victory," *Toronto Star*, 22 April 2006.

70  Ontario Secretariat for Aboriginal Affairs, *Press Release: Frequent Questions and Answers*, February 2007.

71  Toby Barrett, in "Dozens of Police Contain Caledonia Rally," CBC *News*, 15 October 2006, http://www.cbc.ca/news/canada/dozens-of-police-contain-caledonia-rally-1.608838.

72  Tom Blackwell, "Native Standoff Straining Ontario Police," *National Post*, 20 October 2006.

73 Julian Fantino, in "OPP's Job to 'Preserve the Peace' in Caledonia: Top Cop," CBC News, 30 October 2006, http://www.cbc.ca/news/canada/toronto/opp-s-job-to-preserve-the-peace-in-caledonia-top-cop-1.586493.

74 Dalton McGuinty and David Ramsey, both in "Feds Scrap Planned Caledonia Meeting," CBC News, 31 October 2006.

75 Michael Coyle, "Senate Committee Submission on the Specific Claims Process," 3 October 2006, http://archive-ca.com/page/100213/2012-07-09/ http://www.law.uwo.ca/News/2006/Oct2006_Coyle_Senate_Committee_ Submission.html.

76 Ontario Secretariat for Aboriginal Affairs, Press Release.

77 Gary Lepage, in "Archaeological Finds on Disputed Ont. Land Strengthen Claims, Natives Say," CBC News, 17 January 2007, http://www.cbc.ca/ news/canada/toronto/archeological-finds-on-disputed-ont-land-strength- en-claims-natives-say-1.662001; Ontario Secretariat for Aboriginal Affairs, Press Release. Despite vast media documentation claiming the contrary, these artifacts were discovered in digs during 2002 and 2005, not in the archaeological dig conducted after the occupation of the disputed lands.

78 Hazel Hill, Ava Hill, and Marie Trainer, all in Peter Edwards, "Caledonia Talks, 'Who's in Charge?'; Tensions between Traditional Leaders, Elected Band Officials Simmering for Generations," Toronto Star, 19 March 2007.

79 Tom Keefer, "The Contradictions of Canadian Colonialism: Non-Native Responses to the Six Nations Reclamation at Caledonia," unpublished paper, August 2007. Trade unions and labour organizations included the Canadian Auto Workers, Canadian Union of Public Employees, Ontario Public Service Employees Union, Canadian Union of Postal Workers, and Canadian Labour Congress. In 1990 Oka Park became the rallying point for those supporting the Mohawk at Kanesatake.

80 Taiaiake Alfred, in Margaret Wente, "The New Warrior Class," Globe and Mail, 15 July 2006.

81 Ontario Hansard, Legislative Assembly of Ontario: Oral Questions, 9 May 2006; Renee Berube, "Barrett Adding-Up the Cost of the Aboriginal Occupation in Caledonia," Norfolk News Centre, 22 February 2010.

82 The trial had been scheduled to resume on 4 January 2010, with OPP officers among the listed witnesses. Christie Blatchford, "Two Standards of Policing Failed the Residents of Caledonia," Globe and Mail, 14 November 2009; Christie Blatchford, "Settlement Gives Hope to Others in Caledonia," Globe and Mail, 5 January 2010. Blatchford frequently published editorials and articles on the recent events at Caledonia.

83 Canadian Press, "No Decision on Caledonia Handover, Says Bentley," *CTV News*, 22 February 2010, http://toronto.ctvnews.ca/no-decision-on-caledonia-handover-says-bentley-1.485870.

84 McHale's website is at http://caledoniawakeupcall.com, and Vandermaas's is at http://voiceofcanada.ca.

85 Canadian Advocates for Charter Equality, "CBC National News Stories Vindicate CANACE Founders," 2 March 2010, http://joincanace.wordpress.com/2010/02/03/cbc-news-stories-vindicate-canace-founders.

86 "Illegal Smoke Shack Demolished," *Hamilton Spectator*, 11 January 2011, excerpts, http://www.caledoniawakeupcall.com/updates/110111spectator.html.

87 Julian Fantino, in Christie Blatchford, "Activist Outmatched in Fight with Top Cop," *Globe and Mail*, 14 January 2010; and in Sean Mallen, "'Standing Up and Doing What's Right,' Fantino Says," *National Post*, 21 January 2010. For McHale's perspective on events, see Gary McHale, *Victory in the No-Go Zone: Winning the Fight against Two-Tier Policing* (St Catharines, ON: Freedom Press, 2013).

88 Julian Fantino and Gary McHale, both in Timothy Appleby, "Crown Withdraws Charge against Fantino," *Globe and Mail*, 3 February 2010.

# Contributors

YALE D. BELANGER is an associate professor in the Department of Political Science and an adjunct associate professor in the Faculty of Health Sciences, University of Lethbridge. His books include *Gambling with the Future: The Evolution of Aboriginal Gaming in Canada* (2006), *Aboriginal Self-Government in Canada: Current Trends and Issues* (editor, 2008), *Ways of Knowing: An Introduction to Native Studies in Canada* (2010, 2014), and *First Nations Gaming in Canada* (editor, 2011).

TOM FLANAGAN, FRSC, is a Distinguished Fellow in the School of Public Policy, University of Calgary, and the author of several books on Louis Riel, the Northwest Rebellion, and Aboriginal land claims. His book *First Nations? Second Thoughts* received both the Donner Prize for the best Canadian book on public policy and the Canadian Political Science Association's Donald Smiley Prize for the best book on Canadian politics published in the year 2000.

VICTOR GULEWITSCH teaches anthropology and First Nations issues at the University of Guelph and Wilfrid Laurier University. He has conducted land claims research and has provided negotiation/litigation support for various Ontario First Nations since 1992.

SARAH J. KING is an assistant professor in the Liberal Studies Department at Grand Valley State University, Michigan, where she is also appointed to the Environmental Studies and Religious Studies Programs. Her book *Fishing in Contested Waters: Place and Community in Burnt Church/Esgenoôpetitj* (2014) explores the post-Marshall dispute as it was experienced by the communities of Esgenoôpetitj and Burnt Church, New Brunswick.

P. WHITNEY LACKENBAUER is an associate professor and chair of the Department of History at St Jerome's University in the University of Waterloo. He has written or edited more than a dozen books on Native-newcomer relations and northern history, including *Battle Grounds: The Canadian Military and Aboriginal Lands* (2007), *Arctic Front: Defending Canada in the Far North* (co-authored 2008, winner of the 2009 Donner Prize for the best Canadian book on public policy), *A Commemorative History of Aboriginal People in the Canadian Military* (co-authored 2010), and *The Canadian Rangers: A Living History* (2013).

DAVID A. ROSSITER is an associate professor at Huxley College of the Environment at Western Washington University. Much of his research explores the intersection of Aboriginal claims and historical resource geographies, with articles appearing in journals such as *Cultural Geographies*, the *Journal of Historical Geography*, and the *Canadian Geographer*. He is also editor of the *American Review of Canadian Studies*.

JOHN SANDLOS is an associate professor in the Department of History at Memorial University of Newfoundland. In 2012–13 he was a Visiting Fellow at the Rachel Carson Center for Environment and Society in Munich, Germany. His research interests include the history of national parks, conservation, and mining in Canada. He is the author of *Hunters at the Margin* (2007) and co-author of several articles on abandoned mines in northern Canada.

NICK SHRUBSOLE holds a doctorate in religious studies from the University of Waterloo. His dissertation, "Religion, Land and Democracy in Canadian Indigenous-State Relations" (2013) examines the political and legal structures inhibiting the protection of Indigenous religious freedom in contemporary Canada. He currently teaches as a contract academic staff instructor in the Department of Religious Studies at St Jerome's University in the University of Waterloo and in the Social Justice and Peace Studies Program at Western University.

TIMOTHY C. WINEGARD served nine years as an officer in the Canadian Forces, including a two-year attachment to the British Army while completing his doctorate at the University of Oxford. His recent books include *Oka: A Convergence of Cultures and the Canadian Forces* (2008); *Indigenous Peoples of the British Dominions and the First World War* (2011); and *For King and Kanata: Canadian Indians and the First World War* (2012). He currently teaches history and political science at Colorado Mesa University.

# Select Bibliography

## BOOKS

Alfred, Gerald R. (Taiaiake). *Heeding the Voice of Our Ancestors: Kahnawake Mohawk Politics and the Rise of Native Nationalism.* Toronto: Oxford University Press, 1995.

– *Peace, Power, Righteousness: An Indigenous Manifesto.* Toronto: Oxford University Press, 1999.

– *Wasáse: Indigenous Pathways of Action and Freedom.* Peterborough, ON: Broadview, 2005.

Allen, Robert S. *His Majesty's Indian Allies: British Indian Policy in the Defence of Canada, 1774-1815.* Toronto: Dundurn, 1992.

Bland, Douglas L. *Uprising.* Toronto: Blue Butterfly Books, 2009.

Blatchford, Christie. *Helpless: Caledonia's Nightmare of Fear and Anarchy, and How the Law Failed All of Us.* Toronto: Doubleday Canada, 2010.

Cairns, Alan. *Citizens Plus: Aboriginal Peoples and the Canadian State.* Vancouver: UBC Press, 2000.

Churchill, Ward, ed. *Indians Are Us? Culture and Genocide in Native North America.* Monroe, ME: Common Courage, 1994.

Ciaccia, John. *The Oka Crisis: A Mirror of the Soul.* Dorval, QC: Maren, 2000.

Coates, Ken S. *The Marshall Decision and Native Rights.* Montreal and Kingston: McGill-Queen's University Press, 2000.

Devries, Laura. *Conflict in Caledonia: Aboriginal Land Rights and the Rule of Law.* Vancouver: UBC Press, 2011.

Edwards, Peter. *One Dead Indian: The Premier, the Police, and the Ipperwash Crisis.* Toronto: Stoddart, 2001.

Flanagan, Tom. *First Nations? Second Thoughts*. Montreal and Kingston: McGill-Queen's University Press, 2000.

Francis, Daniel. *The Imaginary Indian: The Image of the Indian in Canadian Culture*. Vancouver: Arsenal, 1993.

George-Kanentiio, Douglas M. *Iroquois on Fire: A Voice from the Mohawk Nation*. Lincoln: University of Nebraska Press, 2008.

Glenn, Jack. *Once Upon an Oldman: Special Interest Politics and the Oldman River Dam*. Vancouver: UBC Press, 1999.

Goddard, John. *Last Stand of the Lubicon Cree*. Vancouver: Douglas and McIntyre, 1991.

Goldleaf, Donna. *Entering the Warzone: A Mohawk Perspective on Resisting Invasions*. Penticton, BC: Theytus Books, 1995.

Hall, Louis Karoniaktajeh. *Rebuilding the Iroquois Confederacy*. Kahnawake, QC: L.K. Hall, 1985.

– *Warrior's Handbook*. Kahnawake, QC: L.K. Hall, 1985.

Harris, R. Cole. *Making Native Space: Colonialism, Resistance, and Reserves in British Columbia*. Vancouver: UBC Press, 2002.

Hedican, Edward J. *Ipperwash: The Tragic Failure of Canada's Aboriginal Policy*. Toronto: University of Toronto Press, 2013.

Hill, John Boncore (Splitting the Sky), with Sandra Bruderer (She Keeps the Door). *The Autobiography of Dacajeweiah, Splitting the Sky: From Attica to Gustafsen Lake, Unmasking the Secrets of the Psycho-sexual Energy and the Struggle for Original Peoples' Title*. Chase, BC: John Pasquale Boncore, 2001.

Hodgins, Bruce W., and Jamie Benidickson. *The Temagami Experience: Recreation, Resources, and Aboriginal Rights in the Northern Ontario Wilderness*. Toronto: University of Toronto Press, 1989.

Hodgins, Bruce W., Ute Lischke, and David T. McNab, eds. *Blockades and Resistance: Studies in Actions of Peace and the Temagami Blockades of 1988–89*. Waterloo, ON: Wilfrid Laurier University Press, 2003.

Hornung, Rick. *One Nation under the Gun: Inside the Mohawk Civil War*. Toronto: Stoddart, 1991.

Johansen, Bruce E. *Life and Death in Mohawk Country*. Golden, BC: North American Press, 1993.

Johnson, Bruce E., Joane Nagel, and Duane Champagne. *American Indian Activism: Alcatraz to the Longest Walk*. Urbana: University of Illinois Press, 1996.

Johnson, Troy R. *The Occupation of Alcatraz Island: Indian Self-Determination and the Rise of Indian Activism*. Urbana: University of Illinois Press, 1996.

Kalant, Amelia. *National Identity and the Conflict at Oka: Native Belonging and Myths of Postcolonial Nationhood in Canada*. New York: Routledge, 2004.

Keller, Robert H., and Michael F. Turek. *American Indians and National Parks*. Tucson: University of Arizona Press, 1998.

King, Sarah J. *Fishing in Contested Waters: Place and Community in Burnt Church/Esgenoôpetitj*. Toronto: University of Toronto Press, 2014.

Koenig, Edwin C. *Cultures and Ecologies: A Native Fishing Conflict on the Saugeen-Bruce Peninsula*. Toronto: University of Toronto Press, 2005.

Lackenbauer, P. Whitney. *Battle Grounds: The Canadian Military and Aboriginal Lands*. Vancouver: UBC Press, 2007.

Ladner, Kiera, and Leanne Simpson, eds. *This Is an Honour Song: Twenty Years since the Blockades*. Winnipeg: Arbeiter Ring, 2010.

Lambertus, Sandra. *Wartime Images, Peacetime Wounds: The Media and the Gustafsen Lake Standoff*. Toronto: University of Toronto Press, 2004.

Landsman, Gail H. *Sovereignty and Symbol: Indian-White Conflict at Ganienkeh*. Albuquerque: University of New Mexico Press, 1988.

MacLaine, Craig, Michael Baxendale, and Robert Galbraith. *This Land Is Our Land: The Mohawk Revolt at Oka*. Montreal: Optimum, 1990.

May, Elizabeth. *Paradise Won: The Struggle for South Moresby*. Toronto: McClelland and Stewart, 1990.

McNab, David. *No Place for Fairness: Indigenous Land Rights and Policy in the Bear Island Case and Beyond*. Montreal and Kingston: McGill-Queen's University Press, 2009.

Miller, J.R. *Lethal Legacies: Current Native Controversies in Canada*. Toronto: McClelland and Stewart, 2004.

– *Skyscrapers Hide the Heavens: A History of Indian-White Relations in Canada*. 3rd ed. Toronto: University of Toronto Press, 2000.

– *Compact, Contract, Covenant: Aboriginal Treaty-Making in Canada*. Toronto: University of Toronto Press, 2009.

Pasquaretta, Paul. *Gambling and Survival in Native North America*. Tucson: University of Arizona Press, 2003.

Pertusati, Linda. *In Defense of Mohawk Land: Ethnopolitical Conflict in Native North America*. Albany: State University of New York Press, 1997.

Reid, Gerald F. *Kahnawà:ke: Factionalism, Traditionalism, and Nationalism in a Mohawk Community*. Lincoln: University of Nebraska Press, 2004.

– *Mohawk Territory: A Cultural Geography*. Kahnawake, QC: Center for Curriculum Development, Kahnawake Survival School, 1981.

Richardson, Boyce, ed. *Drumbeat: Anger and Renewal in Indian Country*. Toronto: Summerhill Press for the Assembly of First Nations, 1989.

Richter, Daniel K. *The Ordeal of the Longhouse: The Peoples of the Iroquois League in the Era of European Colonization*. Charlotte: University of North Carolina Press, 1993.

Salisbury, Richard. *A Homeland for the Cree: Regional Development in James Bay, 1971–1981*. Montreal and Kingston: McGill-Queen's University Press, 1986.

Sandlos, John. *Hunters at the Margin: Wildlife Conservation in the Northwest Territories*. Vancouver: UBC Press, 2007.

Swain, Harry. *Oka: A Political Crisis and Its Legacy*. Vancouver: Douglas and McIntyre, 2010.

Switlo, Janice G.A.E. *Gustafsen Lake: Under Siege*. Peachland, BC: TIAC Communications, 1997.

Treaty 7 Elders and Tribal Council, with Walter Hildebrant, Sarah Carter, and Dorthy First Rider. *The True Spirit and Intent of Treaty 7*. Montreal and Kingston: McGill-Queen's University Press, 1996.

Turner, Dale. *This Is Not A Peace Pipe: Toward a Critical Indigenous Philosophy*. Toronto: University of Toronto Press, 2006.

Valaskakis, Gail Guthrie. *Indian Country: Essays on Contemporary Native Culture*. Waterloo, ON: Wilfrid Laurier University Press, 2005.

Wadden, Marie. *Nitassinan: The Innu Struggle to Reclaim Their Homeland*. Vancouver: Douglas and McIntyre, 1991.

Willow, Anna J. *Strong Hearts, Native Lands: Anti-Clearcutting Activism at Grassy Narrows First Nation*. Albany: State University of New York Press, 2012.

Winegard, Timothy C. *Oka: A Convergence of Cultures and the Canadian Forces*. Kingston: Canadian Defence Academy Press, 2008.

York, Geoffrey, and Loreen Pindera. *People of the Pines: The Warriors and the Legacy of Oka*. Toronto: Little, Brown, 1991.

### ARTICLES AND BOOK CHAPTERS

Alcantara, Christopher. "Explaining Aboriginal Treaty Negotiation Outcomes in Canada: The Case of the Inuit and the Innu in Labrador." *Canadian Journal of Political Science* 40, no. 1 (2007): 185–207.

Anderson, Mark, and Carmen Robertson. "The 'Bended Elbow' News, Kenora 1974: How a Small-Town Newspaper Promoted Colonization." *American Indian Quarterly* 31, no. 3 (Summer 2007): 410–40.

Armitage, Peter. "Indigenous Homelands and the Security Requirements of Western Nation-States: Innu Opposition to Military Flight Training in

Eastern Quebec and Labrador." In *Pentagon and the Cities*, ed. A. Kirby, 126–53. Newbury Park, CA: Sage, 1992.

Armitage, Peter, and John C. Kennedy. "Redbaiting and Racism on Our Frontier: Military Expansion in Labrador and Quebec." *Canadian Review of Anthropology and Sociology* 26, no. 5 (1989): 798–817.

Ashini, Daniel. "Innu Opposition to Low-Level Flying." *Native Issues*, August 1987, 7–9.

Barker, Mary. "Low-Level Military Flight Training in Quebec-Labrador: The Anatomy of a Northern Development Conflict." In *Aboriginal Autonomy and Development in Northern Quebec and Labrador*, ed. Colin H. Scott, 233–54. Vancouver: UBC Press, 2001.

Beauregard, Claude. "The Military Intervention in Oka: Strategy, Communication and Press Coverage." Trans. Graham Timms. *Canadian Military History* 2, no. 1 (Spring 1993): 23–47.

Blomley, Nicholas. "'Shut the Province Down': First Nations Blockades in British Columbia, 1984–1995." *BC Studies* 111 (Autumn 1996): 5–35.

Borrows, John. "An Analysis of and Dialogue on Indigenous and Crown Blockades." In *Philosophy and Aboriginal Rights: Critical Dialogues*, ed. Sandra Tomsons and Lorraine Mayer, 101–22. Toronto: Oxford University Press, 2013.

Campbell, Robert, and Leslie Pal. "Feather and Gun: Confrontation at Oka/Kanesatake." In *The Real Worlds of Canadian Politics: Cases in Process and Policy*, 2nd ed., ed. Robert M. Campbell and Leslie Pal, 267–333. Toronto: Broadview, 1991.

Carroll, William K., and R.S. Ratner. "Master Frames and Counter-Hegemony: Political Sensibilities in Contemporary Social Movements." *Canadian Review of Sociology and Anthropology* 33, no. 4 (1996): 407–35.

Castree, Noel. "Differential Geographies: Place, Indigenous Rights and 'Local' Resources." *Political Geography* 23, no. 2 (2004): 133–67.

D'Arcus, B. "Contested Boundaries: Native Sovereignty and State Power at Wounded Knee, 1973." *Political Geography* 22, no. 4 (2003): 415–37.

Dickson-Gilmore, Jane. "Always about the Land: The Oka Crisis of 1990." In *Canada: Confederation to Present*, ed. Bob Hesketh and Chris Hackett. CD-ROM. Edmonton: Chinook Multimedia, 2001.

Flanagan, Tom. "The Lubicon Lake Dispute." In *Government and Politics in Alberta*, ed. Allan Tupper and Roger Gibbins, 269–303. Edmonton: University of Alberta Press, 1992.

– "Some Factors Bearing on the Origin of the Lubicon Lake Dispute, 1899–1940." *Alberta: Studies in the Arts and Sciences* 2, no. 2 (1990): 47–62.

Gallagher, John, and Cy Gonick. "The Occupation of Anicinabe Park." *Canadian Dimension* 10, no. 5 (November 1974): 21–40.

Grenier, Marc. "Native Indians in the English-Canadian Press: The Case of the 'Oka Crisis.'" *Media, Culture and Society* 16, no. 2 (1994): 313–36.

Hall, Tony. "Blockades and Bannock: Aboriginal Protests and Politics in Northern Ontario, 1980–1990." *Wicazo Sa Review* 7, no. 2 (Autumn 1991): 58–77.

Helwig, Maggie. "Low-Level Flight Testing: Innu Women Fight Back." *Canadian Women Studies* 13, no. 3 (Spring 1993): 52–3.

Jhappan, C. Radha. "Indian Symbolic Politics: The Double-Edged Sword of Publicity." *Canadian Ethnic Studies* 22, no. 3 (1990): 19–39.

Johnston, Moira. "Canada's Queen Charlotte Islands: Home of the Haida." *National Geographic*, July 1987, 102–27.

Keene, Tony. "Guns among the Mohawks." *Sentinel* 24, no. 4 (1988): 2–4.

Keller, Robert. "Haida Indian Land Claims and South Moresby National Park." *American Review of Canadian Studies* 20, no. 1 (Spring 1990): 7–30.

Lackenbauer, P. Whitney. "Combined Operation: The Appropriation of Stoney Point Reserve and the Creation of Camp Ipperwash." *Journal of Military and Strategic Studies* 2, no. 1 (Fall 1999): 1–31.

Lackenbauer, P. Whitney, and Andrew F. Cooper. "The Achilles Heel of Canadian International Citizenship: Indigenous Diplomacies and State Responses in the Twentieth Century." *Canadian Foreign Policy Journal* 13, no. 3 (2007): 99–119.

Laurin, Serge. "Les 'troubles d'oka' ou l'histoire d'une résistance (1760–1945)." *Recherches amérindiennes au Québec* 21, nos 1–2 (1991): 87–92.

Long, A. David. "Culture, Ideology, and Militancy: The Movement of Native Indians in Canada, 1969–1991." In *Organizing Dissent: Contemporary Social Movements in Theory and Practice*, ed. William K. Carroll, 118–34. Toronto: Garamond.

Maloney, Sean M. "Domestic Operations: The Canadian Approach." *Parameters* 27, no. 3 (Autumn 1997): 135–52.

McDougall, Allan K., and Lisa Phillips Valentine. "Selective Marginalization of Aboriginal Voices: Censorship in Public Performance." In *Interpreting Censorship in Canada*, ed. Klaus Petersen and Allan C. Hutchinson, 334–50. Toronto: University of Toronto Press, 1999.

Miller, J.R. "Great White Father Knows Best: Oka and the Land Claims Process." *Native Studies Review* 7, no. 1 (1991): 24–5.

Morris, Martin J. "Overcoming the Barricades: The Crisis at Oka as a Case Study in Political Communication." *Journal of Canadian Studies* 30, no. 2 (Summer 1995): 74–90.

Penashue, Elizabeth, and Rose Gregoire. "Nitassinan: Our Land, Our Struggle." *Peace Magazine*, August-September 1989, 14.

Ponting, J. Rick. "Internationalization: Perspectives on an Emerging Direction in Aboriginal Affairs." *Canadian Ethnic Studies* 22, no. 3 (1990): 85–109.

Ramos, Howard. "What Causes Canadian Aboriginal Protest? Examining Resources, Opportunities, and Identity, 1951–2000." *Canadian Journal of Sociology* 31, no. 2 (2006): 211–34.

Rojas, Alejandro, Lorenzo Magzul, Gregory P. Machildon, and Bernardo Reyes. "The Oldman River Dam Conflict: Adaptation and Institutional Learning." *Prairie Forum* 34, no. 1 (2009): 235–60.

Rossiter, David A. "The Nature of Protest: Constructing the Spaces of British Columbia's Rainforests." *Cultural Geographies* 11, no. 2 (2004): 139–64.

– "Negotiating Nature: Colonial Geographies and Environmental Politics in the Pacific Northwest." *Ethics, Place and Environment* 11, no. 2 (2008): 113–28.

Rossiter, David A., and Patricia K. Wood. "Fantastic Topographies: Neo-liberal Responses to Aboriginal Land Claims in British Columbia." *Canadian Geographer* 49, no. 4 (2005): 352–66.

Sandlos, John. "Federal Spaces, Local Conflicts: National Parks and the Exclusionary Politics of the Conservation Movement in Ontario, 1900–1935." *Journal of the Canadian Historical Association* 16, no. 1 (2005): 293–318.

– "Not Wanted in the Boundary: the Expulsion of the Keeseekowenin Ojibway Band from Riding Mountain National Park." *Canadian Historical Review* 89, no. 2 (2008): 189–221.

Skea, Warren H. "The Canadian Newspaper Industry's Portrayal of the Oka Crisis." *Native Studies Review* 9, no. 1 (1993–94): 15–31.

Spaven, Malcolm. "Environmental State, Military State, and Society: The Goose Bay Low Flying Controversy." *British Journal of Canadian Studies* 6, no. 1 (1991): 155–71.

Strange, Carolyn, and Tina Loo. "Holding the Rock: The 'Indianization' of Alcatraz Island, 1969–1999." *Public Historian* 23, no. 1 (Winter 2001): 55–74.

Tronnes, Libby R. "'Where Is John Wayne?': The Menominee Warriors Society, Indian Militancy, and Social Unrest during the Alexian Brothers Novitiate Takeover." *American Indian Quarterly* 26, no. 4 (Fall 2002): 526–58.

Usher, P.J. "Environment, Race and Nation Reconsidered: Reflections on Aboriginal Land Claims in Canada." *Canadian Geographer* 47, no. 4 (2003): 365–82.

Valentine, Lisa Phillips, and Alan K. McDougall. "A Separation Agreement Forty Years in the Making." In *Papers of the Thirty-Third Algonquian*

*Conference*, ed. H.C. Wofart, 392–413. Winnipeg: University of Manitoba, 2002.

– "Unveiling the Hegemon: Political Imag(in)ing of Stoney Point (Ipperwash)." In *Papers of the Thirtieth Algonquian Conference*, ed. David H. Pentland, 397–410. Winnipeg: University of Manitoba, 1999.

Vest, Jay Hansford C. "The Oldman River and the Sacred: A Meditation upon Aputosi Pii'kani Tradition and Environmental Ethics." *Canadian Journal of Native Studies* 25, no. 2 (2005): 571–607.

Wilkes, Rima. "First Nation Politics: Deprivation, Resources, and Participation in Collective Action." *Sociological Inquiry* 74, no. 4 (2004): 570–89.

– "A Systematic Approach to Studying Indigenous Politics: Band-Level Mobilization in Canada, 1981–2000." *Social Science Journal* 41, no. 3 (2004): 447–57.

Wilkes, Rima, Catherine Corrigal-Brown, and Danielle Ricard. "Nationalism and Media Coverage of Indigenous People's Collective Action in Canada." *American Indian Culture and Research Journal* 34, no. 4 (2010): 41–59.

Wilkes, Rima, and Danielle Ricard. "How Does Newspaper Coverage of Collective Action Vary? Protest by Indigenous People in Canada." *Social Science Journal* 44, no. 2 (2007): 231–51.

Winegard, Timothy C. "The Forgotten Front of the Oka Crisis: Operation Feather/Akwesasne." *Journal of Military and Strategic Studies* 11, nos 1–2 (2009): 1–50.

## REPORTS

Alfred, Gerald R. (Taiaiake), and Lana Lowe. "Warrior Societies in Contemporary Indigenous Communities." Paper prepared for the Ipperwash Inquiry, May 2005. http://www.attorneygeneral.jus.gov.on.ca/inquiries/ipperwash/policy_part/research/index.html.

Armitage, Peter. *Homeland or Wasteland? Contemporary Land Use and Occupancy among the Innu of Utshimassit and Sheshatshit and the Impact of Military Expansion*. Naskapi Montagnais Innu Association, Northwest River, Labrador, 31 January 1989.

Borrows, John. "Crown and Aboriginal Occupations of Land: A History and Comparison." Paper prepared for the Ipperwash Inquiry, 15 October 2005. http://www.attorneygeneral.jus.gov.on.ca/inquiries/ipperwash/policy_part/research/index.html.

Darling, Graham. *Land Claims and the Six Nations in Caledonia*. Centre for Constitutional Studies, University of Calgary, September 2006.

Dickson-Gilmore, E.J. *Communities, Contraband and Conflict: Considering Restorative Responses to Repairing the Harms Implicit in Smuggling in the Akwesasne Mohawk Nation*. Research and Evaluation Branch, Royal Canadian Mounted Police, Ottawa, 2002.

Dickson-Gilmore, E.J., and Chris Whitehead. *Aboriginal Organized Crime in Canada: Developing a Typology for Understanding and Strategizing Responses*. Research and Evaluation Branch, Royal Canadian Mounted Police, Ottawa, 2005.

Gilbert, Guy. *Rapport d'enquête du coroner Guy Gilbert sur les causes et circonstances du deces de Monsieur Marcel Lemay*. Coroner's Bureau, Government of Quebec, Quebec City, 1995.

Indian Claims Commission. *Inquiry into the 1927 Surrender Claim of the Chippewas of Kettle and Stony Point First Nation*. Indian Claims Commission, Ottawa, March 1997.

*The Ipperwash Papers: The Untold Story*. 14 March 2007. http://www. ipperwashpapers.com/IW-documents.htm.

Linden, Sidney B. *Report of the Ipperwash Inquiry*. 4 vols. Attorney General of Ontario, Toronto, 2007. http://www.attorneygeneral.jus.gov.on.ca/inquiries/ ipperwash/index.html.

Murrell, David. "A Balanced Overall View? Media Reporting of the Labrador Low-Flying Controversy." Paper for the Mackenzie Institute for the Study of Terrorism, Revolution and Propaganda, Toronto, 1990.

Royal Commission on Aboriginal Peoples. *Final Report*. 5 vols. Ottawa, 2006.

Standing Senate Committee on Aboriginal Peoples. *Negotiation or Confrontation: It's Canada's Choice*. Senate, Ottawa, December 2006.

Thompson, John C. "The Long Fall of the Mohawk Warriors." Paper for the Mackenzie Institute for the Study of Terrorism, Revolution and Propaganda, Toronto, 2006, http://www.numberswatchdog.com/THE%20LONG%20 FALL%20OF%20THE%20MOHAW%20WARRIORS.htm.

Tugwell, Maurice, and John C. Thompson. "The Legacy of Oka." Paper for the Mackenzie Institute for the Study of Terrorism, Revolution and Propaganda, Toronto, 1991.

### THESES AND DISSERTATIONS

Alcantara, Christopher. "Deal? Or No deal? Explaining Comprehensive Land Claims Negotiation Outcomes in Canada." PhD diss., University of Toronto, 2008.

Bisha, Timothy. "Seeds of Conflict on a Southwestern Ontario Reserve." MA thesis, University of Western Ontario, 1996.

Bryant, Michael J. "Legal Aspects of Chiapas, Oka and Wounded Knee Conflicts: Intranational Armed Conflicts between Indigenous Peoples and States." LLM thesis, Harvard Law School, 1994.

Cooper, Shannon J.C. "Analysis of the Inquiry as a Conflict Management System: Case Study – The Ipperwash Inquiry." MA thesis, Royal Roads University, 2006.

King, Sarah J. "Contested Place: Religion and Values in the Dispute, Burnt Church/Esgenoôpetitj, New Brunswick." PhD diss., University of Toronto, 2008.

Larose, Roger. "La crise d'Oka à la television: L'éloge du barbare." PhD diss., Concordia University, 2000.

Niemans, M.J. "'For the Future for Every One of Us': Innu Women on Community, Country and Military Low-Level Flying in Labrador." MA thesis, University of Amsterdam, 1995.

Ramos, Howard. "Divergent Paths: Aboriginal Mobilization in Canada, 1951–2000." PhD diss., McGill University, 2004.

Roos, Helen. "It Happened as If Overnight: The Expropriation and Relocation of Stoney Point Reserve #43, 1942." MA thesis, University of Western Ontario, 1998.

Scholtz, Christa. "Negotiating Claims: Recognition, Citizenship, and the Emergence of Indigenous Land Claim Negotiation Policies in Australia, Canada, New Zealand, and the United States." PhD diss., Princeton University, 2004.

Stuart, Charles. "The Mohawk Crisis: A Crisis of Hegemony." MA thesis, University of Ottawa, 1993.

Trevethick, Scott. "Conflicting Outlooks: The Background to the 1924 Deposing of the Six Nations Hereditary Council." MA thesis, University of Calgary, 1998.

Wilkes, Rima Catherine. "Competition or Colonization? An Analysis of Two Theories of Ethnic Collective Action." PhD diss., University of Toronto, 2001.

Williamson, Peter. "So I Can Hold My Head High: History and Representations of the Oka Crisis." MA thesis, Carleton University, 1997.

Winegard, Timothy C. "The Court of Last Resort: The 1990 Oka Crisis and the Canadian Forces." MA thesis, Royal Military College of Canada, 2006.

# Index

Standing Senate Committee on
Aboriginal Peoples, 104, 264, 342
Sûreté du Québec (SQ), 175, 177–9,
181–3, 191–5, 202
Syncrude project, 95–6

Taku River case, 246
Tékakwita Island, 192
Temagami Band, 98–9
Treaty 2, 53
Treaty 3½, 384, 386
Treaty 5, 98
Treaty 6, 98
Treaty 7, 225–6
Treaty 8, 91–3, 95–6, 98–100, 103,
105, 107, 112
Treaty 9, 98
treaty entitlement, 100, 106, 107, 111,
112
Trudeau, Pierre Elliott, 10, 101
Ts'peten. See Gustafsen Lake
Turton Penn Lease, 385, 390–1
Two-Row Wampum, 18, 83–4, 206,
387, 413, 423
Tyendinaga, 384–90, 392, 395, 398–
402, 405; Police Service, 392, 401,
402

Union of British Columbia Indian
Chiefs (UBCIC), 4, 316, 331

United Nations (UN), 82, 97, 179,
181, 228, 334, 426; Committee on
the Elimination of All Forms of
Racial Discrimination, 286; Convention on the Non-applicability
of Statutory Limitations to War
Crimes against Humanity, 231;
Human Rights Committee, 104,
108, 111, 286; Permanent Forum
on Indigenous Peoples, 426; Working Group on Indigenous Peoples,
185
usufructory rights, 415

Vagrancy Act (1824), 226
Valaskakis, Gale, 16

War of 1812, 12, 53, 57, 61, 254
Waterland, Thomas, 80
White Paper (1969), 10, 11, 95, 170,
316
Wilkes, Rima, 13
Wolfe, James, 360
Woodland Cree, 35, 108
World Council of Churches, 101–2
Wounded Knee, 16, 52, 232

Yellowhorn, Peter, 229, 233
Yovanvic, Ada, 79